DICKENS STUDIES ANNUAL

DICKENS STUDIES ANNUAL

Essays on Victorian Fiction

DICKENS
STUDIES
ANNUAL

Essays on Victorian Fiction

VOLUME
33

Edited by
Stanley Friedman, Edward Guiliano,
Anne Humpherys, and Michael Timko

AMS PRESS
NEW YORK

DICKENS STUDIES ANNUAL
ISSN 0084-9812

COPYRIGHT © 2003 by AMS Press, Inc.
Dickens Studies Annual: Essays on Victorian Fiction is published in cooperation with Queens College and the Graduate Center, CUNY.

International Standard Book Number
Series: 0-404-18520-7
Vol. 33: 0-404-18933-4

Dickens Studies Annual: Essays on Victorian Fiction welcomes essay- and monograph-length contributions on Dickens and other Victorian novelists and on the history of aesthetics of Victorian fiction. All manuscripts should be double-spaced and should follow the documentation format described in the most recent *MLA Style Manual.* The author's name should appear only on a cover-page, not elsewhere in the essay. An editorial decision can usually be reached more quickly if two copies of the article are submitted, since outside readers are asked to evaluate each submission. If a manuscript is accepted for publication, the author will be asked to provide a 100- to 200-word abstract and also a disk containing the final version of the essay. The preferred editions for citations from Dickens's works are the Clarendon and the Norton Critical when available, otherwise the Oxford Illustrated or the Penguin.

Please send submissions to The Editors, *Dickens Studies Annual*, Ph.D. Program in English. The Graduate Center, CUNY, 365 Fifth Avenue, New York, NY 10016-4309. Please send inquiries concerning subscriptions and/or the availability of earlier volumes to AMS Press, Inc., Brooklyn Navy Yard, Bldg. 292, Suite 417, 63 Flushing Ave., Brooklyn, NY 11205.

Manufactured in the United States of America

All AMS books are printed on acid-free paper that meets the guidelines for performance and durability of the Committee on Production Guidelines for Book Longevity of the Council on Library Resources.

Contents

List of Illustrations

Preface

Since this volume offers a particularly wide range of subjects and approaches, we may be tempted to invoke the words of that well-known educator Wackford Squeers, "here's richness!"

In assembling this issue, we have been dependent on the assistance of many persons. First, of course, we thank all who submitted essays, and we also thank the many outside reviewers whose detailed reports aided us in our decisions and at times helped contributors to strengthen their articles.

This volume contains a number of review essays: we are indebted to Professor Duane K. DeVries for his meticulous, extremely informative examination of bibliographical and textual studies of Dickens; to Ms. Robyn L. Schiffman for her stimulating, helpful discussion of psychological studies of Dickens during the last two decades; and to Professor Goldie Morgentaler for her incisive, thoughtful survey of Dickens studies published in 2001.

In addition, we thank Professor Robert J. Heaman, who has provided an updating of *Our Mutual Friend: An Annotated Bibliography*, compiled by Professors Joel J. Brattin and Bert G. Hornback (New York: Garland, 1984), and we are grateful to Professor DeVries, the General Editor of The Dickens Bibliographies (now being published by AMS Press, Inc.), for helping to make this bibliographical supplement available to us and for assisting with its editing. (This bibliography includes its own index.)

For valuable practical assistance, we thank the following administrators: President Frances Degen Horowitz; Provost William P. Kelly; Ph.D. Program in English Executive Officer Joan Richardson; and Marilyn Weber, Assistant Program Officer, Ph.D. Program in English, all of The Graduate Center, CUNY; and President James L. Muyskens; Acting Dean of Arts and Humanities Tamara S. Evans; and Department of English Chair Nancy R. Comley, all of Queens College, CUNY.

We thank, too, Professor John O. Jordan, Director of The Dickens Project at the University of California, Santa Cruz, and JoAnna Rottke, Project Coordinator for The Dickens Project, for placing on the Project's website the tables of contents for volumes 1–27 of *DSA*, as well as abstracts for subsequent volumes. (These materials are included in the Project's Dickens Electronic Archive.) The Dickens Project can be reached at http: // humwww.ucsc.edu/ dickens/index.html

We appreciate the generous support and consistent interest of Gabriel Hornstein, President of AMS Press, and we gratefully acknowledge the cordial cooperation given by Jack Hopper, Editor-in-Chief at AMS Press. Finally, we thank our two editorial assistants for ably performing numerous essential tasks for this volume: Janine Utell, for her help during the earlier and middle stages of preparation, and Evan Brier, for his work in the later phases.

—The Editors

Notes on Contributors

PHILIP V. ALLINGHAM holds Master's degrees in Educational Administration and English from the University of Victoria, British Columbia. After completing a doctorate on the dramatic adaptations of the Christmas Books of Charles Dickens at the University of B. C. (Vancouver), he served for three years as a coordinator in the Provincial Examinations Branch, Victoria. In August, 2000, after three decades working in British Columbia's secondary and post-secondary systems, Dr. Allingham took up the post as Assistant Professor, Secondary English Curriculum and Instruction, in the Faculty of Education at Lakehead University in Thunder Bay, Ontario. Currently, he is Contributing Editor to George Landow's Victorian Web and one of the vice presidents of the Thomas Hardy Association (North America); he has numerous publications on the works of Charles Dickens and Thomas Hardy.

ALLAN W. ATLAS is Distinguished Professor of Music at The Graduate Center of The City University of New York. His *Renaissance Music* (W. W. Norton, 1998) is the standard undergraduate text on the subject. He has published on various aspects of music in the works of both Wilkie Collins and George Gissing, and as a player of the English concertina gives lecture-recitals featuring the original Victorian repertory for the instrument.

ELLEN MILLER CASEY, Professor of English at the University of Scranton, has published on the *Athenaeum*'s reception of both women and American novelists, as well as on Dickens as editor of the weekly serial. She is currently working on the *Athenaeum* reviewers' presentation of themselves and on their reception of George Eliot.

JEFFREY CASS is Associate Provost at Texas A & M International University. His fields of interest include nineteenth-century women writers and popular culture. He has published articles on Mary Shelley, Maria Edgeworth, and Elizabeth Gaskell. An essay on the Luxor Las Vegas and Postmodern Orientalism will appear in a collection on architecture and tourism (Berg Publishers, 2004).

DUANE DEVRIES is Associate Professor Emeritus of Humanities at Polytechnic University, Brooklyn, NY. He is the author *of Dickens's Apprentice Years: The Making of a Novelist* (1976), former editor of *Dickens Studies Newletter* (1974–1982), and general editor of the Garland Dickens Bibliographies (11 volumes, 1981–93) and The Dickens Bibliographies (AMS Press), 1998–. He is currently working on a four-volume edition of *General Studies of Charles Dickens and His Writings and Collected Editions of His Works: An Annotated Bibliography*, volume one of which, *Bibliographies, Catalogues, and Bibliographical and Textual Studies*, will be published this year.

ROBERT J. HEAMAN is Emeritus Professor of English at Wilkes University and currently serves as Secretary/Treasurer to the Dickens Society. In addition to publishing on Dickens, he has published on Aeschylus and Hemingway.

MARK M. HENNELLY, JR. is English Department Chair at California State University, Sacramento, and has published widely on Victorian fiction, particularly Dickens. His most recent work appears or is forthcoming in *Dickens Quarterly, College Literature, Contemporary Literature, The Thomas Hardy Yearbook*, and MLA's *Teaching Approaches to Gothic Fiction*. He is currently working on a liminal reading of *Wuthering Heights* and a carnivalesque reading of *Adam Bede*.

MONIQUE R. MORGAN is Assistant Professor of English literature at McGill University. She is currently writing a book on time, lyric, and narrative in the nineteenth-century long poem.

GOLDIE MORGENTALER is Associate Professor of English at the University of Lethbridge. She is the author of *Dickens and Heredity: When Like Begets Like* (2000), and she has published articles on Dickens in *SEL* and *Dickens Quarterly*, as well as *Dickens Studies Annual*. Her essay on Dickens in Canada appeared in the September 2002 issue of *Dickens Quarterly*. She has also published translations from and articles on Yiddish literature and is the author, most recently, of three essays on Yiddish writers in *Holocaust Literature* (Routledge, 2002).

ROBYN L. SCHIFFMAN is writing a dissertation on reading practices in sentimental fictions in the Department of Comparative Literature at the University of Chicago. She had previously published an article on *Bleak House* and the uncanny in Volume 30 of *DSA*.

KATHERINE WILLIAMS, Associate Professor of English at New York Institute of Technology, Manhattan Campus, has published articles in *Hellas* and *Research in African Literature*. She is currently at work on a cultural history of glass windows.

A Rabelaisian View from Todgers's Backside, Or "Partly Spiritual, Partly Spiritous" in *Martin Chuzzlewit*

Mark M. Hennelly, Jr.

The troubling confrontation between old Martin and Sairey Gamp near the conclusion of Martin Chuzzlewit *typifies the tensions between Lenten and carnivalesque extremes which significantly inform the entire novel and which archetypally appear in* Gargantua and Pantagruel. *In fact, understanding the crucial relationships between Dickens and Rabelais's bawdy epic helps readers better evaluate the miraculous but often melancholy comedy of* Chuzzlewit. *Specifically, it clarifies the text's confusing medley of carnivalesque motifs: cornucopian (and dialogic) plentitude, grotesque matter, prandial and Pantagruelian excesses, billingsgate rhetoric, and the paradox of "pregnant death." Ultimately, it provides a novel and refreshing perspective on the textual "problems" of* Chuzzlewit's *preface, American chapters, and representation of Mrs. Gamp's boozy expertise in both "births and berryins."*

When you come into your world, do not fail to affirm and witness, that the greatest treasures, and most admirable things, are hidden underground; and not without reason.—Rabelais, *Gargantua and Pantagruel*

But the grand mystery of Todgers's was the cellarage, approachable only by a little back door

---

1

and a rusty grating: which cellarge within the
memory of man had no connexion with the
house, but had always been the freehold property
of somebody else, and was reported to be full
of wealth.—Charles Dickens, *Martin Chuzzlewit*

The genesis of this reading of Charles Dickens's *Martin Chuzzlewit* (1843–44) is my recurring dissatisfaction with old Martin's ultimate moral censure of Sairey Gamp, that expert on both "births and berryins" (387; 25), and his "word or two of good advice" to her: "the expediency of a little less liquor, and a little more humanity, and a little less regard for herself, and a little more regard for her patients, and perhaps a trifle of honesty" (761; 52). It's not just that this *sentence*—especially following priggish Betsey Prig's denial of Sairey's beloved alter ego Mrs. Harris (708 ;49)—appears to be too cruel a cut of murderous logic and moral law. It's not even that Martin's zealously zeugmatic (and falsely binary) "less liquor" and "more humanity" seems to crush Mrs. Gamp's boozy, comic paganism with sober, classical sententiousness. No, it's more that the scene leaves *something to be desired*, and this desire cries out for fairer play, or at least a fairer fight, between the two parties.

Mrs. Gamp's subsequent seizing on "fresh air" and gasping "Less liquor!—Sairey Gamp!—Bottle on the chimley-piece, and let me put my lips to it, when I am so dispoged" provide some creative creature comfort as does her performative "swooning" exit with "the revolving Bailey." Old Martin's following "smile,"—and then "he smiled the more" (761; 52), however, adds only more unsettling discomfort, as does his dinner party for the remaining mutual friends, his compassionate orchestration of their table talk, and his ultimate and genuine care for Mercy Chuzzlewit, née Pecksniff.

I am not the first, of course, to be bothered by this scene. James Kincaid's dismissive response proves both typical and telling, but its *reductio*, though insightful, itself leaves something to be desired: "When old Martin denounces [Mrs. Gamp] at the end and tells her to take less liquor, our consolation is the assurance that she will surely ignore this stupidity. She does, in fact, transform his moral rigidity into something so plastic and artful as to repudiate immediately old Martin's code" (*Dickens and the Rhetoric of Laughter* 160). Kincaid's later analysis of the novel's "splendid parody of moralistic solemnity" relevantly notes the possible value of the carnivalesque here, but then dismisses it: "The force of this anarchic parody completely subverts the moralistic center provided by the theme of selfishness and suggests not righteous reconciliation but carnival. Or does it? Of course not. . . ." (" 'All the Wickedness in the World is Print' " 263).

Unpredictably, though, *A Christmas Carol*, which Dickens composed in the midst of writing *Chuzzlewit*, provides a clue as to just what might be desired in old Martin's dismissal of Sairey (and Kincaid's different dismissal of old Martin) when the charitable gentleman reveals to Scrooge that "We choose this time [for charity], because it is a time, of all others, when Want is keenly felt, and Abundance rejoices" (18; st. 1). In a very meaningful sense, this dialectic between *Want* and *Abundance* is allegorically related to that between the usually miserable miser old Martin and the usually merry midwife Mrs. Gamp, which itself is even closer to the dialogism between Lent and Carnival (in some traditions even between Lent and *Christmas*) variously performed in Rabelais's *Gargantua and Pantagruel* (1532–64). As Samuel Kinser describes this central "Carnival-Lent theme,"

> Thus, although [Rabelais] transforms nearly every element of the old combat theme, he nevertheless preserves the schema. And although he derives the qualities of representation almost entirely from the Carnival, secular side and scarcely at all from Lenten, churchly views, the comic ideology supporting the representation affably accepts both kinds of institution, even with their common tendency to encourage excess. Both institutions are necessary to provide the dynamics driving either of them. (121–22)

In this carnivalesque sense, the key to fathoming the inchoate comedy (and related seriousness) of *Martin Chuzzlewit*—and much of Dickens—is not so much the view from Todgers's head, as Dorothy Van Ghent famously argues, but the Rabelaisian view from Todgers's backside. Mixing carnivalesque metaphors and defying allegorical "signs," or better, moving to the central carnivalesque metaphor of mixing sacred and profane "spirits," the reader should therefore keep at least one eye on the artful Mrs. Gamp and her own zany zeugma: "With a leer of mingled sweetness and slyness; with one eye on the future, one on the bride; and an arch expression in her face, partly spiritual, partly spiritous, and wholly professional and peculiar to her art; Mrs Gamp rummaged in her pocket again, and took from it a printed card, whereon was an inscription copied from her sign-board. . . . 'it's my card, Gamp is my name, and Gamp my nater' " (403–04; 26).

In order to comprehend Sairey's "name" and her "nater" and, more significantly, the crucial relationships between Lenten and Carnivalesque *spirits* in the novel, we need to summarize Dickens's own relationships to the carnivalesque in general and Rabelais in particular, discuss the text's medley of significant carnivalesque motifs, and finally view three central textual problems through a Rabelaisian lense: the almost unreadable "prologue," the allegedly extraneous "American chapters," and again the apparent dismissal of Mrs. Gamp and her various carnivalesque "spirits." Such an approach can help us better appreciate the relationships between Rabelais's novel, which holds at one point that "laughing" is "the action that is most peculiar to man" (603; II; v, 25) and which M. A. Screech believes to include "the profoundest statements of philosophical comedy ever conceived" (13), and the supreme comedy (not to mention supreme melancholy) of *Chuzzlewit*, which Steven Marcus calls a "comedy of soul-making" (259), Kincaid "Dickens's funniest novel" (*Rhetoric* 132), R. C. Churchill "the greatest work of comic genius in the whole of English literature" (120), and about which Robert Polhemus confides that "I can think of no other novel in the language before Joyce's *Ulysses* that has so much fantastic, suggestive, and astonishingly original comic language as *Chuzzlewit*" (89). In sum, such an approach can answer George Gissing's early criticism that "a novel more shapeless, a story less coherent than *Martin Chuzzlewit*, will not easily be found in any literature" (54), besides both honoring and healing "the structural dissonances" (158) which Terry Eagleton more recently notes in the novel.

I

As especially dramatized by the giants, dwarfs, Punch performers, and various other strolling players in *The Old Curiosity Shop* (1840–41) and documented generally in Paul Schlicke's *Dickens and Popular Entertainment* and more particularly in Edwin Eigner's *The Dickens Pantomime*, Dickens was himself passionately devoted to carnivalesque pastimes. One of his favorite playwrights was Ben Jonson, whose *Bartholomew Fair* enshrines carnivalism and whose *Every Man in His Humour* provided Dickens's favorite dramatic role in the somewhat Panurgic and somewhat Pecksniffian Captain Bobadil. His favorite—and his culture's favorite—clown and performative idol was Joseph Grimaldi, whose bittersweet *Memoirs* (1838) Dickens edited and extensively revised. In the words of Schlicke (who never invokes Bakhtin or the "carnivalesque" specifically), "at the very outset of the Victorian era, the amusements of the people were under attack from many directions, and Dickens, the great popular entertainer, was their champion" (3). In the words of Eigner (who does sporadically invoke both Bakhtin and the carnivalesque), "Like carnival, Dickens and pantomime are associated with traditional holiday times of the year, but they do not serve tradition." Rather, their goal is gnostic: "to provide the anarchical holiday space that Bakhtin saw as essential for the rethinking of ingrained moral and political systems and that Dickens perceived as an opportunity for changing his readers' basic stories about the nature of reality" (41).

More relevantly, Dickens owned a copy of Sir Thomas Urquhart's celebrated 1653 English translation of *Gargantua and Pantagruel* (completed by Peter Motteux), which featured Theodore Martin's "Introductory Notice and Life of Rabelais" (Stonehouse 96), whose own inimitable "life" and vision the Inimitable Dickens often seemed to imitate. Even more to the point, as editor of *Bentley's Miscellany* in November of 1838, Dickens helped P. W. Banks prepare his "Rabelais article" (*Letters* I: 455, 459), which unaccountably did not appear in *Bentley's* but did reach print under the title "Of Rabelais" in three lengthy installments in *Fraser's Magazine* (November 1839, February and July 1840). This pivotal piece serves as a kind of tricky testament to Dickens's, if not his Victorian culture's, general take on Rabelais.

Banks's long-winded, often digressive, and heavily citational essay provides a running comparison of Rabelais with Homer and Shakespeare, though its primary purpose is "to say something about Rabelais, his life, and works" (Nov. 514). Banks repeatedly documents Rabelais's "omnigenous knowledge" (Nov. 523) and "omnigenous learning" (Feb. 218) in (his vocational) areas like religion, education, medicine, linguistics/semiotics, law, and politics in such a way that the syncretistic background and expertise (Screech 2–3) of this prototypical Renaissance man and Christian humanist anticipate those of the Victorian polymath Dickens. In fact, Rabelais and Dickens both famously invoke prandial or banquet metaphors to capture the sedimented, polysemous richness of their art. As Banks cites this "allegorical sense," Rabelais compares a dog devouring its bone to reach the juicy marrow to a reader digesting his book, who "must, by sedulous lecture, and frequent meditation, break the bone, and suck the marrow" of the blessedly bawdy epic, which "then will disclose unto you the most glorious sacraments, and dreadful mysteries, as well in what concerneth your religion, as matters of the publicke state, and life œconomical" (Nov. 517). In *Oliver Twist*, Dickens similarly compares his melodramatic "tragic and . . . comic scenes" to "the layers of red and white in a side of streaky bacon," suggesting that "[t]he transitions in real life . . . from mourning weeds to holiday garments, are not a wit less startling" (168–69; 17). To use a favorite Dickensian word that appears both in *Chuzzlewit* and in Urquhart's translation of Rabelais, both writers thus "feast . . . with store[s] of *gammon*" (246; I: ii, 5; emphasis added)—both foodstuffs and tomfoolery—to fight the gammon of humbug and hypocrisy.

Both democratic reformers also attempt to feed and *heal* "the multitude" and its "world of [chill] reality" with "the world of imagination" (Nov. 529). And again, the imagination of both is *multitudinous*, that is, it invariably invokes the rhetoric of *copiae* in exercising "our noble and copious tongue" (Nov. 523, though Banks is specifically referencing Urquhart here). And again (and again), both employ "monstrous buffoonery" to expose and excoriate "Every [Pecksniffian] hypocrite, every base or bad man" (Nov. 517–18). "[F]rom the commencement to the close" of their lives, both also betray a *curious* restlessness—"not merely freedom, but waywardness of locomotion and of will, which no professed enemy of humbug ever could have accomplished without the aid of ample pecuniary means" (Nov. 524). In fact,

Rabelais's carnivalesque and dialogized "motley groups" countered the same kind of mechanized and monologic groups that Dickens later condemns: "the new-fangled schools of your professed utilitarians" (Nov. 526). In Rabelais's own carnivalesque words, " 'bodily refection,—that is, . . . eating and drinking' " (Nov. 516) is worth much more than such official policies and pronouncements: a lively party defeats the party line every time because in Pecksniff's immortal phrasing, it's "a carnal universe" (207; 12).

At the same time, the genius of both writers preaches and practices a golden mean of moderation (July 79–80) typified by the *gentleness* of the "Thelemites" and Tom Pinch—"Gentleness is the same in all climates, in all ages" (Nov. 519)—and by the "cheerful, genial feeling" (Nov. 518) of that jolly giant Pantagruel and that even more jolly gent Mark Tapley. In other words, though each "riots" in comedic "Humour"—satiric as well as psychological—both also respond to *lacrimae rerum* in "the condition of the Fall." Consequently, as one of Banks's citations insists of Rabelais, readers can find " 'beneath the surface of [Carnival] gaiety' " (in both) a significant " 'substratum of [Lenten] melancholy,' " or in Banks's own Dickensian rhetoric, "that heavenly sorrow which purifies the heart" (Nov. 520), whether it appears in the death of Gargantua's wife in childbirth and the moral doldrums of Panurge or the sentimental masochism of Augustus Moddle and the (musical) pathos of Tom Pinch.

More specifically, Banks cites Molière's *Tartuffe* (Feb. 221), which many Dickensians have also noted as the source of Pecksniff's hypocrisy and which falling text famously appears (along with *Paradise Lost*) in Phiz's illustration of the fall of Pecksniff (751; 52). Further, Banks's citation of "what the Greeks call 'circle-learning' " (July 65) anticipates both Bahktin's discussion of this primary carnivalesque movement, captured in clowning cartwheels, which profoundly joins heaven and earth—"the theme of descent into hell is implicit in this simple acrobatic feat" (397)—and which is also personified in the recurring rotary movements of "the revolving Bailey" (761; 52). In his discussion of Rabelais's liberal educational theory, Banks even cites Bacon's dictum " 'Keep your authority wholly from your children—*not so your purse!*' " —the same advice Dickens levels at both elder Chuzzlewit brothers as well as Pecksniff.

Finally, Banks's essay provides an unexpected surprise in its remarks on the Gampian Panurge (and, as we'll see, another surprise in its remarks on America). Although Michael Heath contends that Rabelais was the "scourge of Victorian vicarages" (1) and that "Victorian England . . . was on the whole infertile ground for [Rabelais's] boisterous humor, in public"(124), I have previously tried to historicize a very vital Victorian interest in *Gargantua and Pantagruel* (see "Victorian Carnivalesque"). Indeed, Rabelais remained popular enough to inspire Walter Besant's Victorian "Rabelais

Club,'' of which Thomas Hardy and Henry James were charter members (*Autobiography* 240–42). And although archdeacon Grantly in Trollope's *The Warden*(1855) does keep his ''volume of Rabelais'' hidden in ''a secret drawer beneath his table'' in the study—his ''sacred room''—he also (ironically and repeatedly) retires there ''to amuse himself with the witty mischief of Panurge'' (98–99; 8). In fact, most Rabelaisians, including Heath, believe this ribald rascal to be Rabelais's most ''complex and evolving figure who,'' like Sairey Gamp, ''incarnates much that is dark and intimidating in the human psyche. His gradual decline [from 'the once-resourceful trickster'] into melancholic madness is remorselessly unfolded'' (68). Depending on one's point of view, it is consequently remarkable (or not) that the Victorian Banks considers Panurge to be ''the author's own pet character. . . . Panurge is, in my opinion, to Rabelais what Falstaff was to Shakespeare. He has been wrought out of the poet's brain with all the labour of love, and decked with the rarest flowers of fancy'' (Feb. 223). One could easily say the same of Mrs. Gamp.

Despite, then, Heath's undocumented claim that ''Dickens . . . shared none of Balzac's enthusiasm for Rabelais'' (124), Dickens's intimate acquaintance with Banks's essay as well as with *Gargantua and Pantagruel,* plus his even more intimate participation in the carnivalesque tradition itself, suggests that from the dwarfs and giants in *The Old Curiosity Shop* (1840) to the dipsomaniacal Mr. Dolls's ''Gargantuan order for a dram'' (788; V: 8) in *Our Mutual Friend* (1864), Dickens's fiction, as I have argued in a series of essays (see *Works Cited*), is drenched in Rabelaisian *spirits*. The inspiring aeolian imagery which blows a gale through *Gargantua and Pantagruel* and similarly ventilates *Martin Chuzzlewit*—beginning with its proleptic pratfelling of Pecksniff—even recalls the etymological link between *wind* and *spirit*. Nevertheless, Rabelais and Dickens are much more than just comparative ''kindred spirits,'' though the Rabelaisian influence grows more displaced and subtle as Dickens's career develops. The very notion of *communality*, which the Banks connection clearly connotes, also implies that a post-Bakhtinian awareness of the ''cultural'' powers of both Carnival *and* Lent provides a necessary complement to Bakhtin's more formalist/structuralist focus on specific carnivalesque categories. For example, in Dickens's carnivalesque name game, Pecksniff's daughters are (mis)named both Cherry *and* Charity, both Merry *and* Mercy. Indeed, Kinser's ''unfamiliar'' sense of Rabelais, or at least of his narrator Alcofribas, as a ''good-time-Charley'' (which he distinguishes from Bakhtin's reading) and his repeated identification of ''Pantagruelism . . . with conviviality'' (240–41), uncannily recalls the ''familiar'' notion of the Dickensian ''spirit and tradition of convivialism'' (258), which W. Walter Crotch traced through the novels as early as 1915.

At this point, then, we are ready to explore some of Bakhtin's more significant, overlapping carnivalesque motifs in the text—cornucopian and dialogic plentitude, grotesque (especially carnal) matter, prandial and Pantagruelian values, billingsgate rhetoric, and the paradox of "pregnant death"—before we take up post-Bakhtinian solutions to the problems of the genealogical preface, the American chapters, and finally, again, the "nater" of Sairey Gamp.

II

Both Rabelais and Dickens hymn mutability cantos to Nature's principle of plentitude. For Rabelais, "according to the course of nature, . . . all things, you know, are subject to change" (505; II: 2); for Dickens, "the natural laws of change" dictate that "change begets change" (288; 18). For Bakhtin, the carnivalesque glorifies this changing universe in its "very act of becoming and growth, the eternal incomplete unfinished nature of being. Its images present simultaneously the two poles of becoming: that which is receding and dying, and that which is being born; they show two bodies in one" (52). Similarly, the cornucopian and "carnal universe" in *Martin Chuzzlewit* wills and wants *more* as at "the Bacchanalian" feast at Todgers where repeatedly "More punch is called for, and produced, and drunk." Here the various carnival principles of plentitude are characteristically and convivially *(en)-listed*, as they are in Rabelais, against the despondency of Lent: "Then more wine came on; red wines and white wines; and a large china bowl of punch, brewed by the gentleman of a convivial turn, who adjured the Miss Pecksniffs not to be despondent on account of its dimensions, as there were materials in the house for the concoction of half a dozen more of the same size. Good gracious, how they laughed!" (148–50: 9). Besides the repeated emphasis on cornucopian containers like the "large china bowl of punch" here, the "basket" Mrs. Lupin abyssally loads with surprises for Tom Pinch's famous coach ride (530; 36), or Sairey Gamp's bottomless bag of provisions, Dickens like Rabelais continually taps into carnivalesque "monstrous profusion" (431; 28) by linking it with infinite numbers (Bakhtin 464–65) as when Mark Tapley loads more and more kisses on the more than willing Mrs. Lupin:

> "Fifteen more!" said Mr Tapley. "How handsome and how young you look! Six more! The last half-dozen warn't a fair one, and must be done over again. Lord bless you, what a treat it is to see you! One more! Well, I never was so jolly. Just a few more, on account of there not being any credit in it!"
>
> (617; 43)

Initially, this kind of "beautiful confusion" (679; 47) and profusion represents the inexhaustible variety and generosity of the shape-shifting carnivalesque universe where, as in the view from atop Todgers, the universal "host of objects" can hospitably "thicken and expand a hundredfold" (134; 9) but can never be absolutely pinned down to one measure or meaning. Indeed, then, the most humanizing response is Mark Tapley's equally "inexhaustible cheerfulness" (357; 23), which itself also recalls the Romantic credo of *genial faith* ("Resolution and Independence") or *genial spirits* ("Dejection: An Ode") with its own suggestions of *genesis, genius, genuine, gentleness, congeniality,* and even *genital.* Such fulsome resources can thus make humanity eminently resourceful so that it finds the "comfort and consolation" Tom Pinch seeks when he unsuccessfully scans the job ads and voices the universal lament " 'I want such and such a thing, and I can't get it, and I don't expect I ever shall!' " In fact, by healing the schism between high and low, the carnivalesque creates the leveling sense of *community* that Kinser argues is so primary to Rabelais and that Tom finds so lacking in his contemporary society: "Here are all kinds of employers wanting all sorts of servants, and all sorts of servants wanting all kinds of employers, and they never seem to come together" (535–36; 36). Even Tom's chiasmus, which trope is also very dear to Rabelais, syntactically binds together the classes that seem semantically separate.

In this sense, the textual universe which, based on rhetorical evidence, John Bowen rightly dubs "a world of endless metamorphoses" (210), is also a world bound by a seemingly infinite series of "sets of twins" (759; 52) or dialogic doubles like old and young Martin Chuzzlewit, Montague Tigg/Tigg Montague, "the two profiles of Zephaniah Scadder" (343; 21), Sairey Gamp/ Mrs. Harris and "her" ability to become "two people" (394; 25), and even Pecksniff's "double eye-glass" (473; 31). Such uncanny repetition compulsion again coordinates metaphysical categories, "Swans" and "Oysters" (67; 4) and even "Capricorn" and "Cauliflower," in a "reversed" version of the "old axiom" that like cures like since in the carnivalesque, dialogic opposites attract: "like clings to unlike more than to like" (106; 7). And so both *différance* and similitude in dissimilitude prevail in "the dual-bodied world of becoming" (Bakhtin 420) as, like Tom Pinch with his library post, one must serially defer making sense of all the "double meaning" (585; 40) in the universe. Instead, as Besant emphasizes in his 1877 article on Rabelais, one must imitate the author of *Gargantua and Pantagruel*'s deathbed utterance and "go to seek the great Perhaps" (107). Or, like Pantagruel in Lanternland and Mark in America, one must become "seasoned to the place" even though "the season was a sickly one" (488; 33); for, as the servant Mark's partially prandial metaphor tells his dear double and employer Martin, "It's only a seasoning; and we must all be seasoned, one way or another. That's religion, that is, you know" (366; 23).

Like the related "Philosophy of Vegetables," the carnivalesque "Philosophy of Matter" (284; 17) is preached and practiced in England as well as

America. In this grotesque *sense*, Pecksniff follows Heraclitus in finding that "Beautiful Truth!" ironically "live[s] in a well" (627; 43), just as Rabelais also discovers truth at "the bottom of that undrainable well" (346; I: ii, 18). In placing matter over mind, this brand of gnosticism reverses official hierarchies for establishing the grounds of knowledge or "groundwork of belief" (181; 11). Consequently, it often reveals itself in subversive images of the *mundus inversus* or so-called *grotto values* like those underground in Todgers and all the other wine cellars in *Chuzzlewit*. For example, Montague Tigg's reappearance as Tigg Montague re-presents him as "turned and twisted upside down, and outside out" (408; 27); and during the spirited sea storm, Mark Tapley finds himself standing "on my head all night" in "a nearly perpendicular elevation" (241; 15). Indeed, all of the novel's *grotesque* characters, like the resurrected Bailey, characteristically "retire underground" (145; 9). Mrs. Gamp's favorite figure of "this wale of life" (588; 40), like the chapter 52 title "In which the Tables are Turned, completely Upside Down" (743) during Old Martin's rise and Pecksniff's fall, ultimately preaches a carnivalesque version of the fortunate fall, one in which both Carnival and Lent, malt and Milton, justify man's ways to God.

We will return to this kind of grotesque *prima materia* in the American chapters, but we should stress here that significant lower-body references appear almost as frequently, if not quite as graphically, in *Martin Chuzzlewit*'s "anatomical point of view" (417; 27) as they do in *Gargantua and Pantagruel*. And, in fact, Robert E. Lougy has noted *Chuzzlewit*'s fascination with bodily "orifices and protuberances" in connection with "Rabelais's fascination with the grotesque body" (38). Dickens, though, seems more particularly concerned with "[t]he process of digestion" (126; 8), especially that "important organ" the stomach and its "gastric juices" (413, 415; 27), whose prandial cultivation leads to remarkable "spirits" (602; 41). Like digesting tripe in Rabelais (Bakhtin 162–64), this circulatory process again suggests carnivalesque correspondences and the self-renewing cycle of life, which turns from eating, to digesting, to defecating, to fertilizing. Similarly, the fertility of Sairey Gamp, who cyclically attends "a lying-in or a laying-out with equal zest and relish," is represented by her carnivalized body, her clownish "nose in particular—[which] was somewhat red and swoln, and it was difficult to enjoy her society without becoming conscious of the smell of spirits" (303; 19). At the other end of the body, liminal limbs, especially legs, become significant carnivalesque zones of transformation when they are grotesquely *grounded*. As the viscount's boy suggests to Pip, the absence of such grotesque realism seriously impairs any art, even the Bard's: "There's a lot of feet in Shakespeare's verse, but there an't any legs worth mentioning in Shakespeare's plays" (431; 28). Game gams, however, do ground Sairey Gamp's grotesque "name" and her grotesque "nater" as "her whole being resolved itself into an absorbing anxiety about her pattens, with which she played innumerable games at quoits, on Mr Pecksniff's legs'' (302; 19).

Thirdly, the multitude and magnitude of the feastings in *Martin Chuzzlewit* are genuinely Gargantuan. The grotesque body cannot survive, of course, without ''eatables and drinkables'' (92; 6), without prandial and Pantagruelian (''all-thirsty'') satisfaction; and all the grotesque characters ''eat and drink in high good humour'' (393; 25). Tom Pinch, for instance, repeatedly styles himself ''a great eater'' (32; 2) and then practices the carnivalesque philosophy he preaches when he ''fell to work upon a well-cooked steak and smoking hot potatoes, with a strong appreciation of their excellence, and a very keen sense of enjoyment. Beside him, too, there stood a mug of most stupendous Wiltshire beer; and the effect of the whole was so transcendent, that he was obliged every now and then to lay down his knife and fork and think about it'' (79–80; 5). Like Rabelais's celebrated grotesque description of his books as *ces beaux livres de haulte gresse* (Auerbach 245–46) and Pecksniff's characteristic ''grace after meat''—though minus the Falstaffian pun on *grace/grease* in his accompanying ''greasy expression of countenance, indicating contentment, if not repletion'' (126; 8)—Tom also joins mardi gras and Lenten motifs in his meditation on the transcendental quality of the table and its ''stupendous'' spirits. Again at ''Bacchanalian'' Todgers, as so often in Rabelais, the meal becomes the kind of symposium appearing ''in that dialogue of Plato's, which is entitled, 'The Banquet,' '' in which ''bodily refection, that is, . . . eating and drinking'' (Rabelais xxxiii, xxxvii; I:i, Author's Prologue) transform into a communal love feast, if not comic communion rite where providential *provisions* repeatedly provide proof of God's limitless bounty and blessings: ''Quarts of almonds; dozens of oranges; pounds of raisins; stacks of biffins; soup-plates full of nuts.—Oh, Todgers's could do it when it chose! mind that'' (148–49; 9). And just as the hiccupping Aristophanes' more earthy myth of the circle people transcends Eryximachus' more abstract and turgid treatise on love in Plato, drunken Pecksniff's cyclically comic return from passing out in his room to woo Mrs. Todgers with carnivalesque compliments on the ''legs of the human subject'' transcends his treatises on ''moral responsibilities'' (153–54; 9).

The text's repeated Pantagruelian emphasis on ''exciting liquids'' (25; 2) and ''enlivening fluid''—always linked with ''more spirit'' (126; 8)—approaches a kind of carnivalesque flow theory when Mark and Martin return to England; and significantly like ''two grateful-tempered giants,'' they ''regaled upon a smoking steak, and certain flowing mugs of beer, as only men just landed from the sea can revel in the generous dainties of the earth'' (517; 35). When Mrs. Lupin mimes Bacbuc, the high priestess of the Subterranean Temple in Rabelais, and becomes the ''high priestess of the temple'' at the Blue Dragon, the shape-shifting metaphysical flow animates her dish to run away with the spoon or, at least, the "plethoric cherry-brandy [to begin] winking at a foaming jug of beer upon the table" (619; 43), just as we seem to find "[t]he pudding having taken a chair" during Ruth Pinch's "high [comic] art" of creating "a beef-steak pudding"(571, 565; 39). As at the Subterranean Temple, the Pantagruelian solution to the twin mysteries of life and love here seems boldly to belch out the old French "TRINC" (674; II: v,44) from the *Dive Bouteille*, that is, joyfully to drink life's cocktail in all its manifold manifestations, especially love. The many flowing "fountains" that mark the mystic "subterranean rule" (683; II: 47) of the Rabelaisian Temple consequently seem reprised in the repeated references to "The Temple fountain" in *Chuzzlewit*, though why Ruth and John Westlock "came towards the Fountain at all is a mystery. It was quite out of their way. They had no more to do with the Fountain, bless you, than they had with—Love" (762; 53).

Lest we be blinded by these benign prandial and Pantagruelian blessings, though, we should note other more grotesque, if not cannibalistic, examples that support Michael André Bernstein's post-Bakhtinian reflections in *Bitter Carnival*: "when the tropes of a Saturnalian reversal of all values spill over into daily life, they usually do so with a savagery that is the grim underside of their exuberant affirmations. It is precisely the festival's bitter side, the relationship between its celebratory and its rage-filled aspects, that I want to probe" (6). For example, at Anthony's *funferall* "everyone, except poor Chuffey, who came within the shadow of Anthony Chuzzlewit's grave, feasted like a Ghoule" in "a round of dismal joviality and grim enjoyment" (309; 19). Tom Pinch even worries lest John Westlock fear he has become unholy communion for Sweeney Todd, that "I have strayed into one of those streets where the countrymen are murdered; and that I have been made meat pies of, or some horrible thing" (544; 36). Carnivalesque "spirits" become much more existentially *bitter*, if not hallucinogenic, during Jonas Chuzzlewit's "diabolical fun" on the coach with Tigg when Jonas's "mirth was of such a savage and extraordinary character" (608–09; 42) that he attempts to bludgeon him with a wine bottle. Such cautionary carnivalism (what Umberto Eco terms "cold carnival") not only admonishes extreme carnal self-indulgence, but also implicitly invites Lenten self-restraint. Perhaps, though, Sairey Gamp's spirited recollection of Mrs. Harris's discovering her foetal niece "kep in spirits in a bottle; and that sweet babe she see at Greenwich Fair, a travellin in company vith the pink-eyed lady, Prooshan dwarf, and livin skelinton" (760; 52) most grotesquely recalls the significant Pantagruelian implications of carnivalesque bottles. Indeed, its version of foul fairness and fair foulness ambivalently suggests related tropes of doubling self-discovery and self-renewal through pregnant death, what Bakhtin defines as "ambivalent images [that] are dual-bodied, dual-faced, pregnant" (409).

Next, Bakhtin analyzes ambivalently "abusive language as a special genre of billingsgate" (16), the London fish market which featured grotesquely fluid and fertile grammatologies and which sometimes appears in Dickens's novels as in the "old Billingsgate market with its oyster-boats" (*Great Expectations* 413; 54). Jonas, for example, will invoke nay-by-yea ambivalence to keep Mercy in check: "one such threatening affirmative being sufficient, in defiance of English grammar, to express a negative"(601; 41). Seedy Pip further "invented a new oath for the introduction of everything he said" (431; 28), while Montague Tigg characteristically creates carnivalesque praise-abuse heteroglossia as he feels "inspirited to swear a few round oaths, and hum the fag-end of a song" (614; 42). And Tom Pinch reads alphabetized newspaper ads in terms of their amorphous anarchy and self-deconstruction: "Even those letters of the alphabet who are always running away from their friends and being entreated at the tops of columns to come back, never *do* come back, if we may judge from the number of times they are asked to do it, and don't" (536; 36). Playing the Clown in *Hamlet*, who metatextually muses that "An act hath three branches—it is to act, to do, and to perform" (V: i, 11–12), Mark Tapley clarifies, indeed embodies, all these protean and perverse verbal performances as vital speech acts when Tom promises to "swear at" him if Mark doesn't accept his jolly welcome:

> It's a considerable invasion of a man's jollity to be made so partickler welcome, but a Werb is a word as signifies to be, to do, or to suffer (which is all the grammar, and enough too, as ever I wos taught); and if there's a Werb alive; I'm it. For I'm always a bein', sometimes a doin', and continually a sufferin'.
> (687; 48)

As in *Gargantua and Pantagruel*, name games in *Martin Chuzzlewit* are integral to the carnivalesque play with language and identity. For instance, the 104 names of cooks in *Quart Livre* include silly sobriquets like Greedy-gut, Cock-broth, Lick-sauce, Fat-lard, Suck-gravy, Long-tool, and Prick-pride (380; II: iv, 40). Similar "Playful little name[s]" and puns like "Cherrywer-rychigo" (636; 44) appear throughout Dickens's text: for example, *Tigg* is etymologically related to playing *tag*, *Tapley* anticipates Mark's Pantagruelian vocation at the Jolly Tapley's *tap*, and *Gamp*, not only implies game *gams*, but also the fluid *damp* associated with "Mrs Gamp's twofold profession" (402; 26) of sex and death. In this sense, "Gammy" (710; 49) Gamp personifies a venal Venus Geneatrix, the Lady of Misrule whose paradox Julia Kristeva locates at the heart of carnival: "The carnival exteriorizes the structure of reflective literary productivity, then inevitably brings to light this structure's underlying unconscious: sexuality and death" (78). On the other hand, the versatile Bailey Junior is "known by a great variety of names" like Benjamin, Uncle, Uncle Ben, Barnwell, Mr. Pitt, and Young Brownrigg. And in carnivalesque fashion, the motives behind these nominations unite low and high, convict and church goer: "The gentlemen at Todgers's had a merry habit . . . of bestowing upon him, for the time being, the name of any notorious malefactor or minister" (145–46; 9).

Beyond suggesting *chiselers*, *Chuzzlewit* itself may recall the *Guzzlers* repeatedly invoked in Rabelais. In fact, besides devoting entire episodes to diction, like the "Unfrozen Words" chapters in *Quart Livre* and America's developing deconstruction of "the name of Freedom" (345; 21), each text seems in quest of a single word. Again in Rabelais, it appears to be *Trinc*, "*le mot de la dive Bouteille*"; in Dickens, it seems to be *Hypocrite*, as old Martin suggests when he asks, "What signifies that word, Pecksniff? Hypocrite! Why, we are all hypocrites" (123; 8). And *hypocrisy* is a favorite Rabelaisian source of carnivalesque satire as on Hypocrites Island in book 5, and it is homophonically played off against the healer *Hippocrates* who so "inspired" (Screech 430) Rabelais. Still, other words are also nominated; for example, Nadgett correctly insists that plumbing the well of "Truth" invariably "depends on your judgment and construction of it" (556–57; 38)—and so its depths may be Lenten as well as carnivalesque. As Tom tells Cherry when asking for *forgiveness*, "oh can you think, that what I said just now, I said with any but the true and plain intention which my words professed? I mean it, in the spirit and the letter. If I ever offended you, forgive me" (549; 37). Gradually, though, the word search turns more joyfully carnivalesque and seems ultimately complete when Martin and Mark reverse master-servant roles, Martin calling Mark "the best master in the world" and Mark doubly indicating "sharp's the word, and Jolly!" (524; 36).

Lastly, as I have suggested in " 'Playing at Leap-Frog with the Tombstones,' " the paradoxical motif of *pregnant death*, which Bakhtin invokes to thematize so much of the carnivalesque, helps to coordinate much of the above with much that appears below. In fact, after discussing the relevant danse-of-death motif as a "funny monstrosity," Bakhtin adds that "[t]he theme of death as renewal, the combination of death and birth, and the pictures of gay death play an important part in the system of grotesque imagery in Rabelais' novel" (50). In *Martin Chuzzlewit*, pregnant death appears in "the fat atmosphere of funerals" (310; 19) as well as the "new mound" marking the churchyard after old Chuffey's funeral: "Time, burrowing like a mole below the ground, had marked his track by throwing up another heap of earth" (314; 19). In displaced form, it even appears in the "big butts of beer in . . . a cellar" (763; 53) below London's streets as well as in the *danse macabre* "compound figure of Death and the Lady" (343; 21) which resembles "the two profiles of Zephaniah Scadder" (343; 21) in America.

The appropriately named undertaker *Mould* and his family particularly personify this motif, which tends to integrate carnival with Lent, Fat Tuesday with Ash Wednesday, and thus resolve Panurge's liminal worry, "Suppose we find ourselves pent up between the Chitterlings [Carnival] and Shrovetide [Lent]" (346–47; II: iv, 29): "Plump as any partridge was each Miss Mould, and Mrs. M. was plumper than the two together. So round and chubby were their fair proportions that they might have been the bodies once belonging to the angels' faces in the shop below, grown up, with other heads attached to make them mortal." No matter how "large" Mr. Mould's (né Death's) "stock in trade," his daughters could be found "[s]porting behind the scenes of death and burial from cradlehood." And carnivalesque grins can outwit the grim reaper when "from the distant shop a pleasant sound arose of coffin-making" (383–84; 25). But nothing makes the carnivalesque point regarding the cycles of pregnant death more poignantly than the final resurrection of that "clown, *redivivus*" (Pratt 197), Bailey Junior. With his boon companion Poll Sweedlepipe "half-laughing and half-crying" like *democratizing* and *heraclitizing* Gargantua upon the death of his wife and the birth of his son, "a something in top-boots, with its head bandaged up, staggered into the room, and began going round and round and round, apparently under the impression that it was walking straight forward." At once Poll portentously parrots, again "laughing and crying in the same breath," "Here he is! That'll soon wear off, and then he'll be all right again. He's no more dead than I am. He's all alive and hearty. Ain't you, Bailey?" (759–60; 52). Here at last Bailey, like Panurge, seems to have discovered "the first precept of philosophy, which is, *Know thyself*'" (64; II: iii, 25).

II

Albert Guerard echoes the feelings of many readers when he writes that "*Martin Chuzzlewit* begins as badly as any important English novel, with a chapter of random and juvenile garrulity on the forebears of the Chuzzlewits" (239). Nevertheless, the Adamic pedigree, the wordplay, and the "grounds" of (grotesque) knowledge issues all also suggest that Rabelais is a forebear of Dickens since both fiction writers similarly "play very strange and extraordinary tricks" (18; 2) with these carnivalesque motifs.

Returning to Banks's essay, we should note that during a digression on Urquhart (a polymath like Rabelais and Dickens), he cites a commentary which implicitly links Rabelaisiana to Dickens's own "digression" on the Chuzzlewits' descent "in a direct line from Adam and Eve" (15; 1). In fact, Urquhart—like Alcofribas with " 'the genealogy and antiquity of Gargantua' " (Feb. 225)—' "has traced his family descent in an unbroken series up to the red earth, out of which Adam the Protoplas was created' " (Nov. 523). Throughout their texts, both writers play fast and loose with such a quest for utopian and paradisal (or is it dystopic and infernal?) origins. Gargantua's genealogy is grotesquely discovered in a tomb "sealed on the top with the mark of a goblet" and with the inscription "HIC BIBITUR," though "hardly could three letters together there be perfectly discerned" (2–3; I: i, 1). The "ancient origin" of the Adamic Chuzzlewits is also "hardly" traced—through "fragments of correspondence [that] have escaped the ravages of moths"—to "their Great Ancestor" and, by extension, to "the genealogy of every ancient family," the spurious origin of which significantly returns in America's Eden. The "Great Ancestor," however, serially devolves through Cain, William the Conqueror, Guy Fawkes, Lord No Zoo (Lord Knows Who?), to the ultimate "probability of the human race having once been monkeys" (16, 18; 1). In both texts, then, farcical filiation grounds absolute knowledge in grotesque nonsense which, like Jabberwocky, provides an ironic gnostic gospel: "If it came within the scope of reasonable probability that further proofs were required, they might be heaped upon each other until they formed an Alps of testimony beneath which the boldest scepticism should be crushed and beaten flat" (17; 1). Indeed, such sentiments actually invite "the boldest scepticism" about any single branch of knowledge and thereby again echo Rabelais's "great Perhaps." In this sense, one can only "trinc" multiple sources of knowledge, but even more importantly, one must drink the wellsprings of life itself.

Patricia Ingham, editor of the Penquin *Chuzzlewit*, notes many of the name games and word plays in the novel's opening, like, again, the possible pun on the *Chuzzlewits* as *chiselers* (793–94). But I would like to pursue the Rabelaisian significance of just one of these: the extended conceit linking the "Chuzzlewit Fawkes," " 'The Match Maker,' " and the references to "a dark lantern of undoubted antiquity" (14–15; 1). Alan Burke has insightfully discussed the thematic relationships between Fawkes's "Gunpowder Plot and the Great [London] Fire" (34) of 1666, which the Monument by Todgers memorializes and which all "The fire references surrounding Mrs. Gamp" and other characters reinforce, "suggest[ing] that some catastrophe is imminent, that some revelation is at hand" (22). Such suggestions may immediately recall all Rabelais's apocalyptic references to fire, especially Friar John's portentous advice to Panurge regarding his fear of drowning: "I pray thee never be afraid of water; thy life . . . art threatened with a contrary element" (328; II: iv, 24), that is, fire, and *Tiers Livre*'s ultimate account of the magical "Herb Named Pantagruelion" (chs. 49–52) and how this all-thirsty "Asbeston" will "not only not be consumed nor burnt" (206; II: iii, 52), but will also provide protection against soul-consuming fire.

At the same time, *Quart Livre*'s related account of the voyage to Lanternland is sprinkled with references to (black and white) magical lanterns, of which Kinser writes "Such divergent references to Lanterners and lanternizing are Rabelais's way of communicating different perspectives upon one verbal sign by juxtaposing the points of view of author, narrator, and narrative actor'' regarding issues as diverse as Carnival, the Council of Trent, any "dreamy trust" in human institutions, and even penises, for which "lanterning" is "a slang word" (71). Read within this Rabelaisian context, the Chuzzlewit genealogy not only previews the polysemy of coming carnivalesque attractions in the text, but also implies that "Pantagruelism" can prevent a London holocaust of the soul, which symptomatic Chuzzlewit concupiscence portends—especially when old Martin suspects young Martin to be another Guy Fawkes and so intones "A new plot; a new plot! Oh self, self, self! At every turn, nothing but self!" as he scatters "the ashes of the burnt [will leaving his money to Martin] in the candlestick" (51; 3).

Ever since an early British review of *Chuzzlewit* labeled the American episodes an "unaccountable excrescence" (Monod 51), these eight chapters (15–17, 21–23, 33–34) have provided a rallying call for subsequent supporters and detractors alike. Unexpectedly, Banks's essay on which Dickens collaborated, like modern supporters, addresses America as a kind of photographic (and Rabelaisian?) negative of Europe: "I go to America, and there I find a visible and living history, and map of European civilization" where a typical citizen like "An American judge . . . . curses, draws his knife to call counsel to order, squats himself on the bench, with his heels flung aloft—spits, smokes, and drinks brandy, in the judgment-seat" (Nov. 527). Such a representation immediately recalls Dickens's own (in)famous representations of America in his letters, *American Notes* (1842), and *Martin Chuzzlewit*, where citizens like Hannibal Chollop characteristically swill sherry-cobblers, spit, shoot, and slash with Bowie knives and "sword-sticks"—"Rippers" and "Ticklers" for "the gratification of [their] tickling and ripping fancies" (492–93; 33) as they dole out hypothetical frontier injustice. More to the point, Alice Fiola Berry's response to Foucault's response to *Don Quixote* (and, comparatively, to *Gargantua and Pantagruel*) could just as well describe Dickens's response to *Quart Livre* since both Pantagruel and Panurge and Martin and Mark ultimately travel to "the Far West" (262; 16):

> Could not [Foucault's] description be applied, word for word to Rabelais's *Quart livre*? His characters, too, confront the ruins of lost identities—those terrible islands. His odyssey also functions as an ongoing dialectic between a master and a servant who are "seekers" [endnote omitted]. Their psychology launches them on a quest to recover or to discover life's lost totality. And, if Rabelais does not perceive that totality "bookishly," he surely perceives it verbally. His characters pursue a Word, "le mot de la dive Bouteille." On this Word he envisions the establishment of a new Eden, "Jardin et Paradis terrestre" (Ch.lvii), where the writer as Adam, will dispense original, appropriate names to creation, where words and things will once again blissfully coincide.   (472).

The seasoning process that Martin suffers in "edenic" America as he loses and rediscovers both his identity and ''life's totality'' is suggested here, as is the reversibility of the master/servant dialectic or dialogic. And, again, Dickens likewise stages a quest for the carnivalesque ''Word,'' which in *Chuzzlewit* ultimately becomes *Jolly* personified in Mark, especially in America. Further, the Foucault reference also recalls his concept of the *heterotopia*, which is related to Bakhtin's notion of the *heteroglossia*. Like Bakhtin with the carnivalesque, Foucault opposes the ''hierarchized ensemble of places'' in ''medieval space'' with *other*, more playful ''emplacements,'' especially *utopias*, or ''emplacements having no real place'' and *heterotopias*, or ''actually realized utopias,'' both of which, like both Pantagruel's native land ''of Utopia'' (391; I: ii, 29) and the Subterranean Temple and like both Todgers and utopian/dystopic America, ''have the curious property of being connected to all the other emplacements'' (176–78). Foucault further maps so-called *heterotopias of illusion* and *compensation*, the first of which ''denounces all real space, all real emplacements within which human life is partitioned off,'' the second of which creates ''a different real space as perfect, as meticulous, as well-arranged as [the heterotopia of illusion] is disorganized, badly arranged, and muddled.'' Although for Foucault, the ''first wave'' of American colonies represents these ''absolutely perfect places'' (184), in *Chuzzlewit*, the contrast between Phiz's illustrated and mapped ''thriving City of Eden, as it appeared on paper'' (339; 21), and his illustrated and muddled ''thriving City of Eden, as it appeared in fact'' (365; 23), suggests that Dickens's America—like his England—dialogically teeters somewhere betwixt and between *illusion* and *compensation*.

The ''Spirit searching'' Idealism of the ''two L.L's'' (Literary Ladies) puts it only slightly differently and suggests the Carnival-Lent combat by *grotesquely* parodying Emerson's operational definition of Transcendentalism in ''Nature'' (1836) as one negotiating ''[t]his relation between the mind and matter'' (20). '' 'Mind and matter,' said the lady in the wig, 'glide swift into the vortex of immensity. Howls the sublime, and softly sleeps in the calm Ideal, in the whispering chambers of Imagination. To hear it, sweet it is. But then, outlaughs the stern philosopher, and saith to the Grotesque, 'What ho! Arrest for me that Agency. Go bring it here!' And so the vision fadeth'' (512–13; 34). Again, the point involves ''Grotesque'' grounds of knowledge and grounding grotesque knowledge issues. And Dickens's subversive (per)-version of America appears more Thoreauvian than Emersonian, more the ''Philosophy of Matter'' than the ''Philosophy of the Soul'' (284; 17), as it gnostically celebrates matter over mind in Eden's Underworld or ''underwood: not divisible into their separate kinds, but tangled all together in a heap; a jungle deep and dark, with neither earth nor water at its roots, but putrid matter, formed of the pulpy offal of the two, and of their own corruption.'' Here, the trees, ''forced into shapes of strange distortion'' (363; 23), suggest a carnivalization of space or what Bakhtin terms *gay matter*, a patch-work medley that's "neither earth nor water" but an uncategorizable, promis-cuous mixture of both like America's "wonderful invention" of "Sherry cobbler" (287; 17) or the *tripe* image in Rabelais.

Involving "obsessive [word] play" (Newman 120), Dickens's more recur-ring name for America's "crop of vegetable rottenness" (486; 33), though, is *slime*, which, with typical Rabelaisian antonomasia (45; II: iii, 22) or interchange between proper and common nouns, he puns with the British Chevy *Slyme*, "the American aloe of the human race" (113; 7). And, indeed, one can read "foul slime" (501; 33) as the defining mark of American democracy which homogenizes heteroglossia and difference so that General Fladdock appears decarnivalized "like a dead Clown" (280; 17): cloned Americans "did the same things; said the same things; judged all subjects by, and reduced all subjects to, the same standard" (335; 21). Or like Sairey Gamp, one can read "slime drafts" (440; 29) as possibly spiritual or spiritous restoratives which signify fortunate falls to the American Underworld, thus prompting the genuine "regeneration of man" from his "primeval state" (334; 21). In either case, Mr. Bevan's charge that no "Juvenal or Swift" or other "satirist could breathe" American "air" is countered by Dickens's own brand of Mennippean satire; and Victorians like Besant clearly under-stood that "La Satyre Ménippée" was, indeed, carnivalesque "after the man-ner of Rabelais" (*French Humorists* 148).

Finally, the double *spirits* of Sairey Gamp have intoxicated and inspired our entire discussion, and so it has proved impossible to keep her silent until this last gasp. In fact, her spirits paradoxically embody Rabelaisian grave and gay matter as, again, "she went to a lying in or a laying-out with equal zest and relish" (303; 10). Like midwife Sally Thingummy and the other "bab-bling drabs" (397; 51) in *Oliver Twist*, Sairey particularly personifies the relevant Rabelaisian motif of *caquets* or the "female chatter" of midwives "gathering at the bedside of a woman recovering from childbirth. The tradi-tion of such gatherings is very old." And as with Sairey and Betsey's table talks, "they were marked by abundant food and frank conversation, at which social conventions were dropped" (Bakhtin 105). In Rabelais, such "mid-wives" preside over Badebec's delivery of "great loads of gammons of bacon" (besides the baby giant Pantagruel himself) as they drink both "la-zily" and "lustily" (237–38; I: ii, 2). Later, at the "Queendom of Whims" in book 5, such "old, weather-beaten, over-ridden, toothless, blear-eyed, tough, wrinkled, shrivelled, tawny, mouldy, phthysiky, decrepit hags" are literally reborn and "made young again . . . , recovering at once the beauty, shape, size, and disposition which they enjoyed at sixteen" (587; II: v, 21). And Mrs. Gamp's repeated connections with self-renewing food, drink, and "wales" similarly promise her (and life's) eternal return.

For instance, Sairey's figurative association with "The Philosophy of Vegetables" (284; 17), particulary her talismanic "nightcap, of prodigious size,
in shape resembling a cabbage" (394; 25), recalls the alchemist at the Queendom of Whims who holds an equally talismanic "doctor's cap" in one hand
and a "huge cabbage-stump" (572–73; II: v, 18) in the other, the former of
which functions as a kind of fountain of youth, the latter as a transforming
philosopher's stone. And it's not just that the magical "bottle on the chimley-
piece" with its "little sip of liquor" lends Sairey spiritual and spiritous
"nerve" (303–04; 19), it's also that her trademark "tea-pot," the talismanic
holy grail or *Dive Bouteille* of the British Empire, is even more rich in
"spiritual" and "spiritous" resources "as if it were a talisman against all
earthly sorrows" (711; 49). In fact, outside of the mad tea party in Wonder-
land, never in English literature has such a tea service been so wonderfully
performed as Sairey's miraculous tea-time symposium for those gathering
around Old Chuffey's sick-bed, which "ministration" finally "restored her
to herself" (662; 46).

The matter of "earthly sorrows" again recalls Sairey's famous Rabelaisian
"Philosophy of Matter": "what a blessed thing it is—living in a wale—to
be contented!" (393; 25)—*Rabelaisian* because this "Piljian's Projiss of a
mortal wale" (385; 25) or "travell[ing] into this wale of life" is also imaginatively related to "Jonadage's belly, . . . appearing to confound the prophet
with the whale in this miraculous aspiration" (588; 40). In this sense and
beyond Joseph Gold's insightful reading of the "Living in a Wale" image,
Sairey's *wale* seems clearly related to the related *vale/whale* word play in
Motteux's translation of Rabelais, where Panurge's comically cruel drowning
of Dingdong and his sheep is satirically presented as a viable alternative to
"living in this vale of misery." That is, Dingdong "might have the good
luck to meet with some kind of whale which might set them ashore safe and
sound, on some land of Gotham, after a famous example," namely, as explained in the note citing Rabelais's original French, "*l'example de Jonas*"
(268; II: iv, 8).

It seems to me, then, that Jonathan Arac's perceptive reading of the crucial
"decrowning of the king of carnival, the Lord of Misrule" implicitly clarifies
"Gammy" Gamp's role as the queen of carnival, the Lady of Misrule, and
at the same time helps satisfy my initial dissatisfaction with old Martin's
rejection of her by reinforcing the Rabelaisian context of her promised rebirth
after a period of Lenten "sadness":

> In full carnival festivities the primary performance is the mock crowning and
> subsequent uncrowning of the king of carnival, the Lord of Misrule, who over-
> sees sexual license and alcoholic indulgence. In this cyclical process the pathos
> within the jollity becomes evident, the sadness of vicissitude and death as well
> as the promise of change and renewal. . . . [Carnival] is thus hostile to any final
> ending. Every end is only a new beginning, for the carnival images are born
> and reborn again and again.   (487)

Whether one agrees with post-Bakhtinians like Kinser that Rabelais dialogically dramatizes an equal and eternal contest between Lent and carnival, or whether one more optimistically holds, perhaps with Bahktin himself, that Carnival absorbs both Lenten "sadness" and carnival "jollity"—but like Mark Tapley, tips the tap decidedly in favor of the latter—the Truth always already resides in the "great Perhaps" or at least rests at the bottom of a bottomless well. What seems certain, though, is that after her "uncrowning" and fortunate fall, Sairey Gamp, like Bailey Junior, will rise again to return eternally since "the greatest treasures, and most admirable things, are hidden underground." In this sense, Sairey perhaps most recalls the references to Proserpine (an earth diver and heaven climber like Christ) at the end of *Gargantua and Pantagruel* when Friar John and Panurge indulge in dueling, dialogic rhyming. Panurge's coupling couplet proclaims that the good Friar shall end up in a Rablelaisian hell which dovetails sex and death: "E'en there, I know, thou'lt play some trick,/And Proserpine shan't scape a prick" (677; II: 5, 54). But better yet is Alcofribas's own grotesque prophecy "forseeing that Proserpine would meet with more excellent things, more desirable enjoyments, below, than she her mother could be blessed with above" (682; II: 5, 57). This Rabelaisian view from the backside also gloriously promises the same grotesque enjoyments both for Mrs. Gamp and for the reader of *Martin Chuzzlewit*.

WORKS CITED

Arac, Jonathan. "The Form of Carnival in *Under the Volcano*." *PMLA* 92 (1977): 481–89.

Auerbach, Erich. *Mimesis: The Representation of Reality in Western Literature*. Trans. William Trask. Garden City: Doubleday, 1957.

Bakhtin, Mikhail Mikhailovich. *Rabelais and His World*. Trans. Hélène Iswolsky. Forward Krystyna Pomorska. Cambridge: MIT Press, 1968.

Banks, P. W. "Of Rabelais." *Fraser's Magazine* 20 (Nov. 1839): 513–29; 21 (Feb. 1840): 212–27; 21 (July 1840): 60–80.

Berry, Alice Fiola. " 'Les Mithologies Pantagruelicques': Introduction to a Study of Rabelais's *Quart livre*." *PMLA* 92 (1977): 471–80.

Besant, Walter. *The Autobiography of Walter Besant*. London: Hutchinson, 1902.

———. *The French Humorists From the Twelfth to the Nineteenth Century*. Boston: Roberts Brothers, 1877.

Bernstein, Michael André. *Bitter Carnival:* Ressentiment *and the Abject Hero.* Princeton: Princeton UP, 1992.

Bowen, John. *Other Dickens: From Pickwick to Chuzzlewit.* Oxford: Oxford UP, 2000.

Burke, Alan R. "The House of Chuzzlewit and the Architectural City." *Dickens Studies Annual: Essays on Victorian Fiction* 3 (1974): 14–40, 232–33.

Crotch, Walter W. *The Pageant of Dickens.* New York: Haskell House, 1972.

Churchill, R. C. "Charles Dickens." *From Dickens to Hardy.* vol. 6. *The Pelican Guide to English Literature.* Ed. Boris Ford. Middlesex: Penguin, 1958. 119–43.

Dickens, Charles. *A Christmas Carol.* London: Penguin, 1984.

———. *The Oxford Illustrated Dickens.* 21 vols. London: Oxford UP, 1951–59.

———. *The Letters of Charles Dickens.* 11 vols. to date. Eds. Madeline House, Graham Storey, and Kathleen Tillotson. Oxford: Clarendon, 1965–.

———. *The Life and Adventures of Martin Chuzzlewit.* Ed., intro, and annotat. Patricia Ingham. London: Penguin, 1999.

———. *Our Mutual Friend.* Ed. and intro. Stephen Gill. Harmondsworth, Middlesex: Penguin, 1977.

Eagleton, Terry. "Ideology and Literary Form: Charles Dickens." *Charles Dickens.* Ed and intro. Steven Connor. London: Longman, 1996. 151–58.

Eco, Umberto. "The Frames of Comic 'Freedom.' " *Carnival.* Ed. Thomas A. Sebeok. Approaches to Semiotics 64. Berlin: Mouton, 1984. 1– 9.

Eigner, Edwin M. *The Dickens Pantomime.* Berkeley: U of California P, 1989.

Emerson, Ralph Waldo. "Nature." *Selected Prose and Poetry.* Intro. Reginald L. Cook. New York: Holt, 1966. 3–46.

Foucault, Michel. "Different Spaces." *Aesthetics, Method, And Epistemology. Essential Works of Foucault 1954–1984.* vol 2. Ed. James D Faubion. Trans. Robert Hurley, et al. New York: New Press, 1998. 175–85.

Gissing, George. *Charles Dickens: A Critical Study.* London: Blackie, 1898.

Gold, Joseph. " 'Living in a Wale': *Martin Chuzzlewit. Dickens Studies Annual: Essays on Victorian Fiction* 2 (1972): 150–62, 362.

Guerard, Albert J. *The Triumph of the Novel: Dickens, Dostoevsky, Faulkner.* New York: Oxford UP, 1976.

Heath, Michael J. *Rabelais.* Tempe, Arizona: Medieval & Renaissance Texts & Studies, 1996.

Hennelly, Mark M., Jr. "Carnivalesque 'Unlawful Games' in *The Old Curiosity Shop.*" *Dickens Studies Annual: Essays on Victorian Fiction* 22 (1993): 67–120.

———. "Courtly Wild Men and Carnivalesque Pig Women in Dickens and Hardy." *Dickens Studies Annual: Essays on Victorian Fiction* 26 (1998): 1–32.

———. " 'Playing at Leap-Frog with the Tombstones': The *Danse Macabre* Motif in Dickens." *Essays in Literature* 22 (1995): 227–43.

———. "Victorian Carnivalesque." *Victorian Literature and Culture* 30 (2002): 365–81.

Ingham, Patricia. "Annotations." *The Life and Adventures of Martin Chuzzlewit.* 793–94.

Kincaid, James R. " 'All the Wickedness in the World is Print': Dickens and Subversive Interpretation." *Victorian Literature and Society: Essays Presented to Richard D. Altick.* Ed. James R. Kincaid and Albert J. Kuhn. Columbus: Ohio UP, 1984. 258–75.

———. *Dickens and the Rhetoric of Laughter.* Oxford: Clarendon, 1971.

Kinser, Samuel. *Rabelais Carnival: Text, Context, Metatext.* Berkeley: U of California P, 1990.

Kristeva. Julia. *Desire in Language: A Semiotic Approach to Literature.* Ed. Leon S. Roudiez. Trans. Thomas Gora, Alice Jardine, and Leon S. Roudiez. New York: Columbia UP, 1980.

Lougy, Robert E. "Repressive and Expressive Forms: The Bodies of Comedy and Desire in *Martin Chuzzlewit.*" *Dickens Studies Annual: Essays on Victorian Fiction* 21 (1992): 37–61.

Marcus, Steven. *Dickens from Pickwick to Dombey.* New York: Simon and Schuster, 1968.

Monod, Sylvère. *Martin Chuzzlewit.* London: Allen & Unwin, 1985.

Newman, S. J. "*Martin Chuzzlewit*: the Novel as Play." *Dickens at Play New York:* St. Martin's, 1981. 101–23.

Polhemus, Robert M. *Comic Faith: The Great Tradition from Austen to Joyce.* Chicago and London: Chicago UP, 1980.

Pratt, Branwen Bailey. "Dickens and Freedom: Young Bailey in *Martin Chuzzlewit.*" *Nineteenth-Century Fiction* 30 (1975): 185–99.

Rabelais, François. *The Complete Works of Doctor François Rabelais Abstractor of the Quintessence Being an Account of the Inestimable Life of the Great Gargantua, and of the Heroic Deeds, Sayings and Marvellous Voyages of his Son the Good*

Pantagruel. Trans. Sir Thomas Urquhart and Peter Motteux. Intro. J. Lewis May. Illus. Frank C. Papé. 2 vols. London: John Lane and the Bodley Head Ltd., 1927.

Schlicke, Paul. *Dickens and Popular Entertainment.* London: Allen, 1985.

Screech, M. A. *Rabelais.* Ithaca: Cornell UP, 1979.

Shakespeare, William. *Hamlet.* Eds. Louis B. Wright and Virginia A. LeMar. The Folger Library General Reader's Shakespeare. New York: Washington Square Press, 1973.

Stonehouse, J. H. *Catalogue of the Library of Charles Dickens from Gadshill, Catalogue of His Pictures and Objects of Art, Catalogue of the Library of W. M. Thackeray, and Relics from His Library.* London: Piccadilly Fountain, 1935.

Trollope, Anthony. *The Warden.* New York: George Macy, 1955.

Van Ghent, Dorothy. ''The Dickens World: A View from Todgers's.'' *Sewanee Review* 58 (1950): 419–38.

Lighthousekeeping: *Bleak House* and the Crystal Palace

Robert Tracy

Esther Summerson is the housekeeper at Bleak House and the partial narrator of Bleak House. *Her duties are to order Jarndyce's house and Dickens's novel. Like Mrs. Rouncewell at Chesney Wold, she also catalogues the contents of the house of fiction she controls, and on occasion exhibits them by bringing us into the presence of the other narrative voice. Esther shepherds the reader as he/she confronts the evils of contemporary England presented by that other, unnamed reader: Chancery, Tom-All-Alone's, the disease-breeding graveyard. With* Bleak House *Dickens answers his own call, in* Household Words, *for "a great exhibition of England's sins and negligence" to set beside the Great Exhibition of industrial and material progress that was displayed in the Crystal Palace, and so reminds his readers of the need for comparable social and political progress.*

> Now it came to pass in the days of Ahasuerus
> ... in the third year of his reign ... he shewed
> the riches of his glorious kingdom and the hon-
> our of his excellent majesty many days ...
>
> Esther 1.1–4
>
> "I am in the first throes of a new book, and
> am spasmodically altering and arranging a new
> house besides ..."
>
> Dickens to the duke of Devonshire,
> 28 September 1851

Dickens Studies Annual, Volume 33, Copyright © 2003 by AMS Press, Inc. All rights reserved.

In chapter 36 of *Bleak House*—the first chapter of the twelfth number—Esther performs and describes a series of characteristic acts. She is at Boythorn's house near Chesney World, recuperating after her illness. She narrates the chapter, thus carrying out one of her principal functions in the novel, that of writing about her own adventures, observations, and feelings, and those of her associates. Temporarily relieved of her housekeeping duties at Bleak House, she creates similar duties for herself at Boythorn's house, which he has turned over to her for her convalescence. And she continues her housekeeping duties toward *Bleak House* the novel, narrating and controlling the narrative, and so keeping Dickens's house of fiction in order and smoothly functioning.

Arriving at Boythorn's house, prepared for her as "If a good fairy had built the house for me with a wave of her wand" (36: 444)—a hint that she is in a kind of palace of the imagination, which *Bleak House* is—her first act is to write a narrative of her journey for Ada. Her next act is to tour the house and examine the "many preparations . . . made for me" and to note the "endearing remembrance . . . shown of all my little tastes and likings." She then conducts Charley on a tour of the house, enjoying her maid's "delight" and exhaustion of "her whole vocabulary of admiring expressions."

The tour done, she turns again to written narration. She writes a note of thanks to Boythorn—in her written narration that is *Bleak House* she narrates the writing of another narration. Her "little note" to Boythorn contains a catalogue of the house's splendors: "I wrote . . . telling him how all his favourite plants and trees were looking." As is Esther's habit, this catalogue turns into a narrative, complete with a little mystifying or limiting of what can be told; she tells Boythorn "how the most astonishing of birds had chirped the honours of the house to me in the most hospitable manner, and how, after singing on my shoulder, to the inconceivable rapture of my little maid, he was then at roost in the usual corner of his cage, but whether dreaming or no I could not report."

All this precedes her moment of self-examination in the mirror, when she confronts the changes wrought by her illness. As usual, Esther leaves her personal issues and crises until last. The mirror shows her to herself with an unfamiliar face, in a moment of self-scrutiny that is also an encounter with a stranger, a face at once her own and not her own. She studies the changes until they "became more familiar" (445), and accepts them. Though "never . . . a beauty," she tells us, she "had been very different from this." The change has erased her past—that betraying resemblance to Lady Dedlock, her only legacy—and robbed her of her future, since she decides that she can no longer hope for Allan Woodcourt's love. Her time before the mirror is pure present, a single static moment created by the glass artifice.

A few pages later, Esther is to have her emotional reunion with Lady Dedlock, and learn that Lady Dedlock is her mother. But before she writes about that, she writes again about her own activities as a writer. She tells us how she writes "long letters to Ada every day," and even becomes a writer-illustrator by writing a letter for an old woman to an absent grandson, drawing

> at the top of it the chimney-corner in which she had brought him up, and where his old stool yet occupied its old place. This was considered by the whole village the most wonderful achievement in the world . . . an answer came back all the way from Plymouth, in which he mentioned that he was going to take the picture all the way to America, and from America would write again.
>
> (36: 446–47)

Esther's letter is at once a narrative and an illustrated catalogue to part of the old woman's tiny cottage. A little later, she catalogues the contents of Mr. Grubble's parlor:

> a neat carpeted room, with more plants in it than were quite convenient, a coloured print of Queen Caroline, several shells, a good many tea-trays, two stuffed and dried fish in glass cases, and either a curious egg or a curious pumpkin (but I don't know which, and I doubt if many people did) hanging from his ceiling.   (37: 458)

A few pages more, and she records Mr. Skimpole's descriptive catalogue of the family portraits at Chesney Wold:

> There were such portentous shepherdesses among the Ladies Dedlock dead and gone, he told us, that peaceful crooks became weapons of assault in their hands. They tended their flocks severely in buckram and powder, and put their sticking-plaster patches on to terrify commoners . . . There was a Sir Somebody Dedlock, with a battle, a sprung-mine, volumes of smoke, flashes of lightning, a town on fire, and a stormed fort, all in full action between his horse's two hind legs: showing, he supposed, how little a Dedlock made of such trifles. The whole race he represented, as having evidently been, in life, what he called 'stuffed people,'—a large collection, glassy eyed, set up in the most approved manner on their various twigs and perches, very correct, perfectly free from animation, and always in glass cases.   (37: 468–69)

These are by no means Esther's first catalogues. Arriving at Bleak House by night, she almost immediately offers a description of the house's interior and an inventory of its contents, from the "Native-Hindoo chair, which was also a sofa, a box, and a bedstead" to "real trout in a case . . . the death of Captain Cook," and "the whole process of preparing tea in China, as depicted by Chinese artists" (6: 116). Next morning, she itemizes the things she can see from her window (8: 85).

Esther has already been appointed housekeeper of Bleak House. Jarndyce sends the household keys—with all their phallic implications—to her bedroom on her first night, making her mistress of Bleak House and hinting at his plan to make her his wife. She half-senses his intention, and, not surprisingly, the keys enter her dreams, in a passage Dickens removed from proofs. "I was in such a flutter about my two bunches of keys that I had been dreaming for an hour before I got up," she tells us, "that the more I tried to open a variety of locks with them, the more determined they were not to fit any. No dream could have been less prophetic" (*Bleak House,* Textual Notes, 825).

On that first morning, she is "dressed before daylight" to watch the darkness withdraw, a process she compares to her own "memory over my life" and so implicitly to her own task as narrator/cataloguer of *Bleak House.* Her description prefigures the novel's gradual dissipation of mysteries, its processes of discovery and clarification, and celebrates the coming of light: "the dark places in my room all melted away, and the day shone bright upon a cheerful landscape." Then she opens all the locked cupboards and storerooms and makes an inventory of their contents. She also gives her first order, telling the gardener to roll the drive in order to obliterate the marks made by the carriage in which she arrived (8: 85–86). She deliberately obliterates the traces of her own past. Later she determinedly evades her own genealogical past, as Mr. Jarndyce evades the lawsuit which represents the destructive past of the Jarndyce family.

When she prepares for Caddy Jellyby's wedding, Esther does so by excavating and destroying the past of the Jellyby family:

> Caddy and I were attempting to establish some order among all this waste and ruin . . . such wonderful things came tumbling out of the closets when they were opened—bits of mouldy pie, sour bottles, Mrs. Jellyby's caps, letters, tea, forks, odd boots and shoes of children, firewood, wafers, saucepan-lids, damp sugar in odds and ends of paper bags, footstools, blacklead brushes, bread, Mrs. Jellyby's bonnets, books with butter sticking to the binding, guttered candle-ends put out by being turned upside down in broken candlesticks, nutshells, heads and tails of shrimps, dinner-mats, gloves, coffee-grounds, umbrellas.
>
> (30: 373)

The Jellyby past, which is ruin and confusion—" 'Ma' is ruinous to everything,' " Caddy exclaims—must be destroyed to create Caddy's future. Mr. Krook's shop burns, and Lady Dedlock's letter about Esther's past must be burned (36: 453). The past must be suppressed to create the future.

Esther's inventories or catalogues are often associated with a repudiation of the past, and are thus central to her role in the novel as housekeeper narrator. She writes of herself writing an inventory of Bleak House, and her completed narrative is an inventory of *Bleak House* the novel, as she brings before us the various characters and locales of the story, orchestrates their appearances, and links them together. At the same time, she offers us an inventory of contemporary England's social failures and their roots in an inability to change the forms and usages of the past.

Esther's functions of housekeeping and cataloguing are linked, and are among the duties of a housekeeper. A housekeeper must list and describe the objects under her charge; she must keep them in order; and she is also responsible for guiding others among them and presenting them in coherent narrative form. Dickens reminds us that housekeepers are cataloguers and guides in chapter 7, when Mrs. Rouncewell conducts Mr. Guppy and Mr. Jobling on a tour of the house at Chesney Wold and listens "with stately approval to Rosa's exposition" of the house's splendors. Rosa deputizes for Mrs. Rouncewell, explaining the uses of the various rooms and pointing out the most valuable items, identifying the subjects of the portraits, and guiding the viewer's responses: Lady Dedlock's portrait'' 'is considered a perfect likeness,' '' the terrace called " 'The Ghost's Walk' '' is " 'much admired' '' (7: 81–82). That chapter, and the tour it describes, occurring "While Esther sleeps and while Esther wakes'' (7: 76), is interposed between Esther's first tour of Bleak House and her second more formal inventory.

Touring, cataloguing, guiding, narrating, writing. *Bleak House*, as J. Hillis Miller has pointed out, is a text about texts, full of readers and writers (*Victorian Subjects* 179–88). But it is a special kind of text, written by a housekeeper who is keeping both the fictional Bleak House and the fiction that is *Bleak House* in order. As a housekeeper's narrative, it is shaped by a commitment to ordering chaos, and Esther deals with the events of her story as she dealt with Bleak House, by creating a catalogue or inventory. It also contains that guiding and explaining element that Mrs. Rouncewell delegates to Rosa. *Bleak House* the novel is in fact an inventory and guide to an exhibition of what is wrong with contemporary England: the neglect and ignorance of the poor, unsanitary slums which breed disease, irrelevant projects for reform, the inefficiencies and cruelties of Chancery.

Dickens probably had many models for *Bleak House* as guide or catalogue, but there are three that seem particularly influential in shaping his approach to his narrator and her material. One is the format of parts publication itself, as employed for *Bleak House* and other Dickens novels, which placed the chapters comprising each part between many pages of advertisements, presenting a kind of exhibition of new books, devices, and services, which constitute a guide to the preoccupations and aspirations of contemporary England: the House of Things. The second is another enterprise which occupied Dickens before, during, and after the writing of *Bleak House*, his journal *Household Words,* itself a verbal exhibit of new inventions, new ideas, exotic places, and old abuses: the House of Words. Finally, and most important, there was the most conspicuous event of the early eighteen-fifties, the Great Exhibition of 1851, formally "The Great Exhibition of the Works of Industry of all

Nations, 1851'' (Gibbs-Smith 32), which celebrated the technological wonders of the new machine age in a structure of iron and glass that was itself a
technological wonder, Sir Joseph Paxton's Crystal Palace- the House of Light.

Dickens's uneasiness about the triumphalism of the Great Exhibition seems
to have been a major element in shaping *Bleak House* and determining both
its themes and its form. Against the Crystal Palace he sets up ''Bleak
House''—not Mr. Jarndyce's cheerful residence, but the novel *Bleak House*
itself, presented both as a House of Darkness—''a great display of England's
sins and negligences'' (*DJ* 2. 313) which call out for a committed housekeeper—and as a kind of lighthouse, warning England of the shoals and
wrecks which may destroy her in all her triumphant pride of industry and
science.

The novel, then, is at once a work of fiction and a critical guide to contemporary reality, in Dickens's phrase ''in part forensic and in part romantic''
(39: 491). Fiction and reality become each other's context and continually
invoke once another. This deliberate division of purpose is characteristic
of Dickens, whose novels often comment on contemporary issues. Here he
emphasizes the division not only by the conventional device of contrasting
rich and poor, generous and selfish, but by the novel's divided narration. At
the same time, these divisions unite in the achieved structure of the work
itself. It is less a division than a pairing, two voices, two pictures placed side
by side to reinforce and comment upon one another.

Phiz made this paired aspect of the novel graphic through a convention of
serial publication in parts, by which the two plates normally accompanying
each number preceded the text and faced one another. So placed, the plates
could sometimes be used to comment on one another (readers who later had
the parts bound were advised to insert the plates into the text, as close as
possible to the scene depicted). Pairs of mutually commenting plates are
common in Bleak House. In Part XVI, for example, the left hand plate is
entitled ''Light'' and the right hand plate ''Shadow.'' In each plate, a printed
and posted legal document is at the center, and is out of place: a legal calendar
over Richard Carstone's fireplace, the reward poster on Sir Leicester's stair-
case. In Part XVIII, the left hand plate, ''The Night,'' confronts ''The Morning,'' both plates black in mood and black in execution.

Other contrasts are more subtle. For Part II, Coavins's man, an intruder
ostentatiously out of place in the pretty Bleak House parlor (left plate), is set
against Esther in Krook's squalid shop, where she clearly does not belong.
Mr. Chadband strikes an attitude over Jo in VIII (left); facing him, Mr.
Turveydrop strikes another attitude as he graciously permits Prince and Caddy
to marry. Both men exist only as posed stances, empty words, and voracious
appetites, and the placement of the plates emphasizes their similarity. The
left plate for Part XVII depicts a prison cell, but it is full of light, and

the scene—Mrs. Bagnet reuniting Mrs. Rouncewell with George—celebrates motherly love, in contrast to the very dark facing print, "The Lonely Figure," a mother fleeing through a bleak landscape because her motherhood is her disgrace.

The plates establish a visual context for each other. Text and plates establish each other's context. And the two narrating voices, Esther's and her unidentified collaborator's, also establish each other's context. Phiz's plates have often been praised for their fidelity to Dickens's intentions. In this novel especially, their conventional placement becomes a way of reinforcing the novel's narrative form and its content, that bringing of "squalor among the upper classes" (12: 149) which Sir Leicester so much deplores. Jo does not belong at Bleak House, and yet he does. Lady Dedlock does not belong at the squalid graveyard where Hawdon lies buried, and yet she does—and she is at once Lady Dedlock, her own maid, and a mysterious stranger. Later she is at once Lady Dedlock, the brickmaker's wife Jenny, and a lonely fugitive.

Dickens continually manipulates these incongruities or uncertainties to question identities or stability. Esther is at once a young woman and "Old Woman . . . Little Old Woman . . . Mother Hubbard, and Dame Durden, and so many names of that sort, that my own name soon became quite lost among them" (8: 90). Hallucinating during her fever, she can discern "little or no separation between the various stages of my life which had been really divided by years . . . At once a child, an elder girl, and the little woman I had been so happy as, I was not only oppressed by cares and difficulties adapted to each station, but by the great perplexity of endlessly trying to reconcile them" (35: 431).

We can glimpse other contexts within the text, for many of the characters appear trailing clouds of story. The great case of Jarndyce and Jarndyce is one. We never fully understand the case or its issues, but it controls the lives of some of the characters, or threatens to do so. Mr. Jarndyce and his benevolence exist in contrast to and in the context of Tom Jarndyce, who blew out his brains after allowing himself to be entangled in the suit, and in the context of all those others who have been attracted, ensnared, and devoured by Chancery. Tom Jarndyce's story is but one of the many half-glimpsed stories—dimly perceived alternate novels—which shape the characters and events of the novel we are reading. What was the love story of Honoria and Captain Hawdon? Of Boythorn's thwarted love for the other Miss "Barbary"? Jo's story stretches further back than we can see, a grim alternative version of *Oliver Twist* or *David Copperfield.* There is a hidden tale of military life in Trooper George, an odyssey in Mrs. Bagnet's journey from "another quarter of the world—with nothing but a grey cloak and an umbrella—to make [her] way home to Europe' " (27: 343). We have the cloak and the umbrella, but not the story. Again and again we glance down an enticing narrative vista, but Dickens calls us away. There are more stories than even he can tell, but he continually invokes them as context for the story he does tell. As on a guided tour of a rich museum, we are hurried past exhibits we would like to examine more closely, and connect to one another.

These tantalizing internal contexts are matched by external contexts for *Bleak House*. Dickens's use of current events and issues in his novels is well known: workhouse reform in *Oliver Twist*, the scandal of the Yorkshire schools in *Nicholas Nickeby*. *Bleak House* is rich in contemporary issues. Mrs. Pardiggle, with her sons named after Saxon saints, is a negative commentary on the Oxford Movement of Pusey and Newman. Guster has survived the notorious "baby farm" at Tooting, where the proprietor, Drouet, let 150 children die of cholera in 1849 (10: 117). Mrs. Jellyby's Borrioboola-Gha project recalls an 1840s expedition to establish English settlers on the Upper Niger (House 86-88). Mrs. Bagnet's virtues contrast with the contemporary notion that soldiers' wives were usually immoral creatures; the army made it difficult for privates to marry, and treated their wives as camp-followers, issues explored by W. H. Wills and Henry Morley in *Household Words* (No. 76. 6 September 1851; Butt and Tillotson 198–99).

Even that startling and anachronistic Megaloosaurus in the novel's first paragraph is a contemporary allusion. In *Household Words* (38: 14 December 1850) Frederick Knight Hunt described the Hunterian Museum in Lincoln's Inn Fields, close by Lincoln's Inn Hall, where the Lord Chancellor is sitting on that first foggy November afternoon. The Museum contained, among other things, "relics of the huge monsters who roved in the primeval wilds of our earth long before the Flood," among them the glyptodon, the mylodon, and the Megatherium, "more ancient than either."

Dickens's themes of housekeeping, houses in disorder, and putting England's house in order are also related to his personal affairs as he began *Bleak House*. He started writing in November 1851. That June he had moved out of Devonshire Place, and spent the summer at Broadstairs, waiting for his new house in Tavistock Place to be ready. His letters are full of references to the new book and the new house, frustrations at the slowness of the workmen, meticulous directions about the placement, construction, and finish of bookcases and other furnishing. "Wait till I get rid of my workmen and get to my work," he writes (26 September), "and see if we don't raise the (East) wind!"; "I am in the first throes of a new book, and am spasmodically altering and arranging a new house besides,—and am walking by the sea every day, endeavouring to think of both sets of distraction to some practical end" (28 September); "I am wild to begin a new book, and can't until I am settled" (6 October); "the distraction of the new book, the whirling of the story through one's mind, escorted by workmen . . . the wild necessity of beginning to write, the not being able to do so" (7 October); "I am three parts distracted and the fourth part wretched in the agonies of getting into a new house . . . I can not work at my new book—having all my notions of order turned completely topsy-turvy . . .'' (9 October; *Letters* 6. 495-513). Among the ordered decorations was a false bookcase lined with imaginary titles (''Steele. By the Author of 'Ion' . . . Lady Godiva on the Horse''). Dickens wanted a prominent place for ''the History of a Short Chancery Suit'' (22 October; *Letters* 6. 524-25).

The House of Things

If the story of *Bleak House* exists in a context of the novel's other untold stories, of contemporary issues, and of events in Dickens's own life, in parts publication it also exists in the context of each serial part, that is, in a specific relationship to the usual arrangement of a printed number. Each number combined Dickens's fiction with advertisements, an exhibition of items currently available, and so embedded Dickens's text in a display of goods. This arrangement is especially appropriate for *Bleak House*, placing the text as it does amid an exhibition of manufactured items, some of which had also been seen at the Crystal Palace Exhibition.

The reader began with the wrapper, or cover, repeated from number to number, and hinting at the novel's only partially disclosed plots. Like most Phiz wrappers for Dickens's novels, that of *Bleak House* juxtaposes events from the story and allegorical references to its themes. We can identify Miss Flite releasing her birds, Mr. Krook tracing letters, Nemo copying, and Lady Dedlock with her footman. But most of the cover's vignettes are allegorical, and hint that the novel is also an allegory, a hint Dickens reinforces with his frequent references to the allegorical figure painted on Tulkinghorn's ceiling. We see a crowd of lawyers engaged in a boisterous game of blindman's buff around the mace and Woolsack—the Lord Chancellor's official insignia and seat. Two lawyers play battledore and shuttlecock with clients for shuttlecocks. Two more play chess with clients for chessmen. There is a crowd outside a gabled house, presumably Bleak House, among them a jester carrying a scroll marked ''Humbug'' and another wearing a sandwich board advertising Exeter Hall—the favorite platform for launching ''missions.'' In a little cart marked ''Bubble'' and ''Tin'' a man blows a toy trumpet; elsewhere a woman embraces two black children, a boy and a girl. As readers read on from installment to installment, they were able to decipher more of the cover's meanings even as the story itself offered revelations. The cover creates enigmas which the text is to solve, and prepares us for the gradual revelations that comprise the plot of *Bleak House*.

Each part's first pages are given over, first to publishers' advertising, then to miscellaneous advertisements. The many pages of book lists, often carried over from number to number, remind us how much Victorian England was a reading culture. But they also hint at aspects of Dickens's novel. We find, along with notices of then-recent books which are still sometimes read, Carlyle's *Life of John Sterling* (1851) and Thackeray's *Pendennis* (1848-50), books that offer versions of the "fashionable intelligence" in their preoccupation with aristocratic behavior: Craik's *Romance of the Peerage,* Burke's *Romantic Records of Distinguished Families.* Accounts of aristocratic families and their legends or scandals anticipate the Dedlocks' Ghost's Walk and Lady Dedlock's secret. Mrs. Crowe's *Adventures of a Beauty* is suggestive. *The Female Jesuit* and *The Perverter in High Life: a True Narrative of Jesuit Duplicity* evoke that alleged Catholic conspiracy to subvert England so stoutly resisted in the Ecclesiastical Titles Act of 1851; the restoration of a Catholic hierarchy in England provoked riots, and was seen as a consequence of the Oxford Movement and of that High Church "dandyism" represented by Mrs. Pardiggle. There are technical books about how things work: *The Mine, The Ship, The Steam Engine.*

Many books advocate or define feminine virtue: in the first number we find *Home Influence: a Tale for Mothers and Daughters*, its sequel, *The Mother's Recompense,* and *Woman's Friendship: A Tale of Domestic Life,* all by Grace Aguilar; *Woman: Her Mission and Her Life,* translated from the French of Monod; Miss Julia Kavanagh's *Women of Christianity Exemplary for Piety and Charity;* and *Home Truths for Home Peace,* recommended to young housewives who wish to become "efficient housekeepers and exemplary wives and mothers." These domestic preoccupations anticipate the domestic failures of Lady Dedlock and Mrs. Jellyby, and Dickens's celebration of housekeeping and feminine modesty in Esther. *Bleak House* Part II advertises *The Gallery of Byron Beauties*, a set of engravings of Byron's heroines, and similar "galleries" of women from Shakespeare, Scott, the British Poets, and the Bible; Jobling, we recall, prizes his "choice collection of copperplate impressions from that truly national work, The Divinities of Albion, or Galaxy Gallery of British Beauty, representing ladies of title and fashion in every variety of smirk that art, combined with capital, is capable of producing" (20:256).

I am not suggesting that Dickens drew on any of these books, nor did he control their presence in the pages preceding his text. But they provided a context for that text, and they catalogue for us some of the preoccupations of the day, to reveal how very much *Bleak House* is a book of 1851-53 in its themes, attitudes, and characters. In so doing they reinforce Dickens's story, if only by chance.

Publishers' advertisements are followed by advertisements for miscellaneous objects: shirts, wigs, hair oil, patent medicines, waterproof coats and leggings. These are tangential to the text in their profusion of objects. Like

Esther's inventories of Bleak House, Mr. Grubble's parlor, and Mrs. Jellyby's closets, they represent a catalogue of things, partly an illustrated catalogue. The sheer accumulation of all these perhaps desirable but certain unrelated objects foreshadows the novel's world. We approach *Bleak House* through a library catalogue and an exhibit of luxuries and necessities. *Bleak House* itself is a catalogue and exhibition of "England's sins and negligences."

The plates and text are followed by more advertisements, another catalogue of things. This later catalogue lists stationers, printing machinery, copying presses—the very items whose product we hold in our hands, and on which the whole literary enterprise depends. They are an ironic counterpoint to the novel's preoccupation with texts and writing, the proliferation of written paper which becomes the waste paper of Krook's shop, and the meaningless documents of Jarndyce and Jarndyce: Dickens the writer suggesting his own anxieties in the lonely death of Nemo the writer, the neglected family of Mrs. Jellyby the writer, and the futility of writings that end as waste paper.

There is even an explicit dialogue between one advertiser and *Bleak House* itself. In each number, the penultimate advertisement, on the inside back cover, is always a full page devoted to E. Moses and Son, Clothiers. In their *Bleak House* advertisements, Moses and Son often responded directly to the novel's text. In the first number their back page is headed "Anti-Bleak House," and declares

> A BLEAK HOUSE that is indeed, where the north winds meet to howl in ignoble concert, and bitter blasts mourn like tortured spirits . . . Woe to the inhabitant of the Bleak House if he is not armed with the weapons of an OVERCOAT and a SUIT OF FASHIONABLE and substantial clothing, such as can only be obtained at E. MOSES AND SONS'S Establishments. . . .

The House of Words

Dickens established *Household Words* and edited its 479 weekly issues, as well as occasional supplements, from 30 March 1850 until 28 March 1859, when he had already begun a new journal, *All the Year Round* (1859-70). During this same period he completed *David Copperfield* and wrote *Bleak House, A Child's History of England, Hard Times, Little Dorrit,* and part of *A Tale of Two Cities.* He also wrote more than a hundred articles and stories for *Household Words,* and there are fifty-eight more which are substantially his, written in collaboration. Dickens was a committed and attentive editor, keeping a "ruthless hand" (Johnson 2: 759) on the journal from day to day. He suggested topics for articles, invited contributions, read hundreds of manuscripts, inserted paragraphs of his own in many articles, sometimes completely rewrote articles, and read proof—which often involved further revisions (*UW* 36-37; Lohrli 15, 250).

Household Words and *Bleak House* were driven in tandem, and it is hardly surprising that journal and novel should share themes and ideas. Dickens's statement in his 1853 preface to the novel—"In Bleak House I have purposely dwelt upon the romantic side of familiar things" (Preface: 4)—echoes "A Preliminary Word," his statement of purpose in the first number of *Household Words:* "To show to all, that in all familiar things, even in those which are repellent on the surface, there is Romance enough, if we will find it out" (1. 30 March 1850/*DJ* 2. 177). The new journal would also mediate between social classes by introducing them to each other, bringing "the greater and the lesser in degree, together, upon that wide field, and mutually dispose them to a better acquaintance and a kinder understanding"—a less melodramatic version of the question that shapes *Bleak House*:

> What connexion can there be, between the place in Lincolnshire, the house in town, the Mercury in powder, and the whereabout of Jo the outlaw with the broom. . . . What connexion can there have been between many people in the innumerable histories of this world, who, from opposite sides of great gulfs, have, nevertheless, been very curiously brought together!   (16: 197)

Articles in *Household Words* discuss issues and situations which also appear in *Bleak House:* the evils of Chancery, women with a Mission, detectives, and even Jo's testimony at the inquest (Butt and Tillotson 182, 196-98; House 32-33). In fact, the parallels are so frequent that journal and novel continually create each other's context, especially for Dickens's contemporaries, who were simultaneously reading both. Dickens's own *Household Words* articles attack middle class indifference to "the filth and misery of the poor" and opposition to Sanitary Reform (2. 6 April 1850/DJ 2. 191). He speaks of the danger of infection from overcrowded City graveyards (11. 8 June 1850; 13.22 June; 140.27 November 1852/*DJ* 3.97), scorns static societies (4.20 April 1850/*DJ* 2.205). He attacks the "Young England" movement and ecclesiastical dandies (12. 15 June 1850; 35. 23 November 1850/ DJ 2. 243-44, 301, 304), which Mrs. Pardiggle represents; Exeter Hall (13.22 June 1850/DJ 2. 255-56); and orators of the Chadband type (74. 23 August/DJ 3. 21-22). One piece, about John Bull's opposition to change, begins on a "November evening at dusk, when all was mud, mist, and darkness, out of doors, and a good deal of fog had even got into the [Bull] family parlour" (35. 23 November 1850/DJ 2. 299), a metaphor for the household of England. A Spirit clearly related to those that visit Scrooge sees "children, hunted, flogged, imprisoned, but not taught" (38 14 December 1850/DJ 2. 307). In "A Sleep to Startle Us" (103. 13 March 1852) Dickens visits a shelter for outcasts and encounters "an orphan boy with burning cheeks and great gaunt eager eyes . . . in pressing peril of death . . . who had no possession . . . but a bottle of physic and a scrap of writing. He brought both from . . . a Hospital . . . too full to admit him . . . He held the bottle of physic in his claw of a hand, and stood, apparently unconscious of it, staggering, and staring with his bright glazed eyes . . . He passed into the darkness with his physic-bottle" (*DJ* 3. 56) to re-emerge in the brickmaker's cottage as Jo, feverish and possessed of "a bottle of cooling medicine" (31. 386). "My Lords and Gentlemen, can you at the present time, consider this," Dickens exclaims (*DJ* 3. 57), as he is to do at Jo's death: "Dead, your Majesty. Dead, my lords and gentlemen. Dead, Right Reverends and Wrong Reverends" (47: 572). Dickens's recollection of an old woman obsessed with the Bank of England (145. 1 January 1853/*DJ* 3. 111) suggests a partial model for Miss Flite.

Dickens collaborated with Caroline Chisholm, the original of Mrs. Jellyby, on "A Bundle of Emigrants' Letters," (*HW* 1. 30 March 1850;/*UW* 1. 85-96): "I dream of Mrs. Chisholm and her housekeeping," he wrote to Miss Coutts (4 March 1850). "The dirty faces of her children are my continual companions" (*Letters* 6. 53). "The Doom of English Wills," written with W. H. Wills (27. 28 September 1850;/*UW* 1. 163-81), reveals how poorly such documents are stored in their legal depositories, the papers thrown in heaps, devoured by rats, foreshadowing the legal waste paper and " 'muddle' " (5: 51) of Krook's shop. "We date from the time of the Prince Regent, and remember picture-books about dandies—satires upon that eminent personage himself, possibly," Dickens exclaims, in a passage added to George Augustus Sala's "First Fruits" (112. 15 May 1852/*UW* 2.413). Mr. Turveydrop reenacts those pictures of dandies "embellishing themselves with artificial personal graces of many kinds."

Such parallels are even present in pieces which Dickens merely accepted for publication and read in proof. In *Household Words* number 27 (28 September 1850), for example, W. B. Jerrold and Wills introduce Lady Bittern, who presumably taught Mrs. Pardiggle how all the members of a family could appear in a subscription list in return for a small contribution (8: 95). In number 28 (5 October 1850), "A Lay of the London Streets" shows a child sleeping in a doorway and an opium addict; character is deduced from handwriting in R. H. Horne's "Mr. Van Ploos on Penmanship." There is a "gorged London graveyard" in F. K. Hunt's "What a London Curate Can Do If He Tries" (*HW* 34. 16 November 1850), and the energetic curate is a preliminary sketch for Allan Woodcourt. A. W. Cole tells a story like Gridley's in "The Martyrs of Chancery" (37. 7 December 1850), and "The Outcast Lady," in the same number, is a version of Lady Dedlock's story. "City Graves" in number 38 (14 December 1850) returns us to Captain Hawdon's noisome resting place, with "Its half-unburied dead," describes such places as sources of disease ("thousands whom, in bygone years,/Our City Graves have slain!"), and attacks telescopic philanthropy:

> I thought of those who bear the sounds
> Of Life across the foam,

In foreign climes, in savage lands,
Who rear Religion's dome;
They might have taught our rulers first
To spare *our* lives at home.

In number 43 (18 January 1851) there are sardonic references to "the Niger expedition of 1841" which we know as Borrioboola-Gha (Dickens himself had written about the Niger Expedition in August 1848, in *The Examiner*), and a reference to a labyrinthine Chancery case about "a piece of dirty land literally not so big as a doorstep." A story in number 47 (15 February 1851) refers to an "estate . . . in Chancery, the manor house in ruins, the lord of it an outlaw." In the same number part two of "The Martyrs of Chancery" quotes Vice Chancellor Shadwell: " 'estates are destroyed, according to law.' "

This is a very brief sampling of *Bleak House* elements in *Household Words*. No doubt there are many more. But, while *Household Words* is an important source or parallel for *Bleak House,* the journal is even more important as a model for the novel's form, and because it offers an important parallel for Esther's role in *Bleak House* as narrator, housekeeper, and guide.

Household Words promised to show its readers the "Romance . . . in all familiar things" and to develop "a better acquaintance and a kinder understanding" between classes (1. 30 March 1850/*DJ* 2. 177). In doing so, it took the form of a Museum or Exhibition in words. Dickens coined the term "process" article (*UW* 1. 53). He showed his readers scientific processes ("The Chemistry of a Candle," "The Mysteries of a Tea-Kettle"), industrial processes ("A Paper Mill," "Pottery and Porcelain"), and the processes which served and fed Londoners ("Valentine's Day at the Post-Office," articles on London's water supply, Smithfield cattle market, Billlingsgate fish market, "Post-Office Money Orders"). Many articles describe exotic foreign places, Australia, the Arctic regions, India, or exotic foreign animals and plants.

These technically or scientifically instructive pieces alternated with morally instructive articles about the miseries of the poor, about prisons, law courts, hospitals, and workhouses. If Dickens's largely middle-class readership (Lohrli 15) learned about elementary chemistry and physics, and vicariously visited the snowy wastes of the Arctic and the steamy jungless along the Niger, they were also shown slums and tenements as remote from their lives as those more exotic places. As in *Bleak House* and so many other Dickens novels, the middle-class reader can safely examine places and people he or she would not dare to visit personally, escorted by *Household Words* as Mr. Snagsby visits Tom-all-Alone's under Mr. Bucket's protection, and as Dickens himself toured slums and doss houses in the company of Bucket's prototype, Inspector Field.

Dickens's "Preliminary Word" spoke of "the stirring world around us . . . . in this summer-dawn of time" and celebrated that technical and industrial progress his journal was to depict. But he also promised to show "social wonders, both good and evil" (*DJ* 2. 177-79). His readers would be forced to recognize how little had been achieved socially and morally despite victorian material progress. Sir Leicester Dedlock objects when Tulkinghorn describes Nemo's wretched life and death, "Not so much shocked by the fact, as by the fact being mentioned . . . he . . . feels that to bring this sort of squalor among the upper class is really—really—" (12: 149). In a passage he added to W. H. Wills's "Idiots," an account of the Park Lane Asylum (167. 4 June 1853), Dickens excoriated "That class of persons . . . so desperately careful to receive no uncomfortable emotions from sad realities or pictures of sad realities, that they become the incarnation of the demon selfishness, and are, by their sickly letting-alone, the most intolerably mischievous people in the community . . . And, madam," he goes on, addressing such a one, "if I may make so bold, I will venture to submit whether such delicate persons as your ladyship may not be laying up a rather considerable stock of responsibility" (*UW* 2. 497). As in *Bleak House,* where he exhibited the brickmaker's cottage and Tom-all-Alone's, as well as the slow cruelty of Chancery and the dangerous insolation of rulers from ruled, Dickens used *Household Words* to show "one half of the world . . . how the other half lives" (I. 30 March 1850/*DJ* 2. 180). In both cases, the reader is shown hitherto avoidable realities, and urged, implicitly or explicitly, to take responsibility for social and moral improvement. To see an evil, Dickens hoped, is to act to end it.

Though this device of showing or exhibiting in *Bleak House* may owe something to Thackeray's device of the showman puppet-master in *Vanity Fair* (1947–48), the most striking parallels are with the show and tell method of *Household Words.* An even clearer parallel is suggested by the title Dickens chose for his journal, after rejecting many, among them *The Household Voice, The Household Guest,* and *The Household Face* (*UW* 1.13). *Household Words,* Dickens hoped, would "be admitted into many homes with affection and confidence" (1. 30 March 1850/*DJ* 2. 178). It would bring those middle-class households news of the larger household of England. These domestic metaphors reappear in Esther Summerson's role as housekeeper, keeping Bleak House in order but also responsible for the smooth running of the story, as Dickens was responsible for running *Household Words.*

Dickens's choice of title suggests how highly he regarded households and housekeeping, private and public. As editor of *Household Words,* he styled himself in such a way as to emphasize that other duty of housekeepers, to show a house by guiding or conducting visitors through it. He did not call himself editor of *Household Words*; every issue instead announced that it was "Conducted by Charles Dickens." Articles often referred to "Mr. Conductor"—one who leads, guides, escorts; "I, the Conductor of this journal" encounters the outcasts in Dickens's "A Nightly Scene in London" (13. 26 January 1856/*DJ* 3. 346). "Mr. Conductor" did not have an obtrusive or idiosyncratic personality to flavor the journal (Lohrli 8), though readers often detected Dickens's energetic style, even when another had written the piece in question. Most pieces were unsigned, and Dickens wanted the journal to sound like the product of a single mind. Articles were to be clear, informative, brief, and above all imaginative, fanciful. Articles were to be clear, informative, brief, and above all imaginative, fanciful. "The swart giants, Slaves of the Lamp of Knowledge, have their thousand and one tales, no less than the Genii of the East; and these, in all their wild, grotesque, and fanciful aspects . . . in all their many moving lessons of compassion and consideration, we design to tell," Dickens declared in "A Preliminary Word" (*DJ* 2. 178).

"Mr. Conductor" gently led his reader from exhibit to exhibit, as Esther's narrating connects the various exhibits in *Bleak House*. The *Household Words* exhibits show themselves and speak for themselves without "Mr. Conductor's" intervention or commentary, and the exhibits in *Bleak House* present themselves in the same way, without Esther's specific involvement. Dickens is everywhere in *Household Words* shaping and arranging what we see, but he is sometimes absent as a personal voice. In *Bleak House* he also conceals himself, disguised now as Esther, now as the voice of an anonymous exhibitor, a portable talking guide of the sort now common in museums, who will show us high life, law life, and low life. "He is not a genuine foreign-grown savage," this other voice announces, inviting us to look at Jo:

> he is the ordinary home-made article. Dirty, ugly, disagreeable to all the senses, in body a common creature of the common streets, only in soul a heathen. Homely filth begrimes him, homely parasites devour him, homely sores are in him, homely rags are on him: native ignorance, the growth of English soil and climate, sinks his immortal nature lower than the beasts that perish. Stand forth, Jo, in uncompromising colours!   (47: 564)

Dickens had imagined a similar anonymous persona, able to go everywhere and reveal what it found, as the controlling voice for *Household Words*. "The original matter to be essays, reviews, letters, theatrical criticisms, &c. & c. as amusing as possible, but all distinctly and boldly going to what in one's own view ought to be the spirit of the people and the time," Dickens wrote to Forster (7 October 1849):

> Now to bind all this together, and to get a character established as it were which any of the writers may maintain without difficulty, I want to suppose a certain SHADOW, which may go into any place, by sunlight, moon-light, starlight, firelight, candlelight, and be in all homes, and all nooks and corners, and be supposed to be cognisant of everything, and go everywhere, without the least difficulty. Which may be in the Theatre, the Palace, the House of Commons,

the Prisons, the Unions, the Churches, on the Railroad, on the Sea, abroad and at home: a semi-omniscient, omnipresent, intangible creature . . . a cheerful, useful, and always welcome Shadow. (*Letters* 5: 622–23)

"Mr. Conductor" is the Shadow as finally developed for *Household Words,* though Dickens also solicited and published several "Shadows" ("The Shadow of Lucy Hutchinson," "The Shadow of Margery Paston"), which allowed the reader to see and hear individuals from past history, as in *Bleak House* we see and hear scenes and characters not accessible to Esther. Dickens also devised "Our Phantom Ship" ("Our Phantom Ship: Negro Land," "Our Phantom Ship: Japan"), which carried the reader instantly to distant places. These devices, and the anonymous ubiquitous other narrator of *Bleak House,* develop out of the Spirits who show Scrooge past, present, and future Christmases in *A Christmas Carol* (1843). Dickens would create another version in the persona of the "Uncommercial Traveller" he employed in *All the Year Round.*

Dickens's working notes for *Bleak House* refer to certain chapters as "pictures." Chapter 2, for example, "In Fashion," is "Open country house picture"; chapter 12, "On the Watch," was "Picture, Chesney Wold," but Dickens crossed out "Picture" (*WN* 207, 213). Jo "munching, and gnawing, and looking up at the great Cross on the summit of St. Paul's Cathedral" (19: 326) is "Closing picture on the bridge/Golden Cross of St. Pauls" (*WN* 217). Later we have "Inn picture," "Night Picture" (chapters 57 and 58), and "Chesney Wold Picture" (chapter 66; *WN* 241. 243).

None of these refer to extant Phiz illustrations, and all save one—"Inn picture"—are associated with the anonymous narrator; "Inn picture" occurs while Bucket and Esther are pursuing Lady Dedlock, and Esther herself has become a kind of phantom observer. The anonymous narrator—a voice-over—provides us with many pictures: Chancery in session; Fashionable Life; Tom-all-Alone's; the Inquest, Guppy, Jobling, and Smallweed at dinner.

In a passage he added to "H. W." (*HW* 160. 16 April 1853), Henry Morley's piece about "the processes by which" *Household Words* was produced, Dickens describes the author's "patient massing of many reflections, experiences, and imaginings for one minute purpose, and the patient separation from the heap of all the fragments that will unite to serve "that purpose (*UW* 2. 467-8). The author's task is to connect or unite, to impose coherence on apparently unrelated fragments. This is Esther's role in *Bleak House.* She connects the various exhibits which the anonymous narrator's voice presents and describes. They are talking exhibits, among which she leads us in an orderly progression, as Little Nell guides visitors through Mrs. Jarley's Wax-Work exhibition. Just as Dickens controlled and "conducted" *Household Words,* Esther controls *Bleak House* as she conducts us through the story.

She alone holds the keys that can open all Bleak House's hidden secret places. She also can reveal the novel's secrets through her own connecting narrative, which she breaks off at intervals to let the exhibits speak for themselves. Without her connecting narrative, there would be no coherence between these disparate exhibits. Mr. Guppy's Entertainment, Mrs. Bagnet's birthday party, Lady Dedlock's last interview with Mr. Tulkinghorn would remain unrelated sketches: dinner at a "Slap-Bang" (20: 246) eating house, a bassoon-player's party, the defiant beauty.

The House of Light

After listing and commenting on some of the contemporary issues and references incorporated into *Bleak House*, John Butt and Kathleen Tillotson point out a significant omission. "In a novel where the life of England in 1851 is otherwise fully represented," they remark, "the Great Exhibition is deliberately, even conspicuously, excluded." They have already commented on the scant attention paid to the Great Exhibition in the pages of *Household Words,* and suggested Dickens's "instinctive feeling against the Exhibition" as a partial exploration for these omissions (Butt 180-82).

For Dickens and *Household Words* to ignore so conspicuous an event as the Great Exhibition, the embodiment of Victorian confidence, optimism, and belief in both technical and moral progress, would indeed be a striking omission. From the first announcement of the project, early in 1850, the Exhibition became a controversial issue in the newspapers and journals of the day. Once Queen Victoria had officially opened the Exhibition, on 1 May 1851, and its success became apparent, the Exhibition became a constant topic for news articles, editorial comment, printed jokes, and cartoons until it closed on 15 October.

"The Great Exhibition of the Works of Industry of all Nations, 1851," was the first international or world's fair. British and foreign manufacturers sent examples of their products: furniture, pottery, cloth, carriages, agricultural implements, shoes, paper, jewelry, as well as such eccentric items as a dressing-table that doubled as a fire escape, the "Registered Alarum Bedstead" that ejected the sleeper into a cold bath, cuffs made from the wool of French poodles, "a shirt cut on mathematical principles," a compartmented drinking-glass that mixed soda and acid "at the moment of entering the mouth" (Gibbs-Smith 32). Manufacturers also exhibited the machinery which made these products possible. There were steam engines, working models of docks and canal locks, printing presses, a model coal mine, locomotives, a hydraulic press, and an envelope-folding machine which produced 2700 envelopes an hour; the public could watch many of these machines in operation. There were also displays of raw material: cotton, iron ore, coal.

Prince Albert and his colleagues wished to create both a trade fair and a moral statement. The Prince called the Exhibition "a living picture of the point of development at which the whole of mankind has arrived" in shaping nature to the human will, but he also insisted that civilization and progress could be maintained and advanced "only by peace, love, and ready assistance, not only between individuals, but between the nations of the earth" (Gibbs-Smith 7). An intelligent visitor to the Exhibition would begin to understand something about the new science and technology. But he or she would also begin to realize how much the England of the eighteen-fifties already depended on these machines and those who operated them, and how the machines all depended on each other, and on the labor and transport that brought them their raw materials. The Exhibition celebrated progress, but it also emphasized the interdependence of classes and nations, though the contemporary press emphasized progress rather than interdependence. Dickens continually reminds us of the interdependence of classes—if not nations—in *Bleak House*: "What connexion can there be, between the place in Lincolnshire . . . and . . . Jo the outlaw with the broom?" (16: 197).

Butt and Tillotson are misleading in suggesting that *Household Words* gave scant attention to the Great Exhibition. There are many references in passing to the Exhibition, and several articles specifically devoted to it, all of them celebratory. Butt and Tillotson do note three sequential articles, "Three May-Days in London," by Charles Knight, without explaining that they emphasize that progress which the Exhibition made manifest. At the first May Day, set in 1517, apprentices riot against free trade and several are killed (56. 19 April 1851); by May Day 1701 the world had progressed, but trade is still restricted, to England's impoverishment (57. 26 April). But May Day 1851 brings a "Palace of Industry" which shows "the general advance of the world in civilisation and happiness," a Palace which would not be possible "If Science had not been at work in every direction for the last fifty years—Political, as well as Chemical and Mechanical Science" (58. 3 May). "The Great Exhibition and the Little One" (67. 5 July 1851) contrasted the Great Exhibition with an exhibition of Chinese arts and manufactures on a junk moored in the Thames. Dickens added a passage contrasting England's progress and China's stasis:

> The true Tory spirit would have made a China of England, if it could. Behold its results in the curious little Exhibition now established close beside the great one. It is very curious to have the Exhibition of a people who came to a dead stop, Heaven knows how many hundred years ago, side by side with the Exhibition of the moving world. It points the moral in a surprising manner.
>
> (*UW* 1: 322)

Household Words discussed designs for the structure that was to house the

Exhibition (17. 20 July 1850), accommodations for visitors (22. 24 August 1850; 81. 11 October 1851), and the procedure for compiling the Catalogue (74. 23 August 1851).

Like many visitors to the Exhibition, *Household Words* was as fascinated with the structure housing the Exhibition as with the Exhibition itself: Joseph Paxton's wonderful creation of cast iron and plate glass which the editor of *Punch,* Dickens's friend Douglas Jerrold, had christened "the Crystal Palace." W. H. Wills's "The Private History of the Palace of Glass" (43. 18 January 1851) described Paxton's career, his successes as a gardener and builder of glass conservatories, and hailed "the Great Giant in Hyde Park . . . an enormous glass-case under which to collect the products of all nations," adding some statistics: the structure would cover eighteen acres, was 1851 feet long, and contained 90,000 square feet of glass, with ingenious devices for carrying off rain water and keeping the floors clean. Dickens collaborated with Wills on "Plate Glass" (45. 1 February 1851), which described the manufacture of the Crystal Palace's crystal, to Dickens "the beautiful substance that makes our modern rooms so glittering and bright; our streets so dazzling, and our windows at once so radiant and so strong" (*UW* 1. 208). Dickens probably added—to a scientific piece by Henry Morley, "The Wind and the Rain" (62. 31 May 1851)—the remark that "the wind has got into some little notoriety of late, for not having blown down Mr. Paxton's Crystal Palace . . . which, it appears, it was bound to do, and ought by all means to have done" (*UW* 1. 285), a reference to dire predictions that the Palace would collapse in a strong wind, that hail stones would smash the glass, that condensation would send a perpetual drizzle down on exhibits and viewers. "What is Not Clear about the Crystal Palace" (69. 19 July 1851), reviews the arguments for keeping the Palace permanently in Hyde Park versus those urging that it be removed as promised.

Butt and Tillotson argue that Dickens's alleged indifference to the Great Exhibition in *Household Words,* and his failure to include it in *Bleak House,* can best be explained by his impatience with such a celebration of progress when so much remained to be done. They cite particularly Dickens's "The Last Words of the Old Year," published in *Household Words* 41 on 4 January 1851, in which the year 1850 looks back at his life and its events, and describes the legacy he is leaving to 1851; inadequate sewers, unsafe steamboats, illiteracy, "a vast inheritance of degradation and neglect in England," the Irish question, the Court of Chancery, and the religious controversies arising out of Puseyism and the Oxford Movement (Butt and Tillotson, 179-82). Most of these dubious legacies find their place in *Bleak House*—which, we must remember, is supposed to have been written by Esther at least seven years after the events she describes (67: 767).

The Old Year's bitterest words are inspired by the impending Great Exhibition " 'I have seen . . . a project carried into execution for a great assemblage of the peaceful glories of the world,' " he declares:

> "I have seen a wonderful structure, reared in glass, by the energy and skill of a great natural genius, self-improved: worthy descendant of my Saxon ancestors: worthy type of industry and ingenuity triumphant! Which of my children shall behold the Princes, Prelates, Nobles, Merchants, of England, equally united, for another Exhibition—for a great display of England's sins and negligences, to be, by steady contemplation of all eyes, and steady union of all hearts and hands, set right? Come hither my Right Reverend Brother . . . and study the Humanities through these transparent windows! Wake, Colleges of Oxford, from day-dreams of ecclesiastical melodrama, and look in on these realities in the daylight, for the night cometh when no man can work! Listen, my Lords and Gentlemen, to the roar within, so deep, so real, so low down, so incessant and accumulative! Not all the . . . Quantities of Prosody, or Law, or State, or Church, or Quantities of anything but work in the right spirit, will quiet it for a second, or clear an inch of space in this dark Exhibition of the bad results of our doings! Where shall we hold it? When shall we open it?" (*DJ* 2. 313: 14)

Bleak House is that other exhibition, Dickens's Great Exhibition of 1852, reminding England that all was not well, that the efficient machines so proudly shown and viewed were not matched by a correspondingly efficient social machinery, and that the light and fresh air of the Crystal Palace did not penetrate the slums. Chancery is a machine that produces nothing save grief, squalor, and waste, a metaphor for all the inefficiency of outmoded government. Government is a meaningless alternating of incompetents. Sir Leicester's family name emphasizes the deadlock that prevents reform or improvement, an inert power that thwarts change, and Chesney Wold, like Tom-all-Alone's, is a place of darkness and shadows.

Like the Dust Heap in *Our Mutual Friend,* the heaps of waste paper in Krook's shop are what this system produces—and Dickens may have invoked Spontaneous Combustion to remind readers that the Houses of Parliament had caught fire in 1834; the fire was caused by the burning of tally-sticks, traditionally used to keep financial records, a primitive form of waste paper. Does Krook's accumulation of written papers, waste paper, also represent Dickens's own anxiety—perhaps every writer's anxiety—about writing itself, especially when we combine it with the Law-Writer Nemo's sordid isolation and Mrs. Jellyby writing, writing, writing, and neglecting her family?

The Crystal Palace and the Exhibition it housed was an allegory of progress, proclaiming that science and technology would make life better, a celebration of order and reason against dirt and chaos. As such—as a created space to display what Victorian civilization had achieved—it evoked a pride which Dickens also felt. It also perhaps asserted Victorian values against Victorian fears that order, reason, cleanliness, and light could not be so easily achieved or imposed outside those walls of glass.

The Exhibition contained works of art as well as technical triumphs. Paintings were excluded (Hobhouse 114) but sculpture was admitted. Many of the statues were patriotic—Queen Victoria, the Duke of Wellington—or represented heroic figures from British history: Richard the Lion-Hearted; King Alfred and his Mother; Lord Chancellor Eldon and his brother, Lord Stowell, carved from a single twenty-ton block of marble (Hobbhouse 114). The statues pictured in the *Art-Journal* catalogue of the Exhibition depict classical, Biblical, or allegorical subjects, with a marked emphasis on maternal love: the Virgin and Child, Eve Nursing Cain and Abel, a tigress defending her cub, Cres and Proserpina (*Art-Journal* 68, 72, 320; 293; 316; 304). Only one statue, "The Bashful Beggar" (282), hints at social issues, but even here the emphasis is on maternal love and the mother and her children are clad in flowing Grecian draperies. There are no Ragged Beggars, no Crossing Sweepers, no Brickmakers' Wives and their sickly Children, no Chancery Suitors.

The Crystal Palace packaged the Victorian dream of progress. It was a dream Dickens shared, but he found the Crystal Palace version inadequate because it excluded misery and want. Unlike Dostoevsky, who condemned the Crystal Palace and its machines as an expression of arid utilitarianism, denying spiritual freedom, Dickens wanted the ingenuity that had created the Exhibition to address itself to social and political issues.

The Old Year 1850's dying speech suggests Dickens's purpose and method in *Bleak House*, and the novel itself obliquely confirms its role as an alternate Exhibition to the one in the Crystal Palace. Dickens's title for his novel seems a deliberate contrast to the optimistic promise of "Crystal Palace": House replies to "Palace," Bleak implies desolation and exposure, unlike the warm sunny enclosure of the Crystal Palace. Some of Dickens's discarded titles for *Bleak House* make the same kind of contrast *Tom-All Alone's/The Ruined House; Tom-All-Alone's./The Ruined Building/Factory/Mill/House; Tom-All Alone's/the Solitary House That was always shut up. Never lighted (WN* 186-205). The occasional address to "Your Highness" (2: 11); 32: 403) speaks to Prince Albert, the originator of the Great Exhibition and one of the very small number of adults in the Britain of 1851 entitled to be so addressed.

The Crystal Palace—built in sections, like a Dickens novel—was designed by Joseph Paxton, who was Dickens's friend and was in certain ways closely connected with the genesis of *Bleak House*. Paxton started life as a gardener's apprentice. He became chief gardener to the sixth duke of Devonshire at Chatsworth. He soon became manager of all the duke's estates and interests, the duke's closest friend and most trusted adviser, and a prominent businessman and railroad developer. Paxton was Dickens's major backer in 1846, when the novelist established and briefly edited the Liberal and pro-Reform

Daily News, and had recruited a number of railway promoters and business-men from the North of England to support the paper (Johnson 1. 574–75; 581–85; 584–85). Knighted in 1851 for his work on the Crystal Palace, he became a Liberal Member of Parliament for Coventry in 1854, and held the seat until his death in 1865. His success made him a Victorian hero, though it was due to aristocratic favor as well as his own considerable talents. His story in fact combines those elements of propertied benevolence and virtuous poverty so often brought together in Dickens's novels.

Dickens had come to know the duke of Devonshire, Paxton's patron, in the spring of 1851, while directing and acting in Bulwer Lytton's *Not So Bad As We Seem* at Devonshire, Paxton's patron, in the spring of 1851, while directing and acting in Bulwer-Lytton's *Not So Bad As We Seem* at Dev-onshire House, the duke's London residence. Dickens's audience sat in the great picture galley at Devonshire House (the pictures had been covered), and the adjacent library became stage and greenroom. Time spent in the gallery and library of a great nobleman's town house clearly suggested some of the settings for *Bleak House,* notably the much frequented library at Sir Leicester's town residence, and perhaps the gallery of ancestral portraits of Chesney Wold.

On the night of the performance, Dickens was aware that Bulwer Lyt-ton's estranged wife had threatened to disrupt the play and embarrass "Sir Liar-Coward Lytton" (Johnson 2. 734). Lady Lytton's threat suggests Lady Dedlock's potential for embarrassing her husband should her story become known. Dickens, like Sir Leicester, hired a detective to deal with the threat: Bucket's prototype, "Inspector Field of the Detective Police . . . in plain clothes" (*Letters* 6. 380; 9 May 1851), would watch for Lady Lytton and prevent her from entering. Great London town house, baronet, library, liveried footmen (Johnson 2. 733), potentially embarrassing wife, and detective on the watch for her, all played their part in the germination of *Bleak House.* They provide a link with the opening of the Great Exhibition two weeks earlier and, through the duke of Devonshire, with Josesph Paxton. In his dependence on Paxton, the duke is a generally accepted partial model for Sir Leicester, especially in his dependence on Mrs. Rouncewell '7: 78; Hill 43). The duke depended on Paxton for practical advice, so much so that after his doctor had diagnosed an illness, he had wished also to have Paxton's opinion.

When Dickens visited the duke at Chatsworth, just before beginning to write *Bleak House,* he found himself at "the Palace of the Peak," as contem-porary guide books described Chatsworth; until Tom Jarndyce's day, we are told, Bleak House was called " 'the Peaks' " (8: 89). At Chatsworth, Dickens would have seen the great glass conservatory which Paxton had built to bring the Victoria Regia lily to blossom by recreating a tropical climate ("The Private History of the Palace of Glass," *HW* 43. 18 January 1851). The conservatory was the prototype for the Crystal Palace.

In his innovative use of iron in building the Crystal Palace, his beginnings as a servant of a great nobleman, and his associations with progress and the liberal industrial North of England, Paxton resembles the Ironmaster, Mr. Rouncewell, another self-made success born to be a servant. Dickens emphasizes the Ironmaster's "strong Saxon face" (28: 352), recalling the Old Year's praise of Paxton as "worthy descendant of my Saxon ancestors" (*DJ* 2. 313) and perhaps invoking the near rhyme of Paxton/Saxon. Paxton's ability to maintain a kind of feudal relationship with his duke, while creating an independent existence as a man of affairs, reconciles in one character Mr. Rouncewell's sturdy independence and the feudal loyalty exemplified by Mrs. Rouncewell, and eventually by her son George.

Paxton raised walls and ceilings of glass to make a space filled with light. Esther is also a light-bringer, as Dickens reminds us by letting her watch the sun rise on her first morning at Bleak House. Her presence at Bleak House fills the place with light, and she illuminates the lives of others by helping them emerge from darkness and squalor. Her presence causes Caddy Jellyby to aspire to order and light, and she teaches Charlie how to read. She even brings sunshine to the gloomy purlieus of Chesney Wold when she visits nearby. Her associations with light contrast with the fog, murk, gloom, and obscurity of all those places associated with the outmoded and ineffectual machinery of English society: Chancery, Tom-all-Alone's, Krook's shop, Chesney Wold, where even the windows are dark, and "old stone lions and grotesque monsters bristled outside dens of shadow, and snarled at the evening gloom" (36: 453-54). Light informed the Crystal Palace, and light and shadow are almost characters in *Bleak House,* associated respectively with orderliness and decay. Paxton made a space filled with light, where progress and craftsmanship can be comfortably examined; Esther controls the space that is the book—separate from the reader's ordinary world—where squalor and inefficiency can be comfortably examined.

Within the book, Rouncewell and Esther together represent those possibilities for change and renewal which Paxton's Crystal Palace and the Great Exhibition itself revealed to Dickens's contemporaries. Rouncewell as representative of progress is essentially unexamined, and Dickens's Great Exhibition in fact omits industrial England and the cruelties and injustices accompanying industrial progress. He will make good that omission in his next novel, the uncharacteristically brief *Hard Times* (1854), which is a kind of appendage to *Bleak House*, another exhibit detached from the rest, reexamining industrialism's claim to be socially liberating.

In ordering Bleak House and *Bleak House,* Esther is, in Skimpole's words, " 'intent upon the perfect working of the whole little orderly system of which [she is] the centre' " (37: 468). Dickens described himself as "accustomed . . . to sit in the midst of a system of Order" (*Letters* 6: 514; 9 October

1851). Esther is Dickens's deputy, and she is also his other self, with his gift for organizing and telling a story. Her narrative is often critical, as when she describes Mrs. Jellyby's housekeeping—where writing is a substitute for action. Esther is ready to tidy what she can at Mrs. Jellyby's, even as she describes the squalor and futile activity she finds there. For Dickens, narrating and housekeeping are closely connected. The narrating voice-over can describe and can call upon us to witness what is shown, but Esther acts. She washes Peepy Jellyby's face and would wash England's face too, given the chance.

Esther narrates the story, or, to put it another way, she conducts us through the Exhibition that is the story, firmly preserving at least the attentive reader from the confusion and oppression to which Guppy and Jobling succumb while touring Chesney Wold, "dead beat before they have well begun. They straggle about in wrong places, look at wrong things, don't care for the right things, gape when more rooms are opened, exhibit profound depression of spirits, and are clearly knocked up" (7: 81).

Esther's guided tour of the *Bleak House* Exhibition enables us to recognize the connections between the apparently unrelated worlds of Chancery, Chesney Wold, Bleak House, and Tom-all-Alone's as the story gradually reveals them, and so to discover the anatomy of England's flawed social structure. She helps us see how England operates, or fails to operate, as the exhibits at the Crystal Palace, and "process" articles in *Households Words* showed Victorians how the machines which already dominated their lives operated. She also shows us those who manipulate the political and social machinery of England, and those who are caught and destroyed by that machinery, categories omitted from the Great Exhibition.

Esther shows us Krook's shop, Caddy Jellyby, Charlie, and gives us access to the other narrative voice that amplifies these examples of individual neglect into a display of the state of England. Esther is haunted by her past, the evidence of which she initially carries in her face, and that past destroys Lady Dedlock—who is married to the embodiment of a nation fixed in its past. The other narrative voice reminds us of how the heavy hand of the past impedes the present. Both narrative voices alternately emphasize the same theme, and carry on the same critical narrative. They develop the novel as a diptych, embodying Disraeli's description of England as "Two nations; between whom there is no intercourse and no sympathy . . . ignorant of each other's habits, thoughts, and feelings . . . THE RICH AND THE POOR" (Disraeli, *Sybil* 2.5.73), and Dickens's emphasis on their mutual interdependence.

As housekeeper and guide, Esther has no family portraits to show, though she is herself a kind of family portrait. She brings us through Dickens's "great display of England's sins and negligences": Chancery, Fashionable Life, Telescopic Philanthropy, Tom-all-Alone's. Each exhibit is presented and commented on by the voice-over, and takes the form of a *tableaux vivants* or *poses plastiques,* a favorite Victorian entertainment, in which live actors and actresses in costume posed to represent a painting, a statuary group, or a scene from a play.

For the Victorians, paintings and statues were stories, to be read or interpreted. The *tableaux* or *poses* mixed art, life, and narrative. Some of the scenes Esther herself describes have an air of being posed in this way, to represent a condition or a situation. Mrs. Jellyby at her correspondence graphically displays Woman with a Mission, and Mr. Turveydrop is a one-man pose of Regency deportment, Jarndyce at Richard's deathbed is "the picture of a good man" (65: 762). "Look at this! For God's sake look at this!' " Jarndyce exclaims, when he discovers Charlie and her siblings in Bell Yard. "It was a thing to look at," Esther goes on. "The three children close together, and two of them relying solely on the third, and the third so young and yet with an air of age and steadiness that sat so strangely on the childish figure" (15: 188). The pursuit of Lady Dedlock is a set of tableaux, a rapid tour of a gallery.

The exhibits the other voice presents are also posed statically for us to contemplate. In the opening scene, Chancery in session, a courtroom full of living men do nothing except reveal their inaction. In chapter 2, Sir Leicester, Lady Dedlock, and Mr. Tulkinghorn are another static picture until reality—the text written by Nemo—breaks in and Lady Dedlock faints. Sir Leicester and Mr. Rouncewell together make a kind of genre picture, "The Old and the New," or "Feudalism and Industrialism." Tom-all-Alone's is a chiaroscuro of ruins and vaguely threatening furtive shapes when Bucket takes Snagsby there. The painted pointing figure on Tulkinghorn's ceiling calls our attention to these posed pictures. Esther does not create the pictures, but she provides us with access to them in the proper order, and links them, appearing after we have been challenged to connect the first pair of pictures, "In Chancery" and "In Fashion."

The nineteenth century invented the museum and the exhibition as we know them. Earlier, museums had usually been private, though respectable visitors were usually admitted on certain days or on request, as Mr. Guppy is admitted to Chesney Wold. Exhibitions grew out of medieval carnivals and fairs, but they had become boisterous and tawdry, as "Three May-Days in London" reminds us; respectable people avoided them. The Great Exhibition was a neutral space where alien activities and objects could be safely viewed. Dickens's *Bleak House* is a similar exhibition space, where the middle class reader can safely look at Chancery in operation, the dangerous " 'Monster' " (5: 441) that draws people in as an unprotected machine might do, or safely tour Tom-all-Alone's, a slum too dangerous to enter in reality without a police escort, as Dickens visited Saint Giles's and Whitechapel with Inspector Field

("On Duty with Inspector Field," *HW* 64, 14 June 1851/*DJ* 2. 356-69), a tour he sometimes organized for friends. *Bleak House* is Dicken's space for exhibiting "England's sins and negligences." *Bleak House* and the Crystal Palace exhibit and contrast England's successes and failures. They create each other's context, and their contrast brings the novel into a dialogue with the real contemporary world. The Crystal Palace was a house full of light where objects exhibited could be clearly seen. *Bleak House* repeats the Crystal Palace's function as exhibition space where ordinary objects are isolated and so revealed, showing contemporary readers those hidden social concerns which can bring England to disaster.

NOTES

All references to *Bleak House* are to the Ford-Monod edition (Norton), cited by
　　chapter and page.
DJ: Dickens' Journalism, ed. Michael Slater.
HW: Household Words as originally published, cited by number and date. If reprinted
　　in *DJ* or *UW* that citation is added: 1. 30 March 1850/*DJ* 2. 177.
UW: Dickens's Uncollected Writings from "Household Words", ed. Harry Stone.
WN: Dickens' Working Notes for His Novels, ed. Harry Stone.

WORKS CONSULTED

Art-Journal, The. The Crystal Palace Exhibition Illustrated Catalogue. London:
　　George Virtue, 1851; repr. New York: Dover, 1970.

Butt, John, and Kathleen Tillotson. *Dickens at Work.* London: Methuen, 1957.

Dickens, Charles. *Bleak House.* Ed. George Ford and Sylvère Monod. New York:
　　Norton, 1977. All citations to the novel are to this text, cited by chapter and page:
　　35: 441.

———. *Bleak House.* Original parts publication; 20 numbers in 19 monthly parts,
from March 1852 to September 1853. London: Bradbury and Evans.

———. *Dickens' Journalism.* Ed. Michael Slater. 3 vols. Columbus: Ohio State UP,
1994–99.

———. *Dickens' Working Notes for His Novels.* Ed. Harry Stone. Chicago: U of
Chicago P, 1987.

———. Letters. Ed. Graham Storey and K. J. Fielding. Vol. 5. Oxford: Clarendon, 1981.

———. *Letters*. Ed. Graham Storey, Kathleen Tillotson and Nina Burgis. Vol. 6. Oxford: Clarendon, 1988.

———. *Uncollected Writings from "Household Words,"* 2 volumes. Ed. Harry Stone. Bloomington: Indiana UP, 1968.

Delespinasse, Doris Stringham. "The Significance of Dual Point of View in *Bleak House." Nineteenth-Century Fiction,* 23: 3 (December 1968): 253-64.

Disraeli, Benjamin. *Sybil, or: The Two Nations.* 1845; repr. Penguin, 1954.

Frazee, John P. "The Character of Esther and the Narrative Structure of Bleak House." *Studies in the Novel* 17: 3 (Fall, 1985): 227-40.

Garis, Robert. *The Dickens Theatre: A Reassessment of the Novels.* Oxford: Clarendon, 1965.

Gibbs-Smith, C. H. *The Great Exhibition of 1851: A Commemorative Album.* London: Her Majesty's Stationery Office, 1964.

Hill, T. W. "Notes on *Bleak House." Dickensian* 40 (1943-44): 39-44; 65-70; 133-41.

Hobhouse, Christopher. *1851 and the Crystal Palace.* London: John Murray, 1937.

House, Humphry. *The Dickens World.* second edition, 1942. London: Oxford UP, 1961.

Household Words. Conducted by Charles Dickens. Volume 1, numbers 1–26 (30 March 1850–21 September); Vol. 2: 27–52 (28 September 1850–22 March 1851); Vol. 3: 53–78 (29 March–20 September 1851); Vol. 4: 79–103 (27 September 1851-13 March 1852); Vol. 5: 104–29 (20 March-11 September 1852); Vol. 6: 130-153 (18 September 1852–26 February 1853); Vol. 7: 154–79 (5 March 1853-27 August 1853); Vol. 8: 180–203 (3 September 1853–14 February 1854).

Johnson, Edgar. *Charles Dickens: His Tragedy and Triumph.* 2 volumes. New York: Simon and Schuster, 1952.

Lohrli, Anne. *Household Words.* Toronto: U of Toronto P, 1973.

Miller, J. Hillis. *Charles Dickens: The World of His Novels.,* 1958; repr. Bloomington: Indiana UP, 1969.

———. "Interpretation in Dickens' *Bleak House." Victorian Subjects.* Durham: Duke UP, 1991. This originally appeared as the introduction to *Bleak House,* ed. Norman Page (Harmondsworth, Middlesex: Penguin, 1971).

Monod, Sylvére. "Esther Summerson. Charles Dickens and the Reader in *Bleak House." Dickens Studies* 5 (May 1969): 5-25.

Newsom, Robert. *Dickens on the Romantic Side of Familiar Things: "Bleak House" and the Novel Tradition.* New York: Columbia UP, 1977.

Shatto, Susan. *The Companion to "Bleak House".* London: Unwin Hyman, 1988.

Stone, Harry. "Dickens and the Uses of Literature." *Dickensian* 69 (1973): 139–47.

Zwerdling, Alex. "Esther Summerson Rehabilitated." *PMLA* 88: 3 (May 1973): 429–39.

Glass Windows: The View
from *Bleak House*

Katherine Williams

Conceived and written in the immediate aftermath of the 1851 Great Exhibition, Bleak House *has been mined by critics for allusions to that event and to the Crystal Palace that housed it. Although Paxton's "bundle of transparency" is never mentioned, another version of transparency abounds: the glass window. In* Bleak House, *Dickens uses windows as what Philip Hamon calls "character particles." Windows, in other words, not only serve as metaphors and plot devices, but also as characters, fostering misprision and understanding, exclusion and inclusion, stability and change, constraint and freedom, blindness and insight. Windows provide light, air, and vision, but also boundaries and limitations. Rather than the illusion of "utter transparency," a modernist, utopian value inaugurated by Paxton's edifice, Dickens opts for the imperfect view from windows.*

Light and air are the first essentials for our being. Among the facts demonstrated by Physical Science, there is not one more indisputable, than that a large amount of Solar Light is necessary to the development of the nervous system. Lettuces, and some other vegetables, may be grown in the dark, at no greater disadvantage than a change in their natural colour; but, the nervous system of Animals must be developed by Light. The higher the Animal, the more stringent and absolute the necessity of a free admission to it

of the sun's bright rays. All human creatures
bred in darkness, droop, and become degenerate.
Among the diseases distinctly known to be engendered and propagated by the want of Light,
and by its necessary concomitant, the want of
free Air, those dreadful maladies, Scrofula and
Consumption, occupy the foremost place.

—Charles Dickens, "Red Tape," *Household
Words*

Have you any printed particulars in any Reports,
concerning the more obvious absurdities & evils
of the Window Tax? If you have, and can send
them up to me (in Devonshire Terrace) in the
course of tomorrow forenoon, I think I can do
great service to the Repeal cause.

—Dickens, letter to Henry Austin

Counting Windows

Like death and English fog, taxes sometimes linger. Such was the case in the
eighteenth and nineteenth centuries for British householders unlucky enough
to be found with windows. From 1697 to 1851, the notorious "Window Tax"
(levied by William III as a financing tool for military operations) produced
tidy annual revenues. In 1825, some light-deprived householders got a break:
dwellings with fewer than eight windows were exempted. Still, the tax continued to stifle the English glass industry and shape housing construction. It
discouraged builders from creating or adding windows, encouraged landlords
to brick up existing windows, and effectively limited natural illumination and
ventilation in the domestic housing of the poor and working classes.[1] No
windows, no light, no air, no hope: "so these ruined shelters have bred a
crowd of foul existence that crawls in and out of gaps in the walls and
boards . . . ", writes Dickens in *Bleak House*, describing the blighted slum
known as Tom-all-Alone's (236: 16).

Dickens attacked the Window Tax in a strident *Household Words* article
called "Red Tape," published on February 15, 1851 (2: 481–84). For Dickens, the window tax exemplified the bureaucratic impulse that strangled all
reform efforts—whether legal or hygienic or political. Attempts to repeal the
tax had so far failed, less on account of its (sizeable) revenue provisions than
in the face of parliamentary inertia. Dickens saw the repeal effort as a moral
battle against the spirit of oppression and in favor of health and cleanliness.
He turned to his brother-in-law Henry Austin for relevant facts and figures
on light and ventilation, but he needed no help stoking his own emotional
fires on the subject.

At the time, Dickens had architecture very much in mind. For one thing, he was searching for a house—not an unusual state of affairs. His previous lease was to expire at the end of 1851, and he spent the early part of the year anxiously searching for, bidding on, and losing promising properties. At last, just north of the British Museum, he discovered Tavistock House. It was large, unkempt, just vacated, and ripe for renovations by Austin. Although Dickens was beginning to tire of London, the prospect of a well-situated, spacious, and (once the blinds were taken down) sunny dwelling soon launched him into high-spirited (if erratic) supervision of the renovations. Beyond hunting for his own house, Dickens also had his eye out for another suitable dwelling; this search, undertaken with Miss Coutts, aimed to find suitable housing for young prostitutes. The project engaged him sporadically through the 1850s. In 1852, he found an appropriate building, and architects (including Austin) were promptly engaged, although work was not begun until 1859, owing to legal impediments. And finally, sometime in November 1851, with architectural matters abounding in his personal life, Dickens began work on *Bleak House*, his most overtly ''architectural'' novel.[2]

Not that architecture is absent elsewhere in Dickens, whether as metaphor or plot device. Take, for instance, *Dombey and Son* and *Little Dorrit*. In both novels, architectural forms determine plot, shape (and misshape) character, and define social condition. We have only to think of the formidable prison walls of the Marshalsea or Mrs. Clennan's lopsided, doomed house or Dombey's ''panopticon'' glass conservatory to see that in Dickens architecture is often fate.

Still, in *Bleak House*, as in no other Dickens novel, architecture takes central stage—a place of dwelling being the titular subject and how to dwell without sinking into the dark vortexes and muck of London life being the operative question. Topics of sociology, psychology, aesthetics, and politics of place and architecture are woven into the novel. Moreover, a remarkable number of buildings—Bleak House itself, Chesney Wold, Krook's shop, Tulkinghorn's rooms, Chancery, and the dank slums of Tom-all-Alone's—are integral to the plot. Even more distinct than individual buildings is the architectural aura of the city as a whole. London is a place of decomposition and mystification, its architectural decay spreading outward from Chancery, its edifices adorned by hieroglyphic markings (like the inscrutable Allegory in Tulkinghorn's chamber), and its constructions raw reminders of class distinction and psychological disjunction.

In this article, I focus on a particular architectural detail—glass windows. In *Bleak House,* windows are useful not only because of what they do (mark and transcend boundaries, focus, exude and invite light, permit and deny seeing, puncture otherwise stifling walls), but also because of how we—and Dickens—feel about them. Windows tend to attract the eye more than any other architectural detail. Whether to provide natural light and ventilation, or contact with the world, windows are so essential to our psychological well-being that modern building codes require them in domestic housing. Of all architectural details, windows are arguably the most emotive since they mitigate an unwanted effect of architecture: its semblance to the cave, from which we first escaped into architecture. The window, then, defines architecture as "other" than the cave in a way that no other detail can. Indeed, architecture without light and ventilation is worse than the cave. It is the tomb.[3]

Like other critics interested in Dickens and the Window Tax,[4] I see his anti-tax activities as social activism driven especially by his interest in sanitation and health. I also believe that Dickens was viscerally attracted to windows and viscerally repulsed by their absence. In *Bleak House*, he evokes for us the horror of the dark (Nemo in his room), the pathos of the captive (Lady Dedlock cornered by Tulkinghorn), the stench of poverty (Tom-all-Alone's) by playing on our shared experience of windows. We imagine Nemo in his shuttered room, Lady Dedlock gazing past Tulkinghorn at freedom beyond her reach, and Jo sleeping like a "maggot" in the "tumbling tenements" (236: 16).

Windows are, of course, part of an architectural context. Thus, although my focus is on windows, it seems appropriate to comment briefly on the uses in fiction of architecture as a whole. Simply put, buildings function as metaphor and as theatrical site. These two functions are especially useful for the urban novel, where intercourse among characters takes place on the street, on doorsteps, through windows, up and down winding stairs, and in and out of drawing rooms or parlors or the bare rooms of squalid hovels.

Architecture works as metaphor because of its aesthetic appeal and its central function in our lives. We live in architecture, and inevitably we try to make it our own, whether by modification or accommodation. Like landscape, a building may represent a psychic state. But unlike landscape, a building is wholly constructed by humans and modified continually by its inhabitants. Bleak House, for example, is an elastic, gothic edifice whose psychic disposition matches that of John Jarndyce. Its structure is irregular and delightfully messy without being chaotic. With its many turns and hidden passageways, Bleak House is like a maze. It gives inhabitants the space to dream, to explore, and to be lost, momentarily, to the world. It functions both as a focal point for the contest of wills between Jarndyce and Richard, and as a haven for escape, if fleeting, from the juridical tentacles. Not that escape is always positive: Skimpole's evasion of domestic responsibility is deplorable, and even Jarndyce's retreats to the Growlery are evidence of psychic disjunction.[5] The architectural imperfections of Bleak House, however, seem to meet with Dickens's approval; the house is neither an unrealistic utopian vision nor an edifice utterly permeated by its ugly history. It seems to thrive in a society otherwise debilitated by Chancery.

Architecture also organizes action in novels. Events revolve around edifices and architectural interiors—especially architectural elements like entryways, rooms, and windows. The edifices of *Bleak House*—Chancery, Chesney Wold, Krook's shop, Nemo's room, Tom-all-Alone's, and Tulkinghorn's apartment—enable and constrain the movements and interactions of characters. Indeed, Nemo, Lady Dedlock, Richard Carstone, Jo, and Miss Flyte, trapped by their socio-histories, are equally ensnared by architectural forms—whether these forms are stifling rooms, luxurious mansions, Chancery, Tom-all-Alone's, or the upper garret of Krook's house, with its bird cages and prowling cat.

Like architecture as a whole, the window spawns metaphors and facilitates stagecraft. Its structural uses (ventilation and illumination) give rise to a variety of metaphoric possibilities. It provides access to the outside (the intersection of human space and nature); it is variously the eye (and thus, the "I") and the lens; it is a frame for what is inside and what is outside (evoking comparison with pictorial art); it is a point of exit or entrance at its most fragile and furtive (indeed, locked-door mysteries often find their solution through some quixotic penetration of a window). It is a device that lets characters or the narrator or even the reader carry out various activities, often invisibly, either as observer or voyeur: focusing, interpreting, defining, analyzing, excluding, including, imagining, and connecting.[6] And, of course, the window is useful in a narrative. The window allows characters to see in and out; it reveals and conceals; it may even seem to have a "viewpoint" and, as a consequence, display attitude or emotion. (In the trope that equates building with the human form, windows always represent the most expressive feature of the face: the eyes.[7])

Windows in fiction generally fall into three categories of function: (1) to frame an outside world that is seen and analyzed from an interior (carceral) space; (2) to frame an interior space that is seen and analyzed from the outside; and (3) to focus sight and transform that sight into power. I argue that windows in *Bleak House* fulfill these functions, and that in doing so they become what Philip Hamon calls "character particles"—nearly animate aspects of the drama. Like the painting of Allegory in Tulkinghorn's rooms, which generates narrative information (though in this case for the reader and the anonymous narrator only), windows also generate narrative information through their interaction with characters.

If I argue for the importance of windows in *Bleak House,* I do so not only because of their analytical and emotive force, but also because of their historical development in nineteenth-century England, and especially in the decade preceding publication of *Bleak House*. Within a short generation, glass was transformed from limited resource to ubiquitous product, from a manor-house amenity to the embodiment of modernist "transparency." I take this excursion into industrial history because I believe that Dickens's interest in industrial progress—the development of how things are made—bears heavily on the conflict between decay and progress in *Bleak House*. (This conflict is most pointedly laid out in characters of the two Rouncewells: George, the trooper, ultimately opting for the "natural" processes of decay and generation "where there's more room for a Weed" (884: 63), and his elder brother, purveyor of the bare and purposeful ironworks. Glass windows have their foot in both camps, of course: they give us visual access to the "natural," and they are, at the same time, industrialized and industrializing products.)

Railways, bridges, steam, gas lighting, the factory system, and ventilation systems—these new methods of "making" defined Victorian England. As engineering benefited from the development of iron, so did architecture benefit from advances in glass manufacture. Even before the lifting of English tariffs on imported glass in 1845, the glass industry was able to supply sufficient glass to produce enormous conservatories, like Paxton's Great Stove at Chatsworth and Burton and Turner's Palm House at Kew. Glass-covered arcades introduced consumers to a nineteenth-century version of the mall experience; plate-glass windows gave birth to the pastime known as "window shopping." By mid-century, vast iron sheds with glass plating were erected to shelter railway passengers. Finally, in 1851, Paxton and the Great Exhibition Committee drew up plans for a spectacular glass edifice—the Crystal Palace (which loomed in the background as Dickens composed *Bleak House*). From this feat of engineering, architecture gained a new idiom. The (slightly tinted) transparent glass panes of the Crystal Palace anticipated such modernist celebrations of glass as the Lever House and the Seagram Building.

As glass production accelerated, so did the tendency to equate ordinary glass with insight—as if a product that permits transitivity ensures it.[8] Dickens seems lukewarm at best toward this metaphoric equation. True, *Bleak House* teaches us about the value of seeing clearly, even in the midst of psychic, social, political, and juridical muddle. But it also teaches us about the danger of believing in the possibility of absolute clarity. The novel begins in fog and ends with the central confusion of Jarndyce and Jarndyce melting away, and the central mystery of Esther's parentage revealed. These resolutions make things clearer for some: Richard sees the light, though too late; Miss Flyte frees her birds; Trooper George reconciles with his conscience; John Jarndyce, Allan, and Esther settle into a suitable domesticity. But Dickens seems uncomfortable with notions of absolute clarity, a condition he equates with moral absolutism and complacency. The novel is replete with lessons about the limitations of our sight and insight. Sir Leicester, whose station should raise him above the manifold fray, ends up blind; Richard, whose vision has been fixed on the suit, dies; Bucket, whose profession is detection, fails to find Lady Dedlock in time to save her. In a telling and tender scene, Trooper George visits his elder brother at the latter's ironworks, where in "a bare office, with bare windows," the younger Rouncewell looks out at industry: " . . . iron-dust on everything; and the smoke is seen, through the windows, rolling heavily out of the tall chimnies, to mingle with the smoke from a vaporous Babylon of other chimnies" (880: 63). The elder Rouncewell, whose contribution to world pollution is not purposeless fog, but purposeful smoke, is remarkably unassuming about his power over others and his own self-knowledge: " 'You know yourself, George,' says the elder brother, returning the grip of his hand, 'and perhaps you know me better than I know myself. Take your way. So that we don't quite lose one another again, take your way' " (884: 63). In these lines (spoken as the characters gaze out a window), we find the degrees of knowledge and loss linked paradoxically. Rouncewell disclaims omniscience and lets his brother go in the hope of never losing him again. Partial knowledge, like the partial sight we gain through windows, seems more valuable than any pretense of absolute clarity.

The Window Tax targeted houses particularly, the domestic space where, as countless critics have noted, Dickens turned for solace and order. With the confluence of house-hunting, the fight to repeal the Window Tax, and the gestation of *Bleak House,* it is not surprising that, as evidenced by the article "Plate Glass," Dickens cultivated an interest in the subject of glass manufacture, to which topic we now turn.

Plate-Glass to Crystal Palace

Until the late Renaissance, glass was a luxury item. Most windows, outside of cathedrals and manor houses, were shuttered or covered with oiled parchment. By the seventeenth century, glass windows began to appear regularly in domestic and commercial buildings. By the nineteenth century, glass windows could be found in all classes and types of building. Plate glass was handmade in one of two ways: either the crown method (glass spun into a crown shape) or the cylinder method (glass spun into a cylinder, cut, and flattened into a plate). The cylinder method was the more flexible and efficient, though rarely seen in England before being adopted by the Chance Brothers, who used it to glaze the Crystal Palace.

By mid-century, the English glass industry was thriving. In December 1850, Dickens and W. H. Hall visited a glass-manufacturing site and wrote of the experience in an essay entitled "Plate Glass," published in *Household Words* on February 1, 1851 (2: 433–437). At once awestruck and repelled, the visitors evoke a hellish scene in language as vivid as Melville's description of the rendering pots on the Pequod. At the foot of the factory lies the industrial detritus:

Having, by this time, crossed a yard, we stood on the edge of a foul creek of
the Thames, so horribly slimy that a crocodile, or an alligator, or any scaly
monster of the Saurian period, seemed much more likely to be encountered in
such a neighbourhood than the beautiful substance that makes our modern
rooms so glittering and bright; our streets so dazzling, and our windows at once
so radiant and strong.   (*HW* 2: 434)

The "monster of the Saurian period" (who anticipates the Megalosaurus that
ambles through the first paragraph of *Bleak House*) suggests not only the
chemical transformation from sand and limestone to glass, but also the history
of intrigue and industrial espionage associated with glassmaking: "Its mixture
with the other materials is a secret, even to us. We give the man who possesses
it a handsome salary for exercising his mystery" (*HW* 2:434). The visitors
step into the factory itself:

It was a sight indeed. A lofty and enormous hall, with windows in the high
walls open to the rainy night. Down the centre, a fearful row of roaring furnaces,
white-hot: to look at which, even through the chinks in the iron screens before
them, and masked, seemed to scorch and splinter the very breath within one.
At right angles with this hall, another, an immense building in itself, with
unearthly-looking instruments hanging on the walls, and strewn about, as if for
some diabolical cookery. In dark corners, where the furnaces redly glimmered
on them, from time to time, knots of swarthy muscular men, with nets drawn
over their faces, or hanging from their hats: confusedly grouped, wildly dressed,
scarcely heard to mute amidst the roaring fires, and mysteriously coming and
going, like picturesque shadows, cast by the terrific glare. Such figures there
must have been, once upon a time, in some such scene, ministering to the
worship of fire, and feeding the altars of the cruel god with victims. Figures
not dissimilar, alas! there have been, torturing and burning, even in Our Savi-
our's name. But, happily those bitter days are gone. The senseless world is
tortured for the good of man, and made to take new forms in his service. Upon
the rack, we stretch the ores and metals of the earth, and not in the image of
the Creator of all. These fires and figures are the agents of civilisation, and not
of deadly persecution and black murder. Burn fires and welcome! making a
light in England that shall not be quenched by all the monkish dreamers in the
world!   (*HW* 2: 435)

Thus does Dickens moralize and nationalize Victorian industrial progress in
heightened, nearly operatic language. The glassmaking process is an allegory
of industrial alchemy: faceless men in a factory system forge a gleaming,
modern substance out of natural elements melded in vast, mechanized pots
and molded into desired forms, all on a massive commercial scale.

Dickens's visit to the Thames Glass Works was quite timely. His one-time
publishing associate, the self-made engineer-architect Joseph Paxton, was
erecting his Crystal Palace, an engineering feat that would thrust architecture
into the modernist age of mechanical reproduction.[9] Built to house the Great

Exhibition of 1851, the Crystal Palace answered one of the major demands made by commercialism: cheap, effective lighting for factories, railroad stations, department stores, shopping arcades, and office buildings. As architects responded—W. H. Barlow engineered the glazed vaulting of St. Pancras Station in 1864; Eiffel and Boileau constructed the iron and glass Bon Marché in 1867; H. H. Richardson built the Marshall Field Store, with its street-front Chicago windows, in 1885–glass manufacturers strove to keep up with rising demand for size, stability, and transparency. Throughout much of the nineteenth century, glass was handmade, though improved techniques resulted in large-scale manufacture. Only towards the end of the century was glassmaking automated. The result was stunning. Large plate glass windows set in iron skeletons gave way in the twentieth century to the glass curtain and finally to the glass box.

By the beginning of the twentieth century, glass architecture had become an integral part of the urban landscape. On the continent, especially, artists and architects welcomed the machine age and its glass and iron production. Paul Scheerbart, a modernist poet, announced a new "philosophy" of glass in his 1914 manifesto *Glasarchitektur*:

> If we want our culture to rise to a higher level, we are obliged, for better or for worse, to change our architecture. And this only becomes possible if we take away the closed character from the rooms in which we live. We can only do that by introducing glass architecture, which lets in the light of the sun, the moon, and the stars, not merely through a few windows, but through every possible wall, which will be made entirely of glass—of coloured glass. The new environment, which we thus create, must bring us a new culture. (41)

Scheerbart's revolution was, as he himself acknowledges, prefigured in early botanical glasshouses and especially in the Crystal Palace. What Paxton built to house the Great Exhibition turned architecture upside down: "The Crystal Palace is the mid-nineteenth century touchstone, if one wishes to discover what belongs wholly to the nineteenth century and what points forward into the twentieth," writes Nikolaus Pevsner (11). Not that Paxton drew upon glasshouse architecture alone. Some of the magic lay in the architectural heterogeneity: the Crystal Palace was part gothic cathedral, part railway station, part arcade, part winter garden. It seemed, despite this heritage, both "entirely novel" and "admirably adapted for the purpose" of an exhibition dedicated to progress, in the view of the Gothic revivalist architect G. E. Street (qtd. in McKean 40). As glasshouse winter gardens housed tropical plants plundered from the colonies, so did the Crystal Palace house the ideals of industrial and commercial progress. The building embodied Victorian progress and Victorian attributes. It valorized the transitional (progress moving forward), the ephemeral (progress as a spiritual journey), the imperial (globalism in the service of nationalism), and the invisible (progress as an expression of the natural order). And it looked forward to Scheerbart's modernism, where transparency would be seen as a value in itself.

Why, then, does *Bleak House* contain no mention of, nor even a recognizable allusion to, the Crystal Palace, an omission that is a "continuing puzzlement" to its readers?[10] The explanation, according to Philip Landon, lies in the very nature of the opposition: "the architectural and the literary work are in competition with each other, as the parodic echo in Dickens's title strongly suggests" (36). On the one hand, the Crystal Palace and its consumer's paradise of unparalleled material abundance; on the other hand, the London of *Bleak House*, with its poverty, degradation, filth, and hopelessness that was everywhere apparent to Dickens.

True, at least some of the powerful values and aspirations represented by the Crystal Palace resonated with Dickens. Its glass architecture literally embodied fresh air, cleanliness, and light—the very opposite of Tom-all-Alone's. Its rational construction ensured that objects of all sizes, shapes, and purposes could be viewed equally, however packed with exhibitors and visitors. Laid out like a city within a cathedral, including "avenues," a "transept," and a "nave," the Crystal Palace struck most viewers as both orderly and infinite.[11] But unlike the city, John McKean argues, the Crystal Palace was "completely conflict-free" (31).[12] With its palms and flowers, living elms (preserved on the site by Paxton's special design), soaring birds, and centrally located crystal fountain, the building struck some as "fairy-like" —an oasis of unreality, a nineteenth-century pastoral site where discord was banished. The Exhibition experience replicated this "pastoral" effect: the discord many Exhibition critics had feared—working-class intrusions and nationalist squabbles—never materialized. In short, just as winter gardens subsume "nature" into the urban experience, so the Crystal Palace subsumed economic imbalances into its cheerful cathedral of global consumerism.[13]

The very transparency feared by critics of the Crystal Palace (that glass would facilitate industrial espionage, for instance) lends itself to a powerful political theorem: glass architecture lets us see the political process, rendering that process honest and understandable.[14] This argument, so forceful and seemingly self-evident, becomes an idée fixe among modern architects. From Hannes Meyer and Hans Wittwer's League of Nations project to Norman Foster's transparent cupola topping the Reichstag, twentieth-century architects have used glass to lay bare politics to the skies and, presumably, to the populace: "no back corridors for backstairs diplomacy but open, glazed rooms for public negotiation of honest men" (Meyer, qtd. in McKean 32). With glass architecture, the interior is no longer cut off from the exterior; indeed, the interior ceases to exist. All is public and exterior; all is knowable.

In short, glass architecture embodies the enlightenment project, with its universal and knowable subject and its rationalizing structures.

Still, the transparency of the Crystal Palace was, for some Victorian observers, quite troubling. What did that vast nothingness, the Crystal Palace, represent, if not moral neutrality? Said Gottfried Semper, "This glass-covered vacuum will suit anything one wishes to bring into it" (qtd. in McKean 36). Moreover, transparency is itself contradictory and elusive. Take glass as a substance: it is clear, and thus seems to reveal all, opening up whatever lies below the surface. Yet it is also reflective, and thus not revealing, but opaque on its surface. So which is it? Is glass all surface, pretending to reveal, but, in fact, concealing? Or does it reveal the entirety of what lies on the other side? Ironically, the birth of glass curtain architecture coincides with what Stuart Ewen calls the triumph of superficiality: as Ewen argues, the nineteenth century witnessed a "separation of surface and substance" (34), a process nowhere more evident than in architecture. The glass curtain wall, emptied of its load-bearing duties, is mere skin hanging over an iron skeleton, with the promise of utter transparency. But isn't the transparency of glass an ideal rather than a reality? The Crystal Palace, though nominally transparent, certainly had its limits: from a distance, the tinted glass panes were for all practical purposes opaque. Even with clear glass, transparency tends to turn into reflectivity (the opposite of clarity) as light beams hit and bounce off the surface. Further, glass is highly subject to the effects of dust and grime; the elements eat away at its transparency. Thus, glass teeters on the verge of opacity. This functional ambivalence may have contributed to the development of a commercial consciousness, argues Ewen. For the modern consumer,

> . . . the visual juxtaposition of *style* and *self* is continual. Passing by shop window displays, broad expanses of gleaming plate glass, people confront a reflection of themselves, superimposed against the dream world of the commodity. An invidious comparison is instantaneously provoked between the "off-guard" imperfections of ourselves—suddenly on view—and the studied perfection of the display. (85)

Still, glass promised a degree of clarity that no other material could rival, at least in the nineteenth century.[15] Little wonder, then, that *Punch*, its satirical instincts whetted by the controversy over Paxton's design, extolled the "transparency" of the Crystal Palace over the impenetrable Gothic stone of the Houses of Parliament, where Parliamentary shenanigans hid from the light of day.[16]

Does transparency actually make things clearer? Dickens, for one, seems skeptical, at least in regard to the Crystal Palace and its contents. Visiting the Great Exhibition left him more muddled than enlightened: "I find I am 'used up' by the Exhibition. I don't say 'there's nothing in it'—there's too much. I have only been twice. So many things bewildered me. I have a natural horror of sights, and the fusion of so many sights in one has not decreased it'' (*Letters* 6: 428). Indeed, the very flood of illumination produced by the Crystal Palace may have contributed to this "fusion." Missing from the displays were boundaries and shadows, and thus delineation and perspective, since the Crystal Palace bathed everything in equal amounts of light. The building seemed like an "incorporeal space," said Richard Lucae, a contemporary German critic (qtd. in McKean 32), in which transparency overwhelmed perception.

Dickens begins to write *Bleak House* just as Paxton brings transparency to architecture. Yet the language, plot, and imagery of *Bleak House* are overwhelmingly opaque. Even the narratives, Esther's tortured "I" alternating with the "omniscient" narrator's penetrating observation, suggest limits to transparency, for if the narrator *were* omniscient and "his" narration a version of transparency, Esther's narrative would be superfluous or subsumed, instead of standing on its own.[17] Is transparency presented as an ideal in the novel? Indeed, the novel's characters struggle within the labyrinth and fog of London and Chancery. Transparency would certainly end that struggle. Yet even the most insightful character, Bucket, is only moderately successful in seeing through the fog. Utter transparency does not seem possible in *Bleak House*. Instead, "seeing" is provisional and hard earned or even accidental. If no medium in the London of *Bleak House* can assure transparency, if, that is, no device external to the characters embodies transcendent knowledge, then in order to see and gain knowledge, characters must use imperfect tools.

Windows are such tools. Unlike the Crystal Palace, with its (theoretically) universalizing transparency, the window creates distinctive space. It frames the view from within and without, mapping a limited space for the viewer to observe, protecting the viewer from being seen, creating boundaries for vision and access. It controls information among characters and readers; it encourages thematic connections by focusing critical attention on a relatively arbitrary, but heightened view; it represents vision and the limits of vision, both in its symbolic aspect and in its heuristic capacity; and it requires characters to position and reposition themselves. Thus, a window may become an actor, for better or worse, in the manufacture of knowledge. But, as with actors, the window exists within the flux, offering only provisional, partial, and uncertain, rather than absolute vision.

Literary Windows, Functional Windows

Literary windows proliferate in the modern novel, and for good reason.[18] They may, for instance, suggest insight or prophetic vision to the reader or to characters. Camus's twentieth-century doctor gazes out a window at his ordinary village and imagines the horrors of the plague. The act of looking out seems to create the possibility of looking forward, as if the imagination were loosed outward into space and forward in time. Ideally suited to urban settings, windows turn cityscapes into theaters and building facades into proscenia. Zola's Thérèse Raquin looks through the window at the blank wall that is her life; Tolstoy's Levin first spots Kitty displayed in the window of a carriage. Long before Bill Gates, Daniel Defoe imagined windows as axes of communication: those confined to houses "had no way to converse with any of their Friends but out at their Windows, where they wou'd make such piteous Lamentations, as often mov'd the Hearts of those they talk'd with, and of other who passing by heard their Story . . . " (*Journal of a Plague Year*, 125).

Windows help us perceive and communicate. They are camera lenses, focusing and framing, doubling the eye. They magnify: behind plate glass windows, marketable goods seem intense and dramatic. But while focusing our sight, windows also restrict our view from within and from without. In one of the most significant gestures of *Bleak House*, Tulkinghorn does not see Lady Dedlock on her way to Nemo's grave because he does not look out of his window at the very moment that she passes.

Beyond their literary uses, windows are practical devices. They give us ventilation and natural light. For nineteenth-century reformers, these two functions crystallized into the architectural equivalent of preventive medicine and moral reformation, particularly in urban settings. In 1867, the architect Joseph Gwilt lamented the condition of working-class residences: "Workmen . . . have been hitherto strangers not only to the conveniences which render home attractive, but to the barest accommodation necessary to render social life tolerably decent . . . " (1063). He provides his own bottom-line specifications for acceptable light and ventilation:

> The door should open into a porch or vestibule, and be placed at the end of the wall opposite to the window, so that when both are open the air in the dwelling may be effectively changed. The window should be sufficiently large to light every part of the room. It should be fitted with sashes to insure top and bottom ventilation; and its sill should not be more than 2 feet 9 inches from the floor, to prevent high furniture being placed under it. Tolerably large panes of glass will be found to last longer than if the panes be small.   (1063)

But Gwilt's bottom-line was far from the reality. Countless nineteenth-century observers, from Engels to Mayhew, described appalling housing conditions. In *Bleak House,* the abject and even the working poor live in gloomy, ill-ventilated houses. Tom-all-Alone's; Nemo's room; the Jellyby's house, its curtain "fastened up with a fork" (49:4) and its "windows . . . encrusted with dirt'' (58: 5); the brick-maker's house, its window overlooking the pigsty—all intolerably airless and dark.

Chesney Wold, on the other hand, has ample light and air, with its grand windows and vast grounds. As a practical matter, the Dedlocks live in a world of light and air. But their psychological states overwhelm physical reality, transforming mansions into prisons. The house stifles Lady Dedlock:

> The view from my Lady Dedlock's own windows is alternately a lead-colored view, and a view in Indian ink (18: 3); Sir Leicester is apprehensive that my Lady, not being well, will take cold at that open window. My Lady is obliged to him, but would rather sit there, for the air (599: 40); "I wish to hear it at the window, then. I can't breathe where I am" (607: 41); Interposed between her and the fading light of day in the now quiet street, his [Tulkinghorn's] shadow falls upon her, and he darkens all before her   (681: 48).

By contrast, Bleak House feels open and airy to its inhabitants. It is a place of unexpected windows and unimpeded views of nature. True, the house closes up when necessary, particularly during the epidemic, when Esther draws the curtains and shuts herself off from the household. As Charley lies ill, Esther will not see Ada, but instead stands "behind the window-curtain listening and replying, but not so much as looking out!" (459: 31). When Esther herself falls ill, she is at first able to deceive Ada by hiding behind the curtain. But later, she orders Charley to lock the door, and the sickroom seems to collapse into itself: "I had never known before how short life really was, and into how small a space the mind can put it" (513: 35). When Esther regains her sight, the windows regain their normal use.

Looking Out

As Esther explores the many-cornered Bleak House, she finds a window "commanding a beautiful view (we saw a great expanse of darkness lying underneath the stars)" and (according to her presupposition) "lattice windows and green growth pressing through them" (78: 6), as well as John Jarndyce's room with its "window open" (79: 6) and the house's "illuminated windows, softened here and there by shadows of curtains, shining out upon the star-light night" (80: 6). The window views are, like much of Esther's observation, deceptively sweet. The view from Ada's window may be beautiful, but only as a sublime and terrifying landscape of infinite darkness beneath a distant night sky. Like spectacles or binoculars or the camera lens, windows increase both the limits and the acuity of sight. The window frame cuts off our peripheral vision, but what we see is heightened in importance, since it is framed and focused. Indeed, the window, like a lens, seems to play an active part in what we see: in Esther's description, Ada's window looks out, "commanding a beautiful view," as if the view had been ordered up. This seemingly active role in vision suggests the "imaginative" function of windows, as we shall see. As Esther and Ada peer through their window, they gaze into what cannot be seen, the "great expanse of darkness" that is both unknown and presciently ominous. The landscape obviously foreshadows Ada's future pain. Esther sees other equivocal signs as she peers out various windows in her new house: "green growth pressing through" a window (78:6) as if the house were under attack; brightly "illuminated windows" that must be "softened here and there by shadows of curtains" (80: 6) as if the light might overwhelm the world.

These lens-like qualities of windows—focusing and magnifying—are particularly useful in *Bleak House*, since they reflect a similar duality in Esther's narration. Esther is adept at seeing doubly: her sentimentality lives alongside an acute eye for detail. This double vision occurs regularly. For instance, as she leaves Miss Barbary's house, she looks back with longing: "As long as I could see the house, I looked back at it from the window, through my tears . . . .There was to be a sale; and an old hearth-rug with roses on it, which always seemed to me the first thing in the world I had ever seen, was hanging outside in the frost and snow . . . " (31: 6). Like a prism that bends light, Esther's tears invert the reality of her early life: she leaves her life of utter deprivation with "a sorrowful heart," believing herself at fault for the emotional vacuum that has nurtured her. Were those tears to govern her narration, we would be left with impenetrable distortion. Yet her eyes also see and report a very telling detail: the hasty sale of the hearth-rug, evidence that Mrs. Rachael cannot rid herself of Esther and her trappings soon enough. Just as Esther is no longer trapped in her frozen prison, we are not trapped by her distorting sentimentality. As the carriage carries her away, she accepts the architecture of her new situation, turning from one window to another:

> When the house was out of sight, I sat, with my bird-cage in the straw at my feet, forward on the low seat, to look out of the high window; watching the frosty trees, that were like beautiful pieces of spar; and the fields all smooth and white with last night's snow; and the sun, so red but yielding so little heat; and the ice, dark like metal, where the skaters and sliders had brushed the snow away . . . .   (31: 6)

The window frames a scene worthy of romantic poetry: the juxtaposition of snow-white fields and fiery sun, the deadly and deadening metallic ice, the intrusion into nature of the skaters. The words vacillate between rich metaphor and rough realism. This "double" vision—the distorted vision of her heart alongside the clear vision of her eyes—produces a narrative that is at once naïve and knowledgeable, prescient and focused.

Windows may not ensure clear vision, but they make it possible. Although London is a befogged, sinuous, illegible place of deception and secrets, windows offer the possibility of seeing beyond one form of opacity: walls. Still, even the activity of seeing through windows is limited, particularly for women. If any character has a room with a view, and thus, seemingly, the hope of "seeing," it is Miss Flyte, who lives atop Krook's house. Miss Flyte looks out over the rooftops. Hers is literally a "bird's eye view." She and her caged birds gaze upon the avowed agent of their imprisonment, Chancery. "She could look at it, she said, in the night: especially in the moonshine" (66: 5). Miss Flyte does live high enough for light to enter: "There! We'll let in the full light," she proclaims, to the delight of her birds. But she rejects adequate ventilation. "I cannot admit the air freely," she says, fearing Lady Jane, Krook's fierce cat, whom Miss Flyte likens to a wolf at the door (67: 5). Her window looks out over Lincoln's Inn Hall, and for her that is its only purpose. Of the limitations of her life-focus, Miss Flyte seems well aware. She closely identifies with the birds, whose cages contain no portals under their own control. Like them, her vision is limited and effectively alienated. From her garret window, she sees the infinite skies and the very pinnacle of Chancery. But the skies do not free her from Chancery's grasp, and her view of Chancery does not help her understand the futility of her suit.[19]

If Miss Flyte has only a single garret window, Lady Dedlock's houses are full of windows. Yet hers is a "deadened world, and its growth is sometimes unhealthy for want of air" (17: 2). However leaden and drab the view, Lady Dedlock is an inveterate window-gazer. Rarely is she described in a scene without reference to her looking, or attempting to look, from a window. Indeed, the progressive blocking of her vision parallels her psychic descent. As her husband reads from Tulkinghorn's letter announcing his having seen Nemo, Lady Dedlock, "leaning forward, looks out of her window" (168: 12). At Chesney Wold, with Volumnia and Sir Leicester, "Lady Dedlock, seated at an open window with her arm upon its cushioned ledge and looking out at the evening shadows falling on the park, has seemed to attend since the lawyer's name was mentioned" (597: 40). As Tulkinghorn, in full possession of the facts of Esther's birth, dictates his terms, Lady Dedlock says:

> "I wish to hear it at the window, then. I can't breathe where I am."
> His jealous glance as she walks that way, betrays an instant's misgiving that she may have it in her thoughts to leap over, and dashing against ledge and cornice, strike her life out upon the terrace below. But, a moment's observation of her figure as she stands in the window without any support, looking out at the stars—not up—gloomily out at those stars which are low in the heavens—reassures him.   (607: 41)

In any architecture, windows offer a psychological connection to the outside world. As light slowly reveals Lady Dedlock's secret, her own world narrows and her surroundings seem increasingly carceral. In the final interview with Tulkinghorn, her view to the outside is completely blocked: "Mr. Tulkinghorn . . . retires into a window opposite. Interposed between her and the fading light of day in the now quiet street, his shadow falls upon her, and he darkens all before her. Even so does he darken her life . . . " (681: 48). Tulkinghorn has become quite literally the prison bars, his body blocking her escape as surely as does his knowledge. Beyond Tulkinghorn lies the fashionable street that houses Lady Dedlock's carceral society:

> It is a dull street, under the best conditions; where the two long rows of houses stare at each other with that severity, that half a dozen of its greatest mansions seem to have been slowly stared into stone, rather than originally built in that material. It is a street of such dismal grandeur, so determined not to condescend to liveliness, that the doors and windows hold a gloomy state of their own in black paint and dust, and the echoing mews behind have a dry and massive appearance, as if they were reserved to stable the stone chargers of noble statues.   (681: 48)

Stony and oppressive, the houses are as vigilant as Tulkinghorn and as tenacious as Chancery. So imprisoned is Lady Dedlock by the architecture of her class that she is, for all practical purposes, entombed. The carceral space is transformed into carceral time as the Dedlocks linger in a luxuriant, purposeless limbo outside of the present, yet superimposed on it, in "petrified bowers" illuminated by "the upstart gas" (681: 48).

Not even fog is required to create carceral space in London. D. A. Miller notes that Chancery's "operations far exceed the architecture in which it is apparently circumscribed . . . .Though the court is affirmed to be situated 'at the heart of the fog,' this literally nebulous information only restates the difficulty of locating it substantially, since there is 'fog everywhere'(198)." At the most extreme edges of Chancery's grip lie London's most impoverished places. There, carceral space is often defined by the lack of windows. Nemo dies alone in an airless, sunless room. The broken windows of the bricklayer's house, looking out on the adjacent pigsty, neither illuminate nor ventilate. Tom-all-Alone's, putrid and infectious, is a ruin without windows: "It is a street of perishing blind houses, with their eyes stoned out; without a pane of glass; without so much as a window-frame, with the bare blank shutters tumbling from their hinges and falling asunder," says John Jarndyce (109: 8).

Looking Glass

Krook's shop suggests the complexity and porous nature of mid-nineteenth-century commerce, looking forward to mechanical mass production but still tied to pre- and early-industrial manufacture. It lies in the shadows of Lincoln's Inn and, like the Crystal Palace, overflows with goods. But whereas the Crystal Palace displayed wares using an elaborate, rational system, Krook's objects are sorted into obscure categories emblematic of Chancery: books, parchment, keys, and rags all representing scraps from the juridical machine. And, unlike the Crystal Palace, which did not sell wares but certainly aimed to market them, Krook does not intend to give up a thing. He seems the antithesis of a shop-master. In his shop, only Nemo's advertisement enters into an exchange system. Perversely, in Krook's shop, the shop-owner himself consumes, and the shop visitors are eyed for their goods:

> "You see I have so many things here," he resumed, holding up the lantern, "of so many kinds, and all, as the neighbours think (but *they* know nothing), wasting away and going to rack and ruin, that that's why they have given me and my place a christening. And I have so many old parchmentses and papers in my stock. And I have a liking for rust and must and cobwebs. And all's fish that comes to my net. And I can't abear to part with anything I once lay hold of (or so my neighbours think, but what do *they* know?) or to alter anything, or to have any sweeping, nor scouring, nor cleaning, nor repairing going on about me. That's the way I've got the ill name of Chancery. *I* don't mind. I go to see my noble and learned brother pretty well every day, when he sits in the Inn. He don't notice me, but I notice him. There's no great odds betwixt us. We both grub on in a muddle."   (63–64: 5)

The objects in Krook's window are not modern commodities (like those contained in the Great Exhibition), but rather the detritus of early industrialism. His is a self-described "warehouse," not a word we associate with the direct sale of goods. Indeed, not one, but two signs (a redundancy that suggests Krook's intuition that words, like things, are inadequate to their purpose) propose storage as opposed to sales: "KROOK, RAG AND BOTTLE WAREHOUSE," and "KROOK, DEALER IN MARINE STORES" (61: 5). Rags, bottles, and marine stores (ironwork and other material from old ships[20]) seem to have landed in Krook's care as if in some halfway house toward the modern junkyard.

Clearly, the shop participates only nominally in the exchange processes of commerce. We see what Krook has procured, but he advertises to gather, not to sell: "BONES BOUGHT," "KITCHEN-STUFF BOUGHT," "OLD IRON BOUGHT," "WASTE PAPER BOUGHT," and "LADIES' AND GENTLEMEN'S WARDROBES BOUGHT" (61: 5). Behind the window glass, Esther and her companions see bottles intended neither for their original purpose nor for a substitute purpose. They simply collect dust. In theory, the endless flow of goods contained within age-old yet marvelously modern glass bottles should glide without visible effort from the producer to the consumer. Instead, the empty bottles illustrate the problem of supply and demand, and a flaw in the logic of capitalism: once goods have been supplied and demand fulfilled, the two sides of the equation should be equal, with nothing left over. Only Krook, on the margins of the commercial world, reminds us that much remains, unwanted and unusable, once supply and demand have had their turn.

As D. A. Miller has suggested, Chancery is the ultimate consumer, able to penetrate like fog throughout all space, "all-encompassing because it cannot be compassed in turn"(199). Krook's shop is a kind of Chancery-parody. It contains aged law books and parchment scrolls, over which the black contents of numerous inkbottles have at one time spilled. Like Chancery, Krook's appetite is impervious to boundaries: his shop overflows, yet he is still acquisitive. The shop is laden with goods, as was the Crystal Palace, and Esther tries to categorize this riotous confusion. She cannot, however, any more than Dickens himself could take in the spectacle of the Crystal Palace. She imagines that the keys might have "once belonged to doors or rooms or strong chests in lawyers' offices" (keys to unlock legal secrets?) and that the litter of rags "might have been counsellors' bands and gowns torn up" (juridical power frayed and tattered?).

At least Krook's window is penetrable. Chancery, by contrast, lurks behind nearly opaque windows, as foggy as the weather:

> Well may the court be dim, with wasting candles here and there; well may the fog hang heavy in it, as if it would never get out; well may the stained glass windows lose their color, and admit no light of day into the place; well may the uninitiated from the streets, who peep in through the glass panes in the door, be deterred from entrance by its owlish aspect, and by the drawl languidly echoing to the roof from the padded dais where the Lord High Chancellor looks into the lantern that has no light in it, and where the attendant wigs are all stuck in a fog-bank! This is the Court of Chancery; which has its decaying houses and its blighted lands in every shire; which has its worn-out lunatic in every madhouse, and its dead in every churchyard; which has its ruined suitor, with his slipshod heels and threadbare dress, borrowing and begging through the round of every man's acquaintance; which gives to monied might the means abundantly of wearying out the right; which so exhausts finances, patience, courage, hope; so overthrows the brain and breaks the heart; that there is not an honorable man among its practitioners who would not give—who does not often give—the warning, "Suffer any wrong that can be done to you, rather than come here!"   (12–13: 1)

Unlike Krook's more accessible shop, Chancery is neither marginal nor fractional. Its control extends out from its center, the origin of its *logos*, of which the suit of Jarndyce and Jarndyce is one example. It is, D.A. Miller argues, "in all places at once,"—an "unlocalizability" (198) made explicit in the first chapter of the novel. Whereas Esther can observe the contents of Krook's window, no single vision can observe the contents within Chancery. Even the encompassing eye of the anonymous narrator is befuddled by the swirl of gray wigs and the plethora of papers. Normally, a window permits light and images from without to enter and those from within to exit. The Chancery windows do not play by these rules. They pervert physics, as Dickens suggests in his ambiguous syntax: "well may the court be dim . . . ."—which I read to mean either "it is as if" or "it may as well be that." Whatever the intention of the glazier, whatever the physical properties of the glass, the state of mind that is Chancery overwhelms the physical properties and either modifies their influence or trumps them altogether. The "Lord High Chancellor looks into the lantern that has no light in it," says the narrator. In Chancery, elements, even durable glass or light, do not follow nature's laws. They are, instead, outside of nature, transformed from an indifferent providence into a malevolent force.

Looking Through the Glass

From the seventeenth through the late eighteenth centuries, architectural allusions often served as a trope for tradition—technologies of power and practice that govern us from the past. Political power is celebrated in such English poems of place as "On Appleton House" and "Penshurst"; social prestige adheres to Squire Western's country estate; spirituality infuses Herbert's Temple. Starting in the late eighteenth century, however, poets and novelists began to use architecture not as a sign of permanence, but rather as an indication of ruin and decay: Walpole's *Castle of Otranto*, Wordworth's "The Ruined Cottage," Brontë's *Wuthering Heights*, Eliot's *Dorlcote Mill*—and, in painting, Constable and Friedrich. Gothic, haunted, uncanny,[21] unstable, decaying architecture implies corrosion, perhaps to be followed by revolution, transition, and the provision of space for new possibilities, perhaps to fall into nothingness.

In *Bleak House,* architecture is either in transition or headed inevitably for transition (or nothingness), whatever resistance is put forth by its inhabitants. Sir Leicester clings to his social position, but the power that rests upon the feudal past is betrayed by the architecture of Chesney Wold: "The pictures of the Dedlocks past and gone have seemed to vanish into the damp walls in mere lowness of sprits, as the housekeeper has passed along the old rooms, shutting up the shutters" (18: 2). The past, like mildew or mold aggravated by poor ventilation, is absorbed into the aging walls. Architecture deteriorates (Tom-all-Alone's) or survives through reinvention. Tulkinghorn, the character most adept at using traditional mores as technologies of power, lives in a building that is formerly a house of state ... in whose shrunken fragments of its greatness, lawyers lie like maggots in nuts. But its roomy staircases, passages, and ante-chambers, still remain; and even its painted ceilings, where Allegory, in Roman helmet and celestial linen, sprawls among balustrades and pillars, flowers, clouds, and big-legged boys, and makes the head ache—as would seem to be Allegory's object always, more or less.   (145–46: 10)

The apartment serves as both office and home, its "out of date" décor and unobtrusive demeanor suited to this "Oyster"-like inhabitant who feeds on an aging elite (146: 10). Change, for better or worse, permeates the London of *Bleak House*. The dwellings in Tom-all-Alone's crash to the ground. Krook's house mutates from storehouse into gothic horror. Chesney Wold is eventually "abandoned to darkness and vacancy" (910: 66). Bleak House, the one locus of stability (as opposed to permanence), is nevertheless fragile and subject to change, as Jarndyce suggests when he moves to London: "Bleak House ... must learn to take care of itself" (848: 60). In the end, the name "Bleak House" migrates from one dwelling to another. Only Chancery seems to represent encompassing, absolute, unchanging power. Only Chancery claims a kind of permanence, having dispersed its decay outward into "houses and ... blighted lands in every shire" (13: 1).

Not only are the non-Chancery dwellings malleable in name and substance, but they are also limiting in terms of the vision they allow from the interior. Windows are like zoom lenses; depending on one's distance from the glass, one's angle changes from narrow to wide. Windows may be shuttered or simply ignored, as well. Tulkinghorn's window resembles a panopticon with a commanding view of Lincoln's Inns Fields. It is certainly the perfect device for the quintessential observer who desires omniscience and, at the same time, obscurity—all seeing, but never seen, "an Oyster of the old school, whom nobody can open" (146: 10). Encased in his shell, with Allegory pointing helpfully, Tulkinghorn should have perfect oversight of the narrative field.

But Tulkinghorn is not omniscient. He fails to look out of his window at the opportune moment, when Lady Dedlock passes by. Transparency—complete, panoptic vision—does not occur: "Why should Mr. Tulkinghorn, for such no-reason, look out of window?" (238: 16) Causality may be an inexorable path that action clears in a forest of possibilities, but that path cannot be controlled nor even discerned by one person. Tulkinghorn, however powerful, is constrained by the limits of his physical universe—and the window is an aperture, not a glass curtain. He might walk to the window for no reason and peer out or, in tune with his character (which would seem to eschew unmoti-vated action), he might sit meditating on the danger posed to him by Gridley, the outraged suitor. Of course, Allegory points to the window and, in the narrator's view, invites Tulkinghorn to gaze out on Lady Dedlock. But it is the point of allegory to be inscrutable in an age of myth, and to be ignored or marginalized into the realm of mere metaphor in an age of reason. So Tulkinghorn, a man of reason, does not go to the window.

During the Middle Ages, stained-glass windows told stories of revealed truth. The nineteenth century revived Gothic architecture and built new cathedral-like edifices—railway stations, arcades, conservatories, and, of course, the Crystal Palace—of glass and iron. Clear glass revealed new truths and narratives: the narrative of acquisition and fashion, told in the shop windows of Leadenhall Market; the narrative of nature and its submission, told in the conservatories of Chatsworth and Kew; the narratives of geographical mobility and commercial intercourse told in the splendid glass shed at St. Pancras and in the international displays of the Crystal Palace. And in the shop windows of the streets, literate audiences read signs and annotations explaining the commodities of mammon.

If the imagery of stained-glass windows seduced viewers into accepting revealed truth, how does clear glass seduce its passersby into commodity exchange? One answer lies in the twin aspects of glass: transparency and reflectivity. Rather than contain the medium of seduction within the glass, clear glass creates a relationship between the viewer and the objects viewed, as if the glass were a narrator creating a relationship between reader and story. The viewer enters into commercial action, into commercial intercourse, into a community of owners. How natural these relations seem to the moneyed young Jarndyce wards as they walk through London window-gazing! Class markers in *Bleak House* are ranged around commercialism: the Dedlocks are ensconced in the feudal, precommercial past; the younger generation of Jarndyces are firmly in the grip of the modern commercial world and either resist the pull to avarice or succumb (as Richard does); Krook and Jo, illiterate and doomed, live on the margins of commerce, scratching at its doors and its meanings.

One character seems to live (or rather to have died) outside the commercial din: Nemo, who had sealed up the sole window in his room: "discolored shutters . . . drawn together" (151: 10) through which darkness peers in like "gaunt eyes . . . staring down upon the bed" (152: 10). The room contains no possessions save the "rain of ink" (151: 10) on the broken desk and an empty portmanteau. Nemo himself lies barefooted and filthy, his skin, hair, and beard melded and at one with the "scum and mist around him" (151: 10). His is a solitary opium den, coffin-like, lightless. It is the spiritual vortex of London, a spot of hell still within the circumference of bourgeois London, though on its margins. Objectively, we know one thing about Nemo: he has clear handwriting. But unlike Esther, he does not reveal himself through his writing. Rather, he simply reproduces writing. The words he copies do not seek any end; instead, they stall progress, or at least confound it. Legal documents, confusing, self-referential, swirling in on themselves, create a changeless limbo that negates time. Granted, a document somehow rises to the top of the legal pile and produces a moment of "clarity" and a kind of ending to the case and to the novel. But this clarity does not emanate from legal logic; rather, the "argument" sputters out from lack of fuel. Chancery, like some perpetual motion machine, can only be controlled negatively and locally. Once the suit of Jarndyce and Jarndyce is consumed, Chancery simply turns to another case that, we presume, will also resist clarity and transparency.

The most active viewer-through-windows is Inspector Bucket. Like Tulkinghorn, he collects information. But, unlike Tulkinghorn, he ranges far and wide over the urban landscape and its outlying reaches:

> Clattering over the stones at a dangerous pace, yet thoughtfully bringing his keen eyes to bear on every slinking creature whom he passes in the midnight streets, and even on the lights in the upper windows where people are going or gone to bed, and on all the turnings that he rattles by, and alike on the heavy sky, and on the earth where the snow lies thin—for something may present itself to assist him, anywhere—he dashes to his destination at such a speed, that when he stops, the horse half smothers him in a cloud of steam. (796: 56)

If Tulkinghorn inhabits an architectural tower, Bucket is wedded to the ground. He is terrestrial, looking up, around, in, and sometimes through. Even when he ascends to a higher architectural story, he gives the appearance of staying close to the ground:

> Mr. Jarndyce begs him to remain there, while he speaks to Miss Summerson. Mr. Bucket says he will; but, acting on his usual principle, does no such thing—following up-stairs instead, and keeping his man in sight. So he remains, dodging and lurking about in the gloom of the staircase, while they confer.
> (798: 56)

Yet the terrestrial Bucket is singularly capable of vision, signified by mental height: as he awaits Esther at the door of her house,

> he mounts a high tower in his mind, and looks out, far and wide. Many solitary figures he perceives, creeping through the streets; many solitary figures out on heaths, and roads, and lying under haystacks. But the figure that he seeks, is not among them. (798: 56)

Bucket's pursuit of Lady Dedlock after her flight is more active and his task more time-sensitive than Tulkinghorn's persecution of her. From the "tower in his mind," he sees a world that seems perfectly legible—with the exception of Lady Dedlock's thoughts. Again and again, he finds that Lady Dedlock cannot be read, nor even effectively described, as it turns out, since the description that is "sent out upon its travels" (802: 57) does not match her: she has so effectively disguised herself that she is unrecognizable even to her own daughter.

Not that Bucket is easily tricked. He sees through Skimpole's duplicity by analyzing the latter's language:

> Whenever a person says to you that they are as innocent as can be in all concerning money, look well after your own money, for they are dead certain to collar it . . . .Now I am not a poetical man myself, except in a vocal way when it goes round a company, but I'm a practical one, and that's my experience. So's this rule. Fast and loose in one thing, Fast in loose in everything.   (810: 57)

Bucket is a rugged reader, neither hoodwinked by common hypocrisy nor confused by class differences. Dickens undoubtedly sets him up as the master reader of the novel, shrewd and relentless, attentive to subtext and context. But his reading ability is limited in one way, as he acknowledges: he is practical, not "poetical" in nature. And, as it happens, Lady Dedlock's actions are suited to romance and drama, not logic and reason.

As they travel on the circuitous false trail, Bucket and Esther stop at an inn. Bucket has lost the trail. Esther's room, at the corner, has windows that allow her to look "two ways"—first, onto the road, where the road "sign was heavily swinging" and then into a dark pine forest (817: 57). As she peers into the forest, she imagines her mother dying—a vision so vivid that she faints. Here, finally, is a window that provides insight: Esther's vision proves to be literally true. It fails only to specify the location of Lady Dedlock's death. The window does not reveal through its transparency, however, any more than the road signs lead in the right direction. Instead, it works mysteriously, as if it were a modern version of allegory—a metaphor for the way one sees when abstractions and illusions fall away. Esther sees beyond the material into her own heart and mind. Not even Bucket is able to rival this moment of insight. Esther and the anonymous narrator seem to have become one, for a moment, although Esther's vision springs from psychological empathy rather than godlike vision. True, her insight cannot prevent her mother's death (insight is not the same thing as omnipotence). And, indeed, as a woman, her power of insight has social, as well as material, limits. Unfettered by such social limits, Bucket and Tulkinghorn enter and exit houses and rooms, peer through windows, command subordinates, and then act vigorously on the knowledge they have gained.

The Myth of Transparency

One of the founding tenets of Modernism (as a design aesthetic) in the mid-nineteenth century links transparency with honesty. Materials must represent what they are (not be hidden and covered up) and must appear to do only what they can do, what shapes they can form, loads they can bear and so on (and not deceive a viewer). In this view, engineering is more honest than architecture—and some sense of this is indeed what Modernist architects have felt resonate in the Crystal Palace from the start. Here is a building of clarity, transparency, and no deceit.   (McKean 32)

Philip Landon argues that although Dickens rejects the Crystal Palace as an icon of "the industrial spectacle" (38) he re-presents its "panoramic realism" (41). The central repository of this visionary perspective is Esther, who reveals a "habit of perpetually situating herself in a broader picture, soaring above the floundering egotists that populate the London household . . . . Esther has internalized the panoramic faculty that regulates the controlling narrative in which she herself is described in the third person" (41–42). Thus, the sweep of the Crystal Palace is recreated in the sweep of Esther's vision.

Persuasive and insightful as Landon's argument is, I am considering the Crystal Palace (as distinct from the Exhibition it held) as an icon of transparency rather than of "panoramic vision." Against this protomodernist desire for transparency, so integral to the materials and method of the Crystal Palace, Dickens offers the densely layered world of *Bleak House*. In such a world of fog, opacity, and deceit, characters struggle mightily to attain glimmers of knowledge. Some characters are better situated to see beyond themselves and their conditions (Esther, Mr. Jarndyce, Allan Woodcourt, Bucket). Others, whether tethered by subject position or by psychological impediment, are overwhelmed by the task (Richard Carstone, Miss Flyte, Jo). Even knowledge achieved at great cost may prove incomplete or useless. John Jarndyce and Esther see the lawsuit for the monstrous pit it is, but they cannot save Richard from its grip. Insight is, in and of itself, neither malevolent nor beneficent. The malevolent Tulkinghorn lurks in doorways, the ideal location for observing an entire room and gleaning the secrets therein. The beneficent Bucket also slinks in and out, observant and oyster-like in his own way.

Esther is perpetually modest about her ability to see, to understand, to record. "I am not clever," (24: 3) she announces at the beginning of her narration. "I don't know how it is, I seem always to be writing about myself. I mean all the time to write about other people, and I try to think about myself as little as possible . . . " (125: 9). She is, however, perhaps least insightful about herself, preferring distortion and modest evasion even to the end:

"And don't you know that you are prettier than you ever were?"

I did not know that; I am not certain that I know it now. But I know that my
dearest little pets are very pretty, and that my darling is very beautiful, and that
my husband is very handsome, and that my guardian has the brightest and most
benevolent face that ever was seen; and that they can very well do without
much beauty in me—even supposing—.   (914: 67)

However great Esther's "panoramic faculty," it has limits, though modesty
and selflessness also sharpen her ability to observe others.

It is the promise of perfect transparency, of sight without limit, of compass
without boundary, of knowledge without effort, of clarity without doubt, that
I believe Dickens rejects in *Bleak House*. And as he rejects the perfect visual
transparency of the Crystal Palace, he rejects also the idea of transparency
of language, or Adamic language, tainted by the Fall, but still retaining its
originary purity—what Leibniz has in mind when he asserts: "languages are
the best mirror of the human mind" (qtd. in Aarsleff 69). Between the natural
language of Adam and the humanly constructed language of *Bleak House*
lies a gulf as wide as madness and as distant as uncontaminated nature. Miss
Flyte seems to hear some "natural" language when her birds sing, but she
has no access to its meaning:

> "I cannot allow them to sing much," said the little old lady, "for (you'll think
> this curious) I find my mind confused by the idea that they are singing, while
> I am following the arguments in court. And my mind requires to be so very
> clear, you know! Another time, I'll tell you their names. Not at present. On a
> day of such good omen, they shall sing as much as they like. In honor of
> youth," a smile and curtsey; "hope," a smile and curtsey; "and beauty," a
> smile and curtsey. "There! We'll let in the full light."   (67: 5)

From Krook's window, dimly lit but revealing a stew of commercial detritus,
to Miss Flyte's plain room fringed with singing birds, the wards of Jarndyce
and Esther travel from one language paradigm to another. Krook grapples
with humanly constructed language as if it required divine revelation. Miss
Flyte waits for a day of judgment that will harmonize and perfect human
language, even the tangled tongues of the law. Richard is utterly trapped by
these tangled tongues. Esther constructs her own narration, but it is incomplete
without the broader vision of her fellow narrator. The binary structure of the
novel (two narrators, two plots) is itself equivocal, giving roughly equal voice
to both narrators—one limited and human, the other seemingly omniscient.
Dickens, master of the middle way, takes no side in this dispute between
language paradigms. Only the anonymous narrator appears to live above it
all, in the realm of perfect language. The characters with names are indelibly
inscribed in the tortured, layered world of London.

Indeed, transparency cannot exist except as a metaphor that ignores, rather
than solves, the opacity of reality, where in space and time things overlap.

In space, all objects, neighborhoods, and sites crowd one another on the vertical plane and bury one another on the horizontal plane. Over time, systems persist beyond their usefulness; new technologies and objects emerge, but do not always eradicate old ones. People live disproportionate and uneven lives, often impinging unseen or unseeing on other lives.

If the Crystal Palace anticipates the modernist belief in transparency as a guiding metaphor of political and social relations, Dickens's *Bleak House* serves as prolepsis, anticipating the postmodern debunking of that mythos. In this proleptic projection, Bleak House (both the original gothic structure and Esther's cottage) and other dwellings in the novel recall the traditional metaphor of house/body as a hermeneutic device: the human heart is at once profoundly obscure (hidden from the outside as the interior of a house) and yet susceptible of inquiry and information "leakage" through the body's counterparts to doors and windows. Perhaps, then, some of Dickens's anticipatory argument with modernism may be found in architectural details.

Thus, the absence of the Crystal Palace seems to signal Dickens's "belief" in doubt. Unspoken in the novel, but ever-present, is the myth of transparency—that is, the utopian hope for omniscience proffered by the Crystal Palace's glass sheeting, as opposed to the limited vision and leaky apertures proffered by glass windows. In *Bleak House*, the promise of transparency and utter legibility is the illusion that destroys Richard Carstone; it is the false promise of Chancery; it is a misprision of human language, which holds out so much hope to the illiterates Krook and Jo: "those mysterious symbols, so abundant over the shops, and at the corners of streets, and on the doors, and in the windows!" (236: 16).

NOTES

This essay was begun during a sabbatical leave generously awarded by New York Institute of Technology. For helpful comments and suggestions, I would like to thank Stanley Friedman and Diane Marks.
 1. As ever, the wealthy could afford to pay the tax. Indeed, as Dickens points out in "Red Tape," windows were taxed regressively: the fewer the number of windows, the higher the per-window levy.
 2. F. S. Schwarzbach notes the confluence of Dickens as writer, social activist and householder: "Thus, the opening numbers of *Bleak House* were written, perhaps even conceived, in conjunction with this work on a practical project to build clean, sound, healthy and inexpensive housing for the poor" (129).
 3. Denis Hollier cites instances of what Georges Bataille considered "stifling architecture," including the "feudal castle," whose "nooks and crannies," according to Bataille, "could be deeply inaccessible . . . as deeply buried as any tomb" (Hollier 180).

4. Most especially, see Isobel Armstrong, who brilliantly positions glass into both industrial and literary production. Armstrong sees within nineteenth-century glass technology the material basis for a "scopic culture" now eclipsed by the very ubiquity of glass and by automation in glass production. Michael Greenstein comments on the impact of the Window Tax and of its repeal in his study of "transparencies" in Victorian fiction (270–71).

5. F. S. Schwarzbach argues that the Growlery allows Jarndyce to "diffuse his rage . . . . but it also prevents that rage from being directed where it is rightly deserved" (140).

6. In his examination of the intersection of nineteenth-century literature, architecture, and exhibitions, Philip Hamon sees the use of "the architectural object" in literature as having three functions: hermeneutical, discriminating, and hierarchical or constraining (26–28). I have not strictly adopted this classification system, but I have adapted some of its elements. According to Hamon, the hermeneutical function comes into play by virtue of architecture's interior/exterior duality. What is interior is hidden, subject to interpretation based on extracted or inferred evidence. What is exterior is open to scrutiny, opinion, and judgment. Thus, Chancery, by far the most cloistered edifice, extends its control over London by hiding and resisting interpretation. Jarndyce's Bleak House, on the other hand, sports numerous windows that open the interior to the exterior. The discriminating function deploys characters into, and defines them by, space that can be analyzed, since it is subject to partition, separation, and division. Lady Dedlock stares out her window at Chesney Wold, isolated from the world that holds her secret. Tulkinghorn's apartment is the shell to his oyster-like existence, the nexus of his worldly operations. Jo lives on a street imploding with decay and fallen houses. The hierarchical function places characters into social relations. Tulkinghorn, at home in his panoptical apartment, misses the opportunity to see Lady Dedlock with the pauper Jo on their way to the graveyard. Krook's shop is visited by nearly every major character, at one time or another, providing an architectural nexus for plot and class.

7. The word "window" is thought to derive from the Old Norse *vindauga*, a compound of *vindr* (wind or air) and *auga* (eye). See St. George (126) for an examination of the house-body topos.

8. Armstrong proposes that the new "world of multiple transparency very quickly became a highly mediated world, generating different kinds of epistemological confusion out of the very lucidity of glass . . . . The dialectic of glass in the nineteenth century is about mediation, about transitivity and its implications" (152).

9. Architectural critics—contemporary and modern—have argued that the Crystal Palace is not architecture, but pure engineering. Built of materials suited not to artistic statement but to unadorned functionality, it was neither an expression of architectural principles nor intended to be permanent. As McKean notes, the Crystal Palace brazenly breaks the fundamental rule of Alberti, that "nothing can be added, nothing taken away" (41). Indeed, the whole point of the Crystal Palace was its prefabricated, replicable, and flexible structural units. It is, says McKean, "indeterminate" architecture. It is a precursor in architecture of Benjamin's

notion of mechanical reproduction—panes of glass and iron bars endlessly reproducible, a portable structure that, like Tinkertoys, could be disassembled and reassembled.

10. Landon 36. In his article on the Crystal Palace, Landon examines the absent presence in *Bleak House* of the building and the Exhibition alike. Dickens visited the site during its construction; his excursions to the Great Exhibition (which left him headachy and stunned) engendered edgy, sometimes sardonic commentary in *Household Words*. He called the building a "tremendous pile of transparency . . . astounding for its cheapness . . . ." In letters, he professed to being "used up" by the Exhibition: "I don't say 'there's nothing in it'—there's too much" (letter to Mrs. Richard Watson, 11 July 1851, 6: 429). At one point, he vowed to flee the city at the next mention of the exhibition.

11. McKean quotes Lochar Bucher, a German reporter: "We see a fine network of symmetrical lines that do not, however, provide any clues whereby one could estimate its distance from the eye or the actual size of the mesh. The side walls stand too far apart to be taken in at a glance, and instead of meeting a facing wall, the eye moves upwards over an endless perspective, or one whose ends appear diffuse and blue. We do not know whether this enclosure hovers a hundred or a thousand feet above us, or whether the ceiling is flat or formed by a number of small parallel ceilings; this is due to the total absence of shadows, which normally aid the eye in comprehending the impressions received by the optic nerve . . . " (31).

12. In *All That's Solid Melts Into Air,* Marshall Berman comments on the modernism that was presaged by the Crystal Palace: "for most of our century, urban spaces have been systematically designed and organized to ensure that collisions and confrontations will not take place here" (165). Not so the London of *Bleak House,* where "tumbling tenements contain, by night, a swarm of misery" (236: 16) and where "carriages rattle, doors are battered at, the world exchanges calls . . . " (791: 56). The architecture of Dickens's London facilitates bumping and confronting among classes and even among historical moments, as Lady Dedlock and Esther continually bump up against the past.

13. The irony of this architectural purpose—and of the "winter-garden" conceit—is perhaps best illustrated by King Leopold II's glasshouses at Laeken, where the fruits of his slave-state, the Congo, found a winter home. After the world community had finally wrested the Congo from his personal grip, the unspeakable Leopold retreated into his beloved Congo House, spending his final years among tropical plants and fauna, his former colony now recreated in and protected from the chilly European climate by means of glass.

14. Berman locates a notion similar to that of transparency in Marx's "dialectic of nakedness," which marks the dissolution of illusion and the revelation of "new options" in the modern world: "Their the workers' communism, when it comes, will appear as a kind of transparent garment, at once keeping its wearers warm and setting off their naked beauty, so that they can recognize themselves and each other in all their radiance" (109–10).

15. See Wigginton, 78–83, 240, for descriptions of the varieties of glass and of modern composite materials, including plastics.

16. See Davis 90. The name "Crystal Palace," probably coined by *Punch*, was meant to spoof the Palace of Westminster, according to Davis.

17. Landon would disagree with my parsing of point-of-view. In arguing against the "proscribed" omniscience proposed by Audrey Jaffe, Landon says, "To me it seems disingenuous to regard Esther's narrative as a challenge to the third-person narrator with whom she collaborates seamlessly and whose panoramic vision and social conscience she shares. Indeed, Esther's vehicular role as a promoter of model domesticity requires her to internalize the omniscient perspective . . . " (54). I find the existence of collaboration (that is, the fact of two narrators) to be evidence of limitation, despite the anonymous narrator's seeming omniscience. See Jaffe's analysis of competing critical interpretations of the narratives of *Bleak House*.

18. Balzac, Maupassant, Flaubert, Proust, and Zola among the French, notes Hamon (38).

19. Gustave Caillebotte, the French Impressionist, painted a view of Parisian rooftops from his window, a subject relatively rare in its focus on the "overbelly" of urban life (as opposed to street scenes viewed from an upper studio). It was an alien and disconcerting view, especially in a world before elevators. The somber palette of the "Toits sous la neige" reminds us that architects do not build for birds, but for the earthbound.

20. The OED cites Dickens's use of "marine store" in its definition: "old ship's materials as an object of merchandise."

21. See Vidler for an authoritative examination of the uncanny in late nineteenth- and twentieth-century literature.

WORKS CITED

Aarsleff, Hans. *From Locke to Saussure*. Minneapolis: U of Minnesota P, 1982.

Armstrong, Isobel. "Technology and Text: Glass Consciousness and Nineteenth-century Culture." *Culture, Landscape, and the Environment*. Ed. Kate Flint and Howard Morphy. Oxford: Oxford UP, 2000.

Benjamin, Walter. "The Work of Art in the Age of Mechanical Reproduction." *Illuminations*. Ed. Hannah Arendt. Trans. Harry Zohn. New York: Schocken, 1969.

Berman, Marshall. *All That's Solid Melts Into Air*. New York: Penguin, 1982.

Davis, John R. *The Great Exhibition*. Stroud, UK: Sutton, 1999.

Defoe, Daniel. *Journal of a Plague Year*. New York: Norton, 1992.

Dickens, Charles. *Bleak House*. Ed. Stephen Gill. London: Oxford World Classics, 1996.

————. *Household Words: A Weekly Journal.* Vol. 2. London: Bradbury and Evans. 19 vols. 1850–1859.

————. *The Letters of Charles Dickens.* Ed. Madeline House, Graham Storey, Kathleen Tillotson. Vol. 6. Oxford: Clarendon, 1988.

Ewen, Stuart. *Captains of Consciousness.* New York: McGraw Hill, 1976.

Greenstein, Michael. "Magic Casements and Victorian Transparencies: Post-Romantic Modes of Perception." *Dickens Studies Annual* 14 (1985): 267–286.

Gwilt, Joseph. *The Encyclopedia of Architecture.* 1867. New York: Crown, 1982.

Hamon, Philip. *Expositions.* Trans. Katia Sainson-Frank and Lisa Maguire. Berkeley: U of California P, 1992.

Hollier, Denis. *Against Architecture: The Writings of Georges Bataille.* Trans. Betsy Wing. Cambridge: MIT P, 1995.

Jaffe, Audrey. *Vanishing Points: Dickens, Narrative, and Subject of Omniscience.* Berkeley: U of California P, 1991.

Landon, Philip. "Great Exhibitions: Representations of the Crystal Palace in Mayhew, Dickens, and Dostoevsky." *Nineteenth Century Contexts* 20 (1997): 27–59.

McKean, John. *Crystal Palace: Joseph Paxton and Charles Fox.* London: Phaidon, 1994.

Miller, D. A. "Discipline in Different Voices: Bureaucracy, Police, Family, and *Bleak House.*" *Charles Dickens: Modern Critical Views.* Ed. Harold Bloom. New York: Chelsea House, 1987.

Pevsner, Nicolas, *The Sources of Modern Architecture and Design.* London: Thames and Hudson, 1968.

St. George, Robert Blair. *Conversing by Signs: Poetics of Implication in Colonial New England Culture.* Chapel Hill: U of North Carolina P, 1998.

Scheerbart, Paul. *Glass Architecture.* Ed. Dennis Sharp. Trans. James Palmes. New York: Praeger, 1972.

Schwarzbach, F. S. *Dickens and the City.* London: Athlone, 1979.

Vidler, Antony, *The Architectural Uncanny.* Cambridge: Cambridge UP, 1996.

Wigginton, Michael, *Glass in Architecture.* London: Phaidon, 1996.

Conviction in Writing: Crime, Confession, and the Written Word in *Great Expectations*

Monique R. Morgan

Great Expectations *interweaves the themes of literacy and crime to such an extent that writing itself becomes a mark of guilt. Although Dickens frequently blurs the distinctions between written and spoken words, characteristics commonly attributed to writing remain tainted with crime, while those associated with speech provide the hope of confession and forgiveness. These thematic links are rooted in nineteenth-century confession law, and* Great Expectations *provides an alternative to recent accounts of the status of testimony in Victorian legal practice and Victorian fiction. The confluence of writing, guilt, and confession helps explain both this novel's incorporation of* George Barnwell, *and the novel's rhetorical purpose. Like Lillo's play,* Great Expectations *is crafted to prod its audience's guilty consciences, encouraging them to confess and seek forgiveness.*

Charles Dickens's *Great Expectations* presents an abundance of criminal guilt, opening with Pip's first meeting with the convict Magwitch, and closing shortly after Magwitch's death. That crucial first encounter with the convict occurs just after a description of Pip's idiosyncratic attempts to read his parents' tombstones, thus juxtaposing crime with another important theme of the novel — literacy. Both these themes have received ample treatment in

Dickens Studies Annual, Volume 33, Copyright © 2003 by AMS Press, Inc. All rights reserved.

criticism on *Great Expectations*; this essay brings these two strands of criticism together, and places them in the larger context of scholarship on Victorian legal practice, serving as a counter-argument to the work of Alexander Welsh and Jan-Melissa Schramm. The novel's opening juxtaposition of crime and literacy is far from accidental; an examination of *Great Expectations* reveals a whole web of associations between the written word and criminal guilt. These associations, in turn, blur the lines between writing and speech, and reveal that the confession of guilt is important not only *within* the novel, but also as the rhetorical purpose *of* the novel.

While debating what name to call Pip, Herbert Pocket makes this bizarre digression: "I don't take to Philip . . . for it sounds like a moral boy out of the spelling-book, who was so lazy that he fell into a pond, or so fat that he couldn't see out of his eyes, or so avaricious that he locked up his cake till the mice ate it, or so determined to go birds'-nesting that he got himself eaten by bears who lived handy in the neighbourhood" (140–41). A spelling-book is obviously a tool in obtaining access to the written word, in learning to write for oneself. But here the emphasis is not on the acquisition of literacy, but rather on the punishment of vice. Such books threaten their young pupils with poetically apt punishments in order to prevent them from committing the trespasses the books describe. This not only illustrates the heavy-handed moralizing and ideological indoctrination that infused many nineteenth-century spelling and grammar books; in the context of *Great Expectations* it also forms a link in a long chain of direct and indirect associations of writing with guilt. Such associations develop a step further when Pumblechook drags Pip to the magistrate to be bound as an apprentice. Curious onlookers mistake Pumblechook's purpose and assume that Pip is a criminal. Pip recalls, "One person of mild and benevolent aspect even gave me a tract ornamented with a woodcut of a malevolent young man fitted up with a perfect sausage-shop of fetters, and entitled TO BE READ IN MY CELL" (85). Here, the written document deals specifically with criminal guilt and with punishment doled out by the legal system. Instead of serving as a warning to prevent crime, this tract addresses those who have already committed a crime. It likely tries to inspire the repentance that might gain the pardon of God, but doesn't gain the pardon of the English judicial system. The "sausage-shop of fetters" shown in the woodcut gives a striking reminder of the criminal's earthly punishment and his sequestration from society, which might provide some comforting distance for the "person of mild and benevolent aspect" who is so concerned for Pip's soul, if not for Pip's body.

Some written documents in the novel deal not with warnings to prevent crimes, or punishments and pardons after the fact, but with the crimes themselves. For instance, Mr. Wopsle reads aloud, to the delight of fellow tavern patrons, a newspaper account of a crime:

A highly popular murder had been committed, and Mr. Wopsle was imbrued in blood to the eyebrows. He gloated over every abhorrent adjective in the description, and identified himself with every witness at the Inquest. He faintly moaned, "I am done for," as the victim, and he barbarously bellowed, "I'll serve you out," as the murderer.... He enjoyed himself thoroughly, and we all enjoyed ourselves, and were delightfully comfortable. In this cosy state of mind we came to the verdict Wilful Murder. (105)

By "gloat[ing] over every abhorrent adjective," Wopsle's reading emphasizes the enjoyment produced by salacious descriptions of shocking crimes. The tavern audience can share a vicarious pleasure in the vividly rendered murder, while remaining "comfortable" and "cosy" in the knowledge that they have only imagined and not committed such vicious acts. Pip, Wopsle, and their companions can also cosily relish passing judgment without any of the responsibility attendant upon the legal offices of judge and jury. Since *Great Expectations* is itself a written document that deals heavily with crime, several possibilities naturally arise. Dickens's novel may offer the reader vicarious pleasure from identifying with crime or from judging criminals, as Wopsle's reading does. The novel might instead provide a warning against vice and crime before they are committed, as does Herbert's spelling-book. Or *Great Expectations* may offer either punishment or pardon to readers who are already guilty, as in the case of the prisoner's tract. Although all three of these strategies are present in the novel, a detailed analysis of the novel's presentation of writing and guilt reveals a much greater emphasis on pardoning an implied reader who is construed as already guilty.

Such an analysis can begin with the larger context of Wopsle's newspaper reading. Immediately after the tavern-goers pronounce the murderer guilty, Mr. Jaggers enters the scene and questions their decision. This is the lawyer's second appearance in the novel, and it is the first time he is named. Jaggers is the chief representative of the legal system in the novel, and he quite notably distorts and tortures language. He reduces the purpose, and the danger, of communication to the concept of evidence. Jaggers advises Pip, "Take nothing on its looks; take everything on evidence. There's no better rule" (251). The iron rule of evidence governs all of Jaggers's verbal interactions. Conversations become interrogations when he is present. Consider the exchange that begins when Jaggers asks Joe if he expects compensation for relieving Pip from his indentures:

"You would not object to cancel his indentures, at his request and for his good? You would not want anything for so doing?"

"Lord forbid that I should want anything for not standing in Pip's way!" said Joe, staring.

"Lord forbidding is pious, but not to the purpose," returned Mr. Jaggers. "The question is, Would you want anything? Do you want anything?"

"The answer is," returned Joe, sternly, "No."
. . .
"Very well," said Mr. Jaggers. "Recollect the admission you have made,
and don't try to go from it presently."   (108)

Jaggers prods people for answers, exploits inconsistencies, and assumes that
any and all statements could be stored in memory and used against their
speaker at a later date. Jaggers is also very careful about the implications of
his words and the words of others. He studiously avoids saying anything
incriminating that could be used as evidence later, as when he refuses to use
the word "recommendation" instead of "mention" because of the responsibility it might imply (110). As Andrew Gordon has remarked, Jaggers "is a
master-mind at evading personal responsibility, to the point of public, private,
and self-deception . . . .his speech is legalistic and guarded, and his sentences
are usually interrogative or imperative, disclosing nothing and extracting everything" (8). Jaggers tip-toes around self-incrimination by calling close attention to the exact letter of what's spoken and its difference from virtually
synonymous phrases that may have connotations Jaggers wishes to avoid. In
many cases, Jaggers seems concerned that his intention in communicating is
completely explicit and in no danger of being misconstrued; he wants his
language to work with complete accuracy and clarity.

In some instances, however, Jaggers uses the same techniques for disingenuous purposes, to veil thinly a mutually understood meaning that he would
nonetheless later disown if confronted with it. An extreme example is when
Jaggers asks one-eyed Mike what a rather shady defense witness is prepared
to testify. When Mike replies, "In a general way, anythink [sic]," Jaggers
explodes, "You infernal scoundrel, how dare you tell ME that?" (133, 134).
But when Mike revises his answer to "ayther [sic] to character, or to having
been in his company and never left him all the night in question," Jaggers
finds it totally acceptable (134). Both parties clearly understand the falsity of
the testimony, but Jaggers must disavow that knowledge while retaining the
witness. He thus divorces intention and reception from what could later be
proven out of the context of the verbal interaction. This incident with Mike
also illustrates the selectivity of Jaggers's communication: he only wants to
know information that he explicitly seeks out, and only accepts the answers
he anticipates. If he is in danger of learning anything in addition to what he
wants, he immediately silences his interlocutor, as when he cuts off a client
by saying, "I want to know no more than I know" (132). According to
Stephen Sossaman, "Jaggers is a master of carefully chosen indirect statement, of communicating without saying anything, and of using suppositions,
innuendoes, and rhetorical questions to transact business without so much as
a trace of anything quotable. . . . Jaggers wants to be told nothing and yet

know everything'' (67). Although Sossaman sees here an encouraging example of "man's ability to get along without forthright speech'' (67), Dickens seems antagonistic toward Jaggers's methods.

Such methods bear an obvious resemblance to the controlled oral exchanges of courtroom practice, through which Jaggers makes his living. But the sum total of his techniques—having a long-term memory for consistency, showing minute care in choice of language, divorcing meaning from context, carefully selecting only the information wanted—also makes Jaggers's verbal interactions take on some of the characteristics of written documents. Murray Baumgarten notes that for Jaggers "speech consists of cross-examination—that is, of treating oral communication as if it were a written contract'' (70). This important point merits expansion. The written word often seems to have less context than the spoken word. Walter Ong emphasizes this view in his problematic but useful study *Orality and Literacy*: whereas "spoken utterance is addressed by a real, living person to another real, living person . . . at a specific time in a real setting which includes always much more than mere words,'' the written word "establishes what has been called 'context-free' language . . . discourse which cannot be directly questioned or contested as oral speech can because written discourse has been detached from its author'' (101, 78). Writing has often been associated with preserved language that can easily be reexamined after its original use; writing can thus be a substitute for memory, allowing an examination of consistency in communications whose moments of origin can be widely separated. According to Ong, "Writing establishes in the text a 'line' of continuity outside the mind. If distraction confuses or obliterates from the mind the context out of which emerges the material I am now reading, the context can be retrieved by glancing back over the text selectively'' (39). The reader can also use this selective backlooping to verify the understanding and consistency of the author, as well as to aid the reader's own understanding. Jaggers's spoken language takes on these characteristics more commonly attributed to writing. Jaggers forcibly calls attention to how he, and his opponents, could take a spoken word out of context, and reduce it to its bare minimum of denoted meaning. He is quite conscious of how his own speech could be preserved and reexamined, and his impressive memory is capable of storing and comparing the spoken words of others. Perhaps Pip remarks of Jaggers's office, "There were not so many papers about, as I should have expected to see,'' because the lawyer makes spoken language act as written language and gives speech the disingenuousness otherwise associated with legal writing (130). A rather curious description of Jaggers's clerk Wemmick reinforces this distortion of the oral into the written. Wemmick's "mouth was such a post-office of a mouth that he had a mechanical appearance of smiling'' (136), thus changing the instrument of speech into a receptacle for the written word.[1]

The distortion and deceptiveness of writing becomes more prominent, and writing and crime overlap, in the recurrent theme of forgery. Jaggers's office contains two death masks of criminals, one of whom forged wills (156). Among Wemmick's "collection of curiosities" is "the pen with which a celebrated forgery had been committed" (162). While visiting Newgate, Pip and Wemmick have a conversation with a coin forger (200–201). And of course, one of Compeyson's criminal talents and occupations is "handwriting forging" (260–61). His proficiency at such deception is evident in Orlick's boast that his new companion and master "writes fifty hands" (318). Handwriting forgery violently calls to our attention the difficulties of providing written words with the clear context and origin that is expected of speech. A forged note deceives the receiver about such fundamental information as the author of the words and his intent. Forgery creates the closest possible link between writing and crime; it is a case when writing itself *is* a crime.

Successful prosecutions can produce written documents that are just as unreliable as the forged notes which constitute the crime. The most treasured items in Wemmick's collection are "several manuscript confessions written under condemnation—upon which Mr. Wemmick set particular value as being, to use his own words, 'every one of 'em Lies, sir' '' (162). Dickens also shows anxiety about false confessions in Pip's outlandish description of Miss Havisham's house, given while under pressure from his relatives: "I was perfectly frantic—a reckless witness under the torture—and would have told them anything" (57). This concern over false confessions is part of a larger pattern of anxiety about distorted legal discourse, and the concern seems justified given some of the standard practices of the Victorian judicial system.

In his influential study *Strong Representations*, Alexander Welsh argues that "narrative consisting of carefully managed circumstantial evidence" superseded direct testimony in importance and reliability in both law and literature; the method of making "facts speak for themselves . . . became the single most prominent form of narrative in the later eighteenth and nineteenth centuries" (ix). More recently, Jan-Melissa Schramm has contested Welsh's position by arguing that, in the early nineteenth century, defense lawyers gradually gained more scope and power, creating a shift in the legal system that recognized the necessity of a rhetorical presentation of facts (20–21, 61). She traces a change in the model of a trial away from the artless testimony of the accused, toward the skillful rhetoric of criminal lawyers. Nineteenth-century fiction, however, retains the "accused speaks" model, and allows protagonists to declare their own innocence (Schramm 99–100). According to Schramm, Dickens in particular "fear[ed] that representation enabled the guilty to evade responsibility," and in his writings "integrity was equated with a rejection of legal representation and a preference for straightforward narratives of innocence" (121). But there are two key respects in which

Schramm's study seems incompatible with the present analysis of *Great Expectations*. First, this novel may be representative of Dickens's general skepticism toward lawyers, but Pip gives us a straightforward narrative of guilt, not innocence. A more important, and more general, difference, is that despite Schramm's persuasive argument for the "essential orality of English courtroom procedure" (20), the relationship between written communication and spoken communication in the Victorian legal system was much more subtle in the case of information provided by the accused—specifically, confessions.

Henry Joy's 1842 law treatise on the admissibility of confessions openly states as a rule, "A confession is admissible, although it is elicited in answer to a question which assumes the prisoner's guilt, or is obtained by artifice or deception" (42). We might suppose that for a prisoner faced with a magistrate who uses such trickery and entrapment, the wisest recourse is silence. That, however, was not the case for Victorian prisoners. The same law treatise states, "A confession may be inferred from the conduct and demeanor of a prisoner, when a statement is made in his presence, affecting himself" (Joy 77). Indeed, the author mentions a "general rule, that whatever was said to a prisoner on the subject matter of the charge, to which he made no direct answer, was receivable as evidence of an implied admission on his part" (Joy 78). If the legal system takes silence as equivalent to a confession, then the system forces a suspect to engage in the potentially disingenuous wordplay, the "artifice or deception," that can constitute an official interrogation.

As a writer concerned with law and with extensive personal experience of the field, Dickens was all too familiar with a legal system which openly acknowledged its own deceptions, and yet proclaimed its interest in the truth of confessions. Although examiners could unearth or infer a confession through trickery, they could not coerce a confession through threats or promises. Joy's treatise states, "A confession is NOT admissible in evidence where it is obtained by *temporal* inducement, by threat, promise, or hope of favor held out to the party, in respect of his escape from the charge against him, by a person IN AUTHORITY, or where there is reason to presume, that such a person appeared to the party to *sanction* such threat or inducement" (5). The court presumed the existence of a "threat or inducement" unduly coerced the suspect, making the confession involuntary. And an involuntary confession was inadmissible because its veracity was suspect. This rationale of excluding coerced confessions, for the purpose of insuring the truth of confessions that *are* admitted, was clearly established in the judge's ruling in the 1783 case of Rex v. Warickshall. The case record states, "A free and voluntary confession is deserving of the highest credit, because it is presumed to flow from the strongest sense of guilt . . . but a confession forced from the mind by the flattery of hope, or by the torture of fear, comes in so questionable a shape . . . that no credit ought to be given to it; and therefore it is rejected"

(Herman 157). Whereas confessions forced by hope or fear are questionable and should not be admitted as evidence, those that are voluntary are given "the highest credit," and treated as completely credible. Such certainty is afforded to voluntary confessions because they "flow from the strongest sense of guilt," because they originate in the suspect's conviction that he is truly guilty and (presumably) truly repentant. Confessions can then transform the "conviction" of emotional certainty into the "conviction" of criminal punishment. The importance given to a guilty conscience and the implication of repentance link confessions used as legal evidence to religious confessions. The British court system recognized the overlap of the legal with the religious when it declared, "A confession is admissible, where it is induced by *spiritual* exhortation or persuasion to confess, not held out with any view of temporal benefit" (Joy 49). Such spiritual exhortation would likely present confession as a step toward gaining the forgiveness of God, but often was used to gain the condemnation of the court.

The law's ostensible focus on the strength of emotion and the voluntariness of speech, which guarantee the truth of confession, might imply a concern with sincerity in the suspect and sincerity in the law. But in practice, the focus quickly shifted away from voluntariness and reliability, and the law concentrated on more easily identifiable, but less meaningful, criteria:

> Following . . . Warickshall, British courts found that applying the reliability-based voluntariness test could be a difficult task. . . . In some circumstances, a particular inducement might produce an involuntary and untrue confession, but the result could be different with other defendants in other settings. . . . Over time, however, courts became less concerned with the general concepts of voluntariness and reliability in their confession rulings. Instead, they began to substitute a more mechanical analysis in which the inquiry focused on whether the confession followed any threat or promise. Under this approach, confessions were held involuntary and inadmissible based solely on the existence of a threat or promise, but without any real inquiry into whether the suspect exercised freedom of choice and without any considered judgment about the reliability of the statement.   (Berger 9)

Decisions on the admission or exclusion of confessions became so mechanical that in England from 1785 to the mid-nineteenth century, "If an incriminating statement was made, objection to its admissibility in a criminal proceeding on the ground that it was involuntary was virtually a matter of routine, and the objection was often sustained" (Herman 158). Certainly this corroborates Welsh's arguments that Victorian courts often viewed testimony as unreliable, and many prosecutions had to proceed without using confessions. But the legal rhetoric of the time, and Dickens's fascination with the subject, suggest a continued interest in confessions, perhaps *because* of the anxiety they produced.

Victorian law thus encouraged deceptive questioning to elicit truthful confessions, allowed the spiritual inducement of God's forgiveness to obtain
evidence for temporal condemnation, and divorced the justification of voluntariness and veracity at the base of confession law from the actual practice
of it.[2] If an examination of this small branch of English law unearths this
much hypocrisy and duplicity, we need not wonder at Dickens's skepticism
towards legal language in *Great Expectations*. And if Jaggers, as the novel's
representative of convoluted legal language, emphasizes the characteristics
of the written, rather than the spoken, word, we need not be surprised that
actual confession law also put an emphasis on writing. The 1736 edition of
Sir Matthew Hale's *Historia Placitorum Coronae* states:

> Justices of peace and coroners have power to take examinations of the party
> accused, and informations of the accusers and witnesses . . . and are to put the
> same in writing, and are to certify the same to the [court of trial jurisdiction].
> These examinations and informations thus taken and returned may be read in
> evidence against the prisoner, if the informer be dead, or so sick, that he is not
> able to travel, and oath thereof made; otherwise not. But then, 1. Oath must be
> made either by the justice or coroner, that took them, or the clerk that wrote
> them, that they are the true substance of what the informer gave in upon oath,
> and what the prisoner confessed upon his examination.   (Herman 148)

By 1736 British legal practice explicitly required a person with authority to
take down in writing a confession made during an examination of the suspect.
The usual procedure, then, involved the informant taking the stand during
trial and verbally repeating what had previously been taken down in writing.
This process, though it requires a record of the confession to be made in
writing, puts greater weight on the spoken presentation of evidence during
the trial. We may be tempted to infer that the oath serves as spoken evidence
of the truth of writing. But until the Criminal Evidence Act of 1898, the
accused could not be placed under oath, and was hence denied this oral
assertion of truthfulness (Schramm 51). By the mid-nineteenth century there
was further reason to minimize the importance of the accused's speech and
to emphasize the importance of written confessions. Joy's legal treatise of
1842 states, "Parol evidence of a confession made during an examination
before a magistrate is admissible in evidence, although it was taken down in
writing by the magistrate, if from informality the written examination is not
admissible; and such examination, though informal, may be used to refresh
the memory of a witness who was present and took it down" (95). In 1842,
then, courts give the written transcript of a confession primacy when admitting a confession as evidence. A verbal statement of the confession is used
as a substitute when the written statement cannot be admitted, and thus serves
as secondary, rather than primary, evidence. Moreover, the inadmissible written document can be used to "refresh the memory of a witness"; writing

is now the repository of memory and is the guarantor of the accuracy of spoken testimony.

Of course, Wemmick's collection of false confessions would undermine the assumption that writing is any guarantor of the validity of such statements. But Wemmick's curiosities are not the sole instances of confessions in *Great Expectations*. Pip makes the "lunatic confession" to Biddy that he "want[s] to be a gentleman on [Estella's] account" (102). And from his retrospective narratorial vantage, Pip writes, "Let me confess exactly, with what feelings I looked forward to Joe's coming. Not with pleasure, . . . no; with considerable disturbance, some mortification, and a keen sense of incongruity" (168–69). After Pip steals food for Magwitch and must keep silent under the threat that a terrible young man will kill him, Pip considers, "Under the weight of my wicked secret, I pondered whether the Church would be powerful enough to shield me from the vengeance of the terrible young man, if I divulged to that establishment" (24). This passage puts confession in the context of divulging to the church, rather than admitting to the court. Although in this instance the ostensible motivation for divulging is to gain the church's sanctuary from a worldly threat, in most cases the purpose is to obtain God's forgiveness. And certainly in the novel, the desire for forgiveness, from God and from those wronged, is omnipresent. There are several key moments when characters specifically ask to be pardoned, and these moments refocus the tensions and overlaps between written and spoken language in the novel.

Miss Havisham makes what may be the most odd request for forgiveness. She hands Pip a small tablet and says, "My name is on the first leaf. If you can ever write under my name, 'I forgive her,' though ever so long after my broken heart is dust—pray do it!" (297). Miss Havisham specifically wants her forgiveness to be in writing, perhaps because it suggests to her more permanent evidence. But Miss Havisham is often terribly misguided, and the novel undermines and devalues the desire to have forgiveness in writing. Pip makes no mention of his ever complying to the specifics of her request. Instead, he tells her that she can have his forgiveness now. When she deliriously repeats the request after being burned, Pip responds with a kiss. He recounts, "I leaned over her and touched her lips with mine, just as they said, not stopping for being touched, 'Take the pencil and write under my name, "I forgive her" ' " (301). This seems to be the moment when Pip conclusively forgives her. It occurs with her physically present, and Pip kisses her mouth (the part of the body most clearly associated with spoken words) while she is speaking the very words whose meaning Pip is trying to impart. The episode places forgiveness in a very oral context, even though the request was to put it in writing.

The need to hear forgiveness rather than read it gains greater prominence in what is perhaps the most climactic moment of forgiveness in the novel—Pip's long-awaited admission of his ingratitude toward Joe and Biddy and his request for their pardon. Pip exclaims, "Pray tell me, both, that you forgive me! Pray let me hear you say the words, that I may carry the sound of them away with me, and then I shall be able to believe that you can trust me, and think better of me, in the time to come!" (355). The emphasis is clearly on needing to hear the sound of the spoken words. The passage gives oral communication an odd sense of greater permanence than writing, since Pip can "carry the sound of [the words] away," and since they will last in "the time to come." Pip's request also gives the spoken word a sense of greater reliability than writing because it is through *hearing* the words that Pip will be able to believe he is forgiven, to give credence to the pardon. If Dickens gives spoken words greater permanence and reliability than written words, and if he associates the characteristics of written language with highly suspect legal discourse, then what are the implications for Dickens's novel as a written document?

We can approach this larger concern through a further analysis of slippages between, and valuations of, speech and writing within the novel. A key instance of the privileging of speech over writing, and a key instance of forgiveness, occurs during Magwitch's last moments. Pip provides the following description:

> With a last faint effort, which would have been powerless but for my yielding to it and assisting it, he raised my hand to his lips. . . . Mindful, then, of what we had read together, I thought of the two men who went up into the Temple to pray, and I knew there were no better words that I could say beside his bed, than "O Lord, be merciful to him, a sinner!" (342)

Pip asks God to forgive and bless Magwitch, and this is the moment when Pip himself most clearly forgives the convict for everything that had caused Pip fear, revulsion, and shame. A sentiment originally expressed in writing is spoken at this crucial moment. This shift to orality resembles the spoken answer to Miss Havisham's request for written forgiveness. The kiss Magwitch gives to Pip may also echo the kiss Pip gives Miss Havisham. In this case, however, the kiss is placed on the hand, the instrument of writing, rather than the mouth, the instrument of speech. It seems that the kiss here transforms the hand from an outlet for writing to a means of very personal interaction, a vehicle that shares some of the characteristics of orality. Pip's description of his dealings with the dying Magwitch supports this interpretation: "Sometimes he was almost, or quite, unable to speak; then, he would answer me with slight pressures on my hand, and I grew to understand his meaning very well" (341). Pip understands Magwitch's squeezes quite easily. Using hands for squeezing instead of writing allows for physical contact that can be cut off in writing, and it assumes a natural sympathy and mutual

understanding between the silent interlocutors which stands in stark contrast
to the alienation and dissimulation of Jaggers's twisted use of speech.

Pip's ability to understand the speechless Magwitch also stands in contrast
to his inability to understand another speechless invalid—his sister. After
Orlick's attack on her, Mrs. Joe loses the ability to speak, and she communicates by writing on Pip's little slate:

> It was . . . necessary to keep my slate always by her, that she might indicate in
> writing what she could not indicate in speech. As she was (very bad handwriting
> apart) a more than indifferent speller, and as Joe was a more than indifferent
> reader, extraordinary complications arose between them, which I was always
> called in to solve. The administration of mutton instead of medicine, the substi-
> tution of Tea for Joe, and the baker for bacon, were among the mildest of my
> own mistakes.   (98)

We could attribute Pip's incongruous accidental substitutions to the fact that
he and Mrs. Joe are less than fully literate. But this explanation is less
than fully satisfactory. Pip mistakes ''medicine'' for ''mutton,'' and yet with
Magwitch, Pip ''understood his touch to mean that he wished to lift [Pip's]
hand, and lay it on his breast'' (341). For Dickens, the written word not only
can be used for studied and subtle dissimulation, but also can interfere with
simple and straightforward reference. If a sincere understanding of another's
heart is required, and speech is impossible, then squeezing a hand is more
effective than writing with one. And laying a hand on someone's breast
over his heart is perhaps the best way, outside of spoken words, to gain an
understanding of that heart. In the novel, requesting and granting forgiveness
require a sincere understanding of another person's heart, and most characters
avoid writing on such occasions. Even Mrs. Joe avoids writing when, just
before her death, she requests Joe's forgiveness of Pip. Biddy recounts her
last words: ''She presently said 'Joe' again, and once 'Pardon,' and once
'Pip' '' (215–16). This verbal request comes from a woman who has been
unable to speak for years, and is perhaps the strongest evidence that obtaining
forgiveness is of chief importance, and that writing is an inappropriate or
impossible medium for obtaining it.

Although Pip frequently fails to understand Mrs. Joe's written requests,
Biddy is a more successful interpreter, and is an exception to the general
inability to communicate faithfully through writing. It is Biddy who realizes
that the strange 'T' Mrs. Joe has been drawing indicates a desire to see Orlick.
The 'T' isn't a letter at all, but rather a hammer to stand for Orlick, because
''she had lost his name, and could only signify him by his hammer'' (99).
Biddy is successful here because she is able to get beyond the arbitrary
signification of a letter of the alphabet, and beyond the arbitrary name for a
man, to see the mimetic representation of an object that is crucial to Orlick's

chief physical activity—working at the forge. She is able to escape the arbitrary and to create a meaningful context in order to bring a man into Mrs. Joe's physical presence, and hence Biddy is able to escape some of the more negative aspects of writing and give it some characteristics of orality. Pip was once similarly able to escape the arbitrariness of writing. He describes Biddy's first attempt to fulfill her promise to teach him to read and write as a child: "That very evening Biddy entered on our special agreement, by . . . lending me, to copy at home, a large old English D which she had imitated from the heading of some newspaper, and which I supposed, until she told me what it was, to be a design for a buckle" (62). Pip was once able to imagine the letter 'D' to be a mimetic representation of a metal object, a buckle, just as Biddy could later see a hammer in a 'T'. As a young child, Pip, too, could give writing some of the characteristics of speech. The novel opens with his creative interpretation of written words:

> As I never saw my father or my mother, . . . my first fancies regarding what they were like, were unreasonably derived from their tombstones. The shape of the letters on my father's, gave me an odd idea that he was a square, stout, dark man with curly black hair. From the character and turn of the inscription, "*Also Georgiana Wife of the Above*," I drew a childish conclusion that my mother was freckled and sickly. (9)

Pip's inferences based on the shape of the letters add greater context, invoke a sense of the physical, and add a great deal of idiosyncrasy. He also gets away from writing as a formal, denotative, mechanical system, which may be the characteristics that make Dickens so suspicious of writing in the novel. Pip's reading of the tombstones is thus an example of how one might avoid some of the negative aspects of writing, and give writing some of the characteristics more usually associated with speech.

But it is the very young, narrated Pip who performs this escape from some of the dangers of writing, and it is unclear if the older, narrating Pip is capable of a similar feat. In a novel so suspicious of written language and so nostalgic for orality, the status of Pip's autobiography as a written document has troubling implications. What is the motivation for resorting to such a suspect medium? We could certainly see the novel as a whole as motivated by Pip's need to confess.[3] The older, narrating Pip is constantly exposing moments of ingratitude or pretension in his younger self, and these moments sometimes make explicit the purpose of confession. When Pip describes his acquisition of literacy, he admits, "Whatever I acquired, I tried to impart to Joe. This statement sounds so well, that I cannot in my conscience let it pass unexplained. I wanted to make Joe less ignorant and common, that he might be worthier of my society and less open to Estella's reproach" (88). Pip goes out of his way to prevent the reader from inferring a motivation more admirable than was the case. He does so out of the "strongest sense of guilt"

(Herman 157), that the legal system felt must motivate voluntary confessions, since he attributes his admission to a pained "conscience." Pip's revelation of his past egotism is also consistent with the "general tone . . . of candid self-revelation" that marks confession as a literary genre, as Samuel Sipe notes (60). But other instances of Pip's self-revelation suggest a legal or spiritual, rather than a literary, context for his confession. His admission, "It is a most miserable thing to feel ashamed of home. There may be black ingratitude in the thing, and the punishment may be retributive and well deserved; but that it is a miserable thing, I can *testify*," makes his statement into testimony, which is suggestive of a confession reiterated at trial (86, my emphasis). Later Pip describes his love for Estella: "Ah me! I thought those were high and great emotions. But I never thought there was anything low and small in my keeping away from Joe, because I knew she would be contemptuous of him. It was but a day gone, and Joe had brought the tears into my eyes; they had soon dried, God forgive me! soon dried" (187). The interjected plea for God's forgiveness may reveal the intention, not only of this admission, but of the novel in general—to confess his sins and receive pardon.

We can infer another overarching motivation for Pip's narrative from his thoughts while he is Orlick's captive at the limekiln. He worries that if Orlick kills him, "Joe and Biddy would never know how sorry I had been that night; none would ever know what I had suffered, how true I had meant to be, what an agony I had passed through. The death close before me was terrible, but far more terrible than death was the dread of being misremembered after death" (316–17). This implies that Pip wants an accurate record of his transgressions and repentance not for God but for his fellow humans, for Joe and Biddy especially. Yet Pip seems to have Joe and Biddy's unreserved pardon and love by the end of the novel, before Pip could have embarked on the project of autobiography. Indeed, after Pip requests of them, "Pray tell me, both, that you forgive me! Pray let me hear you say the words" (355), Joe and Biddy respond quite definitively:

> "O dear old Pip, old chap," said Joe. "God knows as I forgive you, if I have anythink [sic] to forgive!"
> "Amen! And God knows I do!" echoed Biddy.   (355)

By the end of the novel, Pip has already asked for, and obtained, pardon through speech, and we have no reason to doubt the sincerity and efficacy of the pardon. But Pip presents this oral scene in the written medium of his confession. We might assume that the suspicion given to writing in general also casts suspicion on Pip's writing. Yet most readers of the novel have complete faith in the narrating Pip,[4] whatever doubts we entertain about the younger, narrated Pip.

A focus on the novel as Pip's confession thus fails to explain the motivation for writing, and fails to reconcile the novel's suspicions of writing with the novel's status *as* writing. An explanation and a reconciliation is possible by examining not the narrator's fictional purposes but rather Dickens's implied purposes. For the concerns with writing and confession are more general concerns of his and not limited to his creation of Pip. In the novel immediately preceding *Great Expectations*, for example, Dickens makes a rare first-person digression in an otherwise third-person narration:

> A wonderful fact to reflect upon, that every human creature is constituted to be that profound secret and mystery to every other. A solemn consideration, when I enter a great city by night, . . . that every beating heart in the hundreds of thousands of breasts there is, in some of its imaginings, a secret to the heart nearest it! Something of the awfulness, even of Death itself, is referable to this. No more can I turn the leaves of this dear book that I loved, and vainly hope in time to read it all. . . . It was appointed that the book should shut with a spring, for ever and for ever, when I had read but a page. . . . My friend is dead, my neighbour is dead, my love, the darling of my soul, is dead; it is the inexorable consolidation and perpetuation of the secret that was always in that individuality, and which I shall carry in mine to my life's end. In any of the burial-places of this city through which I pass, is there a sleeper more inscrutable than its busy inhabitants are, in their innermost personality, to me, or than I am to them?   (*Tale* 21)

Pip's concern with being misremembered after death echoes this awfulness of death, an awfulness that Dickens attributes to the impossibility of ever fully knowing a person, to the inevitability of keeping secrets in life and death. Dickens may use Pip's confessional autobiography as an attempt to reveal fully the secret heart of that character, as an attempt to relieve the anxiety revealed in the above passage from *A Tale of Two Cities*. Barry Westburg discusses this motivation behind *Great Expectations*: "Dickens emphasizes, in this novel, the need for confession, the need for destroying the secrecies existing among its characters, which intensify their sense of egoistic individuality. When confession becomes possible, one enters upon life with others, an open . . . life, with secrecies abolished and the heart no longer a fortified citadel" (138). Dickens seems concerned not only with abolishing secrets among characters, but also with abolishing secrets between characters and the reader. Such an interpretation is reinforced by Dickens's comparison of the inability ever to know a person fully to the inability ever to read a book to its end—*Great Expectations* is a book that we can read to the end, and it attempts to give near-complete knowledge of a (fictitious) person.

And yet if writing is so frequently suspect within this novel, how can the written novel itself be a credible vehicle for a purpose so personal and important? A clue lies in Estella's reply to Pip's declaration of love: "When you say you love me, I know what you mean, as a form of words; but nothing more. You address nothing in my breast, you touch nothing there. I don't care for what you say at all'' (270). The implication to the reader is that there should be an intimate connection between words and the heart, a connection that Estella crucially lacks. If Dickens sometimes questions the veracity of writing, perhaps it is because he views writing as more likely than speech to devolve into a mere "form of words." But Dickens may hope to rescue writing from such danger, to make writing speak to the secret hearts of others, to be full of sincere and personal meaning. Such a hope underlies Pip's declaration to Estella, "You are part of my existence, part of myself. You have been in every line I have ever read since I first came here, the rough common boy whose poor heart you wounded even then" (272). Here the connection between the heart and written words is clear and inextricable.

If there is fluidity between speech and writing, if attributes usually associated with one can be given to the other, then this suggests the possibility of Dickens giving his writing the characteristics of speech. And perhaps Dickens was successful in doing so. As David Gervais aptly claims, "To read *Great Expectations* is, first of all, to listen to it" (87). Murray Baumgarten argues that Dickens invests the novel with the feel of speech rather than writing:

> In *Great Expectations*, Dickens explores the ambiguous meanings and values of literacy, in a style which seems not so much to be written as spoken. . . . To read Dickens as we all know is not to decipher and decode the rules of grammar and the laws of syntax but to listen to someone speaking personally to us. His writing has the plenitude of face to face encounters, of speech itself.   (67)

Although the degree to which, and the mechanisms through which, Dickens gives his writing the "plenitude" of speech are open to debate, it is incontestable that Dickens quite literally transformed his novels into spoken events by performing excerpts in public reading tours. Indeed, as he was finishing *Great Expectations*, Dickens began his second series of professional readings in March of 1861. On November 8, 1861 Dickens wrote to John Forster describing his provincial reading tour: "Everywhere I have found that peculiar personal relation between my audience and myself on which I counted most when I entered on this enterprise" (Forster 240). Dickens did feel himself to be "speaking personally" to his audience, perhaps even to be speaking to their secret hearts.[5] And if this was his foremost concern in his public readings of novels, it seems likely that he tried to achieve a similar connection to his audience through the written medium of his novels as well.

Dickens's purpose in establishing such a connection with his readers may lie hidden in an early association of writing with crime. Mr. Wopsle purchases "the affecting tragedy of George Barnwell" for sixpence, and then proceeds to read it aloud in Pumblechook's parlor (93). The play, now known by the title *The London Merchant*, depicts how the young apprentice, George Barnwell, is seduced by a beautiful woman and, at her bidding, robs his master and murders his uncle. The subject matter of an apprentice turned from virtue by a beautiful woman certainly resonates with the plot of *Great Expectations*, but Dickens may have had other reasons for choosing it. In the dedication to the play, its author, George Lillo, makes the claim, "The end of tragedy [is], the exciting of the passions, in order to the correcting such of them as are criminal, either in their nature, or through their excess" (261). Such prevention of crime through the correction of passions could be an important purpose for fiction. Lillo begins to elaborate on how such correction comes about, but quickly adopts instead a second moral justification for drama:

> Plays founded on moral tales in private life may be of admirable use, by carrying conviction to the mind with such irresistible force as to engage all the faculties and powers of the soul in the cause of virtue, by stifling vice in its first principles. They who imagine this to be too much to be attributed to tragedy, must be strangers to the energy of that noble species of poetry. Shakespeare . . . in his *Hamlet* has the following lines:
>
> > *Had he the motive and the cause for passion*
> > *That I have, he would drown the stage with tears*
> > *And cleave the general ear with horrid speech;*
> > . . . .
>
> and farther in the same speech:
> > *I've heard that guilty creatures at a play*
> > *Have, by the very cunning of the scene*
> > *Been so struck to the soul, that presently*
> > *They have proclaimed their malefactions.*
>
> Prodigious! yet strictly just. . . . Such plays are the best answers to them who deny the lawfulness of the stage. (262–63)

Lillo begins by asserting the efficacy of drama in eliciting strong emotions in its audience. This emotional intensity carries "conviction to the mind," creates the certainty of belief that will keep the audience virtuous and eliminate the need for criminal "conviction" of vice. He then quotes a passage from *Hamlet*, presumably meant to illustrate the intensity of emotion that can be evoked from the stage. But Lillo continues to quote *Hamlet*, citing lines that claim guilty men who see their crimes represented on the stage "have proclaimed their malefactions." Implicit in this is a shift in argument about the efficacy of drama: rather than giving further support that plays can prevent crimes, Lillo now gives evidence that plays can detect the guilty *after* crimes have been committed.

The rhetorical purpose of *Great Expectations* becomes clear if we recognize that Dickens shares this latter view of Lillo's: Dickens expects his fiction to inspire readers to "proclaim their malefactions." Such a claim may seem too grandiose to base on the never-explicitly-quoted dedication of a play mentioned only in passing in the novel. But there is other evidence to support it. First, *Great Expectations* prominently features *Hamlet*—the source of literary corroboration for Lillo's claim, and the best-known example of fiction prodding a guilty conscience. Second, the scene of Wopsle's reading of Lillo's play dramatizes the very response Lillo meant to evoke. Pip complains of Wopsle's performance, "What stung me, was the identification of the whole affair with my unoffending self. When Barnwell began to go wrong, I declare that I felt positively apologetic, Pumblechook's indignant stare so taxed me with it" (94). Barnwell is a young apprentice who murders his uncle; Pip is a young apprentice hearing the story in the company of his uncle Pumblechook. Although Pip never commits crimes of the magnitude of Barnwell's, he does feel great anger toward his tyrannical uncle. Clearly Pumblechook suspects the play might be all-too-appropriate for his hostile nephew, and Pip is "stung" by "the identification," an identification which elicits a guilty conscience and "apologetic" feelings. Although Pip doesn't explicitly confess to any wrongdoing in this scene, he does show signs of conscience and remorse that accompany sincere confession. Dickens's use of Lillo's play to show the very effects of fiction discussed in Lillo's dedication suggests a self-conscious and carefully planned incorporation of *George Barnwell*. It also suggests that *Great Expectations* is not only Pip's confession, but also Dickens's attempt to elicit confessions from his readers, to get his audience to recognize in Pip their own wrongdoing and to take the necessary steps for finding atonement and forgiveness in their own lives.

This rhetorical concern is even more explicitly enacted in Dickens's subsequent novel, *Our Mutual Friend*. Near the novel's conclusion, we learn that Mr. Boffin's moral corruption due to his new-found wealth has been an elaborate fiction. Dickens places the ruse in a specifically theatrical context when Mr. Boffin describes himself as "playing a part" (756), one which Bella correctly infers has served as a "glaring instance," a "finger-post . . . pointing out the road that [she] was taking and the end it led to" (754–55). The wished-for (and attained) result of the impersonation is to "correct and amend" Bella's behavior, following her initial failure in the test of character for which the wealthy inheritor John Harmon undertook his impersonation of the penniless Rokesmith (755). Mr. Boffin plays the part of a surly miser who grows increasingly contemptuous of John Rokesmith, in order to make Bella recognize and correct her own overvaluation of money and mistreatment of Rokesmith. By enacting Bella's own faults, before her very eyes, Boffin compels Bella to confess and amend.

Although this embedded story in *Our Mutual Friend* provides an ideal example of the fictional presentation of vice producing real repentance, the process does not work as felicitously in *Great Expectations*. In Pip's case Dickens betrays some doubts, and his anxiety about forged confessions extends even to the effects of fiction. Shortly after Pip hears Lillo's play, he learns of the brutal attack on his sister. Pip recollects, "With my head full of George Barnwell, I was at first disposed to believe that *I* must have had some hand in the attack upon my sister, or at all events that as her near relation, popularly known to be under obligations to her, I was a more legitimate object of suspicion than anyone else" (96). Although Pip had every reason to be hostile towards his sister, he had no direct involvement in the attack on her. His sense of guilt is too strong and extends too far. As Julian Moynahan notes, "Pip has certainly one of the guiltiest consciences in literature. He not only suffers *agenbite of inwit* for his sin of snobbish ingratitude toward Joe and Biddy, but also suffers through much of the novel from what can only be called a conviction of criminal guilt" (60). Pip's "conviction" of guilt, his strong emotional belief in his own guilt, never leads to criminal conviction "because it does not seem to correspond with any real criminal acts or intentions" (Moynahan 60). Pip's case may serve as an example of Peter Brooks's assertion that confession has some truth value as a performance of felt guilt, even if there is no truth to the specific crime that is confessed, and that the psychological dynamics of confession make guilt self-perpetuating (21–22). In the specific context of *Great Expectations*, Moynahan uses Pip's excessive guilt as a basis for his convincing argument that Orlick is Pip's dark double, and hence that Pip feels guilt for Orlick's attack on his sister. But if we shift the emphasis from the psychological realism of the characters to the rhetorical force of a text, we have another explanation. Pip's "conviction" of guilt in this scene has much to do with having a "head full of George Barnwell." The play has been all too successful in creating a guilty conscience in its audience; in fact, it produces *false* feelings of guilt. If Pip is sometimes inclined to make false confessions within his fictional narrative, then it may be possible that his narrative is, as a whole, a false confession. John Jordan remarks, "If, as I believe the novel shows us, there is something 'infected' about the medium of writing, then Pip has no choice but to forge his autobiography. Any written document involves falsification, and Pip's is no exception. His narrative belongs in Wemmick's collection of curiosities" (86). While most readers of the novel wish to avoid such an extreme interpretation, we must admit that Dickens acknowledges the potential for falsehood in confessions, including those inspired by fictional works.

This acknowledgement may seemingly undermine Dickens's assumption that his novel can elicit sincere, beneficial confessions from his readers, showing such an assumption to be sentimental and simplistic. Such an interpretation would be an example of Bernard Shaw's claim that Dickens's "pregnant observations and demonstrations of life are not co-ordinated into any philosophy or religion: on the contrary, Dickens's sentimental assumptions are violently contradicted by his observations'' (29). This essay offers a more generous assessment. Although in *Great Expectations* Dickens does not present a completely satisfactory and self-consistent philosophy, he does offer a very thorough and complex exploration of written and spoken language, and of guilt and forgiveness. If Dickens hopes that his novel may lead to understanding and forgiveness, he does not do so through a simplistically sentimental assumption which he unthinkingly contradicts elsewhere. Rather, he recognizes and illustrates the dangers of evoking confessions, informing his readers of the difficulties of a pursuit that is nonetheless worthwhile. In this respect, Robert Tracy's reading of the novel is astute: ''Dickens writes Pip's truth. In doing so, he implies . . . that fiction need not always be morally destructive. . . . It can also be morally redemptive'' (57). In *Great Expectations*, despite all of Dickens's doubts about the sincerity of the written word, he still tries to achieve emotional conviction in writing, a conviction that may lead to forgiveness.

NOTES

1. I believe that a similar interpretation is implicit in Max Byrd's assertion, ''Facts, not emotions, are for [Jaggers] what is real in reading, and he would understand that instinct of Miss Havisham's to have Pip write down 'I forgive her' as well as speak it. By no accident is his assistant Wemmick's mouth shaped like the slot in a postbox'' (264). But I believe the image of Wemmick's postbox mouth is effective not because Jaggers desires writing in addition to speech, nor because he values writing more highly than speech, but rather because he *transforms* speech into writing, a process that is grotesquely literalized by this description of Wemmick.
2. Peter Brooks discusses these contradictions inherent in the tradition of confessions, largely in the modern American legal context, in *Troubling Confessions.*
3. This aspect of the novel has been noted by many critics, including Baumgarten (62), John O. Jordan (79), Julian Moynahan (64), Samuel Sipe (59), Robert Tracy (57), and Barry Westburg (121).
4. At least two exceptions are Baumgarten 64, and Jordan 86.
5. Robert Tracy has also noted that Dickens used the public readings as a means for attaining ''some immediate relationship with an audience'' (44).

WORKS CITED

Baumgarten, Murray. ''Calligraphy and Code: Writing in *Great Expectations.*'' *Dickens Studies Annual* 11 (1983): 61–72.

Berger, Mark. "Legislating Confession Law in Great Britain: A Statutory Approach to Police Interrogations." *University of Michigan Journal of Law Reform* 24.1 (Fall 1990): 1–64.

Brooks, Peter. *Troubling Confessions: Speaking Guilt in Law and Literature.* Chicago: U of Chicago P, 2000.

Byrd, Max. " 'Reading' in *Great Expectations.*' " PMLA 91 (1976): 259–65.

Dickens, Charles. *Great Expectations.* 1860–61. New York: Norton, 1999.

———. *Our Mutual Friend.* 1865. New York: Penguin, 1997.

———. *A Tale of Two Cities.* 1859. New York: Signet Classic, 1997.

Forster, John. *The Life of Charles Dickens,* Vol. 2. 1872–74. New York: Everyman's Library, 1980.

Gervais, David. "The Prose and Poetry of *Great Expectations.*" *Dickens Studies Annual* 13 (1984): 85–114.

Gordon, Andrew. "Jaggers and the Moral Scheme of *Great Expectations.*" *The Dickensian* 65.357 (Winter 1969): 3–11.

Herman, Lawrence. "The Unexplored Relationship Between the Privilege Against Compulsory Self-Incrimination and the Involuntary Confessions Rule (Part I)." *Ohio State Law Journal* 53.1 (1992): 101–209.

Jordan, John O. "The Medium of *Great Expectations.*" *Dickens Studies Annual* 11 (1983): 73–88.

Joy, Henry H. *On the Admissibility of Confessions, and Challenge of Jurors in Criminal Cases in England and Ireland.* London: Stevens & Norton, 1842.

Lillo, George. *The London Merchant, or the History of George Barnwell. The Beggar's Opera and Other Eighteenth-Century Plays.* Intro. by David W. Lindsay. London: Everyman, J. M. Dent, 1993.

Moynahan, Julian. "The Hero's Guilt: The Case of *Great Expectations.*" *Essays in Criticism* 10.1 (Jan. 1960): 60–79.

Ong, Walter J. *Orality and Literacy: The Technologizing of the Word.* New York: Methuen, 1982.

Shaw, Bernard. "Epistle Dedicatory, to Arthur Bingham Walkley." *Man and Superman.* 1903. New York: Penguin, 1946.

Schramm, Jan-Melissa. *Testimony and Advocacy in Victorian Law, Literature, and Theology.* Cambridge Studies in Nineteenth-Century Literature and Culture. Ed. Gillian Beer. Cambridge: Cambridge UP, 2000.

Sipe, Samuel. "Memory and Confession in *Great Expectations.*" *Essays in Literature* 2.1 (Spring 1975): 53–64.

Sossaman, Stephen. "Language and Communication in *Great Expectations.*" *Dickens Studies Newsletter* 5.3 (Sept. 1974): 66–68.

Tracy, Robert. "Reading Dickens' Writing." *Dickens Studies Annual* 11 (1983): 37–59.

Welsh, Alexander. *Strong Representations: Narrative and Circumstantial Evidence in England.* Baltimore: Johns Hopkins UP, 1992.

Westburg, Barry. *The Confessional Fictions of Charles Dickens.* Dekalb: Northern Illinois UP, 1977.

Charles Dickens's *A Tale of Two Cities* (1859) Illustrated: A Critical Reassessment of Hablot Knight Browne's Accompanying Plates

Philip V. Allingham

Although a number of critics have pilloried Hablot Knight Browne ("Phiz") for his supposed ineptitude in the program of illustration for A Tale of Two Cities, *the fact that he so astutely realized and graphically elaborated so many significant elements of Dickens's letterpress is evidence that his pictorial series reflects an extremely careful reading of the printed text, and that these much-maligned plates that have stood the test of time in the book's publishing history are deserving of further serious scrutiny. The visual twinning of the monthly wrapper designed by Phiz reinforces the fact that the structure of* A Tale of Two Cities, *even as published in thirty-one weekly parts, was influenced by the crucial doubling that eventually resolves the plot. The obvious dualities of the Darnay/Carton likeness and the Paris/London setting not only reflect the binary structure of* All the Year Round's *weekly instalments, but also, in the story's second iteration (as a monthly, illustrated serial), complement the monthly pairing of plates, which obliged readers simultaneously to decode pictorial accompaniments in terms of the letterpress and to visualize their reading of Dickens's text in terms of Phiz's plates. The visual accompaniment was not mere ornamentation, but an aide-mémoire intended to facilitate the monthly reader's keeping track of a discontinuous narrative over a period of seven months.*

Hoping to attract as broad a readership as possible and at least equal the weekly sales of 40,000 which Bradbury and Evans's *Household Words* had averaged, Charles Dickens and his new publishers, Chapman and Hall, decided to issue the numbers of his new weekly journal, *All the Year Round,* without illustration and set the price of that small pulp magazine at only 2d. per issue, as had been the case with his former weekly. To capture the interest of the reading public, as he had in *Household Words* with *Hard Times* (1 April through 12 August, 1854), Dickens decided to run a new novel, *A Tale of Two Cities,* serially from the first number. However, as Edgar Browne says of *A Tale of Two Cities*, Dickens "also issued it independently in the usual green-covered [*sic*] monthly parts, with two illustrations by Hablot K. Browne (alias "N.E.M.O." for his first two *Pickwick* plates, and simply 'Phiz' thereafter). The two issues ran concurrently" (*Phiz and Dickens* 221), the monthly part in the blue-green wrapper costing a shilling. *A Tale of Two Cities*, Dickens's twelfth novel (but only his second venture into the genre of the historical novel), has the distinction of having appeared in three forms: it began its life in the first issue of Dickens's new weekly journal, *All the Year Round*, on 30 April 1859, each instalment averaging four-and-one-half double-columned pages (each column being 2.75 inches wide by 6.25 inches high). Unparalleled in the history of the Dickens canon is the writer's decision to overlap the thirty-one unillustrated weekly and seven illustrated monthly instalments of *A Tale of Two Cities*. These "shilling numbers" were each thirty-two pages of text (that for December being a longer "double-number"), with two steel plates and an eight-page Advertiser. That Dickens undervalued Phiz's work may be deduced from his ordering his own volume (issued by Chapman and Hall in November, 1859) to be bound without the plates, perhaps out of pique that monthly sales did not reach expectation, or that Phiz had not offered his drawings to the novelist for his scrutiny well in advance of publication (*Letters* 9: 136).

One naturally wonders what Dickens felt had gone so wrong with the illustrations for *A Tale of Two Cities* that he determined to sever a collaborative relationship which had lasted twenty-three years, and which had resulted (by Albert Johannsen's calculation, p. vi) in 1603 illustrations. Phiz was much upset at Dickens's strangely silent manner of breaking the connection. Writing to his friend and assistant, Robert Young, shortly before the serial publication of *Our Mutual Friend*, the artist speculates that

> Marcus [Stone] is no doubt to do Dickens. *I* have been a "good boy," I believe. The plates in hand are all in good time, so that I do not know what's "up," any more than you. Dickens probably thinks a new hand would give his old puppets a fresh look, or perhaps he does not like my illustrating Trollope neck-and-neck with him–though, by Jingo, he need have no rivalry *there*! Confound all authors and publishers, say I. There is no pleasing one or t'other. I wish I

had never had anything to do with the lot. (cited in Kitton 113; dated by Harvey as "February or early March, 1864" 227)

Ironically, although subsequent editions of *A Tale of Two Cities* were illustrated by *"new hands"* (Marcus Stone and Fred Barnard in Great Britain, J. McLenan in the *Harper's Weekly* serial in America), it is still Phiz's plates that are most commonly chosen to accompany the text (the most notable examples being the New Oxford Dickens [1954] and Penguin English Library edition of 1970), "remarkably tame and lacking in dramatic spirit" (Hammerton 430) as some, including paratextual critic Michael Steig (311), may find them. The note of bitterness about all publishers and novelists in the closing of his letter to Young suggests that Browne was dissatisfied with his relationship with Dickens specifically and illustrating conditions generally; "it is at least clear that some years before the final break, the partnership of Dickens and Browne had become querulous and unproductive" (Harvey 164). Browne's work for Dickens had become increasingly perfunctory, and he was less in sympathy with *Little Dorrit* (1855–57)[1] than with Dickens's earlier comic novels, for caricature and the grotesque were Phiz's speciality; indeed, the only character in *Tale* who excited his interest was the spikey-haired Jerry Cruncher, whom the illustrator pronounced the novel's only "genuine bit of Dickens" (Browne 219). Perhaps Phiz sensed that he was near the end of his career as an illustrator; in fact, he was already nearing the end of his working life, for in 1867 he suffered a stroke which rendered him incapable of further artistic production, although he did not die until long after Dickens, on 8 July, 1882.

On 16 October, 1859, Dickens complained to his publisher, Edward Chapman: "I have not yet seen any sketches from Mr. Browne for No. 6 [to be published 31 Oct.]. Will you see to this, without loss of time" (*Letters* 9: 136). The Pilgrim editors note that Dickens "may have felt that Browne was dilatory and have resented the fact that he was simultaneously providing numerous illustrations for *Once a Week*" (*Letters* 9: 136, n. 8). The rival weekly was one of the new, illustrated sort, and the other serialized novel on which Phiz had been working was Charles Lever's *Davenport Dunn* (1857–59), the forty-four plates for which Steig pronounces "more interesting than those for Dickens's novel" because of their incisive lines, "greater attention to detail, and a depiction of human figures which is charged with life and energy" (312). Thus, Dickens may well have felt that Phiz's superiorwork for *Once a Week* was preventing the illustrator from adhering to Chapman and Hall's publishing deadlines for the monthly numbers of *Tale*. The established practice was that Phiz would read the instalment and make two sketches, which he would then send to Dickens for criticism and suggested alterations. Only when Dickens had returned the sketches with his comments would the artist prepare the etchings. However, as the October 16th letter indicates, Phiz was failing to clear his conceptions at the draft stage with the novelist, who thus felt alienated from what had previously been a truly artistic collaboration.

Jane Rabb Cohen in *Charles Dickens and His Original Illustrators* (1980) indicates that sales of the monthly parts, though each accompanied by two Phiz plates, "languished" (118). The sales figures offered in *Charles Dickens and His Publishers* (1978) show that, whereas the weekly numbers soared initially to 120,000 and settled down to a steady 100,000, the monthly parts lagged far behind: "15,000 of I, 10,000 of II, 7,000 of III, and 5,000 of the rest were originally published" (Patten 277). In contrast, 36,000 copies of the first monthly instalment of *Little Dorrit* were sold in November-December, 1855. Cohen contends that, since Dickens had eliminated his usual detail in descriptions of characters and settings to accommodate weekly instalments, his style in *A Tale of Two Cities* is "declarative" (118) rather than "evocative," and that therefore Dickens's text failed to provide Browne with sufficient inspiration. Dickens's cast of characters (much more limited than one finds in his usual monthly serializations), she maintains, are "easily recalled without graphic reminders," and therefore she regards illustrations for this novel as "superfluous." She asserts that the artist's renditions of Darnay and Dr. Manette are "too conventional to be memorable" and that his visual realizations of the villains "look too benign to be credible." Browne's interiors and architectural backgrounds, she continues, lack interest, atmosphere, and authenticity: "Since they contain neither draftsmanship to be admired nor detail to be studied, it is hardly worth interrupting the gripping narrative to turn the page around to view" the oblong plates.

Nevertheless, as a narrative series they are not lacking in imaginative power and coherence. Indeed, Kitton pronounced them "full of vigour, as the character of the story justifies" (*"Phiz"* 30). However, Browne's work poses a problem for the reader: how to integrate illustrations and text into a total interpretation when the relationship between the two is not entirely clear. We know little of Dickens's directions for Browne's program since both author and artist subsequently burned much of their correspondence, including (presumably) the novelist's instructions and responses regarding the visual sequence that runs from the second chapter through all but the last three. (That incidents from the last three chapters are not illustrated is probably no accident, since an illustration of any incident in those last chapters would have let the cat out of the bag in terms of plot and suspense).

One must approach Browne's etchings for *A Tale of Two Cities*, then, not individually but as a series or program in which certain poses and objects acquire additional meanings through repetition and placement, and serve to knit individual scenes together. In the plates, characters initially unknown become more and more recognizable as a result of an interaction of text and plate, and of the plates with each other. The pair of plates accompanying each monthly instalment had to serve in part as an inducement to lay additional money out; another advantage of the monthly over the weekly parts is that the former, on superior paper, leant themselves eventually to being bound together as a single text. Throughout their long association, Phiz had supplied the illustrations (visual counterpoint and pictorial commentary to Dickens's texts) as the value-added feature that so much of the Victorian readership appreciated: two full-page plates per serial instalment. The function of these illustrations was initially to provide an anticipatory set for the serial reader, then subsequently a handy aide-mémoire so that, as the date of release for the next number approached, the reader could quickly refresh his recollection of characters and relationships thus far introduced. Perhaps, then, with these functions in mind the modern reader should approach these plates as a sequence and juxtapose them against Dickens's text, just as monthly readers would have from June through November, 1859, the wrapper each month recapitulating themes, movements, and characters, and lending itself to successive reinterpretations as both printed and visual texts unfolded.

Far from being slap-dash and unimaginative, Browne's illustrations for *A Tale of Two Cities* reveal that the artist had carefully read Dickens's text and that he designed the plates as an intact, self-referential series, connecting each plate to the others through symbolic and thematic structures and repetitions. In illustrating the monthly numbers of *A Tale of Two Cities*, the products of melding somewhat Spartan weekly serial instalments lacking the specificity of detail that he had found in Dickens's monthly serializations, Browne had a greater freedom to invent poses and settings, and to depart from the style of caricature he had employed in his earlier work for Dickens. The undated letter of complaint by Phiz to his assistant may also imply that Dickens was becoming dissatisfied with Phiz's work even before *A Tale of Two Cities*, and had made demands that Phiz felt unable to accommodate. On the one hand, his failing to sign any of the novel's plates suggests a certain truculence on the part of Browne, while his failing to send his drafts to Dickens in advance may indicate that the plates represent his artistic interpretations rather than Dickens's. If the latter is the case, this narrative-pictorial sequence is indeed unique among the productions of Browne for Dickens. In the program for *A Tale of Two Cities;* Browne abandoned his light-hearted character comedy and sentimentality for a somber mood, providing plates that emphasized theatrical realism, pathos, and above all suspense. Such artists as Charles Keene, John Everett Millais, Dante Gabriel Rossetti, Arthur Hughes, and Holman Hunt had recently altered the language of book illustration. Undoubtedly, Dickens's text itself forced this stylistic change upon Browne. Although the mob scenes in France and England possess something of the vitality (if not the detail) of those in *Barnaby Rudge*, in the majority of his plates for the 1859 novel we see Browne attempting to adapt his work to the more serious tastes of the late fifties and alter a mode of expression (derived from the visual satire of Gilray and Hogarth) that he sensed would look dated because it reverted to earlier ways of visualizing text.

A significant carryover from his previous work for Dickens is the allegorical design on the wrapper (reminiscent of the designs for such earlier wrappers as those for *Martin Chuzzlewit*, 1843–44). Each of the monthly parts shows scenes from the novel between vignettes of London (top) and Paris (bottom), indicating that Browne had probably read the story in manuscript prior to June, 1859, or at least had received a highly detailed account of the novel from Dickens himself. The top register contains St. Paul's, the Thames, the spires of Wren's late-seventeenth- and early-eighteenth-century city churches, and bales and barrels suggestive of marine commerce[2] "–but just below this, a tree killed by a storm. Across the foot Nôtre Dame, the Pont de Double and Quai St. Bernard" (note to *Letters* 9: 35); the bottom register's Paris cathedral is flanked by symbols of violent revolution, a hatchet-waving male and a pike-wielding female Jacobin, with those emblems of execution, "tumbril and guillotine above"(*Letters* 9: 35, note 2). The reader should regard the contrasting Gothic and Neoclassical cathedrals as social symbols of national character rather "than actual locales in the narrative" (Cohen 118), although these also serve to reinforce Dickens's religious note sounded frequently, especially in Carton's closing monologue.

In the central space, Browne has placed the blasted tree to suggest the devastation caused by the revolution in general and in particular the destruction of the "trees" of two families (Madame Defarge's and the St. Evrémondes). He presents thumb-nail sketches of seven scenes from the novel: the "institutional" scenes of Darnay's Old Bailey trial (upper left) and Tellson's Bank (upper right); Lucie Manette (right: the dutiful, loving daughter) balanced by Therese Defarge (left: the vengeful, hateful sister), the pair both knitting (although Lucie's domestic work will be revealed to be a contrast to Therese's patiently augmenting her secret record of those upon whom she intends to be avenged); a disinterring of a body in a graveyard (lower left) balanced appropriately by Dr. Manette, the Bastille's shoe-making inmate (lower right) recalled to social life after years of being buried alive; and the culminating journey by tumbril to the guillotine (the termination of so many family trees) under the title, center, complementing the blasted tree above. The "golden thread" (of which Dickens speaks in the text as one of love rather than of vengeance) connects all six scenes in the lower register, perhaps reflecting how the love entangled and twisted by hatred (as is the love of Therese Defarge for her dead brother) can be almost as powerful as that animated by self-sacrifice and loyalty (as ultimately expressed by Sydney Carton)."As usual, the cover was intended to excite expectations without giving too much away; by the time it appeared [in monthly form], Ch. 1–6 had been published in *AYR*"(*Letters* 9: 35, note 2). Month by month, the reader of this "second serial" version of the novel would have augmented and adjusted his or her interpretation of those wrapper scenes as further pieces of the narrative puzzle fell into place. All the elements of the simultaneous, backward-forward reading and rereading of a Victorian illustrated novel are present in the monthly instalments: anticipating the moment in the letterpress that the pictorial accompaniment had realized; attempting to integrate details of the text with those in the corresponding plate; and then reverting to a plate when encountering another of similar composition.

In the monthly parts, Browne continued to employ the increasingly unfashionable steel-plate etching that he had used to illustrate previous Dickens novels, maintaining also the comic style of drawing with which Dickens's readers had been familiar ever since the part-publication of *The Pickwick Papers* (1836–37). Andrew Sanders has pronounced the comedy "more subdued, than in [Phiz's] earlier work" (*Companion* 166); in contrast, Phiz has accentuated the elements of melodrama, although as ever his delineation of period costume and selected background details such as the French fountain in the August plates is, as Sanders notes, "generally careful" (*Companion* 166). Michael Steig in *Dickens and Phiz* notes that, while Browne's early Dickens plates are characterized by the artist's "use of iconographic techniques developed by Hogarth and his followers, especially emblematic detail" (13), these diminish after *David Copperfield*, "disappearing entirely from the sixteen illustrations for *A Tale of Two Cities*" (13). However, Cayzer detects subtle (almost subliminal) iconographic messages in plates such as "The Stoppage at the Fountain":

> Both the content and the composition of the illustration work on a symbolic level too. The cherubs adorning the fountain are an ironic comment on the scene–a case of Browne using an architectural motif natural to the picture for other purposes. The cherubs are fat and playful and are blessed with plenty—the water. How different are those objects of stone to the feeble-looking, dead, child. (134)

We shall examine this plate from Book II, Chapter 7, presently.

In the June, 1859, installment, Phiz provides contrasting and complementary scenes in the narrative: in the first, Jerry Cruncher has just stopped the Dover mail to deliver the famous message "Recalled to life"; in the second, Ernest Defarge takes Mr. Lorry and Lucie Manette up to his loft to see the Shoemaker, recently released from the Bastille. Discounting the horses in plate one, each illustration contains four figures and elaborates the message that Jerry has delivered. The polarities of the two plates are obvious: outside versus inside, England versus France, figures muffled versus figures clearly seen. In both, background details are minimized to focus on the poses of the figures, although in what is almost a dark plate Phiz is careful to delineate the guard's blunderbuss, trained on the horseman still. The artist merely hints at the highroad setting of Shooter's Hill by broadly outlined bushes in the rear. The twin focal points are the coach lantern and the reader (Mr. Jarvis Lorry) beneath (center) and the guard with Jerry Cruncher beneath him (left), leaving us to ponder what lies ahead (right). The identities of these figures, of course, depend upon the viewer's becoming a reader who must then mediate between text and picture. Significantly, we have not yet seen enough of either Jerry Cruncher or Mr. Lorry to identify them in subsequent illustrations–pictorially, we remain in the dark until the plate entitled ''The Shoemaker'' reveals the artist's conception of Mr. Lorry. The darkness of plate one, like the presence of Mr. Lorry, makes a visual connection to the wrapper's two dark scenes, mercantile London (above) and revolutionary Paris (below).

Although the second of the first installment's plates, ''The Shoemaker,'' is alluded to in the lower right register of the wrapper (paralleling the robbing of the grave to the left), in other words, in pre-reading, its connection with the other lower register scenes (the female Jacobin, and the arrival of the tumbrils at the guillotine) is made apparent much later in the story. In contrast to the panoramic scene of coach, horses, driver, guard, passenger, and messenger in the first plate, ''The Shoemaker''—itself perhaps a realization of a tableau called ''Roman Charity''[3]—is a close-up that focuses on the reunion of father and daughter. They are surrounded by an aura that visually connects this scene to the lantern of the first, and that hints of the forthcoming Manichaean conflict between the forces of darkness and of light. Here, however, there is no apparent source of illumination; rather, the light seems to emanate from the central figures themselves. Only reading the text will enable the viewer to unmask the characters in ''The Mail'' and to connect that scene to ''The Shoemaker.'' The two horizontal plates are complementary, too, in that the first involves a scene towards the middle of the second chapter while the second describes a scene right at the close of the first instalment, so that, while the reader can quickly resolve the riddles of the first, he or she must peruse almost the entire number to decode the implications of the second.

Finally, the opening scene of his visual program for A Tale of Two Cities reveals once again Browne's capacity for conveying a sinister or mysterious atmosphere, and for depicting nocturnal scenarios—and horses, a feature of his style ever since he was awarded a medal by the Society of Arts for ''John Gilpin's Ride'' in 1833, which in turn led to his being commissioned to provide the plates for Surtees's Jorrocks' Jaunts and Jollities (1838). Apparently, Christmas Book illustrator John Leech envied Phiz for his ability to draw lifelike horses.[4] The heads of the rearing steeds of the marquis's carriage in "The Stoppage at the Fountain" (August) contribute a sense of high drama, and suggest that the horses of the state, the proletariat, once out of their old masters' control, will destroy the innocent as well as the guilty, and will not be easily righted. Although the pair of horses' heads in "The Spy's Funeral" (September) do not make similar contributions to the comic vignette, they do provide a visual connection to the complementary carriage scene in France, "The Stoppage at the Fountain." The English horses, in contrast, are as placid as (despite the rollicking nature of the scene) the London mob is relatively benign. In contrast to those set in England, there is little comedy in the French scenes, but plenty of melodrama.

The third and fourth plates, for July, "The Likeness" and "Congratulations," repeat the small-scale/large-scale dichotomy of the first number's illustrations. In "The Likeness," Cayzer speculates upon the reason behind Browne's departing from Dickens's text:

> Sydney Carton is asked to "lay aside his wig" (Book II, chapter 3) in order that his appearance may be compared with that of Charles Darnay. The artist sensibly leaves Carton with his wig on, in the plate illustrating the scene, as his contribution to the tension caused for the surprised on-lookers.   (141)

The courtroom is in uproar, according to Browne, even prior to the presiding magistrate's instructing his learned friend to lay aside his wig to reinforce the likeness. This is, in fact, not a deviation from the written text, but a demonstration of how carefully Browne has read that text. The judgment that Browne has exercised is evident in his choosing to depict both facial likeness and different roles: the prisoner is in the dock, behind a row of confining spikes; the attorney, however, is in casual pose, hand in pocket, self-possessed, at ease, and free. Finally, on a level with the accused is the reader's analogue, the magistrate, who, receiving competing histories of events on that night in November, 1775, must sort out who is telling the truth and what that truth is. Only later will we apprehend one further continuing character in the *mêlée*.

In both plates of the second number, Carton is alienated: in "The Likeness," he is detached from the others in the court by being depicted almost head to foot, slightly right of center, and dividing the jurymen in their box from the rest of the scene; in "Congratulations," Carton is socially isolated more obviously from the main group, leaning aloofly right-rear, the casualness of the pose again suggestive of a "slovenly if not debauched" nature (104; II, ch.3). Here, however, the similarity in dress between attorney and client becomes much more obvious since Browne has placed Darnay center, and drawn him head to foot. Lucie is positioned exactly between her future husband and her admirer, visually "the golden thread" (110; II, ch. 4).

Major figures from "The Likeness"—except Stryver—are repeated in the final month's frontispiece for the novel, "Under the Plane Tree," in which Carton is presented once again as being outside the charmed circle (although, once dead, he will be ever-present in the survivors' thoughts). The Pilgrim editors note that the plate shows "Lucie and Charles Darnay, after their wedding, with Dr. Manette, Mr. Lorry and Miss Pross, drinking wine under the plane-tree of the Manettes' London garden" (Vol. 9: 136). As in "Congratulations," Carton's listless pose and darkened face (shaded by the arch in the former plate, and by the plane tree in the latter) convey his alienation and depression, in contrast to the joy and contentment of the rest of the company, who are paired off and seated around the sacramental bread and wine. Carton facially is almost a *doppelgänger* for Darnay, a conception Dickens had experimented with ten years earlier in *The Haunted Man* (1848) in giving the gloomy protagonist, Redlaw (who, like Carton and the author himself, suffers from an ennui induced by a painful childhood experience), an even darker genius. In all three plates, Carton is leaning (on the prisoner's dock, against the arch, and against the tree), observing the others rather than joining in, being the most significant background detail in "Congratulations" and "Under the Plane-Tree" and connecting the visual sequence from an earlier month to the last.

As we have seen, structurally as well as thematically, "The Stoppage at the Fountain" (August) and "The Spy's Funeral" (September) are visual complements, for in each case a crowd reacts to a death in a right-to-left movement of a carriage bearing an object of opprobrium—the indignant marquis and the spy. Within these large group, historical genre pictures is a strong sense of violent, swirling, confusing motion complementing each plate's dominant mood; to convey all this, each crowd scene has several focal points. In the Paris street scene, under the characteristic, Baroque fountain (left) the decently-attired women express sincere regard for mother and child; in the background, the rearing horses draw our attention to the driver, who is experiencing difficulty controlling the animals, and his scowling master; from the back rank, our attention moves forward, to Gaspard and Defarge embracing, and the recorder of the pathetic communal scene, the knitting Madame Defarge. The dead child's lack of animation contrasts the lively poses of the stone cherubs of the gushing fountain, suggestive of an outpouring of tears. The English street again involves a communal response, general rejoicing over the death of a spy, whose casket we cannot see, and a shadowy figure just emerging from the doorway, extreme right.

Again, horses, numerous figures (28 in the Paris street, 35 in the English street), and multiple focal points suggest parallel scene construction. Appropriate to the release of animal spirits in "The Spy's Funeral," there is only one woman, as opposed to at least five in "The Stoppage at the Fountain."

In contrast to the sounds of the horses, the consternation of the men, and the lachrymose lamentations of the women in "The Stoppage at the Fountain," in the essentially comedic "The Spy's Funeral" we hear sounds of communal festivity: three "common" musical instruments (proletarian trumpet, drum, and fiddle), and the boisterous play of the leap-frogging street urchins—indeed, as opposed to the marble children of the French fountain, the English scene bubbles over with the youthful vivacity of living children, consistent with Dickens piling present participles on top of each other to describe the scene: "with beer-drink*ing*, pipe-smok*ing*, song-roar*ing*, and infinite caricatur*ing* of woe, the disorderly procession went its way, recruit*ing* at every step, and all the shops shutt*ing* up before it" (186; II, ch. 14; italics added). In the French street scene, the marble children form a second chorus of grief, their physical contortions reflecting the inward agitation of the tragic chorus of women. In Paris, all faces are animated to suggest discord: accusation, shock, disbelief, and grief are written on all faces but those of the detached observers, the watchful, cold-hearted marquis and his lower-middle-class counterpart, Madame Defarge. In the Parisian scene, the fountain, the houses, and in particular the clogs clearly establish the scene's context. The clogs, suggestive of social class as well as nationality, are foiled by the adults' shoes and the children's bare feet in the succeeding month's plate. Finally, the overall movement, right to left, is unimpeded in both scenes: the direction as suggested by the faces of all present is reinforced by the horses' heads, left of center in each plate.

One wonders to what extent these details and the overall conception of both scenes originated in Browne's imagination rather than Dickens's text. The passage of the marquis's carriage, for example, is marked by "women screaming before it, and men clutching each other" (140; II, ch. 7), both of which Phiz's Paris scene includes; "there was a loud cry from a number of voices, and the horses reared" seems to be the precise moment that Phiz has chosen to illustrate. However, while Dickens has "twenty hands at the horses' bridles" (141), Phiz has rendered a single hand, and, more significantly, the "tall man in nightcap" (Gaspard) is not captured in the act of catching up his dead son, depositing the corpse at the fountain's base, and "howling over it like a wild animal." Rather, "some women [are already] stooping over the motionless bundle" (142), "silent, however, as the men." Nowhere in the text does Defarge comfort Gaspard as he does in Phiz's plate. Thus, we can see which textual hints the artist took up, which he disregarded, and how he synthesized several pages of text into a single illustration that impresses its powerful poses and juxtapositions upon the mind of the reader, ready to be called forth in the next month's illustration of a London street scene.

Plates in the following months' instalments similarly invite the reader in a simultaneous forward-backward movement to draw comparisons and contrasts, knitting up the pictorial and print narratives with the golden thread of fancy. Just as "The Stoppage at the Fountain," Book II, chapter 7 (for August), and "The Spy's Funeral," Book II, Chapter 14 (for September), are structurally similar but thematically quite different, so "Mr. Stryver at Tellson's Bank," Book II, Chapter 12 (for August), and "The Wine-Shop," Book II, Chapter 16 (for September), help the reader draw parallels and make differentiations between the two cities and knit up the plot. Both scenes ostensibly concern business—the ledgers in the London counting house (symbolic of British commerce, and, by extension, British society) are paralleled by the bottles of the Defarges' St. Antoine wine-shop. In the background of the Tellson's scene, three men count bags of money, apparently for deposit, the iron grates here (suggestive of the need for security) contrasting the fifteen-paned window of the wine-shop. Outside the Defarges' door, women gossip in the street as a male idler attempts to overhear the conversation between the publicans and the spy. The close-up structure of both scenes does not permit us to see whether there are other patrons, but the rose in Madame Defarge's cap is a detail consistent with the printed text, and we may therefore assume that this signal has momentarily cleared the shop of customers. The precise moment captured seems to be that at which Barsad (seen in the plates for the first time) informs the Defarges that Lucie is to marry Charles Darnay (otherwise, D'Aulnais on his mother's side and St. Evrémonde on his father's), in effect, the present marquis.

Whereas Browne's Defarge seems unperturbed, Dickens's betrays his emotion at this "intelligence": "Do what he would, behind the little counter, as to striking of a light and the lighting of his pipe, he was troubled, and his hand not trustworthy" (214; II, ch. 16). Although Dickens says that the effect of this news is "palpable," Browne has not chosen to reveal it. Rather, he has chosen to depict a tranquil surface whose undercurrents he signals to us through the male idler just beyond the lintel, for his Jacobin cap is a visual reminder of the revolutionary nature of the establishment roughly equivalent to Barsad's hailing Defarge as "Jacques," the code-name for a member of the clandestine Jacquerie. A clear symbol of the coming social cataclysm, the idler is seen through the doorway in roughly the same position in "The Wine-Shop" as the fashionably-dressed gentleman in the greatcoat and sporting a cane who is apparently depositing three bags of coins, details all suggestive of Britain's mercantile establishment, in "Mr. Stryver at Tellson's Bank."

The common activity (the graphic subtext, if you will) in these scenes is recording, for Madame Defarge's knitting is as much a ledger as the large tome on Mr. Lorry's desk, right of center. The chair and large pot of the wine-shop are paralleled by the stool and waste-basket in Tellson's, occupying a similar position in both plates. Despite the differences in their trade and clients, the St. Antoine wine-shop is the counterpart of the bank hard by

Temple Bar, for information as well as coin is exchanged in both establishments, the former run by implacable foes of the aristocracy, the latter superintended by the protector of Lucie Darnay and frequented by French *émigrés* in search of news of home after the outbreak of the Revolution. The aristocratic and monied clientele of Tellson's are in marked contrast to the scarecrow paupers (covert radicals) who haunt the wine-shop, which becomes a grassroots insurrectionist stronghold after the storming of the Bastille (depicted to the right on the Paris skyline of "The Sea Rises," Browne's plate for October). In addition to being centers of recording, the wine-shop and Tellson's are repositories of records. The weighty volumes on the shelf behind Mr. Lorry bespeak years of financial transactions (deposits and withdrawals), and assure the financial survival of those French aristocrats wise enough to deposit in a Parisian bank with a London house. In Madame Defarge's equally copious coded ledgers are accounts of the aristocracy's heinous domestic crimes and familial lineages. Behind these quiet genre scenes lie the essential differences in the societies of the tale; the prosperity of a relatively free trading people implies that they will not experience the mob violence of "The Sea Rises" that proletarian poverty and exploitation across the water have virtually foredoomed.

This reconsideration of Phiz's critically underrated and neglected plates for *A Tale of Two Cities* and how best to read them owes much, as we have seen, to Elizabeth Cayzer's critical reappraisal of seven of the sixteen plates in her 1990 *Dickensian* article. Some of her most perceptive observations occur in her analysis of "The Accomplices," in which an anxious and furtive Miss Pross and Mr. Lorry dismember the shoemaker's bench that was Dr. Manette's sole companion during his confinement in the Bastille:

> Dickens suffuses his prose with irony describing them as feeling 'like accomplices in a horrible crime', with Miss Pross holding 'the candle as if she were assisting at a murder'. The reader would be fully alert to such textual implications by now while, at the same time, comparing this picture with its companion 'The Sea Rises' which does deal with murder. Further echoes with events in Paris are exhibited in the wooden bench (compare the lamp-posts) and the saw (compare the mob's axes and other improvised tools of destruction and murder). Browne, typically, adds his own touch of irony by placing a skull on top of the bookcase, and comments on Lucie's probable anxiety over her friends' actions by the inclusion of an oval portrait-head of a young woman peering down on the scene.   (135–136)

So thorough has Cayzer been in her assessment that there seems little left to say. The skull, a *memento mori* for us all, serves to connect the books and desk with Alexandre Manette, physician, the true identity that the totalitarian regime sought to erase, substituting the more plebeian and docile occupation of shoe-making, as suggested by the artefact of the bench. The skull is both an object appropriate to a doctor's study and a grim foreshadowing of the maniacal forces of destruction (unleashed in the companion plate) that threaten many of the tale's principals. The bench, screen, and books acquire additional meanings when one juxtaposes "The Accomplices" and previous pictures. The inverted cobbler's bench is the same one on which the withdrawn, ill-clad ex-prisoner sits in "The Shoemaker" (June), and resembles that on which Dr. Manette sits in the lower-right register of the monthly wrapper. Later, monthly readers will encounter that same bench in the frontispiece "In the Bastille" (December). Thus, the bench comes to represent an irrepressible past to which in "The Accomplices" the well-meaning vandals attempt to prevent their friend returning. The screen, or one very like it, connects Dr. Manette to the Darnay family grouping in "The Knock at the Door" (November), in which he holds the candle (although Dickens specifies "a lamp" in Book III, Chapter 8), suggesting that he somehow performs something of the function of Miss Pross in "The Accomplices." Both screens imply a need for acting in secret and for concealment in order to preserve (sanity in the earlier plate, life itself in the latter). Finally, the shelves of books in Dr. Manette's private library connect this scene with the scenes at Tellson's and the wine-shop. They remind us that recorded knowledge (here, presumably, medical knowledge) is power.

To clarify why Browne has established these visual resonances in "The Accomplices" and to what extent these originate with Dickens himself, one must turn once again to the printed text. The details of light (Browne is probably wise in his choice of candle over lamp or rush-light), "chopper, saw, chisel, and hammer" (235; II, ch. 19), as well as the "mysterious and guilty manner" of the pair are all there, but everything else in the plate is the artist's invention. The room, we note, is specifically Dr. Manette's, and not just a parlour or drawing-room; thus, the vacant chair that bears witness to the clandestine dismemberment is Dr. Manette's, a metonymy for the usual occupant himself, a man of taste, discernment, and learning, a counterpoint to his other identity, prisoner and automaton. The power of books, of records, for good or ill is thus implied; while Dr. Manette's own document will serve to condemn his son-in-law to the guillotine, the whole text of the story that intertwines the lives of the Defarges, the Evrémondes, and the Manettes memorializes Sydney Carton and his self-sacrifice, intended to preserve and redeem.

In contrast to the behind-the-scenes, close-up study of the destruction of the shoemaker's bench and implements intended to preserve the physician's sanity, "The Sea Rises" is a public panorama of anarchic natural forces that will sweep away innocent and guilty alike. In its composition, it is akin to earlier plates "The Stoppage at the Fountain" and "The Spy's Funeral" with its violent motion from right to left (accentuated in all three crowd scenes by

fine, dense horizontal lines running through the lower half of the plate, suggestive of Shakespeare's "tide in the affairs of men"[5] that, once set in motion,
proves unstoppable) and its swirling figures all gripped by powerful emotion.
However, the female masks of grief and compassion in "The Stoppage at
the Fountain" have been replaced by haggard, jeering masks of sadistic delight, and the benign male drummer of "The Spy's Funeral" has been transformed into an ebullient female waving a bloodied meat-cleaver as she urges
her fellows to commit further acts of bloodshed under the shadow of that
implacable symbol of the ancien régime, the Bastille (stormed earlier in the
same monthly instalment, in chapter 21). It is likely that this is Phiz's realization of the Vengeance, "The short, rather plump wife of a starved grocer"
(251; II, ch. 22) who Dickens indicates carries a drum that she keeps behind
her shop counter. Our eyes are drawn to a glum face in the midst of the
maelstrom, Foulon, then is deftly drawn forward to a woman who calmly
regards him (although we cannot see her face, she is almost certainly intended
to be Madame Defarge, distinguished by her cap while the other furies are
characterized by"streaming hair," 252). Already the crowd is approaching
the fatal lamp standard (extreme left). Present participles ("pant*ing*, bleed*ing*,
yet always entreat*ing* and beseech*ing* for mercy" on p. 254) in the printed
text imply a highly active, groveling Foulon, not the rigid, passive figure
in uniform in Phiz's plate. Nevertheless, Phiz achieves focus by Foulon's
impassivity and the still figure of Madame Defarge who, as in the printed
text, "silently and composedly" (254) regards her prey as he approaches the
lamp-post, pulled on by a musket-carrying male who may be Defarge, for he
is described as carrying such a weapon when he enters Dr. Manette's cell in
the chapter previous to "The Sea Still Rises" (Book II, Chapter 22). Finally,
the lightly sketched-in face of Foulon (left of center) reminds us of another
lightly sketched-in face, that of the Marquis (right of center) in "The Stoppage
at the Fountain"—perhaps Phiz's way of suggesting that both men, like the
system that they represent, are now less substantial than the oppressed masses
who are rising against them.

While Browne obviously felt some interest in many of the plates that close
the pictorial-narrative sequence, "Before the Prison Tribunal" (III, ch. 1;
November) suggests that the graphic artist found this part of the text less
than inspiring; certainly, this section offers few "descriptive passages [that
are] sparkling and effective" (Edgar Browne 233). Indeed, the artist's son,
perhaps implying a bias towards Dickens's earlier monthly serializations,
finds the concluding book of *A Tale of Two Cities* "huddled up, instead of
being spread out and elaborated in the usual Dickens manner" (225). Cayzer
notes that in "Before the Prison Tribunal" Dickens has offered little upon
which the artist can elaborate:

an unadorned catalogue outlining the people, their states and behaviour, and the setting that Darnay finds himself in. The monotony of the prose . . . blots out all personality and only gives Browne a few definite objects to include: the oil-lamps, and the registers lying on the desk. He does what he can, though, with this illustration bringing to mind, in its general composition, his depiction of Darnay's first trial in England, 'The Likeness' (Book II, chapter 3). A corresponding indifference and pitilessness . . . is also evident. But whereas in *that* picture there is a sense of decorum in the courtroom—judge and barristers in wigs, and spectators, in the main, fashionably dressed—Darnay's next ordeal . . . occurs, as Dickens's prose has indicated, under arbitrary circumstances.

(139)

Surely the greatest difference between the two scenes lies in the animation of the court room spectators and the dramatic juxtaposition of Carton and Darnay in "The Likeness" as opposed to a general lack of drama in "Before the Prison Tribunal," in which Browne depicts over half the figures as totally unconcerned about Darnay's arraignment. Browne has found some pictorial interest in the headgear of the figures, for in addition to the omnipresent revolutionary symbols, the Phrygian "red cap and tri-colour cockade" (279; III, ch. 1) that Dickens mentions, the artist has included several examples of the Jacques Louis David-designed feathered hats[6] of the revolutionary dignitaries. Darnay's military judge, "an officer of a coarse, dark aspect" (280) as in the printed text, even wears the color-coordinated taffeta sash designed by the great pictorial chronicler of the French Revolution (these details are not mentioned until the sixth chapter, although the artist may, like Dickens, have consulted Thomas Carlyle's *The French Revolution* III, v, rather than that future chapter). Phiz has chosen to illustrate the precise moment at which Darnay questions the justice of the regime that the fanatics of "The Sea Rises" have installed. Consigned by the magistrate to the old debtors' prison of La Force, now rehabilitated for the reception of political prisoners, the arrested man exclaims as Phiz has him point at the slip of paper on which the sitting officer has been writing: " 'Under what law, and for what offence?' The officer looked up from his slip of paper for a moment" (280). However, Darnay seems no more agitated or impassioned here than he does in "The Likeness." While those about smile grimly, whisper, or regard him with glum expressions, he actually seems to smile faintly. We note that he is distinguished from the rabble of patriots present by his fashionable English dress: caped travelling coat[6]and top hat, held in the left hand (out of respect for what the judges before him ought to represent).

The officer of "dark aspect" in Dickens's text presides over open registers, surely intended to connect him to other documents memorializing the past and that other dark recorder, Madame Defarge. Unfortunately, Phiz has not followed up Dickens's textual description: no such books are evident. While the novelist merely has "certain soldiers and patriots . . . standing and lying about'' (280), Phiz has elected to show them clustered around a table, animat-edly arguing while smoking and drinking and utterly oblivious to the arrest of yet another aristocrat. Another detail Browne has added is the fireplace (center), in front of which a uniformed soldier warms himself.

The hanging lamps, however, are consistent with ''the waning oil-lamps of the night'' (280), although Browne has made the one above the socializing guardsmen clear burning and the other, above Darnay, smokey, an arrange-ment which Cayzer interprets as intended to ''echo the shape of the scales of justice'' (140). Certainly, Darnay's fate at this point remains unclear. In the end, his escape will be facilitated by the dubious figure of Barsad (who, like Darnay, has both French and English identities and fluency), whom in ''The Double Recognition'' Miss Pross recognizes as her lost brother, Solo-mon, who instantly sees that her public exposure of his true identity will almost certainly bring about his death. In that this scene paves the way for the resolution of the main action and resolves the Barsad subplot, it marks a key moment in the story. It prepares us for Darnay's escape and Carton's death, equally exciting moments that the artist has avoided illustrating for fear of giving away the climax before the reader had even opened the accom-panying text. While the November and December parts came out as a single issue early in November, weekly parts encompassing Book III, Chapters 11 through 15 continued to be issued via the pages of *All the Year Round*. Thus, in purchasing the much more expensive final double-number, the monthly reader early acquired knowledge of the story's outcome not available to the weekly reader.

Thus, in the final sequence Phiz uses elements of contemporary, domestic melodrama (particularly physical threats to the hero, a child or young woman in distress, and the possible triumph of evil over good and the foreign over the English) to build suspense without giving away the climax and resolution of the conflict. In ''Before the Tribunal,'' as we have seen, Phiz undercuts the melodrama by having the majority of the plate's figures utterly uncon-cerned about Darnay's plight. The final movement of the pictorial narrative, the plates for November and December, has much less of such muting, al-though the three unconcerned and unrelated jailors to the left of ''After the Sentence'' certainly foil the melodramatic pose of the principal characters, a visual cliff-hanger that only a reading of the printed text will resolve. In this pictorial climax, Lucie faints into Sydney Carton's arms after the courtroom ordeal and parting from her doomed husband, Mr. Lorry sympathetically takes her hand, and her father (not described in the printed text at this moment) tears his hair to exemplify his frustration at his own powerlessness to alter the outcome of events that his secret document, written in blood years before in the Bastille, has enabled Madame Defarge to produce.

This final sequence begins with Darnay's re-arrest by three uncouth figures in ''The Knock at the Door'' (November). Although Phiz's placing two of the arresting party in trousers and clogs rather than the respectable shoes and the breeches of the leader is consistent with the "rude clattering of feet" (319; III, ch. 7), why Phiz has depicted three instead of four is problematic. In number (and possibly by implication moral force) the minions of brutality and oblivion are equal to the family of well-dressed, middle-class adults whom they menace. The three armed men (suggestive perhaps of the Three Fates) form a solid block, separating the pyramidal family (like her child, Lucie leans for protection against her husband, who, relatively unmoved and tower-like, stands head and shoulders above his wife) from the retreat of the roughly sketched-in door behind them. Juxtaposed against the refined furniture and elegant fireplace and mirror of the drawing-room, the heavy-set males seem especially out of place. Phiz depicts the head of the leader as bestial or non-human (implying an absence of both intellect and compassion) and all three as armed to the teeth, the "sabres and pistols" of the printed text augmented by the leader's sword and his followers' shortened spears, which point upward as if denoting the family's fate.

Other, non-Dickensian details that are at variance with the text add to the scene's melodrama. The clock on the mantlepiece is set at five minutes to midnight, signaling the doom that threatens to engulf the family. Dr. Manette's candle (in the printed text, the light is clearly described as a "lamp") has gone out, its smoke without light recalling the smoking lamp in the guardroom of the companion plate, "Before the Tribunal." Although the scene in the text is indeed lit by the fire, the text implies by the departure of Miss Pross and Jerry Cruncher to buy provisions that the hour of the arrest is somewhat earlier. Downstage (and the stage direction is pertinent, considering the tableau poses and the shallowness of the field), nearest us, is Dr. Manette, who will again attempt to intervene, but whose bent figure and gesture towards a reasonable mean (like his snuffed candle) already imply his failure to counteract the anarchic course of events that the Defarges and "one other" as yet unidentified have set in motion.

Dickens ingeniously introduces the solution to Darnay's problem, being consigned to the guillotine, even as he is being re-arrested, and it is this plot-gambit that "The Double Recognition" dramatizes in vignette on a shallow stage. Caught in a moment of *contraposto*, Barsad does a double-take as he twists around to see who has just recalled to life an identity he has submerged in roles created in service of the state. However, his face remains concealed; the viewer must construct its expression and features based on the model Phiz had earlier provided in "The Wine-Shop" in which he wears precisely the same clothes. In this second wine-shop scene, Dickens does not specify what he is wearing, but one assumes that this "thorough Republican" (323; III, ch. 8) has blended in as spies in all ages have done, and is wearing a shaggy spenser and Phrygian cap rather than standard middle-class garb.

Furthermore, in the printed text, he does not turn back to regard Miss Pross; rather, "In going, he had to face Miss Pross" (323), who blocks his exit as the arresting party had blocked Darnay's in the previous plate. She will "be the death" of him unless she is silent as to his real name, and he will have to buy her silence. Thus, in having Barsad twist backward, Phiz exemplifies the present-past-present movement that occurs again and again in plates and text. Barsad writhes and twists, caught in his own devious coils, but remains an enigmatic figure: we do not see his facial expression.

The scene contains a number of by-now familiar elements: a room full of onlookers(as in "Before the Tribunal"), the publican and his wife, behind their bar and situated amidst their bottles and tankards, scrutinizing a well-dressed stranger (as in "The Wine-Shop"), a mixture of uniformed and Phrygian-capped patriots (again as in "Before the Tribunal"), Miss Pross (wearing the same dress as in "The Accomplices"), and, depicted clearly for the first time, Jerry Cruncher. Although the text indicates that the Tellson's functionary who doubles as a Resurrection Man is present in "The Mail," "The Likeness" (indeed, Dickens explores much of the English courtroom scene from Jerry's perspective), and "The Spy's Funeral," this is the first plate in which Phiz gives him center stage. In the monthly version's first plate, "The Mail," he is a muffled figure on horseback who is recognizable only by virtue of the context established by the accompanying text. In "The Likeness" we can identify the wigless figure, center, immediately behind attorney Carton, as Jerry only after we have seen him in "The Double Recognition." In the printed text, we enter the Old Bailey with Jerry (91; II, ch. 2), experience moment by moment what Jerry sees, thinks, and feels "on the floor of the court" (p. 92), and follow the trial proceedings with him (p. 95), so that he mediates between the action and the reader, although he is usually regarded as a minor character throughout the text.

Although young Lucie Manette and her father, witnesses on behalf of the accused, are somewhere in the courtroom as well, according to Dickens's text, their figures (familiar to us as a result of the previous month's plate, "The Shoemaker") are not discernible in Phiz's plate. In "The Spy's Funeral," we initially look for Jerry where Dickens places him, inside the mourning coach, "modestly concealed from the observation of Tellson's" (186; II, ch. 14), which we assume to be the building at the right, in front of which stands a well-dressed gentleman who strongly resembles the client in the background of "Mr. Stryver at Tellson's Bank." The connection between Tellson's and the building in the plate is further reinforced by a scrutiny of the text, which indicates that the mob impresses a bear-leader and his charge "as an additional ornament, before the cavalcade had gone far down the Strand" (p. 186), Tellson's being opposite Temple Bar (Andrew Sanders in *A Companion to* A Tale of Two Cities, p. 35, indicates Dickens based Tellson's in part on Child and Company, which "had premises at 1 Fleet Street and leased rooms over Temple Bar from the City as a repository''). Immediately behind the Tellson's client in Phiz's plate, someone is creeping out of the door to the extreme right; since this figure resembles the Jerry of the other plates, we may assume that the artist has chosen to conflate two different moments in the text, because Jerry is among the first of those rowdies who appropriate seats on the hearse, and so should already be well-concealed ''in the further corner of the mourning coach'' (p. 186) before the bear-leader unwillingly joins the rag-tag funeral procession. Thus, Phiz has attempted to capture two moments in one temporal schema, which can only be fully decoded much later in the pictorial sequence.

The viewer, then, must carefully examine the present (Jerry in the Paris wine-shop) in order to interpret the past correctly (identifying the figure of Jerry in the Old Bailey trial and the spy's funeral). Brown compels readers to move from present to past and then back to the present: revisiting the past critically, searching out meaningful detail in both plates and text, and mediating between the two narrative media. This process of engagement with the past enables the reader to find clues to interpret the present, precisely as Dickens the novelist and Carlyle the historian have proposed. The center of this temporal maelstrom is exemplified in the title-page vignette ''In the Bastille'' (the only such single pictorial character study): ''I, Alexandre Manette, write this melancholy paper in my doleful cell in the Bastille, during the last month of the year 1767''—*Two Cities, Bk. III. ch. x* (Hammerton 440). A ray of light cuts diagonally across the circular picture as the writer folds his communication and prepares to post it towards an uncertain future. The darkness of insanity, of mindlessness, of being buried alive, has not yet engulfed the writer, but it is present, waiting for the light of sanity to fade; to the right and left of the seated prisoner are chains adjacent to the dark fields of the plate, in which Phiz has utilized Baroque *chiaroscuro* to highlight the writer's broad forehead, suggestive of the power of mind that has thus far been able to transform the stone-walled cell into a writer's workshop. The arch is reminiscent of the grotto-like cell in which Dr. Manette is kept for the sake of his sanity by his former servant, Ernest Defarge, in ''The Shoemaker.'' Here, however, his patient labor is directed not towards the production of shoes but to the production of text. Once again, then, Phiz has created a character who is an author or recorder of events because decoding the past is the central activity of *A Tale of Two Cities*. Until Dr. Manette can make contact with that younger self who cursed the St. Evrémondes and mediates that past self with his present self, he cannot be a whole person. Rather, he will be a fractured personality identified by two jobs and (his descent into insanity effected through ten years of imprisonment and isolation) but one name, lost for a time (significantly, he is shown unchained in Phiz's plate because his manacles are becoming, as poet William Blake had remarked of what kept London's underclass economically and politically oppressed, "mind-forged") but recovered through the benevolent operation of memory, the golden thread that connects the quondam shoemaker to his wife and, by extension, to his former life through the medium of his golden-haired daughter, whose tresses recall that past identity as intellectual, physician, husband, and father to the present. Thus, through the accidents of time and chance, Dr. Manette, reunited with his past sentiments, has become a realization of the good Lucius Junius Brutus of Roman antiquity, sacrificing his family (here, not his son, but his son-in-law) and his daughter's happiness to the blood-thirsty Republic which has idolized him. Dr. Manette regains full knowledge of himself, but at what a cost, as he returns to the time when he was shortly to be reduced to a mere agent or mechanism without higher level thinking and poignant feeling, a shoemaker, and craved but one thing as his sanity slipped from him: vengeance. Thus, the monthly readers of the printed and pictorial texts achieved a coherent vision by fusing the separate images of the Bastille prisoner (present in the title page vignette, past in "The Shoemaker") and the venerable Enlightenment scientist and humanist of "The Knock at the Door."

In the final sequence of plates, Phiz uses elements of contemporary, domestic melodrama inherited from the Gothic novels of Matthew G. Lewis and Anne Radcliffe (particularly physical threats to the hero, a child, or young woman in distress, and the possible triumph of evil over good and the foreign over the English) to build suspense without giving away the climax and resolution of the conflict. In "Before the Tribunal," Phiz undercuts the melodrama by having the majority of the plate's figures utterly unconcerned about Darnay's plight. Their utter lack of interest in Darnay's arrest and disposition foil the reader/viewer's engagement with text and plate. That Darnay's initial release is but a "red herring" is revealed immediately by the succeeding plate—one need not even scan the letterpress to understand the twist in the plot. The power to influence the outcome has shifted from Darnay (right in "Before the Tribunal"), pointing his finger at the military judge (reflecting the friendly difference of opinion between two of the carousers, right) to suggest his self-confidence, to the shag-eared villain (right) who points accusatorially at Darnay in "The Knock at the Door." Comparing the juxtapositions and gestures of the characters in these two plates, the viewer notices that the hand that before had lightly held his respectable top-hat now gestures downward, as if he is pleading to remain with his wife and child. At this tense moment, the flame of hope, represented by the smoking taper that Dr. Manette holds, seems to have been irrevocably snuffed. The viewer fully expects that the last, double number will feature a scene depicting either Darnay's being transported by tumbril to his place of execution or his being placed under the ominous blade of Madame de la Guillotine.

The reader of the monthly instalments returns to the Paris of the Reign of Terror, having visited Dr. Manette as he was after ten years' confinement in the Bastille, the writer of the 1767 epistle to the future, encapsulated in the figure of the writer of the narrative of Therese Defarge's family and of his own plight, a narrative that comes to closure in a curse upon his and her persecutors. Dickens and Phiz have transported the reader to a point eight years prior to the novel's opening, and from thence ten years earlier, to the period when the St. Evrémonde brothers had committed their unspeakable crimes that have come back to assault their innocent descendant in the present. As the scene "The Double Recognition" suggests, there is no burying the past; it is always there, ready to erupt when least we expect it, threatening to destroy the present self for past sins, even the sins of past generations. Thus, the justice of history in *A Tale of Two Cities* is not entirely *nemesis*, for although Dickens permits Lucie, her father, child, and husband to escape the vengeance of the Revolution, Therese Defarge, a victim of the Old Regime now a victimizer under the New Order, has suffered in the past, and, but for her persecution of the blameless Darnays, would not deserve her fate any more than the dissolute but self-sacrificing Sydney Carton.

As Linda Hughes and Michael Lund in *The Victorian Serial* remind us, the structure of the story published in weekly parts was influenced by the kind of doubling evidenced in the Darnay/Carton likeness and the dichotomous Paris/London setting: instalments"consisted of two closely-related, often paired chapters" (64). As was usual in Dickens's monthly serials, pairs of plates accompanied thirty-two pages of text, obliging readers to decode plates in terms of text and visualize text in terms of plates. In *A Tale of Two Cities*, the second of Dickens's two historical novels, "The merging of characters and readers in the experience of history is developed further through the figure of Jarvis Lorry" (66), with whom we embark upon the London-Paris road in the opening chapter and with whom we flee Paris at the close. Lorry appears with greater frequency than any other character in the text (he is named 716 times) and in Phiz's plates (see Appendix 2). Although Phiz has been pilloried for his ineptitude in the program of illustration for *A Tale of Two Cities*, the fact that he so astutely gauged the importance of Lorry is yet further evidence that his pictorial series reflects an extremely careful reading of Dickens's letterpress.

Epilogue

In order to keep each journal's purchase price low while maintaining as broad a readership as possible, Dickens had his weeklies printed on inexpensive newsprint. Both the small format and inferior paper of his literary magazines militated against the use of illustrations. As of 1861, Dickens seems not to have recognized the importance of a new publishing phenomenon, the British illustrated literary magazine, the first of which, *Once a Week*, illustrated by Phiz and others, appeared in the same year that Dickens published his melodramatic tale of the French Revolution in *All the Year Round*. Dickens failed to adapt his works to this new form, and seems for a time to have lost his former interest in illustration (the first volume edition of *Great Expectations*, for example, had no illustrations). Only for the Library Edition of 1862 did Dickens decide that his curious story of Pip and the convict needed such embellishment, to be provided by one of the new generation of illustrators, Marcus Stone (all other illustrations for unpirated editions of *Great Expectations* were not executed until after Dickens's death). How strange was this apparent neglect in Dickens, who in producing the Christmas Books in the 1840s had worked so closely with such notable illustrators as John Leech, Clarkson Stanfield, John Tenniel, Richard Doyle, Daniel Maclise, Frank Stone, and Edward Landseer, developing the innovative technique of dropping the plates into the text. By 1862, however, Dickens was considering collaborating with some of the bright, young artists working on the new illustrated magazines.

There would be moving (and, perhaps, technically superior) illustrations for Dickens's *A Tale of Two Cities* in other editions, although these are available today only in such specialized publications as *The Annotated Dickens* (1986). For example, Fred Barnard's series for The Household Edition (1870s) offers more detail and a better three-dimensional sense of space, and occasionally engages us, as in "Miss Pross smoothing Lucie's Hair" and "Still, the Doctor, with shaded forehead, beat his foot nervously on the ground," but he and later artists, one senses, were always laboring under the shadow of Phiz's greatness, reacting to his series as well as to the text, and generally avoiding any subject Phiz had attempted. When Barnard does follow Phiz in his selections, as in "Dragged, and struck at, and stifled by the bunches of grass and straw that were thrust into his face by hundreds of hands" (paralleling Phiz's "The Sea Rises"), the result is decidedly more modern and realistic, but undistinguished because, unlike Phiz, he fails to establish each member of the mob as an individual in a tide of humanity. American illustrator John McLenan's "Revolutionary" (Author's Edition, 1859) possesses the convincing solidity of the sixties' style, but lacks the grace, charm, and wit that underlie all of Phiz's creations. The most significant of the non-Phiz illustrations for *A Tale of Two Cities*, Fred Barnard's occasionally reproduced "The Third Tumbril," lacks the sense of melodrama and pathos found in "The Arrest," and does not give us enough of the expressions of Carton and the little seamstress to render them as sympathetic as Dickens intended.

According to J. R. Harvey, of seventeen editions of Dickens's works published between 1861 (The Library Edition) and 1937 (The Nonesuch Edition), only three do not utilize Browne's original plates in some manner: The Household Edition (1871–79), Nelson's New Century Library (1899), and The Temple Edition (1901–03), the latter two being illustrated by John A. Bacon.[7] After the turn of the century, publishers abandoned any attempt to displace Phiz as Dickens's principal illustrator, and Harvey concludes that "it is more than likely that Browne's plates will still be printed in editions of Dickens one or two centuries from now" (198).

Appendix One:

A Tale of Two Cities: 30 April through 26 November, 1859,
in thirty-one weekly parts in *All the Year Round* and eight monthly instalments—
List of Sixteen Illustrations by Hablot Knight Browne ("Phiz"); including

Frontispiece "Hundreds of People" or "Under the Plane Tree" (Book II, Chapter 6), and *Title-page Vignette* "In the Bastille" (Book III, Chapter 10); neither issued until final, double number (Nov. 26, 1859)*

1A. "The Mail," Book I, Chapter 2 (for June, 1859; issued 30 April weekly)

1B. "The Shoemaker," Book I, Chapter 6 (for June, 1859; issued 21 May)

2A. "The Likeness," Book II, Chapter 3 (for July, 1859; issued 4 June)

2B. "Congratulations," Book II, Chapter 4 (for July, 1859; issued 11 June)

3A. "The Stoppage at the Fountain," Book II, Chapter 7 (for August, 1859; issued 25 June in weekly numbers)

3B. "Mr. Stryver at Tellson's Bank," Book II, Chapter 12 (for August, 1859; issued 16 July in weekly numbers)

4A. "The Spy's Funeral," Book II, Chapter 14 (for September, 1859; c issued 23 July in weekly numbers)

4B. "The Wine-shop," Book II, Chapter 16 (for September, 1859; issued 6 August in weekly numbers)

5A. "The Accomplices," Book II, Chapter 19 (for October, 1859; issued 20 August in weekly numbers)

5B. "The Sea Rises," Book II, Chapter 22 (for October, 1859; issued 3 September in weekly numbers)

6A. "Before the Prison Tribunal," Book III, Chapter 1 (for November, 1859, published 31 Oct.; issued 17 September in weekly numbers)

6B. "The Knock at the Door," Book III, Chapter 7 (for November, 1859; issued 8 October in weekly numbers)

7A. "The Double Recognition," Book III, Chapter 8 (for December, 1859; issued 15 October in weekly numbers)

7B. "After the Sentence," Book III, Chapter 11 (for December, 1859; issued 5 November in weekly numbers).

*7C. "In the Bastille," vignette, Book III, Chapter 10 (for December, 1859; issued 29 October in weekly numbers); issued in the December instalment, a double number (parts 7 and 8), and also as the title-page vignette for first volume edition (Nov. 26);

*7D. *Frontispiece* "Hundreds of People" or "Under the Plane Tree" (Book II, Chapter 6).

Pictures 7B and C in the sequence depict incidents with which readers following the tale in *All the Year Round* but also purchasing the monthly parts would have been familiar.

Appendix Two:

From Concordance.com *Tale of Two Cities* Frequency Word Search, versus Appearances in the Novel's Plates

Lorry:	339
Mr. Lorry:	358
Jarvis Lorry:	19
Total	716

7: "The Mail," "The Shoemaker," "Congratulations," "Mr. Stryver at Tellson's Bank," "After the Sentence," "The Accomplices," "Under the Plane Tree."

Alexandre:	6
Manette:	156
Alexandre Manette:	6
Total	168

6: "The Shoemaker," "Congratulations," "The Knock at the Door," "After the Sentence," "In the Bastille," and "Under the Plane Tree."

Charles:	96
Darnay:	141
Charles Darnay:	59
Total	296

5: "The Likeness," "Congratulations," "Before the Prison Tribunal," "The Knock at the Door," and "Under the Plane Tree."

Lucie:	124	
Lucie Manette:	11	
Miss Manette:	54	
Total	189	

5. "The Shoemaker," "Congratulations," "The Knock at the Door," "After the Sentence," and "Under the Plane Tree."

Carton:	149
Sydney	73
Sydney Carton:	38
Total	260

4: "The Likeness," "Congratulations," "After the Sentence," and "Under the Plane Tree."

Cruncher:	110
Jerry:	106
Jerry Cruncher:	19
Total	235

4: "The Mail," "The Likeness," "The Spy's Funeral," and "The Double Recognition."

Monsieur Defarge:	37
Ernest Defarge:	3
Total	40

4: "The Shoemaker," "The Stoppage at the Fountain," "The Wine-Shop," and "The Sea Rises."

Madame Defarge	127
Therese Defarge:	3
Therese:	4
Total	134

3: "The Stoppage at the Fountain," "The Wine-Shop," and "The Sea Rises."

Stryver:	103
"The Lion":	9
Total	112

3: "The Likeness," "Congratulations," and "Mr. Stryver at Tellson's Bank."

John:	10
Barsad:	44
Solomon:	24
Solomon Barsad:	1
John Barsad:	5
Total	84

3: "The Wine-shop," "The Double Recognition," and "After the Sentence."

Pross:	150
Miss Pross:	159
Total	309

2: "The Accomplices" and "The Double Recognition."

Gaspard:	7
mender of the roads:	45
Total	52

1: "The Stoppage at the Fountain."

St. Evrémonde:	46	1: "The Stoppage at the Fountain."
Marquis St. Evrémonde:	2	
Total	48	

Vengeance (name):	40	1: "The Sea Rises."

Conclusions

Owing to the variations in the naming of characters in the printed text (note, for example, that in Book III, Chapter 14, Lucie is called variously "she," "the wife," "his wife," "the wife of Evrémonde" and "my Lady-bird," as well as "Lucie," and that in Book I, Chapter 4, she is "Miss Manette") the name frequency derived from Concordance.com is actually approximate, while the frequency of figures in the plates is absolute. Generally speaking, however, the frequency with which a character's name (or names) appears in the printed text parallels the frequency with which that character appears in Phiz's plates. However, Miss Pross, a far more significant character than her brother Solomon in the textual form of *A Tale of Two Cities*, appears in only two of Phiz's illustrations while her scapegrace brother appears in three. Moreover, certain characters who seem relatively minor in the plates, such as the Marquis St. Evrémonde, are actually extremely important in the novel's complicated plot. Surprisingly, the story's main protagonist, Charles Darnay, in terms of both text and plates is less important than Dr. Manette, who seems to be a secondary character until the hidden letter, the inset tale of his Bastille experience, is read into the main text at Darnay's third trial in the book. The frequency with which a character is depicted is not an infallible signifier of that character's importance, of course; Sydney Carton, Jerry Cruncher, and Ernest Defarge, for instance, each appear in four plates, but the first two are far more frequently mentioned by name in the text than is the French publican (who, oddly, is named far more often than the novel's heroine, Lucie, despite her status as a principal in the pictorial-narrative sequence). Nevertheless, both printed and illustrated versions of the story yield pride of place to Mr. Jarvis Lorry, the man of good business (life-long servant of the House of Tellson) who is also a good man of business (using his commercial connections on both sides of the Channel to guard the Manettes).

NOTES

1. As early as the serialization of *Little Dorrit*, Browne had been uncooperative with the novelist in terms of adjusting his artistic productions according to Dickens's

guidelines. In a letter dated 19 October, 1855, to his managing editor at *Household Words*, W. H. Wills, Dickens complains that he has heard nothing from Browne after sending him suggestions for revisions, and asks Wills to have publishers Bradbury and Evans contact Browne's engraver and send the artist his present address (*Letters* 7: 722).

2. The smoke (suggestive, perhaps, of the dark tales of the Defarges and the St. Evrémondes, and of the forces of repression and revolution that animate the bottom register of the wrapper) from the Southwark chimneys, downstage right and left, blows symmetrically from the southeast and southwest, casting a pall over the City, dominated by the dome of St. Paul's Cathedral (designed by Wren, and built between 1675 and 1711). In contrast to the twin, square Gothic towers of Paris's Nôtre Dame below is the Baroque-style dome of St. Paul's, crowned by a lantern, an orb, and a cross. Whereas Browne's Paris is mediaeval, his London is relatively modern, and—despite the dome and steeples—focussed on commerce rather than religion. Although Browne has not shown the quarter-mile of embankment and its buildings in any detail, one may note that, to either side of Wren's dome, rise the steeples of three churches, all of which approximately date from the period of the Glorious Revolution, the cornerstone of eighteenth-century England's parliamentary democracy. Stretching from the sites of the modern-day bridges of Blackfriars (left: 1769) to Southwark (right: 1819), the Thames shoreline is cluttered with wharfs and piers. Fromthe left to the right, the spires (see Pevsner's map, inside cover) probably belong to the following churches, all designed by Sir Christopher Wren: St. Martin Ludgate (1677–87) in the background; St. Andrew-by-the-Wardrobe (1685–95); St. Benet Paul's Wharf (1677–85); St. Nicholas Cole Abbey (1671–81); St. Mary le Bow (1670–83) well back; and St. James Garlickhithe (1674–87). The ramshackle London scene in the foreground is strongly characterized by bales (left), barrels, and a lighter (right), indicative of mercantile activity and material prosperity, but has no figures, in contrast to the Paris scene at the bottom of the wrapper vignette.

3. "Doubtless Dickens encountered the image of Roman Charity in more than one obscure gallery; in the private palaces of Rome, for example, where he thought 'pictures are seen to the best advantage''[*Pictures from Italy*, London , 1846: p. 212] (Meisel, 310).

Earlier, in *A Tour in Italy and Sicily* (London, 1828), Louis Simard had expressed his admiration of Guido's *Roman Charity* in Genoa's Durazzo Palace, a visit to which Dickens alludes in a letter to Lady Blessington (*Letters* 4: 305). Meisel argues that, although there is a Shakespearean parallel in Cordelia's tending Lear, Amy's comforting her father in *Little Dorrit*, and Lucie's rocking her father on her heart "like a child" (I, vi) in *A Tale of Two Cities* are manifestations of Dickens's fascination with such paintings of Roman Charity as Andrea Sirani's (1630–42).

The image of Roman Charity recurs in *A Tale of Two Cities*, in a section entitled "Recalled to Life." It takes form (like a *tableau vivant*) in a prepared fictive setting, designed to accommodate the actual world to the mental world of the prisoner. Dr. Manette, recently released from the Bastille but unable to accept his condition, is

brought together with his daughter, Lucie, in a garret room that has
been darkened and made into a pseudo-cell. The wine-shop keeper,
Defarge, ostentatiously wielding a key, stands for the jailor. Lucie is
required by her father's fragile mental state to restrain her "eagerness
to lay the spectral face upon her warm young breast, and love it both
to life and hope." (Meisel 315)

4. Notes Buchanan-Brown,

> Browne was a keen horseman. The family claimed he would rather
> ride than walk fifty yards. He kept his horses at Croydon and regularly
> hunted with the local pack. His illustrations of horses are always good
> and, after his return to London (oddly enough), he published his
> sporting books *Hunting Bits* (1862) and *Racing and Chasing* (1868)
> (p. 30).

5. Brutus's memorable philosophizing about forces of destiny beyond the control of
even the great men of history seems consistent with Thomas Carlyle's interpretation of events in *The French Revolution* (1837), upon which Dickens draws so
heavily. See William Shakespeare's *The Tragedy of Julius Caesar*, IV, iii, 217.

6. Despite Buchanan-Brown's assertion that Phiz was not much of a hand at "costume [i. e., pre-Victorian] pieces" (26), the late eighteenth-century costumes of
the characters in his plates for *A Tale of Two Cities* are, in the main, correct. In
addition to British magazines and newspapers of the period (1757–1794), Browne
may have consulted some of the material that Dickens borrowed from the historian Carlyle. However, in "Before the Tribunal" the beaver which the fashionably accoutered Charles Darnay holds in his left hand does not closely correspond
to the early 1790s. According to C. Willett Cunnington and Phillis Cunnington,
the various styles of round hat at that period had in common a crown that was
tall and a "brim small and generally rolled up on each side" (*Handbook of
English Costume in the Eighteenth Century* 239). In fact, Darnay's top hat looks
more like the type known as "Lincoln and Bennett" worn by Englishmen at the
time that Dickens penned the novel and Phiz etched the plates, as opposed to the
(then) "Old-fashioned beaver" (*Handbook of English Costume in the Nineteenth
Century* 223–24). The caped great-coat which survives today as the Australian
stockman's coat and the top-boots that Darnay wears in "Before the Tribunal"
are certainly plausible, although the French top-boots that condemned and inquisi-
tor alike wear present a minor problem. The prisoner, attired in fashions of
English manufacture, would more likely be wearing English "jockey" boots with
the "turned-over top sloping down to a point in front" as opposed to the "French
turned-over top, cut straight round" (*Handbook of English Costume in the Eighteenth Century* 230) which Browne depicts in "Before the Tribunal."

Mr. Lorry's somewhat unfashionable mode of dress, including a wig, in "After
the Sentence," set almost twenty years after his initial appearance in the novel,
in "The Shoemaker," is consistent with the tastes of an older, conservative bank-
manager: the coat with close sleeves; small, round cuffs; the skirts ending just
above the knee; the plain waistcoat with flapped pockets below the waist; the
neckcloth; and the three-cornered hat so much in fashion for much of the century
were becoming passé by the 1790s. Lucie's father, like the younger professional

in "After the Sentence," Sydney Carton, is not wearing a wig, although this departure from earlier fashion did not become widespread until after the British government levied a tax on hair-powder in 1795. Dickens specifically mentions wearing "the white riding-coat and top-boots, then in vogue, . . . with his long brown hair, all untrimmed, hanging loose about him" (Book III, Chapter 9, pages 338–39). In both text and plate, Carton seems to be affecting a "Brutus" head—long hair "with a wind-blown, dishevelled appearance" (*Handbook of English Costume in the Eighteenth Century* 247), named after J. L. David's hero of Republican Rome, as seen in "Brutus Condemning His Son" (1789). This figure Dickens himself alludes to in both the name of the wineshop where Miss Pross encounters Barsad, and obliquely at the close of Book III, Chapter 10 ("the questionable virtues of antiquity, and for sacrifices and self-immolations on the people's altar"). Notes Andrew Sanders in the World's Classics edition of the novel, "Carton's not wearing a wig, and letting his long hair hang loose would . . . have rendered him less conspicuous in Paris, where such anti-aristocratic modes were popular" (517). The implied comparison of Sydney Carton and Lucius Junius Brutus is both apt and ironic: although both represent the virtue of sacrifice, David depicts Lucius Junius Brutus as a public official so inspired with love of country that he can stoically sacrifice both his sons to Republican principle, for as consul in 509 B. C. he was officially compelled to sentence his sons to death for conspiring to restore the Etruscan monarchy; the chivalric Carton, on the other hand, gives his own life to preserve the life of the man who has been his rival in love, and thereby cheat the French Republic of an aristocrat whom it has arbitrarily declared an enemy of the state under the "Law of the Suspect" passed on September 19, 1793 (which, by November, led to The Reign of Terror).

7. John Harvey favors the reproductive quality of the plates in Chapman and Hall's Gadshill Edition (1897), "in which the illustrations were printed from the original steels with a beautiful clarity and sensitivity" (197).

WORKS CITED

Allingham, Philip V. " 'We Can Now See That the Days of Illustrated Novels Were Drawing to an End'—Not So." *The Dickens Magazine*. Series 1, Issue 3: 6–7.

Browne, Edgar. *Phiz and Dickens As They Appeared to Edgar Browne*. London: James Nisbet, 1913.

Buchanan-Brown, John. *Phiz! The Book Illustrations of Hablot Knight Browne*. Newton Abbot, London: David and Charles, 1978.

Cayzer, Elizabeth. "Dickens and His Late Illustrators. A Change in Style: Phiz and *A Tale of Two Cities*." *Dickensian* 86, 3 (Autumn, 1990): 130–141.

Cohen. Jane R. *Charles Dickens and His Original Illustrators*. Columbus: U of Ohio P, 1980.

Cunnington, C. Willett, and Phillis Cunnington. *Handbook of English Costume in the Eighteenth Century.* Boston: Plays, 1972.

———. *Handbook of English Costume in the Nineteenth Century.* Boston: Plays, 1970.

Daiches, David, and John Flower. *Literary Landscapes of the British Isles: A Narrative Atlas.* Harmondsworth: Penguin, 1981.

Davis, Paul B. "Dickens, Hogarth, and the Illustrations for *Great Expectations.*" Dickensian 80, 3 (Autumn, 1984): 130–143.

Dickens, Charles. *The Annotated Dickens*, Volume Two: *David Copperfield, A Tale of Two Cities*, and *Great Expectations.* Ed. Edward Guiliano and Philip Collins. New York: Clarkson N. Potter, 1986.

———. *The Letters of Charles Dickens.* Gen. eds. Madeline House, Graham Storey, and Kathleen Tillotson. Vol. 4 (1844–1846), ed. Kathleen Tillotson, 1977; Vol. 7 (1853–1855), ed. Graham Storey, Kathleen Tillotson, and Angus Easson, 1993; Vol. 9 (1859–1861), ed. Madeline House, Graham Storey, and Kathleen Tillotson, 1997; Vol. 11 (1865–1867), ed. Graham Storey. Oxford: Clarendon, 1999.

———. (1859). *A Tale of Two Cities*, ed. Andrew Sanders. World's Classics. Oxford: Oxford UP, 1990.

———. *A Tale of Two Cities*, ed. George Woodcock. Harmondsworth: Penguin, 1970. Unless otherwise noted, all references are to this edition.

Hammerton, J. A. *The Dickens Picture-Book.* London: Educational Book Co., [1910].

Harvey, John R. *Victorian Novelists and Their Illustrators.* London: Sidgwick and Jackson, 1970.

Hughes, Linda K, and Michael Lund. *The Victorian Serial.* Charlottesville: UP of Virginia, 1991.

Johannsen, Albert. *Phiz: Illustrations from the Novels of Charles Dickens.* Chicago: U of Chicago P, 1956.

Leavis, F. R. and Q. D. "The Dickens Illustrators: Their Functions." *Dickens the Novelist.* London: Chatto and Windus, 1970. 332–71.

Kitton, Frederic G. *Dickens and His Illustrators.* 1899. Amsterdam: S. Emmering, 1972.

———. *"Phiz" (Hablot Knight Browne): A Memoir.* 1882. New York: Haskell House, 1974

Meisel, Martin. *Realizations: Narrative, Pictorial, and Theatrical Arts in Nineteenth-Century England.* Princeton, NJ: Princeton UP, 1983.

Muir, Percy. *Victorian Illustrated Books*. London: B. T. Batsford, 1971.

Patten, Robert L. *Charles Dickens and His Publishers*. Oxford: Clarendon, 1978.

————. "Review of Michael Steig, *Dickens and Phiz*. Bloomington: Indiana UP, 1978. x + 340." and "Review of John Buchanan-Brown, *Phiz! Illustrator of Dickens's World*. New York: Scribner's, 1978." *Nineteenth-Century Fiction* 34, 2 (Sept., 1979): 224–28.

Pevsner, Nikolaus. *The Buildings of England: London I: The Cities of London and Westminster*. Harmondsworth: Penguin, 1957.

Sanders, A. *The Companion to* A Tale of Two Cities. London: Unwin Hyman, 1988.

Shakespeare, William. *The Tragedy of Julius Caesar* (1599), ed. Sylvan Barnet. New York: Signet, 1963.

Solberg, Sarah A. "A Note on Phiz's Dark Plates." *Dickensian* 76, 1 (1980): 40–41.

Steig, Michael. *Dickens and Phiz*. Bloomington: Indiana UP, 1978.

Watts, Alan S. "Why Wasn't *Great Expectations* Illustrated?" *The Dickens Magazine*. Series 1, Issue 2: 8–9.

Fig. No. 1A: "The Mail" Book I, Ch. 2
(for June, 1859; chapter issued 30 April in the weekly numbers)

Fig. No. 1B. ''The Shoemaker,'' Book I, Chapter 6
(for June, 1859; chapter issued 21 May in the weekly numbers)

Fig. No. 2A. ''The Likeness,'' Book II, Chapter 3
(for July, 1859; chapter issued 4 June in the weekly numbers)

Fig. No. 2B. ''Congratulations,'' Book II, Chapter 4
(for July, 1859; chapter issued 11 June in the weekly numbers)

Fig. No. 3A. "The Stoppage at the Fountain," Book II, Chapter 7
(for August, 1859; chapter issued 25 June in the weekly numbers)

Fig. 3B. "Mr. Stryver at Tellson's Bank," Book II, Chapter 12
(for August, 1859; chapter issued 16 July in the weekly numbers)

Fig. 4A. "The Spy's Funeral," Book II, Chapter 14
(for September, 1859; chapter issued 23 July in the weekly numbers)

Fig. No. 4B: ''The Wine-shop,'' Book II, Ch. 16
(for September, 1859; chapter issued 6 August in the weekly numbers)

Fig. 5A. ''The Accomplices,'' Book II, Chapter 19
(for October, 1859; chapter issued 20 August in the weekly numbers)

Fig. 5B. "The Sea Rises," Book II, Chapter 22
(for October, 1859; chapter issued 3 September in the weekly numbers)

Fig. 6A. "Before the Prison Tribunal," Book III, Chapter 1
(for November, 1859; chapter issued 17 September in the weekly numbers)

Fig. 6B. "The Knock at the Door," Book III, Chapter 7
(for November, 1859; chapter issued 8 October in the weekly numbers)

Fig. 7A. ''The Double Recognition,'' Book III, Chapter 8
(for December, 1859; chapter issued 15 October in the weekly numbers)

Fig. 7B. "After the Sentence," Book III, Chapter 11
(for December, 1859; chapter issued 5 November in the weekly numbers)

Fig. 7C. ''In the Bastille,'' Book III, Chapter 10
(for December, 1859; chapter issued 29 October in the weekly numbers)

Fig. 7D. Frontispiece "Hundreds of People," or "Under the Plane Tree"
Book II, Chapter 6
(for December, 1859; chapter issued 18 June in the weekly numbers)

A TALE OF TWO CITIES

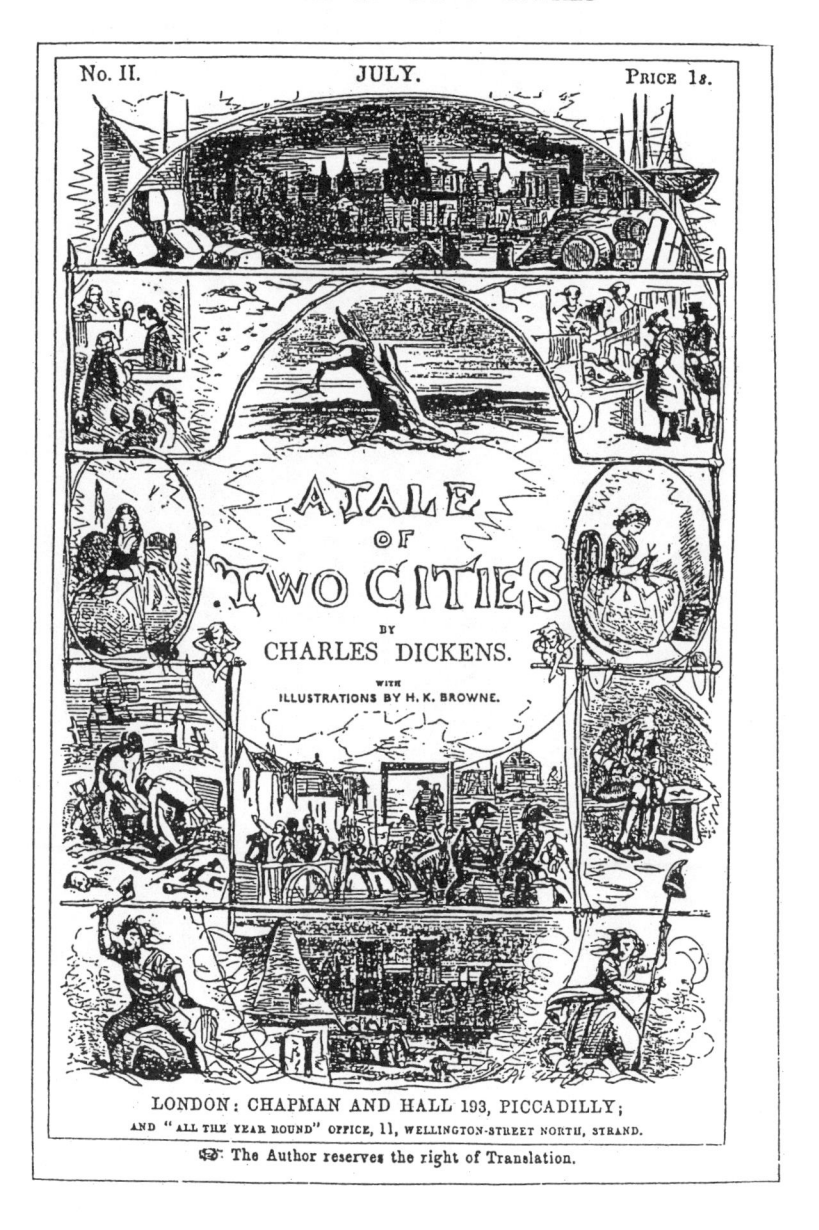

Fig. 8. Monthly Wrapper No. 1 (for June, 1859)
Source: *Dickens Studies Annual* 12 (1983): viii.

"Boz has got the Town by the ear": Dickens and the *Athenaeum* Critics

Ellen Miller Casey

The weekly Athenaeum, *called by its editors "the mirror of Victorian culture," published more than 10,000 reviews of fiction from its inception in 1828 until 1900. While* Athenaeum *reviewers recognized Dickens's ability from the earliest review of* Sketches *by Boz, they had reservations about his vulgarity. They also distinguished between the enthusiastic popular reception and the more sophisticated understanding of the critics. Impressed by Dickens's growing social criticism, however, they came to value both his moral influence and his art. These judgments are apparent not only in the reviews of Dickens himself, but also in the extensive comments on him found in reviews of other novelists.*

> Boz has got the Town by the ear, and he is not so thorough-bred as we imagine, if he lets go his hold in deference to the critics.
>
> Mr. Dickens has obtained the ear of his country more completely than any other man; and, on the whole, he uses his glorious privilege for the noblest ends. His monthly Part carries joy, mourning, laughter, and tears into thousands of households; and this laughter and these tears are such as brighten and purify the heart.
>
> *The Athenaeum*

These two *Athenaeum* quotations, from the anonymous 1836 review of the second series of *Sketches by Boz* (916) and from William Hepworth Dixon's

---

1855 review of the first installment of *Little Dorrit* (1393), epitomize the journal's evaluation of Charles Dickens.[1] The reviews of Dickens in the *Athenaeum* recognized Dickens's great popularity, distinguished between this popularity and the more sophisticated understanding of the critics, and came to value highly his moral influence and his art. But there is more commentary on Dickens in the *Athenaeum* than is contained in these reviews of his own work, for throughout the century the reviewers referred to and commented on Dickens in their reviews of novels by other authors. These indirect reviews of Dickens deepen our understanding of the position that he held in the minds of Victorian readers and reviewers, for they expand on the evaluations of him written during his life and extend them after his death.

Founded on 2 January 1828 as a "Literary and Critical Journal," the *Athenaeum* was called by its editors the "mirror of Victorian culture" and by George Moore "the first literary journal in the English language" (Elwin 83). In his comprehensive and authoritative history of the journal, Leslie Marchand makes it clear that by the time Dickens began publishing, the *Athenaeum* had established itself under the editorship of Charles Wentworth Dilke as an influential journal which prided itself on its independence of authors and publishers and on its staff of competent critics and correspondents. In July 1831 the journal had dropped its price from 8*d* to 4*d*, thereby increasing its sales sixfold. By January 1832 Dilke could accurately proclaim that the *Athenaeum*'s sales exceeded those of any other literary journal (34–37). Its prestige and influence declined after 1846 under the editorship first of Thomas Kibble Hervey and then of William Hepworth Dixon, but when Norman MacColl took over in 1871, "the journal soon . . . surged ahead of all competitors to become an organ of literary criticism with unequalled influence in the late Victorian era" (88–89). Although initially "stodgy" (Jump 42), by the 1880s the *Athenaeum* was more comprehensive and more open to new trends than the other two weeklies, the *Spectator* and the *Saturday Review* (Casey).

Appearing every Saturday, the *Athenaeum* was a quarto-sized journal with three columns of small type per page. It was devoted to reviews and notices of books, exhibitions, concerts, plays, and meetings of learned societies. It published three kinds of fiction reviews. First, a feature review of two to three pages in the front of the journal was occasionally devoted to a novel. Second, after 1849, when novels became more numerous, the *Athenaeum* increasingly dealt with them "collectively" (H. Chorley, "New Novels" 1177) and "in a short compass" (H. Chorley, "New Novels" 459) in the column named first "New Novels," then "Novels and Novelettes" and still later "Novels of the Week." Later in the century, this column was augmented with such specialized columns as "American Novels" and "Short Stories." Third, brief comments of a sentence or two were gathered in "Our Library

Table,'' and occasionally remarks on fiction appeared in "Our Weekly Gossip.'' This essay is based on a systematic analysis of the more than 10,000 reviews in the first two categories which appeared from 1836 to 1900; it also refers to comments on Dickens in "Our Library Table" and "Our Weekly Gossip.''

All of the reviews in the *Athenaeum* were anonymous, a practice to which the journal clung even after many reviews moved to signatures in the 1860s, a change that is thoroughly discussed by Oscar Maurer and Dallas Liddle. J. D. Jump summarizes the arguments for and against this anonymity when he says: "At its worst, anonymous reviewing gave scope to puffing and to irresponsible malignity. At its best, it encouraged the reviewer to subordinate his personal likes and dislikes to judgements dependent upon an impersonal standard of value which he and his colleagues alike respected" (44). In his 1898 article celebrating the *Athenaeum*'s seventieth birthday, Theodore Watts-Dunton acknowledged "the enormous responsibility of anonymous criticism," for "in an unsigned article the speaker is clothed with all the authority of the journal in which he writes" (10). Despite this continuing anonymity, however, Margaret Oliphant praised the *Athenaeum* for its work toward ending the "puffing of particular publishers' books by hireling critics" (622), and Joanne Shattock argues that weeklies like the *Athenaeum* retained the practice until the end of the century because it allowed reviewers to air controversial opinions and editors to control their publications (16).

The *Athenaeum*'s reviews were written by a handful of critics, including whoever was the fiction editor at the time. Recently *The* Athenaeum *Index of Reviews and Reviewers, 1830–1870* (http://web.soi.city.ac.uk) has used the marked copies of the *Athenaeum* to make available the identity of the authors of most of the reviews published from 1830 into 1871.[2] When possible I have indicated reviewers's names, but except in the cases of the reviews of Dickens where I have augmented the *Index*'s information with the aid of the *New CBEL* and Marchand, I have made no methodical effort to expand on this information.

The *Athenaeum*'s recognition of Dickens's popularity can be seen in the frequency, promptness, and length of its reviews of his works. As the chart in the appendix indicates, the *Athenaeum* reviewed virtually everything that Dickens wrote, typically with a lengthy review within two weeks of publication.[3] Moreover, it was common for the journal to review the early installments of Dickens's novels as well as the completed work.

From the first, the *Athenaeum* recognized Dickens's talent. Its earliest mention of him was a one-inch review of *Sketches by Boz* which appeared in "Our Library Table" on 20 February 1836 and praised the sketches for their "admirable truth." By the end of the year, Dickens had moved from one-inch in "Our Library Table" to almost three pages in the lead review. Although the

Athenaeum rarely devoted lead reviews to novels, it dedicated the opening of the 3 December 1836 issue to the first nine installments of *The Posthumous Papers of the Pickwick Club*. Lead reviews were also given to *Barnaby Rudge, American Notes, The Chimes, Bleak House*, and the first installments of *Little Dorrit* and *Edwin Drood*.

The pattern of reviewing early installments, started with *Pickwick*, was repeated with *Nicholas Nickleby, Martin Chuzzlewit, Dombey and Son, David Copperfield, Bleak House, Little Dorrit, Our Mutual Friend*, and *The Mystery of Edwin Drood*. Of these, all but *Pickwick Nickleby*, and *Dombey* were reviewed again when they appeared in book form. The frequency and length of the reviews of Dickens's novels clearly indicate the importance assigned to him by the *Athenaeum*. This importance is underlined by Henry Fothergill Chorley's lengthy obituary of Dickens, by the lengthy reviews devoted to all three volumes of John Forster's *Life of Charles Dickens*, and by the substantial review of Dickens's *Letters*.

Beginning with the comment about *Sketches* that "Boz has got the Town by the ear" (916), the reviewers frequently acknowledged Dickens's popularity. By the time that *Oliver Twist* appeared in three volumes at the end of 1838, the *Athenaeum* pronounced a review superfluous, since everyone had already read the novel. It settled instead for a two-page extract recounting the death of Sykes. In November 1840, Thomas Hood declared, "*Master Humphrey's Clock* has already its thousands upon thousands of readers" (888). Henry Chorley's 1844 review of *Martin Chuzzlewit* acknowledged Dickens's "sudden and brilliant success" which had put his book "in the hands of tens of thousands" (665). In his 1857 review of *Little Dorrit*, Dixon conceded that "to quote from a volume which everybody has read—or will read—is superfluous" (722–23).

Although it acknowledged that the whole town was listening to Dickens, the *Athenaeum* did not wholeheartedly lend him its ear. That first review of *Sketches* reserved judgment—"a suspicion crossed our minds during the perusal, whether the subjects were always worthy of the artistic skill and power of the writer." The review of the opening installments of *Pickwick* introduced two recurrent reservations about Dickens: his lack of originality and his vulgarity. It noted that the "fashion of late days" was "to christen a new favourite in the humorous department of literature, after one of the great pleasant fathers." The *Athenaeum* objected to this practice, for "true wit, or true humour, ought to provoke no trace of relationship." Boz, though clever

> runs closely upon some leading hounds in the humorous pack, and when he gives tongue (perchance a vulgar tongue,) he reminds you of the baying of several *deep dogs* who have gone before. The Pickwick Papers, in fact, are made up of two pounds of Smollett, three ounces of Sterne, a handful of Hook, a dash of a grammatical Pierce Egan—incidents at pleasure, served with an original *sauce piquante*.   (841)

This frequently quoted comment sums up the *Athenaeum*'s response to Dickens's early novels: they are clever and humorous, but too imitative and vulgar.

This review of *Pickwick* also introduced a distinction between popularity and literary worth which the *Athenaeum* reviewers would repeat again and again. It suggested that *Pickwick* was a dish to "tickle the palates of many of the particular, as well as of many of the deeply voracious" (841). Although the terminology varied, this distinction between "the particular" and "the deeply voracious" ran through the *Athenaeum*'s reviews of Dickens. Not surprisingly, the *Athenaeum* reviewers always classed themselves as particular rather than voracious readers.

In reviews of Dickens's early novels they acknowledged his popularity, but held themselves apart from it. The December 1836 review of *Sketches*, for instance, posed a contrast between *Town* and *critics*, asserting that Dickens would not let go his hold on the Town's ear "in deference to the critics" (916). Henry Chorley's review of *Martin Chuzzlewit* opposed *magazines* and *books*, suggesting that Dickens's "freakish and affected" characteristics of style were "tricks for the magazines, but have no place on the library shelf" (666). The very brief notice of *A Tale of Two Cities* couched the distinction in terms of the *public* and the *journalist critic* as it dismissed the novel while acknowledging its popularity: "A hundred thousand readers have followed the exciting adventures of Dr. Manette and his charming daughter. The tale is told, and the audience of a hundred thousand, as the curtain drops, cry—Well done! The public is here before the journalist, and the critic can only echo the public voice."

Gradually, however, the distinction between public and critic took on a different tone. As Dickens's novels darkened, the reviewers increasingly suggested that the general reader did not recognize Dickens's true worth but hankered after his earlier, simpler novels. In his review of *David Copperfield*, for example, Henry Chorley suggested that since the novel was full of "natural truths," it would be less pleasing than other Dickens novels to "the lovers of higher excitement" (1210). Chorley repeated this distinction in his review of *Our Mutual Friend*, framing it this time in terms of "those who, with understanding, as distinct from that wonderment which belongs to the foolish face of praise, have followed Mr. Dickens throughout his career" (569). John Cordy Jeaffreson used the same metaphor of voracious readers in 1867 when he suggested that *Lost at the Winning Post* was "good enough for those numerous devourers of light literature who systematically read all the novels of the season, without discerning any difference between the works of Mr. Dickens and the productions that die as soon as they are born." Dr. John Doran repeated the contrast between the foolish and the discerning reader in his review of the first installment of *Drood*, arguing that although "there are some of Mr. Dickens's critics who have never been able to see in him anything but a caricaturist,'' his defects of exaggeration which are especially prominent in his early novels "disappear in the brilliancy and truthfulness with which other characters are portrayed'' (443).

The *Athenaeum* reviewers viewed themselves as more discriminating than the average reader, a perception which may have contributed to the magazine's dissent from most critics in its evaluation of Dickens. George Ford, for example, notes that the *Athenaeum* was more negative than other journals towards Dickens's early novels, especially in looking down on them for their vulgarity (6, 29). Around 1850, however, Dickens's public split. He retained his wide general popularity, but gradually lost critical acclaim. Ford suggests that after this split the *Athenaeum* was one of the few papers to comment favorably on the social criticism of such novels as *Bleak House* and *Our Mutual Friend* (108). Jump also observes that in the 1850s the *Athenaeum* esteemed Dickens much more highly than the other two weeklies (47). In her article on the *Athenaeum*'s reception of *Little Dorrit*, Charlotte Rotkin argues that after its initial satiric response to *Pickwick*, the *Athenaeum* became progressively more positive in its evaluation of Dickens. She contends that *Little Dorrit* was the first for which it offered "unequivocal praise" and that its review, which anticipates twentieth-century evaluations, was much more positive and sophisticated than most Victorian reviews. Marchand summarizes this movement when he says, "Dickens won his way to favor more slowly in the *Athenaeum* than he did in other magazines" but, unlike the other journals, the *Athenaeum* "took a more kindly interest in him when it perceived that his writing tended to something more than mere amusement" (300).

Certainly, as the century went on, the *Athenaeum* increasingly praised Dickens for his morality and his benevolence. It particularly valued him for using his access to his country's ear for the noble end of informing his readers about the plight of the poor. Hood's 1840 review of *The Old Curiosity Shop*, for example, praised Dickens for enlightening the ignorance of one-half of the world about how the other half lives. Hood went on to identify his reasons for liking the novel: "it is life-like and bustling, and therefore good for one's amusement; it comes from a sound head and heart, and is therefore fitted for one's improvement" (888). In 1843, Henry Chorley praised *A Christmas Carol* because it was "a tale to make the reader laugh and cry—open his hands, and open his heart to charity even towards the uncharitable" (1127).

There was a further shift in the *Athenaeum*'s response to Dickens beginning with Henry Chorley's review of *Chuzzlewit* in 1844. Until this point, he says, "the nature of [Dickens's] compact with the public" was

to make his monthly or weekly hit—here, to make his serviceable truths pleasant, to strew the way with Samivel Weller's flowers of slang, or Richard Swiveller's poetical reminiscences—there to bite in his effect by Miggs's acidity, or to "creep into the easy ear" by the aid of Mrs. Gamp's oily malaprop. We never looked at these tales as having a beginning, middle, and end.　　(655)

Despite their "jerks and chasms, and violent junctures," however, the tales' benevolent purpose made them "worthier a hundred-fold than many a work of art more symmetrically arranged." With *Chuzzlewit*, though, it became necessary to judge Dickens "after a new fashion," as "a literary artist" contributing to "the world's library of Fiction" rather than merely a benevolent entertainer (665).

John Westland Marston continued this double praise of Dickens's morality and art in his review of *The Battle of Life* when he praised him both for giving "lessons in the Philosophy of the Heart" and for being "the Poet of the Actual" (1319). From then on the reviewers spent increasingly more time evaluating and praising Dickens's art. Dixon applauded *Little Dorrit* for its "evidence of an ever-ripening genius and an ever-progressing art" (1893). Henry Chorley announced that in *Great Expectations* "we have to do with a work of Art arranged from the first moment of conception with power, progress, and a minuteness consistent with the widest apparent freedom" (44). By the time Chorley reviewed *Our Mutual Friend*, he praised Dickens as "the greatest novelist living" and summed up his qualities by noting that time and success had not "spoilt, or dimmed, or turned aside his quick sympathies, his power of minute observation, his keen desire to advocate what he deems right, his wondrous force of hand and colour as a painter in words" (569).

The *Athenaeum* reserved its highest praise for a handful of Dickens's novels. Thomas Kibble Hervey proclaimed *Nicholas Nickleby* "perhaps the best of Mr. Dickens's works" (554). Henry Chorley thought *David Copperfield* "in many respects the most beautiful and highly finished work which the world has had from the pen of Mr. Dickens" (1209). Chorley was even more enthusiastic about *Great Expectations*, which he called "the creation of a great artist in his prime" (44), and about *Our Mutual Friend*, which he proclaimed "one of Mr. Dickens's richest and most carefully-wrought books" (570). The review of Dickens's *Letters* in 1881 summed up the *Athenaeum*'s evaluation of him as an artist:

> The man's genius did but ripen and expand with years and labour; he spent his life in developing from a popular writer into an artist. He extemporized *Pickwick*, it may be, but into *Copperfield* and *Chuzzlewit* and the *Tale of Two Cities* and *Our Mutual Friend*, he put his whole might, working at them with a passion and a determination hardly exceeded by Balzac.　　(659)

The review went on to dismiss the recent "cant . . . about art and artists; the

gospel of 'l'art pour l'art' [which] has been preached with so much unprofit-
able iteration'' and to suggest that Dickens was a better model for English
novelists:

> [Dickens] was a man self-made and self-taught; and if he knew anything at all
> about the ''art for art'' theory—which is doubtful—he probably held it cheaply
> enough. But for all that he is found to be a truer artist than the quasi-heroic
> creatures upon whom his countrymen are told to fashion themselves, and whom
> many of them worship . . . . Dickens's claim to be considered an earnest artist
> may be justified without much difficulty. He began as a serious novelist with
> Ralph Nickleby and Lord Frederick Verisopht; he ended by producing such
> masterpieces as Jonas Chuzzlewit, and Doubledick, and Eugene Wrayburn, and
> the Golden May, and Fagin and Sikes, and Sydney Carton, and many another.
> The advance is one from positive weakness to positive strength, from ignorance
> to knowledge, from ineptitude to mastery, from the manufacture of lay figures
> to the creation of human beings.   (659)

This judgment that Dickens worked hard to develop into a great artist was
repeated in the 1888 review of the Victoria edition of *Pickwick Papers*:

> In the beginning Dickens did not always write well, especially when he was
> doing his best to write seriously. He developed into a great artist in words as
> he developed into an admirable artist in the construction and the evolution of
> a story. But his development was his own work, and it is a fact that should
> redound eternally to his honour that he began in newspaper English, and by
> the production of an imitation of the *novela picaresca*—a string of adventures
> as broken and disconnected as the adventures of Lazarillo de Tormes or Pere-
> grine Pickle.   (80–81)

These final reviews of Dickens's own work sum up the *Athenaeum*'s opinion
of him: he developed through much labor from a rather vulgar popular writer
into a great artist. It was his determination to address the issue of urban
poverty that led him to improve, for it was only when he began addressing
social problems instead of imitating his picaresque predecessors that his novels developed artistically. His later novels were more carefully structured,
and his later characters were ''less rouged and ochred, and hacked and
draped'' (Dixon, rev. of *LD* #1 1393).

But if we limit ourselves to the reviews of Dickens's own novels, we have
read only part of what the *Athenaeum* had to say about him. Throughout the
century, the reviewers frequently referred to Dickens when reviewing the
fiction of other authors. Sometimes they simply alluded to a Dickensian character; sometimes they made a more extensive comparison; occasionally they
wrote an extended discussion of Dickens's place in the literary canon. Reading
this material confirms and expands our understanding of the *Athenaeum*'s
opinion of Dickens.

These reviews of novels by authors other than Dickens emphatically confirm the *Athenaeum*'s recognition of Dickens's popularity. In his book *Sociological Aspects of the Literary System*, Karl Erik Rosengren presents a methodology for studying the "climate of opinion" of reviewers. He suggests that one can ascertain the importance of an author to reviewers by counting the number of times they mention an author in reviews of works by other authors. A count of such references in the *Athenaeum* reveals that Dickens occupied an important position on the horizon of critical discourse throughout the century. As can be seen by the following ten-year samples, *Athenaeum* reviewers frequently and persistently referred to Dickens when reviewing the works of others. In 1843 Dickens and Edward Bulwer-Lytton were cited twice, ranking fourth behind Sir Walter Scott (cited seven times), Harrison Ainsworth (cited four times), and Mrs. Trollope, G. P. R. James, and Samuel Richardson (cited three times each). In 1853 Scott was still first with five citations, but Shakespeare and Dickens followed with four each. By 1863 Dickens was cited eight times, more than any other author. (He was followed by Wilkie Collins with four citations and by Mary Elizabeth Braddon and Samuel Richardson with three each.) Dickens still ranked first in 1873 with six citations, followed by George Eliot with five. By 1883 Dickens and Anthony Trollope had moved back to third place with four citations each, behind Henry James's eight and George Eliot's five. In 1893, however, Dickens was back in first place with six citations, followed by Scott with five and James and Thackeray with four each. Obviously a simple accumulation of references does not indicate the attitude of the reviewers, but it does confirm that Dickens occupied a central position in the critical landscape throughout the century.

The quantity of references to Dickens demonstrates his importance; their content gives a sense of which Dickens works were most popular. *Copperfield* was most frequently cited, followed by *Chuzzlewit* (the latter largely because of multiple references to Sarah Gamp and Pecksniff). On the other hand, *A Tale of Two Cities* and *Barnaby Rudge* were mentioned only three times, *Drood* but once, and *Hard Times* not at all.

The variety of these references exemplifies how well *Athenaeum* reviewers knew Dickens's novels and how well they expected their readers to know him. We expect the repeated references to Sam Weller and Pecksniff and Skimpole, but there are also references to lesser-known characters such as Tim Linkinwater (Jewsbury, rev. of *How Could He Help it?*) and Mrs. Wittiterly (Jewsbury, rev. of *Side Winds*) from *Nicholas Nickleby*, the signalman from *Mugby Junction* (rev. of *A Spanish Maid*), and Mrs. Chick from *Dombey and Son* (Romer).

These allusions to Dickens characters were often employed to communicate information and judgments about characters in other novels. Thus reviewers recognized a villain who was "simply our old friend Mr. James Carker" (rev. of *My Time*), another who was "of the Bill Sykes genus" (Jewsbury, rev. of *Mad*), and a third who was "of the Bill Sykes kind, without his bull-dog" (Jewsbury, rev. of *Strange Work*). They noted a heroine who was "a middle-class Little Em'ly" (rev. of *Mr. Spivey's Clerk*), a hero who was "rather too like Carton" (Collyer, rev. of *Earl's Dene*), and another who was "Wilkins Micawber in good health" (rev. of *My Time*). They observed that David Copperfield was "the literary father of a large family of destitute and maltreated boys" (rev. of *Some Stained Pages* 309). They recognized "a new Miss Dartle" (rev. of *In Connection*), "a *fin-de siècle* Uriah Heep" (rev. of *A Valuable Life*), "a Mrs. Nickleby of higher spheres" (rev. of *Margaret Jermine*), "a libertine of the Steerforth type" (rev. of *Old Ship-mates*), an "aristocratic Pecksniff" (rev. of *A Lucky Young Woman*) and a Russian one (rev. of *The Friend* 573), an "Irish Mrs. Gamp" (Collyer, rev. of *Eventide*), as well as a "female Skimpole" (rev. of *A Prince*), "a kind of Skimpolian cynic" (rev. of *Workers*), and "sort of a cross between Micawber and Skimpole" (rev. of *The Three Oxonians*).

The reviewers also used Dickens's characters to comment on authors and readers. Geraldine Jewsbury suggested that "no one but the immortal Mr. Pecksniff could have written anything equal to this last paragraph" (rev. of *The Life*). Jeaffreson likened Charles Stuart Savile to Dickens's "amiable simpletons" like Mr. Dick and Mr. Toots who write for want of thought. Like them, Savile "finds peace of mind in composing romances which no sane man will ever read for pleasure's sake" (rev. of *Beating to Windward* 835). The reviewer of Turgenev's *A Sportsman's Sketches* asserted that "With some people Nihilism is as invariably introduced when Russia is discussed as the head of King Charles I was brought in by the old gentleman in the story by Dickens." Dixon used Dickens to attack Charles Lever's sentences as "simply abominable. Betsey Prig would not write more slipslop paragraphs than Mr. Lever has written in *Luttrell of Arran*" (791). The reviewer of Jeaffreson's *A Woman in Spite of Herself* suggested that to accept the novel's plot "our powers of 'make-believe' must exceed those of the Marchioness of Dick Swiveller's affections" (49). Jeaffreson himself feared that the pro-prietors of *Cassell's Family Paper* had "adopted a course not at variance with the morality of Mr. Pecksniff" in giving a £250 prize to the anonymous *A Good Fight in the Battle of Life* when perhaps it hadn't been chosen by the eminent judges but "by a bookseller's hack" (639).

Sometimes, of course, these resemblances to Dickens were deliberate on the part of other authors, and *Athenaeum* reviewers recognized that Dickens was a source of "undying influence" (rev. of *Settled out of Court*). As early as 1843 Marmion Savage noted that the anonymous author of *The Commissioner* "mimics Mr. Dickens," and as late as 1900 a reviewer noted that Tom Gallon's *Kiddy* was "visibly in the key of Dickens." In 1853 John Rutter

Chorley proclaimed a " 'Boz' School" (rev. of *Eugene Stillfried*); in 1875 a review of *Miss Honeywood's Lovers* declared Dickens "the founder and head" of the "purely narrative school of novelists" (303); in 1897 a reviewer alluded to "the still surviving school of Dickens" (rev. of *Tatterley*); and later that year a reviewer declared that Richard Pryce was "of the school of Dickens, and we do not know that there is a better" (rev. of *Elementary Jane*).

Everyone, it seems, imitated Dickens. Elizabeth Gaskell surpassed the tragedy of Nancy in *Oliver Twist* with the "deep, dreary sadness" of Esther's visit to Mary in *Mary Barton* (H. Chorley 1050). George Eliot inappropriately imitated *Pickwick Papers* in serializing *Middlemarch*. Thomas Hardy seemed in *The Trumpet-Major* "to be in the way to do for rural life what Dickens did for that of the town." Benjamin Farjeon was "a follower of the method of Dickens" (rev. of *Great Porter Square* 692). Frederick Robinson was the subject of an "enormous" influence by Dickens (rev. of *Her Love* 84). Since Rudyard Kipling's use of the supernatural proved "the affinity of his genius to that of Dickens, who excelled in precisely similar *tours de force*" (rev. of *A Spanish Maid*), there was hope that he might become "a second Dickens" (revs. of *Soldiers Three* and *In Black and White*).

Nor was imitation confined to British novelists. Friedrich von Hackländer was "a German Boz" (J. Chorley, rev. of *Stories* 720) and later "the German Dickens" (rev. of *European Slave Life*). Bret Harte "trained his imagination to walk with a Dickensian gait" (rev. of *The Complete Works* 390). In his "Notes from Paris," Edmond About noted that Alphonse Daudet was "the pupil of Charles Dickens, . . . the most fertile and popular of your novelists" (19); a later reviewer said Daudet "had reason to be grateful for the influence of the master" (rev. of *Gideon Fleyce*). Ivan Turgenev "had a great passion for the writings of Dickens," of whom he often reminded the reviewer (rev. of *Torrents*). Even Henry James introduced "some touches of Dickens, refined and subtilized" (rev. of *Lesson* 370).

The *Athenaeum* reviewers, however, found Dickens a dangerous model. Some of their reservations were based on the general problems of imitation, which they judged analogous to wearing mock jewelry (Jewsbury, rev. of *Mildrington*), to having a waistcoat made after another man's fashion (Hannay), or to compounding a salad rather than doing honest cookery (H. Chorley, rev. of *Kingsford*).

Other of their reservations were specifically directed at imitators of Dickens, who rarely equaled the master. They grew tired of "endless imitations of Dickens at his weakest" (rev. of *Mr. Smith* 543) and found "third-rate Dickens . . . perhaps the most depressing of all styles" (rev. of *Jobson's*). These imitators grasped the tricks of the "Dickensesque manner" (rev. of *Marion*) like "ejaculations, broken sentences, replies and rejoinders, neat and regular as anvil strokes" (rev. of *"It is never too late to mend"* 991) and "recurrent refrains, sudden apostrophes and reflections" (rev. of *Humbling*). Too often, however, they produced a style which was "a travesty of Dickens" (rev. of *A Peal* 604) or "desperately diluted Dickens" (rev. of *Skill*). Dickens was a difficult model because it was "fatally easy to imitate some of Dickens's mannerisms, but impossible for anybody to write freely in his style" (rev. of *A Great Mystery*) and because his writing was full of "freaks and phrases and unfinished sentences" (H. Chorley, rev. of *Mount Sorel* 328). Too many imitators failed to recognize that Dickens's genius triumphed in spite of, rather than because of, his "peculiarities" (rev. of *A Young Girl's Life*). As a result, they caught Dickens's vulgarity without his humanity (rev. of *Bishopspool*), his grotesquerie without his pathos, humor, and power (rev. of *Wilbourne Hall*). They managed to reproduce "Dickens's vices of exaggeration and the rest, but how little of his virtues!" (rev. of *The New Faith*).

The reviews of non-Dickensian novels also contain a great deal of material which expands our understanding of the *Athenaeum*'s judgment of Dickens. Frequently these discussed Dickens's virtues, one of the greatest of which was the humor of which he was "so great a master" (Knollys). He "invented" (rev. of *Prinkle*) and made "fashionable" (rev. of *"B"*) a new style of humor. This "jovial" (Dixon, rev. of *LD* #1 1393), "broad" (Jeaffreson, rev. of *Gordian* 882), and "hearty, easy-flowing" (Knollys) humor offered "an air of almost rollicking enjoyment" (rev. of *Island Nights' Entertainments* 468). Though Dickens's humor had become old fashioned by the end of the century (rev. of *A Tiger's Cub*), in mid-century Dickens defined national humor (rev. of *New Year's Cake* 327).

Another of Dickens's virtues was his realism of detail. He manifested "the chief qualification of the novelist"—observation (rev. of *In Love*), using it to "vitalize" incidents (rev. of *Sport*) by providing all the details of a character: "his looks, his gait, his dress, his peculiarities of speech, the dinginess of his office, and the furniture of his house" (rev. of *Maygrove*). Like the great Flemish artists, he steeped his details in a "mellow atmosphere" (rev. of *The Herberts*). Like Scott and Shakespeare, he could make men talk "by virtue of this gift of perception, this intuition of the complexity of human nature" (Collyer, rev. of *Grey and Gold*). Like Homer, he could "delude the reader's imagination into mistaking the picture for real portraiture" (rev. of *The Works of Robert Louis Stevenson* 214). Imitators of Dickens generally missed this detailed realism. They were too prone to create puppet characters with tricks or catchwords (revs. of *Mortomley's Estate* and *The Tale of Chloe* 175). Because their use of caricature was reminiscent of "Dickens at his worst" (rev. of *Laura Ruthven's Widowhood*), their characters were often "several removes further from any likeness to human nature" (Jewsbury, rev. of *How Could He*).

More important than these virtues were Dickens's concern for the poor and his dramatic method of narration. Morally his greatest contribution was his humanizing concern for the poor. He established as a novelistic subject "the struggle between character and that form of hostile and sinister circumstance—an early environment of London's poverty and crime" (rev. of *Her Love* 84). Henry Chorley vividly described Dickens's intimate knowledge of the poor by contrasting it with Disraeli's:

> Then, with all his feeling for the people, Mr. Disraeli appears to have studied them in the pages of the parliamentary or statistical Reports referred to, rather than to have "eaten with them, drank with them, or prayed with them," as Shylock says. A citizen of the world sitting with its "Dandy Micks" over their glasses of "bar mixture," would come to a far different knowledge of their modes of remark and action, as Mr. Dickens knows full well. (rev. of *Sybil* 477)

Just as Eliot had an instinct for observing "the colourless manners of the *bourgeoisie*" and Thackeray one for observing "that class which is called (sometimes in earnest, if sometimes in irony) 'upper,' " Dickens was "born with an instinct for observing the sharply-cut manners of the lower orders" (rev. of *Through the Long Night* 729). Dickens's knowledge of the poor was so impressive that in 1839 Lady Sydney Owenson Morgan suggested that as material for future historians of "the class-morality of the nation," one should bind up the novels of Mrs. Gore "with those of Mr. Dickens, the forthcoming reports of Chartist trials, and a few similar books of fact and fiction" (rev. of *Preferment* 888). She here anticipates Thackeray's famous 1840 comment on *Pickwick*: "I am sure that a man who, a hundred years hence, should sit down to write the history of our time, would do wrong to put that great contemporary history of *Pickwick* aside as a frivolous work. It . . . gives us a better idea of the state and ways of the people than one could gather from any more pompous or authentic histories" (Collins 38).

The *Athenaeum* was concerned, however, that Dickens sometime succumbed to the vulgarity inherent in describing lower-class life. Dixon condemned *Hard Times*, for example, as "coarse, violent, and awkward" ("Our Library Table"). Despite this occasional vulgarity, Dickens was better than other novelists who described the poor because his aim was moral rather than merely sensational. He had an "optimism which discerns good ore latent in uncouth lumps of rough humanity" (Collyer, rev. of *Joshua Marvel* 717). Unlike Wilkie Collins, Dickens was determined "not to show a horror without a suggestion towards its cure" (H. Chorley, rev. of *Armadale* 732). Unlike Arthur Morrison, author of *A Child of the Jago*, "Dickens went straight to a definite point, and had something to reveal" (833).

Dickens's "genial and humanizing work" (rev. of *Winged Words*) was the grounds for an important defense against the charge of vulgarity leveled against him. In 1839, Morgan reviewed Harrison Ainsworth's *Jack Sheppard*. She commented that a critic had suggested that Dickens's popularity resulted from a reaction against the silver-fork novels of ''vapid and languid insipidity'' which created in readers ''a morbid appetite in search of strong excitement'' and led them to ''the coarse manners and vulgar crimes of low life.'' However, she distinguished Dickens from his imitators, from ''the Factory Boys and the Jack Sheppards'' despite his external similarity:

> If Boz has depicted scenes of hardened vice, and displayed the peculiar phasis [*sic*] of degradation which poverty impresses on the human character under the combinations of a defective civilization, he is guided in his career by a high moral object; and in tracing what is most loathsome and repulsive, he contrives to enlist the best feelings of our nature in his cause, and to engage his readers in the consideration of what lies below the surface. In this respect he approaches his great predecessors, Fielding and Gay; for though he proceeds by a different path, he arrives at the same end; and instead of sullying the mind of an intelligent reader, he leaves him wiser and better for the perusal of his tale. But this is precisely the excellence which we suspect the readers of Boz most frequently overlook; and we are certain that it is far less the under-current of philosophy which has sold his book, than the strong flavour of the medium, in which he has disguised the bitterness of its taste.   (803–04)

For Morgan and other readers able to perceive ''the under-current of philosophy,'' Dickens's high moral purpose redeemed him from the charge of vulgarity to which ''the strong flavour'' of his medium lay him open. This entire review is a valuable one for its discussion of the ''signs of the times,'' of contemporary literature, and of the literary marketplace. It also utilizes the distinction so often made by *Athenaeum* critics between the voracious reader who is attracted by the strong flavor of Dickens's medium and the particular one whose palate can taste the underlying philosophy.

The 1876 review of Frederick Robinson's *As Long as She Lived* similarly linked Dickens's realism and his moral purpose, though it had more reservations about the impact of his purpose on his art. In an extended discussion of what it called ''poor-life'' novels, the review traced realism from Defoe through Dickens to contemporary writers such as Robinson, who had published *Owen, A Waif* (1862) and *Mattie, A Stray* (1864), Frederick Greenwood, who wrote *The True History of A Little Ragamuffin* (1866), and Benjamin Farjeon whose *Grif*, the story of a street arab, was published in New Zealand in 1866 and in Britain in 1870. Dickens learned from Defoe a ''mastery over the realism of accessories, and of the mere externals of character,'' and the younger writers succeeded to this. They, however, exceeded Dickens, for they ''sought, besides, an utter truthfulness of characterization, according to the lights within them which Dickens,—whose quest was not the truthful at all, but the striking,—did not even seek, apparently.'' At the same time, Dickens was absolutely unlike Defoe in the aim of his illusion-making: "While Defoe seeks illusion as the 'be-all and end-all' of narrative art, Dickens seeks illusion as a means of 'making people laugh or cry.' " Like Poe, Defoe aimed "to 'lie like truth.' " Dickens, however, "not only writes with a purpose—ethical, humorous, aesthetic, or what not, but he takes care to let you see that he so writes" (76). For the *Athenaeum* reviewer, neither of these two schools was that of the true artist, who should neither paint exactly what he sees nor obtrude his purpose upon the reader. Rather, the artist is the one who

> while really fashioning his characters out of broad general elements,—from universal types of humanity,—at the same time deceives us into mistaking these characters for real biographies—deceives us by appearing (from his mastery over the "properties" of the fictionist) to be drawing from particulars—from peculiar individual traits—instead of from generalities,—and especially by never obtruding, but rather by hiding away from us, all sentimental, humorous, aesthetic, or ethical purposes. (77)

If Dickens differed from Defoe in his aim, he also differed in his narrative method. He followed up on Scott's "purely dramatic method of telling a story by dialogue" (76). The extension and popularization of this method of presenting action through dialogue was for the *Athenaeum* Dickens's most distinctive artistic contribution. It was, as an 1887 reviewer suggested, a mystery how "after the enormous revolution of methods inaugurated by Scott, and carried on by Dickens, Thackeray, Reade, and others, the non-dramatic method, which seemed to have been entirely superseded, has been revived, and successfully revived" (rev. of *In Bad Hands*).

These comments in reviews of novels by others enrich and complicate our understanding of the *Athenaeum*'s response to Dickens. If we read only the reviews of Dickens's works, we can construct a reasonably straightforward description of this response, as indicated in the first part of this essay. When we read all the comments about Dickens, however, this construction becomes less coherent. To take only one example, it is commonly accepted that the *Athenaeum* was opposed to the vulgarity of Dickens's early novels. True enough, but in her 1839 *Jack Sheppard* review Morgan wrote her extended and perceptive defense against the charge, a defense we would not find if we confined ourselves to the reviews of Dickens's own works.

These reviews of others' works contain perceptive and valuable comments about Dickens and his role in the literary canon. Some are quick comments about Dickens himself, like Collyer's 1871 note that "the great master . . . could never quite describe a lady" (rev. of *Fernyhurst Court*). Others are far more extended. John Rutter Chorley's 1852 review of Hackländer's *Stories without a Name*, for instance, tells us as much about Dickens as about

Hackländer. Chorley identified Hackländer as "a German 'Boz,' " but one who is

> more temperate in his abundance than Mr. Dickens; and, at the same time, less idiomatic, racy, and whimsical,—keeping no equal pace with him in the style of broad caricature, in droll exaggerations of imbecility or perverseness, in drawing out odd figures from the back-settlements of Life,—wherein, after all, lies the special *forte* of Boz.   (720)

Hackländer's description is preferable to Dickens's, for it displays "less of native energy" but "a more accomplished taste." He shares Dickens's humanity, "but is not, like the latter, prone to use his invention for didactic purposes." Both authors avoid "unwholesome excitements" but Hackländer has more freedom than Dickens, who "wholly avoids questionable ground" and those "passionate accidents" which English society thinks "undesirable to mention." Both authors are prone to apparently superfluous detail, but the vivacity of Dickens's scenes gives them "a substantive place." Chorley concluded his review with a comment essentially on Dickens: "To conclude the list of resemblances and differences, we may say that Dickens is more racy of his own soil, Hackländer more of a cosmopolite:—that the former, narrower in his range, and, with less of what has been termed "school," is more humorous, robust and idiomatic than the latter" (721).

   Another extended commentary on Dickens is found in the 1875 review of Farjeon's *Love's Victory*, which spent several paragraphs arguing that Dickens's methods of characterization were severely limited:

> Judging from [Mr. Farjeon's] present novel no less than from those which he has already written, we should have said that they belonged unmistakably to that school of fiction of which, of course, Dickens was the great master, and which deals almost exclusively with incident, the "characters" being chiefly specimens more or less recognizable of certain well-known types, broadly drawn, and serving for very little more than the subjects to be variously operated up. Of *character*, as distinct from *characters*, this school would seem to us to know nothing. . . . The other characters are all commonplace where they are not caricatures; indeed, the difficulty of steering between these two dangers has at times wrecked every novelist of the school, not even excepting its founder; and where Dickens could not always succeed, less able writers are pretty sure always to fail.

The obsessive nature of Dickens's imagination was the subject of an extended comment in the 1886 review of *The Courting of Mary Smith*:

> No one will say that it was a lack of fertility which impelled Dickens to ring a dozen changes on the same chimes till at length a large proportion of his work seems to be informed with the same reiterated idea—that of a secret

crime brought at last to light by the watchful skill of a hidden and disguised witness. What was it then? It was a yielding to a fixed habit of imagination.

(109)

Other reviews used Dickens to discuss the fiction of the time. An 1880 reviewer, for instance, proposed that "a style of the present day . . . is an amalgam; it savours of Dickens and Thackeray, and George Eliot and Ouidà; it is pathetic, and cynical, and contemplative, and magniloquent by turns" (rev. of *A Plot*). An 1899 reviewer contrasted the contemporary taste for "Zolaism," which had been made possible by photography and which was manifested by such realistic English writers as Morrison, George Gissing, and Richard Whiteing, with the taste of Dickens's contemporaries:

> Though photography was discovered in Dickens's day, there would then have been no place for such writing, for what the public wanted was not realistic pictures of life, but pictures coloured by sentiment or humour, or both. Although Dickens was fond of inculcating moral and social lessons by fiction, he never forgot the old tradition handed down through Scott, that the final cause of the novel is to amuse. (rev. of *No. 5*)

Despite reservations about certain of Dickens's qualities and a sense by the end of the century that he was somewhat old-fashioned, the *Athenaeum* held him in high esteem throughout the century, an esteem that is evident in reviews of both Dickens's own work and of that of others. The first inch-long review of *Sketches by Boz* spoke of Dickens's "artistic skill and power." He was one of those authors who wrote "words that burn" and "thoughts that breathe," thereby printing "their fancies and creations on the memory" (H. Chorley, rev. of *A Lady*). "One of the best living novelists" (Jeaffreson, rev. of *Wait* 674), he was "first-class" and "a permanent English classic" who was "destined to live in future memory" (Lush) for his "brilliant writing" (Butler). When Dickens died in 1870, Henry Chorley's obituary praised him as "possibly the most original English writer of English domestic fiction who has ever been seen" (804). John Doran's review of *Edwin Drood* later that year reiterated this note, mourning "one more of the few sons of genius gone to his rest" (361).

Though Dickens's reputation generally declined after his death (Graham 22), and critical response was marked by a growing "condescension" (Engel and King 60), we should not overstate this response, for the *Athenaeum* reviewers continued their superlatives until the end of the century, frequently commenting on Dickens's "genius" (rev. of *Philip*) and his "masterhand" (rev. of *Timar's*). Although they found Dickens "a little out of date" as the century drew to a close (revs. of *A Voyage* and *Queen*), they still recognized his "glorious work" (rev. of *Works of Stevenson* 215). They hoped that contemporary novelists would return to Dickens's "saner themes and subtler craftsmanship" (rev. of *Vain* 614), and they praised his "wonderful skill" (rev. of *In the Grip*) which created some of "the greatest characters in fiction" (rev. of *Evelyn Innes* 32). The last mention of him in 1900 called him a "past master" who touched "the strings of pity, humour, love, and fear" (rev. of *Kiddy*).

The *Athenaeum* reviews both of Dickens's own works and of those by other novelists make it clear that while Dickens began by grabbing hold of the "easy ears" of the voracious readers, it was not long before he also held the most demanding ones of the discerning reviewers. He also managed to hold those ears throughout the century, winning praise first for his humor, then for his moral teaching, and finally for his art.

NOTES

1. An earlier version of this essay was presented at the annual meeting of the Research Society for Victorian Periodicals at Birkbeck College, University of London, 20–22 July 2000.
2. The web site indicates that it covers the period from about 1830 through 1870; it in fact identifies the authors of some 1871 reviews as well. It begins in "about" 1830 because, although the *Athenaeum* began publication in 1828, there are no marked files until the middle of 1830. There are also no identifications for 1832, 1835–38, and 1844 (Marchand ix); as a result there are no entries on the site for these years.
3. No single source lists all of these reviews. Within its time limits, Kathryn Chittick's extremely thorough book *The Critical Reception of Charles Dickens, 1833–41,* identifies all the pertinent reviews. Since the *Athenaeum* website includes only the years for which there are marked files, it does not list the reviews for *Sketches, Pickwick, Bentley's Miscellany, OT,* the first installment of *NN,* the one-volume edition of *MC, Chimes,* and *The Mudfog Papers.* In addition the site misses the reviews of *MHC* and *TTC,* the first two installments of *MC,* the first installment of *OMF,* the second reviews of *American Notes* and *Pictures from Italy,* and the German translation of his five Christmas tales. The *New CBEL* identifies most of the reviews, but misses those of *Bentley's, No Thoroughfare* and *Mudfog Papers,* the cheap editions of *NN* and *BR,* the part edition of *MC,* and the German *Christmas Carol.*

WORKS CITED
Athenaeum Reviews and Essays

About, Edmond. "Notes from Paris." *Athenaeum* 2462 (2 Jan 1875): 19–20.

Rev. of *American Notes for General Circulation,* by Charles Dickens. *Athenaeum* 782 (22 Oct 1842): 899–902.

Rev. of *American Notes for General Circulation*, by Charles Dickens, Second Notice. *Athenaeum* 783 (29 Oct 1842): 927–29.

Rev. of *As Long as She Lived*, by F[rederick] W[illiam] Robinson. *Athenaeum* 2542 (15 July 1876): 76–77.

Rev. of *"B.," an Autobiography*, by E[dward] Dyne Fenton. *Athenaeum* 2429 (16 May 1874): 660.

Rev. of *Bentley's Miscellany*, ed. " Boz" [i.e., Charles Dickens]. *Athenaeum* 480 (7 Jan 1837): 4–6.

Rev. of *Bishopspool*, by William Renton, *Athenaeum* 2928 (8 Dec 1883): 736.

[Butler, Arthur John]. Rev. of *The Queen's Sailors*, by Edward Greey. *Athenaeum* 2246 (12 Nov 1870): 623.

Rev. of *A Child of the Jago*, by Arthur Morrison. *Athenaeum* 3607 (12 Dec 1896): 832–33.

[Chorley, Henry Fothergill]. Rev. of *Armadale*, by [William] Wilkie Collins. *Athenaeum* 2014 (2 June 1866): 732–33.

[Chorley, Henry Fothergill]. Rev. of *Bleak House*, by Charles Dickens. *Athenaeum* 1351 (17 Sept 1853): 1087–88.

[Chorley, Henry Fothergill]. Rev. of *The Chimes: a Goblin Story of some Bells that Rang an Old Year out and New Year in*, by Charles Dickens. *Athenaeum* 895 (21 Dec 1844): 1165–66.

[Chorley, Henry Fothergill]. Rev. of *A Christmas Carol; in Prose; being a Ghost Story of Christmas*, by Charles Dickens. *Athenaeum* 843 (23 Dec 1843): 1127–28.

[Chorley, Henry Fothergill]. Rev. of *Great Expectations*, by Charles Dickens. *Athenaeum* 1759 (13 July 1861): 43–45.

[Chorley, Henry Fothergill]. Rev. of *Kingsford*, by the Author of *Son and Heir* [i.e., Emily Spender]. *Athenaeum* 2037 (10 Nov 1866): 603.

[Chorley, Henry Fothergill]. Rev. of *A Lady in her own Right*, by [John] Westland Marston. *Athenaeum* 1701 (2 Jun 1860): 754.

[Chorley, Henry Fothergill]. Rev. of *Martin Chuzzlewit*, by Charles Dickens. *Athenaeum* 873 (20 July 1844): 665–66.

[Chorley, Henry Fothergill]. Rev. of *Mary Barton: A Tale of Manchester Life*, [by Elizabeth Gaskell]. *Athenaeum* 1095 (21 Oct 1848): 1050–51.

Chorley, Henry F[othergill]. "Mr. Charles Dickens." *Athenaeum* 225 (18 Jun 1870): 804–05.

[Chorley, Henry Fothergill]. Rev. of *Mount Sorel; or, the Heiress of the De Veres*, by the Author of *Two Old Men's Tales* [i.e., Sara Anne Marsh-Caldwell (née Caldwell)]. *Athenaeum* 910 (5 Apr 1845): 328–29.

[Chorley, Henry Fothergill]. "New Novels." 1123 (5 May 1849): 459–60.

[Chorley, Henry Fothergill]. "New Novels." 1152 (24 Nov 1849): 1177–78.

[Chorley, Henry Fothergill]. Rev. of *Our Mutual Friend*, by Charles Dickens. *Athenaeum* 1983 (28 Oct 1865): 569–70.

[Chorley, Henry Fothergill]. Rev. of *The Personal History of David Copperfield*, by Charles Dickens. *Athenaeum* 1204 (23 Nov 1850): 1209–11.

[Chorley, Henry Fothergill]. Rev. of *Sybil; or, the Two Nations*, by B[enjamin] Disraeli, M.P. *Athenaeum* 916 (17 May 1845): 477–79.

[Chorley, John Rutter]. Rev. of *Eugene Stillfried—[Eugen Stillfried]*, by F[riedrich] W[ilhelm Ritter von] Hackländer. *Athenaeum* 1349 (3 Sept 1853): 1031–33.

[Chorley, John Rutter]. Rev. of *Stories without a Name—[Namenlose Geschichten]*, by F[riedrich] W[ilhelm Ritter von] Hackländer. *Athenaeum* 1288 (3 Jul 1852): 720–21.

"Christmas Books" [Rev. of *Fünf Weihnachtsegeschichten*, von C[harles] Dickens]. *Athenaeum* 2826 (24 Dec 1881): 849.

[Collyer (Collier?), Robert]. Rev. of *Earl's Dene*, by R[obert] E[dward] Francillon. *Athenaeum* 2258 (4 Feb 1871): 140–41.

[Collyer (Collier?), Robert]. Rev. of *Eventide*, by Mrs. A. Locke. *Athenaeum* 2259 (11 Feb 1871): 173.

[Collyer (Collier?), Robert]. Rev. of *Fernyhurst Court*, by the Author of *Stone Edge* [i.e., Frances Parthenope Verney (née Nightingale)]. *Athenaeum* 2288 (2 Sept 1871): 303.

[Collyer (Collier?), Robert]. Rev. of *Grey and Gold*, by E[mma] J[ane] Worboise [later Guyton]. *Athenaeum* 2219 (7 May 1870): 611.

[Collyer (Collier?), Robert]. Rev. of *Joshua Marvel*, by B[enjamin] L[eopold] Farjeon. *Athenaeum* 2276 (10 June 1871): 717.

Rev. of *The Complete Works of Bret Harte*. *Athenaeum* 2786 (19 Mar 1881): 390–91.

Rev. of *The Courting of Mary Smith*, by F[rederick] W[illiam] Robinson. *Athenaeum* 3065 (24 July 1886): 109–10.

[Dixon, William Hepworth]. Rev. of *Little Dorrit*, by Charles Dickens. *Athenaeum* 1545 (6 June 1857): 722–24.

[Dixon, William Hepworth]. Rev. of *Little Dorrit*, No. 1, by Charles Dickens. *Athenaeum* 1466 (1 Dec 1855): 1393–95.

[Dixon, William Hepworth]. Rev. of *Luttrell of Arran*, No. 1, by Charles Lever. *Athenaeum* 1885 (12 Dec 1863): 791–92.

[Dixon, William Hepworth]. "Our Library Table" [Rev. of *Hard Times*, by Charles Dickens]. *Athenaeum* 1398 (12 Aug 1854): 992.

[Doran, Dr. John]. Rev. of *The Life of Charles Dickens*, Vol 1, 1812–42, by John Forster. *Athenaeum* 2302 (9 Dec 1871): 747–48.

[Doran, Dr. John]. Rev. of *The Life of Charles Dickens*, Vol 1, 1812–42, by John Forster, Second Notice. *Athenaeum* 2303 (16 Dec 1871): 789–90.

[Doran, Dr. John]. Rev. of *The Mystery of Edwin Drood*, by Charles Dickens. *Athenaeum* 2238 (17 Sept 1870): 361–62.

[Doran, Dr. John]. Rev. of *The Mystery of Edwin Drood*, Installment 1, by Charles Dickens. *Athenaeum* 2214 (2 Apr 1870): 443–44.

Rev. of *Elementary Jane*, by Richard Pryce, *Athenaeum* 3627 (1 May 1897): 573.

Rev. of *European Slave Life*, by F[riedrich] W[ilhelm Ritter von] Hackländer, trans. E. Woltmann. *Athenaeum* 2724 (10 Jan 1880): 52.

Rev. of *Evelyn Innes*, by George [Augustus] Moore. *Athenaeum* 3688 (2 Jul 1898): 31–32.

Rev. of *The Friend of the Family: The Gambler*, by Fedor Dostoieffsky. *Athenaeum* 3105 (30 Apr 1887): 573–74.

Rev. of *Gideon Fleyce*, by Henry W[illiam] Lucy. *Athenaeum* 2883 (27 Jan 1883): 119.

Rev. of *A Great Mystery Solved: a Sequel to the Mystery of Edwin Drood*, by Gillan Vase [i.e., Elizabeth Newton (née Palmer)]. *Athenaeum* 2657 (28 Sept 1878): 399.

Rev. of *Great Porter Square: a Mystery*, by B[enjamin] L[eopold] Farjeon. *Athenaeum* 2979 (29 Nov 1884): 691–92.

[Hannay, James]. Rev. of *Nearer and Dearer: a Tale out of School* by Cuthbert Bede, B.A. [i.e., Edward Bradley]. *Athenaeum* 1563 (10 Oct 1857): 261.

Rev. of *Her Love and his Life*, by F[rederick] W[illiam] Robinson. *Athenaeum* 3299 (17 Jan 1891): 84–85.

[Heraud, John Abraham]. Rev. of *The Cricket on the Hearth, a Fairy Tale of Home*, by Charles Dickens. *Athenaeum* 947 (20 Dec 1845): 1219–21.

Rev. of *The Herberts*, by the Author of *Elphinstone* [i.e., Alfred Butler]. *Athenaeum* 755 (16 Apr 1842): 338.

[Hervey, Thomas Kibble]. Rev. of *Barnaby Rudge: A Tale of the Riots of '80*, by Charles Dickens. *Athenaeum* 1122 (28 Apr 1849): 433.

[Hervey, Thomas Kibble]. Rev. of *Bleak House*, No. 1, by Charles Dickens. *Athenaeum* 1271 (6 Mar 1852): 270–71.

[Hervey, Thomas Kibble]. Rev. of *Dealings with the Firm of Dombey & Son; Wholesale, Retail, and for Exportation*, Nos. 1 & 2, by Charles Dickens. *Athenaeum* 992 (31 Oct 1846): 1113–15.

[Hervey, Thomas Kibble]. Rev. of *The Life and Adventures of Nicholas Nickleby*, by Charles Dickens. *Athenaeum* 1075 (3 June 1848): 554.

[Hervey, Thomas Kibble]. Rev. of *The Life and Adventures of Nicholas Nickleby, containing a faithful account of the Fortunes, Misfortunes, Uprisings, Downfallings, and Complete Career of the Nickleby Family*, edited by "Boz" [i.e., Charles Dickens]. *Athenaeum* 544 (31 Mar 1838): 227–29.

[Hervey, Thomas Kibble]. Rev. of *The Personal History, Adventures, Experience and Observation of David Copperfield the Younger, of Blunderstone Rookery (which he never meant to be published on any account)*, No. 1, by Charles Dickens. *Athenaeum* 1123 (5 May 1849): 455–57.

[Hervey, Thomas Kibble]. Rev. of *Pictures from Italy*, by Charles Dickens. *Athenaeum* 969 (23 May 1846): 519–20.

[Hervey, Thomas Kibble]. Rev. of *Pictures from Italy*, by Charles Dickens, Second Notice. *Athenaeum* 970 (30 May 1846): 546–47.

[Hood, Thomas]. Rev. of *Barnaby Rudge* by C[harles] Dickens, Esq. *Athenaeum* 743 (22 Jan 1842): 77–79.

[Hood, Thomas]. Rev. of *Master Humphrey's Clock*, Vol. I [i.e., *The Old Curiosity Shop*], by "Boz" [i.e., Charles Dickens]. *Athenaeum* 680 (7 Nov 1840): 887–88.

Rev. of *Humbling his Pride*, by C[harles] T[homas] C[lement] James. *Athenaeum* 3323 (4 July 1891): 35.

Rev. of *In Bad Hands, and other Tales*, by F[rederick] W[illiam] Robinson. *Athenaeum* 3125 (17 Sept 1887): 363.

Rev. of *In Black and White*, by Rudyard Kipling. *Athenaeum* 3281 (13 Sep 1890): 348.

Rev. of *In Connection with the De Willoughby Claim*, by Frances Hodgson Burnett. *Athenaeum* 3767 (6 Jan 1900): 9.

Rev. of *In the Grip of the Law*, by Dick Donovan [i.e., Joyce Emerson Muddock]. *Athenaeum* 3368 (14 May 1892): 630.

Rev. of *In Love and Honour*, by J. K. Ritchie. *Athenaeum* 3152 (24 Mar 1888): 369.

Rev. of *Island Nights' Entertainments*, by Robert Louis Stevenson. *Athenaeum* 3416 (15 Apr 1893): 468–69.

Rev. of *"It is never too late to mend": a Matter of Fact Romance*, by Charles Reade. *Athenaeum* 1502 (9 Aug 1856): 990–991.

[Jeaffreson, John Cordy]. Rev. of *Beating to Windward; or, Light and Shade: a Novel*, by the Hon. Charles Stuart Savile. *Athenaeum* 2043 (22 Dec 1866): 834–35.

[Jeaffreson, John Cordy]. "Christmas Stories" [Rev. of *No Thoroughfare*, by Charles Dickens and Wilkie Collins]. *Athenaeum* 2095 (21 Dec 1867): 841–42.

[Jeaffreson, John Cordy]. Rev. of *A Good Fight in the Battle of Life*. *Athenaeum* 1881 (14 Nov 1863): 639–40.

[Jeaffreson, John Cordy]. Rev. of *The Gordian Knot*, by [Charles William] Shirley Brooks. *Athenaeum* 1679 (31 Dec 1859): 882–83.

[Jeaffreson, John Cordy]. Rev. of *Lost at the Winning Post*, by H. L. H. [i.e., Harriet Lydia Stevenson]. *Athenaeum* 2065 (25 May 1867): 689.

[Jeaffreson, John Cordy]. Rev. of *Wait for the End*, by Mark Lemon. *Athenaeum* 1882 (21 Nov 1863): 674–75.

[Jewsbury, Geraldine Endsor]. Rev. of *How Could He Help it? Or, the Heart Triumphant*, by A[zel] S[tevens] Row. *Athenaeum* 1700 (26 May 1860): 718.

[Jewsbury, Geraldine Endsor]. Rev. of *The Life of Sir Timothy Graceless, Bart.*, by Himself. *Athenaeum* 1895 (20 Feb 1864): 262–63.

[Jewsbury, Geraldine Endsor]. Rev. of *Mad: a Story of "Dust and Ashes,"* by George Manville Fenn. *Athenaeum* 2153 (31 Jan 1869): 170.

[Jewsbury, Geraldine Endsor]. Rev. of *Mildrington the Barrister: a Romance* [by Percy Hetherington Fitzgerald]. *Athenaeum* 1858 (6 June 1863): 744.

[Jewsbury, Geraldine Endsor]. Rev. of *Side Winds*, by Morton Rae. *Athenaeum* 1759 (13 July 1861): 50.

[Jewsbury, Geraldine Endsor]. Rev. of *Strange Work: A Novel*, by Thomas Archer. *Athenaeum* 2146 (12 Dec 1868): 792.

Rev. of *Jobson's Enemies*, by [John] Edward Jenkins. *Athenaeum* 2862 (2 Sept 1882): 302.

Rev. of *Kiddy*, by Tom Gallon. *Athenaeum* 3787 (26 May 1900): 651.

[Knollys, William Wallingford]. Rev. of *A Ready-Made Family; or, the Life and Adventures of Julian Leep's Cherub: a Story*, [by Frederick Wicks]. *Athenaeum* 2303 (16 Dec 1871): 791.

Rev. of *Laura Ruthven's Widowhood*, by C[harles] J[ames] Wills and John Davidson. *Athenaeum* 3405 (28 Jan 1893): 118.

[Leeds, William Henry]. Rev. of *Mr. Pecksniff, The Life and Adventures of Martin Chuzzlewit*, Nos. 1 & 2 [by Charles Dickens]. *Athenaeum* 801 (4 Mar 1843): 209–210.

Rev. of *The Lesson of the Master, and other Stories*, by Henry James. *Athenaeum* 3360 (19 Mar 1892): 369–70.

Rev. of *The Letters of Charles Dickens*, Vol 3, 1836–70, ed. his Sister-in-Law [i.e., Georgina Hogarth] and his Eldest Daughter [i.e., Mary [Mamie] Dickens]. *Athenaeum* 2821 (19 Nov 1881): 659–70.

Rev. of *The Life of Charles Dickens*, Vol 2, 1842–52, by John Forster. *Athenaeum* 2351 (16 Nov 1872): 625–26.

Rev. of *The Life of Charles Dickens*, Vol 3, 1852–70, by John Forster. *Athenaeum* 2415 (7 Feb 1874): 185–86.

Rev. of *Love's Victory* by B[enjamin] L[eopold] Farjeon. *Athenaeum* 2488 (3 July 1875): 18.

Rev. of *A Lucky Young Woman*, by F[rancis] C[harles] Philips. *Athenaeum* 3055 (15 May 1886): 643.

[Lush, William?]. Rev. of *The Buckhurst Volunteers: a Novel*, by J[ohn] M[oore] Capes. *Athenaeum* 2174 (16 Jun 1869): 857.

Rev. of *Margaret Jermine*, by Fayr Madoc [i.e., Miss Maddock]. *Athenaeum* 3081 (13 Nov 1886): 631.

Rev. of *Marion; or, the Mystery of Robesdale*, by R. Sebright Scholes. *Athenaeum* 3025 (17 Oct 1885): 503.

[Marston, John Westland]. Rev. of *The Battle of Life; a Love Story*, by Charles Dickens. *Athenaeum* 1000 (26 Dec 1846): 1319–21.

[Marston, John Westland]. Rev. of *The Haunted Man and the Ghost's Bargain: A Fancy for Christmas-time*, by Charles Dickens. *Athenaeum* 1104 (23 Dec 1848): 1291–93.

Rev. of *Maygrove: a Family History*, by W[illiam] Fraser Rae. *Athenaeum* 3241 (7 Dec 1889): 777.

Rev. of *Middlemarch*, Book 4—*Three Love Problems*, by George Eliot [i.e., Mary Anne Evans]. *Athenaeum* 2327 (1 June 1872): 681.

"Miscellanea: A Gem out of *Nicholas Nickleby*." *Athenaeum* 570 (29 Sept 1838): 716.

Rev. of *Miss Honeywood's Lovers. Athenaeum* 2497 (4 Sept 1875): 303–04.

[Morgan, Lady Sydney Owenson]. Rev. of *Jack Sheppard: a Romance*, by W[illiam] Harrison Ainsworth, Esq. *Athenaeum* 626 (26 Oct 1839): 803–05.

[Morgan, Lady Sydney Owenson]. Rev. of *Preferment; or, My Uncle the Earl*, by Mrs. [Catherine Grace Frances] Gore [née Moody]. *Athenaeum* 630 (23 Nov 1839): 888–89.

Rev. of *Mortomley's Estate,* by Mrs. [Charlotte Elizabeth Lawson] Riddell [née Cowan]. *Athenaeum* 2447 (19 Sept 1874): 373.

Rev. of *Mr. Smith,* by L[ucy] B[ethia] Walford [née Colquhoun]. *Athenaeum* 2452 (24 Oct 1874): 543–44.

Rev. of *Mr. Spivey's Clerk,* by J[oseph] S[mith] Fletcher. *Athenaeum* 3262 (3 May 1890): 564.

Rev. of *The Mudfog Papers,* by Charles Dickens. *Athenaeum* 2758 (4 Sept 1880): 303.

Rev. of *My Time, and What I've Done with It, An Autobiography,* by F[rancis] C[owley] Burnand. *Athenaeum* 2439 (25 July 1874): 109.

Rev. of *The New Faith,* by Charles T[homas] C[lement] James. *Athenaeum* 3266 (31 May 1890): 701.

Rev. of *The New Year's Cake: A Fantastic Symphony.—[Le Gàteau des Rois, &c],* by M. Jules [Gabriel] Janin. *Athenaeum* 1013 (27 Mar 1847): 326–27.

Rev. of *No. 5, John Street,* by Richard Whiteing. *Athenaeum* 3725 (18 Mar 1899): 334.

Rev. of *Old Shipmates,* by Claud Harding, R.N. *Athenaeum* 3095 (19 Feb 1887): 252.

Rev. of *Oliver Twist; or, the Parish Boy's Progress,* by "Boz" [i.e., Charles Dickens]. *Athenaeum* 577 (17 Nov 1838): 824–25.

"Our Library Table" [Rev. of *A Tale of Two Cities,* by Charles Dickens]. *Athenaeum* 1676 (10 Dec 1859): 774.

"Our Library Table" [Rev. of *Sketches by Boz* [i.e., Charles Dickens]]. *Athenaeum* 434 (20 Feb 1836): 145.

"Our Weekly Gossip" [Rev. of *Our Mutual Friend,* Installment 1, by Charles Dickens]. *Athenaeum* 1905 (30 Apr 1864): 613.

Rev. of *A Peal of Merry Bells,* by Leopold Lewis. *Athenaeum* 2767 (6 Nov 1880): 603–04.

Rev. of *Philip Lyndon's Troubles,* by Edith Owen Bourne. *Athenaeum* 2694 (14 June 1879): 755.

Rev. of *The Pickwick Papers,* Victoria Edition, by Charles Dickens. *Athenaeum* 3143 (21 Jan 1888): 80–81.

Rev. of *A Plot of the Present Day,* by Kate Hope. *Athenaeum* 2764 (16 Oct 1880): 496.

Rev. of *A Prince of Mischance,* by Tom Gallon. *Athenaeum* 3656 (20 Nov 1897): 704.

Rev. of *Prinkle and his Friends,* by James Shearar. *Athenaeum* 2571 (3 Feb 1877): 153.

Rev. of *The Posthumous Papers of the Pickwick Club,* numbers 1–9, ed. "Boz" [i.e., Charles Dickens]. *Athenaeum* 475 (3 Dec 1836): 841–43.

Rev. of *Queen of the Hamlet,* by H[orace] F[rancis] Lester. *Athenaeum* 3505 (29 Dec 1894): 887.

[Romer, Sir Robert]. Rev. of *Not in Vain: A Story of the Day,* by Armar Greye [i.e., Maria J. Greer]. *Athenaeum* 2212 (19 Mar 1870): 385.

[Savage, Marmion W.]. Rev. of *The Commissioner; or, de Lunatico Inquirendo,* [by George Payne Rainsford James]. *Athenaeum* 793 (7 Jan 1843): 11.

Rev. of *Settled out of Court,* by G[eorge] B[rown] Burgin. *Athenaeum* 3707 (12 Nov 1898): 672.

Rev. of *Sketches by Boz* [i.e., Charles Dickens], Second Series. *Athenaeum* 479 (31 Dec 1836): 916–17.

Rev. of *Skill Wins Favour,* by Mrs. George Elliott Kent [i.e., Dorothea S. Kent (née Elliott)]. *Athenaeum* 3220 (13 Jul 1889): 61.

Rev. of *Soldiers Three: Stories of Barrack-Room Life,* by Rudyard Kipling. *Athenaeum* 3261 (26 Apr 1890): 528.

Rev. of *Some Stained Pages,* by the Author of *The New Mistress. Athenaeum* 2993 (7 Mar 1885): 309–10.

Rev. of *A Spanish Maid,* by L[ilian M.] Quiller Couch. *Athenaeum* 3657 (27 Nov 1897): 745.

Rev. of *The Sport of Chance,* by William Sharp. *Athenaeum* 3137 (10 Dec 1887): 780.

Rev. of *A Sportsman's Sketches,* by Ivan Turgenev. *Athenaeum* 3593 (5 Sept 1896): 319.

Rev. of *The Tale of Chloe; The House on the Beach; The Case of General Ople and Lady Camper,* by George Meredith. *Athenaeum* 3511 (9 Feb 1895): 175–76.

Rev. of *Tatterley: the Story of a Dead Man,* by Tom Gallon. *Athenaeum* 3617 (20 Feb 1897): 242.

Rev. of *The Three Oxonians,* by Frank Usher [i.e., Frank Usher Waite]. *Athenaeum* 2389 (9 Aug 1873): 178.

Rev. of *Timar's Two Worlds,* by Maurus Jokai, trans. Mrs. Hegan Kennard. *Athenaeum* 3153 (31 Mar 1888): 395.

Rev. of *The Torrents of Spring, &c.,* by Ivan Turgenev, trans. Constance Garnett. *Athenaeum* 3669 (19 Feb 1898): 246.

Rev. of *The Trumpet-Major,* by Thomas Hardy. *Athenaeum* 2769 (20 Nov 1880): 672.

Rev. of *Through the Long Night,* by E[liza] Lynn Linton. *Athenaeum* 3188 (1 Dec 1888): 729–31.

Rev. of *Vain Fortune,* by George [Augustus] Moore. *Athenaeum* 3341 (7 Nov 1891): 613–14.

Rev. of *A Valuable Life*, by [Emily Frances] Adeline Sergeant. *Athenaeum* 3695 (20 Aug 1898): 251.

Rev. of *A Voyage at Anchor*, by W[illiam] Clark Russell. *Athenaeum* 3764 (16 Dec 1899): 831.

[Watts-Dunton, Theodore]. "Our Seventieth Birthday." *Athenaeum* 3662 (1 Jan 1898): 9–12.

Rev. of *Wilbourne Hall*, by Mrs. [Mary] Caumont. *Athenaeum* 3002 (9 May 1885): 595.

Rev. of *Winged Words*, by [William] Henry Spicer. *Athenaeum* 2755 (14 Aug 1880): 206.

Rev. of *A Woman in Spite of Herself*, by J[ohn] C[ordy] Jeaffreson. *Athenaeum* 2307 (18 Jan 1872): 49.

Rev. of *Workers in the Dawn*, by George R[obert] Gissing. *Athenaeum* 2746 (12 June 1880): 758.

Rev. of *The Works of Robert Louis Stevenson*, Vol 1–24. *Athenaeum* 3642 (14 Aug 1897): 213–15.

Rev. of *A Young Girl's Life* by B[enjamin] L[eopold] Farjeon. *Athenaeum* 3235 (26 Oct 1889): 555.

II. Other Items

Casey, Ellen Miller. "Weekly Reviews of Fiction: The *Athenaeum* vs. The *Spectator* and the *Saturday Review*." *VPR* 23.1 (Sp 1990): 8–12.

Chittick, Kathryn. *The Critical Reception of Charles Dickens, 1833–41*. New York: Garland, 1989.

Collins, Philip, ed. *Dickens: The Critical Heritage*. London: Routledge and Kegan Paul, 1971.

Elwin, Malcolm. *Old Gods Falling*. New York: Macmillan, 1939.

Engel, Elliot D., and Margaret F. King. "*Pickwick*'s Progress: The Critical Reception of *The PickwickPapers* from 1836–1986." *Dickens Quarterly* 3.1 (Mar 1986): 56–66.

Ford, George H. *Dickens and His Readers*. Princeton: Princeton UP, 1955.

Graham, Kenneth. *English Criticism of the Novel 1865–1900*. Oxford: Clarendon, 1965.

Jump, J. D. "Weekly Reviewing in the Eighteen-Fifties." *RES* 24 (1948): 42–57.

Liddle, Dallas. "Salesmen, Sportsmen, Mentors: Anonymity and Mid-Victorian Theories of Journalism." *VS* 41.1 (Aut 1997): 31–68.

Marchand, Leslie A. *The Athenaeum: A Mirror of Victorian Culture.* Chapel Hill: U of North Carolina P, 1941; New York: Octagon Books, 1971.

Maurer, Oscar, Jr. "Anonymity vs. Signature in Victorian Reviewing." *Studies in English* 27 (Jun 1948): 1–27.

Oliphant, Mrs. [Margaret]. *The Victorian Age of English Literature.* New York: Dodd, Mead & Co., 1892.

Rosengren, Karl Erik. *Sociological Aspects of the Literary System.* Stockholm: Natur och Kultur, 1968.

Rotkin, Charlotte. "The *Athenaeum* Reviews *Little Dorrit.*" *VPR* 23.1 (Sp 1990): 25–28.

Schlicke, Paul, ed. *Oxford Reader's Companion to Dickens.* Oxford: Oxford UP, 1999.

Shattock, Joanne, ed. *The Cambridge Bibliography of English Literature, Vol 4: 1800–1900.* 3rd ed. Cambridge: Cambridge UP, 1999.

Shattock, Joanne. *Politics and Reviewers: The* Edinburgh *and The* Quarterly *in the Early Victorian Age.* London: Leicester UP, 1989.

Vann, J. Don. *Victorian Novels in Serial.* New York: MLA, 1985.

DICKENS'S NOVELS: PUBLICATION & REVIEW INFORMATION

For sources, full names of reviewers, and explanations of "Types," see the note after this chart

Title	Format	Publication Date	Date of Review	Type	Length	Reviewer
Sketches by Boz	2 vols.	8 Feb. 1836	434 (20 Feb 1836): 145	OLT	$1/10$	Not Marked
Pickwick Papers	20 (as 19) monthly parts	April 1836–Nov 1837, except June 1837	Installments 1–9:475 (3 Dec 1836): 841–43	Lead Review	$8^1/4$ cols.	Not Marked
	1 vol.	17 Nov 1837				
	1 vol.	Victoria Edn: 1887	3143 (21 Jan. 1888): 80–81	Review	2 cols.	
Sketches by Boz, 2nd Series	1 vol.	17 Dec. 1836	479 (31 Dec 1836): 916–17	Review	$2^1/2$	Not Marked
Bentley's Miscellany (BM)	Monthly magazine, Jan 1837–Feb. 1839	First number: Jan 1837	480 (7 Jan 1837): 4–6	Review	$4^1/2$ cols.	Not Marked
The Mudfog Papers	6 papers in *VM*	Jan, Mar, May & oct 1837, Aug & Sept, 1838				
	1 vol.	Empire Library: 1880	2758 (4 Sept 1880): 393	NofW	$1/2$ col.	
Oliver Twist	24 monthly installments in *BM*	Feb 1837–Apr 1839 (except June & Oct 1837 & Sept 1838)				
	3 vols.	9 Nov 1838	577 (17 Nov 1838): 824–25	Review	4 cols.	Not Marked
Nicholas Nickleby	20 (as 19) monthly parts	Apr 1838–Oct 1839	544 (31 Mar 1838): 227–29 570 (29 Sept 1838): 716	Review Misc.	$5^1/4$ cols.	Hervey
	1 vol.	Cheap Edn: 23 Oct 1839	1075 (3 June 1848): 554	Review	$1/2$ cols.	Hervey
The Old Curiosity Shop	40 weekly installments in *Master Humphrey's Clock (MHC)*	25 Apr 1840–6 Feb 1841	680 (7 Nov 1840): 887–88	Review	$5^3/4$ cols.	Hood
	1 vol.	15 Dec 1841				
Barnaby Rudge	42 weekly installments in *MHC*	13 Feb–27 Nov 1841				
	1 vol.	15 Dec 1841	743 (22 Jan 1842): 77–79	Lead Review	$7^1/4$ cols.	Hood
		Cheap edition: 1849	1122 (28 Apr 1849): 433	Review	1 col.	Hervey

DICKENS'S NOVELS: PUBLICATION & REVIEW INFORMATION

For sources, full names of reviewers, and explanations of "Types," see the note after this chart

Title	Format	Publication Date	Date of Review	Type	Length	Reviewer
American Notes	2 vol.	19 Oct 1842	782 (22 Oct 1842): 899–902	Lead Review	$9^1/2$ cols. $8^1/4$ cols.	Not marked Not marked
			783 (29 Oct 1842): 977–29	Review		
Martin Chuzzlewit	20 (as 19) monthly parts	Jan 1843–Jul 1844	Installments 1–2: 801 (4 Mar 1843): 209–10	Review	$3^3/4$ cols	Leeds
	1 vol.	16 July 1844	873 (20 Jul 1844): 665–66	Review	$3^1/4$ cols.	Chorley
A Christmas Carol	1 vol.	19 Dec 1843	843 (23 Dec 1843): 1127–28	Review	3 cols.	Chorley
	Fünf Weihnachtsgeschichten	1881	2826 (24 Dec 1881): 849	Xmas	$1/10$ col	
The Chimes	1 vol.	16 Dec 1844	895 (21 Dec 1844): 1165–66	Lead Review	$4^1/4$ cols	Chorley
The Cricket on the Hearth	1 vol.	20 Dec 1845	947 (20 Dec 1845): 1219–21	Review	$5^1/2$ cols.	Heraud
Pictures from Italy	1 vol.	18 May 1846	969 (23 May 1846): 519–20	Review	5 cols.	Hervey
			970 (30 May 1846): 546–47	Review	$4^1/4$ cols.	Hervey
Dombey and Sons	20 (as 19) monthly parts	Oct 1846–Apr 1848	Installments 1–2; 992 (31 Oct 1846): 1113–15	Review	$6^1/4$ cols.	Hervey
	1 vol. 12 Apr 1848					
The Battle of Life	1 vol.	19 Dec 1846	1000 (26 Dec 1846): 1319–21	Review	$6^3/4$ cols.	Marston
The Haunted Man	1 vol.	19 Dec 1848	1104 (23 Dec 1848): 1291–93	Review	$6^3/4$ cols.	Marston
David Copperfield	20 (as 19 monthly parts	May 1849–Nov 1850	Installment 1:1123 (5 May 1849): 455–57	Review	5 cols.	Hervey
	1 vol.	15 Nov 1850	1204 (23 Nov 1850): 1209–11	Review	6 cols.	Chorley
A Child's History of England	39 weekly installments in Household Words (HW)	Jan 1851–Dec 1853				
	3 vol: 1852, 1853, 1854					

DICKENS'S NOVELS: PUBLICATION & REVIEW INFORMATION

For sources, full names of reviewers, and explanations of "Types," see the note after this chart

Title	Format	Publication Date	Date of Review	Type	Length	Reviewer
Bleak House	20 (as 19) monthly parts	Mar 1852–Sept 1853	Installment 1: 1217 (6 Mar 1852): 270–71	Review	3 cols.	Hervey
	1 vol.	Sept 1853	1351 (17 Sept 1853): 1087–88	Lead Review	$3^1/4$ cols.	Chorley
Hard Times	20 weekly installments in *HW*	1 Apr–12 Aug 1854				
	1 vol.	1854	1398 (12 Aug 1854): 992	OLT	$^1/2$ col.	Dixon
Little Dorrit	20 (as 19) monthly parts	Dec 1855–Jun 1857	Installment 1: 1466 (1 Dec 1885): 1393–95	Lead Review	8 cols.	Dixon
	1 vol.	30 May 1857	1545 (6 Jun 1857): 722–24	Review	$6^1/2$ cols.	Dixon
A Tale of Two Cities	31 weekly installments in *All the Year Round (AYR)*	30 Apr-26 Nov 1859				
	1 vol.	27 Nov 1859	1676 (10 Dec 1859): 774	OLT	$^1/4$ col.	Not marked
Great Expectations	36 weekly installment in *AYR*	1 Dec 1860–3 Aug 1861				
	3 vols.	Aug 1861	1759 (13 July 1861): 43–45	Review	$3^3/4$ cols.	Chorley
Our Mutual Friend	20 (as 19) monthly parts	May 1864–Nov 1865	Installment 1: 1905 (30 Apr 1864): 613	OWG	$^1/2$ col.	Not Marked
	2 vols.	Nov 1865	1983 (28 Oct 1865): 569–70	Review	$3^1/4$ col.	Chorley
No Thoroughfare	Extra Christmas Number of *AYR*	Dec 1867	2095 (21 Dec 1867): 841–42	Lead Review	$4^3/4$ cols.	Jefferson
The Mystery of Edwin Drood	Monthly parts: 6 of 12 completed	Apr–Sept 1870	Installment 1: 2214 (2 Apr 1870): 443–44	Lead Review	$4^1/2$ cols.	Doran
	1 vol.	1870	2238 (17 Sept 1870): 361–63	Review	$2^1/2$ cols.	Doran

Types:

Lead review: A long review beginning on the first page of the journal

Review: A long review in the front of the journal; rarely used for fiction

NN ("New Novels"): A column of short reviews, increasingly common after 1849. The column first appeared 5 May 1849, when Henry Chorley announced that "the appearance of *David*

Copperfield making the distinguished exception, we must say that the Easter Offering of Fiction for 1849 is not either 'rich or rare.' '' He therefore decreed it "best in a short compass to make a clearance of much that has been 'sitting heavy' on our table for the last month" (459). When the column next appeared in November, Chorley declared, "The month of November generally produces a liberal provision of new novels. Having dealt singly with the most eminent of these, we find it best to notice the remainder collectively" (1177). "New Novels" appeared with increasingly regularity, becoming virtually a weekly event. It was named "New Novels" through 16 Oct 1869, "Novels and Novelettes" from 23 Oct through 11 Dec 1869, "Novels of the Week" (NofW) from 25 December 1869 through 11 December 1892, and "New Novels" from 17 December through the end of the century.

OLT ("Our Library Table"): A column of miscellaneous notices of and brief comments on new books which were presumably not judged worth a full review.

OWG ("Our Weekly Gossip"): Miscellaneous comments on literary matters.

Misc ("Miscellanea"): Various short comments.

Xmas ("Christmas Books"): Short notices of books for children.

Full Names of Reviewers:
Chorley, Henry Fothergill
Dixon, William Hepworth
Doran, Dr. John
Heraud, John Abraham
Hervey, Thomas Kibble
Hood, Thomas
Jeaffreson, John Cordy
Leeds, William Henry
Marston, John Westland

Sources:
Besides the *Athenaeum* web site (http://web.soi.city.ac.uk), the sources for the information in this chart are Chittick; Marchand; Schlicke; Shattock, *The Cambridge Bibliography*; and Vann.

Miltonic Orientalism: *Jane Eyre* and the Two Dalilas

Jeffrey Cass

This essay explores the intertextual relationship between Charlotte Brontë's Jane Eyre *and John Milton's* Samson Agonistes. *Rebutting the largely unchallenged claim of Gilbert and Gubar that Milton is a patriarchal "bogey" against whom women writers struggle to find their voices, the author suggests a far more problematic and complex relationship between the two. In fact, Brontë's position with regard to Milton's influence remains far more unsettled than many of the women writers before and after her, at times criticizing Milton's representations of women, at others incorporating them into her work. In particular, Brontë actually presents two versions of Milton's Dalila in* Jane Eyre: *Bertha, the dark, ruthless, dehumanized Dalila who represents betrayal and deceit and Jane, the servant Dalila, the one who nurses her "Sightless Samson" back to health. Although Samson rejects Dalila's overtures to minister to him, naturally doubting her sincerity, Milton at least voices the possibility of reconciliation, which Brontë allusively weaves into the plot of her novel. Curiously, however, the redemptive process that ultimately sees Rochester submit to Jane resonates strongly with the Orientalist representation of Dalila in* Samson Agonistes. *Indeed, throughout* Jane Eyre, *Jane resists Orientalizing, a process of "othering" that perpetuates her own status as an outsider. Even when she achieves financial independence, appears to break free of such exoticism, and reconciles her Samson to divine authority, the specter of Orientalism haunts the green spaces of Ferndean, threatening the peace and security she and Rochester desire.*

Dickens Studies Annual, Volume 33, Copyright © 2003 by AMS Press, Inc. All rights reserved.

The "Bogey" of Milton's Influence[1]

For over twenty years, the prevailing view regarding Milton's influence on Romantic and Victorian women writers has been that of Sandra Gilbert and Susan Gubar. Theirs is not a positive one. Having successfully transformed Milton into the "bogey" against which women writers struggle to transform their lives and their work, Gilbert and Gubar have been the shadowy furies that persist in demonizing Milton's pervasive influence. Asserting that these women writers read Milton with "painful absorption" (189), Gilbert and Gubar amplify Bloom's argument about Milton as "strong poet" as well as later misprisions of his influence (19). In the case of *Jane Eyre*, Charlotte Brontë's repressed response to the patriarchal values and ideology she inherits is seething anger, the source of her feminist impulses. Thus, for Gilbert and Gubar, Bertha Mason reifies Jane's (and by extension Brontë's) rage; Jane and Charlotte resent their confinement within social, cultural, and political circumscriptions, even if they do little to disavow them publicly.

Following the lead of Gilbert and Gubar, the majority of subsequent critics have explicitly or tacitly endorsed their interpretive bias regarding Milton's influence. For Margaret Homans, dreams of children in the writings of nineteenth-century women writers literalize the latent (if dangerous) desire to transform their social lives and give birth to new ones: "Childbirth enters the figurative structure of the novel as a way of describing the danger that the self will become something other than itself" (90). This imagined "otherness" contravenes the masculine traditions inherited from *Paradise Lost*, traditions that "compel women readers to wish to embody, as Eve does, imaginary ideals, to be glad of this role in masculine life . . . " (109). Deirdre David extends the argument that Gilbert and Gubar make about Jane's necessary castration of Rochester in order to indict the ideals of British imperialism that (for her) *Paradise Lost* tacitly supports. For David, Jane Eyre initially represents the "ideal Victorian woman of empire," but by the end of the novel, she "paradoxically erases class and gender difference and situates them in a precise historical moment of Britannic rule" (117). At the same time, the incorporation of Milton into the colonial curriculum socialized young male Indians "about British moral and cultural values" (133). Reading *Paradise Lost* "wean[ed] Indians from idolatry," inculcating the values that assisted them in "positions of bureaucratic responsibility in the Victorian empire" (133).

Other critical readings of *Jane Eyre* tacitly accept Gilbert and Gubar's reading of Milton. In particular, readings that explore issues of race, class, gender, and sexuality endorse—sometimes intentionally, sometimes not—a belief in Milton's misogyny and how that misogyny translates into traces of his historical influence. But these readings have mischaracterized the relationship between Charlotte Brontë and Milton because they assume a misogyny in Milton's writing, to which Milton scholars have for years roundly objected.[2] Moreover, such a relationship assumes that women writers such as Charlotte Brontë cannot interpellate themselves onto the grid of seventeenth-century patriarchy and still positively interpret Milton's work or construe his women characters for their own writerly ends. Gilbert and Gubar, as well as those who accede to their view of Milton's influence, thus conflate misogyny and patriarchy. That Milton lived in a patriarchal society can hardly be disputed. That he endorses a misogynistic world view—and that women writers "view" Milton as a misogynist—certainly can be.

One of the less myopic readings of *Jane Eyre* (and of Gilbert and Gubar's reading of the novel) is Jerome Beaty's. He contends that "[Gilbert and Gubar's] shift of Brontë's target from Jane to Rochester diverts attention from the increasing intensity of Jane's moral danger, the power of her temptation, the inadequacy of her unaided resources, and the increasingly religious emphasis of her life story . . . " (151). Emphasizing "Jane's moral danger" as well as the "religious" components of Jane's "life story," Beaty questions the presumed radicalism of the novel, a radicalism he believes far too many critics assume. Penny Boumelha, another critic who perceives Gilbert and Gubar's reading as reductionist, insists that readers should "honour what can be honoured of [the novel's] female heroism without suppressing a recognition of the social formation to which, along with her twenty thousand pounds, Jane is heir" (63–64). Boumelha intimates in this passage that Jane's "heroism" does not necessarily enshrine a recurring anger against a patriarchal paradigm; she recognizes that Jane's conservative social formation does not mitigate her heroic behavior, even if that behavior does not, strictly speaking, conform to a more contemporary ideology. Following Politi, Boumelha believes that the novel "reblend[s] the marginality which it initially expose[s], thus securing its survival through the convention of a 'happy ending' " (60). Despite Jane's success at achieving her fiscal independence and gaining the moral high ground, Jane's marginality continues.

Undoubtedly, some readers of *Jane Eyre* may find Jane's retreat into marriage a far too orthodox solution for the stark, social, and political problems that her story raises. After all, on the surface, her submission to marital orthodoxy may be the ultimate reassertion of her conservative and (for Gilbert and Gubar) her Miltonic, social formation. Such an ending may remain unsatisfactory and perhaps unjust because it conveniently sacrifices Bertha Mason's grievances so that Jane Eyre may air and resolve hers. Nevertheless, because Beaty and Boumelha successfully decouple Jane's "heroism" from her "feminism," they problematize not only a particular strain of feminist reading of *Jane Eyre*, but the Miltonic bogey that supposedly underwrites the novel's ideological angst. Unlike much of the work that has explored Milton's influence on Romantic and Victorian women writers, recent Milton scholarship has shattered Milton's image as a brooding, Puritanical tyrant who suppresses women. Indeed, many critics have convincingly argued that Milton's representations of women are positive; they become role models for freedom and not social tyranny or emotional imprisonment. As John Shawcross has amply demonstrated, many women writers in the eighteenth and nineteenth centuries found Milton's work illuminating and challenging. "The upshot of these essays," Shawcross writes in his book *John Milton and Influence*, "is the importance in studying Milton as source and inspiration and presence, and avoiding such study can flirt with superficial reading and understanding. While an anxiety of influence may hang over some of these writers and works . . . the Milton that this influence delineates is an admired force to be enveloped or to be ever like a star apart . . . " (*John Milton and Influence* 4).[3]

Even Connie Eberhart, who insists that Jane Eyre is a "canonical text for feminists" (80), nonetheless acknowledges that "Brontë's utilization of Milton's heroic women for her feminist paradigm calls into question the notion of Milton as an arch-sexist developed by traditional male critics and perpetuated by Sandra Gilbert and Susan Gubar in *The Madwoman in the Attic*" (89). As a reader of Milton, Brontë constructs a narrative inspired by many of Milton's writings but certainly not overshadowed or poisoned by them. Therefore, Jane Eyre is neither complicit with, nor an angry critique of, a perceived Miltonic patriarchy that has "colonized" the woman's imagination, forcibly converting her into orthodox positions. In fact, Brontë's position with regard to Milton's influence remains far more unsettled than many of the women writers before and after her, at times criticizing Milton's representations of women, at others incorporating them into her work. In fact, one may argue that the tension between imagined activism and conservative quietism that governs Brontë's ideology in *Jane Eyre* stems from this persistently ambiguous relationship to Milton, a relationship she often interrogates yet does not truly resolve.

Milton's Women and Jane Eyre

In *Milton and the English Revolution*, Christopher Hill argues that, if "Milton's doctrine of divorce had prevailed, there would have been no plot for Jane Eyre" (140). Hill ironically underscores the fact that while Jane resents being confined by Puritan orthodoxy, she oddly remains reluctant to challenge the divorce laws that would free Rochester from Bertha Mason and allow Jane to marry him. Hill adds, "Jane Eyre accepted exactly Milton's ideal of independence in subordination: the tirade in which she claimed spiritual equality with the socially superior Rochester is one of the crucial—and most

Protestant—passages in the novel. But Jane could see no solution *except in marriage"* (italics mine, 141). Hill reasonably contends that Brontë is not "making an impassioned plea for reform of the divorce law: she takes them as given, and her attitude is quite unfeminist" (140).[4] Of course, Brontë gives no evidence of having read Milton's divorce tracts like *The Doctrine and Discipline of Divorce.* If she had, she would have discovered a convenient theological position for Rochester and Jane, for Milton argues against the grain of Puritan orthodoxy, urging divorce because of incompatibility. Brontë's "unfeminist" response regarding even bad marriages—her seeming acceptance of Protestant orthodoxy—remains at odds with her equally passionate denunciations of the social and cultural coercion that suppresses individual expression and liberty. Ironically, Brontë's "unfeminist" response also unwittingly perpetuates the very social and political hierarchies that subsume the institution of marriage and subordinate women within it, hardly her goal or her mission. Nevertheless, while Brontë may never have been fully cognizant of Milton's abstruse arguments justifying divorce, she is sufficiently aware of the extreme situations in which his literary women find themselves—Comus imprisoning the Lady in his Chair, Satan tempting Eve in the Garden of Eden, Samson rebuking a penitent Dalila in a Gaza prison. Milton's women embody the philosophical ambiguities that attend tough choices as well as the firmness and resolve necessary to untangle and resolve them. Divorce by incompatibility may have legally removed Bertha Mason as an impediment to the marriage of Jane and Rochester, but such an option fails to explain Rochester's obsessive yet pitiable desire to find a scrap of marital happiness at Jane's expense. Yet such obsession results in the rigorous testing of her character and tempering of her obstinacy.

At first glance, Charlotte Brontë would seem to have viewed Milton in the very terms that Gilbert and Gubar describe. For example, Shirley, Brontë's eponymous heroine, criticizes Milton for allowing his great intellect to blind him to the actual conditions women endure:

> "Milton's Eve! Milton's Eve! I repeat. No, by the pure mother of God, she [Nature] is not! Cary, we are alone we may speak what we think. Milton was great; but what was he good? His brain was right; how was his heart? He saw heaven he looked down on hell . . . the long lines of adamantine shields flashed back on his blind eyeballs; the unutterable splendor of heaven . . . Milton tried to see the first woman; but Cary, he saw her not." (315)

Shirley's observation about Milton's "heart" proceeds from her suspicion that Milton's great intellect precludes a real compassion for the plight of women as mothers. He fails to "see" them in their stultified condition. Shirley goes on to reinscribe Milton's Eve within an imagined Greek mythology, making her the mother of the Titans as much as the mother of humanity.

Intending to reshape our perception of Milton's Eve, Shirley contrives this eclectic mythology in order to undermine what she perceives to be the most devastating Miltonic assumption—Eve's guilt in precipitating the Fall. When Joe Scott describes Shirley's new generation of women as "kittle" and "froward" (322), a generation that does not respect the words of St. Paul ("For Adam was first formed then Eve" and "Adam was not deceived; but the woman, being deceived, was in the transgression") [322], Shirley flippantly replies "More shame to Adam to sin with his eyes open!" (322).

It is tempting to read Brontë's interpretation of Milton through Shirley's impassioned speech and decide that Shirley's criticism is precisely Brontë's. But while Brontë identifies, at least in part, with Shirley's emotional fugue, Brontë's sub rosa admiration for Milton still emerges from Shirley's diatribe. Shirley's unquestioned acknowledgment of Milton's "rightness" not only points to the ideological conflicts that Milton's Calvinism raises in Brontë's own ideology, but to the continuing draw Milton has on her literary imagination. Brontë plays out this dynamic between radicalism and orthodoxy through allusions to Milton's most important women—Eve in *Paradise Lost*, the Lady in *A Masque*, and Dalila in *Samson Agonistes*. Milton's women become important intertextual figures, models of liberty and moral action, even if, to borrow a phrase from Christine Froula, they are "informed by patriarchal tradition" (169).

In the case of *Jane Eyre*, the novel becomes a palimpsest, perhaps unintentionally, of all of Milton's important women, their stories piled up and layered to resonate with Jane's story. Embodying her virtuousness and her unwavering temperament, Jane recalls the Lady in *A Masque*, a resonance Connie Eberhart explores in her work. She writes, "In a pervasive way, *Jane Eyre* echoes *Comus*—in its theme of temptation, its climax emphasizing the form of resistance, and its denouement celebrating spiritual triumph" (81). Just as the Lady brusquely pushes aside the lurid hints of Comus, so does Jane vigorously reject the insinuating offer of Rochester to live with him as his mistress. Furthermore, like the Lady, Jane draws upon her own spiritual strength to vanquish the temptations of masculine authority and privilege, but she does require and (also like the Lady) receive outside assistance—the Lady through the divine intervention of Sabrina, Jane in the form of a deus ex machina legacy from her uncle's estate. In the end, Jane's reward is to be the independent woman she has long desired to be, as well as a woman connected to gentility. As a virtuous woman, Jane succeeds in escaping Thornfield's crucible (much as the Lady escapes permanent imprisonment in Comus's chair), but only with some form of help can Jane participate in middle-class privilege and security.[5]

As Eve, Jane ultimately abandons the sterility and barrenness of her origins (the novel opens with Jane walking in "leafless shrubbery," 39) in order to create a new race at Ferndean with Rochester/Adam by regenerating his "green and vigorous" roots so that plants will "lean" toward him, "wind" themselves around him, and prop themselves against him. Moreover, like Milton's Eve, Jane separates herself from Rochester/Adam in order to construct her own identity, exactly Eve's intention when she separates from Adam in *Paradise Lost*, and with this independence Jane refashions Ferndean into an insulated Eden that can protect and nourish a depleted, wrecked Rochester. With the birth of Jane and Rochester's son, Brontë even implies the transmission of original sin, for their son's black eyes, glittering like those of his Byronic father, intimate that the experiences of the parents cannot immunize their son against the dangerous temptations of the world. Notwithstanding Rochester's regeneration as a prelapsarian Adam and Jane as fiercely independent Eve, the son of Adam and Eve remains fallen, prone to the same weaknesses of character and defects of spirit.

Given Charlotte Brontë's eclectic allusiveness to the Lady and to Eve in *Jane Eyre*, it is not surprising that Jane also mirrors Dalila from Milton's last major work, *Samson Agonistes*. Unlike the biblical versions of Samson and Delilah, Milton's Samson and Dalila provide Charlotte Brontë with a man and a woman at a charged moment of conjugal crisis, a marriage that is forced to confront and resolve perceived betrayals and contending loyalties. Moreover, from the narrator's retrospective position, Jane must give voice to the wisdom both she and Rochester achieve through experience—experience that selfish youth foolishly disdains, preferring violent exploits to considered, reasoned actions. In other words, the violent deeds of younger Samson may initially be more appealing than the final submission of an older, wiser (Miltonic) Samson, who learns that caving into anger or vengefulness, however righteous the cause, can never bring divine peace or equanimity. Similarly, the tempestuous, righteous, and conflicted passions Jane vents throughout the novel metamorphose into filtered expressions of controlled emotion by the end. As the concluding words of *Samson Agonistes* attest, all that remains for Rochester and Jane is "calm of mind, all passion spent" (*SA* 1759). Before composing *Jane Eyre*, Charlotte Brontë had probably already seen this version of Milton's "dramatic poem." In an encomium of Milton's *Samson Agonistes*, John Wilson (Christopher North) publishes the following passage in *Blackwood's Edinburgh Magazine*, just before Brontë begins work on *Jane Eyre*.[6]

> The *Samson Agonistes* was, you know, Milton's last work. How suitable, above all other subjects, to the Hebrew soul within him! Their common blindness—the simplicity of a character that is proper to a strong man—the plain heroic magnitude of mind—the absolute dependence on God, that is to say, trustful dependence brought out by blindness—the submission under the visiting hand of heaven provoked by Samson's own disobedience—God's especial selection of

him as his own, a dedicated Nazarite—his call to be a national deliverer—All
these combined to affect his devout imagination; while one might almost think,
that in the youthful Milton the same fancy had delighted in the prowess and
exploits of Samson which rejoiced in the heroes of chivalrous fable.   (506)

The last sentence implies that Milton interprets the ''Samson'' of ''chivalrous
fable'' as someone who has had to relinquish his vitriolic, ''youthful fancy''
and opt instead for the faithfulness and trust that come with age, an interpretive option that moves us far beyond the principal biblical source materials
for the Samson story in the book of Judges. For Brontë, however, this type
of resolution can only end happily if Samson chooses the forgiveness that
the ''Hebrew soul'' demands and which (in Milton's work) his unhappy,
chastened wife offers. In short, Samson should not necessarily follow through
with his plans to slaughter the Philistines, or at least not follow through with
vengeful or suicidal intent, both of which Milton raises as possibilities in
Samson Agonistes. Armed with this interpretation of Milton's work, Brontë
transforms the mere biblical representation of an enraged Samson who asks
God for one last act of carnage into a representation of final acceptance,
submission, and love. In the words of Peter Fjägesund, Brontë radically ''rework[s]'' both the biblical and Miltonic iterations of the ''traditional story''
of Samson and Delilah (450), transforming the essential tragedy of their
relationship into one of ''future fulfillment and revitalisation'' (451).

After achieving her financial independence (as well as her emotional and
intellectual freedom), Jane oddly subordinates herself to the blind and powerless Rochester in Ferndean by embracing her new role as ministering wife to
the ''Sightless Samson.'' In this Miltonic role, she plays a woman whose
story Milton truncates in *Samson Agonistes*, precisely because his sightless
Samson refuses to trust Dalila as ministering wife or as the repository of his
spiritual rebirth. But while Brontë appears to extend and amplify Milton's
Dalila as background story for the fate of Rochester, she also cannily aug-
ments the allusions to *Samson Agonistes* by creating *two* versions of Milton's
Dalila, Bertha Mason and Jane Eyre. Bertha Mason is the dark, mad Dalila,
the colonized other who wreaks vengeance on a husband whose original
intent is a marriage of wealth and convenience. Jane is the penitent Dalila,
the pilgrim who returns to her husband to support and succor him in his blind
distress. Both versions of Dalila are rooted in Milton's text, for in Samson's
presence Milton's Dalila seems at once vulnerable and remorseful, even as
she remains untrustworthy and unpredictable. She can simultaneously suggest
that she ''may serve/To light'n'' Samson's burden (*SA* 743–74) yet shortly
thereafter vehemently conclude that her betrayal ensures her own immortality,
for ''In Ekron, Gaza, Asdod, and in Gath/[she] shall be nam'd among the
famousest/Of Women . . . '' *SA* 981–83). Brontë untangles these contradictory

threads, assigning the darker personality traits to Bertha while endowing Jane with those traits that will truly enable her to tend to her Samson/Rochester with "glad office" (*SA* 924), easing the physical and emotional challenges he now faces. Brontë's Jane becomes the Dalila who returns to her husband and sincerely wishes to ease his burdens, an alternative that Milton offers in his poem, but which Samson stubbornly forecloses. Milton's Samson steadfastly refuses to believe that Dalila wishes to minister to his blindness. By contrast, Jane becomes her husband's eyes; she removes Rochester/Samson from the very worldly battles and concerns that might indeed 'blind' him to her sincerity, shielding him from their continued painfulness and cocooning him within her web of conjugal affection and love.

Bertha Mason as Hyena: Domesticating the Dark Dalila

Recent criticism of *Jane Eyre* has often focused on the colonial themes that lie at the novel's margins; in particular, feminist and post-colonial critics have attempted to interpret Bertha Mason, as Gayatri Spivak indicates, "through the axiomatics of imperialism" (247). Bertha's ferociousness, her animality, have been interpreted as specifically alluding to racist attitudes during the period because she behaves without regard for civilized (and civilizing) virtue, without typically British restraint. Spivak has further written that "Bertha's function . . . is to render indeterminate the boundary between human and animal and thereby to weaken her entitlement under the spirit if not letter of the Law" (249). Despite Bertha's "whiteness," her creole heritage renders her ethnic purity suspicious and subject to imperial domestication. Deirdre David writes that Brontë describes Bertha Mason as having the "obscene propensities of a black woman" (95), while Deirdre Lynch believes that such "domestications of 'foreign females' " buttressed "English state formation" because it depended on "administrating child-bearing women as national, nation-preserving resources" (55). Jenny Sharpe contends that Bertha's madness represents "an idle plantocracy in a state of decline" (46), an implicit criticism of a slave-holding class that continues in its immorality and debauchery. In other words, Bertha is the colonized other who serves the British empire and its interests, as much as she is the colonizing other who profits from the enslavement of her own people by being complicit with the British in Rochester's class. In short, her madness has as much to do with her "otherness" (*other* to both the British *and* to the Jamaicans) as it does her mental degradation, for she cannot ultimately be classified or controlled. She is as much a mystery to her 'native' family as she is to her adopted one.

As a result, Rochester cannot fathom Bertha's actions, any more than Samson comprehends Dalila's, and he demonizes Bertha in the same fashion that Samson demonizes Dalila. Bertha and Dalila remain culturally "other" to Rochester and Samson, finally becoming emblems of exotic, animal passion. Not coincidentally, Rochester describes Bertha as a "clothed hyena" who "rose up, and stood tall on its hind-feet" (321), which Valerie Grosvenor Myer connects to the passage in *Samson Agonistes*, in which Samson shouts: "Out, out Hyaena; these are thy wonted arts. And arts of every woman false like thee . . . " (*SA* 748–49; Myer 318). The "falseness" of Milton's dark Dalila resembles the deceit the Mason family practices on Rochester, cloaking Bertha's genealogy and the likelihood of her descent into madness. Moreover, Samson believes that Dalila's remorseful mien is but another attempt to deceive him into submitting once again to Philistines stratagem, her penitence yet another deceitful trick.

But the hyena also becomes relevant to a discussion of Bertha's role as the dark Dalila because its laugh is a chilling sign of her malevolent intent and a mocking reminder of Rochester's lapses of judgment, first in marrying Bertha for her money and connections, second in becoming himself the deceiver. The laugh also evokes the possibility of very real danger to Jane, and on the night that she saves Rochester from Bertha's arson, Jane hears Bertha's "demonical laugh" at her door (179), behind which Bertha lurks. This laugh becomes her signature throughout the novel, the abiding threat of violence from a woman shielded by Rochester yet also zealously guarded within his dingy, third-story, gothic Panopticon. When Rochester shows the guests from his aborted wedding with Jane, his "mad, bad, and embruted partner" (320), she growls "like some strange wild animal" and grovels "on all fours" (321). Finally, the hyena's laugh foreshadows violent death since the hyena feeds on carrion, and Bertha scavenges off her terroristic mischief. Jane even conceives her as "carrion-seeking" creature (240). Predictably, her greatest feats of physical strength occur at moments when she is most dehumanized: when she stabs Mason with a knife "like a tigress" (241), when she tears at Rochester's throat and rips his cheek with her teeth (321), and when she waves and shouts "above the battlements" of a burning Thornfield Hall, just before she leaps to her death (453).

Bertha's connection to the hyena also explains her androgyny since Bertha manifests both masculine and feminine qualities. Jane describes her as a "big woman" who nearly throttles Rochester with "virile force" (321). Citing Pliny, Myer notes that "The hyena is popularly believed to be bisexual and to become male and female in alternate years . . . " (318). The hyena's mythical bisexuality also seems connected to the creature's ability to deceive, mimicking the voice of men and luring them to their deaths, a belief of which Milton's readers were aware, as Merritt Hughes and Roy Flannagan have noted in their editions of Milton, and Brontë may well have woven such a mythological belief into her presentation of Bertha.[7] Bertha's unmitigated hatred of Rochester resonates strongly with the intensity of Samson's response to the mere presence of Dalila. The irreconcilable differences between Bertha and Rochester (and Dalila and Samson) point to Eccesiastes 13:18–"What peace can there be between hyena and dog?/And what peace between rich man and poor?" For Samson and for Rochester, Dalila remains a dark, deceptive woman who cannot change her hyena spots. There can be no conciliatory gestures, no modus vivendi, "no peace between hyena and dog."

In his essay, "Penance of the Hyaena in *Samson Agonistes*," Samuel Hornsby suggests that Samson unwittingly distinguishes between Dalila's desire for penance and his emerging insistence on penitence because penance represents the satisfaction of an external command while repentance depends upon the strength and determination of the internal (and individual) will. Dalila's stated desire to do "penance," then, suggests to Samson that her change of heart is superficial, nothing more than the outward show of remorse. But Hornsby also implies that despite Samson's insight, he "does not directly apply to himself the distinction between the terms" (354). Only late in Milton's work does Samson embody this interior transformation, when he becomes the Orientalized phoenix:

> But he though blind of sight
> Despis'd and thought extinguish't quite
> With inward eyes illuminated
> His fiery virtue rous'd
> From under ashes into sudden flame . . .
> Like that self-begott'n bird
> In the Arabian woods embost
> What no second knows nor third
> And lay erewhile a Holocaust
> From out her ashy womb now teem'd
> Revives, reflourishes, then vigorous most
> When most unactive deem'd . . . (*SA* 1687–91; 1699–1705)

The hyena reifies the combative sexual politics between Bertha and Rochester, an eerie iteration of the irreconcilable division between Dalila and Samson. Yet Bertha's hyena nature ironically makes possible Rochester's regeneration, for Jane Eyre's reappearance as the loving nurse can occur only when Rochester loses all ability to mask or disguise his unmediated self. When Bertha ignites the Thornfield fire, she forces Rochester to attempt rescue, to throw himself into the "holocaust," to absolutely and publicly accept his role as husband. His actions are sacrificial, and they are, in essence, his "penance" for his acquiescence to a badly conceived and covered-up marriage. Moreover, as the timbers of the house collapse around him, causing his hand to be crushed and his eye to be knocked out, Rochester appears to atone for his previous greed and selfishness. But his handicaps are not merely part of his "penance"; they represent the necessary preconditions for his "repentance," for the recovery of his own "rousing motions." Rochester becomes the confined and watched prisoner within his chosen place of exile, the Ferndean forest. There he waits, for the faithful Dalila to reignite his "fiery virtue": he eventually "revives" and "reflourishes" and grows "vigorous most/ When most unactive deem'd." Brontë alters Milton's Orientalist landscape, betraying an important ideological shift. In brief, Rochester must be rehabilitated by someone. Unlike the phoenix in the Arabian woods, he is not exotically or magically "self-begotten." Instead, he requires actual nurturing, not only to heal his physical and emotional scars, but to discover as well the naked rebirth that comes from penitence. In the end, Jane dissipates Rochester's "othering," a process by which women become objects of his colonialist and Orientalist fantasies, as dangerous as they are unreal, blunting the criticism that Jane Eyre's fullest emergence as the Englishwoman occurs "at the expense of the identity of the colonized woman" (Kennedy 124).

In *The Madwoman in the Attic*, Gilbert and Gubar write that Bertha "is Jane's truest and darkest double: she is the angry aspect of the orphan child, the ferocious secret self Jane has been trying to repress ever since her days at Gateshead" (360). They are surely right when they contend that Bertha represents Jane's "darkest double," for Bertha, literally and figuratively, shadows Jane throughout the novel. But at issue is not Jane's anger but Rochester's. He is angry for marrying the wrong woman and then angry for not being able to marry the right one. And from Rochester's perspective, Jane is Bertha's double that reveals his own "ferocious secret self" because Jane embodies the Dalila to which he clings imaginatively, even as he despairingly remains linked in marriage to the dark Dalila.

Jane Eyre as Nurse: Orientalizing the Redemptive Dalila[8]

After the madwoman's violent attack on Mason (she has not yet been identified as Bertha Mason), Rochester evasively explains his motivations for desiring marriage. He mysteriously alludes to a "capital error" he has made in a "remote foreign land" and speaks of a human "instrument" that will lead to his spiritual regeneration. Vaguely describing the consequences of his youthful error and the measures he has taken to relieve his distress (hypothetically, for he has not yet confessed his indiscretions to Jane), Rochester states

> "Still you are miserable; for the hope has quitted you on the very confines of
> life: your sun at noon darkens in an eclipse, which you feel will not leave it
> till the time of setting. Bitter and base associations have become the sole food

of your memory you wander here and there, seeking rest in exile . . . '' (247)

Brontë appears to have borrowed the description for Rochester's suicidal darkness, the hopeless bleakness of his situation from *Samson Agonistes*. In agony, Samson cries near the beginning of Milton's dramatic poem:

> "O dark, dark, dark, amid the blaze of noon
> Irrecoverably dark, total Eclipse
> Without all hope of day!"

Like Samson, Rochester has married a woman in "a foreign land" and has rued his decision. Both men have embraced despair, finding that their lives resemble a darkened noonday sun, and they interpret their fates through its blackened eclipse. While Samson's blindness literally reifies this darkness, Rochester's obliquely refers to the darkness caused by his marriage to Bertha Mason and to the personal consequences subsequent to that fated marriage. At this point, Rochester's statement that the "sun darkens at noon" becomes symptomatic of an ethical blindness that later becomes an actual moral breach; hence, this statement may be a prolepsis for a fate he must eventually endure. As in Milton's "dramatic poem," however, Samson's initial moments of despair give way to heroic "rousing motions" that undergird the inner strength he requires to defeat the Philistines, an inner strength into which Rochester eventually taps to conquer his own despair.

Further, Milton's Samson and Brontë's Rochester find themselves in exile, although, once again, Samson's has been literalized while Rochester's is at this point only self-fashioned. Rochester is thus in internal exile because he conceives of himself as a pariah even though fashionable women such as Blanche Ingram desire his company and his connections. His desperate determination to be free of Bertha, however, will inevitably lead him to a more literal exile, precisely the condition Jane finds him in Ferndean.

Nevertheless, there is one striking difference. Both the biblical Samson and Milton's Samson are in the habit of telling secrets (first to the woman of Timna and then Dalila). Yet Rochester refuses to disclose his, even to prevent Jane from improperly marrying him, until Mason uncovers his scheme. Rochester attempts to ensnare her within his own rationalizations, denying her the free choice he has regretted having exercised in his marriage to Bertha Mason. Ironically, his desire for intellectual and physical control over Jane (he constantly refers to her "littleness") is another powerful secret, and it unintentionally but perceptibly recapitulates the watchful imprisonment of Bertha Mason.

Rochester's interpellation of Jane within his own imaginative logics surfaces most strongly when he attempts to control her self-image, which he accomplishes by Orientalizing himself as oracle and Jane as his mysterious savior.[9] First, he is the Egyptian "sphinx" whose speech Jane recognizes as being "enigmatical" (169). While his "heart [has been] a sort of charnel," her presence has transformed it into a "shrine" (168). Yet his reference to the sphinx also implies that she must solve the riddle at the heart of Thornfield's mystery, the riddle of Rochester's private passions and history. Because he has described himself as a "disguised deity" (168), Jane must use her shrewdness to decode Rochester's "Egyptian" mystery. This "riddle" may also refer to that which Samson tells the Philistines groomsmen, relations of his first wife, the woman of Timna. In a very real sense, Rochester cannot trust Jane with the truth because, like Samson, he already expects deceit and betrayal. Overtaken by Rochester's Byronic masculinity, Jane loses her normally objective eye, and fails to unravel the mysterious threads of Rochester's life, to solve her Samson/Sphinx's riddle. That failure is nearly her undoing.

Later in the novel, when Rochester gives a party for his friends, he provides an elaborate game of charades for their entertainment. He performs by cross-dressing as a gypsy fortune teller, once again depending on the public fascination with Oriental fashion and entertainment to disguise his true motives. He appears "costumed in shawls, with a turban on his head. His dark eyes and swarthy skin and Paynim features suited the costume exactly: he looked the very model of an Eastern emir . . . " (212). Miss Ingram, Jane's rival for Rochester's affections, is also "attired in Oriental fashion" (212). She appeared to be "some Israelitish princess of the patriarchal day; and such was doubtless the character she intended to represent" (213). Through this charade, Brontë uses the Oriental likeness between Rochester and Miss Ingram to advance the public perception (which is also Jane's view at this point) that Miss Ingram is Rochester's Oriental consort, reinforcing their social resemblances and the public approbation that would ensue if they were to be married. In short, Rochester and Miss Ingram occupy the same class because they have been raised in the same "tribe." Jane is not "Israelitish" because she is the social and cultural other with whom Rochester falls in love and oughtn't; she is the Philistine governess without appropriate social status or connections. She is the Dalila who bewitches Samson and rips him from his "Israelitish" roots, much as Bertha Mason, the West Indian Dalila, has succeeded in doing. Yet Rochester delights in Jane's being his "girl-bride" (287) and in being her "conquest" arising from "witchery" (289). Jane associates his strong passion with Hercules and Samson and their female "charmers" (289), and inasmuch as Rochester attempts to bend Jane to his will, she resists.

As Nancy Workman has demonstrated, Jane's resistance to Rochester's sinister advances evokes another Orientalist motif—Scheherazade.[10] Just as

Scheherazade resists the Sultan's advances so that she will not be executed, so Jane resists Rochester's desire to overpower her and vanquish her fiercely independent spirit. Once smitten by Jane, Rochester wishes to dress her more to his taste and more closely fitting her to his vision of her as mysterious, exotic savior. His smile, Jane suggests, "was such as a sultan might, in a blissful and fond moment, bestow on a slave his gold and gems had enriched" (297). She threatens to wear her "old Lowood frocks" if he continues to gaze at her in such complacency and smug satisfaction. His response is to transform Jane into the perceived Oriental Other:

> "Oh, it is rich to see and hear her! . . . Is she original? Is she piquant? I would not exchange this one little English girl for the Grand Turk's whole sera-glio—gazelle eyes, houri forms, and all!"
> The Eastern allusion bit me again. "I'll not stand you an inch in the stead of a seraglio . . . so don't consider me an equivalent for one. If you have a fancy for anything in that line, away with you, sir, to the bazaars of Stamboul, without delay, and lay out in expensive slave purchases some of that spare cash you seem at a loss to spend satisfactorily here"   (297).

Though Rochester teases her in this scene, Jane rightly senses that even if she were the only woman in the "seraglio," such a position would represent nothing less than confinement and constraint, however exotic the environment. She would no longer have any independence—of thought or of fortune. Paradoxically, in fact, the greater the effort Rochester makes to make Jane conform to his Orientalist expectations, the more he also argues that Jane's exoticism has bewitched him, thereby compromising his free will, and in his mind validating actions that he would ordinarily regard as unseemly and unmanly. She has become a "charmer" of "Samson" who has "conquered" Rochester's heart (289). In *Samson Agonistes*, Samson refers to Dalila as a "sorceress" who has used her arcane arts to ensnare him in a Philistian trap (819).[11] Milton's Dalila looms as the Oriental model that permit Brontë to examine the specious logic of Rochester's rationalizations and to position Jane as the marginalized Other who nonetheless retrieves him from godless despair. When Jane stubbornly resists the marital and social restrictions that Rochester seeks to impose on her freedom and on his own (he wishes to retire from public life and scrutiny), he becomes angry, no longer merely seeing her as a charming sorceress who coyly tempts him into apparent submission. Instead, she has exchanged places with Rochester. Now she is the inscrutable Oriental Other, whose "sphynx-like expression" masks her deeper feelings and sinister intentions. Rochester describes her stubbornness as a "hitch in her character" (340). Her personality is as a "knot" that he wishes to cut through, a "puzzle" whose code he wishes to crack (340). A subtle commentary on his own intractability, Jane's recalcitrance so disturbs

Rochester's equanimity, he exclaims that he "long[s] to exert a fraction of Samson's strength, and break the entanglement like tow!" (340). According to Michael Mason, this statement echoes Judges 16:9, where Samson has at one point escaped from Philistines captivity (525). Rochester's response to being threatened (even if he is later tamed or chastened) is to behave like the desperately enraged, biblical Samson, the one who slaughters Philistines and takes home their foreskins as battle trophies. Like the biblical Samson and the Samson to whom Milton introduces us to at the beginning of his poem, Rochester has not yet accepted the limitations of his existence. He does not accept ethical and moral standards that might govern his personal responsibility, nor does he see how he has not balanced his own passionate drives with reasonable expectations. Without a trace of irony, he cries "Jane! will you hear reason? . . . because if you won't, I'll try violence" (340).

By the end of the novel, Rochester resembles Milton's Samson in his despair, though Rochester transcends this despair, remaining open to renewal and redemption once he realizes that Jane loves him despite his deformities. Moreover, Rochester abandons his crudely Orientalist view of Jane, the elimination of which corresponds to a reinscribed and re-oriented version of Dalila. Brontë has imagined this Dalila as benign, the prop and guide, who in *Samson Agonistes* regrets having caved into pressure, promising to care for Samson with "nursing diligence" (*SA* 924). In *Samson Agonistes*, Samson's understandable lack of trust and Dalila's predictable lack of credibility doom the possibility of reconciliation, but in *Jane Eyre*, Brontë moves her Samson and (second) Dalila beyond this impasse. Rochester finally discerns that Jane has the necessary strength to be his moral compass, rousing him from his blind lethargy and "leading" him "onward with [her] guiding hand" to personal fulfillment and ultimate redemption.[12] He becomes the "Sightless Samson" who has relinquished his rage and his rebellious pride. No longer imperious, Rochester entreats his Redeemer "to give [him] strength to lead henceforth a purer life . . . " (472–3). In effect, they become the reconciled Samson and Dalila, the possibility to which Milton does give voice. Samson (Rochester) is no longer bitterly angry, reviling his wife with terms like "bosom serpent" and "thorn intestine," and Dalila cedes some of her independence to ease his pain and release him spiritually from his "loathsome prison house" (*SA* 921). Ferndean is certainly not the guarantor of social equity and justice, but it does protect the renewed Samson and Dalila from the demoralizing and debilitating encroachments of the outside world, the very encroachments for which in *Samson Agonistes* both Samson and Dalila justify their actions and their dubious rhetoric. The shadows of Ferndean thus disclose the imaginative possibility of marital reconciliation, even between betrayer and betrayed, but the Oriental Other ominously beckons from outside Brontë's hermetic world where real Samsons still subjugate exotic Dalilas, and real Dalilas enslave gullible Samsons.

NOTES

1. Gilbert and Gubar take their cue about Milton's "bogey" from Virginia Woolf. A very interesting exchange on Woolf and Milton's "bogey" has been published in *Critical Inquiry.* See Jane Marcus, "Quentin's Bogey" and Quentin Bell's response, "Reply to Jane Marcus." Unless otherwise indicated, all quotations from *Jane Eyre* are taken from Q. D. Leavis's edition of the novel.

2. Joan Malory Webber indicts Gilbert's "mistake of assuming that a character's viewpoint can be identified with the author's." William Shullenberger suggests in his essay "Wrestling With the Angel: Paradise Lost and Feminist Criticism" that a feminist reading of *Paradise Lost* in which the equation of patriarchy and misogyny obscures elements in Milton's "subtext" which, if discovered, would prove embarrassing to feminists whose "critical idealism," as it turns out, would be "confirmed and encouraged" by Milton, Joseph Wittreich contends that many women writers find in Milton's work subversive solutions. Speaking of Eliza Blackburn and her children. Wittreich remarks "that the platitudes and pieties of a Christian misogynistic tradition are present in *Paradise Lost* but that are there to be silenced" (84). John Shawcross also argues against the perception that Milton is misogynistic. See *John Milton and Influence; John Milton: The Self and the World;* and "Spokesperson Milton."

3. Other important essays on Milton's relationship to nineteenth-century writers can be found in Nyquist and Ferguson, Low and Harding. Two disparate recent essays about the relationship between Charlotte Brontë and Milton are Taylor's "Brontë's *Jane Eyre*" and Simmons, "Jamaica Kincaid."

4. Charlotte Bronte's views on marriage remain far more conservative than Milton's. Milton writes in *The Doctrine and Discipline of Divorce* that "[I]t is less a breach of wedlock to part with wise and quiet consent betimes than still to soil and profane that mystery of joy and union with a polluting sadness and perpetual distemper . . " (Hughes 712). Milton's passage provides a highly reasonable justification for Rochester to divorce Bertha Mason, marry Jane, and still continue to shelter and care for his former wife.

5. In both letters to and by Charlotte Brontë, readers will find echoes to *A Masque* (frequently if mistakenly referred to as *Comus*). In one letter to W. S. Williams, for example, Brontë says she is "grieved and pleased" by Thackeray's *Christmas Books,* worrying that he periodically slides from the angelic to the Satanic: "Alas! Thackeray—I wish your strong wings would lift you often above the smoke of cities into the purer region nearer heaven!" (I, 328) ["Of bright aërial Spirits live inspher's/In regions of mild and calm and serene Air,/Above the smoke and stir of this dim spot. . . ." *A Masque,* 3–6]. In another revealing letter, the unidentified "K.T." clearly connects his reading of *Jane Eyre* to *A Masque*: "Let your sex be what it may I must bring this letter to a climax by saying that no book I have ever read and I am pretty well acquainted with most novels in the English language has ever given me such unqualified pleasure—'such secret and home felt delight' such assurance of a great work greatly 'done' as your Jane Eyre . . . (I, 498)." K.T.'s memory is slightly faulty. In response to Echo's song, Comus

actually says "*sacred* and home felt delight" (italics mine; *A Masque,* 262). Still, K.T. correctly finds a resonance between his appreciation of *Jane Eyre* and Milton's masque.

6. Although Charlotte Brontë does not mention reading *Samson Agonistes* in her letters, the circumstantial evidence has convinced many scholars of her serious intent to allude to Milton's last work in *Jane Eyre.* I discuss elsewhere the work of F.B. Pinion, Valerie Myer, and Paula Sullivan, who argue for connections between *Jane Eyre* and *Samson Agonistes* and who publish their findings, perhaps not coincidentally, prior to the advent of Gilbert and Gubar's famous work. Harold Bloom believes that the conclusion of the novel does not refer to the biblical Samson but to Milton's. Bloom asserts that "despite the author's allusions to Milton's *Samson Agonistes*" (3), the conclusion to the novel, which presents a blind and helpless Rochester dependent on the charity of Jane, is not a kind of Freudian castration. More recently, Peter Fjågesund discusses Charlotte Brontë's use of both the biblical and Miltonic sources for the Samson story in "Samson and Delilah: Chapter 37 of Charlotte Brontë's *Jane Eyre.*" In the forthcoming *Oxford Reader's Companion to the Brontës,* the entry on Milton states: "In her fiction Charlotte quotes from or directly alludes to *Samson Agonistes,* 'L'Allegro,' 'Il Penseroso,' and—in all four of her novels—*Paradise Lost*" [qtd. with permission of the editor, Christine Alexander]. The Brontë Parsonage Museum has listed only a copy of *Paradise Lost* in its collection, although, because that collection of Brontë books is incomplete (136 volumes), it is not inconceivable that *Samson Agonistes* may have been in a now lost volume of their through the Ponden Hall collection, which had a copy of *Paradise Regain'd. A Poem, In Four Books. To which is added Samson Agonistes: and Poems upon Several Occasions.* There is little doubt that she read Milton widely, for she alludes to him frequently (or quotes him verbatim) in her letters, in one recommending only "first rate" poetry to Ellen Nussey, with Milton at the head of a list that included Shakespeare, Pope, Byron, and Wordsworth (I, 130). Finally, throughout the 1840s, *Blackwood's Edinburgh Magazine* references Milton's works, including one important discussion (elaborated above) on *Samson Agonistes* by John Wilson, one of *Blackwood's* regular contributors, and someone whose opinions Brontë and her entire family were very familiar with. For a fascinating discussion of John Wilson, his Toryism, and his career with *Blackwood's,* see Robert Morrision, "*Blackwood's* Berserker."

I am grateful to several people for their assistance and guidance in obtaining some of this information, including Rachel Terry, curator of the Brontë Parsonage Museum in Haworth; Christine Alexander, professor of English at the University of New South Sales; John Maxstadt, one of the reference librarians at Texas A & M International University; and Gabriel Swift, reference librarian at the University of Indiana, Bloomington. I also profusely thank John Shawcross for reading and editing several drafts of this essay.

7. See footnote 748 to *Samson Agonistes* edited by Meritt Y. Hughes (569) and footnote 186 to *Samson Agonistes* edited by Roy Flnnagan (821).

8. One of the first critics to write of the Orientalism in *Jane Eyre* is Joyce Zonana. She suggests that "feminist orientalism is a rhetorical strategy (and a form of

thought) by which a speaker or writer neutralizes the threat inherent in feminist demands and makes them palatable to an audience that wishes to affirm its occidental superiority'' (594). This view suggests that any perceived counter-feminist practices to which Orientalist referencing may attest, in fact, merely becomes the screen that makes ''palatable'' a submerged feminism. Not surprisingly, Zonana allies herself to Gilbert and Gubar's views of the novel, with a feminist Orientalism that subtly undermines the patriarchal ethos. Connecting Brontë's ''diffuse'' Orientalism (Zonana's word) to Milton, however, reveals a more problematic representation of Orientalism, one in which Charlotte Brontë's own ideological positionality is highly ambiguous. Nonetheless, Zonana's essay is useful, with an excellent discussion of Mary Wollstonecraft's Orientalist references in *Vindication of the Rights of Woman.*

9. Interestingly, Charlotte Brontë herself may have been Orientalized by some of her readership. In 1856, *Blackwood's* published a dialogue entitled ''Respectability,'' in which one of the interlocutors, Tlepolemus, says that ''If you want to understand what I mean, read *Jane Eyre, Shirley,* and *Villette.* By the way, Currer Bell is a bit of a female Arab, though in saying so I am venturing on a course where I just owned myself without mark or compass'' (685). Perhaps not coincidentally, the context of this remark is the interlocutors' more general discussion of Philistines and philistinism, as well as oddly racist distinctions between Arabs and Philistines, wherein Arabs embody the search for Truth and Philistines remain ''vulgar impostors'' and snobs (685). At all events, Tlepolemus' representations of Arabs and Philistines in the dialogue exactly reify what Edward Said has classically labeled as Orientalism, a symbolic process of othering that wrests all ''Oriental'' ethnicities from their cultural, political, historical, and geographic specificity in favor of a version that reproduces what Western readers, from an occidentally superior position, believe they already know about them. As Said suggests in *Orientalism:* ''But the phenomenon of Orientalism as I study it here deals principally, not with a correspondence between Orientalism and the Orient but with the internal consistency of Orientalism and its ideas about the Orient (the East as career) despite or beyond any correspondence, or lack thereof, with a 'real' Orient'' (5). Notice how Tlepolemus suggests that he is ''venturing'' on a course that has no ''mark or compass,'' no map that explains how or why he has put Currer Bell (Charlotte Brontë)—the ''female Arab''—in the Orientalized subject position of the subaltern. Finally, Tlepolemus actually transitions his discussion of Philistines and Arabs to his comments about ''Currer Bell'' by quoting Milton's ''L'Allegro'' [line 27]: ''. . . So many little prejudices, 'quips, cranks, and wanton wiles,' truth and falsehood, or rather I should say fiction, interlacing each other so intricately in their constitutions . . . that the task of discrimination, distinction, or classification, is far above my powers'' (685). In the context of a discussion about Brontë and *Samson Agonistes,* Tlepolemus' comments only reinforce the ideological and textual complexities that arise from interpreting Charlotte Brontë's relationship to Milton and, more specifically, to what I have called Miltonic Orientalism. See related discussions of Milton land empire in J. Martin Evans, *Milton's Imperial Epic;* Robert Fallon, *Divided Empire*; and Balachandra Rajan, ''The Imperial Temptation.'' Timothy Morton has

a brilliant discussion on Milton's representations of the spice trade and their connections to Romantic works, Morton briefly discusses Dalila as a merchant ship (See *Samson Agonistes,* 710–14): "But who is this, what thing of Sea or Land?/Female of sex it seems/That so bedeckt, ornate, and gay/Come this way sailing/Like a stately ship/Of Tarsus . . .''). For Morton, Dalila revises Desdemona, "who is described both as a precious cargo *and* the vessel in which she travels . . .'' (72). She is a "paradox''—the "container and the contents'' (72).

10. See Workman, who details the Arabian Nights paradigm as the source for Jane's own storytelling. Workman argues that "by associating her heroine with Scheherazade, Brontë empowers Jane with the ability to confront obstacles that foil her selfhood'' (177).

11. Although Rochester Orientalizes Jane, she does not always find herself in the colonized subject position. She also embodies the colonizer since her own fortune stems from West Indian plantations; she becomes, as Inderpal Grewal says, "the comrade and wife of the Englishman harmed by a colonised, dark woman'' (62). Hence, Jane supports, even as she Orientalizes, both the colonizer and the colonized. For Reina Lewis, the colonial discourse surrounding Bertha Mason, particularly those representations of her madness and degeneracy, "*only* [italics Lewis's] makes sense with imperial discourses of race and heredity'' (30). Cannon Schmitt also acknowledges the "presence of colony as locale, as literal place'' (89) that finances Rochester's activities and Jane Eyre's deus ex machina inheritance. Schmitt also recognizes the Orientalism in Brontë's novel *The Professor.* Finally, see Jenny Sharpe's discussion of *Jane Eyre*: 27–55.

12. F. B. Pinion has identified "A little onward lend thy guiding hand'' as one of the central themes in the novel. He writes that just as "Samson accepted the blame for failure to resist Delilah's wiles, Rochester has condemned himself for the 'prurience, the rashness, the blindness of youth' which made him marry a woman in which he found nothing admirable beyond her physical attractions'' (*Brontë Companion* 114). Another article that touches upon the relation of Jane Eyre to the Samson story is Paula Sullivan's, 192–98.

WORKS CITED

Alexander, Christine and Margaret Smith, ed. *The Oxford Reader's Companion to the Brontës.* Oxford: Oxford UP, 2003 (forthcoming).

Beaty, Jerome. *Misreading Jane Eyre. A Postformalist Paradigm.* Ohio State UP, 1996.

Bell, Quentin. "Reply to Jane Marcus." *Critical Inquiry* 11(3) 1995:486–497.

Bloom, Harold. *The Anxiety of Influence: A Theory of Poetry.* Oxford, New York: Oxford UP 1973.

Boumelha, Penny. *Charlotte Brontë.* New York, London: Harvester Wheatsheaf, 1990.

Brontë, Charlotte. *Jane Eyre.* Ed. Q.D. Leavis. Harmondsworth: Penguin Books, 1984 (1966).

——. *Jane Eyre.* Ed. Michael Mason. Harmondsworth: Penguin, 1996.

——. *The Letters of Charlotte Brontë.* Ed. Margaret Smith. 2 vols. Oxford: Clarendon, 2000.

——. *Shirley.* Ed. Andrew Hook and Judith Hook. Harmondsworth: Penguin, 1977 (1974).

David, Deirdre. "The Governess of Empire: Jane Eyre Takes Care of India and Jamaica." *Rule Britannia: Women, Empire, and Victorian Writing.* Cornell UP, 1995: 77–117.

Dry, Florence Swinton. *The Sources of Jane Eyre.* Cambridge: W. Heffer, 1945; Folcroft, 1973.

Eberhart, Connie. "Jane Eyre—A Daughter of the Lady in Milton's Comus." *University of Mississippi Studies in English* 8 (1990): 80–91.

Evans, J. Martin. *Milton's Imperial Epic. Paradise Lost and the Discourse of Colonialism.* Ithaca: Cornell UP, 1996.

Fallon, Robert, *Divided Empire. Milton's Political Imagery.* University Park, PA: Pennsylvania State UP, 1995.

Fjågesund, Peter. "Samson and Delilah: Chapter 37 of Charlotte Brontë's *Jane Eyre.*" *English Studies* 5 (1999): 449–53.

Flannagan, Roy, ed. *The Riverside Milton.* New York: Houghton Mifflin, 1998.

Froula, Christine. "When Eve Reads Milton Undoing the Canonical Economy." *Canons.* Ed. Robert von Hallberg. U of Chicago P, 1984 (1983).

Gilbert, Sandra, M., and Susan Gubar. *The Madwoman in the Attic: The Woman Writer and the Nineteenth-Century Literary Imagination.* New Haven: Yale UP, 1979.

Grewal, Inderpal. *Home and Harem: Nation, Gender, Empire, and the Cultures of Travel.* Durham and London: Duke UP, 1996.

Hill, Christopher. *Milton and the English Revolution.* New York: Viking, 1978.

Hughes, Merritt Y. *John Milton. Complete Poems and Major Prose.* New York: Macmillan, 1957.

Homans, Margaret. *Bearing the Word. Language and Female Experience in Nineteenth-Century Women's Writing.* Chicago and London: U of Chicago P, 1986.

The Jerusalem Bible. Garden City, NY: Doubleday and Co., 1966.

Kennedy, Valerie. *Edward Said. A Critical Introduction.* Malden, MA: Polity Press, 2000.

Lewis, Reina. *Gendering Orientalism: Race, Femininity and Representation.* London and New York: Routledge, 1996.

Low, Lisa, and Anthony John Harding. *Milton, the Metaphysicals, and Romanticism.* Cambridge UP, 1994.

Lynch, Deirdre. "Domesticating Fictions and Nationalizing Women: Edmund Burke, Property, and the Reproduction of Englishness."

Marcus, Jane. "Quentin's Bogey." *Critical Inquiry* 11(3) 1995: 486–97.

Meyer, Susan. "Indian Ink: Colonialism and the Figurative Strategy of *Jane Eyre.*" *Imperialism at Home: Race and Victorian Women's Fiction.* Ithaca: Cornell UP, 1996:60–95.

Milton, John. *Paradise Regain'd. A Poem, In Four Books. To which is added Samson Agonistes: and Poems upon Several Occasions.* Ed. Thomas Newton. London: W. Strahan, 1777.

Morrison, Robert. "*Blackwood's* Berserker: John Wilson and the Language of Extremity." *Romanticism on the Net* 20 (November 2000) [July 28, 2002] <http: // users.ox.ac.uk/~scat0385/20morrison.html>

Morton, Timothy. *The Poetics of Spice. Romantic Consumerism and the Exotic.* Cambridge: Cambridge UP, 2000.

Myer, Valerie Grosvenor. "Jane Eyer: The Madwoman as Hyena." *Notes and Queries* 35 (233) (3) September 1988: 318.

Nyquist, Mary and Margaret Ferguson, eds. *Re-Membering Milton. Essays on the Texts and Traditions.* New York and London: Methuen 1988 (1987).

Pickrel, Paul. "*Jane Eyre*: The Apocalypse of the Body," *ELH* 531. Spring 1986: 165–82.

Pinion, F. B. *A Brontë Companion: Literary Assessment, Background, and Reference.* London: Macmillan, 1975.

Rajan, Balachandra. "The Imperial Temptation," *Milton and the Imperial Vision.* Ed. B. Rajan and Elizabeth Sauer. Pittsburgh: Duquesne UP 1999.

Said, Edward. *Orientalism.* New York: Vintage, 1979.

Schmitt, Cannon. *Alien Nation. Nineteenth-Century Gothic Fictions and English Nationality.* Philadelphia: U of Pennsylvania P, 1997.

Schullenberger, William. "Wrestling With the Angel: Paradise Lost and Feminist Criticism." *Milton Quarterly* 20 (1987): 69–85.

Sharpe, Jenny. "The Rise of Women in an Age of Progress: *Jane Eyre,*" *Allegories of Empire. The Figure of the Woman in the Colonial Text.* Minneapolis: U of Minnesota P, 1993:27–55.

Shawcross, John T. *John Milton and Influence. Presence in Literature, History and Culture.* Pittsburgh, PA: Duquesne UP, 1991.

———. *John Milton: The Self and the World* Lexington: The UP of Kentucky, 1993.

———. "Spokesperson Milton," *Spokesperson Milton. Voices in Contemporary Criticism.* Eds. Durham, Charles W. and Kristin Pruitt McColgan. London and Toronto: Associated University Presses, 1994:5–17.

Simmons, Diane. "Jamaica Kincaid and the Canon: In Dialogue with *Paradise Lost* and *Jane Eyre,*" *MELUS* 23 (2) 1998:65–86.

Spivak, Gayatri Chakravorty. "Three Women's Texts and a Critique of Imperialism." *Critical Inquiry* 12 (1985): 243–261.

Sullivan, Paula. "Rochester Reconsidered: Jane Eyre in the Light of the Samson Story." *Brontë Society Transactions* 16.3 (1973): 192–98.

Taylor, Susan B., "Brontë's *Jane Eyre,*" *Explicator* 59 (4) 2001:182–85.

Webber, Joan Malory. "The Politics of Poetry: Feminism and Paradise Lost." *Milton Studies* 14 (1980): 3–24.

Wilson, John. "Dryden." *Blackwood's Edinburgh Magazine* 57 (354), Apr. 1845: 503–14.

Workman, Nancy V., "Scheherazade at Thornfield: Mythic Elements in Jane Eyre. *Essays in literature* (15 (2) 1988): 177–92

Wittreich, Joseph. *Feminist Milton.* Ithaca: Cornell UP 1987.

Zonana, Joyce. "The Sultan and the Slave: Feminist Orientalism and the Structure of *Jane Eyre.*" *Signs* 18 (31) 1994:592–617.

Wilkie Collins, Mr. Vanstone, and the Case of Beethoven's "No-Name" Symphony

Allan W. Atlas

For Leo Treitler

Wilkie Collins poses a wonderful musical riddle at the beginning of No Name *(1864). Having attended a concert with his daughters, Mr. Vanstone describes one of the pieces on the program: it lasted forty minutes, "stopped three times along the way," made him think of Jericho, and went "Crash-Bang" (we also learn that there was a female singer on the program). He then asks his daughters what they call such a piece, to which Magdalen replies that it was a Beethoven symphony, without, however, identifying just which one of Beethoven's nine symphonies it was. After reviewing Collins's antipathy to Beethoven's music in general, I use the clues in Mr. Vanstone's description to identify the symphony that he heard. It must have been Symphony No. 7, a conclusion further supported by that number's association with the biblical Mary Magdalen, with whom Magdalen Vanstone, the driving force of the novel, is obviously associated. The unfolding of the mystery is accompanied by incidental information about musical life in Victorian England.*

Intentionally or not, Wilkie Collins poses an interesting music-related riddle at the very beginning of his novel *No Name*.[1] The setting is Combe-Raven, the West Somersetshire country residence of the Vanstone family; it is the

---

morning of 4 March 1846. The previous evening, Mr. Andrew Vanstone, together with his two daughters, Norah and Magdalen, and the family's footman, Thomas, had attended a concert at nearby Clifton.[2] As the morning progresses, Collins dwells upon the concert on three occasions, each time providing a bit more information about one of the pieces performed and, at the same time, distinguishing between levels of discourse suitable to those of different social stations.

The first reference to the concert—without dialogue—involves Thomas and his fellow servants:

> The conversation of the servants . . . referred to a recent family event, and turned . . . on this question: Had Thomas, the footman, seen anything of the concert at Clifton, at which his master and the two young ladies had been present on the previous night? Yes; Thomas had heard the concert; he had been paid for to go in at the back; it was a loud concert; it was a hot concert; it was described at the top of the bills as Grand; whether it was worth travelling sixteen miles to hear by railway, with the additional hardship of going back nineteen miles by road, at half-past one in the morning—was a question which he would leave his master and the young ladies to decide; his own opinion, in the mean time, being unhesitatingly, No. Further inquiries, on the part of all the female servants in succession, elicited no additional information of any sort. Thomas could hum none of the songs, and could describe none of the ladies' dresses. (2)

The second reference features Mr. Vanstone:

> "Thomas!" cried Mr. Vanstone, taking up his old felt hat and his thick walking-stick from the hall table. "Breakfast, this morning, at ten. The young ladies are not likely to be down earlier after the concert last night.—By-the-by, how did you like the concert, yourself, eh? You thought it was Grand? Quite right; so it was. Nothing but Crash-Bang, varied now and then by Bang-Crash; all the women dressed within an inch of their lives; smothering heat, blazing gas, and no room for anybody—yes, yes, Thomas: Grand's the word for it . . . ." (2–3)

Here, then, Mr. Vanstone begins to describe the music, though he tells us only that it went "Crash-Bang," with an occasional "Bang-Crash."

Finally, the third reference takes place at breakfast and involves Mr. Vanstone and his daughters (with Mrs. Vanstone and Miss Garth, the governess, listening in); together they give us as much information about the music as we are going to get:[3]

> Mr. Vanstone sat down composedly under his daughter's flow of language, like a man who was well used to verbal inundation from that quarter. "If I am to be allowed my choice of amusements next time," said the worthy gentleman, "I think a play will suit me better than a concert. The girls enjoyed themselves amazingly, my dear," he continued, addressing his wife. "More than I did, I

must say. It was altogether above my mark. They played one piece of music which lasted forty minutes. It stopped three times by the way; and we all thought it was done each time, and clapped our hands, rejoiced to be rid of it. But on it went again, to our great surprise and mortification, till we gave it up in despair, and all wished ourselves at Jericho. Norah, my dear! when we had Crash-Bang for forty minutes, with three stoppages by the way, what did they call it?''

"A Symphony, papa," replied Norah.

"Yes, you darling old Goth, a Symphony by the great Beethoven!" added Magdalen. "How can you say you were not amused? Have you forgotten the yellow-looking foreign woman, with the unpronounceable name? Don't you remember the faces she made when she sang? and the way she curtseyed and curtseyed, till she cheated the foolish people into crying encore? Look here, mamma—look here Miss Garth!"

She snatched up an empty plate from the table, to represent a sheet of music, held it before her in the established concert-room position, and produced an imitation of the unfortunate singer's grimaces and curtseyings, so accurately and quaintly true to the original, that her father roared with laughter; and even the footman (who came in that moment, with the post-bag) rushed out of the room again, and committed the indecorum of echoing his master audibly on the other side of the door.   (8)

The question, of course, is this: which of Beethoven's nine symphonies—and I shall begin (and end) by assuming that Collins really had one of them in mind—did the Vanstones and their footman hear?

Before turning to this question, however, we should place Mr. Vanstone's wonderfully irreverent "review" into the context of Collins's view of Beethoven's music in general, about which Collins expressed himself on at least two other occasions.

On 12 June 1861, just as *No Name* was beginning to take shape in his mind, Collins wrote to his good friend Nina Lehmann, in whose social-intellectual circle (and that of her husband, Frederick) he was a fixture:[4]

In *one* respect only, I have been the worse for the delightful party at Hal-lé's[5]—the "Great Kreutzer Sonata"[6] has upset me about classical music. I am afraid—I don't like classical music after all—I am afraid I am not the Amateur I once thought myself. The whole violin part of "The Great K.S." appeared to me to be the musical expression of a varying and violent stomach-ache, with intervals of hiccups.   (*Letters* 1: 194)

Collins's meaning cuts through the colorful language in unequivocal fashion: he disliked the sonata.

The other reference to Beethoven appears in the novel *Armadale* (1866), where Miss Lydia Gwilt writes to Mrs. Oldershaw: "I have hired a reasonably good piano. The only man I care two straws about—don't be alarmed; he was laid in his grave many a long year ago, under the name of BEETHOVEN—keeps me company in my lonely hours" (162). Now, there are two ways to read this. Though Collins could be paying Beethoven at least faint praise, I would argue quite the contrary, that we must take Miss Gwilt's diabolical character into consideration—she is a murderer, bigamist, thief, and forger—and that Collins is, in effect, finding Beethoven guilty by association.[7] He had, after all, already begun to associate composers with good and evil in *The Woman in White* (1860), where Laura Fairlie, accustomed to having played "lovely old melodies of Mozart" for her true love, the kind and gentle Walter Hartright, performs only "new music of the dexterous, tuneless, florid kind"—that is, music of Robert Schumann and the "modern German school" —for the sinister Sir Percival Glyde (187).[8]

Finally, perhaps there is another reference to Beethoven in the description of the "Nightmare Sonata" that "the great Bootmann" plays in *Miss or Mrs?* (1873). Here, Lady Winwood says to Natalie Graybrooke: " . . . the great Bootmann is playing the Nightmare Sonata in the next room . . . You have only to shut your eyes, and you fancy you hear four modern German composers playing, instead of one, and not a ghost of a melody among the four" (49). Whereupon the narrator adds: "The great Bootmann had arrived at that part of the Nightmare Sonata in which musical sound, produced principally with the left hand, is made to describe, beyond all possibility of mistake, the rising of the moon in a country churchyard, and a dance of Vampires round a maiden's grave" (50). And, as I have suggested elsewhere, while "Bootmann" is an explicit reference to Clara Schumann—BOOT = SHOE = SCHU(H) + MANN—the "Nightmare Sonata" may well be a veiled reference to one of Beethoven's "titled" (after the fact) piano sonatas, specifically the so-called "Tempest," op. 31, no. 2, which Collins could have heard Clara Schumann perform when she included it on her "Popular Concerts" program of 4 February 1867 (Atlas, "Wilkie Collins" 259–60).[9]

In all, while we might, on first reading, take the comments about the unidentified Beethoven symphony in *No Name* as little more than Collins poking fun at Mr. Vanstone's lack of musical culture, I think he (Collins) had something very different in mind: it is Beethoven who is the real butt of the joke. In fact, it is fair to say that Collins simply did not like Beethoven's music, and that it was to Beethoven that he traced the roots of everything that he disliked—lack of tuneful melody, complicated harmonies and textures, instrumental program music, etc.—in the music of the "modern German school," whether Schumann's in the recital hall or Wagner's in the opera house (Atlas, "Wilkie Collins" 258–63, 267–69).[10]

To return to Collins's riddle, then: if Mr. Vanstone is describing a real Beethoven symphony, which one is it? Fortunately, his conversation with Magdalen and Norah provides a number of clues, though at least one of them (about the singer, see below) may have been designed to mislead us. I list them here in the order in which they appear in the final conversation about the concert: the music lasted forty minutes, it stopped three times along the way, they might have wished themselves at Jericho, the music went crash-bang, and there was a female singer. We may consider these clues one by one, now in the order in which, if taken literally (and I shall take them as such), they proceed along a continuum from the seemingly objective to the almost hopelessly subjective.

Clue No. 1. The yellow-looking foreign woman: If Magdalen's reference to the female singer means that she (the singer) participated in the symphony, our game is over, for then the Vanstones can only have heard the Ninth, where, in the final movement, Beethoven set portions of Friedrich Schiller's famous *An die Freude* for chorus and four soloists; it is the only movement in any Beethoven symphony that incorporates voices.

But is that what Magdalen's reference means? Probably not. First, Magdalen never says that the singer appeared in the symphony itself; rather, she mentions the singer in almost footnote-like fashion, changing the subject from Beethoven to that aspect of the concert that she found amusing (the better, of course, to work in her theatrical impersonation). Second, though Beethoven takes the soprano soloist up to what could be a grimace-causing high b'' on three occasions (188/73–74 and 265/79)[11] and gives her a little cadenza-like flourish just before her final shot at that high note (264/73–265/74),[12] neither female solo part (soprano or alto) provides the singer with a real opportunity to milk the audience for an encore, as neither of them (despite their roles as "soloists") ever sings alone. Rather, whatever applause- or encore-producing vocal writing there might be for solo voice turns the spotlight first on the baritone, with his famous recitative-like entrance on "O Freunde, nicht diese Töne" (176/9), and then shifts—though now dimmed a bit—to the tenor's "Froh, froh, wie seine Sonnen fliegen" a few minutes later (197/45). Finally, it seems odd that Collins would offer a clue that pointed to the Ninth Symphony without mentioning its most specific identifying features: the chorus and Schiller's famous "Ode to Joy." In the end, that Magdalen's "curtsey-ing" singer had used the finale of the Ninth to "cheat" her way to an encore is unlikely.[13]

How, then, might the singer with the "unpronounceable name" (surely German or Italian) have participated in the concert? The most reasonable supposition is that she appeared in one of the other pieces on what was no doubt the long (recall that the Vanstones traveled home at 1:30 A.M.) and mixed-bag type of program that was typical at the time, and that often con-sisted of two symphonies, a pair of overtures, some popular opera arias and scenas, possibly a chamber work, and a concerto or two (or at least some movements therefrom).[14] On the other hand, she might even have appeared "within" the symphony without being "part" of it. As Sir George Grove—of

Dictionary fame[15] —recalled in a letter to his friend Frederick George Edwards on 16 January 1895, he had once heard a performance of Beethoven's Sixth Symphony (the "Pastoral") in "those dim old times"—he seems to be referring to a concert that took place in 1838–in which the aria "Hush ye pretty warbling choirs" from Handel's *Acis and Galatea* (1718) was inserted between the second and third movements of the symphony.[16] And though this practice of mutilating Beethoven's—or anyone else's—symphonies died out as the century wore on, the concert that the Vanstones attended occurred only eight years later, and in the "provinces" to boot, where old traditions and entertaining accomodations to the audience might not have passed away without a struggle.[17]

In all, Magdalen's reference to the singer is at best neutral as far as its evidentiary power is concerned: it points neither to nor away from the Ninth.

Clue No. 2. It stopped three times by the way/three stoppages: Here Mr. Vanstone is clearly referring to the pauses or breaks between the movements of the symphony, which, as he notes, were filled by applause (as they still are at times). Typically, the symphony of the late eighteenth and early nineteenth centuries—thus the so-called "classical" symphony cultivated by the likes of Haydn, Mozart, and, more often than not, Beethoven—consisted of four movements, each separated from the other by a definitive break; thus it had what Mr. Vanstone calls "three stoppages." Table I (page 221) offers a synopsis of the number of movements and the breaks between them in each of the nine Beethoven symphonies.

Assuming that Mr. Vanstone tallied up the number of "stoppages" (three) correctly, we may exclude both the Fifth and the Sixth Symphonies, each of which has only two breaks, from among those that he and his daughters might have heard. (The status of the Ninth Symphony is questionable in this respect; see Table I.)

Clue No. 3. The music lasted forty minutes: Though Mr. Vanstone's reference to the duration of the symphony is undoubtedly nothing more than an estimate and his way of telling us that he was bored and thought the piece a lengthy one—at forty minutes it would be one of Beethoven's longer symphonies (see below)—it carries some clout as evidence, as it serves to exclude those symphonies that either far exceed or fall far short of the mark. Table II (page 222) once again lists the nine symphonies, now with the focus on the precise duration of four (in one instance nine) recorded performances of each one.[18]

What does Table II tell us? Bearing in mind that we have already eliminated the Fifth and Sixth Symphonies on the grounds that they had too few "stoppages" (and the Ninth, too, may fall into this category; see Table I), we can now eliminate the Third and Ninth (the latter now definitively) for being too

Table I. Beethoven's nine symphonies, with an indication of the number of movements and breaks between movements in each; | indicates a break between movements; → indicates that one movement leads directly into the next without a break; dates refer to the year in which the work was completed.

No. 1, Op. 21 (1800)	1		2		3		4				
No. 2, Op. 36 (1802)	1		2		3		4				
No. 3, Op. 55 (1803) ("Eroica")	1		2		3		4				
No. 4, Op. 50 (1806)	1		2		3		4				
No. 5, Op. 67 (1808)	1		2		3	→	4				
No. 6, Op. 68 (1808) ("Pastoral")	1		2		3	→	4	→	5		
No. 7, Op. 92 (1812)	1		2		3		4				
No. 8, Op. 93 (1812)	1		2		3		4				
No. 9, Op. 125 (1824) ("Chorale")	1		2		3	?a	4				

a The break between these two movements is less than definitive, both in Beethoven's score and in performance.

long,[19] as well as the First, Second, Fourth, and Eighth for being too short. Only the Seventh, when not cut (as it is drastically on the Strauss recording), hovers rather consistently around Mr. Vanstone's forty-minute mark (though the Bernstein recording is notably longer). Yet even with this seemingly persuasive evidence that Collins's "No Name" symphony might be the Seventh, our game is hardly over.

The timings given in Table II raise a number of questions: (1) how do the performance times listed there for the Seventh Symphony, all but one of which (the 1926 Strauss recording) date from the second half of the twentieth century, compare with what Mr. Vanstone might have experienced at the fictional concert of 1846 (and with what Collins would really have heard up to the time that he was working on *No Name* in 1861–1862)? (2) the performance times listed in Table II represent the sum of the playing time of the individual movements as preserved on sound recordings, and fail to take into account the seconds or perhaps even minutes that kept ticking away during Mr. Vanstone's three applause-filled "stoppages," something that he would surely have done; and (3) all but one of the recordings of the Seventh Symphony listed in Table II offer performances that are more or less faithful to Beethoven's score; thus while Richard Strauss and Bruno Walter omit the customary repeat of the exposition (of the sonata-allegro form—see the explanation in Table II, note *b*) in the first movement (a common enough cut until fairly recently), only Strauss performs major surgery, while none of the recordings dares to repeat an entire movement as an audience-pleasing encore

Table II. Beethoven's nine symphonies and the duration of four (or more) performances of each one, listed from fastest/shortest to slowest/longest, and with reference to conductor and orchestra, date of recording, CD label, and duration. (Orch = Orchestra, Phil = Philharmonic or Philharmonia, Symph = Symphony; an asterisk denotes a performance on "period" instruments, and thus a performance that claims greater authenticity, including matters pertaining to tempo.)

Symphony	Conductor/Orchestra	Date	CD	Duration
No. 1	Furtwängler/Vienna Phil	1956	EMI CDHE 63606	24'52'
	Harnoncourt/Chamber Orch of Europe*	1991	Teldec ZK 75708	26'27
	Giulini/La Scala Phil	1991	SONY SK 48236	27'29"
	Böhm/Vienna Phil	1972	DG 2GX2 439–681	28'03"
No. 2	Monteux/London Symph	1964	London 2LH2 443–479	31'05"
	Wand/NDR Sinfonieorch	1997	RCA 2RC 66458	32'31"
	Harnoncourt/Chamber Orch of Europe*	1991	Teldec ZK 75712	32'41"
	Walter/Columbia Symph	1959	CBS MK 42013	36'11"
No. 3	Savall/Le Concert des Nations*	1997	Astrée ES 9959 AD 070	44'12"
	Bernstein/Vienna Phil	1978	DG 2GX6 423–481	52'29"
	Celibidache/Munich Phil	1987	EMI CDC 56839	55'30"
	Walter/Columbia Symph	1959	SONY S6K 48099	59'46"
No. 4	Karajan/Berlin Phil	1985	DG 2GX5 429–036	30'56"
	Kletzki/Czech Phil Orch	1965	Supraphon 3453	33'15"
	Mravinsky/Leningrad Phil	1955	Praga PR 256–004	34'15"
	Harnoncourt/Chamber Orch of Europe*	1991	Teldec 9031 75714–12	34'24"
No. 5	Reiner/Chicago Symph	1955	RCA VLS 68976	30'21"
	Mengelberg/ Concertgebouw	1937	Telefunken/Legacy 3984–28408–2	30'26"
	Gardiner/Orch Revolutionaire et Romantique*	1994	DG Archiv 2AHR 439–900	31'47"
	Maazel/Vienna Phil	1980	CBS MDK 44783	33'21"
No. 6	Norrington/London Classical Players*	1988	EMI CDC 7 49746 2	40'05"
	Walter/CBS Symph	1959	CBS MK 42012	40'40"
	Cluytens/Vienna Phil	1955	TESTAMEN SBT 1182	41'54"
	Abbado/Vienna Phil	1987	DG 2GMA 445–542	43'44"
No. 7[a]	Richard Strauss/Berlin State Opera Orch	1926	Naxos Historical 8.110–26	32'23"

(1st movement "exposition"[b] not repeated, thus cutting 2'07"; 4th movement cuts 275 measures (244–418 [of total 467]), thus saving about 3'40", in order to fit the entire movement onto one side of a 78 rpm disc; total cut of about 5'47", without which the duration = 38'10")

Table II. (continued)

Symphony	Conductor/Orchestra	Date	CD	Duration
	Walter/Columbia Symph	1959	CBS MK 42013	38'00"
(1st movement "exposition" not repeated, thus lopping off 2'40", duration = 40'40")				
	Norrington/London Classical Players*	1989	EMI D110622	38'21"
	Kleiber/Vienna Phil	1975	Musical Heritage Society 514501M	38'36"
	Hogwood/Academy of Ancient Music*	1989	L'Oiseau-lyre 425 695–2	39'03"
	Thielemann/Philharmonia	1996	DG 449 981–2	39'31"
	Serkin/Marlboro Festival Orch	1975	SONY SMK 45893	40'02"
	Dorati/London Symph	1963	Mercury EH 462 958	40'37"
	Bernstein/Boston Symph	1990	DG 431 768–2	45'13"
No. 8	Hogwood/Academy of Ancient Music*	1989	L'Oiseau-Lyre 425 695–2	24'07"
	Furtwängler/Vienna Phil	1952	EMI CDHE 63606	25'12"
	Böhm/Vienna Phil	1971	DG 2GX2 437–928	26'14"
	Walter/Columbia Symph	1959	CBS MK 42013	26'25"
No. 9	Toscanini/NBC Symph	1944	Legato LCD 136–1	60'21"
	Goodman/Hanover Band*	1988	Nimbus NI5134	65'46"
	Szell/Cleveland Symph	1961	SONY SBK 46533	66'23"
	Furtwängler/Vienna Phil	1951	Orfeo 533001	75'40"

[a] I offer nine timings on the grounds that it is on the Seventh Symphony that we shall soon focus.

[b] The "exposition" is the first part of the "sonata-allegro" form in which the first movement of a classical symphony is generally cast. Its function is to present the basic thematic material of the movement, with the first theme in the "tonic" (or "home key" = stability) and the second theme (assuming a movement in a major key) in the "dominant" (five steps higher = instability). After being repeated, the exposition is followed by the "development" section, which does precisely what its name implies, and the "recapitulation," which brings back the themes of the exposition, but now in the tonic key from beginning to end.

(something that we can easily do ourselves merely by pressing a button). Yet such cuts—especially the lack of attention to repeat signs—and encores were, as we shall see, standard fare in the nineteenth century. Thus without a legacy of mid-nineteenth-century sound recordings, our answers and responses to these problems must remain speculative and somewhat imprecise.

There is, however, a body of evidence that may provide some help: a series of London Philharmonic Society concert programs that Sir George Smart (1776–1867)—the occasional "conductor" of the Society's orchestra from 1813 to 1843—annotated during the period 1819–1843.[20] Among other things, Smart jotted down the duration (inclusive of the breaks between movements) of many of the works that he directed, and has left us two such records for the Beethoven Seventh: 26 February 1821–thirty-five minutes; and 11 March 1833–forty minutes, with the second movement now played twice (hence, one assumes, the additional five minutes).[21] Thus even with "stoppages" thrown in, Smart's 1821 performance (without the encore of the second movement) is only about 3'20" faster than Roger Norrington's, a discrepancy that is not at all out of line with the differences in duration—precisely measured—among the performances listed in Table II. Stated another way: there is a greater difference between Bernstein and any of the other modern recordings than there is between Smart and Norrington. Finally, even were we to add a minute or two of "stoppage" time to the Table II recordings, all but one of them (Bernstein's) still land comfortably around Mr. Vanstone's forty-minute mark. In all, Smart's testimony, tenuous though it is, does nothing to argue against the answer that seems to be taking shape: if we can trust Mr. Vanstone's remark that the work went on for forty minutes, the Seventh Symphony is beginning to look like our best bet.

Clue No. 4. Nothing but Crash-Bang, varied now and then by Bang-Crash/ Jericho: Here, of course, Mr. Vanstone wallows in subjectivity, since one listener's "Crash-Bang" may well be another's "lite-FM."[22] Yet perhaps we can tease some "soft" evidence out of the remark, especially if we change the point of our questioning: instead of continuing to ask "to which symphony does Mr. Vanstone's description point?" we may refocus the question as "is there anything in Mr. Vanstone's description that points away from the Seventh?"

Example 1 provides a short excerpt from the final movement of the Seventh.

Though today we might characterize the passage as energetic, martial, or, since we are dealing with Beethoven, "heroic," we should try to hear it with Mr. Vanstone's mid-nineteenth-century, West Country ears.

Two features of the orchestra that Mr. Vanstone might have heard, as well as the shape and size of the concert hall in which he may have heard the concert, may help to explain both his description of the music as "nothing but crash-bang" and the reference to Jericho.[23] First, a present-day "world class" symphony orchestra will ordinarily have a string section of approximately 65–70 players. Thus the strings of the New York Philharmonic, Philadelphia Orchestra, and Chicago Symphony number sixty-six, sixty-five, and seventy-one, respectively; more specifically, they are constituted as follows in terms of first + second violins, violas, cellos, and double basses: New York—17+17, 12, 11, 9; Philadelphia—17+14, 13, 12, 9; and Chicago—19+17, 14, 12, 9.[24] On the other hand, the Philharmonic Society of London had string sections of only fifty-seven (16+16, 10, 8, 7), fifty-seven again (15+14, 10, 9, 9), and, owing to economic difficulties, as few as forty-eight (12+12, 8, 8, 8) in 1842, 1846, and 1860, respectively.[25] Yet against

Ex. 1. Beethoven, Symphony No. 7, fourth movement, measures 24–32 (later repeated as 235–243).

Ex. 1. Beethoven, Symphony No. 7, fourth movement, measures 24–32 (later repeated as 235–243).

this smaller—significantly so for 1860—complement of strings, a performance of the Beethoven Seventh requires a constant minimum of woodwinds, brass, and percussion: two each of flutes, oboes, clarinets, bassoons, French horns, and trumpets, as well as a set of two timpani. The point should be clear: the orchestra that apparently blared at Mr. Vanstone had a notably different balance of winds/brass/percussion vs. strings than that of a present-day orchestra, one that would likely have made the combined winds, brass, and percussion seem a good deal louder.[26] And since it may well have been a local—thus provincial—orchestra that Mr. Vanstone heard at Clifton in 1846, one, perhaps, with an even smaller string section than we find in London,[27] the horns and trumpets (quite possibly still without valves) may well have struck him as downright raucous.

The timpanist in particular must have made a racket. Although the 1830s saw timpanists on the Continent regularly begin to wrap soft felt around the hard heads of their drumsticks in order to soften the sound, the innovation caught on only slowly in England, and English timpanists continued to use their old wooden-head (or only slightly softer leather-wrapped) mallets for several decades.[28] Played with wooden heads, the timpani's sixteenth-note figures in Ex. 1 do indeed go "bang."[29]

Finally, about the venue in which Mr. Vanstone heard the concert we can say only the following with certainty: it was terribly hot and uncomfortable (see Mr. Vanstone's description, above). Yet perhaps the concert hall also added to Mr. Vanstone's "crash-bang" impressions, though the remarks that follow represent nothing more than my thinking out loud.[30]

Nineteenth-century concert halls, even those that were home to orchestral forces, were often a good deal smaller—particularly in terms of their width—than those to which we are accustomed today. Thus the Altes Gewandhaus in Leipzig (demolished in 1894), where Mendelssohn held forth from 1835 to 1846, was approximately 76 ft. long x 38 ft. wide, while the main concert hall in London's Hanover Square Rooms (opened in 1775 and decorated in part by Gainsborough), where some of Haydn's "London" symphonies were premiered in 1791–1792 and where the Philharmonic Society performed from 1833 to 1869 (it ceased functioning as a concert hall in December 1874), was even more exaggeratedly rectangular at about 95 ft. x 35 ft.[31] By comparison, Avery Fisher Hall at Lincoln Center, home to the New York Philharmonic, measures approximately 200 ft. x 100 ft. (in its 1976 manifestation) (Forsyth 287).

Now, the acoustics of concert halls vary according to a combination of many things, among them (to cite just some of the basics): dimensions (including height), materials (wood, plaster, drapery, etc.), the shape of the walls (straight, concave, with or without niches, etc.), flat vs. sloping floor, and even, at any given performance, the ratio of filled to unfilled seats (and whether the empty seats are padded or not).[32] In general, though, narrow rooms tend to make the music seem loud, as listeners are closer to the sound that is reflected off the side walls, such proximity having an exaggerated effect the louder the orchestra is playing (Forsyth 39–49).[33] Thus, if Mr. Vanstone heard the symphony in a long and exceptionally narrow room, the *fortissimo* passage shown in Example 1 could well have struck him as being "crash-bangish," especially if performed by an orchestra with a small string section, a proportionally large complement of winds and brass (in comparison to the small string section), and wooden-ended timpani sticks (not to mention the further possibility, given the provincial setting, of some less-than-top-notch players). In all, Mr. Vanstone's description of the work does nothing to hurt our notion that it was Beethoven's Seventh that he and his daughters heard.

Another piece of "evidence": We have exhausted Mr. Vanstone's clues. Yet one more observation about the Seventh Symphony may contribute to the argument that it is the symphony that Collins probably had in mind. Table III shows the number of times that each of Beethoven's nine symphonies was performed at the Philharmonic Society from 1846, the date of our fictional concert, to 1862, when Collins published the novel:[34]

Table III. Frequency of performance of the Beethoven symphonies by the Philharmonic Society, London, 1846–1862 (1846–1855 = eight concerts per season; 1856–1860 = six concerts; 1861 = eight concerts; 1862 = nine concerts).

	'46	'47	'48	'49	'50	'51	'52	'53	'54	'55	'56	'57	'58	'59	'60	'61	'62		
No. 1	x			x				x							x	x		=	5
No. 2		x		x			x	x	x			x		x		x		=	8
No. 3	x	x		x		x	x	x^a	x	x			x		x	x	x	=	13
No. 4	x		x	x	x	x	x	x	x	x	x		x	x		x	x	=	14
No. 5	x	x	x	x	x	x	x	x	x	x	x	x	x	x	x	x	x	=	17
No. 6	x	x	x	x	x	x	x	x	x	x	x	x	x	x	x	x	x	=	17
No. 7	x	x	x	x	x	x	x	x	x	x	x	x	x	x	x	x	x	=	17
No. 8	x	x	x	x	x	x	x	x	x	x		x	x		x	x	x	=	15
No. 9		x		x		x					x				x			=	4

a Performed twice that season.

The Seventh, then, was one of only three Beethoven symphonies performed year in-year out. Nor was its popularity short-lived, for over the course of the Philharmonic Society's first one hundred years, the Seventh proved to be the third most popular of Beethoven's symphonies, its sixty-five performances superceded only by the sixty-nine performances of the Sixth and the seventy-seven of the Fifth (Foster 531). Thus based on the assumption that London's favorite Beethoven symphonies maintained their popularity in the hinterlands, and with the Fifth and Sixth Symphonies out of the running (too few "stoppages"), perhaps sheer statistical probability also points to the Seventh as the symphony that the Vanstones most likely heard at Clinton on the evening of 3 March 1846.

Summing up: That I have offered an answer—and a confident one at that—to Collins's riddle raises three questions, the first of which has been simmering throughout the paper: whose game have we been playing, Collins's or mine? Did Collins really have a specific Beethoven symphony in mind? Obviously, I think the answer is yes! Why else would he have described the piece in as much "detail" as he did? After all, Collins often referred to music in a way that can best be described as "non-committal." Two examples will suffice. In Chapter 10 of *No Name,* Magdalen "trifle[s] away half an hour at the piano; and play[s], in that time, selections from the Songs of Mendelssohn, the Mazurkas of Chopin, the Operas of Verdi, and the Sonatas of Mozart . . . " (69), a description so lacking in detail that it prevents the kind of game that we have been playing here from even getting started; we cannot even begin to guess which mazurkas, operas, or sonatas Magdalen performed. In *Poor Miss Finch* (1872), Madame Pratolungo plays the piano and says: "I played my best. From Mozart to Beethoven. From Beethoven to Schubert. From Schubert to Chopin" (26). Here Collins is even less informative: is Madame Pratolungo playing Mozart sonatas or variations, Chopin mazurkas or waltzes or nocturnes? There is no way of knowing, and there is no game to play. On other occasions, however, Collins is absolutely precise, naming both composers and specific compositions.[35] In fact, the description of the Beethoven symphony in *No Name* seems to be unique in Collins's work: while it stops short of identifying a specific composition by its title, it goes far beyond the non-specific references to the pieces played by Magdalen and Madame Pratolungo.[36]

The second question: why the Seventh? From the point of view of presenting the reader with a game, the Seventh is in some respects singular among Beethoven's nine symphonies: it is at once both anonymous and identifiable. For instance, references to Schiller/chorus or Bonaparte/hero/funeral march would have been dead giveaways to the Ninth and Third Symphonies, respectively. Likewise, had Mr. Vanstone told us that the symphony had only two "stoppages," he would immediately have narrowed the field to the Fifth and Sixth (see Table I), with the latter even more easily identified by means of the extra-musical ("programmatic") references that appear at the head of each movement. Finally, given Collins's lack of sophistication with respect to music and its terminology— Dickens, after all, implied that he was tone deaf[37]—he would probably not have been able to offer sophisticated-enough clues to enable the reader to distinguish between the First, Second, and Fourth Symphonies, all of which have three "stoppages," tend to run within a few minutes of one another in terms of duration, lack explicit extra-musical references, and, without a movement comparably popular to the second movement of the Seventh, never quite endeared themselves to audiences to the extent that the Seventh did (see Table III). The riddle might well have been insoluble.

Yet perhaps there is another reason that Collins chose the Seventh Symphony. In assigning the name Magdalen to his main character, Collins was surely alluding to the Mary Magdalen of the New Testament, who, like Collins's protagonist, had led a wayward life before finding salvation.[38] Now to the extent that the myth of Mary Magdalen can be associated with a numerical attribute, that number is *seven*. Thus, as we read in Mark 16:9 and Luke 8:2, respectively: "Now when Jesus was risen early the first day of the week, he appeared first to Mary Magdalene, out of whom he had cast seven devils," and " . . . Mary called Magdalene, out of whom went seven devils." In addition, the number appears again in the account of her entombment at Ephesus, where her sepulchre was said to have been placed near the entrance to a grotto known as the Cave of the Seven Sleepers (Haskins 107). Moreover, we should not overlook Mr. Vanstone's reference to Jericho, the biblical description of which is saturated with the number seven: "And seven priests shall bear before the ark seven trumpets of rams' horns: and the seventh day ye shall compass the city seven times, and the priests shall blow with the trumpets" (Joshua 6:4). Is all this sheer coincidence, or was Collins aware of and quite intentionally playing with the number seven: Magdalen, Jericho, and the Beethoven symphony? And is there, then, already at the very beginning of the novel, something slightly "wayward" about Magdalen Vanstone's obvious appreciation of the Seventh Symphony? Is this, together with her name, an early hint about her character? I should like to think that Collins knew exactly what he was doing. He usually did!

Finally, if Collins really had the Seventh Symphony in mind, why did he not identify it himself? I can think of two reasons, one from a point of view shared by Magdalen and Norah Vanstone, the other a function of Collins's purpose in referring to the work in the first place. Having described the music as best he could, Mr. Vanstone asks his daughters the following question: "what did they call it?" I take this to mean that, given his naiveté with respect to classical music, Mr. Vanstone was innocently asking what "kind of piece" had they heard, that is, to what genre did it belong. And knowing that their father was an "old Goth," Magdalen and Norah no doubt thought the better of going into detail: enough to say that it was "a Symphony by the great Beethoven!" (and even this is generous when measured by the proverbial present-day standard: "where are you going?" . . . "out!").

As for Collins: whether readers identified the symphony as the Seventh—or even asked the question (and I rather doubt that many have, whether in

Collins's time or in our own)—was probably of little importance. For Collins, I think, had two aims in mind: to poke some gentle fun at the cultural philistinism of Mr. Vanstone and his ilk, and, no less important, to take a swipe at Beethoven, with whom, as I noted above, Collins seemed to associate much of what he disliked in "modern" music. And in the end, Collins's strategy is brilliant in its economy: with one fell swoop, and without being obvious or going into more detail than needed to get a laugh, he snickers at the Mr. Vanstones of his time, sneers at Beethoven, and provides a wonderful little game for those of his readers who wish to play it.

NOTES

1. Serial publication in *All the Year Round* began on 15 March 1862; the first three-volume edition was published in December of that year by Sampson Low; all references are to the World's Classics paperback edition.
2. I assume that the reference to Clifton is to what was already the fashionable suburb of Bristol.
3. There is, in fact, another allusion to the concert involving Thomas and Miss Garth between what I am calling the second and third references; however, it offers no information about the music.
4. Though *Letters* dates the letter unequivocally from 1861, Catherine Peters assigns it more generally to "[1860–62]" (470). We might note that the Lehmanns were themselves fine amateur musicians—Nina a pianist, Frederick a violinist—and may have served as models after whom Collins fashioned Julius and Mrs. Delamayn, who play Mozart sonatas for violin and piano in *Man and Wife* (1870); on this point, see Atlas, "Wilkie Collins" (258).
5. Sir Charles Hallé (1819–1895), conductor-pianist who emigrated to England in 1848, settled in Manchester, and, in 1858, inaugurated that city's famous "Hallé Concerts," which enjoyed an unbroken run of thirty-seven years; for a thumbnail sketch of his career, see Kennedy, "Hallé, Sir Charles" (10: 704–5); and, at greater length, Kennedy, *The Hallé Tradition*.
6. Beethoven's Sonata No. 9 for Violin and Piano, op. 47.
7. I take this position in "Wilkie Collins" (261). I know of only one other reference to the Lydia Gwilt-Beethoven relationship, Edmund Yates's rather non-committal " . . . the devotion to Beethoven of Lydia Gwilt," (532); reprinted in Page (277).
8. I discuss this opposition between Mozart and the "moderns" as one between good and evil in "Wilkie Collins" (267); for further commentary on music in *The Woman in White,* see Losseff, as well as Weliver (99–112).
9. Collins probably derived the Bootmann = Schumann equation from Henry F. Chorley, the influential music critic for the *Athenaeum,* whose nickname for Clara Schumann was the "shoewoman"; on Chorley, see Bledsoe.
10. Robinson, *Wilkie Collins,* also recognizes Collins's dislike of Beethoven: "Neither did he apparently appreciate Beethoven" (156).

11. Page/measure numbers refer to the easily available Edition Eulenburg miniature score, No. 411; *b''* is a half-step beneath what is usually referred to as a soprano's "high C."

12. To a certain extent, the effect of the soprano's flourish in terms of making an impression upon the audience is negated by its being taken up immediately by the other soloists one after another; thus Beethoven permits all four soloists to "show off" as it were.

13. I must confess that Magdalen's reference to the singer did lead me to suggest, on two earlier occasions, that we could be dealing with the Ninth Symphony: "Wilkie Collins" (261); and "Musical References" (18); in both instances, I qualified the suggestion with a question mark.

14. To cite but one example that may stand for many: on 16 March 1846 (thus just two weeks after the fictional concert in *No Name*), the Philharmonic Society orchestra of London, under the direction of its new conductor, Michael Costa, presented the following program:

PART I

SYMPHONY IN B FLAT (No. 9 [= No. 102])	*Haydn*
ARIA, "O cara immagine" (Il Flauto Magico)	*Mozart*
MR. RAFTER	
CONCERTO for Violin in G (No. 11)	*Spohr*
MR. PROSPER SAINTON	
TRIO, "Ti prego"	*Curschmann*[a]
MISSES ANNE and MARTHA WILLIAMS and MR. RAFTER	
OVERTURE, "Oberon"	*Weber*

PART II

SYMPHONY IN E FLAT (No. 3), "Eroica"	*Beethoven*
DUET, "Quis est homo" (Stabat Mater)	*Rossini*
MISSES A. and M. WILLIAMS	
OVERTURE, "Les Deux Journées"	*Cherubini*
Conductor, MR. COSTA	

[a]Karl Friedrich Curschmann (1805–1841)

Cited after Foster (195). Although this type of "miscellany" concert (as it is often called), which had its origins in the late eighteenth century, gradually fell by the wayside during the second half of the nineteenth, it was still frequent enough at century's end to draw the wrath of George Bernard Shaw, who put it as follows on 16 November 1890: "There are few things more terrible to a seasoned musician than a miscellaneous concert . . . [T]he old-fashioned 'grand concert', with an overture here, a scena there, and a ballad or an instrumental solo in between is insufferable . . . " (1: 80); see also Weber.

For general surveys of music in nineteenth-century London, see Temperley, ed., *The Romantic Age*; Temperley, ed., *The Lost Chord*; Sachs; Caldwell; and the excellent series edited by Zon, *Nineteenth-Century British Music Studies*.

15. Grove (1820–1900) first published his four-volume *A Dictionary of Music and Musicians* in 1879–1889; after going through five editions up to 1954, Macmillan (which had published both the original work and all subsequent editions) issued a completely new (from top to bottom), twenty-volume version in 1980 as *The New Grove Dictionary of Music and Musicians* (sometimes called *Grove/6*); a second, revised edition, *New Grove/2*, appeared in 2001.

16. See Young (235).

17. In part, the abandonment of such interpolations came about through a change in the overall shape and dynamic of the symphony itself, as, by mid-century, composers were cultivating the so-called "cyclic" symphony, an organically-unified work in which close thematic relationships across all the movements and the frequent succession of those movements one after another without a break would have made such interpolations downright ludicrous, if not impossible.

18. I should emphasize that the table makes absolutely no pretense of showing historical trends (long- or short-term) with respect to either tempo or duration, something for which we would need a sample that is both far more complete and a good deal wider in its chronological span. (For example, as of September 2000, there were 147 recordings of the Seventh Symphony in print; see *PhonoLog*, 279A-280B.) Rather, it is intended solely to give an idea of approximately how long we might expect a performance of each symphony to run. In addition, the CDs included in the sample were chosen at random on the basis of both easy accessibility and, in most instances, their display of performance durations on the outside of the back cover. My thanks to Mr. Lawrence Shuster, a doctoral candidate in music at The Graduate Center, The City University of New York, for his help in compiling the table. For research that begins to develop methods for using recordings to study long-term trends about tempo and duration, see, especially, Bowen, "Tempo," "Finding."

19. Note, however, that the Savall recording listed in Table II gets through the "Eroica" in under forty-five minutes.

20. On Smart, see Husk and Temperley. What follows is based on Temperley, "Tempo"; unfortunately, *Leaves from the Journals of Sir George Smart* (Cox and Cox) sheds no further light on the matter. We should note that Smart did not quite "conduct" in the modern sense of the term; rather, following eighteenth-century traditions, which wore off a bit more slowly in England than they did on the Continent, he would have done what "conducting" he did from a keyboard instrument, sharing the duties of directing the orchestra with the head of the first violins (the modern concertmaster); on the transition to the modern concept of the conductor, see Galkin (437–520); for a concise summary, see Botstein. In England, the tradition of the conductor who took full responsibility for all aspects of the performance began only in 1846, when the Philharmonic Society appointed Sir Michael Costa as conductor and gave him full control over the orchestra.

21. That the repeat of the second movement added but five minutes to Smart's timing either speaks for an extremely brisk tempo for that movement or may imply that Smart is failing to tell us about a cut or series of cuts made elsewhere in the work. (Among the recordings of the Seventh Symphony listed in Table II, the

second movement runs from about 7'30'' to 9'30''.) The nineteenth-century tradition of repeating the second movement goes back to the very first performances
of the work at Vienna on 8 and 12 December 1813; see Thayer (566).

22. Though we often use the term "crash" with reference to the crashing of cymbals,
    that cannot be what Mr. Vanstone had in mind. Beethoven used cymbals (*piatti*)
    only once in his symphonies: in the "Alla marcia" section of the fourth move-
    ment of the Ninth (194/1), which we have securely eliminated owing to its length.

23. The reference, of course, is to Joshua 6: 4–20, where the walls of Jericho fall
    owing to the "trumpets of rams' horns" and the shouting of the people (see
    below).

24. The numbers reflect the rosters of the three orchestras for their 2001–2002 sea-
    sons, and appear on their "official" websites: *www.nyphilharmonic.org*,
    www.philorch.org, and *www.chicagosymphony.org*.

25. The figures for 1842 and 1846 are taken from Koury (154); those for 1860 appear
    in Ehrlich (267).

26. With their philosophy of performing the music of the Baroque, Classical, and
    even early- to mid-Romantic periods as they believe it would have sounded to
    contemporaries, our present-day "period" orchestras—represented in Table II
    by the likes of the Academy of Ancient Music, the London Classical Players,
    and the Hanover Band—will, among other things, employ a string section that
    is, in terms of size, appropriate to the period in question. (For his recording of
    the "Eroica," Jordi Savall uses a string section of eighteen violins [10 + 8], six
    violas, five cellos, and three double basses, all outfitted with gut strings; see the
    notes that accompany the Savall recording listed in Table II.) And even the major
    symphony orchestras, when moved—or perhaps intimidated—by the spirit of
    "politically (musicologically) correct" performance practice, will do the same.
    As far as I can tell, however, none of the performances by the major symphony
    orchestras listed in Table II do so.

27. We might note that in 1850 the entire orchestra for Manchester's Gentlemen's
    Concerts consisted of only forty players; see Koury (161). On the other hand,
    orchestras could be considerably expanded on special occasions, and perhaps
    Collins's reference to the concert attended by the Vanstones as "described at the
    top of the bills as Grand" (see above) suggests just such an occasion.

28. See Bowles, "The Double" (424–26); Bowles, "The Timpani" (203–04).

29. Among the recordings of the Seventh Symphony listed in Table II, that by
    Norrington/London Classical Players, with its combination of small timpani
    struck by hard sticks (according to the record notes), probably comes closest to
    approximating what Mr. Vanstone might have heard in this respect.

30. Though I cannot be certain about the venue that Collins might have had in mind,
    perhaps, if my identification of Clifton as the suburb of Bristol is correct (see
    note 2), we may imagine that the concert took place either in the New Assembly
    Room, which opened in 1811, or the Victoria Rooms, which opened in 1842; see
    Matthews et al. (4: 360).

31. In both cases, the length includes the platform on which the orchestra was placed.
    For a diagram of the Altes Gewandhaus, see Forsyth (61, 63). The dimensions

reported for the Hanover Square Rooms vary from one source to another depending on whether pre- or post-renovation dimensions are being cited: originally
79 ft. x 32 ft., it eventually grew to the length and width noted above; for diagrams
and discussion, see Forsyth (39, 339); Lewcock et al. (1: 92); Koury (328); Nettel
(173); Landon (29). For an often-reproduced illustration of the interior of the
concert hall as it looked in 1843 (after the *Illustrated London News),* see Forsyth
(37); Musgrave (15: 137); Carse (161). I do not know the dimensions of either
the New Assembly Room or the Victoria Rooms at Clinton, though the latter
could seat between 450 and 750 depending upon the configuration of the stage
(my thanks to Dr. Lesley Mason, University of Bristol, for this information).

32. Forsyth, passim, is a particularly reader-friendly account of the subject, especially
for those like myself without formidable skills in physics and mathematics.

33. This is not to equate such acoustics with poor acoustics. In fact, in a classic
survey, both orchestral conductors and professional music critics, when asked to
identify those concert halls with the best and worst acoustics, consistently favored
small over large and narrow over wide; the preference for narrow over wide has
to do largely with what is called "initial-time-delay gap," as narrow halls minimize the difference (measured in milliseconds) in time between direct (from the
performer) and reflected (from the walls) sound; see Beranek.

34. The statistics are derived from Foster (193–273).

35. For a list of works from both the classical and the vernacular traditions to which
Collins refers specifically, see my "Musical References" (18–24).

36. One of the most interesting of Collins's citations is the reference to the "Air in
A, with Variations," which Mrs. Lucy Crawford plays for Clara Burnham in *The
Frozen Deep* (1874). After identifying the work as being by Mozart and praising
it as "unrivalled," Collins continues: "At the close of the *ninth* variation . . . (my
italics)." Though I have suggested that this was an absent-minded reference to
the first movement of Mozart's well-known Sonata in A, K. 331 (which has only
five variations—see Atlas, "Wilkie Collins" (265), it more likely refers, as Losseff has shown with a stunning piece of detective work, to a similarly titled
composition by the now largely-forgotten Emanuel Aloys Förster (1748–1823),
which, however, circulated widely during the nineteenth century under Mozart's
name (the work is listed as K. Anhang C 26.06 in Köchel (896–97); see Losseff
(539).

Perhaps further support for my contention that Collins had a specific symphony
in mind in *No Name* is suggested by the meticulous attention to detail seen in
connection with other aspects of the work. Thus he wrote to his friend Charles
Ward on at least two occasions in order to ask about such matters as the precise
day of the week on which 4 March fell in 1846 (letter of 11 September 1861)
and the frequency and speed of mail between England and China (letter of 17
March 1862); see *Letters* (1: 202, 205). Collins left few if any such matters
to chance.

37. See Dickens's letter of 21 November 1853 to his wife in *The Letters of Charles
Dickens* (7: 203–05).

38. As noted by Blain in her notes to the World's Classics edition (549); Collins
returns to this allusion in the title of a later work, *The New Magdalen* (1873),

where the "fallen" woman is the one-time prostitute Mercy Merrick. For a discussion of the Magdalen myth in both novels, see Haskins (335–39).

WORKS CITED

Atlas, Allan W. "Musical References in the Works of Wilkie Collins: An Inventory." *The New Collins Society Newsletter* 3/1 (Winter 2000): 15–24.

———. "Wilkie Collins on Music and Musicians." *Journal of the Royal Musical Association* 124 (1999): 255–70.

Beranek, Leo L. "Rating of Acoustical Quality of Concert Halls and Opera Houses," in *Architectural Acoustics. Benchmark Papers in Acoustics*. Vol. 10. Ed. Thomas D. Northwood. Stroudsberg, PA: Dowden, Hutchison & Ross, 1977.

Bledsoe, Robert Terrell. *Henry Fothergill Chorley: Victorian Journalist*. Aldershot: Ashgate, 1998.

Botstein, Leon. "Conducting—§2: History Since 1820." *The New Grove Dictionary of Music and Musicians*. 2nd rev. ed. Ed. John Tyrrell and Stanley Sadie. London: Macmillan, 2001. 264–67 (hereafter *New Grove/2*).

Bowen, José Antonio. "Tempo, Duration, and Flexibility: Techniques in the Analysis of Performance," *Journal of Musicological Research* 16 (1996): 111–56.

———. "Finding the Music in Musicology: Performance History and Musical Works." *Rethinking Music*. Ed. Nicholas Cook and Mark Everist. Oxford: Oxford UP, 1999. 424–51.

Bowles, Edmund A. "The Double, Double, Double Beat of the Thundering Drum: The Timpani in Early Music." *Early Music* 19 (1991): 419–35.

———. "The Timpani and their Performance (Fifteenth to Twentieth Centuries): An Overview." *Performance Practice Review* 10 (1997): 193–203.

Caldwell, John. *The Oxford History of English Music: c. 1715 to the Present Day*. Vol. 2 Oxford: Oxford UP, 1999.

Carse, Adam. *The Orchestra from Beethoven to Berlioz: A History of the Orchestra in the First Half of the 19th Century, and the Development of Orchestra Baton-Conducting*. Cambridge: Heffer & Sons, 1948.

Collins, Wilkie. *Armadale*. 1866. Ed. John Sutherland. New York: Penguin, 1995.

———. *Miss or Mrs?* 1873. Stroud: Alan Sutton, 1993.

———. *No Name*. 1862. Ed. Virginia Blain. Oxford: Oxford UP, 1986.

————. *Poor Miss Finch.* 1872. Ed. Catherine Peters. Oxford: Oxford UP, 1995.

————. *The Woman in White.* 1860. Ed. Julian Symons. New York: Penguin, 1974.

————. *The Letters of Wilkie Collins.* Ed. William Baker and William M. Clarke. London: Macmillan, 1999.

Cox, H. Bertram and C.L.E. Cox. *Leaves from the Journals of Sir George Smart.* London: Longmans, Green, 1907.

Dickens, Charles. *The Letters of Charles Dickens.* Vol. 7. Ed. Madeline House, Graham Storey, and Kathleen Tillotson. Oxford: Clarendon, 1993.

Ehrlich, Cyril. *First Philharmonic: A History of the Royal Philharmonic Society.* Oxford: Clarendon Press, 1995.

Forsyth, Michael. *Buildings for Music: The Architect, the Musician, the Listener from the Seventeenth Century to the Present Day.* Cambridge: Cambridge UP, 1985.

Foster, Myles Birket. *History of the Philharmonic Society of London: 1813–1912.* London: John Lane, 1912.

Galkin, Elliott W. *A History of Orchestral Conducting in Theory and Practice.* New York: Pendragon Press, 1988.

Haskins, Susan. *Mary Magdelen: Myth and Metaphor.* New York: Harcourt Brace, 1993.

Husk, W.H. and Nicholas Temperley, "Smart. English family of musicians." *New Grove/2.* Vol. 23. 533–34.

Kennedy, Michael. *The Hallé Tradition.* Manchester: Manchester UP, 1960.

————. "Hallé, Sir Charles." in *New Grove/2.* Vol. 10. 704–5.

Köchel, Ludwig Ritter von. *Chronologisch-thematisches Verzeichnis sämtliche Tonwerke Wolfgang Amadé Mozarts.* 6th ed. Ed. Franz Giegling, Alexander Weimann, and Gerd Sievers. Wiesbaden: Breitkopf und Härtel, 1964.

Koury, Daniel J. *Orchestral Performance Practices in the Nineteenth Century: Size, Proportions, and Seating.* Ann Arbor: UMI Research Press, 1986.

Landon, H.C. Robbins. *Haydn in England.* Bloomington: Indiana UP, 1976.

Lewcock, Ronald, Rijn Pirn, Jürgen Meyer. "Acoustics—§1, 10: Room Acoustics: 18th and 19th Centuries." *New Grove/2.* Vol. 1. 88–93.

Losseff, Nicky. "Absent Melody and 'The Woman in White'." *Music and Letters* 81 (2000): 532–50.

Matthews, Betty, Ian Stephens, Jill Tucker, John Snelson. "Bristol." *New Grove/2.* Vol. 4. 360.

Musgrave, Michael. "London (i), §VI,2 (i): Concert Life, 1800–1850." *New Grove/ 2.* Vol. 15. 137–41.

Nettel, Reginald. *The Orchestra in England: A Social History.* London: J. Cape, 1956.

Page, Norman. *Wilkie Collins: The Critical Heritage.* London: Routledge, 1974.

Peters, Catherine. *The King of Inventors: A Life of Wilkie Collins.* Princeton: Princeton UP, 1991.

Phonolog 18 (September 2000).

Robinson, Kenneth. *Wilkie Collins: A Biography.* New York: Macmillan, 1952.

Sachs, Joel. "London: The Professionalization of Music." *The Early Romantic Era, Between Revolutions: 1789 and 1848.* Ed. Alexander Ringer. Englewood Cliffs: Prentice Hall, 1990, 201–35.

Shaw, George Bernard. *Music in London, 1890–1894.* 2 vols. London: Constable, 1932.

Temperley, Nicholas. "Tempo and Repeats in the Early Nineteenth Century." *Music and Letters* 47 (1966): 323–38.

————, ed. *The Romantic Age, 1800–1914.* London: Athlone, 1981.

————, ed. *The Lost Chord: Essays on Victorian Music.* Bloomington: Indiana UP, 1989.

Thayer, Alexander Wheelock. *Thayer's Life of Beethoven.* Rev. and ed. Elliot Forbes. Princeton: Princeton UP, 1967.

Weber, William, "Miscellany vs. Homogeneity: Concert Programmes at the Royal Academy of Music and the Royal College of Music in the 1880s," in *Music and British Culture, 1785–1914: Essays in Honour of Cyril Ehrlich.* Ed. Christina Bashford and Leanne Langley. Oxford: Oxford UP, 2000: 299–320.

Weliver, Phyllis. *Women Musicians in Victorian Fiction, 1860–1900: Representations of Music, Science and Gender in the Leisured Home.* Aldershot: Ashgate, 2000.

Yates, Edmund. "The Novels of Wilkie Collins." *Temple Bar* 89 (August 1890): 528–32.

Young, Percy. *George Grove, 1820–1900.* London: Macmillan, 1980.

Zon, Bennett. ed. *Nineteenth-Century British Music Studies,* 3 vols. Aldershot: Ashgate, 1999–.

A Survey of Bibliographical and Textual Studies of Dickens's Works

Duane DeVries

This survey of bibliographical and textual studies of Dickens's works is based on the introduction to my forthcoming General Studies of Charles Dickens and His Writings and Collected Editions of His Works: An Annotated Bibliography. *Volume I:* Bibliographies, Catalogues, and Bibliographical and Textual Studies. *Offered as both a history of Dickensian bibliography and an evaluative guide to research, it examines bibliographies of Dickens's works; bibliographical studies; bibliographies and surveys of translations, readings, dramatic adaptations, plagiarisms and imitations, and illustrations; bibliographies of Dickens studies; library catalogues, catalogues of Dickens collections, and guides to collections; exhibition catalogues; auction and booksellers' catalogues; and studies of manuscripts and textual changes and Dickens at work. A great deal of important work has been done in the field of bibliographical and textual studies over the century and a third since Dickens's death, but much of it is inevitably outdated, and some of the basic bibliographical work needs to be done on Dickens's minor works. With the approach of the bicentennial of Dickens's birth in 2012, it is an appropriate time for younger scholars—and older ones, too—to reevaluate, revise, and update the bibliographical work that has been done and, in the field of textual studies, to continue to work with the number plans, memoranda, manuscripts, and printed texts to provide a better understanding of Dickens's genius for a new century.*

I have three purposes in surveying bibliographical and textual studies of Dickens's works. The first is to provide something of a history of Dickensian bibliography, though not all of the sections that follow are amenable to this approach. I also want to aid students and researchers of Dickens's works by sometimes indicating how to proceed in using the bibliographies and other guides and studies listed here, and sometimes revealing which of these studies are more important and more useful than others. On the other hand, I do not mean to prevent the future bibliographer, or the researcher, for that matter, from searching every nook and cranny of my bibliography. For the mind so swayed, this can be infinitely pleasurable, but for the researcher it can also be valuable, even necessary. The slightest reference may contain just the information needed or generate the spark that will flame into a major discovery or insight. The third purpose is equally important: to stress the value and significance of bibliographical and textual work. Too often it is seen—even, disturbingly, in academic settings—as second-rate scholarship, inferior to literary criticism. It is never that. Bibliographical and textual investigation is where all other scholarly and critical work must begin. Without it, criticism rests on weak or nonexistent foundations, producing brilliant flights of fantasy, perhaps, but nothing more than that. In Dickens's case, bibliographical and textual work establishes both canon and text, or, more frequently, text and its variants, upon which criticism can build. Through studies of manuscript, number plans and memoranda, and proofs, it deals with basic craftsmanship, development of techniques and insight, the importance of influence, and the nature of artistry and genius. Catalogues of collections, auction sales, and booksellers provide an accumulation of materials (manuscripts, letters, documents, relics, and other literary and personal artifacts) that biographers and critics will find essential and that will uncover the richness of a life and a career. Bibliographies of studies of the author's life and works will help to place a critics work in historical perspective, provide a foundation for his or her work, reveal past critical dead ends, and suggest new approaches.

A survey such as this one is will be selective, necessarily, focused on the broad picture rather than the details. The reader who wants to jump headfirst into the sea of bibliographical and textual scholarship on Dickens will want to consult my forthcoming bibliography, *General Studies of Charles Dickens and His Writings and Collected Editions of His Works: An Annotated Bibliography*. Volume I: *Bibliographies, Catalogues, Collections, and Bibliographical and Textual Studies* (8), which is scheduled for publication in 2003 by AMS Press. This survey is based on the introduction to that volume, and the user will find that the bibliography's roughly 2,500 entries form a big sea indeed. This survey is more modest, with its 562 entries listed in the "Works Cited" section at the end.

Bibliographies of Dickens's Works

The bibliography of Dickens's works that John Forster appended to the third volume of his biography of Dickens (14), published in December 1873, three and a half years after Dickens's death, was the first serious effort to catalogue information about the publication of Dickens's works. Forster lists Dickens's writings year by year, beginning with *Sketches by Boz*, and including all separately published works. He indicates as well the monthly and weekly serial publication of the novels and nonfictional works, Dickens's contributions to the Christmas numbers of *Household Words* and *All the Year Round* (but not his journalistic pieces in these two weekly magazines), and some details about the volumes published in the Cheap Edition, the Library Edition, the "Authorized French Translation of the Works of Dickens," and the Charles Dickens Edition of the collected works, all published in Dickens's lifetime. Generally speaking, Forster gets the basic details of publication correct, though his listing of lesser works is not complete, useful details are lacking, and there are some errors.

James Cook's *Bibliography of the Writings of Charles Dickens* (4), published in 1879, the next serious attempt at a bibliography of Dickens's works, was quite detailed for its time. Cook obviously used Forster's bibliography, for he points out that he lists Dickens's chief works separately from the "minor and miscellaneous productions," to avoid the "strictly chronological arrangement observed" by Forster. But he indicates that, nevertheless, he made his compilation "with the aid of a set of various Works as they were originally published, in parts or volumes." If Forster's intent was essentially informational, Cook's was to provide "necessary" particulars for "the Bibliophilist or Collector," a new personage already on the scene only nine years after Dickens's death. Cook's annotations thus needed to be more detailed than Forster's. For example, he frequently quotes information about the writing of a work from Dickens's prefaces, and, where Forster merely noted the original illustrators of the novels, Cook includes much information about the original illustrations, additional plates that were made, and extra illustrations published later, matters that would particularly interest a collector.

Where bibliographical details rather than collecting points are concerned, Cook also modifies and expands upon Forster. He itemizes the *Household Words* and *All the Year Round* articles that Dickens collected in *Reprinted Pieces* (1858) and the three series of *The Uncommercial Traveller* (1861, 1866, 1875 [posthumously]) and devotes a separate section to the Christmas Books. Cook also includes separate sections on *Household Words* and *All the Year Round*. In addition, he provides much bibliographical information about the collected editions that Dickens published in his lifetime (he even itemizes the volumes in the Cheap Edition and the Charles Dickens Edition) and several published after 1870—the Household Edition (1871–79), the Illustrated Library Edition (1873–76), the Shilling series (1877), the Sixpenny series (1878), and the Popular Library Edition (then in process of publication), all by Chapman and Hall. He lists several minor works not mentioned by Forster—the early play *Is She His Wife?* (1837); ''In Memoriam,'' Dickens's eulogy for Thackeray (1864); the Mudfog Papers from *Bentley's Miscellany* (1837–38; first collected 1880); the prologue to J. Westland Marston's *The Patrician's Daughter* (1842); and the introduction to Adelaide Anne Procter's *Legends and Lyrics* (1866)—as well as the People's Edition of Dickens's works (1865), a reissue of the Cheap Edition in green paper boards.

The bibliographical work of Richard H. Shepherd received mixed reviews from his contemporaries. But his 1880 *Bibliography of Dickens* (20) is a full-scale attempt to establish the basic details of Dickens's works. This bibliography appeared in various stages of minor revision through 1885, principally in sections not involving Shepherd's list of Dickens's printed works, a list that remained pretty constant through the 1882 and 1884 revisions. The Dickens House, London, has a copy of the 1880 edition with corrections written into it by A. Wallis, with an introduction in his hand, as unfair as it is vehement, criticizing Shepherd as ''one of those literary ghouls who thrive best upon dead authors'' and complaining that the bibliography is ''of not the least value to anyone above the rank of a mere novice.'' The bibliography would nevertheless hold its own for many years thereafter. Because of its fuller listing of Dickens's works and editions of them published in Dickens's lifetime and because of its greater supply of details about those works, it is much more informative than the bibliographies of Forster and Cook. It contains, for example, the earliest attempt to list the original publication of the early writings that Dickens collected as *Sketches by Boz*, missing only nine of sixty. Shepherd also identifies several additional minor works for the first time.

Shepherd's bibliography contained three other sections—Letters, Speeches, and Ana (reviews of Dickens's works and biographical and critical studies)—all of which he updated in the revised versions. The first two volumes of *The Letters of Charles Dickens*, edited by Georgina Hogarth and Mamie Dickens (560), were published in London by Chapman and Hall in November 1879, just a few months prior to Shepherd's bibliography, and he had time to list the letters in it, note a number not included, and compile a four-page list of errata for the two volumes. In subsequent editions, he omitted the list of letters in the *Hogarth-Dickens Letters*, but included a revised list of published and unpublished letters *not* found there, though he entirely ignored excerpts from Dickens's letters published in Forster's *Life of Dickens*. He accompanied this list with a legitimate complaint that few of the errors noted in his first edition had been corrected in a two-volume revised edition of the letters published in 1882. The number of Dickens's speeches that Shepherd itemized remained at fifty-nine throughout the revisions, but he expanded the "Ana" section.

There is evidence that Shepherd consulted the bibliographies of Forster and Cook; both appear in Shepherd's "Ana" section. Although Shepherd makes no comment on Forster's bibliography, he is surprisingly critical of Cook's volume: "For the more recondite matters which give the chief if not the sole value to a compilation of this kind, the reader will search this bulky *brochure* in vain. Nor is the record of more commonly known and accessible details anywhere thoroughly reliable either as to accuracy or completeness. . . . The pamphlet is also disfigured by a considerable number of *errata*, which should be corrected in a future edition."

Shepherd was more interested in providing bibliographical information for posterity than in serving the new Dickens collectors, but the next group of bibliographies and bibliographical commentary is very much collector-oriented—John F. Dexter's "Hints to Dickens Collectors" (9), published in the *Dickens Memento* in 1884; Charles P. Johnson's *Hints to Collectors of Original Editions of the Works of Charles Dickens* (16), published in 1885; and John H. Slater's chapter on Dickens in his *Early Editions: A Bibliographical Survey of the Works of Some Popular Modern Authors* (22), published a decade later in 1894. Dexter's work is not a bibliography but rather advice to collectors on which editions one should collect, how much they will cost, and how to determine their authenticity. Johnson's small volume (56 pages) is the most thorough of the lot, but also, as his title indicates, for the collector. In his introduction, he finds both Shepherd and Dexter "useful," but adds that he knows of "no volume that will enable a collector or dealer to tell, at a glance, whether any particular volume offered to him is of the genuine, first edition throughout, with the plates in the first state." This, he asserts, "has been my object in preparing these 'Hints to Collectors.' " It is evident from Johnson's comments, written a mere decade and a half after Dickens's death, that the Dickens industry is booming. Not only have book dealers and auction houses entered the picture, but dishonest ones as well, for Johnson feels called upon to warn his readers of the disreputable practice of passing off later editions as first editions. Thus, his plan, he announces, "has been to compare several copies of each work . . . ; to collate them; to note the smallest variations in title-pages, or plates; and to put the information thus gathered in a compact and intelligible form." This plan results in fuller collations of pages and illustrations than had been attempted previously, with commentary on variations in editions, information about the color of cloth bindings in the one-volume editions, and the earliest examination of the different states of the first edition of *A Christmas Carol*. Johnson also includes sections on dramatizations of Dickens's novels, portraits of Dickens (73 items), and Dickensiana. Slater mentions Johnson and Cook in his introduction, but, apart from lengthy annotations for some of Dickens's works, there is not much new in his chapter on Dickens, except for the then current prices for various editions of individual novels.

One other bibliography belongs to the 1884–94 decade, John P. Anderson's "Bibliography," included in Frank T. Marzial's *Life of Charles Dickens* (2), published in 1887. Unlike the others, it is not collector-oriented, and it includes editions of Dickens's collected works, selected works, individual works, and miscellaneous works published between 1870 and 1887 as well as earlier. The information provided about each entry is relatively brief, approximately what one finds in Forster's bibliography. It is, however, historically more important for its listing of studies of Dickens, and so is discussed more fully in the section on bibliographies of Dickens studies, below.

Hard upon the heels of Slater and Anderson came Frederic G. Kitton. An artist, writer, and Dickens collector, he helped to found the Dickens Fellowship in 1902. He died two years later, but his Dickens library eventually became the foundation of the library at the Dickens House in 1926. His earliest bibliography, *Dickensiana: A Bibliography of the Literature Relating to Charles Dickens and His Writings* (235), was published in 1886 and was the first major bibliography of writings about Dickens. This was followed a number of years later by *The Novels of Charles Dickens: A Bibliography and Sketch* (17) in 1897 and the companion volume *The Minor Writings of Charles Dickens* (58) in 1900. Although the former seems more a study of the conception, writing, and publishing of Dickens's major works than a full-fledged bibliography, it does contain the essential bibliographical information, usually in a paragraph or two hidden in the midst of the chapter on each novel. In the twenty-page chapter on *Bleak House*, for example, after commenting on Dickens's initial ideas for his new novel, listing titles (included with the manuscript bequeathed by John Forster to the Victoria and Albert Museum) that Dickens considered before settling on *Bleak House*, discussing Dickens's views on the Court of Chancery, and printing excerpts from Dickens's letters describing both the difficulties and joys of writing the novel, Kitton provides, midway through, the basic bibliographical information:

> "Bleak House" was issued by Messrs. Bradbury and Evans in twenty monthly parts, demy octavo, green wrappers, at one shilling each, commencing in March, 1852, and ending in September, 1853, Parts 19 and 20 forming a double number. The work contained forty etched illustrations by H. K. Browne, and was dedicated, "as a Remembrance of our Friendly Union. To my Companions in the Guild of Literature and Art." The complete story was published in September 1853, in one volume, cloth, at a guinea—*Collation*, pp. xvi., 624. It has often been reissued in the same form, with or without a date, the first Cheap Edition,

with a frontispiece by H. K. Browne, appearing in the Second Series (Messrs. Bradbury and Evans, 1858), cloth, at five shillings.

The original MS and the corrected proofs of "Bleak House" are at South Kensington. A copy of the first edition in parts, as issued, is valued at £2, and in cloth from £1 to £2.

Following this, in the remaining pages of the chapter, Kitton mentions the popularity of the novel (it sold 30,000 copies in March, 40,000 in November), examines its contents (the character of Jo, the repulsive burial ground at St. Mary-le-Strand, the prototype for Mr. Jarndyce's Bleak House, the models for Boythorne and Skimpole), and discusses the attacks on Dickens's portrayal of Chancery and overseas charity. These are obviously not bibliographical matters. Although Kitton makes a minor concession to the book collector in announcing then current prices for first editions in parts and volume form, his bibliographical details are not sufficient for the collector trying to avoid inauthentic copies of the work, and the richness of the chapter lies more in the non-bibliographical than the bibliographical information it provides.

In *The Minor Writings of Charles Dickens* the bibliographical details are of greater importance, and, in the preface, Kitton acknowledges his indebtedness to the bibliographies of Cook, Shepherd, Johnson, and Dexter (in contrast, in the preface to *The Novels of Charles Dickens*, he notes his indebtedness to John Forster's *Life of Charles Dickens* and the *Letters of Charles Dickens* compiled by Georgina Hogarth and Mamie Dickens). But he also indicates the original work he has done in preparing this volume, including "the compilation of a complete list of Dickens's ephemeral contributions to periodical literature, notably to those journals of which he himself was editor." Since almost all of these articles were published anonymously, Kitton relied on internal evidence, the endorsement of Charles Dickens, Jr., autograph manuscripts in the Forster Collection at the Victoria and Albert Museum, and the "office" set of *All the Year Round* with the authors of the articles "inscribed against each article," a set that has since disappeared, though it was then, according to Kitton, in the possession of W. H. Howe, a Dickens collector.

Comparing Kitton's list of Dickens's journalistic writings with the "Complete listing of Dickens's known journalism, December 1833–August 1869" in Michael Slater and John Drew's *The Uncommercial Traveller and Other Papers* (61), published in 2000, is instructive. Kitton missed a number of items since identified: a few early theater reviews and election and other reports for the *Morning Chronicle,* 1834–36 and 1844; several essays in the *Morning Chronicle* and the *Carlton Chronicle*, 1834–36, later included in *Sketches by Boz* (most of these were not identified until 1933 and a few even later); a number of book and theater reviews in the *Examiner,* 1837–49; "The Spirit of Chivalry in Westminster Hall," published in *Douglas Jerrold's*

Shilling Magazine, August 1845; several articles in *Household Words*; and three, mostly debatable, pieces in *All the Year Round*. On the other hand, Kitton identifies a small number of Dickens's writings that Slater and Drew miss, pieces published principally in *Bentley's Miscellany* and the *Daily News*, as well as a few other minor items.

Kitton has chapters on *Sketches by Boz*, *American Notes*, *Pictures from Italy*, *Hard Times* (inexplicably included here rather than in the earlier volume), the Christmas Books, Miscellaneous Prose Writings (*Sunday Under Three Heads*, *Sketches of Young Gentlemen*, *Sketches of Young Couples*, *A Child's History of England*, and, to some extent erroneously, *The Loving Ballad of Lord Bateman*), and other chapters on works Dickens edited or for which he wrote introductions; Dickens's plays; his poems, songs, and other rhymes; and an appendix on plagiarisms of Dickens's novels and "unauthorised continuations, etc.," of *Edwin Drood*. For the chapters dealing with Dickens's full-length "minor" works, Kitton follows pretty much the procedure he used in *The Novels of Charles Dickens* in providing bibliographical information about each work. With *A Christmas Carol* and *The Battle of Life* he does note that there are various issues of the first edition of each work but is not particularly precise about the sequence of publication. These matters would be left for later bibliographers to work out. Kitton's work on the minor writings is a major bibliographical contribution. In addition, Kitton collected a number of Dickens's journalistic pieces in his editions of Dickens's *Old Lamps for New Ones and Other Sketches and Essays Hitherto Uncollected* (90) in 1897, *To Be Read at Dusk and Other Stories, Sketches and Essays, Now First Collected* (90), in 1898, and *The Poems and Verses of Charles Dickens* in 1903 (91).

The *Household Words* Contributors' Book turned up shortly thereafter in the possession of R. C. Lehmann, a great-nephew of W. H. Wills, Dickens's sub-editor on *Household Words* and *All the Year Round*, and was used with Lehmann's permission by B. W. Matz in editing the two volumes of *Miscellaneous Papers, Plays and Poems* (95), published in 1908, in the National Edition of Dickens's Works. This collection also represented the culmination of Matz's and F. G. Kitton's work to identify and recover Dickens's anonymous newspaper and magazine articles. The result was the addition, as Matz notes in his introduction, of "some eighty or so hitherto unknown writings" and two poems to the Dickens canon. This was supplemented in turn by the *Collected Papers* in the Nonesuch Edition (109), published in 1937, edited by Arthur Waugh, Hugh Walpole, Walter Dexter, and Thomas Hatton, which added newer discoveries by Dexter and others (Matz had died in 1925). These included seven articles, one play (the fragment from "O'Thello," a musical burlesque Dickens wrote in 1833), six poems, eight speeches, and *The Loving Ballad of Lord Bateman*, to the last of which Dickens's contribution was minor but definite. Occasionally over the post-Kitton years other individual pieces have been identified or found to be misattributed—see below.

After Kitton, the next attempt at a full bibliography of the Dickens canon was Joseph C. Thomson's *Bibliography of the Writings of Charles Dickens* (25), published in 1904. In a brief introductory note, Thomson modestly announces that he "makes no claim to originality" but hopes that, by coordinating the "labours" of other bibliographers, he can produce "a list of the writings of Dickens to which with some reasonableness the term 'complete' may be applied." Using the chronological approach of Forster and Shepherd, Thomson provides a much fuller account than either, seeming to include every bit of information about each work from virtually every Dickens bibliography published to date, and he includes a section on "Value" under each work in which, using, as he notes in his introductory statement, "the admirable *Book-Prices Current*" (396), he comments at some length on then current and auction prices of various editions and sets of extra illustrations.

Thomson's work was followed by John C. Eckel's *The First Editions of the Writings of Charles Dickens and Their Values: A Bibliography* (11), published in 1913, with a revised edition in 1932. Eckel's work still stands, despite criticism of its writing style and its errors, as the standard modern bibliography of Dickens's writings, though one directed more toward collectors than scholars. Dickens "is essentially a collectors' author," he writes in the introduction to the 1913 edition, "for the reason that his books in their original state make an irresistible appeal." To satisfy this "appeal," Eckel includes, for the first time in Dickensian bibliography, collations that give "a permanent idea of the physical side of a first edition." Although Eckel claims in the introduction to the 1932 edition that the reception of his first edition "was more than flattering," and quotes then recent auction prices to show how valuable it already was as an out-of-print book, critics were not always as happy with either edition as Eckel suggests they were of the first. The *Times Literary Supplement* reviewer (11) of the second edition found the volume ultimately "disappointing" in its scholarship and writing.

One can easily see why the volume is both praised and criticized. On the one hand, it provides far more information about the works it considers than any previous bibliography had, and it covers the entire range of Dickens's works, from the major novels to the smallest contribution to *Household Words*, with information on advertisements in the monthly parts of all the serialized novels and a collation of the advertisements and information on the inside and outside of the back wrappers. On the other hand, the information provided is not always full, not always accurate, and not always consistent from one work to the next. As one might expect, the minor works are given shorter shrift than the major works. But for the major works, the extent of the collation varies from work to work, in accordance, one supposes, with

Eckel's perception of the needs of collectors and booksellers. Thus, *Pickwick Papers* is given forty-two pages, with detailed information about the illustrations (particularly the "first state" of the plates, since many of them were re-etched after the original plates became too worn) and the advertisements in each monthly issue, about the eleven "points" that indicate one has a "perfect," or "prime," set of the original parts, and about auction prices of sets in differing condition. Eckel also includes a briefer collation of the first bound volume of the novel. But all this information is scattered throughout the chapter; it is difficult to pull it together sufficiently to get a clear picture of what makes a "prime Pickwick in parts." It is easier to follow the information in the three-page chapter on *Bleak House* in the 1932 edition, but here all Eckel chooses to give the reader is a short general collation of the parts issue, a little bit of information about illustrations that were duplicated, a vague statement about the advertisements, and brief details about the advertisements for four of the issues. In the chapters on *A Christmas Carol* and *The Battle of Life*, Eckel does discuss the various states of their first editions.

Not more than a year after the publication of the second edition of Eckel's bibliography, Thomas Hatton and Arthur H. Cleaver published *A Bibliography of the Periodical Work of Charles Dickens: Bibliographical, Analytical, and Statistical* (15). They limit their study to the thirteen works that Dickens published in monthly parts, though the monthly publications included of *Sketches by Boz, Master Humphrey's Clock* (containing *The Old Curiosity Shop* and *Barnaby Rudge*), *Oliver Twist*, and *A Tale of Two Cities* were not their first editions. They include full part by part collations of each of these editions, with additional commentary on any peculiar or unique aspects of text, plates, wrappers, and advertisements. One is impressed by the fullness of the content and the logicality of the arrangement of material. Brian Lake, a proprietor of Jarndyce Antiquarian Booksellers, London, and a bibliographer in his own right, calls the Hatton and Cleaver volume "the near-definitive bibliography of the 'part' issues" in a lukewarm review (23) of Walter E. Smith's two-volume bibliography of *Charles Dickens in the Original Cloth* (23, 24). However, had Hatton and Cleaver included the novels first published in weekly installments as well, the work would have been much more satisfying and useful.

The Dickens sections of the first two editions of *The Cambridge Bibliography of English Literature*, compiled by F. J. H. Darton in 1940 (5) and by Philip Collins (as *The New Cambridge Bibliography of English Literature*) in 1969 (3), follow next, with no significant bibliography of Dickens's works in between, and with the Collins section obviously updating the Darton section. They are more expansions on Anderson than on Eckel or Hatton and Cleaver in the information they provide, and therefore more designed for the researcher than the collector. They contain lists of "principal" editions of individual and collected editions, as well as editions of imitations and sequels, dramatizations, and sets of extra illustrations for a few of the novels. The two editors also list collections of Dickens's letters and speeches and, in a very limited way and using an inexplicable selection process, individual letters and speeches.

Walter E. Smith's two-volume *Charles Dickens in the Original Cloth: A Bibliographical Catalogue of the First Appearance of His Writings in Book Form in England with Facsimiles of the Bindings and Titlepages* (23, 24), with *Part One: The Novels with Sketches by Boz*, published in 1982, and *Part Two: The Christmas Books and Selected Secondary Works*, published in 1983, is the essential supplement to Hatton and Cleaver, dealing specifically with the first clothbound editions of all of the novels and *Sketches by Boz* in the first volume and the Christmas Books and other principal nonfictional works in the second. Brian Lake (23) rightly criticizes volume 2 of Smith's bibliography for incompleteness. Smith covers only *Sketches of Young Gentlemen, Sketches of Young Couples, American Notes, Pictures from Italy, A Child's History of England, The Uncommercial Traveller,* and *The Life of Our Lord* in the volume, in addition to the five Christmas Books, leaving scholar, bookseller, and collector still dependent upon Eckel for the shorter journalistic, theatrical, and fictional works.

Most of the bibliographies mentioned so far have been concerned with the English first editions of Dickens's works. The American editions, bibliographically speaking at least, first came to the attention of William Glyde Wilkins, whose *First and Early American Editions of the Works of Charles Dickens* (27), published in 1910, revised and expanded the information in two of his earlier articles in the *Dickensian* (26, 28). Wilkins's work was followed by that of Herman L. Edgar and R. W. G. Vail in their *Early American Editions of the Works of Charles Dickens* (12) in 1929. They list only editions in an exhibition (but obviously a superb one) held at the New York Public Library in 1929 and so add to but do not quite supersede Wilkins. Edgar and Vail include nearly every edition in Wilkins's volume that was published in Philadelphia and New York, but, in most cases, they do not list editions published in Boston. They include additional but sometimes conflicting details, and list a few editions that are not in Wilkins. Wilkins, for example, misses Harper & Brothers's 1844 New York edition of *A Christmas Carol* and does not list any editions of *Cricket on the Hearth, The Battle of Life, The Haunted Man and the Ghost's Bargain, A Child's History of England, Hard Times,* and *The Uncommercial Traveller.* Sometimes, as with editions of *American Notes* and *The Chimes,* the two bibliographies disagree about the order of publication as well. Wilkins lists a few volumes of selections from Dickens's works published after 1870; the Edgar and Vail list ends with an 1871 edition of *A Child's Dream of a Star,* which is in Wilkins, too. Wilkins also identifies a number of American plagiarisms and parodies. Neither bibliography is adequate on early collected editions. Section D, "Books: Collected Editions & Selections," pp. 244–99, in *Dickens and Dickensiana* (297), John D. Podeschi's catalogue of the Richard Gimbel Collection in the Yale University Library, published in 1980, lists far more early American editions of collected works.

Two more recent and more monumental attempts to catalogue American publications, Dickens's among them, seemed initially promising. The first, *A Checklist of American Imprints for 1820[-]*, edited by Richard H. Shoemaker, et al. (21), is now up to 1846 (published in 1997), and so lists American editions of Dickens's works through *Pictures from Italy* and *The Battle of Life*. In the second, *Bibliography of American Imprints to 1901*, compiled by the American Antiquarian Society and the Research Libraries Group (1), volume 46 (published in 1993) contains American editions of Dickens's works. Unfortunately, neither of these publications is as complete as their titles suggest, and they must be used cautiously. They miss editions recorded in Wilkins and in Edgar and Vail, and make strange errors, such as listing an edition of *A Christmas Carol* with illustrations by Arthur Rackham, as being published in Philadelphia in 1843 when it was actually published in 1915. A useful feature (barring such errors) of the *Bibliography of American Imprints to 1901* is that it lists editions published to 1901. Also see Peter S. Bracher's "A Check List of Dickens' Works Published by Harper & Brothers, 1842–70," in his "Harper & Brother: Publishers of Dickens," published in 1976, and his "The Early American Editions of *American Notes*: Their Priority and Circulation" (62), published in 1975, both more specialized studies, and Newbury F. Read's "The American Editions of Pickwick" (54), published in the *Dickensian* in 1936, which lists 127 editions published in the United States, 1836–1936.

Towards the close of the twentieth century, three important bibliographical projects began publication, all aimed more at the researcher than the collector. The first is *The Nineteenth Century Short Title Catalogue*. The English and American editions of Dickens's works published between 1836 and 1870 will be found in volume 12 of *Nineteenth Century Short Title Catalogue. Series II. Phase I, 1816–1870* (10), published in 1988. While the title of the series suggests that the editors are aiming at nothing short of completeness, the publications listed are actually those that are in eight libraries: the Bodleian Library, the British Library, Harvard University Library, the Library of Congress, the Library of Trinity College (Dublin), the National Library of Scotland, the Cambridge University Library, and the University of Newcastle Library. These are, of course, fine libraries, and the final list should be reasonably, if not quite, complete. Of particular concern is the potentially incomplete representation of American editions of Dickens's novels, many fugitive at best, published in Philadelphia and Boston as well as in New York, and even in less populated cities. A number of these may not have made their way to the shelves of these libraries, as a comparison of entries with those in Wilkins and Edgar and Vail will quickly reveal, and others may not be readily identifiable because publishers are not given in the short title catalogue.

The second important project is the third edition of *The Cambridge Bibliography of English Literature*, of which one volume has been published. Fortunately for our purposes, this was the volume for 1800–1900, published in 1999, for which Paul Schlicke did the section on Dickens (19). This is a selective bibliography, one must remember, but in the preface the general editor, Joanne Shattock, announces that the "emphasis is on primary material" and that the aim is to include "all significant English language editions, and where known, American and continental editions." What Schlicke has produced, building of course on his predecessors in the first and second editions, is most impressive. One would not go to the volume for a complete listing of early American editions, but the cataloguing of English editions is sound, and modern editions are well represented. A list of the more important collected editions is also useful.

The third major project is more specialized, though, it is hoped, more comprehensive: *The Garland Dickens Bibliographies* (7), and its successor *The Dickens Bibliographies* (6), published by AMS Press, of which my forthcoming bibliography is one and the present writer the general editor. Thirteen of twenty-one projected volumes and one update have already been published. Eleven were published in the Garland Dickens Bibliographies: the volumes on *David Copperfield*, by Richard J. Dunn (32), published in 1981; *Our Mutual Friend*, by Joel J. Brattin and Bert G. Hornback (48), published in 1984; *Hard Times*, by Sylvia Manning (38), published in 1985; *Dickens's Christmas Books, Christmas Stories, and Other Short Fiction*, by Ruth F. Glancy (30), published in 1985; *Oliver Twist*, by David Paroissien (46), published in 1986; *Great Expectations*, by George J. Worth (37), published in 1986; *Barnaby Rudge*, by Thomas J. Rice (29), published in 1987; *The Old Curiosity Shop*, by Priscilla and Paul Schlicke (45), published in 1988; *Pickwick Papers*, by Elliot Engel (51), published in 1990; *Martin Chuzzlewit*, by Robert E. Lougy (41), published in 1990; and *A Tale of Two Cities*, by Ruth F. Glancy (56), published in 1993. Two have been published in The Dickens Bibliographies series (AMS Press)—*The Mystery of Edwin Drood*, by Don R. Cox (43), published in 1998, and *Dombey and Son*, by Leon Litvack (35), published in 2000—as well as the update of *David Copperfield*, edited by Richard J. Dunn and Ann M. Tandy (33), also published in 2000. My own bibliography (8) is scheduled for publication in 2003, and Robert Hanna's *Dickens's Non-Fictional, Theatrical, and Poetical Writings: An Annotated Bibliography* (57) is in hand and scheduled for publication in 2004. Other updates of volumes in the Garland Dickens Bibliographies will be published over the next few years in *Dickens Studies Annual*, with some being published separately by AMS Press. Robert Heaman's update of Brattin and Hornback's *Our Mutual Friend* bibliography is being published in this issue of *Dickens Studies Annual*. Ruth Glancy's update of her bibliography of the Christmas works and other short fiction and David Paroissien's of *Oliver Twist* are tentatively scheduled for publication in 2004. AMS Press also plans to reprint volumes published in the earlier series. While the authors of the Garland and AMS Press bibliographies do not include detailed collations of the earliest editions of Dickens's works, they do list and annotate all the important English and American editions of a particular work from the first to the most recent.

Also useful is the bibliographical material in the introductory matter and appendices of the volumes in the Clarendon Dickens, yet another major Dickens project, nine of which have been published to date—*Oliver Twist*, edited by Kathleen Tillotson (47), published in 1966; *The Mystery of Edwin Drood*, edited by Margaret Cardwell (42), published in 1972; *Dombey and Son*, edited by Alan Horsman (34), published in 1974; *Little Dorrit*, edited by Harvey P. Sucksmith (39), published in 1979; *David Copperfield*, edited by Nina Burgis (31), published in 1981; *Martin Chuzzlewit*, edited by Margaret Cardwell (40), published in 1982; *Pickwick Papers*, edited by James Kinsley (52), published in 1986; *Great Expectations*, edited by Margaret Cardwell (36), published in 1993; and *The Old Curiosity Shop*, edited by Elizabeth M. Brennan (44), published in 1997. In addition, each volume contains a section titled "Descriptive List of Editions," specifically those published in Dickens's lifetime and under his supervision. These are brief rather than full collations, useful for the scholar if not for the collector.

The best bibliography of Dickens's manuscripts is to be found in volume 4 of Barbara Rosenbaum and Pamela White's *Index of English Literary Manuscripts* (18), published in 1982. The compilers have located 333 manuscripts, not including letters. Their annotations briefly describe each manuscript, indicate its present location, and note whether or not a transcript exists or whether or not the manuscript has been published in whole or in part.

Bibliographical Studies

Bibliographical studies of Dickens's works abound and range from important work on the states of the first edition of *A Christmas Carol* to reports on Dickens exhibitions and book sales, from sales figures for Dickens's novels to the identifying of essays that Dickens published anonymously, from studies of translations and dramatic adaptations of Dickens's works to scrapbooks in the Dickens House library. Here is an enormous body of research work that in many instances backs up and supplements the bibliographies already noted above. A number of these works are of great value to Dickens studies. One important field is the identification of Dickens's lesser-known works. The earlier bibliographers mentioned above established relatively quickly the important bibliographical information about Dickens's volume-length works. But identification of many of Dickens's journalistic pieces was slow in coming. Still, one would have thought the identification of the nonfictional, theatrical, and poetical works in *Collected Papers* in the Nonesuch Edition (109) was definitive, as no doubt Arthur Waugh and his colleagues did. But it was soon discovered that this was not the case. Since 1937, K. J. Fielding and Alec W. Brice have identified a number of Dickens's anonymous pieces, most of them published in the *Examiner* (63–66, 82, 84–85). William J. Carlton has identified fifteen *Morning Chronicle* dramatic reviews (71), and Patrick J. McCarthy (96) and Charles VanNoorden (107–08) have identified other pieces by Dickens in the *Morning Chronicle*, 1835–36. Philip Collins has located still other pieces (74–77), and K. J. Fielding, in his edition of *The Speeches of Charles Dickens* (83), published in 1960 and with additions in 1988, has located more speeches that Dickens gave and better versions of others previously published. Other short pieces were identified by Walter Dexter (79–81), William Long (93), and Graham Storey (105). Harry Stone, in his *Charles Dickens' Uncollected Writings from* **Household Words** *1850–1859* (104), published in two volumes in 1969, has identified numerous short pieces and parts of articles by Dickens in *Household Words*.

Another concern has been the identification of the first publication in magazines and newspapers of the pieces Dickens collected as *Sketches by Boz*. Shepherd, as mentioned above, compiled the earliest list and thought, as did Kitton and Eckel (even in his second edition), that twelve of the pieces were written especially for *Sketches by Boz*, when actually, as it has turned out, only four were. In 1933, Hatton and Cleaver (15), closely followed by Walter Dexter (79), identified five of the eight published earlier. Hilmer Nielsen identified a sixth in 1938 (99). The remaining two were identified by William J. Carlton in 1951 (72) and Graham Mott in 1984 (98). With the exception of Mott's identification of the final previously published piece, Duane DeVries's "Appendix A: The Publication History of *Sketches by Boz*" (55), published in 1976, is the fullest record of previously published pieces and the arrangement of these and the pieces written specifically for the collected edition in the first and subsequent editions published in Dickens's lifetime.

Identifying Dickens's collaborations with other authors and pieces attributed to Dickens but written by others has also occupied scholars, as has identifying authors of articles in *Household Words* and *All the Year Round* not written by Dickens. Anne Lohrli's **Household Words**: *A Weekly Journal,*

1850–1859, Conducted by Charles Dickens (59), published in 1973, and Harry Stone's *Charles Dickens' Uncollected Writing from **Household Words**, 1850–1859* (104), are particularly helpful in identifying authors of articles in Dickens's *Household Words*. Ella A. Oppenlander, in *Dickens' **All the Year Round**: Descriptive Index and Contributor List* (60), published in 1984, has done comparable work with Dickens's contributions to *All the Year Round*, but many authors of articles in the latter remain unidentified. For accounts of the *Household Words* Office Book used by Lohrli, see her study, of course, and also her article, "*Household Words* and Its 'Office Book' " (92), published in 1964. For an account of the *All the Year Round* letter book used by Oppenlander, see her account but also Philip Collins's in *Victorian Periodical Newsletter* (73), published in 1970. In my bibliography, I list a number of studies of Dickens's collaborations with other authors, of incorrect or dubious attributions to Dickens, and of authorship of articles in the two magazines but do not have the space to do so here.

Other bibliographical studies are concerned with the primacy of issues of first editions, particularly of *A Christmas Carol*. Ruth Glancy's "Commentary on the First Issue Problem" in her bibliography of *A Christmas Carol* (30) summarizes the controversy and draws sensible conclusions. Important earlier publications on this issue are E. Allen Osborne's *The Facts about **A Christmas Carol*** (101), published in 1937; Philo Calhoun and Howell J. Heaney's "Dickens' *Christmas Carol* after a Hundred Years: A Study in Bibliographical Evidence" (69), published in 1945; and Richard Gimbel's *Charles Dickens's **A Christmas Carol**. Three States of the First Edition* (86), published in 1955, and his "The Earliest State of the First Edition of Charles Dickens' *A Christmas Carol*" (87), published in 1958. There has also been considerable discussion over the years about what makes up a "Prime Pickwick in Parts" —that is, a set of the monthly numbers of *Pickwick Papers* with the original printing of each part (only 500 copies of Part 2 were printed originally, for example, compared to 20,000 to 40,000 of the later numbers), the earliest etchings of illustrations, and the original advertising inserts. The best of these studies are George W. Davis's *The Posthumous Papers of the Pickwick Club: Some New Bibliographical Discoveries* (78) and John C. Eckel's *Prime Pickwicks in Parts. Census with Complete Collation, Comparison and Comment* (50), both published in 1928, and William Miller and E. H. Strange's "The Original *Pickwick Papers*: The Collation of a Perfect First Edition," reprinted as the "The Bibliography" in their *A Centenary Bibliography of the Pickwick Papers* (53), published in 1936.

Still other bibliographical studies concern publishers' agreements and other publication matters and the characteristics of particular early or later editions of Dickens's works. For publishers' agreements and the publishing history of Dickens's works, see Robert L. Patten's *Charles Dickens and His Publishers*

(102), published in 1978, a mass of information about the writing, printing, and publication of Dickens's works; Newbury F. Read's "On the Writing of *Barnaby Rudge*" (103), published in 1934, on the tangled history of the writing and publication of *Barnaby Rudge*; Gerald Grubb's "On the Serial Publication of *Oliver Twist*" (88), published in 1941; and Kathleen Tillotson's "*Oliver Twist* in Three Volumes" (106), published in 1963. For the difficulties of editing Dickens's works, see particularly John Butt's "Editing a Nineteenth-Century Novelist" (67), published in 1961, sage advice to a prospective editor; Butt and Tillotson's "Preface by the General Editors" to the Clarendon Edition of Dickens's works (68), first published in 1966; and Sylvère Monod's " 'Between Two Worlds': Editing Dickens" (97), published in 1978, on the editing of the Norton Critical Edition of *Bleak House* (447).

Bibliographies and Surveys of Translations, Readings, Dramatic Adaptations, Plagiarisms and Imitations, and Illustrations

There is no full bibliography of translations of Dickens's works, though numerous bibliographies and surveys of varying thoroughness and age have been published (110–69). The only person who ever seems to have tried to collect translations was Marie Roche, Lady Dickens, the wife of Dickens's son Henry. Her collection is now in the British Library (281) and obviously quite outdated. For more modern editions, a variety of bibliographies may be consulted, most dealing with translations into a particular language, although the *Index Translationum* (130), an international bibliography of translations, has tried to cover the field since 1932, gradually increasing the number of countries represented over the years from six at the beginning to over seventy today, according to James Harner's *Literary Research Guide* (233).

In "A First Bibliography of the Reading Editions of Charles Dickens's Works" (183), published in 1921, John Stonehouse compiled the earliest list of the readings that Dickens abridged from some of his novels and used for his reading tours in Great Britain and the United States. Since then, however, they have become, if not quite exclusively, the scholarly property of Philip Collins (171–80), and in 1975 he published the definitive edition of them (178), with a long introduction containing everything one would want to know about them and headnotes and sometimes endnotes to each reading providing additional information. Collins also published facsimile editions of Dickens's readings of *A Christmas Carol* (175) and *Sikes and Nancy*, from *Oliver Twist* (176), in 1971 and 1982, respectively, both with useful notes. John D. Gordan published a facsimile of *Mrs. Gamp*, from *Martin Chuzzlewit* (181) in 1956, with elaborate commentary. Two important studies are of readings Dickens prepared but never performed in public, Jean Callahan's "The (Unread) Reading Version of *Great Expectations* (170), published in 1999, and Michael Slater's "*The Bastille Prisoner*: A Reading Dickens Never Gave" (182), published in 1970.

Dramatic adaptations of Dickens's works have been pretty thoroughly covered by bibliographers and other scholars, particularly film and stage adaptations. Most of the major bibliographies in this area are still relatively up to date. H. Philip Bolton's *Dickens Dramatized* (186), published in 1987, is an impressive, full-scale work, even though Bolton modestly insists that his handlist of some 3,000 items, covering nearly 400 pages, is "by no means a complete listing" of dramatic performances for stage, film, radio, and television. For film versions alone, Ana L. Zambrano's earlier study and bibliography *Dickens and Film* (201), published in 1977, is quite detailed, as is Michael Pointer's even more recent "Catalog of Film, Television, and Video Productions" in his *Charles Dickens on the Screen: The Film, Television, and Video Adaptations* (195), published in 1996. In addition, one may consult numerous general bibliographies of stage and film productions that include adaptations of Dickens's works, such as the impressive, if as yet incomplete *The American Film Institute Catalog of Motion Pictures Produced in the United States* (184), begun in 1971, with six volumes published to date, or the Dickens items located on the Internet Movie Database Web site, http://us.imdb.com (188). Among classic studies of Dickens and the drama are T. Edgar Pemberton's *Charles Dickens and the Stage. A Record of His Connection with the Drama as Playwright, Actor, and Critic* (194), published in 1888; S. J. Adair Fitz-Gerald's *Dickens and the Drama, Being an Account of Charles Dickens's Connections with the Stage and the Stage's Connection with Him* (190), published in 1910; Alexander Woollcott's *Mr. Dickens Goes to the Play* (199), published in 1922; J. B. Van Amerongen's *The Actor in Dickens. A Study of the Histrionic and Dramatic Elements in the Novelist's Life and Works* (198), published in 1926; and F. Dubrez Fawcett's *Dickens the Dramatist: On Stage, Screen and Radio* (189), published in 1952, all of which contain sections, now considerably outdated obviously, on dramatic adaptations of Dickens's works. Many bibliographies and surveys of dramatic productions of individual Dickens works have been published, including, among the more recent and more scholarly, Richard P. Fulkerson's "*Oliver Twist* in the Victorian Theatre" (191), published in 1974; Ana L. Zambrano's "*David Copperfield*: Novel and Film" (200), published in 1977; H. Philip Bolton's "*Bleak House* and the Playhouse" (185), published in 1983; Paul Sammon's *The "Christmas Carol" Trivia Book: Everything You Ever Wanted to Know About Every Version of the Dickens Classic* (196), published in 1994; Elizabeth Brennan's "Little Nell on the Stage, 1840–1841 (187), published in 1997; a number of entries in Paul Schlicke's *Oxford Reader's Companion to Dickens* (197), published in 1999; and Fred Guida's "Filmography" in his *A Christmas Carol and Its Adaptations* (192), published in 2000.

Some work has been done on the imitations and continuations of Dickens's works. Louis James calls them all "plagiarisms" in his account of them in the *Oxford Reader's Companion to Dickens* (206), published in 2000, and in his earlier "The Beginnings of a New Type of Popular Fiction: Plagiarisms of Dickens" (205), published in 1963, and Paul Schlicke lists a number of them in the third edition of the *Cambridge Bibliography of English Literature* (19). J. Cuming Walters, in his *The Complete Mystery of Edwin Drood: The History, Continuations, and Solutions (1870–1912)*, published in 1912 (207), and, more recently, Steven Connor in the new Everyman Library Edition of *The Mystery of Edwin Drood* (203), published in 1996, have tracked the numerous completions of the novel by others and the various proposed solutions to the mystery. Paul Hoggart has located a number of travesties of Dickens works (204), and William Glyde Wilkins has identified American parodies of *American Notes* (208). One should also mention the well-known forgery by Thomas J. Wise of Dickens's minor work *To Be Read at Dusk*—see John Carter and Graham Pollard's *An Inquiry into the Nature of Certain Nineteenth Century Pamphlets* (202), published in 1934.

Scholars have thoroughly catalogued the illustrations in the parts editions of Dickens's works—the "original" illustrations. They are listed part by part in the elaborate collations in Hatton and Cleaver's *Bibliography of the Periodical Works of Charles Dickens* (15), where every plate is itemized by title, and are discussed in detail in Jane R. Cohen's *Charles Dickens and His Original Illustrators* (209), published in 1980. But these are not the only illustrations included in Dickens's works published in his lifetime. In his first volume of *Charles Dickens in the Original Cloth*, Walter E. Smith (23) supplements Hatton and Cleaver by itemizing the plates in the original volume editions of *Sketches by Boz* and *Oliver Twist* and the illustrations inserted in the text in the serial publication of *Master Humphrey's Clock*. In his second volume (24), Smith itemizes the illustrations for *Sketches of Young Gentlemen*, *Sketches of Young Couples*, *Pictures from Italy*, and *A Child's History of England* (only frontispieces for each of the three volumes). He is, however, less specific about the illustrations for the five Christmas Books, merely listing the number of illustrations by each of several artists for each volume, and *The Life of Our Lord*, noting only that eight of the twelve illustrations are paintings, that three are facsimiles of pages of Dickens's manuscript, and that the frontispiece is a portrait of Dickens. Thomas Hatton's list, "A Bibliographical List of the Original Illustrations to the Works of Charles Dickens, Being Those Made Under His Supervision," in *The Nonesuch Dickens: Retrospectus and Prospectus* (100, 212), published in 1937, itemizes the 877 plates made for Dickens's works during his lifetime. These are printed in the volumes of the Nonesuch Dickens, and each set of the collected edition contained one of these plates in a separate boxed volume. J. A. Hammerton's *The Dickens Picture-Book. A Record of the Dickens Illustrators* (211), published in 1910, not only reproduces (though in considerably reduced size) 600 of the original illustrations to Dickens's novels but comments on illustrators of later editions of Dickens's works and on sets of extra illustrations, reproducing a number of these as well. Also see Frederic G. Kitton's *Dickens and His Illustrators* (214), published 1899, for facsimiles of some of the original drawings, lists of illustrators of post-1870 editions of his novels, and sets of extra illustrations, as well as his supplementary *Dickens Illustrations, Facsimiles of Original Drawings, Sketches and Studies for Illustration in the Works of Charles Dickens*, published 1900. Some of the earlier bibliographies mentioned above list sets of extra illustrations to Dickens's novels, some done during Dickens's lifetime and others done after his death. There is, however, no bibliography of illustrations for Dickens's works published after 1870, though reference to illustrated editions of individual works may be found in the Dickens Bibliographies published by Garland and AMS Press (7, 6). Some studies have focused on the illustrations for individual works and on individual illustrators—see particularly Joseph Greco's *Pictorial Pickwickiana* (210), published in 1899; Joan Stevens's " 'Woodcuts Dropped into the Text': The Illustrations in *The Old Curiosity Shop* and *Barnaby Rudge*" (217), published in 1967; Sarah A. Solberg's " 'Texts Dropped into the Woodcuts': Dickens' Christmas Books" (216), published in 1980; Albert Johanssen's *Phiz: Illustrations from the Novels of Charles Dickens* (213), published in 1956; and George S. Layard's studies of plates that were suppressed for several of Dickens's works (215), published in 1899 and 1907.

Bibliographies of Dickens Studies

Here there is richness, particularly in the form of duplication, much that is inevitably outdated, and, to compensate for the outdated, a plethora of serial bibliographies that, in their online versions, at any rate, are quite up to date, if not ever complete. Historically, the interest in compiling lists of Dickens studies began with Cook's 1879 bibliography (4). At the end of his list of Dickens's works, Cook threw in lists of plagiarisms and continuations; portraits, paintings, and sets of extra illustrations; biographies; and a few studies of Dickens. Shepherd (20) includes an "Ana" section that grew from sixty-four in his 1880 bibliography to seventy-nine in the 1884 revision, with a "Supplementary Ana" section of an additional twenty-three studies supplied by W. R. Hughes. Both Dexter and Johnson (9, 16) include small sections of ana, but it was F. G. Kitton who pulled the material together in his *Dickensiana: A Bibliography of the Literature Relating to Charles Dickens and His*

Writings (235) in 1886 in a 511–page edition containing 584 numbered and heavily annotated items, though some of these—in sections labeled Poetical, Anthological, Musical, Dramatic, and Plagiaristic, Etc.— are not biographical or critical, and a few are reviews of John Forster's *Life of Charles Dickens* and *The Letters of Charles Dickens*, edited by Georgina Hogarth and Mamie Dickens. Still, that leaves 374 biographical and critical studies and reviews of individual works published by 1885, Kitton's cut-off date for entries. This figure does not include Kitton's summary of a number of items (unnumbered) published in *Notes and Queries* or his section entitled "Omniana," which he characterizes as "Brief Notes, selected principally from ephemeral literature, relating to Charles Dickens and his Writings." In his introduction, Kitton asserts that the quantity of studies of Dickens is the "surest indication of the nature and extent" of Dickens's popularity and, Kitton suggests, of his enduring fame.

To do something of an analysis of Kitton's bibliography, twenty-six of the biographical and forty-four of the critical studies, as well as seventy-six reviews of individual works by Dickens, for a total of 146, were published before Dickens's death (1840–June 1870). This leaves 105 biographical and sixty-eight critical studies, as well as thirty-two reviews of individual works, for a total of 205, that were published in the fifteen years following Dickens's death. To Kitton's totals, Charles F. Carty, in his "Some Addenda to Kitton's 'Dickensiana' " (218), published in 1902, added sixty-eight numbered items and four unnumbered ones, carried forward to 1901. Only one of these is a pre-1870 biographical sketch, and four are pre-1870 critical studies. Three are biographies published between 1870 and 1885 and five are critical studies. Fifty-three are post-1885 publications and represent what Carty was able to locate for the next fifteen years. Yet, as he acknowledged, he had "missed many."

Hard upon Kitton's bibliographical heels came John P. Anderson's bibliography (2) with twenty-four double-columned pages of appendices to his bibliography of Dickens's works, with subsections labeled "Biographical, Critical, Etc.," "Dramatic" (plays based on Dickens's works), "Musical," "Parodies and Imitations," "Poetical," and "Magazine and Newspaper Articles." Since Anderson lists Kitton's volume, he obviously was indebted to it, but, in some respects, the two works are complementary. Items in one are not necessarily in the other. In comparing, for example, the book-length biographical and critical studies listed in the two works, there are approximately twenty works in Kitton that are not in Anderson and forty or so in Anderson that are not in Kitton, but most are in both.

The next attempts at full-scale bibliographies of Dickens studies would come much later. In the meantime, the earliest serial literary bibliographies began to record the annual (and sometimes monthly, quarterly, and semiannual) production of Dickensiana—*Poole's Index to Periodical Literature,*

1802–81 (249) was published in 1882, revised in 1891, and added five supplementary volumes, 1888–1908, for 1882–1907. The series was continued as the *International Index to Periodicals*, 1907–65; the *Social Sciences and Humanities Index*, 1965–74; and the *Humanities Index*, 1974–). *Poole's Index* was complemented by the *Readers' Guide to Periodical Literature*, 1900– (250), and that in turn by the retrospective *Nineteenth Century Readers' Guide to Periodical Literature, 1890–1899, with Supplementary Indexing, 1900–1922* (224), published in 1944. In the meantime, the *Dickensian* began publication of "Dickensiana Month by Month" from 1905–18 and then "Dickensiana of the Quarter," to reflect its new publication schedule, from 1919 to 1941, followed by "Recent Dickensiana" or "Dickensiana" from 1941 to 1968 (253), and "The Year's Work in Dickens Studies" from 1968–83 (255). The listings are particularly valuable for the earlier decades of the century as a complement to the *International Index to Periodicals* and the *Readers' Guide to Periodical Literature*. By the 1920s, scholarly literary journals were multiplying, and the new serial bibliographies, created to record their output, were gearing up for the great work ahead. The British Modern Humanities Research Association's *Annual Bibliography of English Language and Literature* (247) first appeared in 1921 (for the year 1920) and, the following year, the "American Bibliography" in *Publications of the Modern Language Association of America* (252) appeared (for 1921), though until 1956 it listed only works by American scholars. The "Victorian Bibliography" first appeared in 1933 (for 1932), in *Modern Philology* and, from 1958 on, in *Victorian Studies* (257), with cumulative volumes for 1932–44, 1945–54, 1955–64, 1965–74, and 1975–84, edited, respectively, by W. D. Templeman (240), Austin Wright (244), Robert C. Slack (239), Ronald E. Freeman (229), and Richard C. Tobias (241). This twentieth-century triumvirate of scholarly serial bibliographies was joined in 1970 by "The Dickens Checklist," compiled by Alan M. Cohn and others for the *Dickens Studies Newsletter* and its successor the *Dickens Quarterly* (246), and, even more recently, in 1976, by the Canadian *Annual Bibliography of Victorian Studies* (245), using the Literary Information and Retrieval Database (LITIR). It is edited by Brahma Chaudhuri and was first published, annually, in 1980 (for 1976), and in various cumulative gatherings (1976–1980, 1970–1984, 1975–1989, 1945–1969). It is also available on CD-ROM (1970–1999), and online at the Victorian Database Online Web site, http://www.victoriandatabase.com (245). To these one should add the *Essay and General Literary Index* (248), begun by Minnie E. Sears and Marian Shaw in 1934 (for 1900–33), and the *Subject Index to Periodicals* (251), begun in 1916 (for 1915) by the Library Association, London, which was published as the *British Humanities Index* after 1962. Both of these are still being published, too.

A study by Abigail A. Loomis, "Dickens Duplications: A Study of Overlap in Serial Bibliographies in Literature" (94), published in 1986, concludes that there is no one serial bibliography in the humanities, and particularly in literature, that "provides ongoing comprehensive coverage," despite the need for such. Loomis analyzed the 1980 Dickens entries in the MLA and MHRA bibliographies, *The Year's Work in English Studies* (256), "Recent Dickens Studies" in *Dickens Studies Annual* (254), "The Year's Work in Dickens Studies" in the *Dickensian*, "The Dickens Checklist" in *Dickens Studies Newsletter*, and the "Victorian Bibliography" in *Victorian Studies*. She found that none located all the Dickens studies published in a given year. The *Dickens Studies Newsletter* contained the largest number of entries and the shortest time lag (though about half the entries were published prior to 1980), and, because highly selective, the *Dickensian* and the *Year's Work in English Studies* the smallest number. Loomis also found a high rate of duplication, or overlap, and percentages of unique entries ranging from eight to fifteen percent in the less selective bibliographies. Obviously it is important for a scholar to consult all of these each year.

To return to our history, William Miller's *The Dickens Student and Collector: A List of Writings Relating to Charles Dickens and His Works, 1836–1945* (237), published in 1946, with supplements in 1947 and 1953, was the first major bibliography of Dickens studies to appear since Kitton's *Dickensiana* sixty years earlier. It was severely criticized by Philo Calhoun and Howell J. Heaney in their "Dickensiana in the Rough," published in *Papers of the Bibliographical Society of America* in 1947 (70). One would have liked Miller's ambitious bibliography to have been better. Miller was one of the great Dickensians of the twentieth century and one of the leaders in the exploration of Dickensian bibliographical and textual study centered at the *Dickensian*, which he had helped found. Robert H. Haynes, who wrote the introduction to Miller's bibliography, offers something of an apologia for Miller in noting that he completed his bibliography in the Harvard Library during the Second World War, where he was "separated by the Atlantic from his accumulation of materials," which made the "verifying of many of his references . . . arduous and, in some cases, . . . impossible." Even in 1946 the volume of Dickens material was formidable, though nothing to what it was to become later, and Miller largely omitted newspaper articles to keep his bibliography from becoming too bulky. It ended up being 351 pages long, but seventy of those pages comprised the index.

Miller saw his work as an updating of Kitton's *Dickensiana*, which had been the comprehensive bibliography for its time. However, as Haynes points out, by 1946 Kitton's bibliography was "more or less obsolete because of new material which has made its appearance during the period which has elapsed and because of numberless previously unrecorded items which have been brought to light." Calhoun and Heaney acknowledged that in 1946 a new bibliography was long overdue, and they conceded that Miller's own "unique collection" of Dickensiana, on which much of his volume was based, at least "merited a catalogue" and that "the rest of the book is at least a memorial to the good taste and scholarly instincts of a lifetime." "If its results are faulty and incomplete," they rather condescendingly asserted, "that too is part of a leisurely cultural tradition which, until recently, has held itself aloof from modern standards of utility and thoroughness."

Their principal complaint was lack of thoroughness in the work. They found that Miller missed many items recorded not only in standard serial bibliographies and indexes but also in Kitton's *Dickensiana*, Charles F. Carty's supplement to it (218), and T. W. Hill's catalogue of Miller's own collection of music based on Dickens's works (193), published in 1940. There is "no important source," they concluded, "which does not note a substantial number of books, portions of books or articles of more than trivial interest, which ought to be and are not included in Miller."

Calhoun and Heaney also deplored the arrangement of the bibliography. Although Miller followed Kitton's divisions, Calhoun and Heaney found this grouping "so mussy and confusing, it is difficult to be entirely coherent in criticising it," though they tried. Nor did they find Miller's extremely limited annotations useful. They would have liked more accurate details of editions and other publication information to begin with, but they also proposed that the ideal bibliographer should include annotation that would contain "something in the nature of a critical appraisal of his material." Such commentary, they believed, would "at least have contributed a degree of warmth and color to his basic structure." Their final criticism was of Miller's inadequate index, "one of the most thoroughly irritating examples of that fine art which either of us has yet encountered." Miller's bibliography was, nevertheless, in 1946, the most inclusive bibliography of Dickens studies ever, and not all reviewers condemned it.

Joseph Gold's *The Stature of Dickens: A Centenary Bibliography* (230), published twenty-five years later in 1971, and largely covering the period 1870–1968/69, with a few earlier works, was intentionally a selective bibliography, a "presentation," as Gold explains, of what he found to be "of lasting scholarly value or interest." R. C. Churchill claims in the preface to his *A Bibliography of Dickensian Criticism, 1836–1975* (221), published in 1975, that his is "the most comprehensive" bibliography of Dickens criticism "yet attempted," but "criticism" is the key word here, for Churchill pretty much excludes any work that is not critical, such as bibliographies, biographies, and bibliographical, textual, and biographical studies. Reviewers have generally found the volume verging toward the eccentric—in its selection of material and its structure in particular.

Other bibliographies of Dickens studies, though intentionally of more limited scope, have been ambitious. Among these are the three editions of the

Cambridge Bibliography of English Literature (the second edition was called *The New Cambridge Bibliography of English Literature*), mentioned earlier. While the listing of works by English authors in these volumes attempts to be exhaustive, the secondary literature is quite selective. The Dickens section in the first edition (5) was compiled by F. J. H. Darton, with the "Bibliographies and Catalogues" and the "Biography and Criticism" sections covering only six and one-half double-columned pages of books and chapters in books published through 1937, with approximately another page of studies of individual novels. A supplementary volume by K. J. Fielding (13) added another seven pages of entries, covering 1936–55, a majority of which were journal articles. The Dickens section in the second edition (3), published in 1969, was compiled by Philip Collins and was far more elaborate than the first. By then the Dickens industry was in full swing, and it must have been difficult to put together even a representative selection of biographical and critical studies. The columns in this edition were longer and wider, about doubling the amount of information per page. Collins not only expanded the pre-1955 entries (though a few lesser items disappear), but also extended the bibliography through 1967. The main sections of studies were expanded in number as well as in length, filling thirteen pages (roughly equivalent to twenty-six pages in the first edition), and including a good many journal articles. Of course it was all highly selective. Compare Collins's two-page list of bibliographies and auction catalogues with the considerably larger number of entries in my forthcoming bibliography.

The huge section on Dickens in the third edition (19), published in 1999, and compiled by Paul Schlicke, is both impressive and something of a disappointment, though the latter is not of Schlicke's making. The introductory section on manuscripts, bibliographies, reference works (including Web sites), and studies of manuscripts and editions is, if selective, a useful updating of this section in the earlier editions. It is followed by section 1, which lists editions and studies of individual works, including letters and speeches, with subheadings (where needed) of bibliographies, editions, Dickens's reading adaptations, commentary on the text, imitations, dramatizations, reviews, and studies and appreciations. Section 2 lists personal recollections and memoirs, obituaries, and studies of special periods and aspects, bibliographies and adaptations, Dickens's illustrators and their illustrations, and biographies. The entries are essentially short-title ones, and there are no annotations. The organization throughout is chronological. Section 2 also lists critical and topographical studies, but only those published before 1920. This new and assuredly controversial policy for these two parts of the third edition gives the bibliography a curiously dated look, particularly since the second edition contained critical and topographical studies through 1967–and the first edition publications through 1938. Ironically, one needs to go to the first and second editions to begin to update the third. The justification for this has some sense to it, one must acknowledge. In her "Editor's Preface," Joanne Shattock, editor of the volume (Vol. 4: *1800–1900*), states that the "availability of comprehensive bibliographies of secondary material, both in electronic and volume form," at least back to 1920, meant that the CBEL did not need to "provide a selective list of secondary criticism for each author, as had previously been the case" in the first two editions.

Other selective bibliographies of note or bibliographies limited in scope are George H. Ford and Lauriat Lane, Jr.'s "Bibliography," a twenty-three page list in *The Dickens Critics* (228), published in 1961, "a selection," they point out, "from the impossibly enormous body of material written about Dickens before 1960" that seemed to them to be, "in whole or in part, 'criticism.'" The list contains principally post-1935 studies (though there are some earlier works going back to 1840) and so largely reflects the influence of Edmund Wilson on modern Dickens criticism. Ada Nisbet's bibliographical essay on Dickens in *Victorian Fiction: A Guide to Research* (238), published in 1964, is highly selective but an invaluable guide to Dickens studies prior to 1964, and a testament to what she characterizes as the "phenomenal rise in the number of ardent scramblers over Dickensian terrain" since 1918. Philip Collins provides the supplementary essay in *Victorian Fiction: A Second Guide to Research* (223), published in 1978, covering the next thirteen years (1962–75) of what he terms the "continuing boom" in Dickens studies. J. Don Vann published an intervening update of Nisbet's guide in his "A Checklist of Dickens Criticism, 1963–67" (242), published in *Studies in the Novel* in 1969, and Lauriat Lane, Jr.'s "Dickens Studies, 1958–1968: An Overview" (236) covers essentially the same period. John J. Fenstermaker published his *Charles Dickens, 1940–1975: An Analytical Subject Index to Periodical Criticism of the Novels and Christmas Books* (226) in 1979, in an attempt to make sense out of "post-Wilsonian" criticism of Dickens's novels, but his work, as the title indicates, is restricted to journal articles and excludes the important and rapidly growing body of full-length studies of Dickens's novels.

The last two major bibliographies of limited scope are Alan M. Cohn and K. K. Collins's *The Cumulated Dickens Checklist: 1970–1979* (222), published in 1982, and the Dickens section of Brahma Chaudhuri's *Annual Bibliography of Victorian Studies*, published as *Charles Dickens, a Bibliography: 1970–1986* (219) in 1988. Cohn and Collins's bibliography covers a mere ten years, though thoroughly, and is a cumulation and re-ordering of the checklists published quarterly in the *Dickens Studies Newsletter*. They intended their volume as a supplement to Gold's bibliography, though theirs is far more comprehensive. Since the checklist continued to appear quarterly in the *Dickens Studies Newsletter*, and continues now in the *Dickens Quarterly*, the bibliography remains up to date, in varying degrees of thoroughness, listing editions of Dickens's works, books, articles, reviews, dissertations, miscellaneous items, and, more recently, "Web Sites of Note." This bibliography (and its continuations) is paralleled by Chaudhuri's, which covers only a few more years of work, and is part of an Internet database that has been published in various printed formats as well (see 245). Like many Internet databases, it is not always as accurate as one might like, but it is reasonably thorough in its coverage, though not as thorough as the Cohn and Collins bibliography, which has more entries for a shorter period of time. Like Cohn and Collins, the bibliography stays updated by the continuing database.

There are many other useful bibliographies, more general or more specialized in scope that supplement and, equally as often, duplicate the ones listed here. Some are thematic, some concerned with studies of individual Dickens works (as already noted), some with the works of a particular country or those written in a particular language. Admittedly, any one of these might, at any given time, suit the purposes of a researcher better than the ones singled out here. The bibliographies noted above are the principal sources of studies of Dickens for the modern scholar. Here is a sampling, however, of some of the more important of the specialized bibliographies: William A. Wortman's *A Guide to Serial Bibliographies for Modern Literatures*, 2nd edition (243), published in 1995; James L. Harner's "Databases" and "Internet Resources" (231–32) in his *Literary Research Guide*, 4th edition (233), published in 2002; T. H. Howard-Hill's multi-volume *Index to British Literary Bibliographies* (234), published 1969– ; Frank T. Dunn's *A Cumulative Analytical Index to The Dickensian, 1905–1974* (225), published in 1976; Kathryn Chittick's *The Critical Reception of Charles Dickens, 1833–1841* (220), published in 1989; George H. Ford's "Appendix: Dickens's Awareness of Reviews," in his *Dickens and His Readers: Aspects of Novel-Criticism Since 1836* (227), published in 1955; and, for individual Dickens works, the volumes in the Garland Dickens Bibliographies and The Dickens Bibliographies published by AMS Press (7, 6).

For the twenty-first-century researcher there is now a steadily increasing number of Dickens and Victorian Web sites, each with links to each other and to still other Web sites (surely, a new form of bibliographic resource). Among the best are The Active Portal Project, University of Wisconsin (258), which provides access to "7200 links to pages found on 467 sites" concerning Dickens (as of 17 April 2003); David Perdue's Charles Dickens Page (260); The Dickens Fellowship Web site (261); The Dickens Page Web site, created by Mitsuharu Matsuoka (262); The Dickens Project Web site, University of California, Santa Cruz (263); the Victorian Research Web, Indiana University (264); George Landow's Victorian Web site (265); and The Voice of the Shuttle Web site (266). Many of these provide links to the texts of

Dickens's novels, as well as to a variety of essays, bibliographies, chat rooms—almost anything one could want. There is also a valuable Web site, perhaps not technically a bibliographical reference, that readers will want to know about, www.concordance.com (259), which makes word searches available for fifty-five major and minor Dickens works and offers links to any number of Internet resources.

Library Catalogues and Catalogues of Dickens Collections

These must not be overlooked in working with or locating manuscripts (including letters) and editions of Dickens's works, translations, adaptations, extra illustrations, and book-length studies of Dickens and his works. Of particular value are catalogues of collections specializing in Dickens, such as the collections given or sold to the Dickens House (282), the Dexter Collection in the British Library (271, 302), the VanderPoel Dickens Collection at the University of Texas (276), the Cruikshank and Dickens portions of the library of William Andrews Clark, Jr., at UCLA (280), the Elkins Collection in the Free Library of Philadelphia (283), the J. Pierpont Morgan Library in New York (286), the Berg Collection in the New York Public Library (294), the Gimbel Collection in the Yale University Library (297), Dickens letters in the Henry E. Huntington Library (298), Harry Smith's "Sentimental Library" (301) since dispersed at auction (363), the Widener Collection at Harvard University (299), the Suzannet Collection (303–04), now scattered, but a significant portion of which was donated to the Dickens House (300), and the Forster Collection of manuscripts, page proofs, letters, and other items in the Victoria and Albert Museum, London (305–07). These as well as a number of lesser collections contain valuable manuscripts and rare printed matter and are accessible to the scholar with the necessary credentials.

There is always a thrill in holding in one's hands a beautifully bound manuscript of a Dickens work, whether it is a multivolume set of the manuscript of a major Dickens novel in the Forster Collection of the V & A or a slim article for *All the Year Round* in the Rare Books Division of the New York Public Library. Of course "holding in one's hands" is a bit of a euphemism, since the manuscript is usually placed on a special book rack, and one turns the pages timorously under close supervision of an alert librarian. As Annette Low reveals in "The Conservation of Dickens' Manuscripts" (436), published in 1993, an illustrated report on the recent rebinding of the manuscripts in the Forster Collection, the pages are now hinged at one edge into "blank books of alkaline paper," with the other edge being "held down with a strip of Bondina across the corners." Such binding allows for flex and expansion and contraction, with "generous support leaf margins" preventing any handling of the manuscript pages themselves.

Of equal importance are the Dickens sections of the major national library and union catalogues—The British Museum and Library (270–75), the American Library of Congress (287) and National Union Catalogue (288), the French Bibliothèque Nationale (267–69, 289), the Italian *Catalogo Cumulativo* (278)—and of major city and university libraries, such as the New York Public Library (290–96) and the Houghton and the Widener Libraries, Harvard University (284– 85). The entries in these catalogues are not as fully described as in the often elegant and beautifully illustrated catalogues of special Dickens collections; indeed, they are generally unannotated and without illustrations, and their online catalogue entries are sometimes even more Spartan. In lieu of handling and searching the typically large, heavy volumes of printed library catalogues, one can do the equivalent online at three incredible Web sites: Libweb (312), at http://sunsite.Berkeley.edu/Libweb, providing access to the catalogues of 6,500 libraries in more than 115 countries; libdex, the Library Index Web site, edited and compiled by Peter Scott (317) at http://www.libdex.com, which offers access to the online catalogues of 18,000 (as of 1 April 2003) public, university, and other libraries, as well as links to numerous other interesting sites; and the OCLC WorldCat Web site (315), at http//www.oclc.org/worldcat, which is a database of over 48,000,000 entries from the merged catalogues of innumerable libraries worldwide, available, however, only through subscribing libraries. The advantage of WorldCat is that it is essentially a union catalogue, locating libraries that contain the volume in which one is interested. If one is trying to locate a particular edition of a Dickens novel, say, or a rare bibliographical item, the WorldCat Web site is the one to use, as are two other powerful consortium catalogues available online. The first is the *Catalog collectif de France* (277) at http://www.ccfr.bnf.fr, which accesses more than 14,000,000 documents from the Catalogue des fonds des bibliothèques municipales rétroconvertis and the Catalogue du système universitaire de documentation, in addition to the Catalogue BN-OPALE PLUS of the Bibliothèque Nationale (269). The second is the COPAC Web site of the Consortium of University Research Libraries (279), at http://copac.ac.uk/copac, which provides access to "the merged online catalogues of 22 of the largest university research libraries in the UK and Ireland *plus* the British Library."

Various guides have also been published which list and describe major and minor Dickens collections—see particularly, Lee Ash and William G. Miller's *Subject Collections: A Guide to Special Book Collections and Subject Emphases as Reported by University, College, Public, and Special Libraries and Museums in the United States and Canada* (308), the latest edition published in 1993; Barbara L. Bell's *An Annotated Guide to Current National Bibliographies* (309), published in 1986; Donald L. DeWitt's *Guide to Archives and Manuscript Collections in the United States: An Annotated Bibliography*

(310), published in 1994; Robert B. Downs's *American Library Resources: A Bibliographical Guide*, published in 1951, with later supplements, and his and Elizabeth C. Downs's *British and Irish Library Resources: A Bibliographical Guide* (311), published in 1981; James L. Harner's section on "Research Libraries" in his *Literary Research Guide* (233), published in 2002; Philip M. Hamer's *A Guide to Archives and Manuscripts in the United States* (313), published in 1961; Bonnie R. Nelson's *A Guide to Published Library Catalogs* (314), published in 1982; Keith W. Reynard's *The Aslib Directory of Literary and Historical Collections in the UK* (316), the latest edition published in 1998; and Moelwyn I. Williams's *A Directory of Rare Books and Special Collections in the United Kingdom and the Republic of Ireland* (318), published in 1985 and revised by B. C. Bloomfield and Karen Potts in 1997.

Exhibition Catalogues

These catalogues, too, can be the source of valuable information about Dickens bibliography. The earliest ones track Dickens's post-1870 reputation and the attempts, particularly by the Dickens Fellowship, formed in 1902, to maintain and build that reputation. The first four Dickens exhibitions, held in London between 1903 and 1909, were sponsored by the Fellowship. The Dickens Exhibition held at Memorial Hall for three days in March 1903 (336), was, as its compiler, Frederic G. Kitton, points out in his introduction to the catalogue, the first exhibition "absolutely restricted to Dickens"; it included manuscripts, autograph letters, original editions, translations, relics, portraits, original drawings, and other items. The *Athenaeum* reviewer called the exhibition "an excellent piece of bibliography, which may well become important to collectors," and the London *Times* reviewer, waxing a little more eloquent, asserted that it provided "convincing evidence of Dickens's immense hold upon the feelings and the hearts of the people" (336). The second Dickens exhibition, held at the New Dudley Gallery, 22 July-28 August, only five years later (325), was compiled by two other early Dickensians, B. W. Matz and J. W. T. Ley, the latter of whom asserts in the illustrated catalogue's introduction that "today Dickens is the most popular and most beloved novelist" and that he and Matz had tried to make the exhibition "as comprehensive as possible." The third exhibition was also held at the New Dudley Galleries the following year, 7 August-30 September (339), with a brief introduction to the illustrated catalogue written this time by Percy Fitzgerald, yet another early Dickensian. Intervening between the first and second exhibitions was the first Pickwick exhibition (324), also at the New Dudley Galleries, 22 July-28 August 1907. Its illustrated catalogue was compiled by

Matz and Ley, and is a 116–page listing of the Pickwickiana in the exhibition—English, American, and other foreign editions and translations of the
novel; plagiarisms, parodies, plays, playbills, and music; relics and mementos;
political cartoons and caricatures; postcards, calendars, posters, advertisements; portraits and biographies of Dickens; autograph letters; and a number
of other items.

London celebrated 1912, the centenary of Dickens's birth, with a major
exhibition at the Victoria and Albert Museum, running from March to October. It was the museum's first Dickens exhibition, based on its Forster Collection, the manuscripts, page proofs, number plans, and other items that John
Forster had bequeathed to the museum. The V&A issued a nicely descriptive
and illustrated catalogue (346). A photograph of part of the exhibition can
be seen in Trevor Blount's review of 1970 exhibitions (350). There was also
an exhibition at the Franklin Club, St. Louis, Missouri, 7–12 February 1912
(328), which issued a 49–page catalogue, and one the following year, close
enough to count, perhaps, as a centenary exhibition, at the Grolier Club in
New York (335), 23 January-8 March 1913, which issued a 256–page illustrated catalogue, and included the manuscript of *A Christmas Carol*, thirty-
two pages of the manuscript of *Pickwick Papers*, and manuscripts of lesser
works, as well as editions, sketches, extra illustrations, letters, playbills, relics,
and other items.

Between 1912 and 1970, the centenaries of Dickens's birth and death, there
were a number of exhibitions of lesser importance devoted almost entirely to
specific collections. Interest in Dickens, or at least in Dickens exhibitions,
waned between 1913 and 1936, as to a large extent scholarship did, except
for continuing activity in the Dickens Fellowship and in the pages of the
Dickensian. The only notable exhibition during this period seems to have
been of the Howard Duffield collection of items associated with *Edwin Drood*
(327), mounted at the Grolier Club, New York, in 1932. The year 1936, the
centenary of the beginning of the serialization of *Pickwick Papers*, produced
at least three exhibitions, however. In London, a second major Pickwick
exhibition by the Dickens Fellowship was mounted, this time at the Dickens
House (323), March-April 1936. There were other Pickwick exhibitions of
lesser import at the Southwark Public Libraries and Cuming Museum, London
(343), and at the Public Library, Museums, and National Gallery of Victoria,
in Melbourne, Australia (341), for which catalogues were issued. An exhibition was also held in 1936, and an illustrated catalogue issued (326), of the
Charles J. Sawyer collection of Dickens's manuscripts, letters, presentation
copies, parts editions, and Dickensiana. In 1941, the Henry W. & Albert A.
Berg Collection at the New York Public Library produced its first Dickens
exhibition, but its catalogue was only four pages long (340). In 1946, the
William M. Elkins collection at the Free Library of Philadelphia was featured

in an exhibition there, June-July 1946, for which an illustrated catalogue (329) was issued, and in 1949 and 1958 exhibitions at the New York Public Library featured items from the Berg Collection. The earlier presented first editions of first books by English writers, including *Sketches by Boz*, and the later exhibited prompt books of Dickens's public readings and related materials, with catalogues for both by John D. Gordan (333–34). In February 1962, items from the Richard Gimbel collection were exhibited in the Sterling Memorial Library, Yale University (332), and Gimbel's entire Dickens collection went to Yale University at his death in 1970.

The year 1970, however, was another matter. If interest in Dickens, or at least in major Dickens exhibitions, waned after 1913, with a brief revival in 1936, the centenary of Dickens's death certainly renewed it. A flurry of exhibitions opened in 1970, most in England, but there were also exhibitions in the United States at Loras College in Dubuque, Iowa (321), at the University of Texas (331), at the University of California in Los Angeles (347), at the Pierpont Morgan Library in New York (349), and in the Berg Collection, New York Public Library (344). At the New York Public Library, there were also a smaller exhibition of "Dickens in America" and one of illustrations of Dickens's characters by a number of artists (349). In Belgium, the University of Liège sponsored an exhibition organized by the British Council (322).

In England, Malcolm Andrews reported in the *Dickens Studies Newsletter* (348), there were "seventy or more exhibitions mounted by libraries." He names only the major ones, but does single out as "one of the most interesting" an exhibition at Liverpool University on "Pickwick and Pickwickiana" based on the "extensive holdings of an anonymous local collector," whom Michael Slater (352) identifies as F. S. Bradburn, and whose catalogue, Richard A. Vogler (353) finds, from an examination of it (338), to be "not necessarily of a wealthy, but certainly of a devoted and astute collector." G. Chandler, the librarian at the Liverpool Central Library also reports on an exhibition there (351). Another, smaller exhibition was held at Knebworth House in Hertfordshire (337) of letters and other items associated with the friendship of Dickens and Edward Bulwer-Lytton. And Trevor Blount, in a review of centenary exhibitions for the *Dickensian* (350), describes an exhibition in Eastgate House in Rochester of "various items from the Percy Fitzgerald Collection."

Exhibitions in London were numerous. Trevor Blount characterizes an exhibition in the King's Library in the British Museum (320) as a "notable assemblage of material" from the John F. Dexter Collection. Several reviewers liked the exhibition on "Dickens and Medicine" at the Wellcome Institute of the History of Medicine (330); Blount, for example, found it "a relatively small exhibit but an informative one" and "a great pleasure to visit." The British Council held a small "centenary book exhibition" in London (319).

The major London exhibitions, however, were at the Dickens House and the Victoria and Albert Museum. The Dickens House featured, as the title of its catalogue, compiled by Michael Slater (342), indicates, *Treasures from the Dickens Collection Formed by the Late Comte Alain de Suzannet* of letters, playbills, drawings and sketches, rare editions, manuscripts, and other materials donated to it by Suzannet between 1930 and 1950, and by his widow in 1966 and 1971. Many of the items are now on permanent exhibition in the two Suzannet Rooms in the museum. The Victoria and Albert Museum exhibition (345) was nothing less than sensational, if one can say this about a museum exhibition. It was the first major Dickens exhibition at the museum since its 1912 show. Running from 10 June to 20 September, it was designed by Christopher Firmstone to reflect the purpose announced by John Pope-Hennessey, museum director, in the foreword to the catalogue: "to portray one of the greatest creative artists of the nineteenth century against the background of the life and social history of his time." The exhibition twisted and turned theatrically like a Dickensian street, and the earlier portions of it were confined and dim, as Dickens imagined his childhood to be, with the spaces lightening and opening up as his career developed. The manuscripts of ten of his novels, page proofs, letters, editions of his works, playbills, drawings, paintings, photographs, relics, and a plethora of other items were worked into the dramatic physical structure. As I said in my review of the exhibition (349), the museum, "apart from mounting a major exhibition exciting in itself, has provided a great service for scholars in showing the range and depth of the material available, much of it relatively unexplored to date, for further investigation into the life and works of a great author."

The history of Dickens exhibitions pretty much ends here, at least for the time being. The Dickens exhibition scene has been relatively quiet since 1970, but will no doubt come alive again in 2012, the bicentennial of Dickens's birth.

Because of space restraints, I am not including here the numerous reports on Dickens exhibitions, collections, and library accessions of Dickens materials. nor am I listing Dickens scrapbooks (most at the Dickens House) and Dickens museum guides. All of these will, however, be found in my forthcoming bibliography. Many of these are as interesting in themselves as they are informative and useful.

Auction and Booksellers' Catalogues

One last area of bibliographical significance needs to be covered. Occasionally auction and booksellers' catalogues have shown up in Dickens bibliographies, principally in the three editions of the *Cambridge Bibliography of*

English Literature, and there very selectively, and to an even lesser extent in the volumes of T. H. Howard-Hill's *Index to British Literary Bibliography* (234). Though such catalogues are by no means error-proof, a perusal of the more important of them will quickly reveal their value to Dickens scholarship. The editors of the twelve-volume *Pilgrim Letters* (561) used them extensively, for at least two important reasons. First, since lists of purchase prices (occasionally with the names of purchasers) printed after the sale are often inserted in sale catalogues deposited in libraries, and just as frequently written in by a collector or curator who was at the auction, it is sometimes possible to locate the current owners. A number of sale catalogues in the British Library are auctioneers' copies, with manuscript notes and prices, that were apparently donated by the principal London auction houses. Major collections of auction catalogues will also be found in the New York Public Library and the Library of Congress, as well as, according to David Pearson in his *Provenance Research in Book History: A Handbook* (410), published in 1994, in the Cambridge University Library, the Bodleian Library at Oxford University, and the National Art Library in the Victoria and Albert Museum. Second, most sale as well as booksellers' catalogues will give excerpts from letters or manuscripts or even print or include a photographic facsimile of a letter, a page of manuscript, a title page, or book cover. Having even the partial text of a letter that has disappeared after an auction or been subsequently destroyed is of inestimable value to the scholar. At one point in working on my forthcoming bibliography, out of curiosity I examined the letters in the first ten volumes of the *Pilgrim Letters*, then all that had been published, to see what sources the editors had used for the text of letters for which the autograph manuscripts were unavailable. Some of these letters had been published in books and articles, but the text of a far greater number, in the vicinity of 900, came from auction and booksellers' catalogues. Unfortunately, and uncharacteristically for this thoroughly scholarly enterprise, many of the catalogues are so inadequately identified as to make locating of them impossible.

James Harner, in the fourth edition of his *Literary Research Guide* (233), pp. 612–13, rightly declares that booksellers' and auction catalogues "are among the most underutilized scholarly resources." They are valuable, he adds, for "identifying hitherto unrecorded printed works, editions, or manuscripts," for "finding descriptions (and sometimes reproductions or transcriptions) of unique items no longer locatable," for "tracing the provenance of a copy (and thus possibly locating it)," and for "reconstructing an individual's library." Michael Hunter, in his "Auction Catalogues and Eminent Libraries" (402), published in 1972, also holds that auction catalogues "are mainly interesting for showing what books eminent men owned" but cautions that the listings in catalogues are not always complete since many volumes in a collection may not be offered in a sale.

Auction catalogues do indeed provide a record of some great Dickens collections, and frequently give detailed descriptions of important items in the collection, from elaborate collations of prime Pickwicks in parts to itemizing of large collections of letters. These should find a place among the catalogues of great Dickens collections mentioned, particularly since these were dispersed at auction rather than donated intact to a library, and the auction catalogue remains the sole published record of a great collector's library, even if incomplete. A few of the more important sale catalogues are those of the collections of George McCutcheon (354); William F. Gable of Altoona, Pennsylvania (355); Mr. and Mrs. Edward Daoust (356, 359); George Ulizio, of Pine Valley, New Jersey (360); Ogden Goelet, New York (361–62); Harry B. Smith, New York (363); Augustin Daly (364); Edwin Lapham, Chicago (365), best known for his set of prime Pickwick in parts, the Lapham Pickwick; Edwin W. Coggeshall, New York (366, 369); Ralph T. Jupp, London (367, 393); Jerome Kern, New York (371); Theodore N. Vail, New York (370); Lewis A. Hird, Englewood, New Jersey (376); Comte de Suzannet, Lausanne, Switzerland (380–81), and see also his published catalogues (303–04); H. W. Bruton, Gloucester, England (388); William Wright (387); Richard Manney (391); and, most recently, Horace N. Pym (390).

Other dispersed libraries are of interest for other reasons. First there are the catalogues of the sale of Dickens's property—the furnishings and other effects of Gad's Hill, his last residence, in 1870 (394); his pictures and objets d'art, also in 1870 (373); and his library (392), in 1878. In 1939, Lady Dickens (his son Henry's wife) and her children sold the manuscript of *Life of Our Lord* (384), and, very recently, in 1999, a collection of valuable legal papers then still held by the Dickens family (389) and termed the "Dickens Archive" by Sotheby's was offered at auction. In a disappointing sale, few items found purchasers, but, fortunately, the bulk of the archive eventually ended up in the British Library, as reported by Malcolm Andrews in the *Dickensian* in 2001 (389). Also interesting are sales of the property of old friends or publishers of Dickens—Samuel Rogers (372), including eleven of Dickens's novels, three of which were presented to Rogers by Dickens; William Macready (374), including eight novels, five of which were presented to Macready or his wife; Angela Burdett-Coutts (385), including presentation copies, the autograph manuscript of *The Haunted Man, and the Ghost's Bargain*, and a collection of "upwards of 600 letters" from Dickens, and others from members of the Dickens family and circle; Edmund Yates (386), including letters from Dickens to Yates, one of his writers for *All the Year Round*; and Richard Bentley (375), including correspondence between Dickens and Bentley, one of his earliest publishers, and seven publishing agreements. Still other catalogues reveal the collections of prominent Dickens scholars—for example, John C. Eckel (358), William Glyde Wilkins (368), Herman LeRoy Edgar

(377), A. Edward Newton (378), and Thomas Hatton, who sold his collection in parts over the years (357, 379, 382–83).

Book auction records can sometimes be helpful. The most useful is probably *Book-Prices Current* (396), which was published from 1888 (for 1886/87) to 1957 (for 1955/56), giving the auction house, the date of the sale, the price, and frequently the purchaser of numerous Dickens items, manuscripts as well as books, from 1921 on and American as well as English sales from 1916 on. *Book-Auction Records* (395) lists the auction house and price but not the purchaser or specific date of sale from 1903 on, beginning with just London houses and gradually increasing its range to include all British, then American, and then houses of other countries (the last since 1968). *American Book-Prices Current* (397) gives prices of Dickens items but not the sellers or purchasers, and so is less useful.

Supplementing the sale and booksellers' catalogues and the auction records are innumerable reports of these sales (see items 2071–2197 in my forthcoming bibliography) in such publications as the *Times Literary Supplement*, the London *Times*, and the *New York Times* (though not so much in recent years). These help to identify important sales and, where catalogues are not easily located, at least give some idea of what was in the sale.

Many books have been published as guides for the beginning collector of books, some of which contain brief sections on collecting Dickens's works. A few of the earliest are mentioned above in the section on bibliographies of Dickens's works. More recent or interesting ones are Charles J. Sawyer and J. Harvey Darton's *English Books, 1475–1900: A Signpost for Collectors*, an introduction to book collecting, with a chapter on Dickens (416), published in 1927; Allen and Patricia Ahearn's *Collected Books: The Guide to Values, 1998 Edition* (398), published in 1997; Colton Storm and Howard Peckham's *Invitation to Book Collecting, Its Pleasures and Practices* (419), published in 1947, and John T. Winterich and David A. Randall's *A Primer of Book Collecting*, 3rd edition (420), published in 1966. Others are more personal, such as William H. Arnold's *Ventures in Book Collecting* (399), published in 1923; Percy Fitzgerald's *The Book Fancier, or The Romance of Book Collecting* (401), published in 1886; A. Edward Newton's *The Amenities of Book Collecting, and Kindred Affections* (408), published in 1918; Horace N. Pym's *A Tour Round My Book-Shelves* (411), published in 1891; A. S. W. Rosenbach's *A Book Hunter's Holiday: Adventures with Books and Manuscripts* (412), published in 1936; and Walter T. Spencer's chapter on ''Dickensiana'' in his *Forty Years in My Bookshop* (418), published in 1923.

Biographies or biographical studies of the great Dickens collectors are always fascinating—see, for example, Leslie A. Morris's ''Harry Elkins Widener and A. S. W. Rosenbach: Of Books and Friendship'' (407), published in 1995; Edwin Wolf, 2nd, and John F. Fleming's *Rosenbach, a Biography*

(421), published in 1960; and sketches of Rosenbach (405), Widener (406), George Ulizio (403), Jerome Kern (417), Charles Sessler (404), Harry B. Smith (409), and William Andrews Clark, Jr. (415), in *American Book-Collectors and Bibliographers*, edited by Joseph Rosenblum in two series (413–14), published in 1994 and 1997. Also see "Collecting Charles Dickens," a special issue, published September 1997, of *Firsts: The Book Collector's Magazine* (400), which contains five articles by Lee Biondi, proprietor of The Heritage Book Shop, Los Angeles, written from a bookseller's point of view. In "Strategies of Collecting," he begins with the premise that "a nice 'Dickens Collection' is do-able at various paces and price levels, and with a reasonable degree of difficulty," and then surveys the problems and difficulty of collecting the principal works. Three of the other articles look at bibliographical matters concerning the collecting of editions of *Great Expectations*, *Pickwick Papers*, and *Sketches by Boz*, while the remaining piece, "The Charles Dickens Reference Shelf," is an annotated list of Dickens reference works.

Studies of Manuscripts and Textual Changes/Dickens at Work

One might say that the study of Dickens's manuscripts, page proofs, and number plans, as well as the significance of textual changes between manuscript and published text began with John Butt and Kathleen Tillotson's *Dickens at Work* (430) in 1957, so important and valuable, such a classic, has this study become in modern Dickens scholarship. The volume was based to a considerable extent on work both authors had done in the late 1940s and early 1950s (425, 427–28, 467–68, 472, 476; also see 426, 429, and 475 for three later studies). Scholarly interest in the manuscripts goes back, however, to the nineteenth century. As early as 1874 articles were appearing in the United States (529, 531–34) describing the manuscript of *Our Mutual Friend*, which was then in the possession of George W. Childs, a Philadelphia publisher and collector and former acquaintance of Dickens. Surprisingly, Dickens had given the manuscript and the number plans to E. S. Dallas, a literary critic, whose qualification for such a gift seems to have been that he had written a favorable review of the novel for the London *Times*. The manuscript and its number plans had passed through two other owners before Childs purchased them from the second of these. Then the only major Dickens manuscripts in the country, they are now in the Pierpont Morgan Library, New York.

It was John Forster who, in his *Life of Charles Dickens* (14), published in 1871–73, first emphasized the importance of the manuscripts, number plans, and proofs to an understanding of Dickens's craftsmanship and artistry. He included facsimiles of a page each of the number plans for *David Copperfield* and *Little Dorrit*, as well as facsimiles of the last page of the manuscripts of *Edwin Drood* and *Oliver Twist*. In the biography, Forster also indicated a number of changes, mainly minor ones, that Dickens made in preparing his novels for publication and printed some manuscript material, including Dickens's extant fragment of his autobiography and the original ending for *Great Expectations*. He mentioned in passing that a number of Dickens's manuscripts, page proofs, and number plans were in his possession, but he did not discuss textual changes and their significance.

At Forster's death in 1876, the manuscripts, number plans, and page proofs of the thirteen Dickens manuscripts in his possession went to the South Kensington Museum, now the Victoria and Albert Museum, where scholars soon had access to them. In 1877, in "Charles Dickens's Manuscripts," *Chambers's Journal* published a description of them for its readers (431), an article sufficiently popular to be reprinted in the *Eclectic Magazine, Littell's Living Age*, and *Potter's American Monthly*, the last of which added a paragraph criticizing the way in which the manuscripts and page proofs were displayed in cases in the library. In 1880 the museum published a *Handbook of the Dyce and Forster Collections in the South Kensington Museum* (305) in which the manuscripts and proofs were described. In 1885, J. A. H. Murray pointed out in a *Notes and Queries* piece (486) that he had discovered variant readings in editions of *Hard Times* and wondered whether or not there were any more such variants in other Dickens works. In 1896, J. Holt Schooling published an article, "Charles Dickens's Manuscripts," in the *Strand Magazine* (439), centered on twenty-six illustrations of pages from the manuscripts, page proofs, number plans, and original illustrations, in which he commented on some of the interesting alterations that Dickens had made in the course of composing his novels.

F. G. Kitton, too, was fascinated by the manuscripts and what they revealed about Dickens's creativity. He published a facsimile of the manuscript of *A Christmas Carol* in 1890 (89) and included descriptions of a number of the manuscripts in *The Novels of Charles Dickens* (17) in 1897 and in *The Minor Writings of Charles Dickens* (58), in 1900. The bibliographical notes he wrote for the six novels published in the Rochester Edition (435), 1900–01, contained information about the manuscripts, and he described the manuscripts of the Christmas Books in an article in the *Library Review* (456) in 1893.

Over the years, in the first half or so of the twentieth century, a series of commentaries on cancellations in and additions to the manuscripts and page proofs kept interest in the subject of Dickens's craftsmanship alive. As early as 1910, M. H. Spielmann, in "How Dickens Improved His Style" (441), commenting on a group of accompanying photographic facsimiles of pages from the manuscripts of *Oliver Twist, Martin Chuzzlewit, David Copperfield*, and *Bleak House*, found that the increasingly smaller, cramped hand and the

increasingly larger number of corrections showed "the more careful craftsman." Between 1951 and 1955, Leslie C. Staples, then editor of the *Dickensian*, printed a number of passages that, largely because of his self-imposed
length restrictions (exactly thirty-two full pages per number), Dickens can-
celed in page proof (442). Most articles, however, concentrated on a single
novel, sometimes, as in Alain de Suzannet's "The Original Manuscript of
'The Pickwick Papers' " (540), published in 1932, locating scattered pages
of the novel, or, as in William Miller's "The Manuscript of *Oliver Twist*"
(521), published in 1915, locating portions of the work. Other studies, such
as Gerald G. Grubb's "Dickens's Marchioness Identified" (518), published
in 1953, showed how cancellations or additions in manuscript or page proofs
modified or deepened a character, or, as in Albert A. Dunn's "The Altered
Endings of *Great Expectations*: A Note on Bibliography and First-Person
Narrative" (480), published in 1978, changed the emphasis of an ending. In
his *Dickens romancier*, published in Paris in 1953 (437), Sylvère Monod was
the first biographer/critic to use the manuscripts, number plans, and page
proofs extensively to study, as he expressed it in his 1968 English translation
of his work, how the novels were "conceived, constructed, and written."
These materials, Monod concluded, "provide evidence of Dickens' earnest,
conscientious, even anxious work, and particularly of his passionate, lifelong
interest in language and style."

   But scarcely anyone else paid any attention to the number plans, except
for *Edwin Drood* scholars who were, from virtually 1870 on, desperately
seeking out solutions to the "Mystery," and looking everywhere. This led
W. Robertson Nicoll, in his *The Problem of "Edwin Drood": A Study in the
Methods of Dickens* (509), published in 1912, to print, "now for the first
time" the complete number plans for parts 1–6, as well as a page in Dickens's
hand containing characters' names and proposed titles for the novel. Percy
Carden printed facsimiles of the number plans for *Drood* in 1931 (500). The
immediate predecessor of Butt and Tillotson was Ernest Boll, who printed,
in "The Plotting of *Our Mutual Friend*" (525) in 1944, a transcription of
the number plans for Dickens's last complete novel, and, as Butt and Tillotson
were to do, used the number plans to reveal Dickens's working methods,
craftsmanship, and artistry in "the weaving of the story." Corrections in
Boll's transcription were noted by Joan D. Winslow in 1978 (538).

   The importance of Butt and Tillotson was not so much that they extensively
explored the number plans, page proofs, and manuscripts of Dickens's novels,
because they did not do that much of this—they sampled rather than feasted.
Their purpose, as they stated in the preface, was to represent "different stages
of [Dickens's] career and different kinds of work." It was their approach to
Dickens as a working craftsman rather than an inspired genius that was the
astonishing and innovative element of their approach, "the process," as they

put it, "rather than the result," the "craft" rather than the "art." Yet they also insisted that "the inspiration and justification of our work is none the less a conviction of Dickens's greatness as a creative artist." In the heyday of the New Criticism, they dared to suggest, and illustrate convincingly, that, like Shakespeare, Dickens had control of his craft, and this control became the art of writing the novel, or at least the specific form at which Dickens excelled, the novel in parts. A careful study of Dickens's letters, particularly those to John Forster, and of his manuscripts, page proofs, and number plans would reveal this in great detail, they were convinced, and would prove to be as valid an approach to understanding Dickens critically as ignoring an author's background and working methods and letting the works, and words, speak for themselves.

Accordingly, the introductory chapter, "Dickens as a Serial Novelist," written largely by Butt, examines Dickens's "habits at the desk," developed mostly from his letters and his memoranda, in producing the mainly monthly installments of his novels—only six of fifteen were not produced this way. Chapter 2, "*Sketches by Boz*: Collection and Revision," largely by Tillotson, compares the text of the various magazine and newspaper pieces that Dickens wrote between 1833 and 1836 with his revisions and arrangements of them when he included them in the first and subsequent editions of *Sketches by Boz* (no manuscripts have survived). Chapter 3, "From Sketches to Novel: *Pickwick Papers* (1836–7)," also principally by Tillotson, examines, "largely by inference," since only a few pages of manuscript, no proofs or number plans and very few letters on the subject exist, how Dickens wrote his first novel. The evidence for the writing of *Barnaby Rudge*, the subject of chapter 4 (Tillotson's), "*Barnaby Rudge*: The First Projected Novel," comes largely from Dickens's letters and some comparison of the text of the manuscript with that of the earliest printed text, since neither proof sheets nor memoranda have survived.

Chapter 5, "*Dombey and Son*: Design and Execution," a major chapter in the work, explores the writing of the first novel with extant number plans, showing that, at least from this point on, Dickens "planned each instalment on paper before he began writing." Here Butt and Tillotson, working together—the chapter originally appeared "in substantially its present form" in *Essays and Studies 1951* (472)—use the title, the design of the monthly cover, Dickens's letters to John Forster, the manuscript and number plans, and the proof sheets to "throw light" on Dickens's design for the novel and the "degree of consistency with which he maintained his purpose." Chapter 6, "*David Copperfield* Month by Month" (largely Butt's), uses another innovative approach, a close, and fascinating, examination of a full set of number plans, with a month by month transcription of them included, and accompanied by a month by month explanation of what they reveal of Dickens's interweaving of the strands of the novel into the finished text. In chapter 7, "The Topicality of *Bleak House*," Tillotson, this time *without* consulting any of the available textual apparatus, studies the integration by Dickens of a "diversity of detail," social and political in nature, "into a single view of society." In the next chapter, "*Hard Times*: The Problems of a Weekly Serial" (largely Butt's), attention turns to the problems of weekly publication of the parts of the novel, though Butt indicates that Dickens actually planned the novel more as five monthly installments than as twenty weekly ones, a scheme that did not work well in practice because he found the frame and space of a weekly installment restricting and frustrating. At the same time, it reveals, Butt illustrates, with a number of excerpts from the number plans, "the attention which Dickens was now paying to construction." In the final chapter, "From 'Nobody's Fault' to *Little Dorrit*," Tillotson, the principal author, again illustrates her interest in the "conditions of publication of Victorian fiction," as noted in the preface, in the connection between text and social problems, particularly, as she illustrates, between planning (in the number plans) and dominant "political, social, and ethical themes." There is no concluding chapter. The nine chapters in the volume are offered as examples only of what can be done with textual criticism to shed light on Dickens as conscious craftsman and, ultimately, as artist.

Thus, much more remained to be mined in the archives of the Victoria and Albert Museum and in the other museums holding number plans, manuscripts, and page proofs. It took eight to nine years after the publication of *Dickens at Work*, however, for scholars to publish further investigations into this rich lode of unpublished material. Tillotson followed up her work on *Dickens at Work* with her edition of *Oliver Twist* (523), published in 1966. It was the first volume in the Clarendon Dickens, of which she and Butt served as general editors. The Clarendon Edition, as they announced in a "Preface by the General Editors" (68), which is printed in all the volumes in the series, was to establish a critical text, one "free of the numerous corruptions that disfigure modern reprints, with an apparatus of variants that will exhibit Dickens's progressive revision." See below under my commentary on textual studies of individual Dickens works for *Oliver Twist* and other volumes published in the Clarendon Edition. One of the earlier studies to deal with the manuscripts more generally was Harvey P. Sucksmith's *The Narrative Art of Charles Dickens: The Rhetoric of Irony and Sympathy in His Novels* (444), published in 1970, and related, obviously, to Sucksmith's earlier work on *Bleak House* (450). In this full-length study, Sucksmith makes frequent use of textual variants to study Dickens's "conscious and rhetorical art." Burt Hornback, in his *"The Hero of My Life": Essays on Dickens* (434), published in 1981, likewise studies Dickens's craftsmanship through frequent reference to manuscript materials. Joel J. Brattin was later to publish several textual studies of individual novels (see below), growing out of his doctoral dissertation, "Reading between the Lines: Interpreting Dickens's Later Manuscripts" (424), completed in 1986. In his "A Map of the Labyrinth: Editing Dickens's Manuscripts," which he published in *Dickens Studies Annual* in 1985 (423), Brattin makes a case for using the manuscript of a Dickens novel as the copytext for the most authoritative edition of the novel and contemplates the difficulties and desirability of actually making transcripts of the manuscripts. Susan Shatto's series, The Dickens Companions (440), designed to provide elaborate notes on individual novels, is now well along, with notes on *Our Mutual Friend* by Michael Cotsell (530), published in 1986; *The Mystery of Edwin Drood* by Wendy S. Jacobson (508), published in 1986; *Bleak House* by Susan Shatto (449), published in 1988; *A Tale of Two Cities* by Andrew Sanders (545), published in 1988; *Oliver Twist* by David Paroissien (522), published in 1992; *Hard Times* by Margaret Simpson (487), published in 1997; *Great Expectations* by David Paroissien (481), published in 2000; and *Martin Chuzzlewit*, by Nancy A. Metz (495), published in 2001. Notes in these useful volumes contain the number plans (where they exist), as well as textual variants. Significant textual variations are also noted in the elaborate annotations in *The Annotated Dickens* (433), two large volumes edited by Edward Giuliano and Philip Collins and published in 1986, containing the texts of *Pickwick Papers, Oliver Twist, A Christmas Carol, Hard Times, David Copperfield, A Tale of Two Cities*, and *Great Expectations*. In his 1987 doctoral dissertation, "Proof Revisions in Three Novels by Charles Dickens: *Dombey and Son, David Copperfield*, and *Bleak House*" (432), Philip A. Everson closely studies the revisions Dickens made in the three novels to show that "as his novels became more complex, his proof revisions became increasingly significant."

Where the number plans are concerned, Harry Stone's beautifully produced *Dickens' Working Notes for His Novels* (443), published in 1987, is the masterwork. It contains photographic facsimiles, as well as Stone's transcriptions of all the number plans and other memoranda for *The Old Curiosity Shop* (three pages of notes for the closing chapters of the novel), *Martin Chuzzlewit* (pages of trial titles and two pages of number plans, for No. IV, chapters 9 and 10, and No. VI), *Dombey and Son* (a complete set of number plans, a title page, and a sheet of memoranda, both sides filled), *David Copperfield* (several pages of trial titles and a complete set of number plans), *Bleak House* (several pages of trial titles and a complete set of number plans), *Hard Times* (a double page of memoranda and a full set of number plans divided into weekly and monthly parts), *Little Dorrit* (two pages of memoranda for the concluding double number and a complete set of number plans), *Great Expectations* (three pages of memoranda concerning dates, general notes, and titles), *Our Mutual Friend* (a complete set of number plans, with a page of notes on the back of the plan for No. XIX/XX), and *The Mystery of Edwin Drood* (a page of notes and the number plans for Nos. I-VI, those completed at his death). Finally, Paul Schlicke's *Oxford Reader's Companion to Dickens* (438), published in 1999, is filled with textual information. The highlighted sections on the individual novels and other works (all written by Schlicke himself) contain information about the manuscripts, number plans, and page proofs, as well as other textual information. Also included is an entry by Joel J. Brattin, "Composition, Dickens's Methods of" (422), that is a concise, knowledgeable description of Dickens at work. The number plans, manuscripts, and page proofs in the Forster Collection, Victoria and Albert Museum, are available on microfilm, a set that should be available in major research libraries (562). A color microfilm of the manuscript of *Great Expectations* in the Wisbech and Fenland Museum, Cambridgeshire, England (562), has also been produced, though George Worth, in his bibliography of the novel (37), complains that it "is almost impossible to read." In their bibliography of *Our Mutual Friend* (48), Brattin and Hornback indicate that a microfilm of the manuscript of the novel is available from the Pierpont Morgan Library, New York.

A number of the important textual studies published from the 1960s on were concerned with individual works, often closing gaps left by Butt and Tillotson. It is best to look at these studies work by work.

Sketches by Boz

No manuscripts or memoranda exist for Dickens's earliest work. Two major studies of this work were published in the 1970s, Virgil Grillo's ***Sketches by Boz: End in the Beginning*** (542) in 1974 and Duane DeVries's *Dickens's Apprentice Years: The Making of a Novelist* (541) in 1976. Both study the revisions that Dickens made when he collected his early newspaper and magazine sketches and tales as *Sketches by Boz* and those he made in later editions of the work. DeVries does this perhaps more thoroughly than Grillo, if only because he devotes more space to his analysis; the second half of Grillo's book is concerned with Dickens's later works. Cary D. Ser's 1974 doctoral dissertation, "*Sketches by Boz*: A Collated Edition" (543), deserves notice, though one might question his use of the 1839 edition as copy-text rather than the first edition of 1836–37. Also valuable are Michael Slater's introduction and headnotes to his edition of *Dickens's* ***Sketches by Boz** and Other Early Papers, 1833–39* (544), published in 1994.

Pickwick Papers

Only forty-six pages of the manuscript of *Pickwick Papers* are extant, identified in Elliot Engel's bibliography of *Pickwick Papers* (51), pp. 14–16. There

are no number plans, other memoranda, or proofs. Given the ease and sponta-
neity with which Dickens wrote in the 1830s (the evidence is in the manuscripts, which are only lightly corrected), one would not expect number plans
this early. Dickens seems first to have used them in writing *The Old Curiosity
Shop*. James Kinsley's introduction to the Clarendon Edition of *Pickwick
Papers* (539) is the principal study of what is known about the composition
of *Pickwick Papers*. Kinsley comments at length on the initial scheme for
Pickwick Papers and Dickens's development of the work, on textual variations in the editions published in Dickens's lifetime, and on the location of
the extant fragments of the manuscript. In "The Original Manuscript of 'The
Pickwick Papers'" (540), published in 1932, Alain de Suzannet identifies
and describes the extant manuscript pages of the novel.

Oliver Twist

The manuscript of *Oliver Twist* is incomplete, and a brief history of what
remains and what was lost will be found in David Paroissien's bibliography
of the novel (46), p. 6, as will a list of commentaries on textual matters,
pp. 27–34. No memoranda or proofs are extant. There are two important
examinations of textual matters concerning *Oliver Twist*. The earliest is Kathleen Tillotson's lengthy and valuable introduction to the Clarendon Edition
of the novel (523), published in 1966, in which she comments on the composition, publication, and reception of the work, examines textual variations in
the editions published in Dickens's lifetime, and describes the incomplete
manuscript of the novel. Although Burton M. Wheeler, in "The Text and
Plan of *Oliver Twist*" (524), published in 1983, disagrees with the belief of
Tillotson and others that *Oliver Twist* was planned as a novel from the beginning, his study is textually important because he looks particularly at Dickens's revision of the novel when he published the work, which he had been
serializing in *Bentley's Miscellany*, in a three-volume edition in 1838. He
looks at a number of "significant deletions" that show that the work was
"the product of a radical change of plans" on Dickens's part as he struggled,
after the fourth installment, and over the next three installments, with the
need to change what started as a "short serial" into a full-fledged novel. Also
see Philip Horne's Penguin Classics Edition of the novel (520), published in
2002, for textual variants.

Nicholas Nickleby

According to Paul Schlicke, in *The Oxford Reader's Companion to Dickens*
(438), p. 405, "only fragments survive" of the manuscript of this novel, and
nothing else. Michael Slater has done some valuable work on the textual

variants, in his *The Composition and Monthly Publication of Nicholas Nickleby* (512), published in 1973, and in his Penguin English Library Edition of the novel (513), published in 1978, where he also gives the locations of the six extant chapters of the novel. Paul Schlicke examines some of the textual variations in editions published in Dickens's lifetime in his World's Classics Edition of the novel (511), published in 1990, as does Mark Ford in his Penguin Classics Edition (510), published in 1999.

The Old Curiosity Shop

As Priscilla and Paul Schlicke note in their bibliography of this novel (45), pp. 5–7, the complete manuscript (including the *Master Humphrey's Clock* chapters), the corrected proofs for chapters 33–67, and other notes are in the Forster Collection, Victoria and Albert Museum, as are the number plans for chapters 66–72 ("the first extant number plans for a Dickens novel"), and galley proofs for chapters 29–31 and 37 are in the Dexter Collection, British Library, London. The principal textual study of the extant number plans, manuscript, and proofs is Angus Easson's impressive "*The Old Curiosity Shop*: From Manuscript to Print" (517), published in 1970. The changes Easson analyzes show, he asserts, the way Dickens's "imagination was fired," as well as his active creativity and the developing comedic element in the work. They also indicate, he concludes, that Dickens was hampered by serial publication and that he wrestled with "the Protean shape of his material." In "'The Story-Weaver at His Loom': Dickens and the Beginning of *The Old Curiosity Shop*" (519), published in 1970, Robert Patten uses Dickens's textual changes between manuscript and published text, as well as Dickens's letters, to show how he modified his original plans for *Master Humphrey's Clock* as he expanded the story of Little Nell and her grandfather from a short tale to a long serial novel. In his article entitled "Some Old Curiosities from *The Old Curiosity Shop*" (514), published in 1990, Joel J. Brattin hypothesizes about why Dickens made a large number of cancellations and revisions in manuscript and page proof. Elizabeth Brennan covers similar territory in the Clarendon Edition and the Oxford World's Classics Edition of the novel (515–16), published in 1997 and 1998, respectively.

Barnaby Rudge

The complete manuscript and the corrected proofs for chapters 17 and 18 are in the Forster Collection, Victoria and Albert Museum, as Thomas J. Rice notes in his bibliography of the novel (29), pp. 4–6. Also see his section on the "History of *Barnaby Rudge*'s Composition and Publication," pp. 10–24. The only important study of textual matters, apart from the chapter in Butt and Tillotson, is Joel J. Brattin's "Secrets Inside . . . Readings from Dickens's Manuscript of *Barnaby Rudge*, Chapter 75'' (445), published in 1991, which concerns the fifteen percent of text for chapter 75 that Dickens deleted in order to make the chapter exactly twelve pages long.

Martin Chuzzlewit

As Robert Lougy indicates in his bibliography of *Martin Chuzzlewit* (41), pp. 6–8, the complete manuscript, some pages of preliminary notes, the number plans for parts IV and VI, and corrected proofs for parts I and V are in the Forster Collection, Victoria and Albert Museum, and small portions of proofs are elsewhere. The only significant commentaries on textual matters will be found in chapter two, "The Text and Its Variations," of Sylvère Monod's study of the novel (496), published in 1985; in Margaret Cardwell's editions of the novel in the Clarendon Edition (493) and the World's Classics Edition (492), published in 1982 and 1984, respectively; and in Patricia Ingham's Penguin Classics Edition (494), published in 1999.

The Christmas Books

As noted earlier, the entire manuscript of *A Christmas Carol*, now a star attraction of the Pierpont Morgan Library, New York, was first published in facsimile in 1890. It has been reproduced more than twice since, most recently by Frederick B. Adams, Jr., in 1967 (452), with brief commentary on the manuscript, and by John Mortimer in 1993 (458). In his introduction, "Meeting the Manuscript," Mortimer comments on what the manuscript revisions reveal about Dickens's working methods. In *The Annotated Christmas Carol* (455), published in 1976, Michael Hearn comments on the writing and publication of the novel and includes textual commentary in his marginal notes. The manuscript of *The Chimes*, Dickens's second Christmas Book, is in the Forster Collection, Victoria and Albert Museum, with "proof copies" in the Forster Collection and in the Dexter Collection in the British Library, as noted in Ruth F. Glancy's bibliography of *Dickens's Christmas Books, Christmas Stories, and Other Short Fiction* (30), pp. 144–45. Michael Slater has done the principal textual work on this novel—see his "Dickens (and Forster) at Work on *The Chimes*" (462), published in 1966, based on his 1965 doctoral dissertation, *"The Chimes*: Its Materials, Making, and Public Reception" (461), and see appendices in his edition of *The Christmas Books* (460), published in 1971, which include six passages of political satire that Dickens deleted in the manuscript at John Forster's suggestion. The manuscript of *The Cricket on the Hearth*, Dickens's third Christmas Book, is in the Pierpont Morgan Library, and a facsimile reproduction of it and two leaves on which

Dickens tried out titles and names of characters was published in 1981, along with a brief note on the manuscript by Verlyn Klinkenborg (457) and a more elaborate introduction by Andrew Sanders (459), commenting on the origin, writing, publication, and reception of the work. Glancy also describes the manuscript, p. 194. The manuscript of the fourth Christmas Book, *The Battle of Life*, is likewise in the Pierpont Morgan Library (see Glancy, p. 240). The only important textual study to date of this work is Glancy's "The Shaping of *The Battle of Life*: Dickens' Manuscript Revisions" (454), published in 1988, which compares the manuscript with the first edition to reveal what changes Dickens made in the non-extant proofs. The manuscript of *The Haunted Man, and the Ghost's Bargain*, the last Christmas Book, is in the Carl H. Pforzheimer Library, New York (Glancy, pp. 266–67), and, again, Glancy has done the only important textual work on the novel. Her "Dickens at Work on *The Haunted Man*" (453), published in 1986, is a fascinating study of Dickens's planning and writing of the work, based on his letters, the three pages of notes he made for the story, and the manuscript itself. Also see Glancy's sections in her bibliography on "Commentary on the Manuscript, Publication, Textual Matters, Illustrations" for each of the five Christmas Books, pp. 7–9, 146–49, 195–97, 240–42, 267–68.

Dombey and Son

As Leon Litvack notes in his bibliography of the novel (35), pp. 7–10, this is "the first of Dickens's novels for which a detailed series of preparatory notes survive." There is also a complete manuscript and "various portions of four sets of proof" for the novel. All of these are in the Forster Collection, Victoria and Albert Museum. Also see Litvack's section on "Scholarship Concerning Composition and Publication," pp. 13–22, for a number of textual studies. The principal post-1957 research on *Dombey and Son* is that of Paul D. Herring, in his "The Number Plans for *Dombey and Son*: Some Further Observations" (473), published in 1970. Herring's essay is intended as a supplement to the chapter on *Dombey and Son* in Butt and Tillotson, but it is also valuable because Herring prints for the first time a full transcription of the number plans, with interspersed commentary on how Dickens used them in crafting his novel. The plans are not as structured as later number plans, Herring indicates, but they show Dickens's "growing awareness of the necessity for skillful craftsmanship in the planning and composition of his novels." In "New Readings in *Dombey and Son*" (475), published in 1968, Kathleen Tillotson examines in detail Dickens's revisions in the manuscript and proofs of one installment of the novel. Alan Horsman, in the Clarendon Edition of the novel (474), published in 1974, provides further commentary on the writing and design of the novel, describes the manuscript and the page proofs, and examines textual differences in the various editions published during Dickens's lifetime.

David Copperfield

The manuscript, number plans, pages of titles Dickens considered, galley proofs for the first three numbers, and page proofs for the rest are extant in the Forster Collection, Victoria and Albert Museum, as Richard Dunn points out in his bibliography of *David Copperfield* (32). Also see his section on "Commentary on the Text," pp. 6–13. The number plans are reproduced in full in Butt and Tillotson. Philip Gaskell, in his "The Textual History of *David Copperfield*" (471), published in 1972, looks at Dickens's writing, proofreading, and publishing of the novel, through the six editions published in his lifetime, a process he repeats in his "Dickens, *David Copperfield*, 1850" (470) in 1978. Nina Burgis does the same in the Clarendon Edition (466) and the World's Classics Edition (465) of the novel, published in 1981 and 1983, respectively, as does Jerome H. Buckley in the Norton Critical Edition (464), published in 1990. In "'Let Me Pause Once More': Dickens' Manuscript Revisions in the Retrospective Chapters of *David Copperfield*" (463), published in 1998, Joel J. Brattin investigates the manuscript revisions in the four chapters in which David "looks back over significant phases of his life." Also see George Ford's Riverside Edition of the novel (469), published in 1958, for passages Dickens cancelled in the monthly proof sheets.

Bleak House

In his *Oxford Reader's Companion to Dickens* (438), p. 48, Paul Schlicke notes that the "manuscript, trial titles, and corrected proofs" are in the Forster Collection, Victoria and Albert Museum, but so are the complete number plans. Harvey P. Sucksmith printed the first transcription of the number plans for *Bleak House* in his "Dickens at Work on *Bleak House*: A Critical Examination of His Memoranda and Number Plans" (450) in 1965. Sucksmith was particularly interested in showing how Dickens used them in planning and writing his novel to create pathos, "moral sympathy," and irony in the novel, a theme he was to take up again in his *The Narrative Art of Charles Dickens* (444), published in 1970. In "Dickens at Work on His Manuscript and Proof: "Bleak House' and "Little Dorrit'" (451), published in 1976, J. L. Watson studies the manuscript, number plans, and page proofs of *Bleak House* and *Little Dorrit* to show Dickens's strong "sense of artistic control." The Norton Critical Edition of the novel, edited by George H. Ford and Sylvère Monod (447) and published in 1977, recorded a number of the textual variations from the manuscript to the 1868 edition, as well as reprinting the number plans and the various titles Dickens wrote down for the novel. These will also be found in Duane DeVries's Crowell Critical Library Edition of the novel (446), published in 1971. An interesting article by Sylvère Monod, "'When the Battle's Lost and Won ... ': Dickens *v.* the Compositors of *Bleak House*" (448), published in 1973, concerns Dickens's corrections in proof of over 700 errors made by at least forty different compositors who set the novel into type (and Dickens missed 159 other errors). Monod also discusses errors made in later editions of the novel.

Hard Times

In her bibliography of *Hard Times* (38), p. 6, Sylvia Manning indicates that the manuscript, number plans, and sets of proofs are in the Forster Collection, Victoria and Albert Museum. Also see the section on "Commentary on the Text," pp. 7–9. Ford and Monod also produced the Norton Critical Edition of *Hard Times* in 1966 (484), with textual notes, and in it transcribed for the first time the complete number plans for the novel. In a 1968 essay in the *Dickensian*, "Dickens at Work on the Text of *Hard Times*" (485), Monod reflects on his work with the text of the novel for the Norton Edition.

Little Dorrit

In his *Oxford Reader's Companion to Dickens* (438), p. 336, Paul Schlicke points out that the number plans, manuscript, and most of the corrected proofs are in the Forster Collection of the Victoria and Albert Museum, while other proofs are in the Dexter Collection of the British Library. Paul D. Herring printed the first transcription of the number plans in 1966 in his "Dickens' Monthly Number Plans for *Little Dorrit*" (489) and also commented on how Dickens used the month by month plans to develop and keep track of the "interlocking plots" and the numerous characters he needed for his portrayal of society as a world of imprisonment. In the Clarendon Edition of the novel (490), Harvey P. Sucksmith provides considerable information about textual variants between manuscript and the 1868 edition of the novel. Stephen Wall and Helen Small in the Penguin Classics Edition (491), published in 1998, and Angus Easson in the Everyman Dickens Edition (488), published in 1999, comment on textual matters, and Wall and Small include a transcription of the number plans as well. Also see J. L. Watson under *Bleak House*, above.

A Tale of Two Cities

There are no number plans or proofs for this novel. The manuscript is in the Forster Collection, Victoria and Albert Museum, as Ruth Glancy notes in her bibliography of the novel (56), p. 7. Also see her section "Commentary on the Manuscript, Publication, Textual Matters, Illustrations," pp. 7–11. David Tucker's "Dickens at Work on the MS of *A Tale of Two Cities*" (546), published in 1979, is the only major commentary on textual matters for this novel. He examines three passages that Dickens cancelled in manuscript by pasting slips of paper over them. The revisions, Tucker believes, were "a considerable improvement" over the original drafts and are evidence that Dickens "took considerable pains" with the novel.

Great Expectations

The manuscript, working notes, and other memoranda are in the Wisbech and Fenland Museum in Cambridgeshire, George J. Worth notes in his bibliography of *Great Expectations* (37), pp. 4–6, while galley proofs for chapters 1–4 and 51–58 are in the Forster Collection, Victoria and Albert Museum, and for the entire novel in the Pierpont Morgan Library, New York. Also see the "Commentary on the Text" section of Worth's bibliography, pp. 6–15. A considerable amount of textual work has been done on this novel since 1965, much of it centering on Dickens's original ending and later, happier variations on it. See the ninety-three entries in Worth's index under "Conclusion" for commentary on the ending of the novel up to 1986. There have been more studies since. The working notes, two pages of "Names" and two of "General Mems," were first printed by John Butt in "Dickens at Work" (425) and "Dickens's Plan for the Conclusion of *Great Expectations*" (476) in the late 1940s. Much of the textual commentary has come from Edgar Rosenberg, beginning with his "A Preface to *Great Expectations*: The Pale Usher Dusts His Lexicons" (483), published in 1972, and concluding with his recent and long anticipated Norton Critical Edition of *Great Expectations* (482), published in 1999. A substantial portion of the "Backgrounds" and "Contexts" sections of this annotated edition is the culmination of his textual studies of the novel, an impressive compilation of material, and supersedes his previous publications as well as those of other scholars, though Margaret Cardwell's textual work in the Clarendon Edition (479) and the World's Classics Edition (478), published in 1993 and 1994, respectively, is also valuable, as are the appendices in Angus Calder's Penguin English Library edition of the novel (477), published in 1965.

Our Mutual Friend

As Joel J. Brattin and Bert G. Hornback indicate in their bibliography of *Our Mutual Friend* (48), pp. 6–7, the manuscript and number plans of the novel are in the Pierpont Morgan Library, and the page proofs are in the Berg

Collection, New York Public Library. Also see the section on "Commentary on the Text" in the Brattin-Hornback bibliography, pp. 22–28. As noted above, Ernest Boll published the transcription of the number plans in 1944 (525). Since then, the principal textual studies have been by Francis X. Shea and Brattin. Shea began his work on the novel in his 1961 doctoral dissertation, "The Text of *Our Mutual Friend*: A Study of the Variations between the Copy Text and the First Printed Edition" (537), and followed it with "No Change of Intention in *Our Mutual Friend*" (536), published in 1967, on what the notes and manuscript reveal about Dickens's characterization of Mr. Boffin, and with "Mr. Venus Observed: The Plot Change in *Our Mutual Friend*" (535) in 1968. In "Dickens' Creation of Bradley Headstone" (526), published in 1985, Brattin examines what the number plans and the manuscript revisions reveal about Dickens's gradual development of the character Bradley Headstone. In "'I Will Not Have My Words Misconstrued': The Text of *Our Mutual Friend*" (527), published in 1998, Brattin analyzes the different kinds of variants he has found between the first edition (1864–65) and the Charles Dickens Edition (1868) of the novel, a total of 2,203 "corrections, alterations, and mistakes." He concludes, however, that probably most of these changes were made by someone other than Dickens and are, therefore, not particularly significant. Also see Brattin's Everyman Dickens Edition of the novel (528), published in 2000, for a further study of the textual variants and Dickens's use of his Book of Memoranda and the number plans in constructing the novel.

The Mystery of Edwin Drood

As Don R. Cox notes in his bibliography of the novel (43), pp. 7–10, the manuscript (with one page missing), number plans, list of projected titles, the "Sapsea Fragment," and the proofs for part 5 of *Edwin Drood* are in the Forster Collection, Victoria and Albert Museum, London. A complete set of corrected proofs, with some additional pages of proofs, is in the Gimbel Collection, Yale University Library, and a set of proofs for the third monthly number (chapters 10–12) is in the Houghton Library, Harvard University. Also see the section on "Textual Issues, Illustrations, Editing Problems," pp. 13–42, in Cox's bibliography. W. Robertson Nicoll, as mentioned above, printed a transcription of the number plans in his *The Problem of "Edwin Drood,"* published in 1912 (509), and *Drood* scholars have continued over the years since to use the number plans, manuscript, and proofs, and whatever else they could find, including Dickens's letters and entries in his Memoranda Book (551), to speculate about how Dickens intended to end the novel. Butt and Tillotson wisely did not attempt to do anything with the novel in their *Dickens at Work*, but since the 1950s other scholars have. Felix Aylmer, in

The Drood Case (497), published in 1965, reprints the number plans and examines them, the manuscript, the monthly cover, and the illustrations in once again confronting the "Mystery" in the work. In "The *Drood* Remains" (504), published in 1966, Arthur J. Cox studies changes Dickens made in the manuscript to show problems he had with writing to length. In the introduction (502) to the Clarendon Edition of the novel, published in 1972, Margaret Cardwell compares the manuscript with the published version and describes the manuscripts and the proofs and records textual variants in footnotes to the text. She also uses some of this material in the World's Classics edition of the novel (501), published 1982. Arthur J. Cox covers roughly the same ground in two editions he edited, the Penguin English Library Edition (505) in 1974, and the Folio Society Edition (506) in 1982, as does Steven Connor in the new Everyman Library Edition (503), published in 1996. William M. Burgan, in "The Refinement of Contrast: Manuscript Revision in *Edwin Drood*" (499), published in 1977, studies Dickens's revisions in the manuscript of the novel. They show, he asserts, that Dickens was primarily "engaged in augmenting rather than curbing his initial ideas." In "*Edwin Drood* and the Mystery of Apartness" (498), published in 1984, John Beer uses Dickens's notes and textual revisions in examining where critics from John Forster on thought Dickens meant to go with the plot of the novel. Don R. Cox's "The *Every Saturday* Page Proofs for *The Mystery of Edwin Drood*" (507), published in 1994, is an important supplement to Cardwell's introduction to the Clarendon Edition. Cox describes and gives the provenance of a previously unnoted, if incomplete, set of page proofs in the Harvard University Library, that Dickens sent to Boston as advance sheets for the serialization of the novel in *Every Saturday*. The proofs, Cox concludes, "verify some of the changes we know took place between the first version" of the text and the final printed version.

Shorter Fiction, Nonfictional Works, and the Book of Memoranda

Ruth Glancy's bibliography of *Dickens's Christmas Books, Christmas Stories, and Other Short Fiction* (30) is useful in locating manuscripts of Dickens's Christmas stories and the other shorter fiction and in identifying what few textual studies of these have been published. Likewise, Michael Slater, in the four volumes he edited (the last with John Drew) in the Dent Uniform Edition of Dickens's Journalism (544, 555–57), published 1994–2000, locates existing manuscripts and occasionally notes manuscript revisions and textual variations, as does Harry Stone in his two-volume *Charles Dickens's Uncollected Writings from Household Words, 1850–1859* (104). Robert Hanna will also do this in his forthcoming bibliography of Dickens's nonfictional, theatrical, and poetical writings (57). However, not a great deal of textual scholarship has been devoted to individual minor works. Richard F. Batterson has done a thorough study of ''The Manuscript and Text of Dickens's 'George Silverman's Explanation' '' (547), published in 1979. David Paroissien compared the text of ''Travelling Letters, Written on the Road'' with the first edition of *Pictures from Italy* in his 1968 doctoral dissertation (552), in an article obviously based on his dissertation, ''Dickens's 'Pictures from Italy': Stages of the Work's Development and Dickens's Methods of Composition'' (554), published in 1971, and in ''A Note on the Text,'' in his 1973 edition of *Pictures from Italy* (553). Walter E. Smith also itemizes textual variations, in side by side columns, between the *Daily News* pieces and the first bound edition in Part Two of his *Charles Dickens in the Original Cloth* (24), published in 1983. Also see Kate Flint's Penguin Classics Edition of the work (549), published in 1998. In their Penguin English Library Edition of *American Notes* (558), published in 1972, John S. Whitley and Arnold Goldman include textual notes identifying changes that Dickens made in the Cheap Edition, published in 1850, and the Charles Dickens Edition, published in 1868–as does Patricia Ingham in her Penguin Classics Edition of the work (550), published in 2000. Finally, though technically not a published work of Dickens, the Book of Memoranda that Dickens kept between 1855 and sometime in the 1860s was reproduced in photographic facsimile, accompanied by a printed transcription, by Fred Kaplan in 1981 (551). In his introduction, Kaplan describes the notebook, gives its provenance, and lists the previous publication of excerpts from the manuscript. He also includes nearly thirty pages of elaborate editorial notes and comments on how Dickens used memoranda entries in his writings. Kathryn Chittick, in ''The Meaning of a Literary Idea: Dickens's Memoranda Notebook'' (548), published in 1982, intelligently explores Dickens's creative use of the memoranda notes in writing his later works.

It has been a long journey to this point. Obviously a great deal of important scholarly work has been done for both the researcher and the collector in compiling bibliographies of Dickens's works, translations of them, and every variety of adaptation of them. Bibliographical studies are more than numerous, and bibliographies of studies of Dickens's works fill library shelves, and are sometimes quarterly, or semiannually, and always yearly updated by an impressive list of serial bibliographies. Equally useful work has been done in recording union, national, and public and private library collections of Dickens's works and Dickensiana, as well as in cataloguing and reporting on important exhibitions. Numerous auction and booksellers' catalogues document major and minor private collections (unfortunately usually after the demise of the collector) and often contain transcriptions of Dickens letters, or at least portions of them, that even the alert editors of the *Pilgrim Letters* have occasionally not managed to locate. Textual studies of Dickens's number plans and other memoranda, manuscripts, and page proofs are verifying his craftsmanship and his artistry and asserting the importance of this approach to an understanding of his creativity. Surely there is not much more to be done.

I suppose, however, that nothing is ever sufficiently complete for the scholar/researcher. Inevitably, to begin with, bibliographies are out of date from the moment they are published, for, even then, they are at least a year or two behind. Still, bibliographies and bibliographical and textual studies are generally reliable in the recording of data, if usually annoyingly incomplete, though, in the mass, such work is cumulative and, where necessary, corrective. Many of the individual Dickens bibliographies, it is true, are, in themselves, quite outdated by now. This is particularly true of bibliographies of translations of Dickens's works—because these were often one-time events that have not been updated. From a collector's or bookseller's point of view, some of the basic bibliographical work remains to be done on the minor works and that on the major works needs to be reexamined, if not much at this point corrected or updated. Bibliographers were somewhat slow to understand the complexities of Victorian mass publication and of the relationship of Dickens's serialization of his works to their volume publications, but these matters are now pretty much understood, though the question of what constitutes a true first edition or the best copy-text remains a matter of perennial debate.

While a number of important textual studies have been published, spurred on by the outstanding work of John Butt and Kathleen Tillotson, much remains to be investigated—and used in creative, insightful studies of the relationships between text, creativity, inspiration, and genius. Now, at least, a number of primary documents are available for significant textual and critical work. The editors of the *Pilgrim Letters* have just completed the twelve volumes of known Dickens letters, and plans are in place for publishing in the *Dickensian* new letters that turn up. Michael Slater has recently published (1994–2000) the four volumes in the Dent Uniform Edition of Dickens's Journalism (544, 555–57), the last volume with John Drew. The Clarendon Edition of Dickens's works is in progress, providing more authoritative texts for the scholar to use. The Dickens Companion series, also in progress, is supplementing the strictly textual notes in the Clarendon volumes with explanatory as well as additional textual notes. The manuscripts themselves, at least of the novels, have been available on microfilm for a number of years.

Bibliographies of Dickens studies have never been as complete, as detailed, and as informative as Philo Calhoun and Howell J. Heaney desired, even bibliographies published after their cautionary "Dickensiana in the Rough" (70) appeared more than half a century ago. I think they would have liked the volumes in the Garland Dickens Bibliographies and the Dickens Bibliographies currently being published by AMS Press, two series designed to comprise, together, the most comprehensive, and annotated, bibliography of Dickens's works and Dickens studies every attempted. In criticizing William Miller's *The Dickens Student and Collector* for a half-hearted effort, Calhoun and Heaney concluded that doing it right "is worth doing." They never attempted the task themselves, however, nor has anyone else—until the Garland and AMS Press series of Dickens bibliographies. Our constant and continuing aim is to do it right, and we hope that, for ourselves as well as for future generations of Dickens students and scholars, we are making some success of it.

A new century, a new millennium for that matter, has begun. The computer and the Internet have begun to revolutionize publishing and scholarship, and are opening up new approaches to bibliographical and textual scholarship. The 200th anniversary of Dickens's birth is rapidly approaching, and museum and library directors are undoubtedly beginning to plan their 2012 exhibitions. These exhibitions will take advantage of all this scholarly activity and show us a Dickens more creative, more troubled, something of a victim of the intense perusal of his life and writings that has been going on, but a Dickens whose reputation remains not only intact but considerably more enhanced than earlier.

It now remains for young Dickens scholars and critics, and perhaps even some older ones, to use this newly accumulated body of information and these new electronic tools to gain and disseminate a better understanding of Dickens's artistry and genius for a new age.

Works Cited

Bibliographies of Dickens's Works

1. American Antiquarian Society and the Research Libraries Group, Inc. "Dickens, Charles, 1812–1870." *Bibliography of American Imprints to 1901: Author Index.* Vol. 46. New York, Munich, London, Paris: K. G. Saur, 1993, pp. 246–53, and passim.

2. Anderson, John P. "Bibliography." In *Life of Charles Dickens.* By Frank T. Marzials. Great Writers series. London: Walter Scott, 1887; reprinted Folcroft, PA: Folcroft Library Editions, 1973, pp. i-xxxiii.

3. C[ollins], P[hilip] A. W., comp. "Charles Dickens, 1812–70." In *The New Cambridge Bibliography of English Literature.* Vol. 3: *1800–1900.* Ed. George Watson. Cambridge: Cambridge University Press, 1969, cols. 779–850; reprinted

separately as *A Dickens Bibliography*. By Philip Collins. [London]: Dickens Fellowship by arrangement with the Cambridge University Press, 1970, cols. 779–850.

4. Cook, James. *Bibliography of the Writings of Charles Dickens, with Many Curious and Interesting Particulars Relating to His Works*. London: Frank Kerslake; Paisley, Scotland: J. and J. Cook, 1879. 88 pp.

5. D[arton], F. J. H., comp. "Charles Dickens (1812–1870)." In *The Cambridge Bibliography of English Literature*. Vol. III. *1800–1900*. Ed. F. W. Bateson. Cambridge: Cambridge University Press, 1940, pp. 435–55.

6. DeVries, Duane, gen. ed. *The Dickens Bibliographies*. New York: AMS Press, 1998–. See Dunn and Tandy (33), Litvack (35), and Cox (43) for volumes published in this series, and DeVries (8) and Hanna (57) for volumes to be published in 2003. Other volumes projected are on *Nicholas Nickleby* (Paul Schlicke), *Bleak House* (Angus Easson), *Little Dorrit* (Tony Williams), biographies, letters, and biographical studies (Duane DeVries), critical studies (Duane DeVries), and special studies and collected editions of Dickens's works (Duane DeVries). Over the next few years AMS Press is also planning to issue reprints of the volumes in the Garland Dickens Bibliographies, below, along with updates, the latter of which will first appear in issues of the *Dickens Studies Annual* and then, perhaps, as separate publications. Robert Heaman's update of the *Our Mutual Friend* bibliography is in this volume of *Dickens Studies Annual*, and David Paroissien's updating of his *Oliver Twist* bibliography and Ruth Glancy's updating of her volume on the Christmas Books, Christmas Stories, and other short fiction will follow. Others have not yet been scheduled.

7. DeVries, Duane, gen. ed. *The Garland Dickens Bibliographies*. 11 vols. New York and London: Garland Publishing, 1981–93. See Rice (29), Glancy (30), Dunn (32), Worth (37), Manning (38), Lougy (41), Schlicke and Schlicke (45), Paroissien (46), Brattin and Hornback (48), Engel (51), and Glancy (56) for volumes published in this series.

8. DeVries, Duane. *General Studies of Charles Dickens and His Writings and Collected Editions of His Works: An Annotated Bibliography*. Volume I: *Bibliographies, Catalogues, Collections, and Bibliographical and Textual Studies*. New York: AMS Press, 2003 (forthcoming), approx. 800 pp.

9. Dexter, John F. "Hints to Dickens Collectors." In *Dickens Memento, with Introduction by Francis Phillimore [Wilfred Meynell?], and "Hints to Dickens Collectors" by John F. Dexter, [and] Catalogue with Purchasers' Names & Prices Realised of the Pictures, Drawings, and Objects of Art of the Late Charles Dickens, Sold by Auction in London by Messrs. Christie, Manson, & Woods on July 9th, 1870*. London: Field & Tuer; New York: Scribner & Welford, [1884]; reprinted Folcroft, PA: Folcroft Library Editions, 1978, pp. 7–35.

10. "Dickens, Charles." In *Nineteenth Century Short Title Catalogue. Series II. Phase I. 1816–1870*. Vol. 12. Newcastle-upon-Tyne: Avero, 1988, pp. 109–50.

11. Eckel, John C. *The First Editions of the Writings of Charles Dickens and Their Values: A Bibliography.* London: Chapman and Hall, 1913; reprinted Folcroft, PA: Folcroft Library Editions, 1973; Havertown, PA: R. West, 1976; Norwood, PA: Norwood Editions, 1976. xviii + 296 pp.; 2nd ed., revised and enlarged as *The First Editions of the Writings of Charles Dickens, Their Points and Values: A Bibliography.* New York: Maurice Inman; London: Maggs Brothers, 1932; reprinted New York: Haskell House, 1972. xvi + 272 pp. Reviewed in *Times Literary Supplement*, 26 January 1933, p. 64.

12. Edgar, Herman L., and R. W. G. Vail. "Early American Editions of the Works of Charles Dickens." *Bulletin of the New York Public Library*, 33 (1929), 302–19; reprinted in the two-part publication *Charles Dickens: His Life as Traced by His Works*. By Cortes W. Cavanaugh [and] *Early American Editions of the Works of Charles Dickens*. By Herman Edgar and R. W. G. Vail. New York: New York Public Library, 1929, pp. 14–31.

13. F[ielding], K[enneth]. J., comp. "Charles Dickens (1812–1870)." In *The Cambridge Bibliography of English Literature*. Vol. 5. *Supplement: A. D. 600–1900*. Ed. George Watson. Cambridge: Cambridge University Press, 1957, pp. 623–30.

14. Forster, John. "Appendix. I. The Writings of Charles Dickens." In his *The Life of Charles Dickens*. 3 vols. London: Chapman & Hall, 1872–74 (actually published November 1871, November 1872, and December 1873), III, 505–15; slightly revised as "Appendix. The Writings of Charles Dickens, Published During the Period Comprised in This First Volume" and "Appendix. I. The Writings of Charles Dickens, Published During the Period Comprised in This Second Volume." In his revised *The Life of Charles Dickens*. 2 vols. Library Edition. London: Chapman & Hall, 1876, I, 525–28; II, 522–25.

15. Hatton, Thomas, and Arthur H. Cleaver. *A Bibliography of the Periodical Works of Charles Dickens, Bibliographical, Analytical, and Statistical.* London: Chapman and Hall, 1933; reprinted New York: Haskell House, 1973; Cambridge, MA: Maurizio Martino, [1992]. xix + 384 pp.

16. Johnson, Charles P. *Hints to Collectors of Original Editions of the Works of Charles Dickens.* London: George Redway, 1885. 56 pp.

17. Kitton, Frederic G. *The Novels of Charles Dickens: A Bibliography and Sketch.* The Book-Lover's Library. London: Elliot Stock, 1897; reprinted New York: AMS Press, 1975. ix + 245 pp.

18. Rosenbaum, Barbara, and Pamela White, comps. "Charles Dickens, 1812–1870." In their *Index of English Literary Manuscripts*. Vol. IV. *1800–1900*. Part I. *Arnold-Gissing*. London and New York: Mansell, 1982, pp. 705–42.

19. S[chlicke], P[aul]. "Charles Dickens 1812–70." In *The Cambridge Bibliography of English Literature*, Volume 4: 1800–1900. 3rd. ed. Ed. Joanne Shattock. Cambridge: Cambridge University Press, 1999, cols. 1181–1273.

20. [Shepherd, Richard H.]. *The Bibliography of Dickens: A Bibliographical List Arranged in Chronological Order of the Published Writings in Prose and Verse of Charles Dickens (from 1834 to 1880)*. Manchester: A. Ireland; London: Elliot Stock, [1880]; reprinted Folcroft, PA: Folcroft Press, 1970; Norwood, PA: Norwood Editions, 1976; Philadelphia, PA: R. West, 1977. viii + 107 pp.; 2nd ed., revised and enlarged as *The Bibliography of Dickens: A Bibliographical List Arranged in Chronological Order of the Published Writings in Prose and Verse of Charles Dickens (from 1833 to 1882)*. [London: Printed for private circulation, 1882]. 70 pp.; also included as "The Bibliography of Dickens: A Bibliographical List Arranged in Chronological Order of the Published Writings in Prose and Verse of Charles Dickens (from 1833 to 1882)," in *The Plays and Poems of Charles Dickens, with a Few Miscellanies in Prose. Now First Collected*. Ed. Richard Herne Shepherd. 2 vols. London: W. H. Allen, 1882 (and reprinted unchanged, 1885), II, 337–406; further revised as "The Bibliography of Dickens: A Bibliographical List of the Published Writings in Prose and Verse of Charles Dickens from 1833 to 1883 (Including His Letters)," in *The Speeches of Charles Dickens (1841–1870), With a New Bibliography Revised and Enlarged*. Ed. Richard Herne Shepherd. London: Chatto and Windus, 1884, pp. 325–73.

21. Shoemaker, Richard H., [et al.], comps. *A Checklist of American Imprints for 1820[-]*. New York and London: Scarecrow Press, 1964– , passim.

22. Slater, J[ohn] H. "Charles Dickens." In his *Early Editions: A Bibliographical Survey of the Works of Some Popular Modern Authors*. London: Kegan Paul, Trench, Trübner, 1894, pp. 76–106.

23. Smith, Walter E. *Charles Dickens in the Original Cloth: A Bibliographical Catalogue of the First Appearance of His Writings in Book Form in England with Facsimiles of the Bindings and Titlepages. Part One: The Novels with **Sketches by Boz***. Los Angeles: Heritage Book Shop, 1982. xvi + 120 pp. Reviewed by Brian Lake, *Antiquarian Book Monthly Review*, 9 (1982), 229–31.

24. Smith, Walter E. *Charles Dickens in the Original Cloth: A Bibliographical Catalogue of the First Appearance of His Writings in Book Form in England with Facsimiles of the Bindings and Titlepages. Part Two: The Christmas Books and Selected Secondary Works*. Los Angeles: Heritage Book Shop, 1983. xvi + 95 pp.

25. Thomson, J[oseph] C. *Bibliography of the Writings of Charles Dickens*. Warwick, Eng.: J. Thomson; New York: G. E. Stechert, 1904. 108 pp.

26. Wilkins, William Glyde. "First and Early American Editions of the Works of Charles Dickens." *Dickensian*, 3 (1907), 186–88.

27. Wilkins, William Glyde. *First and Early American Editions of the Works of Charles Dickens*. Cedar Rapids, IA: Privately Printed [Torch Press], 1910; reprinted New York: Burt Franklin, 1968. 51 pp.

28. Wilkins, William Glyde. "More about Early American Editions of the Works of Dickens." *Dickensian*, 4 (1908), 190–91.

Barnaby Rudge

29. Rice, Thomas J. *Barnaby Rudge: An Annotated Bibliography*. Garland Dickens Bibliographies, 6; Garland Reference Library of the Humanities, 630. New York and London: Garland Publishing, 1987. xxxvii + 351 pp.

Bleak House

Note: See entries 1–28.

Christmas Novels, Christmas Stories, and Other Stories

30. Glancy, Ruth F. *Dickens's Christmas Books, Christmas Stories, and Other Short Fiction: An Annotated Bibliography*. Garland Dickens Bibliographies, 4; Garland Reference Library of the Humanities, 479. New York and London: Garland Publishing, 1985. xxxiii + 610 pp. See "Commentary on the First Issue Problem [of *A Christmas Carol*]," pp. 10–16.

David Copperfield

31. Burgis, Nina. "Descriptive List of Editions 1849–1867." In Dickens's *David Copperfield*. Ed. Nina Burgis. Clarendon Edition. Oxford: Clarendon Press; Oxford, London, Glasgow, New York, etc.: Oxford University Press, 1981, pp. lxiii-lxv.

32. Dunn, Richard J. *David Copperfield: An Annotated Bibliography*. Garland Dickens Bibliographies, 8; Garland Reference Library of the Humanities, 280. New York and London: Garland Publishing, 1981. xxv + 256 pp.

33. Dunn, Richard J., and Ann M. Tandy. "*David Copperfield*: An Annotated Bibliography. Supplement I—1981–1998." *Dickens Studies Annual*, 28 (1999), 345–467; published separately, The Dickens Bibliographies, AMS Studies in the Nineteenth Century, 23. New York: AMS Press, 2000. xx + 117 pp.

Dombey and Son

34. Horsman, Alan. "Descriptive List of Editions 1846–1867." In Dickens's *Dombey and Son*. Ed. Alan Horsman. Clarendon Edition. Oxford: Clarendon Press; Oxford, London, Glasgow, New York, etc.: Oxford University Press, 1974, pp. xlvii-xlix.

35. Litvack, Leon. *Charles Dickens's **Dombey and Son**: An Annotated Bibliography*. The Dickens Bibliographies, AMS Studies in the Nineteenth Century, 19. New York: AMS Press, 1999 [2000]. xxxv + 399 pp.

Great Expectations

36. Cardwell, Margaret, "Descriptive List of Editions 1861–1868." In Dickens's *Great Expectations*. Ed. Margaret Cardwell. Clarendon Edition. Oxford: Clarendon Press; Oxford, New York, etc.: Oxford University Press, 1993, pp. lxiv-lxvii.

37. Worth, George J. *Great Expectations: An Annotated Bibliography*. Garland Dickens Bibliographies, 5; Garland Reference Library of the Humanities, 555. New York and London: Garland Publishing, 1986. xxii + 346 pp.

Hard Times

38. Manning, Sylvia. *Hard Times: An Annotated Bibliography*. Garland Dickens Bibliographies, 3; Garland Reference Library of the Humanities, 515. New York and London: Garland Publishing, 1984. xxiii + 296 pp.

Little Dorrit

39. Sucksmith, Harvey P. "Descriptive List of Editions 1855–1868." In Dickens's *Little Dorrit*. Ed. Harvey P. Sucksmith. Clarendon Edition. Oxford: Clarendon Press; Oxford, London, Glasgow, New York, etc.: Oxford University Press, 1979, pp. l-lii.

Martin Chuzzlewit

40. Cardwell, Margaret. "Descriptive List of Editions 1843–1867." In Dickens's *Martin Chuzzlewit*. Ed. Margaret Cardwell. Clarendon Edition. Oxford: Clarendon Press; Oxford, London, Glasgow, New York, etc.: Oxford University Press, 1982, pp. lxi-lxii.

41. Lougy, Robert E. *Martin Chuzzlewit: An Annotated Bibliography*. Garland Dickens Bibliographies, 6; Garland Reference Library of the Humanities, 1033. New York and London: Garland Publishing, 1990. xxx + 290 pp.

The Mystery of Edwin Drood

42. Cardwell, Margaret. "Descriptive List of Editions 1870–1875." In Dickens's *The Mystery of Edwin Drood*. Ed. Margaret Cardwell. Clarendon Edition. Oxford: Clarendon Press; Oxford, London, Glasgow, New York, etc.: Oxford University Press, 1972, pp. li-liii.

43. Cox, Don R., *Charles Dickens's* **The Mystery of Edwin Drood**: *An Annotated Bibliography*. The Dickens Bibliographies. AMS Studies in the Nineteenth Century, 17. New York: AMS Press, 1998. xxxvi + 669 pp.

Nicholas Nickleby

Note: See entries 1–28.

The Old Curiosity Shop

44. Brennan, Elizabeth M. "Descriptive List of Editions." In Dickens's *The Old Curiosity Shop*. Ed. Elizabeth M. Brennan. Clarendon Edition. Oxford: Clarendon Press; Oxford, New York, etc.: Oxford University Press, 1997, pp. xcvi-ciii.

45. Schlicke, Priscilla, and Paul Schlicke. **The Old Curiosity Shop**: *An Annotated Bibliography*. Garland Dickens Bibliographies, 9; Garland Reference Library of the Humanities, 708. New York and London: Garland Publishing, 1988. xxi + 495 pp.

Oliver Twist

46. Paroissien, David. **Oliver Twist**: *An Annotated Bibliography*. Garland Dickens Bibliographies, 2; Garland Reference Library of the Humanities, 385. New York and London: Garland Publishing, 1986. xxxi + 313 pp.

47. Tillotson, Kathleen. "Descriptive List of Editions 1838–1867." In Dickens's *Oliver Twist*. Ed. Kathleen Tillotson. Clarendon Edition. Oxford: Clarendon Press; Oxford, London, Glasgow, New York, etc.: Oxford University Press, 1966, pp. xlviii-lvi.

Our Mutual Friend

48. Brattin, Joel J., and Bert G. Hornback. **Our Mutual Friend**: *An Annotated Bibliography*. Garland Dickens Bibliographies, 1; Garland Reference Library of the

Humanities, 481. New York and London: Garland Publishing, 1984. xxi + 197 pp.

Pickwick Papers

49. *Collation of the Famous Lapham-Wallace Pickwick.* New York: Privately printed by Harry F. Marks, n. d. 8 pp.

50. Eckel, John C. *Prime Pickwicks in Parts. Census with Complete Collation, Comparison and Comment.* New York: E. H. Wells; London: C. J. Sawyer, 1928. [xii] + 91 pp.

51. Engel, Elliot. **Pickwick Papers**: *An Annotated Bibliography.* Garland Dickens Bibliographies, 7; Garland Reference Library of the Humanities, 568. New York and London: Garland Publishing, 1990. xxxii + 345 pp.

52. Kinsley, James. "Descriptive List of Editions 1837–1867." In Dickens's *The Pickwick Papers.* Ed. by James Kinsley. Clarendon Dickens. Oxford: Clarendon Press; Oxford, New York, etc.: Oxford University Press, 1986, pp. lxxxvi-xc.

53. Miller, William, and E. H. Strange. "The Original *Pickwick Papers*: The Collation of a Perfect First Edition." *Dickensian,* 29 (1932/33), 303–09; 30 (1933/34), 31–37, 121–24, 177–80, 249–59; 31 (1934/35), 35–40, 95–99, 219–22, 284–86; reprinted as "The Bibliography." In their *A Centenary Bibliography of the Pickwick Papers.* London: Argonaut Press, 1936, pp. 1–65.

54. Read, Newbury F. "The American Editions of Pickwick." *Dickensian,* 33 (1936/37), 21–26.

Sketches by Boz

55. DeVries, Duane. "Appendix A: The Publishing History of *Sketches by Boz.*" In his *Dickens's Apprentice Years: The Making of a Novelist.* Hassocks, Eng.: Harvester Press; New York: Barnes & Noble Books/Harper & Row, 1976, pp. 147–57.

A Tale of Two Cities

56. Glancy, Ruth F. **A Tale of Two Cities**: *An Annotated Bibliography.* Garland Dickens Bibliographies, 12; Garland Reference Library of the Humanities, 1339. New York and London: Garland Publishing, 1993. xxviii + 236 pp.

Nonfictional, Theatrical, and Poetical Works

57. Hanna, Robert. *Dickens's Nonfictional, Theatrical, and Poetical Writings: An Annotated Bibliography*. The Dickens Bibliographies. New York: AMS Press, 2003 (forthcoming), approx. 700 pp.

58. Kitton, Frederic G. *The Minor Writings of Charles Dickens: A Bibliography and Sketch*. The Book-Lover's Library. London: Elliot Stock, 1900; reprinted New York: Haskell House, 1970; New York: AMS Press, 1975. xi + 260 pp.

59. Lohrli, Anne. ***Household Words: A Weekly Journal***, *1850–1859, Conducted by Charles Dickens: Table of Contents, List of Contributors and Their Contributions, Based on the Household Words Office Book in the Morris L. Parrish Collection of Victorian Novelists, Princeton University Library*. Toronto and Buffalo, NY: University of Toronto Press, 1973. x + 534 pp.

60. Oppenlander, Ella A. *Dickens'* ***All the Year Round****: Descriptive Index and Contributor List*. Troy, NY: Whitston, 1984. 752 pp.

61. Slater, Michael, and John Drew. "Appendix D: Complete Listing of Dickens's Known Journalism, December 1833–August 1869." In their edition of Dickens's ***The Uncommercial Traveller*** *and Other Papers, 1859–70*. Dent Uniform Edition of Dickens' Journalism. Volume 4. London: J. M. Dent; Columbus: Ohio State University Press, 2000, pp. 436–46.

Bibliographical Studies

62. Bracher, Peter S. "The Early American Editions of *American Notes*: Their Priority and Circulation." *Papers of the Bibliographical Society of America*, 69 (1975), 365–76, and "Harper & Brothers: Publishers of Dickens." *Bulletin of the New York Public Library*, 79 (1975/76), 315–35 (includes "A Check List of Dickens' Works Published by Harper & Brothers, 1842–70," pp. 332–35).

63. Brice, Alec W. "'Ignorance and Its Victims': Another New Article by Dickens." *Dickensian*, 63 (1967), 143–47.

64. Brice, Alec W. "'A Truly British Judge': Another Article by Dickens." *Dickensian*, 66 (1970), 30–35.

65. Brice, Alec W., and K. J. Fielding. "A New Article by Dickens: 'Demoralisation and Total Abstinence.'" *Dickens Studies Annual*, 9 (1981), 1–19.

66. Brice, Alec W., and K. J. Fielding. "On Murder and Detection—New Articles by Dickens." *Dickens Studies*, 5 (1969), 45–61.

67. Butt, John. "Editing a Nineteenth-Century Novelist (Proposals for an Edition of Dickens)." In *English Studies Today: Second Series. Lectures and Papers Read at the Fourth Conference of the International Association of University Professors of English Held at Lausanne and Berne, August 1959*. Berne: Francke Verlag, 1961, pp. 187–95; reprinted in *Art and Error: Modern Textual Editing*. Ed. Ronald Gottesman and Scott Bennett. Bloomington and London: Indiana University Press, 1970, pp. 155–66.

68. Butt, John, and Kathleen Tillotson. "Preface by the General Editors." In Dickens's *Oliver Twist*. Ed. Kathleen Tillotson. Clarendon Edition (47), pp. v-vii.

69. Calhoun, Philo, and Howell J. Heaney. "Dickens' *Christmas Carol* after a Hundred Years: A Study in Bibliographical Evidence." *Papers of the Bibliographical Society of America*, 39 (1945), 271–317.

70. Calhoun, Philo, and Howell J. Heaney. "Dickensiana in the Rough." *Papers of the Bibliographical Society of America*, 41 (1947), 293–320; reprinted separately as *Dickensiana in the Rough*. Portland, ME: Antheonsen Press, 1947. 30 pp.

71. Carlton, William J. "Charles Dickens, Dramatic Critic." *Dickensian*, 56 (1960), 11–27.

72. Carlton, William J. "'The Story Without a Beginning': An Unrecorded Contribution by Boz to the *Morning Chronicle*." *Dickensian*, 47 (1950/51), 67–70.

73. Collins, Philip. "The *All the Year Round* Letter Book." *Victorian Periodicals Newsletter*, no. 10 (November 1970), 23–29.

74. Collins, P[hilip]. A. W. "Dickens as Editor: Some Uncollected Fragments." *Dickensian*, 56 (1960), 85–96.

75. Collins, Philip. "Dickens on Ghosts: An Uncollected Article, with Introduction and Notes." *Dickensian*, 59 (1963), 5–14.

76. Collins, Philip. "Some Uncollected Speeches by Dickens." *Dickensian*, 73 (1977), 89–99.

77. Collins, Philip. "Some Unpublished Comic Duologues of Dickens." *Nineteenth-Century Fiction*, 31 (1976/77), 440–49.

78. Davis, George W. *The Posthumous Papers of the Pickwick Club: Some New Bibliographical Discoveries*. London: Marks & Co., 1928; reprinted Folcroft, PA: Folcroft Press, 1971; New York: Haskell, 1972; Folcroft, PA: Folcroft Library Editions, 1973; Norwood, PA: Norwood Editions, 1976; Philadelphia, PA: R. West, 1977. 20 pp.

79. Dexter, Walter. "The Genesis of *Sketches by Boz*." *Dickensian*, 30 (1933/34), 105–11.

80. Dexter, Walter. "A New Contribution to 'The Monthly Magazine' and an Early Dramatic Criticism in 'The Morning Chronicle.'" *Dickensian*, 30 (1933/34), 223–25.

81. [Dexter, Walter]. "An Unpublished Prologue." *Dickensian,* 37 (1940/41), 5.

82. Fielding, K[enneth] J., ed. "A New Article by Dickens: Scott and His Publishers." *Dickensian,* 46 (1949/50), 122–27.

83. Fielding, K[enneth] J. "Textual Introduction," "Notes on Text and Sources," and Headnotes. In *The Speeches of Charles Dickens.* Ed. K[enneth] J. Fielding. Oxford: Clarendon Press, 1960, pp. xv-xviii, 423–43, and passim; reprinted, with an additional introduction, as "Revised Edition: 1988." In *The Speeches of Charles Dickens: A Complete Edition.* Ed. K[enneth] J. Fielding. Hemel, Eng.: Harvester/Wheatsheaf; Atlantic Highlands, NJ: Humanities Press International, 1988, pp. xv-xviii, xxv-xxxii, 423–43, and passim.

84. Fielding, K[enneth] J. "Two Prologues for the Amateur Players." *Dickensian,* 56 (1960), 100–02.

85. Fielding, K[enneth] J., and Alec W. Brice. "Charles Dickens on 'The Exclusion of Evidence.' " *Dickensian,* 64 (1968), 131–40; 65 (1969), 35–41.

86. Gimbel, Richard. *Charles Dickens's A Christmas Carol. Three States of the First Edition.* N.p.: Privately printed, 1956 [1955]. 8 pp.

87. Gimbel, Richard. "The Earliest State of the First Edition of Charles Dickens' *A Christmas Carol." Princeton University Library Chronicle,* 19 (1957/58), 82–86.

88. Grubb, Gerald G. "On the Serial Publication of *Oliver Twist." Modern Language Notes,* 56 (1941), 290–94.

89. Kitton, F. G. "Introduction." In Dickens's *The [sic] Christmas Carol: A Facsimile Reproduction of the Author's Original Manuscript.* London: Elliot Stock; New York: Brentano, 1890, pp. iii-viii.

90. Kitton, Frederick [sic] G. "Introduction." In Dickens's *Old Lamps for New Ones and Other Sketches and Essays Hitherto Uncollected.* New York: New Amsterdam Book Co., 1897, pp. v-vii; revised as "Introduction." In Dickens's *To Be Read at Dusk and Other Stories, Sketches and Essays. Now First Collected.* London: George Redway, 1898, pp. xi-xxiii.

91. Kitton, F[rederic] G., ed. *The Poems and Verses of Charles Dickens.* London: Chapman and Hall; New York: Harper & Brothers, 1903; reprinted Kennebunkport, ME: Milford House, 1974. 206 pp.

92. Lohrli, Anne. "*Household Words* and Its 'Office Book.' " *Princeton University Library Chronicle,* 26 (1964/65), 27–47.

93. Long, William F. "Dickens and the Coming of Rail to Deal: An Uncollected Speech and Its Context." *Dickensian,* 85 (1989), 67–80.

94. Loomis, Abigail A. "Dickens Duplications: A Study of Overlap in Serial Bibliographies in Literature." *RQ* (Reference and Adult Services Division, American Library Association), 25 (1985/86), 348–55.

95. Matz, B. W. "Introduction." In Dickens's *Miscellaneous Papers, Plays and Poems*. Ed. B. W. Matz. Vols. XXXV and XXXVI. The National Edition. London: Chapman and Hall, 1908, XXXV, ix-xvii.

96. McCarthy, Patrick J. "Dickens at the Regent's Park Colosseum: Two Uncollected Pieces." *Dickensian*, 79 (1983), 154–61.

97. Monod, Sylvère. "'Between Two Worlds': Editing Dickens." In *Editing Nineteenth-Century Fiction: Papers Given at the Thirteenth Annual Conference on Editorial Problems, University of Toronto, 4–5 November 1977*. Ed. Jane Millgate. New York and London: Garland Publishing, 1978, pp. 17–39.

98. Mott, Graham. "The First Publication of 'Our Next Door Neighbours.'" *Dickensian*, 80 (1984), 114–16.

99. Nielsen, Hilmer. "Some Observations on *Sketches by Boz*." *Dickensian*, 34 (1937/38), 243–45.

100. Nonesuch Press, Bloomsbury [London]. *The Nonesuch Dickens: Retrospectus and Prospectus*. Bloomsbury [London]: The Nonesuch Press, 1937. 130 pp.

101. Osborne, E. Allen. *The Facts about A Christmas Carol*. London: Printed for the Author by The Bradley Press, 1937. 33 pp.

102. Patten, Robert L. *Charles Dickens and His Publishers*. Oxford: Clarendon Press, 1978, passim.

103. Read, Newbury F. "On the Writing of *Barnaby Rudge*." *Dickensian*, 30 (1933/34), 53–57.

104. Stone, Harry, ed. *Charles Dickens' Uncollected Writings from Household Words 1850–1859*. 2 vols. Bloomington and London: Indiana University Press, 1968; as *The Uncollected Writings of Charles Dickens: Household Words, 1850–1859*. 2 vols. London: Allen Lane, Penguin Press, 1969. xx + 359 pp; xii + pp. 361–716.

105. Storey, Graham. "An Unpublished Satirical Sketch by Dickens." *Dickensian*, 74 (1978), 6–7.

106. Tillotson, Kathleen. "*Oliver Twist* in Three Volumes." *Library*, 5th ser., 18 (1963), 113–32.

107. Van Noorden, C[harles]. "Dickens as a Reporter." *Bookman* (London), 47 (1914/15), 148–49.

108. Van Noorden, C[harles], ed. "A New Bit by Dickens: A Dramatic Critique Which Has Never Been Reprinted Until Now." *Book Monthly*, 15 (1920), 231–32.

109. W[augh], A[rthur], H[ugh] W[alpole], W[alter] D[exter], and T[homas] H[atton]. "Introduction." In their edition of Dickens's *Collected Papers*. 2 vols. The Nonesuch Dickens. Bloomsbury [London]: Nonesuch Press, 1937, I, v-vi.

Bibliographies and Surveys of Translations, Readings, Dramatic Adaptations, Plagiarisms and Imitations, and Illustrations

Bibliographies of Translations

110. Axon, William E. A. "Dickens in Welsh." *Notes and Queries*, 9th ser., 3 (1899), 225.

111. Bachman, Maria. "Dickens Plagiarisms in Poland." *Kwartalnik Neofilologiczny*, 21 (1974), 227–31.

112. Bick, Wolfgang, Bärbel Czennia, and Sybille Rohde-Gaur. "Bibliographie der deutschen Übersetzungen der Romane von Charles Dickens." *Anglia*, 107 (1989), 65–88, 430–51.

113. Bielecka, D[aniela]. "Dickens in Poland." *Dickens Studies Annual*, 17 (1988), 195–223.

114. Carlton, W[illiam] J. "Dickens in Shorthand." *Dickensian*, 44 (1947/48), 205–08.

115. Casotti, Francesco M. "Italian Translations of Dickens." *Dickensian*, 95 (1999), 19–23.

116. *Charles Dickens. Bibliography of the Romanian Translations Published in Volume (1898–1966)*. Bucharest: Romanian Institute for Cultural Relations with Foreign Countries, 1967. 32 pp.

117. *Clio: Catalogo dei libri italiani dell' Ottocento (1801–1900)/Catalogue of Nineteenth Century Italian Books (1801–1900)*. 19 vols. Milan: Editrice Bibliografica, 1991, II, 1602–03.

118. Delattre, Floris. "II.—Dickens en France: Traducteurs et Critiques." In his *Dickens et la France: Étude d'une interaction littéraire Anglo-Française*. Paris: Librairie Universitaire, 1927, pp. 43–88, 179–92.

119. *Deutsche Bibliographie, 1945–1950: Verzeichnis aller in Deutschland erschienenen Veröffentlichungen und der in Österreich und der Schweiz im Buchhandel erscheinenen deutschsprachigen Publikationen sowie der deutschsprachigen Veröffentlichungen anderer Länder*. 4 vols. Frankfurt: Buchhändler-Vereinigung GMBH, 1953–60, passim; continuations published annually and then semi-annually in multi-volume editions, and in 5–year cumulations to date.

120. Devonshire, M[arian] G. "Dickens" and "Dickens (1848–1870)." *The English Novel in France, 1830–1870*. London: University of London Press, 1929; rpt. London: Frank Cass; New York: Octagon Books, 1967, pp. 289–97, 312–29.

121. Diakonova, Nina. "Russian Dickens Studies, 1970–1995." *Dickens Quarterly*, 12 (1995), 181–86.

122. Dontchev, Nicolaï. "Dickens en Bulgarie." Special Dickens Number. *Europe*, no. 488 (December 1969), 130– 35.

123. Duțu, Alexandru, and Sorin Alexandrescu. *Dickens in Rumania: A Bibliography for the 150th Anniversary*. Bucharest: National Commission of the Rumanian People's Republic for UNESCO, 1962. 6 pp.

124. Dyboski, Roman. "Dickens w Polsce" [Dickens in Poland]. In his *Charles Dickens: Życie i twórczość* [Charles Dickens: Life and Works]. Lwów-Warszawa: Ksiaznica-Atlas, 1936, pp. 103–07.

125. Fridlender, I. V., and I. M. Katarsky. [*Charles Dickens: Bibliography of Russian Translations and Critical Literature in Russian, 1838–1960*]. Moscow: Vsesoiuznaia Gosudarstvennaia Biblioteka Inostrannoi Literatury, 1962. 327 pp.

126. Gattégno, Jean. "Les premiéres traductions françaises des romans de Dickens." In special issue: "Studies in Charles Dickens." *Cahiers victoriens et edouardiens*, no. 20 (October 1984), 107–14.

127. Gilenson, Boris. "Dickens in Russia." *Dickensian*, 57 (1961), 56–58.

128. Gummer, Ellis N. "List of German Critical Works on Dickens, 1870–1937," "List of Articles on Dickens in German Periodicals, 1837–1870," "Notes on Some Early German Translators of Dickens' Works," and "General Bibliography." In his *Dickens' Works in Germany, 1837–1937*. Oxford: Clarendon Press; New York: Oxford University Press, 1940; reprinted New York: Octagon Books, 1976, pp. 175–79, 180–84, 185–93, 194–97.

129. Harper, Kenneth E., and Bradford A. Booth. "Russian Translations of Nineteenth-Century English Fiction." *Nineteenth-Century Fiction*, 8 (1953/54), 188–97.

130. *Index Translationum. Repertoire International des Traductions. International Bibliography of Translations*, no. 1 (1932)-no. 31 (1940), published quarterly. Paris: International Institute of Intellectual Cooperation, 1932–40, passim; the first thirty-one numbers reprinted, 4 vols., Vaduz, Liechtenstein: Kraus Reprint, 1964, passim; continued as ns 1 (1948)-39 (1986), published annually. Paris: UNESCO, 1948– , passim; on CD-ROM, 1994– , passim, and on the Internet, passim.

131. Izzo, Carlo. "Bibliografia Generale." In his *Autobiografismo di Charles Dickens*. Collezione di Varia Critica, 11. Venice: Neri Pozza Editore, 1954, pp. 173–90.

132. Katarsky, I[gor]. [Bibliography]. In his *Dikkens v Rossii: seredina XIX veka*. Moscow: Nauka Press, 1966, pp. 404–07.

133. Kogztur, Gizella. "Dickens en Hongrie." Special Dickens Number. *Europe*, no. 488 (December 1969), 124–30.

134. Kong, Haili. "Dickens in China." *Dickens Quarterly*, 4 (1987), 39–41.

135. Lary, N[ikita] M. "Select Bibliography." In his *Dostoevsky and Dickens: A Study of Literary Influence*. London and Boston: Routledge and Kegan Paul, 1973, pp. 162–65.

136. Lindblad, Ishrat. "Dickens in Swedish." *Stockholm Papers in English Language and Literature*, Publication 4 (April 1984), 1–68. Includes "Bibliography of Translations," pp. 53–68.

137. Lzwińska, Maria, and Andrzej Weseliński. "Dickens in Poland: 1839–1981." In *Anglica: Studies in English and American Literature*. Warsaw: Wydawnictwa uniwersytetu Warsawskiego, 1988, pp. 123–40.

138. Makowiecki, Stefan, et al., comps. "Dickens, Ch[arles]." In *Bibliografia anglistyki polskiej, 1945–1975/Bibliographies of Writings on English Language and Literature in Poland, 1945–1975*. Ed. Jacek Fisiak. Warsaw: Państwowe Wydawnictwo Naukowe/Polish Scientific Publishers, 1977, pp. 122–24.

139. Matsumura, Masaie. "Dickens in Japan." In *Charles Dickens: Our Mutual Friend: Essays from Britain and Japan*. Tokyo: Nan'Un-Do, 1983, pp. 173–204.

140. Matsumura, Masaie. "Dickens in Japan." *Michi, a Journal for Cultural Exchange*, 1, i (Spring 1978), 34–54.

141. Mikdadi, F. H. "*David Copperfield* in Arabic." *Dickensian*, 75 (1979), 85–93.

142. Munch-Peterson, Erland. "Dickens, Charles." In his *Bibliografi over oversaettelser til dansk 1800–1900 af prosafiktion fra de germanske og romanske sprog* [A Bibliography of Translations into Danish 1800–1900 of Prose Fiction from Germanic and Romance Languages]. Copenhagen: Rosenkilde og Bagger for the Kongelige Bibliotek, Nationalbibliografisk afdeling [Rosenkilde and Bagger for the Royal Library, Department of National Bibliography], 1976, pp. 74–84.

143. Naumov, Nićifor. In his *Dikens kod Srba I Hrvata* [Dickens in Serbia and Croatia]. Philological Faculty of Belgrade University Monographs, 9. Belgrade: Philological Faculty of Belgrade University, 1967. 174 pp. Also see "Bibliografija," pp. 155–68.

144. Nielsen, Jørgen E. "Charles Dickens in Denmark." In *Proceedings from the Second Nordic Conference for English Studies* (Helsinki, 19–21 May 1983). Ed. Håkan Ringbom and Matti Rissanen. Meddelandan från Stiftelsens för Åbo Akademi Förskningsinstitut (Publications of the Research Institute of the Åbo Akademi Foundation), 92. Åbo, Finland: Åbo Akademi, 1984, pp. 489–96.

145. Nielsen, Jørgen E. "The Danish Translations of *A Tale of Two Cities*." In *A Literary Miscellany Presented to Eric Jacobsen*. Ed. Graham D. Caie and Holger Nørgaard. Copenhagen: University of Copenhagen, 1988, pp. 388–405.

146. Nielsen, Jørgen E. "Lexicography and the Establishment of Translation Norms." In *Symposium on Lexicography III*. Ed. Karl Hyldgaard-Jensen and

Arne Zettersten. Lexicographica Series Maior, 19. Tübingen, Ger.: Max Nie-
meyer, 1988, pp. 355–64.

147. Pagliaini, Attilio, comp. "Dickens, Carlo." In *Catalogo Generale della Libreria
Italiana dall'anno 1847 a tutto il 1899*. 3 vols. Milan: Associazione tipografico-
librarià italiani, 1901–03; reprinted Vaduz, Liechtenstein: Kraus Reprint, 1964,
I, 794–95; also see supplements for 1900–1910, 1911–1920, 1921–1930,
1931–1940, passim.

148. Parchevskaya, B. M. List of Russian translations of Dickens's works and publications about Dickens, 1960–80. In *Taina Charl'za Dikkensa*. By E[katerina] Y.
Genieva. Moscow: Izd-vo "Knizhnaia patata," 1990, pp. 62–123, 490–511.

149. Piscopo, Ugo. "Dickens en Italie." Trans. from the Italian by Camille Sinaï.
Special Dickens Number. *Europe*, No. 488 (December 1969), 116–24.

150. Prades, Juana de José. "Los Libros de Dickens en España." *El Libro Español*,
1 (1958), 515–24.

151. Prager, Leonard. "Charles Dickens in Yiddish (A Survey)." *Jewish Language
Review*, no. 4 (1984), 158–78. Includes his "Checklist of Translations," pp.
170–73.

152. Sadrin, Anny. "French Studies of Dickens since 1970." *Dickens Quarterly*, 12
(1995), 187–98.

153. Sadrin, Anny. "Traductions et Adaptations Françaises de *A Tale of Two Cities*."
In *Charles Dickens et La France: Colloque International de Boulogne-sur-Mer,
3 Juin 1978*. Ed. Sylvère Monod. Lille, France: Presses Universitaires de Lille,
[1981], pp. 77–91.

154. S[adrin], A[nny]. "Translations of Dickens." In *Oxford Reader's Companion
to Dickens*. Ed. Paul Schlicke (197), pp. 567–69.

155. Schmuck, Hilmar, and Willi Gorzny, gen. eds. "Dickens, Charles." In their
Gesamtverzeichnis des deutschsprachigen Schrifttums (GV), 1700–1910. Vol. 28.
München, New York, London, and Paris: K. G. Saur, 1981, pp. 387–96; also
Gorzny, Willi, and Reinhard Oberschelp, gen. eds. "Dickens, Charles." In their
Gesamtverzeichnis des deutschsprachigen Schrifttums (GV), 1911–1965. Vol. 27.
München: Verlag Dokumentation, 1977, pp. 36–53.

156. Sherif, Nur. *Dickens in Arabic (1912–1970)*. Beirut, Lebanon: Beirut Arab University, 1974. 36 pp.

157. Soto Vasquez, Adolfo Luis. *El Inglés de Charles Dickens y su Traducción al
Español*. La Coruña: Universidade da Coruña, Servicio de Publicacións, 1993.
221 pp. See his "Bibliografía," pp. 209–21.

158. Suzannet, A[lain] de. "The First German Translation of *Nicholas Nickleby*."
Dickensian, 28 (1931/32), 60–62.

159. Tschumi, Raymond. "Bibliography." Appended to his "Dickens and Switzerland." *English Studies*, 60 (1979), 456–61.

160. Uhrström, W. "*Pickwick* in Sweden." *Dickensian*, 32 (1935/36), 117–18.

161. van Kessel, J. C. "Dickens in het Nederlands." *Dutch Dickensian*, 6, xv (December 1976), 31–51.

162. Vereş, Grigore. "Dickens and His Romanian Readers: A Tentative Approach." *Analele Stiintifice ale Universitatii "al. i Cuza" din Iasi*, ns 24, section 3f, Literatură (1978), 109–13.

163. Vereş, Grigore. *Opera lui Charles Dickens în România*. Bucharest: Editura Minerva, 1982. 315 pp.

164. Wellens, Oscar. "The Earliest Dutch Translations of Dickens (1837–1870): An All-Inclusive List." *Dickensian*, 93 (1997), 126–32.

165. Wilkins, W[illiam] Glyde. "Early Foreign Translations of Dickens's Works." *Dickensian*, 7 (1911), 35–37.

166. Williams, Aneurin. "Dickens's 'David Copperfield' in Welsh." *Notes and Queries*, 12th ser., 9 (1921), 445.

167. Zentella Mayer, Arturo. "Carlos Dickens en México." In *Charles Dickens, 1812–1870: Homenaje en el primer centenario de su muerte*. Mexico City: Univ. Nacional Autónoma de México, Facultad de Filosofia y Letras/Departamento de Letras Inglesas, 1971, pp. 161–82. Also see Carlos Villalobos's "Bibliografia de Charles Dickens," pp. 193–204.

168. Zhang Ling and Zhang Yang. "Dickens in China." *Dickens Quarterly*, 16 (1999), 191–98.

169. Zhang Yu. "Chinese Translations of 'David Copperfield': Accuracy and Acculturation." *Dissertation Abstracts International*, 53 (1992/93), 485A (Southern Illinois University, Carbondale, 1991).

Bibliographies, Surveys, and Studies of Dickens's Readings

170. Callahan, Jean. "The (Unread) Reading Version of *Great Expectations*." In *Charles Dickens's Great Expectations: Authoritative Text, Backgrounds, Contexts, Criticism*. Ed. Edgar Rosenberg (482), pp. 543–56.

171. Collins, Philip. "Appendix C: Dickens's Readings from the *Christmas Books*." In Dickens's *The Christmas Books*. Ed. Michael Slater (460), II, 355–58.

172. Collins, Philip. "The Dickens Reading-Copies in Dickens House." *Dickensian*, 68 (1972), 173–79.

173. Collins, Philip. "Dickens Reading-Copies in the Beinecke Library." *Yale University Library Gazette*, 46 (1971/72), 153–58.

174. Collins, Philip. "Dickens' Public Readings: Texts and Performances." *Dickens Studies Annual*, 3 (1974), 182–97, 242–44.

175. Collins, Philip. "Introduction." In Dickens's *A Christmas Carol: The Public Reading Version. A Facsimile of the Author's Prompt-Copy*. Ed. Philip Collins. New York: New York Public Library, 1971, pp. ix-xxiii.

176. Collins, Philip. "Introduction." In Dickens's *Sikes and Nancy: A Facsimile of a Privately Printed Annotated Copy, Now in the Dickens House, Presented by Dickens to Adeline Billington*. Ed. Philip Collins. London: Dickens House, 1982, pp. iii-vi.

177. Collins, Philip. "Introduction." In Dickens's *Sikes and Nancy and Other Public Readings*. Ed. Philip Collins. World's Classics Edition. Oxford and New York: Oxford University Press, 1983, pp. vii-xx and passim.

178. Collins, Philip. "Introduction," Headnotes, Endnotes, and Footnotes. In *Charles Dickens: The Public Readings*. Ed. Philip Collins. Oxford: Clarendon Press, 1975, pp. xvii-lxix and passim.

179. Collins, Philip. "The Texts of Dickens' Readings." *Bulletin of the New York Public Library*, 74 (1970), 360–80.

180. Collins, Philip. "The Texts of Dickens' Readings: A Postscript." *Bulletin of the New York Public Library*, 75 (1971), 63.

181. Gordan, John D. "Introduction," "A Guide for Readers," "Notes on the Text," and "Appendix." In *Mrs. Gamp by Charles Dickens: A Facsimile of the Author's Prompt Copy*. New York: New York Public Library, 1956, pp. 1–18, 20, 81–114, 115–20.

182. Slater, Michael. "*The Bastille Prisoner*: A Reading Dickens Never Gave." *Etudes Anglaises*, 23 (1970), 190–96.

183. Stonehouse, John H. "A First Bibliography of the Reading Editions of Charles Dickens's Works." In Dickens's *Sikes and Nancy: A Reading*. Ed. John H. Stonehouse. London: Henry Sotheran, 1921, pp. 49–57.

Bibliographies, Surveys, and Studies of Dramatic and Other Adaptations

184. *The American Film Institute Catalog of Motion Pictures Produced in the United States*. 1971– .

Volume A: *Film Beginnings, 1893–1910: A Work in Progress*. Ed. Elias Savada. 2 parts. Metuchen, NJ, and London: Scarecrow Press, 1995, passim.

Volume F1: *Feature Films, 1911–1920*. Ed. Patricia K. Hanson. 2 parts. Berkeley: University of California Press, 1988.
Volume F2: *Feature Films, 1921–1930*. Ed. Kenneth W. Munden. 2 parts. New York: Bowker, 1971.
Volume F3: *Feature Films, 1931–1940*. Ed Patricia K. Hanson and Alan Grevinson. 3 parts. Berkeley: University of California Press, 1993.
Volume F4: *Feature Films, 1941–1950*. Ed. Patricia K. Hanson and Amy Dunkleberger. 3 vols. Berkeley, Los Angeles, and London: University of California Press, 1999.
Volume F6: *Feature Films, 1961–1970*. Ed. Richard P. Krafsur. 2 parts. New York: Bowker, 1976.

185. Bolton, H. Philip. *"Bleak House* and the Playhouse." *Dickens Studies Annual*, 12 (1983), 81–116.

186. Bolton, H. Philip. *Dickens Dramatized*. London: Mansell; Boston: G. K. Hall, 1987. xviii + 501 pp.

187. Brennan, Elizabeth M. "Appendix E: Little Nell on the Stage, 1840–1841." In Dickens's *The Old Curiosity Shop*. Clarendon Edition (515), pp. 630–34, and Oxford's World Classics Edition (516), pp. 580–84.

188. "Dickens, Charles." The Internet Movie Database Web site. http://us.imdb.-com/Name?Dickens,+Charles#11920(IMDb).

189. Fawcett, F. Dubrez. *Dickens the Dramatist: On Stage, Screen and Radio*. London: W. H. Allen, 1952. xiii + 278 pp. See "Appendix A: Plays and Adaptations of the Works of Charles Dickens for Stage, Screen and Television," pp. 232–54.

190. Fitz-Gerald, S[hafto]. J. Adair. *Dickens and the Drama, Being an Account of Charles Dickens's Connection with the Stage and the Stage's Connection with Him*. London: Chapman and Hall, 1910; reprinted New York: Benjamin Blom, 1971. xxiii + 352 pp.

191. Fulkerson, Richard P. *"Oliver Twist* in the Victorian Theatre." *Dickensian*, 70 (1974), 82–95.

192. Guida, Fred. *"A Christmas Carol" and Its Adaptations: A Critical Examination of Dickens's Story and Its Productions On Screen and Television*. Jefferson, NC, and London: McFarland, 2000. xi + 264 pp. See "Filmography" and "Bibliography," pp. 171–231, 245–49.

193. Hill, T[homas] W. "A Unique Collection of Music." *Dickensian*, 37 (1940/41), 43–54. See "A Catalogue of the [William] Miller Collection of Dickens Music at the Dickens House," pp. 48–54.

194. Pemberton, T. Edgar. "Chapter V. Adaptations and Impersonations." In his *Charles Dickens and the Stage. A Record of His Connection with the Drama as Playwright, Actor, and Critic*. London: Redway, 1888, pp. 136–85.

195. Pointer, Michael. *Charles Dickens on the Screen: The Film, Television, and Video Adaptations*. Lanham, MD, and London: Scarecrow Press, 1996. vii + 207 pp.

196. Sammon, Paul. *The "Christmas Carol" Trivia Book: Everything You Ever Wanted to Know About Every Version of the Dickens Classic*. Secaucus, NJ: Carol Publishing Group, 1994. xvii + 237 pp.

197. Schlicke, Paul, ed. Adaptations of Dickens's Works. In *Oxford Reader's Companion to Dickens* (438), passim. See particularly A[lan] S. W[atts], "Abridgements of Dickens's Works," pp. 1–2, "Adaptations of Dickens's Works," p. 4, and "Sequels and Continuations," pp. 513–14; G[illian] A[very], "Children's Versions of Dickens," pp. 92–93; H. P[hilip] B[olton], "Dramatizations and Dramatizers of Dickens's Works," pp. 195–99; G[rahame] F. S[mith], "Films and Film-Makers of Dickens," pp. 233–36, and "Television Adaptations of Dickens," pp. 548, 554; and R[obert] T. B[ledsoe], "Dickens's Works," pp. 385–86. The pagination varies somewhat in the 2000 paperback edition—see, respectively, pp. 1–2, 4–5, 525–26, 96–97, 198–202, 241–44, 565, and 394–95.

198. Van Amerongen, J. B. "Appendix: Dickens on the Stage." In his *The Actor in Dickens. A Study of the Histrionic and Dramatic Elements in the Novelist's Life and Work*. London: Palmer, 1926; New York: D. Appleton, 1927; reprinted New York: Benjamin Blom, 1969; New York: Haskell House, 1970, pp. 261–73, 295–96.

199. Woollcott, Alexander. "The Dramatizations of Dickens." In his *Mr. Dickens Goes to the Play*. New York and London: G. P. Putnam's Sons, 1922; reprinted Port Washington, NY: Kennikat Press, 1967, pp. 221–36.

200. Zambrano, Ana L. "*David Copperfield*: Novel and Film." *University of Hartford Studies in Literature*, 9 (1977), 1–16.

201. Zambrano, Ana L. "Feature Motion Pictures Adapted from Dickens: A Checklist—Part I" and "Feature Motion Pictures Adapted from Dickens: A Checklist—Part II." *Dickens Studies Newsletter*, 5 (1974), 106–09; 6 (1975), 9–13; adapted as "Feature Motion Pictures Adapted from Dickens: A Chronological Checklist." In her *Dickens and Film*. Gordon Press Film Series. NY: Gordon Press, 1977, pp. 399–41. Also see "Modern Film Adaptations of the Novels of Dickens," pp. 241–379.

Surveys of Plagiarisms, Imitations, Etc., of Dickens's Works

202. Carter, John, and Graham Pollard. "Part III. Dossiers: Charles Dickens." In their *An Enquiry into the Nature of Certain Nineteenth Century Pamphlets*. London: Constable; New York: Charles Scribner's Sons, 1934; reprinted New York: Haskell House, 1971, pp. 183–87; 2nd ed., as *An Enquiry into the Nature*

of Certain Nineteenth Century Pamphlets, with an Epilogue. Ed. Nicolas Barker and John Collins. London and Berkeley, CA: Scolar Press, 1983, pp. 183–87 and p. 15 of added section.

203. Connor, Steven. "Appendix C: Unfinished Business: The History of Continuations, Conclusions and Solutions." In Dickens's *The Mystery of Edwin Drood.* Ed. Steven Connor. Everyman Library. London: Dent, 1996, pp. 286–307.

204. Hoggart, Paul. "Travesties of Dickens." In *English and Cultural Studies: Broadening the Context. Essays & Studies, 1987,* ns 40 (1987). Ed. Michael Green. Atlantic Highlands, NJ: Humanities Press; London: John Murray, 1987, pp. 32–44.

205. James, Louis. "The Beginnings of a New Type of Popular Fiction: Plagiarisms of Dickens." In his *Fiction for the Working Man, 1830–50: A Study of the Literature Produced for the Working Classes in Early Victorian Urban England.* London: Oxford University Press, 1963, pp. 45–71; Harmondsworth, Eng., and Baltimore, MD: Penguin, University Books, 1974, pp. 51–82.

206. J[ames], L[ouis]. "Plagiarisms of Dickens." In *Oxford Reader's Companion to Dickens.* Ed. Paul Schlicke (438), pp. 443, 452–54.

207. Walters, J. Cuming. "The Sequels and Solutions." In his *The Complete Mystery of Edwin Drood. The History, Continuations, and Solutions (1870–1912).* London: Chapman and Hall, 1912; Boston: Dana Estes, 1913; rpt. Folcroft, PA: Folcroft Library Editions, 1974; Norwood, PA: Norwood Editions, 1978, pp. 205–54.

208. Wilkins, W[illiam] Glyde. "American Parodies on Dickens's 'American Notes.'" *Dickensian,* 4 (1908), 214–18.

Bibliographies and Surveys of Illustrations for Dickens's Novels

209. Cohen, Jane R. *Charles Dickens and His Original Illustrators.* Columbus: Ohio State University Press, 1980, passim.

210. Grego, Joseph, ed. *Pictorial Pickwickiana. Charles Dickens and His Illustrators.* 2 vols. London: Chapman and Hall, 1899. xxiii + 493 pp; xii + 509 pp.

211. Hammerton, J. A. *The Dickens Picture-Book. A Record of the Dickens Illustrators.* Vol. XVII of the Charles Dickens Library. London: Educational Book Company, [1910]. viii + 466 pp.

212. Hatton, Thomas, comp. "A Bibliographical List of the Original Illustrations to the Works of Charles Dickens, Being Those Made under His Supervision." In *The Nonesuch Dickens: Retrospectus and Prospectus* (100), pp. 55–78.

213. Johannsen, Albert. *Phiz: Illustrations from the Novels of Charles Dickens*. Chicago: University of Chicago Press, 1956; Cambridge: Cambridge University Press, 1957. xi + 442 pp.

214. Kitton, Frederic G. "Appendix I: Illustrators of Cheap Editions," "Appendix II: Concerning 'Extra Illustrations,'" and "Appendix III: Dickens in Art." In his *Dickens and His Illustrators: Cruikshank, Seymour, Buss, "Phiz," Cattermole, Leech, Doyle, Stanfield, Maclise, Tenniel, Frank Stone, Landseer, Palmer, Topham, Marcus Stone, and Luke Fildes. With Twenty-Two Portraits and Facsimiles of Seventy Original Drawings Now Reproduced for the First Time*. London: George Redway, 1899; reprinted Amsterdam: S. Emmering, 1972; New York: Abner Schram, 1972; New York: AMS Press, 1973, pp. 219–26, 227–40, 240–42. Also see Kitton's *Dickens Illustrations, Facsimiles of Original Drawings, Sketches and Studies for Illustration in the Works of Charles Dickens*. London: George Redway, 1900. viii pp. + 30 plates.

215. Layard, George S. "Suppressed Plates: The Suppressed Portrait of Dickens, 'Pickwick,' 'The Battle of Life,' and 'Grimaldi'" and "Suppressed Plates: III.—Dickens['s] Cancelled Plates: 'Oliver Twist,' 'Martin Chuzzlewit,' 'The Strange Gentleman,' 'Pictures from Italy,' and 'Sketches by Boz.'" *Pall Mall Magazine*, 17 (1899), 254–60, 341–48; reprinted with minor additions as "The Suppressed Portrait of Dickens, 'Pickwick,' 'The Battle of Life,' and 'Grimaldi'" and "Dickens's Cancelled Plates: 'Oliver Twist,' 'Martin Chuzzlewit,' 'The Strange Gentleman,' 'Pictures from Italy,' and 'Sketches by Boz.'" In his *Suppressed Plates, Wood Engravings, &c., Together with Other Curiosities Germane Thereto, Being an Account of Certain Matters Peculiarly Alluring to the Collector*. London: Adam and Charles Black, 1907, pp. 26–42, 43–58.

216. Solberg, Sarah A. "'Text Dropped into the Woodcuts': Dickens' Christmas Books." *Dickens Studies Annual*, 8 (1980), 103–18.

217. Stevens, Joan. "'Woodcuts Dropped into the Text': The Illustrations in *The Old Curiosity Shop* and *Barnaby Rudge*." *Studies in Bibliography*, 20 (1967), 113–34.

Bibliographies of Dickens Studies

General Bibliographies of Dickens Studies

218. Carty, Charles F. "Some Addenda to Kitton's 'Dickensiana.'" *Literary Collector*, 5 (1902/03), 12–14, 43–46.

219. Chaudhuri, Brahma, comp. and ed. *Charles Dickens, a Bibliography: 1970–1986*. Bibliography on Demand Series. Edmonton, Can.: LITIR Database, 1988. xii + 223 pp.

220. Chittick, Kathryn. *The Critical Reception of Charles Dickens, 1833–1841.* New York: Garland Publishing, 1989. xvi + 277 pp.

221. Churchill, R. C. *A Bibliography of Dickensian Criticism, 1836–1975.* London: Macmillan; Garland Reference Library of the Humanities, 12. New York and London: Garland Publishing, 1975. xiv + 314 pp.

222. Cohn, Alan M., and K. K. Collins, comps. *The Cumulated Dickens Checklist: 1970–1979.* Troy, NY: Whitston, 1982. vi + 391 pp.

223. Collins, Philip. "Charles Dickens." In *Victorian Fiction: A Second Guide to Research.* Ed. George H. Ford. New York: Modern Language Association, 1978, pp. 34–113.

224. "Dickens, Charles." In *Nineteenth Century Readers' Guide to Periodical Literature, 1890–1899, with Supplementary Indexing, 1900–1922.* Ed. Helen G. Cushing and Adah V. Morris. 2 vols. New York: H. W. Wilson, 1944, I, 725–26.

225. Dunn, Frank T., comp. *A Cumulative Analytical Index to The Dickensian, 1905–1974, Together with an Index to the Illustrations, Compiled by Mary Ford and Michael Slater.* Hassocks, Eng.: Harvester Press, 1976. x + 199 pp.

226. Fenstermaker, John J., comp. *Charles Dickens, 1940–1975: An Analytical Subject Index to Periodical Criticism of the Novels and Christmas Books.* Boston: G. K. Hall; London: Prior, 1979. xix + 302 pp.

227. Ford, George H. "Appendix: Dickens' Awareness of Reviews" and "Bibliography." In his *Dickens and His Readers: Aspects of Novel-Criticism since 1836.* Princeton, NJ: Published for the University of Cincinnati by Princeton University Press; London: Oxford University Press, 1955; reprinted New York: Norton; Toronto: George J. McLeod, 1965 (paperback); New York: Gordian Press, 1974, pp. 263–66, 303–05.

228. Ford, George H., and Lauriat Lane, Jr. "Bibliography." In their *The Dickens Critics.* Ithaca, NY: Cornell University Press, 1961; reprinted in paperback, 1966, pp. 387–410.

229. Freeman, Ronald E., ed. *Bibliographies of Studies in Victorian Literature for the Ten Years 1965–1974.* New York: AMS Press, 1981, passim.

230. Gold, Joseph, comp. *The Stature of Dickens: A Centenary Bibliography.* Toronto and Buffalo, NY: Published for University of Manitoba Press by University of Toronto Press, 1971. xxix + 237 pp.

231. Harner, James L. "Databases." In his *Literary Research Guide* (233), pp. 30–31.

232. Harner, James L. "Internet Resources." In his *Literary Research Guide* (233), pp. 72–74.

233. Harner, James L. *Literary Research Guide: An Annotated Listing of Reference Sources in English Literary Studies.* 4th ed. New York: Modern Language Association of America, 2002. x + 802 pp. Also see "Research Libraries," pp. 22–25.

234. Howard-Hill, T[revor] H., comp. *Index to British Literary Bibliography.* 9+ vols. Oxford: Clarendon Press, 1969– .

> Volume I: *Bibliography of British Literary Bibliographies*, 1969; 2nd ed., revised and enlarged, 1987.
> Volume II: *Shakespearean Bibliography and Textual Criticism: A Bibliography.* 1971.
> Volume III: *The Early British Book: A Bibliography to 1890.* In preparation.
> Volume IV: *British Bibliography and Textual Criticism: A Bibliography.* 1979.
> Volume V: *British Bibliography and Textual Criticism: A Bibliography (Authors).* 1979.
> Volume VI: *British Literary Bibliography and Textual Criticism, 1890–1969: An Index.* 1980.
> Volume VII: *British Literary Bibliography, 1970–1979: A Bibliography.* 1992.
> Volume VIII: *British Literary Bibliography, 1980–1989: A Bibliography.* 1999.
> Volume IX: *British Literary Bibliography, 1980–1989: A Bibliography (Authors).* 1999.

235. Kitton, Fred[eric] G. *Dickensiana: A Bibliography of the Literature Relating to Charles Dickens and His Writings.* London: George Redway, 1886; reprinted New York: Haskell House, 1971. xxxii + 511 pp.

236. Lane, Lauriat, Jr. "Dickens Studies 1958–1968: An Overview." In "Charles Dickens Special Number." *Studies in the Novel*, 1, ii (Summer 1969), 240–54.

237. Miller, William. *The Dickens Student and Collector: A List of Writings Relating to Charles Dickens and His Works, 1836–1945.* Cambridge, MA: Harvard University Press, 1946. xii + 351 pp. Also see *Supplement to "The Dickens Student and Collector: A List of Writings Relating to Charles Dickens and His Works."* Brighton: Privately printed, 1947. 12 pp. and *A Second Supplement to "The Dickens Student and Collector: A List of Writings Relating to Charles Dickens and His Works."* Hove, Sussex: Privately printed, 1953. 15 pp.

238. Nisbet, Ada. "Charles Dickens." In *Victorian Fiction: A Guide to Research.* Ed. Lionel Stevenson. Cambridge, MA: Harvard University Press, 1964, pp. 44–153.

239. Slack, Robert C., ed. *Bibliographies of Studies in Victorian Literature for the Ten Years 1955–1964.* Urbana: University of Illinois Press, 1967, passim.

240. Templeman, William D., ed. *Bibliographies of Studies in Victorian Literature for the Thirteen Years 1932–1944*. Urbana: University of Illinois Press, 1945, passim.

241. Tobias, Richard C., ed. *Bibliographies of Studies in Victorian Literature for the Ten Years 1975–1984*. New York: AMS Press, 1991, passim.

242. Vann, J. Don. "A Checklist of Dickens Criticism, 1963–1967." In "Charles Dickens Special Number." *Studies in the Novel*, 1, ii (Summer 1969), 255–78.

243. Wortman, William A. *A Guide to Serial Bibliographies for Modern Literatures.* Selected Bibliographies in Language and Literature, 3. New York: Modern Language Association of America, 1982; 2nd ed. New York: Modern Language Association of America, 1995, passim.

244. Wright, Austin, ed. *Bibliographies of Studies in Victorian Literature for the Ten Years 1945–1954*. Urbana: University of Illinois Press, 1956, passim.

General Serial Bibliographies Containing Dickens Studies

245. Chaudhuri, Brahma, comp. and ed. "Charles Dickens." In his *Annual Bibliography of Victorian Studies [1976–]*. Edmonton, Can.: LITIR Database, 1980– , passim. Harner (233) notes that Chaudhuri "expanded and cumulated" these bibliographies as *A Comprehensive Bibliography of Victorian Studies, 1970–1984*, 3 vols. (Edmonton: LITIR Database, 1984–85), which in turn was "corrected and expanded" as *Cumulative Bibliography of Victorian Studies, 1970–1984*, 2 vols. (Edmonton: Access Elite, 1988). There was also an earlier *Cumulative Bibliography of Victorian Studies: 1976–1980* (Edmonton: LITIR, 1982). Chaudhuri has since published additional five-year cumulations, for 1985–89, 1990–94, and 1995–99 (the last compiled and edited by Brahma Chaudhuri, James Mulvihill, and Fred Radford), as well as *Cumulated Index to Reviews of Books on Victorian Studies, 1975–1989* (Edmonton: LITIR, 1990). Also recently published is *Cumulative Bibliography of Victorian Studies: 1945–1969*, 2 vols. (Edmonton: LITIR, 1999). The bibliography is also available in other forms as *Victorian Database on CD-ROM* (1970–99) and *Victorian Studies on the Web*, www.victoriandatabase.com. A number of author and subject bibliographies, 1970–85/86, drawn from these bibliographies have been made available in a Bibliographies on Demand series, published by Access Elite. For Dickens, see Chaudhuri (219).

246. Cohn, Alan M., et al., comps. "The Dickens Checklist." In *Dickens Studies Newsletter*, 1, ii (September 1970)-14, iv (December 1983), passim; continued in *Dickens Quarterly*, 1, i (March 1984)-6, ii (June 1989), passim; continued from June 1989 by William G. Wall, Karen Kurt, Diane Hébert, Patricia Matthew, Karen Droisen and, most recently, Danny Siegel.

247. "Dickens, Charles." In *Annual Bibliography of English Language and Literature for 1920[-]*. Modern Humanities Research Association. Cambridge, Eng.: Bowes and Bowes, 1921–35; Cambridge: Cambridge University Press, 1936–64; London: Modern Humanities Research Association, 1965– , passim.

248. "Dickens, Charles." In *Essay and General Literature Index, 1900–1933[-1985–1989]*. Ed. Minnie E. Sears and Marian Shaw et al. 11 "Permanent Cumulations" vols. New York: H. W. Wilson, 1934–90, passim; continued thereafter in half-yearly and yearly accumulations, 1990– . New York: H. W. Wilson, 1991–, passim.

249. "Dickens, Charles." In *Poole's Index to Periodical Literature, 1802–81*. Ed. William F. Poole and William I. Fletcher. 2 vols. Boston: Houghton, Mifflin, 1882; revised 1891; also five supplementary volumes that continue the index to January 1907. Boston: Houghton, Mifflin, 1888–1908; reprinted in 6 vols. (actually 7, with the 2 vols. for 1802–81 designated as Vol. 1, Parts 1 and 2). Gloucester, MA: Peter Smith, 1963, passim; continued as "Dickens, Charles (1812–1870)." In *International Index to Periodicals*. Vol. 1 (1907–15)-Vol. 18 (April 1964–March 1965). New York: H. W. Wilson, 1916–65, passim; further continued in *Social Sciences & Humanities Index (Formerly International Index)*. Ed. J. Doris Bart et al. Vol. 19 (April 1965–March 1966)-Vol. 27 (April 1973–March 1974). New York: H. W. Wilson, 1966–74, passim; further continued in *Humanities Index*. Ed. Elizabeth E. Pingree et al. Vol. 1 (April 1974–March 1975)- . New York: H. W. Wilson Co., 1975– (issued monthly as well as in annual cumulations), passim.

250. "Dickens, Charles." In *Readers' Guide to Periodical Literature, 1900– *. Ed. Anna L. Guthrie et al. Vol. 1– . Minneapolis [and, later, New York]: H. W. Wilson, 1901– , passim.

251. "Dickens (Charles)." In *Subject Index to Periodicals [1915–1961]*. London: The Library Association, 1916–62, passim; continued as *British Humanities Index [1962–]*. Ed. Peter Ferriday et al. London: The Library Association, 1963–90; London: Melbourne, Munich, and New York: Bowker-Saur, 1991–, passim.

252. ["Dickens, Charles (1812–1870)"]. In "American Bibliography for 1921[-49]" and "1950[-55] American Bibliography." In *Publications of the Modern Language Association of America*, 37 (1922)-71 (1956), passim; continued as "1956[-62] Annual Bibliography." *Publications of the Modern Language Association of America*, 72 (1957)-78 (1963), passim; reprinted as *1921–25[-1954–55] MLA American Bibliography of Books and Articles on the Modern Languages and Literatures* and *1956[-1962] MLA International Bibliography of Books and Articles on the Modern Languages and Literature*. 8 and 7 vols. Millwood, NY: Kraus Reprint, 1976, passim; further continued as "1963[-82] MLA International Bibliography of Books and Articles on the Modern Languages and Literatures." *Publications of the Modern Language Association of America*, 79 (1964)-83 (1968), passim; also published separately as *1963[-]*

MLA International Bibliography of Books and Articles on the Modern Languages and Literatures. New York: New York University Press, 1964–68; New York: Modern Language Association of America, 1969– , passim.

253. "Dickensiana Month by Month." *Dickensian*, 1 (1905)-14 (1918), passim; "Dickensiana of the Quarter," 15 (1919)-37 (1940/41), passim; "Recent Dickensiana" or "Dickensiana," 38 (1941/42)-64 (1968), passim.

254. Kaplan, Fred, et al. "Recent Dickens Studies." In *Dickens Studies Annual: Essays on Victorian Fiction.* Vol. 8– . New York: AMS Press, 1980– , passim.

255. S[later], M[ichael], et al. "The Year's Work in Dickens Studies, 1967[-1976]." *Dickensian*, 64 (1968)-73 (1977), passim; "The Year's Work in Dickens Studies, 1977[-81]: A Survey of Periodical Literature." *Dickensian*, 75 (1979)-79 (1983), passim.

256. Summers, Montague, et al., comps. "The Nineteenth Century and After." In *The Year's Work in English Studies [for 1919–1920–].* Ed. Sir Sidney Lee et al. Published for the English Association. Vol. 1– . London: Oxford University Press, 1921–63; London: John Murray, 1964 (for 1962)-83 (for 1980); London: John Murray, and Atlantic Highlands, NJ: Humanities Press, 1984 (for 1981)-89 (for 1986); Oxford, Eng., and Cambridge, MA: Blackwell, and Atlantic Highlands, NJ: Humanities Press, 1990 (for 1987)-95 (for 1992); Oxford, Eng., and Cambridge, MA: Blackwell Publishers, 1996 (for 1993)- , passim. Vols. 1–32 (1919–51), reprinted New York and London: Johnson Reprint, 1966, passim; vols. 1–43 (1919–62), reprinted New York and London: Johnson Reprint, 1970, passim.

257. "Victorian Bibliography for 1932[-]." Ed. W. D. Templeman, *Modern Philology*, 30 (1932/33)-42 (1944/45); ed. Charles F. Harrold, *Modern Philology*, 43 (1945/46); ed. Austin Wright, *Modern Philology*, 44 (1946/47)-53 (1955/56); ed. Francis G. Townsend, *Modern Philology*, 54 (1956/57), and *Victorian Studies*, 1 (1957/58)-2 (1958/59); ed. Robert C. Slack, *Victorian Studies*, 3 (1959/60)-8 (1964/65); ed. Ronald E. Freeman, *Victorian Studies*, 9 (1965/66)-18 (1974/75); ed. Richard C. Tobias, *Victorian Studies*, 19 (1975/76)-28 (1984/85); ed. Edward H. Cohen, *Victorian Studies*, 29 (1985/86)- , passim.

Web Sites

258. The Active Portal Project. University of Wisconsin, Madison. http://www.active-portal.com/dickens.

259. Concordances of Great Books Web site. Ed. William A. Williams, Jr. http://www.concordances.com.

260. David Perdue's Charles Dickens Page: Dedicated to Bringing the Genius of Dickens to a New Generation of Readers Web site. Ed. David Perdue. http://www.fidnet.com/~dap1995/dickens/index.html.

261. The Dickens Fellowship Web site. London. http://www.dickensfellowship.btint-ernet.co.uk.

262. The Dickens Page Web site. Ed. Mitsuharu Matsuoka, Nagoya University, Nagoya, Japan. http://www.lang.nagoya-u.ac.jp/~matsuoka/Dickens.html.

263. The Dickens Project Web site. University of California, Santa Cruz. http://humwww.ucsc.edu/dickens.

264. Victorian Research Web: Scholarly Resources for Victorian Research Web site. Ed. Patrick Leary, History Department, Indiana University, Bloomington. http://www.indiana.edu/~victoria.

265. The Victorian Web. Ed. George P. Landow, Brown University. http://www.victorianweb.org.

266. Voice of the Shuttle Web site. Ed. Alan Liu, et al. English Department, University of California, Santa Barbara. http://vos.ucsb.edu.

Library Catalogues, Catalogues of Dickens Collections, and Guides to Collections

Library Catalogues and Catalogues of Dickens Collections

267. Bibliothèque Nationale. ''Dickens (Charles).'' In *Catalogue général des livres imprimés: Auteurs, collectivités—auteurs, anonymes, 1960–1969.* Série 1–Caractères Latins. Vol. 6. Paris: Bibliothèque Nationale, 1974, pp. 759–63.

268. Bibliothèque Nationale. ''Dickens (Charles).'' In *Catalogue général des livres imprimés, 1879–1959: Supplément sur fiches, avec corrections et annotations.* Paris: Chadwyck-Healey France, 1986, fiches 258–59.

269. Bibliothèque Nationale de France. ''Dickens (Charles).'' In BN-OPALE PLUS Online Catalogue. http://www.bnf.fr.

270. BLPC: The British Library Public Catalogue, online catalogue. http://portico.bl.uk or http://www.bl.uk (The British Library home page).

271. British Library. *Charles Dickens: The J. F. Dexter Collection: Accessions to the General Catalogue of Printed Books, Manuscripts, Prints and Drawings.* London: Published for the British Library Board by the British Museum Publications, 1974. 120 columns; reprinted in Storey (302), below.

272. British Library, Department of Manuscripts. ''Dickens, Charles.'' In *Index of Manuscripts in the British Library.* Vol. 3. Cambridge: Chadwyck-Healey, 1984, pp. 290–91.

273. British Library, Department of Printed Books. "Dickens (Charles)." In *The British Library General Catalogue of Printed Books to 1975*. Vol. 82. London, München, New York, Paris: K. G. Saur, 1981, pp. 349–447; also supplements, *1976 to 1982*. Vol. 12, 1983, pp. 409–13; *1982 to 1985*. Vol. 7, 1983, pp. 487–90; *1986 to 1987*. Vol. 5., 1988, pp. 274–77; *1988 to 1989*. Vol. 7, 1990, pp. 175–77; *1990 to 1992*. Vol. 7, 1993, pp. 77–80; *1993 to 1994*. Vol. 7, 1995, pp. 148–50; *1995 to 1996*. Vol. 7, 1997, pp. 80–82.

274. British Museum. *Charles Dickens. An Excerpt from the General Catalogue of Printed Books in the British Museum*. London: British Museum; printed by William Clowes and Sons, 1926. 29 pp.

275. British Museum. *Dickens. An Excerpt from the General Catalogue of Printed Books in the British Museum*. London: The Trustees of the British Museum, 1960, cols. 236–378 [72 pp.].

276. Carr, Sister Mary Callista, comp. *Catalogue of the Dickens Collection at the University of Texas*. Austin: University of Texas Humanities Research Center, 1961. ix + 195 pp.; revised as *A Catalogue of the VanderPoel Dickens Collection at the University of Texas*. By Sister Lucile Carr. Tower Bibliographical Series, 1. Austin: University of Texas Press, 1968. xi + 274 pp.

277. Catalogue collectif de France (ccfr). http://www.ccfr.bnf.fr. Accesses more than 14,000,000 documents from the Catalogue des fonds des bibliothèques munici-pales rétroconvertis and the Catalogue du système universitaire de documenta-tion, in addition to the Catalogue BN-OPALE PLUS, the online catalogue of the Bibliothèque Nationale (269).

278. Centro Nazionale per il Catalogo Unico delle Biblioteche Italiane e per le In-formazioni Bibliografiche, Rome. *Catalogo Cumulativo, 1886–1957, del Bollet-tino delle Pubblicazioni Italiane Ricevute per Diritto di Stampa dalla Biblioteca Nazionale Centrale di Firenze*. Vol. 13. Nendeln, Liechtenstein: Kraus Reprint, 1968, pp. 77–84.

279. Consortium of University Research Libraries (CURL). COPAC web catalogue. http://copac.ac.uk/copac. Online catalogue of the British Library (above) merged with 22 university libraries in the UK and Ireland.

280. Cowan, Robert E., and William A. Clark, Jr., comps. *The Library of William Andrews Clark, Jr.: Cruikshank and Dickens. In Two Parts: Part I: Cruikshank. Part II: Dickens*. 2 vols. San Francisco, CA: John Henry Nash, 1921 (vol. I), 1923 (vol. II); reprinted as two vols. in one, New York: Johnson Reprint Corp., 1969. 145 + 94 pp.

281. [Dickens, Marie Roche, Lady]. Manuscript Material Forming Part of the Dick-ens-Roche Gift of Translations of Dickens's Works. In British Library, London. L. R. 106. b. 22. [1935, etc.]. 30 unnumbered pp.

282. The Dickens House, London. Library Collections. These include The Suzannet Collection, completed 1971; the Farrer-Ouvry Papers, 1994; the F. G. Kitton

Collection, 1908; the B. W. Matz Collection, 1925–26; the Dr. Howard Duffield Collection of Droodiana, 1937–38; the William Miller Collection of Dickens Music, 1940; the Dr. Sydney A. Henry and Miss M. Henry Collection, 1959; the William J. Carlton Bequest, 1974; the Noel C. Peyrouton Bequest, 1976; the Gladys Storey Papers, 1980; the Philip F. Skottowe Papers, 1980; the Sir Felix Aylmer Papers, 1981; the Leslie C. Staples Bequest, 1981; and the Nina Burgis Papers. The museum also has a photographic collection, a glass negative and film negative collection, a 35 mm. Slide collection, a magic lantern slide collection, a post card collection, a clippings collection, an objects photographic collection, and a film, video, and audio collection.

283. Free Library of Philadelphia. *The Collections of William M. Elkins in The Free Library of Philadelphia: A Brief Description.* Philadelphia: Free Library of Philadelphia, 1949. 14 pp.

284. Harvard University, Houghton Library. "Dickens, Charles, 1812–1870." In *Catalogue of Manuscripts in the Houghton Library, Harvard University.* Vol. 2. Alexandria, VA: Chadwyck-Healey, 1986, pp. 446–48.

285. Harvard University Library. *English Literature.* 4 vols. Part of *Widener Library Shelflist.* Vols. 35–38. Cambridge, MA: Harvard University Library, 1971, passim.

286. Klinkenborg, Verlyn, Herbert Cahoon, and Charles Ryskamp. *British Literary Manuscripts: Series II, from 1800 to 1914.* New York: Pierpont Morgan Library, in Association with Dover Publications, 1981, pp. [121–26] and 275.

287. Library of Congress. Online Catalogue. http://catalog.loc.gov or http://www.lcweb.loc.gov, the Library of Congress home page.

288. Library of Congress and the National Union Catalog Subcommittee of the Resources Committee of the Resources and Technical Services Division, American Library Association. "Dickens, Charles, 1812–1870." In *The National Union Catalog: Pre-1956 Imprints: A Cumulative Author List Representing Library of Congress Printed Cards and Titles Reported by Other American Libraries.* Vols. 142, 143. London and Chicago: Mansell, 1971, CXLII, 574–698; CXLIII, 1–61; *Supplement,* 1980, DCCXVIII, pp. 28–68.

289. Ministère de l'Instruction publique et des Beaux-Arts. "Dickens (Charles)." In *Catalogue général des livres imprimés de la Bibliothèque Nationale: Auteurs.* Vol. 40. Paris: Imprimerie Nationale, 1910, pp. 338–67; also available on microfiche, revised, in *Catalogue général des livres imprimés, 1879–1959, avec corrections et annotations.* Paris: Chadwyck-Healey, 1986.

290. New York Public Library, New York. *The Arents Collection of Books in Parts and Associated Literature: A Complete Checklist.* Comp. Sarah A. Dickson, assisted by George Solovieff. New York: New York Public Library, 1957. 88 pp.

291. New York Public Library, New York. *The Arents Collection of Books in Parts and Associated Literature: A Supplement to the Checklist, 1957–1963.* Comp. Perry O'Neil. New York: New York Public Library, 1964, pp. 13, 27–28.

292. New York Public Library. CATNYP: The Research Libraries Online Catalog. http://catnyp.nypl.org. The online catalogue for LEO: The Branch Libraries Online will be found at http://webpac.nypl.org/leo.htrml. Both online catalogues may also be accessed at http://www.nypl.org/catalogues/index.html.

293. New York Public Library, New York. "Dickens, Charles, 1812–1870." In *Dictionary Catalogue of the Research Libraries of the New York Public Library, 1911–1971.* New York: New York Public Library, Astor, Lenox and Tilden Foundations, 1979, vols. CXC, 477–553, and CXCI, 1–22. Also see supplements for 1972–79 (published 1980), vol. XIV, 540–43, and for 1972–88 (published 1989), vol. XVIII, 471–76.

294. New York Public Library, New York, Astor, Lenox & Tilden Foundations, The Research Libraries. "Dickens, Charles." In *Dictionary Catalog of the Henry W. and Albert A. Berg Collection of English and American Literature.* 5 vols. Boston: G. K. Hall, 1969, I, 777–812, and passim; also *First Supplement.* 1975, pp. 123–24, 595, 730, and *Second Supplement.* 1983, pp. 138, 544, 673.

295. New York Public Library, New York, Astor, Lenox & Tilden Foundations, The Research Libraries. "Dickens, Charles, 1812–1870." In *Dictionary Catalog of The Rare Book Division.* 21 vols. Boston: G. K. Hall, 1971, VI, 141–51.

296. New York Public Library, New York, Research Libraries. *Dictionary Catalog of the Manuscript Division.* 2 vols. Boston: G. K. Hall, 1967, I, 239.

297. Podeschi, John B. *Dickens and Dickensiana: A Catalogue of the Richard Gimbel Collection in the Yale University Library.* New Haven, CT: Yale University Press, 1980. xxiii + 570 pp.

298. Rolfe, Franklin P. "The Dickens Letters in the Huntington Library." *Huntington Library Quarterly,* 1 (1937/38), 335–63.

299. Rosenbach, A. S. W. *A Catalogue of the Writings of Charles Dickens in the Library of Harry Elkins Widener.* Philadelphia: Privately Printed, 1918; reprinted New York: Arno Press, [1968]. vii + 111 pp.

300. Slater, Michael, ed. *The Catalogue of the Suzannet Charles Dickens Collection.* London and New York: Sotheby Parke Bernet Publications in Association with the Trustees of the Dickens House, 1975. xvi + 299 pp.

301. Smith, Harry B. "Charles Dickens." In his *A Sentimental Library, Comprising Books Formerly Owned by Famous Writers, Presentation Copies, Manuscripts, and Drawings.* [New York]: Privately printed, 1914, pp. 66–108.

302. Storey, Graham, et al., editorial board. *The Charles Dickens Research Collection from the J. F. Dexter Collection in The British Library and Other Major Holdings in Great Britain and the United States of America.* Cambridge, Eng., and Alexandria, VA: Chadwyck-Healey, 1990. ix + 116 pp.

303. Suzannet, A[lain] de. *Catalogue des manuscrits, livres imprimés et lettres autographes composant la bibliothèque de la Petite Chardière. Oeuvres de Charles Dickens.* 3 vols. Lausanne: Imprimeries Réunies, 1934. 94 + 244 + 239 pp.

304. Suzannet, A[lain] de. *Oeuvres de Charles Dickens.* In his *Catalogue d'un choix de livres, imprimés et manuscrits, lettres, autographes, dessins originaux et gravures, provenant de ma bibliothèque de Biarritz.* Vol. I. Biarritz: Privately printed, 1925. 83 pp.

305. [Victoria and Albert Museum, London]. South Kensington Museum, London. "The Forster Collection." In *Handbook of the Dyce and Forster Collections in the South Kensington Museum.* South Kensington Museum Art Handbooks. London: Published for the Committee of Council on Education by Chapman and Hall, 1880, pp. 53–94.

306. [Victoria and Albert Museum, London]. South Kensington Museum, Science and Art Department of the Committee of Council on Education, London. "Dickens (Charles)." In *Forster Collection. A Catalogue of the Printed Books Bequeathed by John Forster, Esq., LL.D.* London: Printed for Her Majesty's Stationery Office by Eyre and Spottiswoode, 1888, pp. 138–41.

307. [Victoria and Albert Museum, London]. South Kensington Museum, Science and Art Department of the Committee of Council on Education, London. *Forster Collection. A Catalogue of the Paintings, Manuscripts, Autograph Letters, Pamphlets, Etc., Bequeathed by John Forster, Esq., LL.D.* London: Printed for Her Majesty's Stationery Office by Eyre and Spottiswoode, 1893. 261 pp.

Guides to Collections

308. Ash, Lee, and William G. Miller, et al., comps. "Dickens, Charles, 1812–1870." In their *Subject Collections: A Guide to Special Book Collections and Subject Emphases as Reported by University, College, Public, and Special Libraries and Museums in the United States and Canada.* 7th ed., rev. and enl. 2 vols. New Providence, NJ: R. R. Bowker, 1993, pp. 622–23.

309. Bell, Barbara L. *An Annotated Guide to Current National Bibliographies.* Government Documents Bibliographies. Alexandria, VA: Chadwyck-Healey, 1986, passim.

310. DeWitt, Donald L., comp. *Guides to Archives and Manuscript Collections in the United States: An Annotated Bibliography.* Bibliographies and Indexes in Library and Information Science, 8. Westport, CT, and London: Greenwood Press, 1994, passim.

311. Downs, Robert B. *American Library Resources: A Bibliographical Guide*. Chicago: American Library Association, 1951, passim; also *Supplement, 1950–1961* (1962), *Supplement, 1961–1970* (1972), and *Supplement, 1971–1980* (1981), passim, and Downs, Robert B., and Elizabeth C. Downs. *British Library Resources: A Bibliographical Guide*. Chicago: American Library Association; London: Mansell, 1973; revised, updated, and expanded as *British and Irish Library Resources: A Bibliographical Guide*. London: Mansell; Bronx, NY: Distributed in the United States and Canada by H. W. Wilson, 1981, p. 338.

312. Libweb. Library Servers via WWW Web site. Berkeley Digital Library SunSITE. http://sunsite.berkeley.edu/Libweb.

313. National Historical Publications and Records Commission. *A Guide to Archives and Manuscripts in the United States*. Ed. Philip M. Hamer. New Haven, CT: Yale University Press, 1961, passim.

314. Nelson, Bonnie R. *A Guide to Published Library Catalogs*. Metuchen, NJ, and London: Scarecrow Press, 1982, pp. 113–22 and passim.

315. OCLC Worldcat Web site. http://www.oclc.org/worldcat.

316. Reynard, Keith W., ed. *The Aslib Directory of Literary and Historical Collections in the UK*. London: Aslib, the Association for Information Management, 1993, passim.

317. Scott, Peter, ed. and comp. LibDex: The Library Index. Internet: http://www.libdex.com.

318. Williams, Moelwyn I., ed. *A Directory of Rare Books and Special Collections in the United Kingdom and the Republic of Ireland*. London: Library Association, 1985, pp. 38, 73, 89, 122, 175–77, 366; revised by B. C. Bloomfield, with the assistance of Karen Potts. 2nd ed. London: Library Association Publishing, 1997, pp. 41, 87, 109, 149–50, 207–08, 410, 558, 577.

Exhibition Catalogues and Reports on Exhibitions

Exhibition Catalogues

319. British Council. *Charles Dickens 1812–1870*. London: British Council, 1970. 22 pp.

320. British Museum, King's Library, London. *Charles Dickens, 1812–1870*. London: British Museum, 1970.

321. *Charles Dickens, 1812–1870: An Exhibition of His Works Held at the Wahlert Memorial Library, October 18 to November 20, 1970.* Dubuque, IA: Loras College, 1970. 15 pp.

322. *Charles Dickens, 1812–1870: Exposition organisée par le British Council en commémoration du centième anniversaire de la mort de Dickens du 18 mars au 27 mars 1970.* Liège: Bibliothèque Générale de l'Université de Liège, [1970]. 16 unnumbered pp.

323. Dickens Fellowship, London. *Catalogue of a Pickwick Exhibition Held at the Dickens House, 48 Doughty Street, London, W. C. 1, March-April, 1936, under the Auspices of the Pickwick Centenary Celebrations Committee.* Arranged by William Miller. London: The Dickens Fellowship, [1936]. 47 pp.

324. Dickens Fellowship, London. *The Pickwick Exhibition, Held at the New Dudley Gallery, 169 Piccadilly, W., from July 22nd to August 28th, 1907, under the Auspices of the Dickens Fellowship: Catalogue of Exhibits.* Comp. and ed. B. W. Matz and J. W. T. Ley. London: The Dickens Fellowship, [1907]. 116 pp.

325. Dickens Fellowship, London. *The Second Dickens Exhibition, Held under the Auspices of the Dickens Fellowship, at the New Dudley Gallery, 169, Piccadilly, London, W. 1, July 29th to September 19th, 1908: Catalogue of Exhibits.* London: New Dudley Gallery, [1908]. 48 pp.

326. *A Dickens Library: Exhibition Catalogue of the Sawyer Collection of the Works of Charles Dickens, Comprising Manuscripts, Autograph Letters, Presentation Copies, the Issues in Original Parts, Dickensiana, Etc.* Letchworth, Eng.: Privately Printed by the Garden City Press, 1936. 108 pp.

327. Duffield, Howard. *A Catalogue of the Curious Literature Created by the Unfinished Novel of Charles Dickens "The Mystery of Edwin Drood" . . . Exhibited at the Grolier Club in the City of New York, State of New York, U. S. A.* Unpublished typescript in the Dickens House, London, 1938. 132 pp.

328. Franklin Club, St. Louis. *An Exhibition of Books, Prints, Drawings, Manuscripts & Letters Commemorative of the Centenary of Charles Dickens.* St. Louis: Franklin Club, 1912. vi + 49 pp.

329. Free Library of Philadelphia. *The Life and Works of Charles Dickens, 1812–1870: An Exhibition from the Collection of William M. Elkins, Esq., of Philadelphia, Held at The Free Library, June-July, 1946.* Philadelphia: Free Library of Philadelphia, 1946. xiii + 58 pp.

330. Gaskell, E. *Dickens and Medicine: An Exhibition of Books, Manuscripts and Prints to Mark the Centenary of His Death: With an Introduction and Bibliography.* Exhibition Catalogues of the Wellcome Institute, 5. London: The Library, The Wellcome Institute of the History of Medicine, 1970. 32 pp.

331. Genet, Malcolm. *Charles Dickens, 1812–1870: An Exhibition of Books and Manuscripts from the VanderPoel Dickens Collection, Miriam Lutcher Stark*

Library, The University of Texas at Austin, Texas, 15 September-31 December 1970. [Austin: Humanities Research Center, University of Texas, 1970]. 48 pp.

332. Gimbel, Richard. "An Exhibition of 150 Manuscripts, Illustrations, and First Editions of Charles Dickens to Commemorate the 150th Anniversary of His Birth Selected from His Collection and Described by Colonel Richard Gimbel, 1920." *Yale University Library Gazette*, 37 (October 1962), 46–93.

333. Gordan, John D. "First Fruits: An Exhibition of First Editions of First Books by English Authors in the Henry W. and Albert A. Berg Collection." *Bulletin of the New York Public Library*, 53 (1949), 159–72, 227–47; reprinted as *First Fruits: An Exhibition of First Editions of First Books by the English Authors in the Henry W. and Albert A. Berg Collection*. New York: New York Public Library, 1949. 36 pp.

334. Gordan, John D. "Reading for Profit: The Other Career of Charles Dickens." *Bulletin of the New York Public Library*, 62 (1958), 425–42, 515–22; reprinted as *Reading for Profit: The Other Career of Charles Dickens: An Exhibition from the Berg Collection*. New York: New York Public Library, 1958. 28 pp.

335. Grolier Club, New York. *Catalogue of an Exhibition of the Works of Charles Dickens*. New York: Grolier Club, 1913; reprinted Folcroft, PA: Folcroft Library Editions, 1973. xxvi + 230 pp.

336. Kitton, F. G, comp. and ed. *The Dickens Exhibition Held at the Memorial Hall, London, March 25th, 26th, and 27th, 1903: Catalogue of Exhibits*. London: Dickens Fellowship, [1903]. 67 pp. See reviews in *Athenaeum*, 121 (1903), 530, and *Times* (London), 26 March 1903, p. 5.

337. Knebworth House, Hertfordshire. *Dickens Centenary Exhibition of Letters and Other Items Resulting from the Lifelong Friendship between Charles Dickens and Edward Bulwer Lytton and the Story of the Guild of Literature and Art at Knebworth House*. Hertfordshire, Eng.: Knebworth House, [1970]. 42 pp.

338. Liverpool University Harold Cohen Library, Liverpool, Eng. *Pickwick and Pickwickiana*. A dittoed list. Liverpool, Eng.: Liverpool University Library, 1970. 7 typewritten pp.

339. New Dudley Galleries, London. *The Third Dickens Exhibition. Scenes from His Life, Works & Characters. Illustrated by Well-Known Artists. Also a Collection of Portraits (at Various Periods of His Life). His Homes and Haunts*. London: New Dudley Galleries, 1909. 79 pp.

340. New York Public Library, Henry W. & Albert A. Berg Collection. *Charles Dickens: The First Exhibition from the Collection, December 16, 1941*. New York: New York Public Library, 1941. 4 pp.

341. Public Library, Museums, and National Gallery of Victoria, Victoria, Australia. *Dickens Exhibition, 1936. Guide to the Books, Autographs, Letters, and Pictures*

Exhibited in Celebration of the Centenary of the Publication of The Pickwick Papers on March 31, 1836. Melbourne: Printed for the Trustees by Fraser & Jenkinson, 1936. 18 pp.

342. Slater, Michael, comp. *Catalogue of Treasures from the Dickens Collection Formed by the Late Comte Alain de Suzannet on Exhibition at the Dickens House 1 June-12 September 1970.* London: The Dickens Fellowship, [1970]. 42 pp.

343. Southwark Public Libraries and Cuming Museum, London. *Catalogue of Books, Portraits, Illustrations and Miscellaneous Exhibits. An Exhibition Arranged to Commemorate Publication of Pickwick Papers by Charles Dickens in 1836. Inaugurated by Walter Dexter, Esq., 19th March, 1936.* London: Southwark Public Libraries and Cuming Museum, 1936. 27 pp.

344. Szladits, Lola L., ed. *Charles Dickens 1812–1870: An Anthology.* New York: New York Public Library and Arno Press, 1970. 166 pp.; 2nd ed., as *Charles Dickens 1812–1870: An Anthology from the Berg Collection.* New York: New York Public Library, 1990. ix + 179 pp. Originally published in association with the Berg Collection's centenary exhibition of Dickensiana. The second edition was redesigned and rearranged in connection with a 1990 exhibition at the New York Public Library that was a revival, in memory of Szladits, of the 1970 exhibition that had been prepared by her.

345. Victoria and Albert Museum, London. *Charles Dickens: An Exhibition to Commemorate the Centenary of His Death, June-September, 1970.* London: Victoria and Albert Museum, 1970. 123 pp.

346. Victoria and Albert Museum, London. *Dickens Exhibition, March to October, 1912.* London: H. M. Stationery Office, 1912. 63 pp.

347. Vogler, Richard A. *An Oliver Twist Exhibition: A Memento for the Dickens Centennial, 1970: An Essay.* Los Angeles: University Research Library, University of California, 1970. 16 pp.

Reports on Exhibitions

348. Andrews, Malcolm Y. "Museum Exhibitions." *Dickens Studies Newsletter,* 1, ii (September 1970), 10–12.

349. [Andrews, Malcolm, and Duane DeVries]. "Museum Exhibitions." *Dickens Studies Newsletter,* 1, ii (September 1970), 10–16.

350. Blount, Trevor. "'Inimitable' Exhibitions." *Dickensian,* 66 (1970), 231–35.

351. Chandler, G. "Liverpool Dickens Exhibition." In *Dickens and Fame 1870–1970: Essays on the Author's Reputation.* Ed. Michael Slater. Centenary Number of *Dickensian,* 66, ii (May 1970), 187.

352. [Slater, Michael]. "Editorial Note on Exhibitions." *Dickensian*, 66 (1970), 235–36.

353. Vogler, Richard A. "Exhibition Catalogues." *Dickens Studies Newsletter*, 1, iii (December 1970), 15–18.

Auction and Booksellers' Catalogues, Auction Records, Collecting Dickens

Auction and Booksellers' Catalogues

354. American Art Association, New York. *The Renowned Collection of First Editions of Charles Dickens and William Makepeace Thackeray Formed by George Barr McCutcheon.* New York: American Art Association, [1926]; reissued New York: G. A. Baker, [1930?], passim.

355. American Art Association, New York. *The Renowned Collection of the Late William F. Gable of Altoona, Pennsylvania.* 8 parts. New York: American Art Association, 1923–25, passim.

356. American Art Association, New York. *The Renowned Collection of the Works of Charles Dickens Formed by Mr. and Mrs. Edward C. Daoust.* New York: American Art Association, [1929]. 45 pp.

357. American Art Association, New York. *The Renowned Collection of the Works of Charles Dickens Formed by Thomas Hatton of Leicester, England.* New York: American Art Association, [1927]. Pages unnumbered.

358. American Art Association, Anderson Galleries, New York. "Dickens (Charles)." In *The Library of John C. Eckel, Author of The First Editions of the Writings of Charles Dickens, Etc.* New York: American Art Association, Anderson Galleries, 1935, pp. 15–22 and passim.

359. American Art Association, Anderson Galleries, New York. "A Fine Series of Dickens Items." In *English and American First Editions, Autograph Letters, and Manuscripts, Including Selections from the Libraries of Francis K. Swartley [and Others] ... [and Including] Remarkable Dickens Mementos, and Fine Sets, from the Library of Edward C. Daoust, Cleveland, Ohio. . . .* New York: American Art Association, 1936, pp. 95–104.

360. American Art Association, Anderson Galleries, New York. *The Library of George Ulizio, Pine Valley, N. J. Part I. First Editions of English Authors.* New York: American Art Association, Anderson Galleries, 1931, pp. 26–50.

361. American Art Association, Anderson Galleries, New York. "A Superb Collection of Autograph Letters, Drawings, and First Editions by Charles Dickens,

Together with a Splendid Series of Original Watercolor Drawings by Hablot Knight Browne ('Phiz'), Numbers 109–146.'' In *The Library of the Late Ogden Goelet of New York. Part One. Public Sale January 3 and 4.* New York: American Art Association, Anderson Galleries, 1935, pp. 54–83.

362. American Art Association, Anderson Galleries, New York. ''A Superb Collection of A. L. s. and First Editions by Charles Dickens, Together with a Splendid Series of Original Watercolor Drawings by Hablot Knight Browne ('Phiz'), John Leech, and F. W. Pailthorpe, Numbers 137–192 [actually 194].'' In *The Library of the Late Ogden Goelet of New York. Part Two. Public Sale January 24 and 25.* New York: American Art Association, Anderson Galleries, 1935, pp. 59–86.

363. American Art Association, Anderson Galleries, New York. ''A Superb Collection of First Editions, Autograph Manuscripts, Autograph Letters, and Ephemera by or Relating to Charles Dickens.'' In *First Editions, Association Books, Autograph Letters and Manuscripts by the Brownings, Dickens, Byron, Thackeray, Swinburne, Lamb, and Other Esteemed Nineteenth Century English and French Authors . . . Collected and Catalogued by the Late Harry B. Smith.* New York, American Art Association, Anderson Galleries, 1936, pp. 88–117.

364. American Art Galleries, New York. *Catalogue of the Valuable Literary and Art Property Gathered by the Late Augustin Daly, Part II: Books.* New York: American Art Galleries, 1900, pp. 74–91.

365. Anderson Auction Co., New York. *Catalogue of the Library of Edwin M. Lapham of Chicago, Ill. A Remarkable Collection, Principally of English Authors of the Georgian and Victorian Eras, in Specially Choice Condition, with a Number of Autograph Letters and Original Manuscripts.* New York: Anderson Auction Co., [1908], pp. 38–47.

366. Anderson Galleries, New York. *Association Books Collected by Edwin W. Coggeshall of New York City.* New York: Anderson Galleries, 1920, pp. 7–19, 26.

367. Anderson Galleries, New York. *The Dickens Collection Formed by the Late R[alph] T. Jupp of London.* New York: Anderson Galleries, 1922. 74 pp.

368. Anderson Galleries, New York. *The Dickens Collection of the Late William Glyde Wilkins of Pittsburgh, Pa.* New York: Anderson Galleries, 1922. 65 pp.

369. Anderson Galleries, New York. *Dickens Collection, Thackeray Collection, and Other Rare Books and Autographs from the Library of Mr. Edwin W. Coggeshall of New York.* 2 vols. New York: Anderson Galleries, 1916, passim.

370. Anderson Galleries, New York. *The Splendid Library of the Late Theodore N. Vail of New York, Comprising a Large Variety of the Choicest Colored Plate Books by Aiken, Cruikshank, and Rowlandson; an Extensive Collection of the First Editions of Dickens and Thackeray, the Former with Manuscripts and Original Drawings . . . .* New York: Anderson Galleries, 1922, pp. 66–79.

371. Anderson Galleries, New York. *The Library of Jerome Kern, Part I, A-J.* New York: Anderson Galleries, 1929, pp. 114–61.

372. Christie and Manson, Messrs., London. *Catalogue of the Library of the Late Samuel Rogers, Esq.* London: Christie and Manson, 1856. 86 pp.; reprinted in facsimile in *Sale Catalogues of Libraries of Eminent Persons. Volume 2: Poets and Men of Letters.* Ed. A. N. L. Munby. London: Mansell, 1971, pp. 217–340.

373. Christie, Manson, and Woods, London. *Catalogue of the Beautiful Collection of Modern Pictures, Water-colour Drawings, and Objects of Art, of Charles Dickens, Deceased.* London: Christie, Manson, and Woods, [1870]. 11 pp.; reprinted, "with the names of the Purchasers and Prices realised appended to each lot." London: Field and Tuer, 1870, 1885; also reprinted in *Dickens Memento* (9), 1884, and *Catalogue of the Library of Charles Dickens from Gadshill, Reprinted from Sotheran's "Price Current of Literature," Nos. CLXXIV and CLXXV; Catalogue of His Pictures and Objects of Art, Sold by Messrs. Christie, Manson & Woods, July 9, 1870; Catalogue of the Library of W. M. Thackeray Sold by Messrs. Christie, Manson & Woods, March 18,1864; and Relics from His Library, Comprising Books Enriched with His Characteristic Drawings, Reprinted from Sotheran's "Price Current of Literature," No. CLXXVII.* London: Piccadilly Fountain Press, 1935; reprinted London: Sotheran, 1936, pp. 121–32.

374. Christie, Manson, & Woods, London. *Catalogue of the Library of William Charles Macready, Esq., Deceased. . . .* London: Christie, Manson, & Woods, 1873, p. 7; reprinted in facsimile in *Sale Catalogues of Libraries of Eminent Persons. Volume 12: Actors.* Ed. James F. Arnott. London: Mansell, 1975, p. 437.

375. Hodgson & Co., London. *A Catalogue of Interesting Autograph Letters and Manuscripts from the Collection of the Late Richard Bentley, Esq., of Upton Park, Slough (Sold by Order of the Trustees), Including an Important Series of Over One Hundred Autograph Letters of Charles Dickens. With Several Signed Agreements. . . .* London: Hodgson & Co., 1938, passim.

376. Parke-Bernet Galleries, New York. *The Distinguished Collection of First Editions, Autographs, Manuscripts, Original Drawings by and Relating to Dickens Formed by Lewis A. Hird, Englewood, New Jersey.* New York: Parke-Bernet Galleries, 1953. 55 pp.

377. Parke-Bernet Galleries, New York. *First Editions, Manuscripts, Autograph Letters of Charles Dickens: The Renowned Collection Formed by the Late Herman LeRoy Edgar, Dobbs Ferry, New York [Together with Another Collection].* New York: Parke-Bernet Galleries, 1944, pp. 30–114.

378. Parke-Bernet Galleries, New York. *Rare Books, Original Drawings, Autograph Letters and Manuscripts Collected by the Late A. Edward Newton, Removed From His Home, Oak Knoll, Daylesford, Pa.* 3 vols. New York: Parke-Bernet Galleries, 1941, I, 185–223.

379. Parke-Bernet Galleries, New York. "Splendid Collection of the Writings of Charles Dickens." In *A Complete Set of "Annals of Sporting," First Editions of English Authors, Dickens, Including "Pickwick Papers," Surtees, Ainsworth, Lever, Thackeray, and Others, Mainly in Original Parts or Cloth, Property of Thomas Hatton, Leicester, England.* New York: Parke-Bernet Galleries, 1938, pp. 19–42.

380. Sotheby & Co., London. *Catalogue of a Further Portion of the Well-Known Library, the Property of the Comte de Suzannet, La Petite Chardière, Lausanne, Comprising the Celebrated Collection of Material Concerning Charles Dickens, Including Upwards of One Thousand Autograph Letters, Several Autograph Manuscripts, Letters Relating to Him, Presentation Copies of His Works, and the Earliest Known Portrait of Him.* London: Sotheby & Co., 1938. 111 pp.

381. Sotheby & Co., London. *Catalogue of Autograph Manuscripts and Letters, Original Drawings and First Editions of Charles Dickens, from the Collection of the Late Comte Alain de Suzannet (Removed from La Petite Chardière, Lausanne), the Property of the Comtesse de Suzannet.* London: Sotheby & Co., [1971]. 121 pp.

382. Sotheby & Co., London. *Catalogue of the Important Collections Mainly of the Writings of Charles Dickens and of Other XIX Century Authors Forming a Part of the Library of Thomas Hatton, Esq., at Anstey Pastures, Leicester.* London: Sotheby & Co., 1931, pp. 8–23.

383. Sotheby & Co., London. *Catalogue of the Remaining Library of Thomas Hatton, Esq., Removed from Anstey Pastures, Leicester.* London: Sotheby & Co., 1933, pp. 8–18.

384. Sotheby & Co., London. *Catalogue of the Valuable Printed Books, Autograph Letters & Historical Documents, Etc., Comprising . . . the Property of Thomas Hatton, Esq . . . and the Holograph Manuscript of Dickens' Life of Our Lord, the Property of Lady Dickens and of Her Children.* London: Sotheby & Co., 1939, pp. 49–54, 79–80.

385. Sotheby, Wilkinson & Hodge, London. *The Burdett Coutts Library. Catalogue of the Valuable Library, the Property of the Late Baroness Burdett Coutts.* London: Dryden Press: J. Davy & Sons, 1922, passim.

386. Sotheby, Wilkinson & Hodge, London. *Catalogue of the Library of the Late Edmund Yates, . . . [With] Works by Tennyson, Thackeray, and Dickens, Including a Portion of Charles Dickens' Correspondence with Edmund Yates . . . .* Sotheby, Wilkinson & Hodge, 1895, passim.

387. Sotheby, Wilkinson & Hodge, London. *Catalogue of the Valuable Library and Collections of Engraved & Other Portraits and Autograph Letters, the Property of the Well-Known Amateur William Wright, Esq.* London: Dryden Press: J. Davy & Sons, 1899, passim.

388. Sotheby, Wilkinson & Hodge, London. *The H. W. Bruton Collections. Catalogue of the Very Choice Collection of Printed Books, Autograph Letters and Book Illustrations, the Property of the Late Henry William Bruton, Esq., Bewick House, Gloucester . . . .* London: Sotheby, Wilkinson & Hodge, 1921, pp. 21–34 and passim.

389. Sotheby's, London. *The Dickens Archive.* London: Sotheby's, 1999. 84 unnumbered pages. Also see report by Malcolm Andrews in "Editorial," *Dickensian,* 97 (2001), 3.

390. Sotheby's, London. *The Library of Horace N. Pym (1844–1896).* London: Sotheby's, 1996, passim.

391. Sotheby's, New York. *The Library of Richard Manney.* New York: Sotheby's, [1991], passim.

392. Sotheran, Henry, & Co., London. "Catalogue of the Library of Charles Dickens, Esq., Author of *The Pickwick Papers,* Etc., Comprehending His Entire Library as Existing at His Decease," and "Charles Dickens's Library (Continued from Preceding Catalogue)." In *Sotheran's Price Current of Literature: A Catalogue of Second Hand Books, Ancient and Modern, in All Classes of Literature . . . ,* Nos. 174 and 175 (November and December 1878), 9–27 and 1–18; reprinted in *Catalogue of the Library of Charles Dickens from Gadshill, Reprinted from Sotheran's "Price Current of Literature," Nos. CLXXIV and CLXXV; Catalogue of His Pictures and Objects of Art, Sold by Messrs. Christie, Manson & Woods, July 9, 1870; Catalogue of the Library of W. M. Thackeray Sold by Messrs. Christie, Manson & Woods, March 18, 1864; and Relics from His Library, Comprising Books Enriched with His Characteristic Drawings, Reprinted from Sotheran's "Price Current of Literature," No. CLXXVII.* Ed. J. H. Stonehouse. London: Piccadilly Fountain Press, 1935; reprinted London: Sotheran, 1936, pp. 1–120.

393. Sotheran, Henry, & Co., London. *Illustrated Catalogue of Books in Beautiful Old Bindings; The Dr. R[alph] T. Jupp Collection of Charles Dickens's Works: Autographs, Mss., Etc.: Also of a Collection of Letters and Relics of the Original Dora of David Copperfield . . . .* Sotheran's Price Current of Literature, No. 775. London: Henry Sotheran & Co., 1920, passim.

394. Thomas & Homan, Messrs., auctioneers, Rochester, Eng. *Catalogue of the Household Furniture, Linen, about 200 Dozen of Superior Wines and Liquors, China, Glass, Horse, Carriages, Green-house Plants, and Other Effects of the Late Charles Dickens.* Rochester, Eng.: Messrs. Thomas and Homan, [1870]. 40 pp.

Auction Records

395. *Book-Auction Records (Formerly Known as "Sales Records"): A Priced and Annotated Record of London, Book Auctions*; later entitled *Book-Auction Records: A Priced and Annotated Annual Record of London, New York and Edinburgh Book-Auctions, Comprising Books from the Invention of Printing to the*

Current Year, Bindings, Early Manuscripts, and Rare Sets of Engravings. London: Karslake, 1903–19; succeeded by Henry Stevens, Son, & Styles, 1920–68, and then by Dawson's of Pall Mall, 1969– , passim.

396. *Book-Prices Current: A Record of the Prices at Which Books Have Been Sold at Auction From December, 1886, to November 1887[-August 1956].* 64 vols. London: Elliot Stock [succeeded by other publishers], 1888–1957, passim.

397. Livingston, Luther S., [et al.], comps. *American Book-Prices Current: A Record of Books, Manuscripts and Autographs Sold at Auction in New York, Boston and Philadelphia, from September 1st, 1894, to September 1st, 1895[-], with the Prices Realized.* New York: Mead [succeeded by other publishers], 1895– , passim. Also on the Internet, http://lola.olywa.net/abpc/index.cfm.

Collecting Dickens

398. Ahearn, Allen, and Patricia Ahearn. *Collected Books: The Guide to Values.* New York: G. P. Putnam's Sons, 1991, pp. 167–69; revised as *Collected Books: The Guide to Values, 1998 Edition.* New York: G. P. Putnam's Sons, 1997, pp. 195–98.

399. Arnold, William H. *Ventures in Book Collecting.* New York: Charles Scribner's Sons, 1923, pp. 62–74, 84–86, 314–17, and passim.

400. Biondi, Lee. "Collecting Charles Dickens." In "Charles Dickens Special" issue of *Firsts: The Book Collector's Magazine,* 7, ix (September 1997), 24–57. Consists of "Strategies of Collecting," pp. 24–39; "In the Beginning . . . Charles Dickens Makes a Pseudonym for Himself: A Bibliographical Background to Dickens' *Sketches by Boz*," pp. 40–46; "Rise to Fame: *Pickwick* Triumphant," pp. 47–50; "The Charles Dickens Reference Shelf," pp. 51–53; and "Great Complications," pp. 54–57.

401. [Fitzgerald, Percy]. "The Romance of Old Books." *Tinsley's Magazine,* 36 (1885), 446–67; somewhat expanded as part of "Of Grangerising and Dickensiana." In his *The Book Fancier or The Romance of Book Collecting.* London: Sampson Low, Marston, Searle, & Rivington, 1886; New York: Scribner & Welford, 1887, pp. 168–92.

402. Hunter, Michael. "Auction Catalogues and Eminent Libraries." *Book Collector,* 21 (1972), pp. 471–88.

403. Keller, Dean H., and Matthew J. Bruccoli. "B. George Ulizio (2 February 1889–29 September 1969)." In *American Book-Collectors and Bibliographers, First Series.* Ed. Joseph Rosenblum (413), pp. 282–88.

404. Klappholz, David. "Charles Sessler (5 November 1854–4 September 1935)." In *American Book-Collectors and Bibliographers, Second Series.* Ed. Joseph Rosenblum (414), pp. 272–78.

405. Morris, Leslie A. "A. S. W. Rosenbach (22 July 1876–1 July 1952)." In *American Book-Collectors and Bibliographers, First Series*. Ed. Joseph Rosenblum (413), pp. 220–29.

406. Morris, Leslie A. "Harry Elkins Widener (3 January 1885–15 April 1912)." In *American Book-Collectors and Bibliographers, First Series*. Ed. Joseph Rosenblum (413), pp. 311–18.

407. Morris, Leslie A. "Harry Elkins Widener and A. S. W. Rosenbach: Of Books and Friendship." *Harvard Library Bulletin*, 6 (1995), 7–28.

408. Newton, A[lfred] Edward. *The Amenities of Book Collecting, and Kindred Affections*. Boston: Atlantic Monthly Press, 1918; 2nd ed., 1919; 3rd ed., 1920; reprinted in Essay and General Literature Index Reprint Series. Port Washington, NY: Kennikat Press, 1969, passim.

409. Overmier, Judith A. "Harry B. Smith (28 December 1860–1 January 1936)." In *American Book-Collectors and Bibliographers, Second Series*. Ed. Joseph Rosenblum (414), pp. 279–85.

410. Pearson, David. *Provenance Research in Book History: A Handbook* (London: British Library, 1994), pp. 144–46.

411. Pym, Horace N. "Chapter II. On Charles Dickens." In his *A Tour Round My Book-Shelves*. [Edinburgh]: Privately Printed for Author by Ballantyne, Hanson, 1891, pp. 7–14.

412. Rosenbach, A. S. W. *A Book Hunter's Holiday: Adventures with Books and Manuscripts*. Boston and New York: Houghton Mifflin, the Riverside Press, Cambridge, 1936; reprinted in facsimile in Essay Index Reprint Series. Freeport, NY: Books for Libraries Press, 1968, pp. 18–19, 64–67.

413. Rosenblum, Joseph, ed. *American Book-Collectors and Bibliographers, First Series*. Dictionary of Literary Biography, 140. Detroit, Washington, DC, and London: A Bruccoli Clark Layman Book, Gale Research, 1994, passim.

414. Rosenblum, Joseph, ed. *American Book-Collectors and Bibliographers, Second Series*. Dictionary of Literary Biography, 187. Detroit, Washington, DC, and London: A Bruccoli Clark Layman Book, Gale Research, 1997, passim.

415. Rosenblum, Joseph. "William Andrews Clark, Jr. (29 March 1877–14 June 1934)." In *American Book-Collectors and Bibliographers, Second Series*, Ed. Joseph Rosenblum (414), pp. 30–39.

416. Sawyer, Charles J., and F. J. Harvey Darton. "Charles Dickens." In their *English Books, 1475–1900: A Signpost for Collectors*. 2 vols. London: Charles J. Sawyer, 1927, II, 237–92.

417. Spahn, Theodore. "Jerome Kern (27 January 1885–11 November 1945)." In *American Book-Collectors and Bibliographers, Second Series*. Ed. Joseph Rosenblum (414), pp. 185–91.

418. Spencer, Walter T. "Dickensiana." In his *Forty Years in My Bookshop*. Ed. Thomas Moult. London: Constable; Boston and New York: Houghton Mifflin, 1923; London: Constable, 1927, pp. 89–161 and passim.

419. Storm, Colton, and Howard Peckham. *Invitation to Book Collecting, Its Pleasures and Practices, with Kindred Discussions of Manuscripts, Maps, and Prints.* New York: R. R. Bowker, 1947, pp. 175–83.

420. Winterich, John T., and David A. Randall. *A Primer of Book Collecting*. 3rd edition. New York: Crown, 1966, pp. 19–20, 43–44, 171–72.

421. Wolf, Edwin, 2nd, with John F. Fleming. *Rosenbach, a Biography*. Cleveland and New York: World Publishing Co., 1960; London: Weidenfeld and Nicholson, 1961, passim.

Studies of Manuscripts and Textual Changes: Dickens at Work

General Studies

422. B[rattin], J[oel] J. "Composition, Dickens's Methods of." In *Oxford Reader's Companion to Dickens*. Ed. Paul Schlicke (438), pp. 111–19.

423. Brattin, Joel J. "A Map of the Labyrinth: Editing Dickens's Manuscripts." *Dickens Quarterly*, 2 (1985), 3–11.

424. Brattin, Joel J. "Reading between the Lines: Interpreting Dickens's Later Manuscripts." *Dissertation Abstracts International*, 47 (1986/87), 534A (Stanford University, 1986).

425. Butt, John. "Dickens at Work." *Durham University Journal*, 40, ns 9 (1947/48), 65–77.

426. Butt, John. "Dickens's Manuscripts." *Yale University Library Gazette*, 36 (1961/62), 149–61.

427. Butt, John. "Dickens's Notes for His Serial Parts." *Dickensian*, 45 (1948/49), 129–38.

428. Butt, John. "New Light on Charles Dickens." *Listener*, 47 (1952), 341–42.

429. Butt, John. "The Serial Publication of Dickens's Novels: *Martin Chuzzlewit* and *Little Dorrit*." In his *Pope, Dickens and Others: Essays and Addresses*. Edinburgh: Edinburgh University Press, 1969, pp. 149–64.

430. Butt, John, and Kathleen Tillotson. *Dickens at Work*. London: Methuen, 1957; Fair Lawn, NJ: Essential Books, 1958; new edition (University Paperbacks,

257), London: Methuen, 1968; reprinted London and New York: Methuen, 1982, passim.

431. "Charles Dickens's Manuscripts." *Chambers's Journal*, 54 (1877), 710–12; reprinted in *Eclectic Magazine*, ns 27 (1878), 80–82; *Littell's Living Age*, 136, 5th ser., 21 (1878), 252–54; and, with minor variations, *Potter's American Monthly*, 10 (1878), 156–58.

432. Everson, Philip A. "Proof Revisions in Three Novels by Charles Dickens: *Dombey and Son*, *David Copperfield*, and *Bleak House*." *Dissertation Abstracts International*, 48 (1987/88), 1459A (University of Delaware, 1987).

433. Guiliano, Edward, and Philip Collins. Annotations. In *The Annotated Dickens*. Ed. Edward Guiliano and Philip Collins. 2 vols. New York: Clarkson N. Potter; London: Orbis Book Publishing Corp., 1986, passim.

434. Hornback, Bert G. *"The Hero of My Life"*: *Essays on Dickens*. Athens, OH: Ohio University Press, 1981, passim.

435. Kitton, F[rederic] G. "Bibliographical Note." In the initial volume each of the six novels published in *The Works of Charles Dickens*. Rochester Edition. 11 vols. London: Methuen, 1900–01, passim.

436. Low, Annette. "The Conservation of Charles Dickens' Manuscripts." *V&A Conservation Journal*, no. 9 (October 1993), 4–7. Also on the Internet, http://www.nal.vam.ac.uk/pubs/lowecons.html.

437. Monod, Sylvère. *Dickens romancier: Etude sur la création littéraire dans les romans de Charles Dickens*. Paris: Hachette, 1953, passim. Translated by Monod as *Dickens the Novelist*. Norman: University of Oklahoma Press, 1968.

438. S[chlicke], P[aul] V. W. Entries for all of Dickens's novels, other major works, and most of his minor works, excluding individual Christmas Stories. In *Oxford Reader's Companion to Dickens*. Ed. Paul Schlicke. Oxford and New York: Oxford University Press, 1999, passim; paperback ed., ibid., 2000, passim.

439. Schooling, J. Holt. "Charles Dickens's Manuscripts." *Strand Magazine*, 11 (1896), 29–40.

440. Shatto, Susan, gen. ed. *The Dickens Companions*. London, Boston, and Sydney: Allen & Unwin (and, later, Edinburgh: Edinburgh University Press and Mountfield, Eng.: Helm Information; Westport, CT: Greenwood Press), 1986– . For volumes published in the series, see *Oliver Twist* by David Paroissien (522), *Martin Chuzzlewit*, by Nancy A. Metz (495), *Bleak House* by Susan Shatto (449), *Hard Times* by Margaret Simpson (487), *A Tale of Two Cities* by Andrew Sanders (545), *Great Expectations* by David Paroissien (481), *Our Mutual Friend* by Michael Cotsell (530), and *The Mystery of Edwin Drood* by Wendy S. Jacobson (508).

441. Spielmann, M. H. "How Dickens Improved His Style: His Tell-Tale Manuscripts." *Graphic* (London), 81 (1910), 360.

442. [Staples, Leslie C.]. "Shavings from Dickens's Workshop: Unpublished Fragments from the Novels." *Dickensian*, 48 (1951/52), 158–61 (*David Copperfield*); 49 (1952/53), 37–43, 65–68 (*Dombey and Son*), 169–74 (*Little Dorrit*); 50 (1953/54), 17–23, 63–66, 132–36 (*The Old Curiosity Shop*), 188–91 (*Bleak House*).

443. Stone, Harry, ed. *Dickens' Working Notes for His Novels*. Chicago and London: University of Chicago Press, 1987. xxxv + 393 pp.

444. Sucksmith, Harvey P. *The Narrative Art of Charles Dickens: The Rhetoric of Sympathy and Irony in His Novels*. Oxford: Clarendon Press, Oxford University Press, 1970, passim.

Individual Works

Barnaby Rudge

445. Brattin, Joel J. "'Secrets Inside . . . to Strike to Your Heart': New Readings from Dickens's Manuscript of *Barnaby Rudge*, Chapter 75." *Dickens Quarterly*, 8 (1991), 15–28.

Bleak House

446. DeVries, Duane. "Introduction," "The Discarded Titles of *Bleak House*," and "The Number Plans for *Bleak House*." In Dickens's *Bleak House*. Ed. Duane DeVries. The Crowell Critical Library. New York: Thomas Y. Crowell, 1971, pp. xiii-xix, 833–35, 837–75.

447. Ford, George, and Sylvère Monod. "A Note on the Text" and "Textual Notes." In Dickens's **Bleak House**: *An Authoritative and Annotated Text, Illustrations, a Note on the Text, Genesis and Composition, Backgrounds, Criticism*. Ed. George Ford and Sylvère Monod. Norton Critical Edition. New York: W. W. Norton, 1977, pp. 773–813, 815–80.

448. Monod, Sylvère. "'When the Battle's Lost and Won . . . ': Dickens *v.* the Compositors of *Bleak House*." *Dickensian*, 69 (1973), 3–12.

449. Shatto, Susan. *The Companion to **Bleak House***. The Dickens Companions. London: Unwin Hyman, 1988, passim.

450. Sucksmith, H[arvey] P. "Dickens at Work on *Bleak House*: A Critical Examination of His Memoranda and Number Plans." *Renaissance and Modern Studies*, 9 (1965), 47–85.

451. Watson, J. L. "Dickens at Work on Manuscript and Proof: 'Bleak House' and 'Little Dorrit.'" *Journal of the Australasian Universities Language and Literature Association*, 45 (May 1976), 54–68.

Christmas Novels and Christmas Stories

452. Adams, Frederick B., Jr. "Preface." In Dickens's *A Christmas Carol: A Facsimile of the Manuscript in the Pierpont Morgan Library.* Ed. Frederick B. Adams, Jr. New York: James H. Heineman, 1967; reprinted London: Folio Press, 1970; New York: Dover; London: Constable, 1971, pp. v-vii.

453. Glancy, Ruth. "Dickens at Work on *The Haunted Man.*" *Dickens Studies Annual*, 15 (1986), 65–85.

454. Glancy, Ruth. "The Shaping of *The Battle of Life*: Dickens' Manuscript Revisions." *Dickens Studies Annual*, 17 (1988), 67–89.

455. Hearn, Michael, ed. *The Annotated Christmas Carol: A Christmas Carol by Charles Dickens*. New York: Clarkson N. Potter, distributed by Crown Publishers, 1976; reprinted as *A Christmas Carol*. New York: Crown, 1989. 182 pp.

456. Kitton, F[rederic] G. "Some Famous Christmas Stories." *Library Review*, 1 (1892/93), 705–17.

457. Klinkenborg, Verlyn. "A Note on the Manuscript." In Dickens's *The Cricket on the Hearth: A Fairy Tale of Home*. Guildford, Eng.: Genesis Publications, 1981, p. 19. Also see Introduction" by Andrew Sanders (459).

458. Mortimer, John. "Meeting the Manuscript." In Dickens's *A Christmas Carol: A Facsimile Edition of the Autograph Manuscript in the Pierpont Morgan Library*. New York: Pierpont Morgan Library; New Haven, CT: Yale University Press, 1993, pp. ix-xiii.

459. Sanders, Andrew. "Introduction." In Dickens's *The Cricket on the Hearth: A Fairy Tale of Home* (457), pp. 11–17.

460. Slater, Michael. "Appendix A: The Deleted 'Young England' Passages from *The Chimes*," "Appendix B," and "Appendix D." In Dickens's *The Christmas Books*. 2 vols. Penguin English Library. Harmondsworth, Eng., Baltimore, MD, and Ringwood, Austral.: Penguin Books, 1971, I, 247–52, 253–55; II, 359–61.

461. Slater, Michael. "*The Chimes*: Its Materials, Making, and Public Reception; With an Assessment of Its Importance as a Turning-Point in the Works of Dickens." *Index to Theses Accepted for Higher Degrees in the Universities of*

Great Britain and Ireland, 15 (1964/65), 16 (Balliol College, Oxford University, 1965).

462. Slater, Michael. "Dickens (and Forster) at Work on *The Chimes*." *Dickens Studies*, 2 (1966), 106–40.

David Copperfield

463. Brattin, Joel J. "'Let Me Pause Once More': Dickens' Manuscript Revisions in the Retrospective Chapters of *David Copperfield*." *Dickens Studies Annual*, 26 (1998), 73–90.

464. Buckley, Jerome H. "Number Plans for *David Copperfield*." In Dickens's *David Copperfield: Authoritative Text, Backgrounds, Criticism*. Ed. Jerome H. Buckley. Norton Critical Edition. New York and London: W. W. Norton, 1990, pp. 741–62.

465. Burgis, Nina. "Appendix B: The Trial Titles" and "Appendix C: The Number Plans." In Dickens's *David Copperfield*. Ed. Nina Burgis. World's Classics Edition. Oxford and New York: Oxford University Press, 1983, pp. 719–21, 722–37; reprinted as "Appendix C: The Trial Titles" and "Appendix D: The Number Plans." In Dickens's *David Copperfield*. Ed. Nina Burgis. With Introduction and Notes by Andrew Sanders. Ibid., 1997, pp. 871–73, 874–89.

466. Burgis, Nina. "Introduction." In Dickens's *David Copperfield*. Ed. Nina Burgis. Clarendon Edition (31), pp. xv-lxii.

467. Butt, John. "The Composition of *David Copperfield*." *Dickensian*, 46 (1949/50), 90–94, 128–35, 176–80; 47 (1950/51), 33–38.

468. Butt, John. "*David Copperfield*: From Manuscript to Print." *Review of English Studies*, ns 1 (1950), 247–51.

469. Ford, George H. "Appendix: Passages Omitted from the Proof Sheets of *David Copperfield*." In Dickens's *David Copperfield*. Ed. George H. Ford. Riverside Editions. Boston: Houghton Mifflin, Riverside Press, Cambridge, MA, 1958, pp. 673–78.

470. Gaskell, Philip. "Dickens, *David Copperfield*, 1850." In his *From Writer to Reader: Studies in Editorial Method*. Oxford: Clarendon Press, 1978, pp. 142–55.

471. Gaskell, Philip. "The Textual History of *David Copperfield*." In his *A New Introduction to Bibliography*. New York and Oxford: Oxford University Press, 1972, pp. 384–91 and passim.

Dombey and Son

472. Butt, John, and Kathleen Tillotson. "Dickens at Work on *Dombey and Son.*" *Essays and Studies, 1951*, ns 4 (1951), 70–93; reprinted, with minor revisions, as Chapter 5, "*Dombey and Son*: Design and Execution," of *Dickens at Work* (430), pp. 90–113.

473. Herring, Paul D. "The Number Plans for *Dombey and Son*: Some Further Observations." *Modern Philology*, 68 (1970/71), 151–87.

474. Horsman, Alan. "Introduction." In Dickens's *Dombey and Son*. Ed. Alan Horsman. Clarendon Edition (34), pp. xiii-xlvi.

475. Tillotson, Kathleen. "New Readings in *Dombey and Son.*" In *Imagined Worlds: Essays on some English Novels and Novelists in Honour of John Butt*. Ed. Maynard Mack and Ian Gregor. London: Methuen, 1968, pp. 173–82.

Great Expectations

476. Butt, John. "Dickens's Plan for the Conclusion of *Great Expectations.*" *Dickensian*, 45 (1948/49), 78–80.

477. Calder, Angus. "Appendix A: The End of the Novel," "Appendix B: 'Dates,'" and "Appendix C: Biddy's Letter." In Dickens's *Great Expectations*. Ed. Angus Calder. Penguin English Library, EL3. Harmondsworth, Eng., and Baltimore, MD: Penguin Books, 1965, etc., pp. 494–96, 497, 498.

478. Cardwell, Margaret. "Appendix A: The Original Ending," "Appendix B: Dickens's Working Notes," and "Appendix C: *All the Year Round* Instalments and Chapter-Numbering in Different Editions." In Dickens's *Great Expectations*. Ed. Margaret Cardwell. World's Classics Edition. Oxford and New York: Oxford University Press, 1994, pp. 481–82, 483–86, 487–89.

479. Cardwell, Margaret. "Introduction." In Dickens's *Great Expectations*. Ed. Margaret Cardwell. Clarendon Edition (36), pp. xiii-lxiii.

480. Dunn, Albert A. "The Altered Endings of *Great Expectations*: A Note on Bibliography and First-Person Narrative." *Dickens Studies Newsletter*, 9 (1978), 40–42.

481. Paroissien, David. *The Companion to Great Expectations*. The Dickens Companions. Mountfield, Eng.: Helm Information; Westport, CT: Greenwood Press, 2000, pp. 1–14, 453–55, and passim.

482. Rosenberg, Edgar. "Preface," "The Original Ending," "Adopted Readings," "Textual Notes," "Launching *Great Expectations*," "Writing *Great Expectations*," "A Note on Dickens's Working Plans," "The Descriptive Headlines,"

and "Putting an End to *Great Expectations*." In Dickens's **Great Expectations**: *Authoritative Text, Backgrounds, Contexts, Criticism*. Ed. Edgar Rosenberg. Norton Critical Edition. New York and London: W. W. Norton, 1999, pp. xi-xix, 359, 361–66, 367–88, 389–423, 427–68, 469–88, 489–90, 491–527.

483. Rosenberg, Edgar. "A Preface to *Great Expectations*: The Pale Usher Dusts His Lexicons." *Dickens Studies Annual*, 2 (1972), 294–335, 374–78.

Hard Times

484. Ford, George, and Sylvère Monod. "A Note on the Text," "Dickens' Working Plans," "The Running Headlines," and "Textual Notes." In Dickens's **Hard Times**: *An Authoritative Text, Backgrounds, Sources, and Contemporary Reactions, Criticism*.. Ed. George Ford and Sylvère Monod. Norton Critical Edition. New York: W. W. Norton, 1966, pp. 228–30, 231–40, 241–42, 243–68; 2nd ed. New York and London: W. W. Norton, 1990, pp. 221 (and 231–35), 221–31, 233–34, 237–64; 3rd ed., ed. Fred Kaplan and Sylvère Monod, ibid., 2001, pp. 223–41, 243–71, 273–74.

485. Monod, Sylvère. "Dickens at Work on the Text of *Hard Times*." *Dickensian*, 64 (1968), 86–99.

486. Murray, J. A. H. "Various Readings in Dickens." *Notes and Queries*, 6th ser., 12 (1885), 289.

487. Simpson, Margaret. *The Companion to **Hard Times***. The Dickens Companions. Mountfield, Eng.: Helm Information; Westport, CT: Greenwood Press, 1997, passim.

Little Dorrit

488. Easson, Angus. "Introduction" and "Notes on the Text." In Dickens's *Little Dorrit*. Ed. Angus Easson. Everyman Dickens. London: J. M. Dent; Rutland, VT: Charles E. Tuttle, 1999, pp. xxiii-xxxv, xxxvi-xxxvii.

489. Herring, Paul D. "Dickens' Monthly Number Plans for *Little Dorrit*." *Modern Philology*, 64 (1966/67), 22–63.

490. Sucksmith, Harvey P. "Introduction." In Dickens's *Little Dorrit*. Ed. Harvey P. Sucksmith. Clarendon Edition (39), pp. xiii-xlix.

491. Wall, Stephen, and Helen Small. "Appendix B: The Number Plans." In Dickens's *Little Dorrit*. Ed. Stephen Wall and Helen Small. Penguin Classics Edition. London, New York, etc.: Penguin Books, 1998, pp. 791–833.

Martin Chuzzlewit

492. Cardwell, Margaret. "Appendix B: Preliminaries and Number Plans." In Dickens's *Martin Chuzzlewit*. World's Classics Edition. Oxford and New York: Oxford University Press, 1984, pp. 723–26.

493. Cardwell, Margaret. "Introduction." In Dickens's *Martin Chuzzlewit*. Ed. Margaret Cardwell. Clarendon Edition (40), pp. xv-lx.

494. Ingham, Patricia. "A Note on the Text and Its History," "Appendix B: Some of Dickens's Working Papers for *Martin Chuzzlewit*," and "Notes." In Dickens's *The Life and Adventures of Martin Chuzzlewit*. Ed. Patricia Ingham. Penguin Classics Edition. London, New York, etc.: Penguin Books, 1999, pp. xxx-xxxiii, 785–88, 793–826.

495. Metz, Nancy. *The Companion to Martin Chuzzlewit*. The Dickens Companions. Mountfield, Eng.: Helm Information; Westport, CT: Greenwood Press, 2001, pp. 499–502 and passim.

496. Monod, Sylvère. "Chapter 2: The Text and Its Variations" and "Chapter 11: External and Additional Material." In his *Martin Chuzzlewit*. London, Boston, and Sydney: George Allen & Unwin, 1985, pp. 9–17, 173–85.

The Mystery of Edwin Drood

497. Aylmer, Felix. *The Drood Case*. London: Rupert Hart-Davis, 1964; New York: Barnes & Noble, 1965. x + 218 pp.

498. Beer, John. *"Edwin Drood and the Mystery of Apartness." Dickens Studies Annual*, 13 (1984), 143–91.

499. Burgan, William M. "The Refinement of Contrast: Manuscript Revision in *Edwin Drood*." *Dickens Studies Annual*, 6 (1977), 167–82, 198–99.

500. Carden, P[ercy] T. "Dickens's 'Number Plans' for *The Mystery of Edwin Drood*." *Dickensian*, 27 (1930/31), 183–85, 200–01, 266–69, 284–85, 300–01.

501. Cardwell, Margaret. "Appendix A: Manuscript List of Projected Names and Titles," "Appendix B: The Number Plans," and "Appendix C: The Sapsea Fragment." In Dickens's *The Mystery of Edwin Drood*. Ed. Margaret Cardwell. World's Classics Edition. Oxford and New York: Oxford University Press, 1982, pp. 218, 219–31, 232–33.

502. Cardwell, Margaret. "Introduction." In Dickens's *The Mystery of Edwin Drood*. Ed. Margaret Cardwell. Clarendon Edition (42), pp. xiii-l.

503. Connor, Steven. "Notes on the Text and Illustrations" and "Appendix A: The 'Sapsea Fragment.' " In Dickens's *The Mystery of Edwin Drood*. Ed. Steven Connor. Everyman Library. London: Dent, 1996, pp. xxxvii-xxxix, 275–80.

504. Cox, Arthur J. "The *Drood* Remains." *Dickens Studies*, 2 (1966), 33–44.

505. Cox, Arthur J. "Introduction." "Appendix A: Dickens's Notes and Number Plans," "Appendix B: The 'Sapsea Fragment,'" and "Notes." In Dickens's *The Mystery of Edwin Drood*. Ed. Arthur J. Cox. Penguin English Library. Harmondsworth, Eng.: Penguin Books, 1974, 1985, pp. 11–30, 281–95, 296–301, 302–14, and passim.

506. Cox, Arthur J. "A Note on the Text," "Appendix A: Dickens's Notes and Number Plans" and "Appendix B: The 'Sapsea Fragment.'" In Dickens's *The Mystery of Edwin Drood*. Ed. Arthur J. Cox. London: Folio Society, 1982, pp. xvii-xviii, 231–45, 246–51.

507. Cox, Don Richard. "The *Every Saturday* Page Proofs for *The Mystery of Edwin Drood*." *Dickensian*, 90 (1994), 95–101.

508. Jacobson, Wendy S. *The Companion to The Mystery of Edwin Drood*. The Dickens Companions. London: Allen & Unwin, 1986, pp. 185–92 and passim.

509. Nicoll, W[illiam] Robertson. "The Text of 'Edwin Drood,'" "Notes for the Novel," and "The Illustrations on the Wrapper." In his *The Problem of "Edwin Drood": A Study in the Methods of Dickens*. London, New York, and Toronto: Hodder and Stoughton, 1912; reprinted New York: Haskell House, 1972, pp. 3–19, 56–68, 69–81.

Nicholas Nickleby

510. Ford, Mark. "A Note on the Text," "Appendix 2: Running Titles Added in 1867," and "Appendix 3: Significant Revisions Made in the 1848 and 1867 Editions." In Dickens's *Nicholas Nickleby*. Ed. Mark Ford. Penguin Classics Edition. London, New York, etc.: Penguin Books, 1999, pp. xxxii-xxxiii, 783–88, 789–96.

511. Schlicke, Paul. "Appendix A: The *Nickleby* Proclamation," "Appendix B: Running Heads for the 1867 Edition," and "Textual Notes." In Dickens's *Nicholas Nickleby*. Ed. Paul Schlicke. World's Classics Edition. Oxford and New York: Oxford University Press, 1990, pp. 832–34, 835–43, 865–70.

512. Slater, Michael. *The Composition and Monthly Publication of Nicholas Nickleby*. Menston, Eng.: Scolar Press, 1973; also published as the final installment of *The Life and Adventures of Nicholas Nickleby. Reproduced in Facsimile from the Original Monthly Parts of 1838–9*. Menston, Eng.: Scolar Press, 1972–73. iv + 43 pp.; also published as part of a boxed set; reprinted as "The Composition

and Monthly Publication of *Nicholas Nickleby.*'' In *The Life and Adventures of Nicholas Nickleby.* 2 vols. London: Scolar Press; Philadelphia: University of Pennsylvania Press, 1982, I, vii-lxxxvi.

513. Slater, Michael. ''A Note on the Text,'' ''Appendix A: The Manuscript of *Nicholas Nickleby,*'' and ''Appendix C: Descriptive Headlines Added in 1867.'' In Dickens's *Nicholas Nickleby.* Ed. Michael Slater. Penguin English Library. Harmondsworth, Eng., New York, etc.: Penguin Books, 1978, pp. 35–37, 935–39, 943–51.

The Old Curiosity Shop

514. Brattin, Joel. ''Some Old Curiosities from *The Old Curiosity Shop* Manuscript.'' *Dickens Quarterly*, 7 (1990), 218–34.

515. Brennan, Elizabeth M. ''Introduction.'' In Dickens's *The Old Curiosity Shop.* Ed. Elizabeth M. Brennan. Clarendon Edition (44), pp. xiii-xcv.

516. Brennan, Elizabeth M. ''Note on the Text,'' ''Appendix A: Passages Deleted from MS and Proofs,'' and ''Appendix B: Dickens's Number Plans and Memoranda.'' In Dickens's *The Old Curiosity Shop.* World's Classics Edition. Ed. Elizabeth M. Brennan. Oxford and New York: Oxford University Press, 1998, pp. xxxiii-xxxvii, 555–68, 569–73.

517. Easson, Angus. ''*The Old Curiosity Shop*: From Manuscript to Print.'' *Dickens Studies Annual*, 1 (1970), 93–128, 286–87.

518. Grubb, Gerald G. ''Dickens's Marchioness Identified.'' *Modern Language Notes*, 68 (1953), 162–65.

519. Patten, Robert. ''‘The Story-Weaver at His Loom’: Dickens and the Beginning of *The Old Curiosity Shop.*'' In *Dickens the Craftsman: Strategies of Presentation.* Ed. Robert B. Partlow, Jr. Carbondale and Edwardsville: Southern Illinois University Press; London and Amsterdam: Feffer & Simons, 1970, pp. 44–64, 191–93.

Oliver Twist

520. Horne, Philip. ''A Note on the Text'' and ''Selected Textual Variants.'' In Dickens's *Oliver Twist, or, The Parish Boy's Progress.* Ed. Philip Horne. Penguin Classics Edition. London, New York, etc.: Penguin Books, 2002, pp. l-liii, 530–54.

521. Miller, W[illiam]. ''The Manuscript of *Oliver Twist.*'' *Dickensian*, 11 (1915), 222–23.

522. Paroissien, David. *The Companion to **Oliver Twist***. The Dickens Companions. Edinburgh: Edinburgh University Press, 1992, passim.

523. Tillotson, Kathleen. "Introduction." In Dickens's *Oliver Twist*. Ed. Kathleen Tillotson. Clarendon Edition (47), pp. xv-xlvii.

524. Wheeler, Burton M. "The Text and Plan of *Oliver Twist*." *Dickens Studies Annual*, 12 (1983), 41–61.

Our Mutual Friend

525. Boll, Ernest. "The Plotting of *Our Mutual Friend*." *Modern Philology*, 42 (1944/45), 96–122.

526. Brattin, Joel J. "Dickens' Creation of Bradley Headstone." *Dickens Studies Annual*, 14 (1985), 147–65.

527. Brattin, Joel J. "'I Will Not Have My Words Misconstrued': The Text of *Our Mutual Friend*." *Dickens Quarterly*, 15 (1998), 167–76.

528. Brattin, Joel J. "Introduction," "Notes on the Text and Illustrations," "Notes," "Appendix A: *Our Mutual Friend* and Dickens's Book of Memoranda," and "Appendix B: Running Titles in the Charles Dickens Edition." In Dickens's *Our Mutual Friend*. Ed. Joel J. Brattin. Everyman Dickens. London: J. M. Dent; Rutland, VT: Charles E. Tuttle, 2000, pp. xxiii-xxxi, xxxii-xxxviii, 875–904, 905–07, 908–13.

529. Childs, George W. "Recollections of George W. Childs. III." *Lippincott's Monthly Magazine*, 44 (1889), 216–20; reprinted in his *Recollections*. Philadelphia: J. B. Lippincott, 1890, etc., pp. 33–36.

530. Cotsell, Michael. *The Companion to **Our Mutual Friend***. The Dickens Companions. London: Allen and Unwin, 1986, pp. 1–7 and passim.

531. [Field, Kate]. "'Our Mutual Friend' in Manuscript." *Scribner's Monthly*, 8 (1874), 472–75.

532. Hawthorne, Julian. "The Recollection of a Famous Editor." *Pall Mall Gazette*, 52 (18 May 1891), 6.

533. "The Ms. of 'Our Mutual Friend,' by Charles Dickens." *Notes and Queries*, 5th ser., 2 (1874), 139.

534. S., J. B. "The Skeleton of 'Our Mutual Friend.'" *Notes and Queries*, 7th ser., 11 (1891), 65.

535. Shea, F[rancis] X. "Mr. Venus Observed: The Plot Change in *Our Mutual Friend*." *Papers on Language & Literature*, 4 (1968), 170–81.

536. Shea, F[rancis] X. "No Change of Intention in *Our Mutual Friend*." *Dickensian*, 63 (1967), 37–40.

537. Shea, Francis X. "The Text of *Our Mutual Friend*: A Study of the Variations between the Copy Text and the First Printed Edition." *Dissertation Abstracts International*, 22 (1961/62), 2007 (University of Minnesota, 1961).

538. Winslow, Joan D. "The Number Plans for *Our Mutual Friend*." *Dickens Studies Newsletter*, 9 (1978), 106–09.

Pickwick Papers

539. Kinsley, James. "Introduction." In Dickens's *The Pickwick Papers*. Ed. by James Kinsley. Clarendon Dickens (52), pp. xv-lxxxv.

540. S[uzannet], A[lain de]. "The Original Manuscript of 'The Pickwick Papers.'" *Dickensian*, 28 (1931/32), 193–96.

Sketches by Boz

541. DeVries, Duane. *Dickens's Apprentice Years: The Making of a Novelist*. Hassocks, Eng.: Harvester Press; New York: Barnes & Noble Books/Harper & Row, 1976. iv + 195 pp.

542. Grillo, Virgil. "Chapter Five: Revisions for Synthesis." In his *Charles Dickens' Sketches by Boz: End in the Beginning*. Boulder: Colorado Associated University Press, 1974, pp. 85–117.

543. Ser, Cary D. "*Sketches by Boz*: A Collated Edition." *Dissertation Abstracts International*, 40 (1979/80), 4013A (University of Florida, 1974).

544. Slater, Michael. "Introduction," "Dickens's Prefaces to *Sketches by Boz*," and Headnotes. In his edition of Dickens's *Sketches by Boz and Other Early Papers, 1833–39*. Dent Uniform Edition of Dickens' Journalism. [Vol. 1]. London: J. M. Dent; Columbus: Ohio State University Press, 1994, pp. xi-xxii, xxxix-xlii, and passim.

A Tale of Two Cities

545. Sanders, Andrew. *The Companion to A Tale of Two Cities*. The Dickens Companions. London, etc.: Unwin; Boston: Unwin Hyman, 1988, passim.

546. Tucker, David. "Dickens at Work on the MS of *A Tale of Two Cities*." *Etudes Anglaises*, 32 (1979), 449–57.

Short Fiction, Nonfictional Works, and the Book of Memoranda

547. Batterson, Richard F. "The Manuscript and Text of Dickens's 'George Silverman's Explanation.'" *Papers of the Bibliographical Society of America*, 73 (1979), 473–76.

548. Chittick, Kathryn. "The Meaning of a Literary Idea: Dickens's Memoranda Notebook." *Dalhousie Review*, 62 (1982/83), 473–84.

549. Flint, Kate. "Further Reading" and "A Note on the Text." In Dickens's *Pictures from Italy*. Ed. Kate Flint. Penguin Classics Edition. London, New York, etc.: Penguin Books, 1998, pp. xxxv, xxxvi-xxxvii.

550. Ingham, Patricia. "A Note on the Text" and "Appendix I: Dickens's Unpublished Introduction of 1842." In Dickens's *American Notes for General Circulation*. Ed. Patricia Ingham. Penguin Classics Edition. London, New York, etc.: Penguin Books, 2000, pp. xxxv-xxxvi, 275–77.

551. Kaplan, Fred, ed. *Charles Dickens' Book of Memoranda: A Photographic and Typographic Facsimile of the Notebook Begun in January 1855*. New York: New York Public Library, 1981. x + 107 pp.

552. Paroissien, David H. "A Critical Edition of Charles Dickens's *Pictures from Italy*." *Dissertation Abstracts International*, 29 (1968/69), 1876A-77A (UCLA, 1968).

553. Paroissien, David. "A Note on the Text" and "Bibliography." In Dickens's *Pictures from Italy*. Ed. David Paroissien. London: André Deutsch, 1973; New York: Coward, McCann & Geoghegan, 1974; reprinted London: Robinson, 1989, pp. 244–46, 258–60.

554. Paroissien, David H. "Dickens's 'Pictures from Italy': Stages of the Work's Development and Dickens's Methods of Composition." *English Miscellany*, 22 (1971), 243–62.

555. Slater, Michael. "Note on the Provenance, Selection and Treatment of the Text," "Appendix A: Descriptive Headlines Added by Dickens to Articles in this Volume from *HW [Household Words]* Which Were Included in *RP [Reprinted Pieces]*," and Headnotes. In his edition of Dickens's *"The Amusements of the People" and Other Papers: Reports, Essays and Reviews, 1834–51*. Dent Uniform Edition of Dickens' Journalism. Vol. 2. London: J. M. Dent; Columbus: Ohio State University Press, 1996, pp. xxvii-xxviii, 370–71, and passim.

556. Slater, Michael, "Textual Note," "Appendix B: Descriptive Headlines Added by Dickens to Articles in this Volume Which Were included in *RP [Reprinted Pieces]*," and Headnotes. In his edition of Dickens's *"Gone Astray" and Other Papers from Household Words, 1851–59*. Dent Uniform Edition of Dickens'

Journalism. Vol. 3. London: J. M. Dent; Columbus: Ohio State University Press, 1998, pp. xxiii, 507–08, and passim.

557. Slater, Michael, and John Drew. "Note on the Text and Illustrations," "Appendix C: Descriptive Headlines Added by Dickens to Articles in this Volume Which Were Included in *UT1 [The Uncommercial Traveller* (1868)*]*," and Headnotes. In their edition of Dickens's *The Uncommercial Traveller and Other Papers, 1859–70* (61), pp. xxvii, 432–35, and passim.

558. Whitley, John S., and Arnold Goldman. "Appendix 1: Dickens's Discarded Introduction" and "Textual Notes." In Dickens's *American Notes for General Circulation.* Ed. John S. Whitley and Arnold Goldman. Penguin English Library. Harmondsworth, Eng., Baltimore, MD, and Ringwood, Austral.: Penguin Books, 1972, pp. 297–300, 359–61.

Dickens's Works

559. Butt, John, and Kathleen Tillotson, general editors. *The Clarendon Dickens.* Oxford: Clarendon Press, 1966– . For published volumes, see *Pickwick Papers*, edited by James Kinsley (52); *Oliver Twist*, edited by Kathleen Tillotson (47); *The Old Curiosity Shop*, edited by Elizabeth M. Brennan (44); *Martin Chuzzlewit*, edited by Margaret Cardwell (40); *Dombey and Son*, edited by Alan Horsman (34); *David Copperfield*, edited by Nina Burgis (31); *Little Dorrit*, edited by Harvey P. Sucksmith (39); *Great Expectations*, edited by Margaret Cardwell (36); and *The Mystery of Edwin Drood*, edited by Margaret Cardwell (42)

560. [Hogarth, Georgina, and Mamie, or Mary, Dickens, eds.]. *The Letters of Charles Dickens.* Edited by His Sister-in- Law and His Eldest Daughter. In 2 vols.: Vol. I. *1833 to 1856*; Vol. II. *1857 to 1870.* London: Chapman and Hall, 1880 [actually 21 November 1879]. ix + 463 pp.; 464 pp. (errata slips in both vols.); Vol. III. *1836 to 1870.* London: Chapman and Hall, 1882 [actually 2 November 1881]. iii + 308 pp.; Vols. I and II, New York: Charles Scribner's Sons, 1879, 544 + 536 pp; Vol. III, New York: Charles Scribner's Sons, 1881. 285 pp.; revised Edition. 2 vols. London: Chapman and Hall, 1882 (uniform with the Charles Dickens Edition of Dickens's Works). Vol. I. *1833 to 1855*. viii + 400 pp.; Vol. II. *1855 to 1870.* 432 pp.; Third Edition (one volume). London and New York: Macmillan, 1893; reprinted 1903 and 1909. ix + 763 pp.

561. House, Madeline, Graham Storey, et al., eds. *The Letters of Charles Dickens.* The Pilgrim Edition (vols. 8–12: The British Academy: The Pilgrim Edition). 12 vols. Oxford: Clarendon Press, 1965–2002.

562. *Manuscripts of the Works of Charles Dickens: From the Forster Collection in the Victoria and Albert Museum, London.* Wakefield, Eng.: Micro Methods,

1970. 10 reels; also *Manuscripts, Correspondence, and Papers of Charles Dickens from the Forster Collection, V&A Museum.* Brighton: Harvester Microform, 1987. 4 reels. See *The Forster and Dyce Collections from the National Art Library of the Victoria and Albert Museum, London* (Brighton: Harvester Microform, 1987), II, 97–124, for detailed list of contents. Also see *Great Expectations.* London: Scolar Press, 1978, for a color microfilm of the manuscript and related papers.

Review Essay: Psychological Criticism on Dickens, 1982–2001

Robyn L. Schiffman

Perhaps psychoanalysis has become a modern equivalent of a contested site of contradiction and paradox, much like "poetry" in the Renaissance or the "novel" in the eighteenth century. Psychoanalysis is generally discussed in at least two ways: as a therapeutic method and as a system of inquiry. It is commonly understood that what brings psychoanalysis and literature together —indeed, what allows the one to serve the other—is that the structures of both the mind and literature are the same. As a methodology, this form of criticism has certainly had its detractors. Yet, and more importantly, it remains a very compelling and profitable mode of criticism, particularly when analyzing the vast body of work of Charles Dickens. This essay reports on some of these critical conversations that attempt to figure out why we never seem to tire of observing the uncanny in Bleak House *or guilt in* Great Expectations. *I present here a selected review of the psychological critical literature on Dickens and his fiction as it has appeared in print since 1982. Ultimately, the results of such an attempt illuminate both Dickens scholarship and psychological criticism in general.*

> Shakespeare was, of course, present, along with Sophocles and Wilhelm Fliess, at the birth of Psychoanalysis in October 1897.
>
> Ned Lukacher, 1994

Charles Dickens and Sigmund Freud cannot really be considered contemporaries in any meaningful sense of the word. While their lives did overlap for a period of fourteen years (Freud was born in 1856, just one year after the first issue of *Little Dorrit* appeared), the British author did not live to see the birth of psychoanalysis as Dickens died in 1870; for that matter, he also never saw a unified Germany or, perhaps more to the point, Dickens also never knew that the Viennese doctor claimed *David Copperfield* as his favorite Dickens novel.[1] Yet Dickens criticism of the late twentieth century has brought these two figures ever closer together in new and illuminating ways, ways that I think profitably impact both Dickens scholarship and psychological criticism in general.

Let me first offer some general remarks on the preparation of this piece, a standard movement in review essays. I have tried to limit myself only to those articles and books that announce explicitly a psychological approach, and I define, rather loosely, psychology here as that which studies the mind and its behavior. More often than not, this psychological approach becomes a bit narrower as most of the authors presented here use psychoanalysis as their methodology, more specifically of a Freudian kind. Psychoanalysis is generally discussed in at least two ways: as a therapeutic method and as a system of inquiry. It is commonly understood that what brings literature and psychoanalysis together—indeed, what allows the one to serve the other—is that the structures of both the mind and literature are the same. What follows is my attempt to present some of the critical conversations as they have appeared in relation to Dickens and his fiction since 1982.[2]

In the case of many articles, their inclusion in my review has been rather simple: methodology is indicated pointedly either by title (*"A Christmas Carol*: A Literary Psychoanalysis"*) or by place of publication (the journal *Literature and Psychology*). Operating within these bounds necessitates that I overlook countless contributions to the field which elaborate psychological language and its relation to Dickens and his work but which largely form part of longer and more complex arguments. Thus, I have tailored my focus specifically. As it is, some of the contributions I examined from book-length studies are not exclusive to Dickens or his work but analyze one of his novels in a more general project about hysterical fiction, nineteenth-century novels, or moments of anxiety in Victorian narrative. This review of psychological literature does not include those seminal articles which were reprinted and republished after 1982, as the 1980s and 1990s brought about new editions of Dickens's novels or as individual critics newly collected their essays in book form.[3] Additionally, given that, to take just one example, the adjective "post-Freudian" is so pervasive in our world, and is commonly understood, one would be hard pressed to find any critical work that does not at least on some level make use of a set of crystallized yet useful interpretive categories, especially as psychoanalysis has been so carefully and substantially revised and rethought in the late twentieth century.

Perhaps consistent with the psychological pieces of the 1970s and earlier, and maybe Dickens scholarship in general, if we believe Philip Collins's famous 1978 iteration concerning its heroine,[4] *Bleak House* is the novel that attracts the most attention from psychoanalytic critics. For this reason, I begin my discussion with *Bleak House*. Rather than proceed in order of publication date, I continue with other critical pieces that focus on a single Dickens novel, with *Great Expectations* receiving the next highest amount of attention. I then group studies of more than one novel together. I end with brief mention of seven critics whose primary critical thrust lies outside of psychology and/ or literature.

Bleak House

G. D. Arms's fine article, "Reassembling *Bleak House*: 'Is there *three* of 'em them?' " revises a popular characterization in studies of Esther as he suggests that Esther is not the emotionally starved and abused child critics have long claimed. If that were the case, he argues, following convincing clinical evidence, she would be angry and her rage at father figures would dominate the text. But, by focusing on the relationship developed and sustained between Esther and John Jarndyce, Arms sees how Esther is complicit in the seduction posed by the possible father/daughter incest narrative and she thus emerges as only a half-accurate portrait of an abused child. Arms also considers how Lady Dedlock and Sir Leicester Dedlock's relationship is the first incestuous pairing in the novel and, as the sins of the parents are visited on the children, the Summerson/Jarndyce pairing refigures this earlier one even as it is not, ultimately, carried to fruition.

Brenda Marshall's "Dickens and Another Modernity: The Eruption of the Real" is a complicated but suggestive piece which sees how Dickens inherits and comments upon his French contemporary Charles Baudelaire's reflections on the modern city and the attendant issues of commodity, disease, the law. With departures into Walter Benjamin and Jacques Lacan, her primary Baudelaire and Freud interlocutors, Marshall spends just a brief amount of time on Dickens but in a very interesting movement reads the character of Jo as a Dickensian *flâneur*, who is produced as such by his city and his home in Tom-all-Alone's. Marshall renews analysis of Dickens's city, marked by trauma, chaos, illiteracy, dirt, and madness, to suggest future implications for the study of modernity and its beginnings, and the accompanying death drive which characterizes all modern subjects, literary and otherwise.[5]

My own essay, "Wax-Work, Clock-Work, and Puppet-Shews: *Bleak House* and the Uncanny," continues the project of Robert Newsom, Maria Tatar, and others in elaborating a theoretical framework of the uncanny toward understanding this novel. I parallel a scene related in a footnote from Freud's essay on "The 'Uncanny'," where he reluctantly recognizes himself in a train compartment window, to the famous moment in the novel where Esther views her much changed self in the mirror. Thus, I closely align Freud and the heroine he had little patience for. But the uncanny, as I argue, ultimately, has less to do with Esther than it has to do with her doll. Instead, I consider "Dolly," as she is called, as the uncanny figure in the text and newly examine those moments when Dolly is spoken to, alluded to, and remembered by Esther. Esther's burial of Dolly allows Esther to emerge as an adult sexual woman and author. Charting Dolly's presence in the novel enables a reconsideration of Esther's own humanness and returns discussion of the uncanny back toward things.

There are a few novel studies that use *Bleak House* as one example of larger points and I group these here together. Christine von Boheeman's book, *The Novel as Family Romance: Language, Gender, and Authority from Fielding to Joyce,* surveys three novelists from the last three centuries to think about how novel-writing and narration devices are early articulations of Freud's concept of the family romance (in a simple formulation, the fantasy expressed by saying, "I am actually an orphan and my real parents are of noble birth." The desire to construct this romance about the child's real family has its roots in the Oedipus complex). Her middle chapter contains a reading of *Bleak House*. In suggesting that Esther's story is a version of this "myth of the birth of the hero," whereby the foundling's quest for and fantasy about origin is enacted through the plot of the novel, Boheeman claims that Esther's initiation includes being able to confront her mother's sexuality, which in turn leads to her own sexual self-knowledge as she becomes a wife and mother. Boheeman's strength is less her individual reading of *Bleak House* or *Tom Jones* than her linking up the overall project of the genre of the novel (its construction, its development, etc.) in psychoanalytic terms. That is, the novel by its very definition, she writes, reflects and is driven by its author's and character's primal fantasies and quests for origin.

Katherine Cummings's analysis of *Bleak House* in a short middle chapter of her *Telling Tales: The Hysteric's Seduction in Fiction and Theory* is a forceful and sustained examination of Esther's fantasies of parentage. Cummings's book connects female foundling narrators with seduction and the telling of tales, two contemporary and fundamental debates ongoing in psychoanalytic communities, by noting outright that in hysteria it is the daughter who does all the talking. In giving the female narrator primary importance, Cummings's more interesting point demonstrates that while Esther is a paragon of Victorian virtue and servitude, she is also a parody of herself. Cummings skillfully weaves Freud, Lacan, Derrida, and a host of more modern psychoanalytic interlocutors into her analysis, which privileges the female narrative subject and the many ways in which she seduces through the act of writing and reading, even as she struggles with writing and reading.

Karen Chase makes a compelling point in discussing *Bleak House* in her *Eros and Psyche: The Representation of Personality in Charlotte Brontë, Charles Dickens and George Eliot*, a study of psychological novels in mid-Victorian fiction. The central occupation of this novel, what she calls the tragic sense, is how the various negotiations of double identities, narrators, and plots are worked out with ambivalence, aggression, and confusion when they come together—but they do come together. Chase reveals that the search and discovery of two seemingly separate things that are in fact one (the narrators who come together in presenting *Bleak House* or the realization that "Nemo" comes to have a name and is in fact someone) also underlies the tragedy of Oedipus: wife and mother are similarly revealed to be one and the same. Though her focus is not on how Oedipus's tragedy is rewritten in Dickens, this point, I think, is suggestive in understanding both the fungibility of identities in *Bleak House* and applying their distillation toward a larger, psychoanalytically driven point.

Carolyn Dever's *Death and the Mother from Dickens to Freud* analyzes selected mid-nineteenth-century texts with absent or dead mothers who then return in order to revise psychoanalytic theories that state that maternal absence dominates the life of the adult. The return of the mother is indeed uncanny, but it also illustrates a repetition and reworking of the initial trauma of loss, worked out, or attempted to be worked out, in the form of the fictional autobiographic and detective novels Dever uses. Dever calls for and develops, using object relations theory, a more presence-based maternal theory. If the death of the mother produces the birth of the authorial and narrating subject, Lady Dedlock's repeated "deaths" complicate Esther's relationship to her own narrating self and explain the neuroses of her adult, writing self. If writing and the mother are so closely liked, as Dever contends, it is surprising that Dever has nothing to say about Esther herself as a mother at the end of the novel.

Great Expectations

Shuli Barzilai's "Dickens's *Great Expectations*: A Motive for Moral Masochism" rethinks why guilt is a central theme in this novel, connecting this oft-noticed preoccupation with Freud's concept of moral masochism. Barzilai uses Kenneth Burke's concept of "symbolic incest" in reading Pip, Estella, and Miss Havisham as versions of the same character, each wanting that which is taboo. Carrying this burden results in frustrated and sublimated desires, and this provides the motive for moral masochism. Barzilai has a provoking if brief section in this article that places recurring imagery of spiders in *Great Expectations* within the context of both literary history (her examples range from Edmund Spenser, and Kafka's well-known metaphor, to lesser-known German writers) and psychoanalytic commentary to suggest how we might rethink how guilty sons are produced by dangerous, spider-mothers (Miss Havisham, Mrs. Joe).

Douglas Stewart's "Anti-Oedipalizing *Great Expectations*, Masochism, Subjectivity, Capitalism" takes up where Barzilai leaves off by continuing to think about, and review, previous studies of masochism in Dickens's novel. Stewart quotes passages from the Marquis de Sade and Leopold von Sacher-Masoch in order to parallel clinical and fictional masochistic descriptions. Stewart suggests that Dickens anticipates two late-twentieth-century critiques in this novel: that of capitalism and of Oedipus. He investigates how masochism and the anti-oedipal (à la Deleuze and Guattari) are interpretive models useful in postmodern culture. His concluding section analyzes an actual postmodern novel that rewrites Dickens: Kathy Acker's *Great Expectations* of 1982.

Psychology and economics become strange bedfellows in Ronald R. Thomas's *Dreams of Authority: Freud and the Fictions of the Unconscious*. Thomas makes the case for a capitalist psychology in psychoanalysis; he links Freud's project in the dreambook to an economic vocabulary in maintaining that psychic economy is one of the goals of psychoanalysis. He brings this to bear on his analysis of *Great Expectations*, a novel centrally concerned with how Pip wrestles and negotiates with his psychic (and sexual) indebtedness. In examining some of Pip's dreams, Thomas sees how the material in the dreams not only represents day residue and repressed wishes but also engages with other fiduciary and moral narratives of worth and value.

David Copperfield

Virginia Carmichael's "In Search of *Beein'*: *Nom/Non Du Père* in *David Copperfield*" continues earlier Freudian psychoanalytic critiques of *David Copperfield* (by Leonard Manheim, J. Hillis Miller, and Dianne Sadoff) but introduces Lacanian elements heretofore excluded from studies of this novel. Carmichael skillfully unpacks Lacan's ideas of the Imaginary or pre-linguist realm and the Symbolic or patriarchal linguistic order as a way of understanding exactly how David struggles with writing and loving through the novel. David's attempt at finding a vocation and a wife is imbued with a kind of violence and sexual ambivalence that Carmichael feels Freudian psychoanalysis has not accounted for. David's negotiations of both the Imaginary and the

Symbolic realms test his acceptance and resistance of the "name" and the "no" of the father (the pun is more explicit in French: *le nom du père*; *le non du père*). Carmichael opens up the possibility of using Lacanian ideas as a way of thinking also about some central questions in Victorian society which get articulated in fiction: appropriate love object choices (e.g., David's sexual love for Dora versus his nonsexual love for Agnes) and the prevalence of orphaned children who go in search of parent replacements.

The Old Curiosity Shop

G. Cordery's "The Gambling Grandfather in *The Old Curiosity Shop*" refocuses critical study of this work toward Grandfather Trent, a character, according to Cordery, long neglected by critics in favor of Little Nell or Quilp. Cordery considers how similar Quilp and the grandfather are, especially in their parasitic and sexual relations vis-à-vis Nell. But it is gambling that most intrigues Cordery as he investigates how the activity serves as a metaphor for frustrated sexuality in a seemingly sexless novel, particularly through the figure of the old man who symbolically rapes his granddaughter when he forcefully enters her bedroom and steals her money. Through his continual rationalizations, denial about his addiction, and dependence on the game, the grandfather fits the model of a compulsive gambler and also a sexual predator. The brief survey of psychological literature presented here considers how gambling is a form of masturbation and also mental illness (see Freud's essay on Dostoevsky as one example).

Our Mutual Friend

Karen C. Gindele's "Desire and Deconstruction: Reclaiming Centers" is a complicated critique of the psychoanalytic category of lack (at once anatomical as in Freud and epistemological or existential as in Lacan and Derrida) as it has been discussed by theorists and mobilized in literary studies. After demonstrating recent critical preoccupation with lack, and certain feminist responses, Gindele suggests that we need to shift the focus of our concerns to think how desire derives from energy and productivity and not lack or absence. She then analyzes *Our Mutual Friend* where she is clearer and where we are on more familiar ground. Her interesting claim is that *Our Mutual Friend* is the first novel to incorporate systematically ideas laid out in Darwin's *Origin of the Species*. Gindele sees how this novel negotiates social, sexual, and class-based hierarchies as she reads a set of concrete post-Darwin elements in Dickens.

The Pickwick Papers

Jean Harris's " 'But He Was His Father': The Gothic and the Impostorious in Dickens's *The Pickwick Papers*" focuses on the many interpolated tales of this first novel. In considering them already as Gothic narratives (a category often deployed by psychoanalytic critics), Harris is then allowed to suggest that these stories reveal anxieties about the father and fantasies of patricide that abound in *Pickwick*. This movement also situates Dickens within a discernible literary tradition that connects him with perhaps previously unconsidered company: Horace Walpole, Matthew Lewis, and Ann Radcliffe. However, Dickens subverts and liberates this older trajectory of the Gothic horror in two ways: through comic relief in an ultimately picaresque novel and by his trenchant critique of the economic and juridical systems vocalized by his characters.

Studies of More Than One Novel

Dirk den Hartog's *Dickens and Romantic Psychology* begins its study of Dickens with possibly an unlikely source: William Wordsworth. Romantic psychology is here read as Wordsworthian psychology; for den Hartog, Wordsworth had already made the transition from childhood to adulthood, and the writing of these memories, a literary subject. The major thrust of den Hartog's book, then, is a sort of influence study; he reads closely Wordsworth alongside *Dombey and Son*, *Little Dorrit*, and *Great Expectations* in his exploration of self-continuity in nineteenth-century fiction, but in some ways the analyses of Wordsworth are the more interesting parts of the book.

Malcolm Andrews's *Dickens and the Grown-Up Child* is largely concerned with tracing theories and problematics of childhood both in Dickens's fiction and Victorian culture. While less focused on considering these characters psychologically, Andrews divides Dickensian children into five rather compelling categories: the professional infant; the portrait of arrested development; the premature adult; the child heroine; and the childlike gentleman. Andrews's comprehensive listing finds those characters, such as Miss Ninetta Crummles, Master Kidderminster, the Artful Dodger, Little Nell, and Joe Gargery, who fit these suggestive characterizations. While Andrews gestures toward connecting his results with larger and contemporary Victorian discourses about child rearing, he leaves open the possibility for analyzing how these characters allow for, break with, or reinscribe any kind of psychological reading.

Dianne Sadoff has one article and a book-length study devoted to psychoanalytic readings of Dickens's (and others') fiction. Her "*Locus Suspectus:*

Narrative, Castration, and the Uncanny'' begins by rehearsing Freud's essay "The 'Uncanny','' and the E. T. A. Hoffmann story "The Sandman'' contained in his analysis, in order to connect how the uncanny is rooted in the expression of unconscious desires, proving that the uncanny is still a profitable interpretive category for unlocking texts (I mean both fiction and, in the case of even Freud's essay, nonfiction). Fiction, perhaps we should be reminded, is one of the ways to access the unconscious and Sadoff focuses on three modes of Dickens's fictional autobiography (*David Copperfield, Great Expectations*, and *Oliver Twist*), and attendant moments of reading and writing in these novels, to discuss a series of complicated oedipal scenarios whereby narrator sons are produced by castrating fathers and phallic mothers. In this subtly argued piece, she reads hanging and beheading as metaphoric castration; to her way of thinking, the body, in death by hanging and beheading, goes limp.

Her *Monsters of Affection: Dickens, Eliot & Brontë on Fatherhood* thinks about why the search for paternal origin is a central concern in Victorian fiction and how psychoanalysis helps us to begin to answer that question. There are many layers to Sadoff's discussion of the father: each author in her book's title is discussed in relation to his or her own father as well as the many depictions of fathers and children as they are represented in the fictional works. With respect to plot patterns in Dickens, Sadoff explains that the identity of the father is revealed in two ways: at the end, as in *Nicholas Nickleby* and *Barnaby Rudge*, and once removed, that is, narrated through another (in *Little Dorrit, A Tale of Two Cities,* and *The Old Curiosity Shop*). Paternal discovery is then linked to novel-writing both in and out of the novels; the sense of an ending, of a novel having been written, maps onto ontological concerns about the father and origin. In a simple formulation, form joins content but ambivalence abounds: *The Old Curiosity Shop* is at once a novel about literary beginnings and the search for origin even as its narrative carefully works through a series of disguised and unanswered genealogical concerns (is Quilp really the father of the Marchioness?). David Copperfield himself is shy in speaking about his own career as a writer, and Sadoff reads this as an example of the larger themes at work in the novel that bears his name and also a reflection of his own search for suitable love-object choices. In other words, Sadoff claims that the fictional children write, as it were, to get back at the father.

Lawrence Frank's *Charles Dickens and the Romantic Self* begins with a useful outline describing how the literary critic benefits from psychoanalytic theory. While Frank's claim that Dickens is proto-Freudian is not new, what is suggestive is the trajectory of authors he places Dickens in the middle of: Rousseau, Goethe, and Freud. Rousseau emerges as one of the first psychologically nuanced writers to posit the self [6] out of which romantic autobiography

(*Faust*, in a problematic certain sense, *David Copperfield*, De Quincey, even Thomas Carlyle) emerges. Frank connects these four very different figures who span many years as well as countries by their own myths of self- creation as expressed in their writings. A thoroughly modern dilemma is then revealed as these selves are also fictions; the romantic self is the autobiographical self which is invested in its own self-generation and production, and, because of this, the genre does not matter—novels, essays, and psychoanalytic case histories are treated on the same level. Because Frank analyzes seven of Dickens's later novels, from *Dombey* to *Drood*, I will just highlight the more interesting aspects of his analyses of *Dombey and Son, David Copperfield,* and *A Tale of Two Cities.*

In the chapter on *Dombey and Son*, Frank focuses on James Carker, a slightly neglected yet fascinating character, one who is the true ''Son and Heir'' to the novel and firm. Carker, caught in the domestic tragedy of the oedipal and family romance, is a version of the romantic self in isolation who struggles with his place in the world and who dies as his father/rival looks on. Frank's chapter on *David Copperfield* concentrates on the character of Steerforth to demonstrate how, as his name suggests, many characters rotate and revolve around him and his movements (just as, we might consider, Dick Swiveller occupies a similar position in *The Old Curiosity Shop*). Additionally, Frank suggests that *Copperfield* takes up the autobiographical imperative of Rousseau's *Confessions* whereby the novel is an autobiography about the writing of autobiographies. Frank's commentary on *A Tale of Two Cities* shows how the nation's struggle maps onto generational conflict. Concentrating on Charles Darnay, and not Sydney Carton, Frank reads anew the overthrow of the tyrannical father/nation state by the son. Frank is quick to point out other common psychoanalytic tendencies in analyzing this novel. While Carton and Darnay represent Dickens's most sophisticated and sustained iteration on the theme of the double, this line of inquiry is less profitable as the relationship between the two men does not have the kind of dramatic tension and subtext of other Dickensian friendships and doubles (e.g., Copperfield and Steerforth). In a very interesting next point, Frank sees how the downfall of the king and father in the figure of Old Foulon (the call for his head, his dismemberment) parallels the band of brothers who kill and devour the father described toward the end of Freud's *Totem and Taboo*. Frank also links the production and composition of this novel to Wilkie Collins's *The Frozen Deep*, noting that Dickens performed the part of the character of Richard Wardour, a precursor to Sydney Carton. The novel *A Tale of Two Cities*, then, itself has a double, though Frank does not go so far as to say this.

Michael Kearns enters into the contemporary psychological discourse of Victorian England to rethink characters and their ongoing and evaluative relations to the external world. Though his *Metaphors of Mind in Fiction and*

Psychology is an elaboration upon an earlier article he published in this journal in 1986, entitled "'Associationism, the Heart, and the Life of the Mind in Dickens' Novels," this earlier discussion is clearer and treats the cases in more depth, and so I will focus on it. Associationism, an idea first developed by John Locke in 1700, is generally held to be a system of thought contending that the mind is blank and is then subjected to shaping and formation by outside forces. Placing the mind in obvious distinction to the heart, this mode of inquiry also, hard as it may be to remember, comes before any understanding of the "'unconscious mind" as such. Kearns's essay is, not surprisingly, character-driven as he analyzes Pip, David Copperfield, Mr. Dombey, and Eugene Wrayburn through associationist mentionings or tendencies in order to recast psychological interpretations around this forgotten applied philosophy.

Honorable Mention[7]

Here are seven authors who deserve only brief mention, mostly because the interpretive methodology and focus are largely non-psychological or, in the last two examples, not exclusively literary. Despite its announced interest in the theme of the double, Stephen Bernstein's "Oliver Twisted: Narrative and Doubling in Dickens's Second Novel" is more a survey of the critical literature which analyzes themes of story-telling and character-doubling than a new reading *Oliver Twist* in these terms.

Though his focus lies primarily in newly analyzing the paralleled failed domestic and industrial economies of *Hard Times*, Richard Fabrizio, in his "Wonderful No-Meaning: Language and the Psychopathology of the Family in *Hard Times*" briefly extends the failure to the family unit as well. Some of the evidence of the pathological family structure includes Bounderby's renunciation of his true self and the incest narrative between Tom and Louisa.

Anna Wilson's very good essay "On History, Case History, and Deviance: Miss Wade's Symptoms and Their Interpretation" focuses on two common Victorian vocational and psychological categories for women: the governess and the madwoman. Discussion of Miss Wade's character is here presented in symptomatic terms, that is, as a symptom of neurosis, which has cultural implications and corollaries, rather than exclusively sexual (i.e., lesbian) terms, a staple in Miss Wade/*Little Dorrit* studies.

Nathalie Shainess's "Charles Dickens: The First (Interpersonal) Psychoanalyst; Or, *A Christmas Carol*: A Literary Psychoanalysis" is a brief and not altogether convincing article claiming that *A Christmas Carol* represents a transcript of an analytic session whereby Dickens (called Dr. Dickens by Shainess) is the analyst and Scrooge the patient who suffers from multiple neuroses, nightmares, and delusions.

H. M. Daleski's "Dickens and the Proleptic Uncanny" considers how the Freudian (and later Todorovian) uncanny serves as a characterization device running through Dickens's fiction. Expansive in its scope, and limited in its claims, Daleski uses examples from six novels, from *Oliver Twist* to *Great Expectations,* to read closely those passages that illuminate moments of, among other things, castration complex, oedipal desires, or déjà vu.

Though it is very brief, Sander L. Gilman comments on "A Curious Dance Round a Curious Tree" which appeared in *Household Words* in 1852. Gilman uses this mostly written by Dickens essay as a way of talking about representations of madness in Victorian asylums in his *Disease and Representation: Images of Illness from Madness to AIDS.* Gilman locates Dickens as one of the vehicles through which debates around asylum reform in the nineteenth century were made accessible to a British public, and finds contemporary models for the various portrayals of insanity scattered throughout his fiction.

Richard A. Currie's "*All the Year Round* and the State of Victorian Psychiatry" s another critical intervention into representations of contemporary insanity in Dickens's and Collins's writing. Currie concludes by saying that this particular periodical occupied a very important role in Victorian society as it served as a conduit for presenting a more humane and compassionate treatment of the mentally ill.

NOTES

1. He discusses its virtues in an October 5, 1883, letter to his future fiancée, Martha Bernays.
2. Leonard Manheim's "Dickens and Psychoanalysis: A Memoir," appearing in this journal in 1983, chronicles psychoanalytic scholarship on Dickens and his fiction until 1981. My essay takes up where he left off.
3. For example, Peter Brooks's very good psychoanalytic examination of repetition and plotting in *Great Expectations* first appeared in the journal *New Literary History* in 1980, but many may recognize it from its inclusion as a chapter in his 1984 *Reading for the Plot: Design and Intention in Narrative.*
4. "The character much the most written about, however," writes Philip Collins, "is Esther Summerson" (97).
5. Another work that briefly uses Benjamin to illuminate Dickens is the chapter on "Dialectical Images: Benjamin/Dickens/Freud" in Ned Lukacher's *Primal Scenes: Literature, Philosophy, Psychoanalysis.* Lukacher's most provocative point contends that not only did *David Copperfield* have a large impact on Freud's life and courtship (as is well known and documented), but this novel also played an important role in Freud's method of interpretation. Lukacher brilliantly parallels the biting scene in the case of the Rat-Man and David's biting of Mr. Murdstone's hand to suggest that the earlier Dickensian incident provided a model for

Freud's understanding of the Rat-Man, in fact enabling the unpacking of the biting scene to evince a cure.

6. In German idealist philosophical terms, Johann Gottlieb Fichte (whom Frank does not cite but whose *Wissenschaftslehre* [Theory of Science or Doctrine of Knowledge] comes between Rousseau and Dickens) called this *das absolute Ich,* the absolute ego. In simple formulation, Fichte describes this to mean that the self posits the self.

7. I want to signal here two critics whose work I have read but have omitted in the main body of my text (but who appear in the Works Cited). Mark M. Hennelly's five-part series, " 'Deep Play' and 'Women's Ridicules' in *Oliver Twist,*" appeared from 1997–1999 in *Journal of Evolutionary Psychology.* Difficult to follow, Hennelly's articles weave back and forth between cultural anthropology, structuralism, Freudian, Lacanian, and feminist psychoanalysis, to name just a few methodologies at work in his pieces, to analyze *Oliver Twist.* Also, Annabeth Naef-Hinderlings's dissertation, published in 1983 as the *Search for the Culprit: Dickens's Conflicting Self- and Object Representations,* rehearses those earlier critics of *The Old Curiosity Shop* and *Little Dorrit* who write on Dickens's traumatic childhood and his life as a prolonged ritual of mourning.

WORKS CITED

Andrews, Malcolm *Dickens and the Grown-Up Child.* London: Macmillan, 1994.

Arms, G. D. "Reassembling *Bleak House*: 'Is There Three of 'Em Then?' " " *Literature and Psychology* 39.1–2 (1993): 84–96.

Barzilai, Shuli. "Dickens's *Great Expectations*: The Motive for Moral Masochism." *American Imago: Studies in Psychoanalysis and Culture* 42.1 (Spring 1985): 45–67.

Bernstein, Stephen. "Oliver Twisted: Narrative and Doubling in Dickens's Second Novel." *Victorian Newsletter* 79 (Spring 1991): 27–34.

Boheeman, Christine von. *The Novel as Family Romance: Language, Gender, and Authority from Fielding to Joyce.* Ithaca: Cornell UP, 1987.

Carmichael, Virginia. "In Search of Beein': *Nom/Non du Père* in *David Copperfield.*" *English Literary History* 54 (1987): 653–67.

Chase, Karen. *Eros and Psyche: The Representation of Personality in Charlotte Brontë, Charles Dickens and George Eliot.* New York: Methuen, 1984.

Collins, Philip. "Charles Dickens." *Victorian Fiction: A Second Guide to Research.* Ed. George Ford. New York: Modern Language Association, 1978. 34–113.

Cordery, G. "The Gambling Grandfather in *The Old Curiosity Shop.*" *Literature and Psychology* 33.1 (1987): 43–61.

Cummings, Katherine. *Telling Tales: The Hysteric's Seduction in Fiction and Theory.* Stanford, CA: Stanford UP, 1991.

Currie, Richard A. "*All the Year Round* and the State of Victorian Psychiatry." *Dickens Quarterly* 12.1 (March 1995): 18–24.

Daleski, H. M. "Dickens and the Proleptic Uncanny." *Dickens Studies Annual* 13 (1984): 193–206.

den Hartog, Dirk. *Dickens and Romantic Psychology: The Self in Time in Nineteenth-Century Literature.* New York: St. Martin's, 1987.

Dever, Carolyn. *Death and the Mother from Freud to Dickens: Victorian Fiction and the Anxiety of Origins.* Cambridge: Cambridge UP, 1998.

Fabrizio, Richard. "Wonderful No-Meaning: Language and the Psychopathology of the Family in *Hard Times.*" *Dickens Studies Annual* 16 (1987): 61–94.

Frank, Lawrence. *Charles Dickens and the Romantic Self.* Lincoln: U of Nebraska P, 1984.

Gilman, Sander L. *Disease and Representation: Images of Illness from Madness to AIDS.* Ithaca: Cornell UP, 1988.

Gindele, Karen C. "Desire and Deconstruction: Reclaiming Centers." *Dickens Studies Annual* 29 (2000): 269–301.

Harris, Jean. " 'But He Was His Father': The Gothic Plot and the Impostorious in Dickens's *The Pickwick Papers.*" In *Psychoanalytic Approaches to Literature and Film.* Eds. Maurice Charney and Joseph Reppen. Cranbury, NJ: Associated UP, 1987. 69–79.

Hennelly, Mark M., Jr. " 'Deep Play' and 'Women's Ridicules' in *Oliver Twist*: Part I." *Journal of Evolutionary Psychology* 18.1–2 (March 1997): 102–11.

———. " 'Deep Play' and 'Women's Ridicules' in *Oliver Twist*: Part II." *Journal of Evolutionary Psychology* 18.3–4 (August 1997): 143–55.

———. " 'Deep Play' and 'Women's Ridicules' in *Oliver Twist*: Part III." *Journal of Evolutionary Psychology.* 19.1–2 (March 1998): 116–31.

———. "Deep Play' and 'Women's Ridicules' in *Oliver Twist*: Part IV" *Journal of Evolutionary Psychology* 19.3–4 (August 1998): 165–74.

———. "Deep Play' and 'Women's Ridicules' in *Oliver Twist*: Part V." *Journal of Evolutionary Psychology* 20.1–2 (March 1999): 92–102.

Kearns, Michael S. "Associationism, the Heart, and the Life of the Mind in Dickens' Novels." *Dickens Studies Annual* 15 (1986): 111–144.

————. *Metaphors of Mind in Fiction and Psychology.* Lexington: UP of Kentucky, 1987.

Lukacher, Ned. "Chiasmatic Reading, Aporetic History: Freud's *Macbeth.*" In *Reading Freud's Reading.* Ed. Sander Gilman, et al. New York: New York UP, 1994. 152–79.

————. *Primal Scenes: Literature, Philosophy, Psychoanalysis.* Ithaca: Cornell UP, 1986.

Manheim, Leonard F. "Dickens and Psychoanalysis: A Memoir." *Dickens Studies Annual* 11 (1983): 335–45.

Marshall, Brenda. "Dickens and Another Modernity: The Eruption of the Real." *Literature and Psychology* 37.4 (1991): 29–46.

Naef-Hinderling, Annabeth. *The Search for the Culprit: Dickens's Conflicting Self- and Object-Representations.* Bern: Francke Verlag, 1983.

Sadoff, Dianne F. "*Locus Suspectus:* Narrative, Castration, and the Uncanny." *Dickens Studies Annual* 13 (1984): 207–30.

————. *Monsters of Affection: Dickens, Eliot & Brontë on Fatherhood.* Baltimore: Johns Hopkins UP, 1982.

Schiffman, Robyn L. "Wax-Work, Clock-Work, and Puppet-Shews: *Bleak House* and the Uncanny." *Dickens Studies Annual* 30 (2001): 159–71.

Shainess, Natalie. "Charles Dickens: The First (Interpersonal) Psychoanalyst; Or, *A Christmas Carol*: A Literary Psychoanalysis." *American Journal of Psychoanalysis* 52.4 (Dec. 92): 351–62.

Stewart, Douglas. "Anti-Oedipalizing *Great Expectations*: Masochism, Subjectivity, Capitalism." *Literature and Psychology* 45.3 (1999): 29–50.

Thomas, Ronald R. *Dreams of Authority: Freud and the Fictions of the Unconscious.* Ithaca: Cornell UP, 1990.

Wilson, Anna. "On History, Case History, and Deviance: Miss Wade's Symptoms and Their Interpretation." *Dickens Studies Annual* 26 (1998) 187–201.

Recent Dickens Studies—2001

Goldie Morgentaler

The following review essay deals with works on Dickens published primarily in the year 2001. It is organized into four sections, depending on the form of publication: Section A deals with books devoted entirely to Dickens and his work, both reference and monograph. Section B discusses books in which the main focus is not on Dickens per se, but which contain a chapter or chapters devoted to his work. Section C discusses collections of essays on Dickens, which have appeared in book form and have one editor but numerous contributors. Finally, Section D deals with a selection of journal articles that appeared in 2001.

I began my work on the 2001 annual review with a heavy heart, dreading the amount of reading that lay ahead. I have ended instead with a sense of gratitude—gratitude to the editors of *Dickens Studies Annual* for having asked me to undertake this review and to all the writers of articles, chapters, and monographs on Dickens and his work who have taught me so much in the course of all my reading. It is a sad but true fact of an academic's life that the amount of time one has to give over to reading anything outside one's immediate research or teaching concerns is limited, so I do not believe that under ordinary circumstances I would have had such an opportunity to survey the field as I have just had. If it has been a great deal of work, it has also been enormously educational and—more often than one might suppose—great fun. It is endlessly amazing to me that with so much having been written on Dickens in the past, there is still so much that is fresh and interesting remaining to be said.

My essay deals with works on Dickens that came out primarily in 2001, although I have included reviews of two books that appeared in the early months of 2002. I have organized the essay according to type of publication, beginning with books devoted entirely to Dickens's life or work. This section includes the only reference book on Dickens to appear in 2001, Nancy Metz's *The Companion to "Martin Chuzzlewit."* The discussion of monographs that follows is arranged alphabetically by author. This first section is followed by Section B, which contains a discussion of chapters on Dickens to be found in books whose main focus is not on Dickens but on other subjects. The third section deals with collections of essays devoted either in whole or in part to Dickens. In this section, I also discuss the essays in *Dickens Studies Annual* 30. The final section is a review of select journal articles that appeared in various publications during the course of 2001. This last section is in no sense comprehensive, the sheer volume of periodical essays in 2001 being a reliable indication that Dickens studies has experienced no diminishment of output or interest in these first years of the twenty-first century.

If I may be permitted a few general remarks before launching into a closer focus on individual contributions, I would say that if the year 2001 proved anything, it proved the continued dominance of Foucault as the literary theorist most quoted and most influential in assessing Dickens. Foucault's *Discipline and Punish,* with its emphasis on the panopticon, appears over and over again as a theoretical springboard for several of the authors under review here. Thematically, 2001 was notable for continuing a trend of the last few years by focusing on the theatrical aspects of Dickens's work. Theatricality, specifically melodrama, is the focus of Juliet John's *Dickens's Villains* and of Susan Ferguson's essay in *SEL,* "Dickens's Public Readings and the Victorian Author." Another aspect of Dickens's life that got more than one reading in 2001 was his relationship to Wilkie Collins, which is the subject of Anthea Trodd's *SEL* essay "Messages in Bottles and Collins's Seafaring Man," as well as of Lillian Nayder's full-length study, *Unequal Partners: Charles Dickens, Wilkie Collins and Victorian Authorship.*

By far the most popular topic of 2001, judging by the number of books and articles devoted to it, was Dickens and his problematic relationship to America, as expressed in both *American Notes* and *Martin Chuzzlewit.* Nancy Metz's *Companion to "Martin Chuzzlewit"* contains wonderful notes to the American portions of that novel, and Jeremy Tambling devotes more than a third of his *Lost in the American City: Dickens, James, Kafka* to Dickens's experiences in the United States. Three of the thirteen essays published in *Dickens Quarterly* in 2001 deal with this topic, including Iain Crawford's on "Dickens and the Whaling City," Jerome Meckier's on Mark Twain's comments on *Great Expectations* in *Life on the Mississippi,* and Nancy Metz's on "Nostalgia and the 'New' Emigrant in *Martin Chuzzlewit.*"

Interestingly, 2001 also saw the publication of two significant journal articles analyzing Dickens's relationship to trains and specifically to the Staplehurst railway disaster, Norris Pope's "Dickens's 'The Signalman' and Information Problems in the Railway Age," which appeared in the journal *Technology and Culture,* and Jill Matus's "Trauma, Memory and Railway Disaster: The Dickensian Connection," which appeared in *Victorian Studies.*

If I have a general complaint, it is that some writers seem not to have learned that communication of even the most sophisticated thought—perhaps especially of the most sophisticated thought—requires clarity. In more than one case, I simply could not make out what was being said on the page. When one has as much reading to do as I did for this essay, leaden prose can become a serious problem indeed. The only good thing about it is that it makes one appreciate lucid writing all the more.

Finally, a note on stylistics for any publishers reading this essay: I find footnotes infinitely preferable to endnotes, because they require so much less time to locate and read, and I appreciated all the more those texts that featured footnotes. But the advantage of ease of access is decidedly undermined when the text in which the note is written is so small that one needs a magnifying glass to make it out, Juliet John's *Dickens's Villains* and Lillian Nayder's *Unequal Partners* being two cases in point.

A) Books

Reference

Nancy Metz's ***Companion to "Martin Chuzzlewit"*** is a wonderful book and a good example of how scholarship at its best can be both enlightening and fun to read. Metz's *Companion* more than fulfills the guidelines for this series, whose purpose is—as the editors write in their preface—to "provide the most comprehensive annotation of the works of Dickens ever undertaken."

Metz's *Companion* is a treasure-trove of material on all aspects of nineteenth-century life that appear in the pages of *Martin Chuzzlewit.* The volume includes a short section at the beginning which highlights such broad themes as the novel's chronology; its literary, social, and philosophical context; America; architecture; and emigration. The bibliography is extensive and will prove of great use to scholars looking for material on even the most esoteric subjects, such as English organs (the kind you play). There are appendices on Dickens's number plans for the novel, on nineteenth-century American English, and on maps relating to *Martin Chuzzlewit.* (Actually the plural is misleading. There is only one map in this section.) Of the three appendices,

I found the section on nineteenth-century American English and how it differed from the English spoken in Britain at this time to be the most informative and useful.

However, the heart of this *Companion* lies in the notes to individual chapters. These are great fun to browse through and often make for fascinating reading, even without reference to the novel that gives rise to them. They also range far in scope, touching on everything from fashions to food to burial customs. To give just a short list: Metz explains the origins of leather jerkins, the link between widows and pubs, the make-up of candles (usually mutton fat), the rules for the games of skittles and quoits, the history of oil lamps, the prevalence of oranges in mid-Victorian England, floor cloth as the predecessor of linoleum and what it was made of, the proper way to serve cheese in the nineteenth century (cubed and handed round in a glass cheese dish), the fact that champagne was by reputation "the people's drink," rather than the drink of the elite, and was popularly associated with radicalism, fast living, and democracy. Metz also describes the living conditions that prevailed in nineteenth-century boarding houses like Todgers', remarking on the particular challenge that these establishments were to run, especially for female proprietors.

I found the material on America in the early nineteenth century particularly informative, especially the section on the uncertainties of American banking practices, and the chilling account of the high level of violence in American public life at this time, when gouging out eyes and dueling were acceptable methods for settling disputes. Metz illuminates conditions on board ships and on American trains. She is also very good at illuminating apparently minor details, such as the popularity of American rocking chairs, which British travelers tended to assume were a totally American invention, whereas in fact they originated and were just as popular in certain parts of England. Metz elucidates the kinds of culture clashes between Americans and the English that gave impetus to much of the anti-American animus in *Martin Chuzzlewit*. For instance, she explains that American boarding houses tended to set on the table all the courses of each meal at once, so that lodgers were required to help themselves, as opposed to the European habit of eating sequentially in courses brought out by servants. The American plan obviated the need for servers, and represented to English travelers like Dickens all that was most reprehensible about American democracy—its leveling spirit and its aggression.

The sampling I have given here is only designed to whet the appetite. There is much much more. Metz's *Companion* is beautifully produced and the text is punctuated by some eighteen illustrations. While not all of Metz's material will be new to scholars, enough of it was new to me to make me suspect that I will be consulting this *Companion* for years to come.

Metz's *Companion* makes central the kind of material that is usually relegated to the endnotes of annotated editions of Dickens's novels. This transforms it into an endless treat for obsessive note-readers like myself. But it also means that the volume is intended for scholars rather than for the casual reader, since it requires a certain familiarity with the text of *Martin Chuzzlewit* itself. I wonder how many first-time or casual readers will actually consult Metz's book while making their way through Dickens's novel. But for those who are familiar enough with the novel not to mind being interrupted in their reading to look up Metz's notes, this book is a feast! Metz writes in clear, concise prose and the quality and quantity of the information she provides makes this reference book a pleasure to read through, even from cover to cover.

Monographs

Juliet John, *Dickens's Villains: Melodrama, Character, Popular Culture*

Juliet John's study of Dickens's villains is both fascinating and oddly unsatisfying. John's monograph seeks to redress the lack of critical attention that has been accorded Dickens's villainous characters. She suggests that the reason these negative kinds of characters have been overlooked in the critical literature is their association with melodrama. John's purpose in this book is thus twofold—to reclaim Dickens's villains for critical discussion and to rescue melodrama as a viable literary and dramatic genre, and one which had a great influence on Dickens. Or, to quote her directly: "I aim to illuminate the crucial symbiosis that exists between the 'deviant' and the 'theatrical' aspects of Dickens's writing" (2).

John claims that Dickens dramatizes rather than analyzes the psyche (3). The reason for this, she suggests, is Dickens's belief in cultural inclusivity. For Dickens, the theatre is "ideally a crucial site of communal imaginative experience." She goes on to argue that "the imagination as it exercises itself in dramatic experience—whether this involves the actor or the spectator—takes one outside rather than inside the self." This is a most suggestive way of understanding what has often been turned into the bugbear of Dickens studies—the apparent superficiality of his characters.

John is very good, not only at explaining the sources of this apparent superficiality in Dickens's method of characterization, but also at arguing that we post-Freudians are too apt to assign a false value to interiority. Critics of Dickens, from Henry James and George Eliot on, have upheld and perpetuated "the Romantic elevation of 'depths' over surfaces, and of conscious intelligence over spontaneous emotion"(16). But for much of his career, Dickens was not an admirer of the inwardly focused personality (13). This is why melodrama is so critical in understanding Dickens's method, according to John, because melodrama is an "anti-intellectual genre which sets out to subvert . . . the value system most commonly used to condemn it" (26). "The emotional basis of melodrama and its compulsion to externalize emotional states largely account for the perceived excess of the genre" (30). As a genre, John argues, melodrama relies on the assumption that surfaces are synonymous with depths.

This seems right to me and John's argument for the importance of drama—and especially melodrama—as a source of Dickens's fiction is convincing. John devotes a great deal of space to theoretical trends in the evaluation of both Dickens's novels and of melodrama, complaining that "there has been only limited appreciation in Dickens criticism of the extent to which Dickens's novelistic villains are shaped by the confluence of his great interest in these two topics, crime and theatre" (70). She also makes the important point that while Dickens felt strongly that art should be inclusive, his desire to be popular did not necessarily imply a belief in democracy.

John's discussion includes chapters on the history of melodrama, dandyism (a discussion which focuses primarily on Skimpole), the Byronic villain (e.g. Steerforth), and deviant women. The range of John's scholarship is impressive, and her discussion of both melodrama and Dickens demonstrates a vast knowledge of both subjects. Yet, ultimately, this book is unsatisfying, because it seems never to really deal with its topic. For instance, the last chapter is ostensibly about Dickens's female villains, but these are defined as "sexually deviant women" and the focus of discussion is Edith Dombey and Lady Dedlock. I wonder how many readers would identify these two characters as the "villains" of their respective novels. At the same time, *Dombey and Son's* most obvious villain, James Carker, never receives a full discussion, despite the fact that he seems a perfect example of the melodramatic villain. When I say that John's book is ultimately unsatisfying this is what I mean: that the title "Dickens's Villains" seems to promise just that, but most of Dickens's villains do not appear here. There is no discussion of Uriah Heep, for instance. And while the Veneerings are offered up as examples of villainous dandyism in *Our Mutual Friend,* Fascination Fledgeby, the obvious dandy from the same novel, does not even rate a mention. Having said which, however, I should add that when John does focus on a particular villain, she invariably has interesting things to say. Her analysis of Fagin, for instance, as a character who is aware from the first that fiction, drama, and comedy have the power to corrupt, is first-rate.

John justifies her neglect of such villainous characters as Quilp and Pecksniff on the grounds that they are comic and pantomimic and therefore less relevant to the tensions between the psychological and theatrical that she wishes to focus on (12). This is fair enough as a limitation, and John is certainly not obliged to discuss characters who do not fit her critical parameters. Nor can she be faulted for excluding many of Dickens's vast array of villainous characters from her discussion. But the focus still seems to me to be askew. The problem may lie in the expectations raised by the title "Dickens's Villains." There are just too many villains left out of the discussion whom one might reasonably expect to see there.

All in all, however, this is a valuable book because it forces a rethinking of our assumptions about Dickens's method of characterization, and because it goes a long way towards rehabilitating that much maligned theatrical genre, the melodrama, and presenting it as a fit subject for serious discussion and analysis.

Rod Mengham, *Charles Dickens*

I am baffled by both the purpose and the intended readership of Rod Mengham's *Charles Dickens,* which is actually a study of Dickens's fiction rather than his life. The book is part of the Northcote series entitled Writers and Their Work, but it is far too sophisticated in its analysis of the novels to serve as an introduction to the works for those who have not yet read Dickens or have just newly discovered him. Mengham's book not only assumes a familiarity with the novels on the reader's part, but also with some of Dickens's less-commonly read stories, like "Dr. Marigold's Prescriptions." On the other hand, the book does not seem to be intended for a specialist readership either. It begins with a biographical outline, which will add nothing new to the knowledge of most Dickensians. It has almost no notes, many of Mengham's interpretations echo the readings of other scholars, usually without attribution, and it makes some odd errors. For instance, Mengham twice claims that John Forster was Dickens's son-in-law (56, 129). The bibliography at the back gives the address of *Dickens Studies Annual* as Carbondale, Illinois, not New York, and only one date for its appearance—1970!

It is not only Mengham's bibliography and biographical information that show evidence of inattention and haste, but the entire structure of this book reads as if it were put together in slapdash fashion. So, for instance, *Hard Times* is discussed in the same chapter as *Barnaby Rudge, American Notes,* and *Martin Chuzzlewit,* while the very skimpy discussion of *A Tale of Two Cities* get wedged in between two sections devoted to *Our Mutual Friend.* What makes these kinds of chronological lapses particularly annoying is that, in the main, Mengham discusses the novels in the order in which they were written, and this doubles the discomfiture when that order is disturbed.

The ostensible reason for the anachronisms is that Mengham has organized his discussion by theme rather than chronology. In his brief introduction he states that, "For those readers who prefer to be given a sense of the writer's development, there is this rough chronological sequence; otherwise, the various chapters could be regarded as preliminary discussions of concerns and compulsions that recur at every stage, and in every aspect, of Dickens's work" (1). This would be fine, except for the fact that Mengham nowhere actually identifies and enumerates these concerns and compulsions, leaving the reader to tease them out on her own. Chapter titles like "Taking the Roof Off" do not really help. (The latter deals with *Bleak House* and *Little Dorrit*, not, as one might expect, *Dombey and Son*.) Since the book lacks any overarching argument, chronology becomes the only obvious organizing principle. Once that too is violated, the result gives the impression of a hodge-podge.

In his introduction Mengham also writes that rather than comment briefly about each of Dickens's novels, he has chosen to give "relatively comprehensive readings of a few" and that these fall "wholly or in part" into the category of first-person narratives. Fair enough, but I cannot help feeling that things have gone seriously askew when the only thing to be said about the vast *Dombey and Son* takes up a page and a half of text on the water imagery that accompanies the death of little Paul.

To be fair, when Mengham is good, he is good. This is especially true of the discussion of *Barnaby Rudge* and *American Notes*. Mengham reads *Barnaby Rudge* in terms of the houses that are described and laid waste in the novel, beginning with the Maypole Inn and ending with the suggestion that John Chester's sexual adventuring in his youth has subverted the dynastic principle by producing an offspring whose gypsy blood threatens miscegenation as well as illegitimacy (38). Mengham also does a fine job of teasing out the libidinal energy inherent in Dickens's descriptions of the rioting mob. He notes that the tone of the passage in which Dolly Varden and Emma Haredale are abducted by the rioters does not permit any discrepancy between the rioters' lasciviousness and that of the narrator, thereby, Mengham argues, drawing the reader into complicity with the spectators' voyeurism. "The willingness to be aroused is typical of the mob, but the contagious nature of its subversive desires finds a textual equivalent in this implication of the reader" (40). This strikes me as an accurate way of expressing what is most impressive and most discomfiting about Dickens's narrative stance in *Barnaby Rudge*.

Mengham suggests that Dickens's non-fictional account of his trip to America in *American Notes for General Circulation* is dominated by Dickens's sense of panic at not being able to control the situations in which he finds himself, and he relates what he calls Dickens's "over-enthusiasm for blindness" (44) to his overall obsession with issues of surveillance, which also underlies *American Notes's* emphasis on prisons and asylums.

But even this third chapter of Mengham's book, with its strong readings of *Barnaby Rudge* and *American Notes,* is spoiled by a too-quick jump to a rather superficial discussion of *Martin Chuzzlewit* and an even more superficial analysis of *Hard Times,* which seems pointlessly tacked on to the end of a chapter that discusses three of Dickens's books in chronological order and then jumps ten years for no apparent reason.

The problem with Mengham's critical approach can be seen most clearly in his discussion of *Oliver Twist.* This begins with a general discussion of hunger in the novel and Oliver's famously asking for more. Mengham notes that Oliver experiences a feeling of revulsion when a dish of sheep's heads is placed in front of him, a revulsion that is all the more surprising because sheep's heads was a not-unusual meal in the nineteenth century. "Why," Mengham asks, "does Dickens fix on sheeps' heads for the meal over which Oliver's appetite hesitates?" It is a good question and arouses an appetite in the reader to know the answer. But answer comes there none. Instead, Mengham goes on to give more examples from the novel of characters, like Monks, like Grimwig, like Nancy, who are constantly engaged in eating parts of their own anatomy. The evidence is laid out and it is intriguing, but it never goes anywhere. Mengham never answers his own question about the sheeps' heads, and he never really goes beyond noticing the instances of self-eating to suggest a reason for them. We jump from a laying out of the evidence for self-ingestion to a discussion of failing to organize experience, with no way of knowing how we got from one topic to the other. In sum, there are good things in this book, but not enough to make it a worthwhile study of Dickens's fiction.

Lillian Nayder, *Unequal Partners: Charles Dickens, Wilkie Collins and Victorian Authorship*

Lillian Nayder's *Unequal Partners: Charles Dickens, Wilkie Collins and Victorian Authorship* chronicles the complex relationship between Dickens and Wilkie Collins as it played out in their collaborative writing. By focusing on the stories and dramas that Dickens and Collins wrote together, Nayder sketches in the philosophical and temperamental differences between the two writers. Her book is full of interesting details about publishing and especially about the unvoiced struggle for literary supremacy between Dickens and Collins.

Dickens was nearly forty years old when he first met Collins in 1851. He was an established author and the editor of *Household Words,* while Collins had only one novel under his belt and was working on the second. Collins was thus clearly Dickens's inferior in terms of age, fame, and accomplishments. While Collins at first accepted his subordinate status, Nayder chronicles how his willingness to do so eventually gave way to resentment. In an informative first chapter, Nayder describes the ups and downs of the friendship between the two men, a friendship in which literary rivalry functioned as a barely submerged leitmotif, especially after Collins's extraordinary success with *The Woman in White.*

While she acknowledges that both writers benefited from their collaborations, Nayder's sympathies are firmly on the side of Collins. As she writes in her introduction, her intention is to ''consider the inequities built into their working relationship at *Household Words* and *All the Year Round,* which both men recognized and that Collins sometimes accepted but increasingly came to resist.'' Another purpose of Nayder's book is to consider the two writers' collaborations within the larger context of Victorian labor disputes and political unrest, to which the stories explicitly and self-consciously respond.

By focusing on the Dickens/Collins collaborations, Nayder performs a valuable service by highlighting works that have generally received very little critical attention. She is also very good at describing and analyzing which sections were written by which author and relating these to the tensions that bubbled just beneath the surface of their apparently harmonious working relationship. These tensions were exacerbated not only by the inherent inequality between the two writers in terms of age, experience, and position, but also by their divergent political and ideological views. Nayder is particularly good at analyzing where the young Collins went along with the philosophy of his older mentor and where he rebelled and set out on his own path. Collins's politics were more radical than Dickens's, and this too accounted for the increasing level of friction between them, so that by the time Dickens died, he and Collins had become, to all intents and purposes, estranged.

Nayder is unmincing in her criticism of Dickens's editorial practices on his journals, singling out his habit of insisting that contributors remain anonymous as particularly egregious. Dickens's own name was, of course, nowhere hidden. The masthead of each issue of *Household Words* proclaimed that the journal was ''Conducted by Charles Dickens.'' The result was that Dickens's journals gave the impression of having, not only one editor, but one writer as well, so that Dickens was often credited with authoring the work of other writers. It is difficult not to sympathize with Collins's anger at the request from Dickens's publishers after the latter's death that Collins identify those parts of ''No Thoroughfare'' which he had written so that they might be eliminated from future editions of Dickens's works.

In a superb first chapter that is hard to put down, Nayder dissects the periodical publishing business of the mid-nineteenth century, and especially Dickens's monetary practices as regards the journals he edited. The section on Dickens's (mis)treatment of women writers is particularly chilling. Nayder amplifies her condemnation of Dickens's editorial practices by arguing that in constructing scenarios for the collaborations, Dickens often used the relationships among the fictional characters to represent and justify his authority

over contributors, whose indebtedness to their editor became the unacknowledged subtext of the stories. To demonstrate this hypothesis, Nayder's subsequent chapters focus on such collaborative efforts as the Christmas story
"The Wreck of the Golden Mary," which was written in response to the
problem of labor unrest among sailors in the British merchant marine, and
the play *The Frozen Deep,* written in response to published reports that
members of the disastrous Franklin expedition had resorted to cannibalism
in order to stay alive. Dickens conceived of *The Frozen Deep* as a refutation
of the charges of cannibalism and a defense of the national honor. However,
Nayder argues, the play's theme of male rivalry also alludes to the antagonism
between the two collaborators, Dickens and Collins. Nayder also uses the
textual history of the writing of *The Frozen Deep* to demonstrate the extent
to which Collins's radicalism was contained by Dickens through his revisions
and excisions of Collins's early drafts.

Another chapter focuses on "The Lazy Tour of Two Idle Apprentices"
and "The Perils of Certain English Prisoners." While the second of these
has long been identified as a response to the Indian Mutiny, Nayder argues
that "The Lazy Tour," which appeared in the same year, is such a response
as well. She also suggests that *The Mystery of Edwin Drood* is Dickens's
attempt to rework Collins's *The Moonstone* along lines that Dickens found
more palatable.

Nayder's discussion of all of these works is consistently illuminating and
intelligent. She is particularly good at teasing out the gender implications in
the two writers' fictions, and relating these to their divergent attitudes towards
class and race. In filtering the collaborative efforts of Dickens and Collins
through the prism of their actual lives and beliefs, Nayder manages to shine
a new light on their relationship as well as on the literary works that complicated that relationship.

David Parker, *The Doughty Street Novels: Pickwick Papers, Oliver Twist,
Nicholas Nickleby, Barnaby Rudge*

Another book that uses the biographical to illuminate the fictional is David
Parker's *The Doughty Street Novels.* Parker has hit on the idea of using the
four novels that Dickens wrote, or mostly wrote, while living at Doughty
Street as the organizing principle behind a book that shines a light on Dickens's early life as a way of understanding his early fiction. As the former
curator of the Dickens House Museum, located in Dickens's former home on
Doughty Street, Parker is in the unique position of being able to apply his
knowledge of Dickens's house and the artifacts in it to his knowledge of the
novels. The Doughty Street residence was the home where Dickens first took
control of his life and settled down, as a householder, a husband, a father,

and a writer, having married Catherine Hogarth just a year before moving there. It is Parker's contention that the three years Dickens spent at Doughty Street—before moving on to still more high-class accommodations at 1 Devonshire Terrace—afforded Dickens the artistic stability and sense of direction he needed to write his first novels, and that both the stability and the sense of direction were related to the domestic happiness that he experienced at Doughty Street. Parker has no doubt that for the first years of their marriage—that is, the years he spent at Doughty Street—Dickens was in love with his wife and was content with his marriage.

This is an enjoyable book. Parker's style is easy to read and informative. The opening two chapters are especially fine. The first of these is full of piquant details about Dickens's garish taste in home decoration and the fact that Dickens seems to have decorated the Doughty Street house mostly by himself, leaving his wife only the option of being "amazed" at the results. This is in keeping with the information that the cash book recording domestic expenditures at Doughty Street is in his hand, not in hers. Parker's second chapter does a fine job of highlighting three traumatic episodes in Dickens's early life that most influenced his fiction. These episodes—the months Dickens spent working at Warren's Blacking Warehouse when he was twelve years old, his courtship of and rejection by Maria Beadnell, the subsequent marriage to Catherine, and the death of Mary Hogarth—have been extensively written about before and will not be new to Dickensians. However, Parker draws on his detailed knowledge of Dickens's life to enhance his retelling, and his account of these events is fresh and consistently interesting. He is especially good at teasing out the class implications behind events, such as the reasons for Dickens's extraordinarily rude behavior to an American woman who committed the social error of calling her husband "darling" in public. His account of what may have gone wrong in Dickens's marriage and his chronicle of the stages by which Dickens came first to mourn, then to idealize, and finally to idolize Mary Hogarth after her death make for excellent reading.

Parker needs to retell the biographical events in Dickens's life because his subsequent chapters, which discuss the novels, draw on these events as a way into the fictions. On the whole, the analysis of the novels is less compelling than the biographical material, although Parker has interesting things to say about each of the novels he discusses. For instance, I was intrigued by his discussion of horsiness and its links to class in *Pickwick Papers,* and Parker is also very good on the prevalence of misogyny in that novel and the way in which this early manifestation of anti-female bias differs from Dickens's subsequent renditions of the same prejudice.

Parker has interesting things to say about *Oliver Twist* and *Nicholas Nickleby* as well, noting that the first of these contains not one instance of an exemplary family, unless one wants to count Fagin and his gang of boys. Given that Dickens was recently married and the father of two young children during the time when he was writing *Oliver Twist,* there is, in Parker's words "a striking lack of correspondence between the events in Dickens's life when he was writing *Oliver Twist* and what is to be found in the novel" (122).

My one serious disagreement with Parker comes in his analysis of *Barnaby Rudge,* a novel which he clearly dislikes, so much so that he falls into the temptation of overstating his case. To say, as Parker does on page 187, that the novel's preoccupation with fathers and sons scarcely amounts to a theme, because the coverage of the topic is too thin, and that therefore *Barnaby Rudge* is a novel without a theme is to assert something that is simply not so. The theme surely is that of rebellion, rebellion in the public sphere of the Gordon riots and in the private sphere of father-son relationships. The novel suggests that there is a connection between these public and private spheres, that the Gordon riots represent the same kind of tensions writ large as do the more private disagreements of fathers and sons. This certainly looks like a theme to me. Parker is also very critical of Dickens's narrative strategy in this novel, and here I believe some of his criticism is justified, although again his obvious dislike of *Barnaby Rudge* skews the discussion away from a balanced assessment. There is much to be said in favor of this novel, and to dismiss it as thematically void and little more than an entertaining yarn is not to do it justice.

But while I may disagree with Parker's negative assessment of *Barnaby Rudge,* I would still wholeheartedly recommend his book as providing a reading of Dickens's early life and early novels that is fresh, insightful and provocative.

Nicolà Barber, *Dickens*

Finally there is Nicolà Barber's study, a colorful, soft-cover, pamphlet-style book, obviously intended for younger readers and containing numerous illustrations on each page. Because each page contains so many illustrations, the text is printed in small letters, which are not easy to read. Nevertheless, Barber manages to get a lot of information on each page. The book is organized thematically, including such topics as "The Writer and his Times," "The World of Charles Dickens," "Dickens's Contemporaries," and "The Writer's Life." The thematic organization means that we are told about the Staplehurst wreck, Ellen Ternan, and Gad's Hill before we read about Dickens's first house, which comes in a later section called "Dickens's London." Barber's book is pleasant to look through and should serve as a good introduction to Dickens for a young reader, although the young reader should not be too young. Judging by the sophistication of the text, I would think that twelve and older might be about right. There is a curious ambiguity on the last page. Barber writes that Dickens "recreated the old Maria [Beadnell] in the character of Flora in *Little Dorrit.*" It is unclear if "the old Maria" is meant to indicate the Maria of old, that is, the younger Maria, or if Barber intended the "old" to refer to the Maria of twenty years later, who would only have been in her mid-forties at the time.

Chapters or Sections in Books

John Peck, *Maritime Fiction: Sailors and the Sea in British and American Novels*

The chapter devoted to Dickens in John Peck's *Maritime Fiction: Sailors and the Sea in British and American Novels* is well worth reading, especially the section on *Dombey and Son.* Peck discusses *Dombey* and *David Copperfield* as the two Dickens novels that deal most extensively with the sea and with seafaring, noting that there are fewer maritime themes in subsequent novels. Peck interestingly interprets the concentration on the sea in these two novels as indicative of "a particular moment during the middle of the century when Dickens was trying to make sense of Britain in a way that needed to acknowledge the maritime identity of the country" (73).

Peck begins his chapter by establishing Dickens's personal ties to the sea, including the fact that both his father and his maternal grandfather worked as clerks in the Navy Pay Office. The Dickens family's economic dependence on the navy was an accurate reflection of the importance of maritime activity to large sections of the population of early nineteenth-century Britain. Peck notes that Dickens was writing during the period when steamships were being introduced and there was no longer any real challenge to Britain's maritime domination of the world, a fact which permitted the expansion of British trade. Dickens's novels therefore reflect the psychology of a trading nation rather than that of a fighting one.

The best example of this is *Dombey and Son,* which is not, Peck notes, just a novel about the sea, but a novel that complicates its vision of maritime economic activity by describing the advent of the railroad. In Peck's analysis *Dombey and Son* is an accurate reflection of the historical moment when reliance on maritime trade gave way to greater reliance on the transportation of goods by rail. The sea in this novel thus represents a kind of security, as when Walter Gay comforts the girl Florence, who has been wandering lost and forlorn through the streets of London by telling her that she is as safe in his company as if she were guarded by a whole boat's crew from a man-of-war (75). The navy has everything under control, a control that is underlined by the novel's extensive focus on measuring instruments, especially in the description of Solomon Gill's shop. Peck nicely notes that part of the appeal of *Dombey and Son* is that it never forces its perception of the navy and of maritime matters on the reader, thereby "reflecting the way in which maritime concerns might be almost invisible but permeate every aspect of the nation's life" (75). Peck is also alive to the mystical aspects of the sea that the novel presents, for example in little Paul's unanswerable question about what the waves are always saying.

At the heart of Peck's discussion of *Dombey* lies what he calls a recurrent theme of Victorian literature, namely, that everything is changing and that all traditional points of reference have disappeared. "The capitalist system has a logic of its own which seems to bear no relation to the maritime activity that has brought the capitalist system into being" (77). It is no longer the sailor but the entrepreneur who occupies center stage, and even this is changing as the enterprising individual trader at the head of a family firm, like Mr. Dombey, gives way to joint stock companies. Peck sees this change as embodied in the railway, since railways required a level of investment that prevented them from being run as individual family businesses. The railway is the new form of transport, which, as the century progresses, will replace shipping as the backbone of trade. The fortunes of the House of Dombey have been built on water, both literally and figuratively. Future fortunes will depend on rail.

Peck's reading of *Dombey and Son* in terms of British economic history at the middle of the century is fascinating. His reading of *David Copperfield* is less suggestive, but again the maritime focus yields some rewarding insights, not least that this novel describes the time when the sea goes from being a place where men fight and work to being, by mid-Victorian times, a place where rich men like Steerforth play.

Peck finishes his discussion of Dickens and the sea with a quick glance at Dickens's reaction to the news of possible cannibalism among the members of the Franklin expedition. Peck argues that the anxieties which Dickens was prepared to confront in his novels were the same anxieties that he tried to deny in everyday life. He labels as racist Dickens's outraged refusal to believe that the members of Franklin's expedition might have sought to prolong their lives through eating the bodies of their dead comrades: "[Dickens's] stance is, obviously, very simple: all problems are eliminated when one denies the possibility that an Englishman might resort to cannibalism. It is as if Dickens, in the end, refuses to believe the more alarming things that he is prepared to imply in a work of fiction" (88). Unfortunately, Peck does not expand on this perception, so that the section on Dickens and Franklin seems tacked on like an afterthought to the end of the chapter on Dickens, serving merely as a transition to the following chapter on American sea fiction. This is too bad, because Peck always has intriguing things to say, and especially in the section on *Dombey and Son* gives a good idea of how rewarding a narrowly focused thematic approach to Dickens's fiction can be.

Cathy Shuman, *Pedagogical Economies: The Examination and the Victorian Literary Man*

Cathy Shuman's *Pedagogical Economies: The Examination and the Victorian Literary Man* begins with an interesting chapter on the new importance of examinations in the mid-Victorian era. Shuman argues that educational testing endows knowledge with exchange value in the form of a grade. And it is by focusing on this exchange value that her book analyzes the "economy" of learning. While examinations of one sort or another have been around forever, and have their origins in religious beliefs and ritual (the Judeo-Christian notion of Judgment Day, for instance), Shuman claims that it is the Victorians who first gave a central role to testing as "an ordeal of questions and answers about acquired knowledge or skills, sanctioned by an institutional framework and resulting in some kind of assessment" (5). In this way, the Victorians endowed cultural capital with exchange value. Furthermore, the mid-Victorian culture of testing established what Shuman calls "the flexible and powerful idea" of an unspecific "ability" or "talent," originally associated with aristocratic privilege, which became known as "intelligence." Examinations thus contested earlier assumptions that linked abilities to social status and income. In this way, they reconfigured class distinctions, and, in the process, as Shuman argues, enforced distinctions between different kinds of labor.

Interestingly, *Hard Times* is not, as one might expect, the Dickens novel that Shuman uses to prove her case. Rather, it is *Our Mutual Friend.* Unfortunately, Shuman's discussion of this novel is less rewarding than her introductory chapter leads one to expect, largely because the writing is in spots dense and unclear, and she has a tendency to push her analogies further than seems profitable, for instance when she compares Gaffer's catching and assessing his prey with John Harmon's catching and assessing the Harmon fortune and with the reader catching and assessing both of them while reading. Nevertheless Shuman does make one rethink this novel in terms of its pedagogical economies. She argues that in *Our Mutual Friend,* figurative examinations feature "a feminine student who evaluates and places the masculine intellectual worker by producing and containing a reified knowledge immune from the risks of exchange" (123).

Shuman begins by discussing *Our Mutual Friend* in terms of its categories of work, with a particular emphasis on the novel's scavengers—Gaffer Hexam, Mr. Venus, and Jenny Wren. She argues that the novel demonstrates "the failure of categorizations based on class, mode of production, and the division between the economic and the extraeconomic to classify the laborer'' (125). For instance, if Gaffer is not stealing but working when he scavenges the bodies of those drowned in the Thames, then his labor as a scavenger can be translated into normative categories.

The main focus of Shuman's discussion, however, is on the sexual dynamics involved in the testing relationships of Bella Wilfer and John Harmon, on the one hand, and Lizzie Hexam, Eugene Wrayburn, and Bradley Headstone, on the other. Shuman is especially good at analyzing Bradley Headstone and his ''mechanical'' knowledge. She singles out the scene in which Rogue Riderhood visits Headstone's schoolroom as an example of an examination which translates knowledge into money even more directly than the payment-by-results inspections. Payment-by-results inspections refers to the fact that schoolmasters were paid a specific amount for each student's passing grade. This meant that the masters' jobs depended on their students' correct answers on exams. It is thus not difficult to appreciate the tensions that school inspections must have produced for both teachers and students. Shuman argues that in parodying this style of examination, Dickens suggests that Rogue Riderhood is threatening Headstone's literal as well as his scholastic bank account (156).

Shuman's analysis is occasionally confusing, and her prose style tends to be leaden, but despite these flaws her discussion is often provocative and illuminating, casting a new light on some of the crucial scenes in *Our Mutual Friend.*

Jeremy Tambling, *Lost in the American City: Dickens, James, Kafka*

Jeremy Tambling devotes about half of *Lost in the American City: Dickens, James, Kafka* to Dickens's *American Notes* and *Martin Chuzzlewit,* arguing that subsequent depictions of American cities in the novels of Henry James and Franz Kafka owe a debt to Dickens. Tambling suggests that prisons, and in particular the panoptical structure of the Philadelphia prison, became for Dickens a trope which ''draws towards itself much of the American experience.'' According to Tambling, the fact that Dickens was a British novelist meant that he suffered from an inability to read certain specific aspects of American life, for instance its feminism, its city culture, and the way in which both of these related to the ''color line.''

Tambling maintains that, in negatively describing America, Dickens was really recording the failure of the writer to describe it. In *American Notes,* Tambling writes, Dickens does not take the American city seriously, but he does take seriously American institutions. Drawing a link between *Bleak House,* the novel Dickens wrote some ten years after his visit to America, and *American Notes,* Tambling suggests that Dickens describes London in the later novel in the same decentering terms that he used to describe Cairo in *American Notes,* thereby aligning *Bleak House* with "the language generated by the sense of America" (19). Thus the London of *Bleak House* relapses into the primeval mud and fog that Dickens first noted in his description of Cairo.

Tambling's most interesting chapter—and also the best written—is his fourth, where he discusses the limitations of English ideology in encountering or responding to the American other. Specifically, Tambling accuses Dickens of not being attuned enough to gender issues in his view of America and of not understanding how the women's movement of the nineteenth century was linked to the abolitionist movement. "The text," Tambling writes, "cannot think of an alternative [to slavery]; while mocking slavery its antagonism to women will not allow for a sustained critique that thinks through the implications of both types of oppression and relates them to each other" (82).

Tambling's chapters include an analysis of *American Notes,* a discussion of Dickens's treatment of architecture in *Martin Chuzzlewit,* and then a chapter comparing Dickens's understanding of America to that of Thackeray and Trollope. In the second part of his book, Tambling goes on to analyze the way in which Henry James treats *American Notes* as a tutor text for his own work, *The American Scene* (1907). Tambling's book ends with a discussion of Kafka's posthumous novel about America, published as *Amerika,* but here renamed as *The Man Who Never Was Heard of Again.* Tambling argues that in this novel Kafka is engaged in a dialogue with Dickens's *David Copperfield,* especially with *Copperfield's* first chapter.

While Tambling has much to say that is of interest, this book is difficult to read and the argument often hard to follow. The discussion jumps from the work of one writer to that of another without discernible connection or chronological coherence. The second chapter, which is supposed to be devoted to a discussion of *American Notes*, wanders off into apparently unrelated discussions of Poe and Melville, although Tambling does try to bring Dickens back into the picture by suggesting that "perhaps" Melville read *American Notes* and this inspired him to end the life of Bartleby the Scrivener within the walls of the Tombs. Well, perhaps yes and perhaps no, but the relevance of Melville to Dickens at this point in the chapter is too ephemeral to be of much value. In fact, the chapter on *American Notes,* while starting off strongly, quickly degenerates into vagueness. And Tambling is rather too fond of that "perhaps," which suggests conjecture rather than fact.

Another problem lies with Tambling's convoluted prose style. For instance: "In reading America in the early years of the twentieth century, feminist matters, for which the British writers had shown a certain incapacity, enlarge into gender-questions" (xv). And I challenge anyone to make sense of the following: "The fate of being an American meeting Dickens is to be a postcolonial subject meeting someone from the center of English culture, and hence to provide another in the *Sketches by Boz;* and if you have read it, to know exactly how Dickens will do it, how much comic obsessionalism is its metier'' (26). Or, ''Architecture confirms the subject-position of the 'criminal' whose position is reified in that he is not able to act any part relative to the crowd in a public hanging'' (37). Or, ''Dickens on architecture draws on buildings autobiographically associated'' (50). There are, unfortunately, far too many sentences like this in Tambling's book, and they tend to obscure many of his most interesting observations. Furthermore, some of Tambling's connections seem questionable. For instance, he tries to get some analytical mileage out of the fact that Dickens describes the prisoners' faces in *American Notes* as haggard, a word that is also used to describe the gas lighting in *Bleak House.* Yes. So?

In particular, the chapter devoted to *American Notes* is a disappointment, partly because some of the worst writing occurs there and partly because it is superficial in its analysis of the later sections of the *Notes.* The following chapter, which contains an analysis of *Martin Chuzzlewit,* is similarly hard to follow and does not seem to have any strong connection to the theme of the book, which the title suggests is the American city. I do not mean to suggest that what Tambling says here is not of interest. Some of the sections, such as the one on nineteenth-century American feminism, are excellent. But the best sections in this book are undermined by its poor organization, its convoluted writing style, and a tendency on Tambling's part to show off what he knows rather than to integrate it into a coherent argument.

Jane Wood, *Passion and Pathology in Victorian Fiction*

The chapter devoted to Dickens in Jane Wood's *Passion and Pathology in Victorian Fiction* contains an excellent analysis of *Little Dorrit's* Mrs. Clennam, an analysis that profits greatly from Wood's overall focus in her book on the links between Victorian medicine and literature.

Beginning with the premise that scientific explanations of human experience rose to new prominence in the nineteenth century, with ''medicine and literature looking at each other for elucidation and illustration'' (1), Wood's study aims to examine the ambivalences and points of contention that arose out of the exchange of ideas between the medical world and the literary. The branch of medicine that is of most concern to her is neurology, which posits a physical mechanism for explaining psychological states. Wood's book examines the work of the major British authors of the nineteenth century. The chapter on Dickens is called ''From passion to paralysis: hysterical pathology and Dickens's women.''

Wood focuses her discussion primarily on Mrs. Clennam, while glancing briefly at Miss Havisham of *Great Expectations,* noting that both of these characters represent "the negative images of embittered resentful women who punish their own bodies into warped and wasted figures of hatred and jealousy" (44). Of Mrs. Clennam, Wood notes that we are given very little sense with this character of an inner experience of suffering, and she suggests intriguingly that it is the revelation of suffering, as opposed to its quiet endurance, that is the focus of Dickens's disapproval.

At the same time as she makes a show of her suffering, Mrs. Clennam is clearly the possessor of a strong will, and it is here that her condition intersects with medical opinion of the time. According to Wood, doctors attempting to interpret the inappropriate social behavior of women located the problem in the "troublesome" question of female will. Since it was a cultural given that women by nature did not initiate but rather reacted, doctors were puzzled when confronted with manifestations of female will that were not reactive. At the same time, the belief in the supposed weakness of women's will coexisted throughout the century with the suspicion that some women had too strong a will. Medical writing of the time often linked a strong will in women to moral transgression. Strong-willed and assertive women under-mined the preferred image of passive Victorian womanhood.

Wood notes that in *Little Dorrit,* the matter of Mrs. Clennam's will is repeatedly addressed as those around her try to make sense of her impressive resolve. Mrs. Clennam's fault, Wood suggests, is not so much that she cuts herself off from the world as that she tries to make the world conform to her own needs by running the affairs of Clennam and Co. from her sickroom. At the same time, Mrs. Clennam sins against the ideal of womanhood by persis-tently demonstrating in the physical weakness of her body the toll that a lifelong devotion to doing one's duty can exact. Since a life of dedication to the moral and spiritual welfare of others was supposed to be woman's special privilege and not a hardship, Mrs. Clennam's invalidism is a further insult to the ideology of the time. Wood argues that Dickens's portrayal of Mrs. Clen-nam's hysterical paralysis as an inability to let go of the past (a portrayal he would repeat with Miss Havisham) was in keeping with nineteenth-century medical views on hysteria, which suggested that dwelling on past emotions was a prime cause of psychosomatic disease. Thus the views of the fiction writer and the physician on the pathological consequences of female memory were mutually confirming. Wood's analysis of Mrs. Clennam is full of rich insights about Victorian medical thinking, and is all the more illuminating because it focuses on a character who has not received as much attention from critics as she deserves.

Collections of Essays

Suzy Anger, Ed., *Knowing the Past: Victorian Literature and Culture.*

As the title implies, Suzy Anger's collection of essays addresses the question of the extent to which we can know the past, and her book of collected essays is designed to present a series of alternative responses to questions of how the Victorians represented themselves in their writings. Two of the essays in Anger's collection deal with Dickens.

The first of these is "How to Be a Benefactor without Any Money: The Chill of Welfare in *Great Expectations,*" by Bruce Robbins. Robbins's approach is heavily theoretical, taking issue with Michel Foucault's view of history and invoking the work of Hegel, Nietzsche, and Moretti to underpin his analysis of *Great Expectations* as "the classic narrative of chastened, self-critical upward mobility" (175). Because of this theoretical focus and Robbins's care in spelling out the philosophical premises of his analysis, it takes a long time before we get to a discussion of Dickens's novel, and by the time we do get there much of the force of the argument has been side-tracked by asides to the various theorists, so that the actual analysis of Dickens's novel reads a little like a by-the-by. What is more, the discussion of *Great Expectations* occurs within a frame of reference that, somewhat anachronistically, includes the film *Silence of the Lambs.*

Robbins has some interesting things to say about *Great Expectations,* for instance, about the distinctions between mentor/ master relationships in the novel, and how in this novel the master is superseded by the mentor. Robbins argues that Pip's relations with his two benefactors—Magwitch and Miss Havisham—are eroticized by Dickens, especially the homosocial bond with Magwitch. However, it is not clear to me where Robbins sees the eroticism of Miss Havisham's role as a benefactor, except in the off-hand and overly hypothetical speculation that if *Great Expectations* had been a French novel Miss Havisham would have been younger and Pip might have had an affair with her (181).

More to the point, Robbins suggests that the theme of social mobility in the novel is not located in the protagonist, but rather in his mentor and benefactor. Robbins then goes on to discuss Magwitch and his relationship to the circulation of money in the novel, suggesting that upward mobility is here founded on Pip's rescuing Magwitch a second time from the hands of the law. By doing this, Robbins writes, Pip is acting like a democratic state at its best, "self-consciously recognizing himself in and tending to another orphan, generalizing the individualized uplift of the upward mobility story into a rescue of all by all'' (190). It is an interesting idea, as is Robbins's attempt to ''salvage the upward mobility story . . . a story there are many reasons not to love.'' However, I do find problematic Robbins's contention that, ''though the genre [of upward mobility stories] favours the individual at the expense of the social, it is actually about democracy . . . and about making democracy real to imperfect, desiring individuals'' (191). Somehow, the idea of Pip's acting like a democratic state evokes absolutely no image in my mind, and while salvaging the upward mobility story from its current loveless state is probably an honorable thing to do, I do not really understand what makes it democratic, nor what notions of democracy have to do with *Great Expectations.*

The only other essay in Anger's collection to deal with Dickens is Rosemarie Bodenheimer's ''Knowing and Telling in Dickens's Retrospects.'' This essay takes as its subject retrospective narrative, which, ''selects its past and suffuses it with the language and consciousness of the present,'' so that, as Bodenheimer states, ''both inside and outside the original text . . . someone is claiming to know more about a past than that past knows about itself'' (215).

Bodenheimer begins her discussion with the assertion that of all the canonical Victorian novelists, Dickens has always been the easiest to condescend to in the matter of knowledge, because his kind of knowledge is ''wrapped up in metaphor'' and very rarely abstracted or theorized (215). By revisiting the retrospective narratives which Dickens wrote during the years 1848–1850—the autobiographical fragment, *David Copperfield* and ''The Haunted Man''—she hopes to show what Dickens ''knew'' by arguing that his narratives dramatize ''the constructedness of bourgeois subjectivity.'' They thereby demonstrate a deep awareness of the instability of class identification.

Dickens first began to write about his childhood experiences at Warren's Blacking Factory during the years 1848 to 1850, some twenty-four years after the event. The revelation of an event suppressed since childhood makes for a tension between past and present in the sense, as Bodenheimer aptly puts it, that the child's own knowledge and feeling is both concealed and overwhelmed by the outrage of the adult narrator (218). Bodenheimer identifies issues of secrecy, revelation, and control as central to Dickens's construction of his former self. For instance, in the episode where Dickens remembers complaining to his father about being lodged at too great a distance from his family, the father immediately provided the child with a lodging much nearer the Marshalsea, an act of parental kindness that undermines the fragment's presentation of Dickens's childhood self as abandoned and neglected.

Turning to fiction, Bodenheimer finds the same autobiographical issues arising in ''The Haunted Man,'' which Dickens wrote at the same time as he wrote the fragment. Bodenheimer sees this fable of a man haunted by his own past, but incapable of recounting that past, as suggesting that autobiography may play the role of exorcism. The act of retelling the past is left to Redlaw's Phantom, who is also his exact replica. But this same Phantom who retells Redlaw's past also offers to rid him of it, thus turning the story into a conflict about whether it is best to confront or to forget the past. Bodenheimer suggests that the story may be read as an allegory of autobiographical anxiety, as an allegory of the "uncontrollable damage [that] might result from 'giving away' ineradicable memories" (221).

Turning to *David Copperfield,* Bodenheimer takes issue with the current critical consensus that the novel celebrates its hero's gradual achievement of a middle-class identity through the bourgeois virtues of hard work and self-discipline, rewarded by success in the domestic sphere. Bodenheimer argues that such an interpretation is only plausible if the novel is read backwards from its ending. Instead, she argues that David's progress is really a perpetual recycling, that every new occurrence calls forth a character who in some way recalls or repeats the past, thus making the past always present. In this way, too, memory begins to act like prediction. Through the proliferation of cyclical repetitions, Bodenheimer sees *David Copperfield* as posing the question of how to compose a narrative relation between past and present. Rather than being about repression, *David Copperfield,* she argues, is about the impossibility of repression, since it views the past and the knowledge that the past contains as constantly recurring.

This is a excellent essay. Bodenheimer is not the first critic who has tried to account for the double perspective of past and present in *David Copperfield,* but her insights are invariably fresh and she gives several suggestive readings of key aspects of the novel. She also writes beautifully and her analysis is a pleasure to read. The thread of argument is never obscure, and while Bodenheimer takes into account, and sometimes takes issue with recent scholarship on *David Copperfield,* she wears her erudition lightly and her essay never gives the impression of being weighed down by its secondary sources.

John O. Jordan, Ed., *The Cambridge Companion to Charles Dickens*

This fine collection of fourteen essays is divided into three sections. The first section deals with Dickens's novels in chronological order. This is followed by a cluster of five essays focusing on such Dickensian themes as childhood, the city, and Dickens's use of language. The final section consists of three essays that explore Dickens's relationship to the other arts, specifically illustration, theater, and film.

On the whole, the essays in the second and third sections are more satisfying than the ones in the first chronological grouping, possibly because when the novels are discussed chronologically they do not always lend themselves to easy comparison. This difficulty is apparently sensed by some of the writers of these essays, who omit novels that do not fit with what they want to say, as Robert Patten does with *Oliver Twist* in his essay on Dickens's early novels. In her article on the "middle novels" Kate Flint must deal with *Martin Chuzzlewit, Dombey and Son,* and *David Copperfield,* all in one short section of fifteen pages. Any one of these three novels could easily be the focus of a single essay. In addition, the book's structure gives rise to certain anomalies: *Bleak House* rates an essay all to itself, but *Barnaby Rudge* is barely mentioned, not even in the chronological section, which also skips *The Old Curiosity Shop.*

In his preface, editor John Jordan writes that Dickens is unusual among canonical English-language authors in being both a vital focus of academic research and a major figure in popular culture. The essays in this collection seek to straddle the two communities of Dickens lovers, and largely succeed, although my sense is that the volume as a whole seems aimed more at university students and specialists than at casual readers seeking an introduction to Dickens and his work.

Grahame Smith's introductory essay on "The Life and Times of Charles Dickens" does a fine job of filtering Dickens's biography through a history of theoretical approaches to the lives of writers. These range from prototypical studies which sought to identify the "real" human beings behind the fictional characters through to the new criticism which relegated the author to second place, or to no place. Smith notes with relief that after years of being ignored by literary studies, "the author is struggling back into life" (2). Using this as his starting point, he goes on to give some of the details of Dickens's life, foregrounding especially his thematic concern with incarceration, a theme that grows out of Dickens's childhood experiences in Warren's Blacking Factory. None of this material will be new to Dickens scholars, but Smith writes engagingly and this opening essay serves as a good introduction to the essays that follow.

The first five of those essays comprehend most of Dickens's novelistic output, with the exceptions, as noted above, of *The Old Curiosity Shop, Barnaby Rudge,* and *The Mystery of Edwin Drood.* (While some of the thematic essays do discuss the first and the last of these, *Barnaby Rudge* gets no sustained discussion anywhere in this collection.) There is a diversity of approaches in these five essays which addresses the collection's double mandate of appealing to both specialist and non-specialist readers. Robert Patten's "From Sketches to Nickleby" is more of an overview than an analysis of the works that he discusses, but it is no less valuable for that. Focusing his discussion on biographical facts, Patten outlines the story behind the stories of Dickens's early writings, suggesting that the young Dickens had contradictory responses to his own literary career, and that these contributed to his use of more than one pseudonym. For instance, Patten notes that, at a time when he was desperately poor, Dickens was submitting his stories to the *Monthly Magazine,* which did not pay contributors and published their pieces anonymously. The reason for this, Patten suggests, was that Dickens's stories in the magazine received complimentary notices, while his paid journalism, although it earned money, was never reviewed anywhere. Patten also chronicles the vagaries of Dickens's dealings with publishers and his shedding all pseudonyms to emerge as the author of *Oliver Twist* under his own name when Bentley brought out the three-volume edition of *Oliver Twist* in 1838. Patten's essay is useful for the light it sheds on some of Dickens's early works, such as *Sketches by Boz* and *Pickwick Papers.* While he credits scholars such as Edmund Wilson with rescuing Dickens's early works from opprobrium and dismissal, Patten suggests that the credit for this renewal of interest really belongs to theater and film. He singles out David Lean's 1948 movie of *Oliver Twist* and the Royal Shakespeare Company's nine-hour presentation of *Nicholas Nickleby* in 1980 as particularly effective in reawakening interest in Dickens's early fictions.

Kate Flint's essay on the middle novels skips *The Old Curiosity Shop* and *Barnaby Rudge* to begin with *Martin Chuzzlewit.* Flint argues that there is ''a conspicuous restlessness'' about the novels which Dickens wrote in the 1840s. In them, travelers voyage from England to the Continent, as well as to the U.S., Australia, and India. With these novels, Flint argues, Dickens's fiction begins to explore in sustained fashion the dialogue between consciousness and the world, and between consciousness and the unconscious. In this sense the travel that figures so prominently in these novels becomes a metaphor for individual growth.

The frequent voyaging mirrors the actual travels in Dickens's own life. He visited America and Canada in 1842, and in 1844 he moved his household through France to Italy. The result was that a trip to America plays a central part in *Martin Chuzzlewit,* while European travel figures in the predominantly English settings of *Dombey and Son* and *David Copperfield.* ''Travel,'' writes Flint, ''was for Dickens both flight and quest; in both cases, internal and external restlessness fuse'' (35).

Flint also suggests that all three of the novels possess a contradictory dynamic: a pull towards domestic contentment on the one hand, and on the other, ''a powerful imaginative involvement with the abuse, the manipulation, and the cruelty that homes can contain'' (40). For instance, Flint finds disconcerting Dickens's use of hyperbole in *Martin Chuzzlewit,* since it serves as both a means of attack and of sentimental endorsement (especially in the Tom and Ruth Pinch sections). She also notes that Dickens's praise for harmonious home life is counterpointed by his lively interest in strong angry women, such as Edith Dombey or Rosa Dartle. By focusing on the theme of restless-ness, Flint manages to unify her discussion of these three large novels with-out strain.

J. Hillis Miller's "Moments of Decision in *Bleak House*" concentrates solely on that novel. In this essay, Miller revisits his influential introduction to the 1971 Penguin edition of the novel, in which he looked at the text as a document about the interpretation of documents. After enumerating some of the other critical approaches to *Bleak House* that have since influenced his thinking, Miller returns to reassess his own earlier essay, suggesting that he had missed something in his earlier approach, namely, that *Bleak House* is punctuated by moments of decision that form turning points in the action. Two such moments precede the action of the novel. The first concerns Lady Dedlock's acquiescence to the love affair with Captain Hawdon, the result of which is the birth of their illegitimate daughter Esther. The other moment of decision occurred when the will or wills were signed by the first Jarndyce, thereby initiating the interminable case of Jarndyce vs Jarndyce. These two preceding actions, which Miller calls "moment of decision registered as speech acts" (51) give rise to the two strands of the novel's plot, each with its own narrator. Miller suggests that the text of *Bleak House* itself is a speech act, because Dickens hoped that the novel would be a way of doing something good with written words, that it would persuade readers to detest Chancery enough either to reform or to abolish it.

Miller's essay is followed by Hilary Schor's assessment of the novels of the 1850s: *Hard Times, Little Dorrit,* and *A Tale of Two Cities.* Schor delin-eates two opposing strands of critical thought about these novels. The first strand claims that the novels of the 1850s prove that Dickens was becoming ever more conservative and reactionary in his outlook on social problems. The second strand, represented by George Bernard Shaw and T. A. Jackson, argued that in these novels Dickens proved himself to be a socialist (Shaw) or a Marxist (Jackson). Schor unifies her discussion by suggesting that all three novels address the same social and political concerns—poverty, class conflict, and family disruption. And she has much to say that is of interest about all three of these themes and how they are played out in each of the novels she writes about.

Her essay is followed by Brian Cheadle's on Dickens's last completed works, *Great Expectations* and *Our Mutual Friend.* This is a first-rate analy-sis, which is especially strong on the repressions of sexuality in both of these late novels. Cheadle begins with a few biographical statements. He suggests that Dickens in the 1860s was a disappointed man, with a failed marriage, a domestic life in tatters, and an illicit relationship with a young actress that he was obliged to keep secret. After a brief summary of various critical approaches to *Great Expectations,* Cheadle suggests that his own analysis will be neo-Marxist or new historicist, aimed not so much at interpreting the novel's intentions as at suggesting how its ideas and assumptions are politically conditioned (79–80).

One of the several strengths of Cheadle's essay is the attention he pays to the sexual undertones in *Great Expectations,* especially in his discussion of Molly, the murderess whom Jaggers forces into domesticity in what Cheadle terms "a weird parody of the angel in the house" (84). Cheadle is very good at teasing out the sado-masochistic implications behind Jaggers's "disciplining" and "binding" of Molly to his household, as well as in his display of her to his guests.

Turning to *Our Mutual Friend,* Cheadle writes that this novel foregrounds the city as the primary locus of modern existence and foregrounds work as the city's dominant condition and imperative, in contrast to *Great Expectations,* which had suppressed work by distancing Pip's rise in wealth and status from the source of his funds. Cheadle relates the Lizzie-Eugene strand of the plot to Dickens's own real-life involvement with Ellen Ternan, suggesting that the liaison with Ellen made Dickens "acutely aware of the realities of a serious involvement with a person as low on the social scale as Lizzie, and of how easy it was to become socially trapped" (88).

Cheadle sees both *Great Expectations* and *Our Mutual Friend* as qualifying Dickens's earlier belief in innate goodness, and suggests that in these two novels, written towards the end of his career, Dickens was echoing the sentiment expressed by the ambiguous Mr. Jaggers in *Great Expectations,* namely, that there is an uncompromising evil in life. This sentiment undermines the moral sentimentality that had played such a large role in Dickens's earlier novels.

Cheadle's essay is the last in the series that deals with the novels chronologically. These now give way to essays on significant Dickensian themes, beginning with Robert Newsom's comprehensive and provocative study of the fictions of childhood. Some of this ground has been covered before, as when Newsom notes the number of bad parents in the novels, especially bad mothers, and in his suggestion that Dickens's children are not merely the victims of neglect, they are also the victims of abuse and potentially of sexual abuse, Little Nell being a case in point. But Newsom also ventures into less fully explored territory. Dickens's new conception of the child went along with a new conception of the grownup, he writes, adding that "Dickens stands the Romantic child on its head by making so many of his children precociously responsible and acute" (96). Newsom is particularly interesting on the influence of *Jane Eyre* on Dickens's conception of *David Copperfield,* since Brontë's novel pioneered the idea of the memory of childhood living on in the adult.

Newsom's essay is followed by Murray Baumgarten's on "Fictions of the City," which chronicles the changes in London during Dickens's lifetime and suggests that until the publication of *Sketches by Boz,* London had rarely figured prominently in fiction (107). Catherine Waters's essay on gender, family, and ideology contains a particularly strong reading of both Little Nell and Lady Dedlock, while Nicola Bradbury, writing on forms of the novel, has some interesting things to say about the prevalence of adultery as a plot device in Dickens's fiction. Garrett Stewart's essay on Dickens and language sometimes gets too technical to be truly enjoyable, a problem which seems to be endemic to all essays that attempt to elucidate the magic behind Dickens's prose. Take, for instance, Stewart's explication of the last paragraph of *Great Expectations:* "The passage has immediately moved, that is, to activate its inversion of subject/object relations across the delayed logic of its transitive grammar, laying further stress on the continuing subjectivity of desire's double negation" (150). This is breaking a butterfly on a wheel. As the author of one of the most accessible, inventive, and lucid prose styles in the English language, Dickens deserves an analysis of his style that is at least as clear as what he himself wrote.

The last group of essays in this collection looks at Dickens in relation to the other arts, beginning with Richard Stein's "Dickens and Illustration." Stein's essay focuses primarily on the illustrations to *Bleak House,* a number of which are reproduced here. John Glavin takes up the subject of Dickens and theatre, provocatively arguing that, contrary to common belief, Dickens would have been a failure had he followed his original impulse of pursuing a life in the theatre. Glavin asserts that Dickens both loathed and longed for the playhouse, and that he transmuted that longing into a fictional style that is essentially theatrical. Joss Marsh rounds out the collection of essays with an interesting study of Dickens and film. Asserting that more films have been made of Dickens's works than those of any other writer, Marsh's essay chronicles the history of Dickens's fictions on film, and in the process gives a thumbnail history of British cinema. The main focus of her discussion is David Lean's 1940s adaptations of *Great Expectations* and *Oliver Twist.* Her description of the directorial decisions which led to Lean's *Oliver Twist* being the most anti-Semitic of all the filmed versions of this novel is fascinating, as is her analysis of the way in which subsequent cinematic renderings tried to fix the damage by sanitizing Fagin, which has often meant de-Judaizing him. It is too bad that Marsh's essay is as short as it is, conforming as it does to the fifteen-page limit of all the essays in this volume. This does not really leave her enough space to do justice to her topic. I would happily have read more about Dickens and cinema.

The selected bibliography at the end of the Cambridge Companion is helpfully divided into categories such as "biography," "reference material," "critical studies," and "general," and is as up-to-date as possible. It should prove very useful to anyone wanting to pursue further study on Dickens.

Stanley Friedman, Edward Guiliano, Michael Timko, Eds. *Dickens Studies Annual: Essays on Victorian Fiction.* Vol. 30 (2001)

The 2001 edition of *Dickens Studies Annual* contains eighteen essays. Of these, fifteen are devoted to Dickens's work, including Michael Lund's review essay of Recent Dickens Studies for 1999. The essays are arranged chronologically beginning with the only essay published in 2001 that deals specifically with *Sketches by Boz,* Amanpal Garcha's ''Styles of Stillness and Motion: Market Culture and Narrative form in *Sketches by Boz.''* Garcha's essay establishes a dichotomy by dividing his discussion between the two kinds of writings that make up the *Sketches,* the imaginative Tales and the journalistic Sketches. Garcha argues that Dickens's switch from writing his early short stories to writing the sketches—that is, from writing narrative to writing non-narrative—corresponded to a change in Dickens's focus from the suburbs to the city and from the comfortable middle class to the struggling lower class.

Garcha suggests that Dickens's sketches, while giving the illusion of being very busy, actually lack a sense of meaningful progression. They create a picture out of life by stopping it, and this stasis is enhanced by the fact that the sketches' dominant mode is description, a description of a specific moment in time and place. The main thrust of Garcha's essay is to rebut J. Hillis Miller's contention in ''The Fiction of Realism'' that Dickens's literary career marks a progression from the sketches to the tales to the novels. Not so, Garcha argues. It is in fact the other way around—the journalistic sketches, not the fictional tales lead directly to the novels. Garcha supports this contention by noting that the tales were published before the sketches. What Dickens needed in order to get to the point where he could write his novels was a rest from the constant change required by narrativity. The static nature of the sketches, their timeless quality, and their emphasis on description, as well as their altered focus on the city and the lower middle classes and away from the suburban and middle-class orientation of the tales, permitted the young Dickens to undergo an apprenticeship that, Garcha argues, served him well in his later fiction. Given that *Sketches by Boz* tends not to receive as much critical attention as most of Dickens's other work, this essay is welcome, not only as a timely reminder of the seminal relationship that the early work has to the later, but also as a way of rethinking the connections between sketch and narrative, between journalism and fiction.

If *The Cambridge Companion to Charles Dickens* omits *Barnaby Rudge,* that omission is more than made up for by the 2001 edition of *Dickens Studies Annual,* which takes up the slack with a cluster of five essays devoted to this most maligned and problematic of Dickens's novels. The cluster begins with Robert Tracy's wonderful ''Clock Work: *The Old Curiosity Shop* and *Barnaby Rudge.''* In this essay, Tracy discusses the framing narrative of *Master*

Humphrey's Clock, in which the two novels originally appeared. *Master Humphrey's Clock* has received scant literary analysis, largely because Dickens abandoned it after writing *Barnaby Rudge,* and later published both *The Old Curiosity Shop* and *Barnaby Rudge* without it. Thus, Tracy's essay is not only informative, but also breaks new ground with his contention that elements from *Master Humphrey's Clock* played an important role in shaping both *The Old Curiosity Shop* and *Barnaby Rudge.* Tracy's essay includes sustained analysis of the metafictional content of *Master Humphrey's Clock* and considers how Dickens intended it originally as a means of portioning out the role of narrator between several different characters, in much the same way as Chaucer does in *The Canterbury Tales.* Master Humphrey himself is the fictional author of *The Old Curiosity Shop* and also plays a role in that narrative, while another member of his storytellers' club, Jack Redburn, is the author of *Barnaby Rudge.*

By exploring the intricate structural and thematic relationships between Dickens's original conception of the club and the actual novels that were intended to be the the the work of the club, Tracy repositions some of the narrative elements of the two novels—their Gothic dimension, for instance, and the fact that both novels take place primarily at night, since Master Humphrey (like Dickens himself) is a night-walker. And although Dickens soon dropped the fiction that Master Humphrey and Redburn are the authors of their respective novels, it nonetheless played an important part in shaping the two works, by "imply[ing] a certain interplay between author and audience" (34). The stories were not only supposedly written by the members of Master Humphrey's club, but read aloud to them, thus anticipating Dickens's own need for public readings in front of a live audience.

Tracy suggests that the various plots and manipulations that form the narrative of *Barnaby Rudge* permit Dickens to address the issue of artistic manipulation. Dickens hints ambiguously at the similarity between the creation of fictional plots and political conspiracies, as well as at the questionable morality that underlies the manipulations of both. "The novelist," Tracy writes, "is licensed to concoct and tell a tale, but in doing so develops some affinity with more sinister types of plotters, whose actions have consequences in the real world" (41).

My own essay on "Dickens and the Aesthetics of Death" is also concerned with Dickens's method of characterization. My argument is that Dickens's notorious reticence on the subject of aesthetics indicates an unease about the value of artistic endeavor, especially as this relates to novel-writing. This unease is demonstrated by the fact that the few times Dickens raises issues of aesthetics in his fiction occur within the context of violent death, and that those few Dickensian characters who are self-proclaimed as artists, such as Dennis the Hangman in *Barnaby Rudge* and Mr. Venus in *Our Mutual Friend,* are both dealers in death. The essay explores the association of art, extinction, and execution in Dickens's fiction, suggesting that by yoking all three, Dickens was speaking indirectly of his own artistic enterprise, and that Dickens's fascination with the gruesome topics of dismemberment, dissection, and decapitation had implications for his literary style.

Patrick Brantlinger's "Did Dickens Have a Philosophy of History? The Case of *Barnaby Rudge*" argues that *Barnaby Rudge* represents Dickens's first attempt to articulate a philosophy of history. Brantlinger labels this philosophy "grotesque populism," defining the term as follows: Populism refers to the belief that all moral virtue and political legitimacy reside in the common people. "But populism turns grotesque when it focuses on the ways the people themselves have been crippled or deformed by history—that is, by centuries of misrule" (65). Brantlinger further suggests that this kind of grotesque populism informs all of the novels that Dickens wrote after *Barnaby Rudge.*

By suggesting that Dickens had a philosophy of history, Brantlinger seeks to counter the often expressed belief (by Walter Bagehot, among others) that Dickens was not a systematic or deeply intellectual thinker, and that all his historical notions derived from Carlyle. Brantlinger argues that the very fact that Dickens tried to write historical fiction so early in his career meant that he held some definite opinions about history. Furthermore, Dickens did not share all of Carlyle's historical opinions, however much he may have been influenced by him generally.

Brantlinger not only discounts the influence of Carlyle on Dickens's historical thinking, he discounts that of Walter Scott as well. By placing Dickens within the context of other historical writers and novelists of the time, Brantlinger demonstrates the differences between them. For instance, unlike Macaulay, Dickens had no faith in any of the existing laws and institutions of government "except for the police, the post office, and the Bank of England" (64). Nor did he think that any past government was better than the present one. Arguing that "there is no more monstrous grotesque distortion of the common people than the sort of mob violence depicted in *Barnaby*" (65), Brantlinger suggests that Dickens had no faith in the democratic ideal of the sovereignty of the people, that he believed instead that the sovereignty of the people might be the ultimate nightmare.

Brantlinger also takes issue with another commonplace about Dickens's historical fiction, namely, that both *Barnaby Rudge* and *A Tale of Two Cities* are not really about the past but about the present. Such readings argue that *Barnaby Rudge* is really about Chartism and trade unionism, not the Gordon Riots, while *A Tale of Two Cities* is actually intended as a warning that the threat of revolution had not died out in mid-Victorian England. Brantlinger argues that such parallels between past and present suggest that history has the potential to repeat itself, and, indeed, *Barnaby Rudge* is full of such anachronisms, which distort the meaning of time and suggest that the past haunts the present. Here Brantlinger contrasts Dickens's understanding of the past to Walter Scott's, arguing that Scott differs from Dickens in presenting history as a straightforward linear narrative of progress with an enlightened present as its outcome. For Dickens, however, past and present are grotesquely entangled, with an uncertain future hanging in the balance.

Brantlinger's essay on Dickens's philosophy of history is followed by Judith Wilt's weird but wonderful "Masks of the English in *Barnaby Rudge*," which also addresses the historical dimension of *Barnaby Rudge*. This time, however, the analysis focuses on the conflict between Catholics and Protestants that was the ostensible cause of the Gordon riots. Some of Wilt's contentions—such as her claim that John Chester is really a Jesuit under the skin—are certainly open to argument, but her essay is endlessly fascinating and even its more dubious and provocative assertions force a rethinking of assumptions because her scholarship is so wide ranging and solid.

Wilt begins with a lengthy analysis of the 1998 film *Elizabeth,* focusing specifically on the way in which that film portrays "the striding black-cloaked figure of a priest who need not be named, so loudly do the echoes of English history supply the name—the Jesuit" (76). While Wilt admits that patient scrutiny has failed to turn up a single Jesuit in the text of *Barnaby Rudge,* this does not deter her from suggesting that in most particulars—except, unfortunately, his religion—John Chester qualifies for this role. Wilt uses Chester as a way of demonstrating her contention that there was an anxiety in British culture, going all the way back to what Wilt calls "the Elizabethan/ Jacobean witches' cauldron" of the sixteenth and seventeenth centuries, that "the Catholic" was the authentic Englishman and the Protestant was merely a shell. "Scratch a Protestant and you find a hollow or a Catholic," Wilt writes (77).

Wilt goes on to give a history of Catholicism in England, focusing on the Gunpowder Plot of 1605, which she suggests was very much in Dickens's mind when he created John Chester. The result of all the tension between Protestants and Catholics, according to Wilt, was a "decided nostalgia" for the Catholic, a nostalgia that would see the reinstatement of the Jesuit Order in England in 1829, Catholic Emancipation in 1829, and the Oxford Movement of the 1830s, whose Tract 90, arguing that in terms of doctrine Anglicans already were Catholics, came out in 1841, the same year *Barnaby Rudge* was running in weekly installments (83).

As I said, some of Wilt's assertions are questionable, to say the least. John Chester is not the only Protestant whom Wilt construes as Catholic. Sim Tappertit is also described this way; he is, in Wilt's phrase, "a kind of latter-day Knight Templar" (85). Which raises the question—if all the characters in *Barnaby Rudge* are really Catholics under the skin, then who are the Protestants and what is all the rioting about?

Wilt's style is lively and provocative, and I would like to give a taste of it:

> If there are three men in a cellar in Westminster in any moment for the next
> 250 years [after the Gunpowder Plot of 1605], one of them has to be a Jesuit.
> If all the men are gentlemen but one the most visibly gentlemanly of all, he is
> the Jesuit. If one of the three claims he was "a promising young Protestant at
> that time, sent to learn the French tongue" at St. Omer . . . well, the breathtak-
> ing laughability of this idea—on second thought the brilliant equivocation of
> this idea—makes him for sure the disguised Jesuit.   (79)

Wilt's character analyses are excellent, and she is especially fine in her
analysis of John Chester's manner of speaking on page 86. Chester himself
she evocatively describes as "a glittering show wrapped around an existential
hollow" (86). Similarly, her characterization of the one scene in which Emma
Haredale comes to life (in her encounter with John Chester) is first-rate. This
is that rare thing in the world of supposedly dispassionate scholarly analysis
where cool objectivity is the ideal—a passionately written essay. Wilt occasionally falls into the trap of such writing by overstating her case, but her
scholarship is impeccable and while some of her assertions may be problematic, the whole of this essay makes for provocative reading. The great contribution Wilt makes, it seems to me, is to remind us of the Catholic dimension
of *Barnaby Rudge,* a novel that takes anti-Catholic rioting as its subject. By
arguing for the place of Catholicism in the collective memory of the English,
Wilt shines a new light on the novel.

Wilt's essay is followed by the last in the series on *Barnaby Rudge,* John
Glavin's "Politics and *Barnaby Rudge:* Surrogation, Restoration, and Revival." Where Patrick Brantlinger attempted to define Dickens's philosophy
of history through a reading of *Barnaby Rudge,* Glavin uses the same novel
to raise the question of Dickens's understanding of politics. Towards this end,
Glavin co-opts the distinction between the terms "restoration" and "revival"
from the vocabulary of nineteenth-century architecture to convey the sense
of Dickens's politics. He then asks whether Dickens is out to restore (i.e.,
memorialize, reestablish in a complete state) the past in *Barnaby Rudge,* or
to revive it, by "presenting [the Gordon riots] anew as a subject if not for
emulation then at least for nostalgia" (96). Glavin answers his own question
by suggesting that Dickens in fact never wrote a political novel and that
throughout his fiction the state is presented as fundamentally bogus. "For
Dickens," Glavin writes, "the state, any state, is an imposition on the inherent liberty of the subject" (97).

Glavin divides his essay into several sections: "theater," "ceremony,"
"festival," "fascism," all of which discuss various aspects of the political
in Dickens's novel. Of these four categories, it is fascism to which Glavin
gives most of his attention, although, because it is anachronistic, this last

category is also, it seems to me, the most problematic. It is problematic, not so much because what Glavin says about the fascistic elements of *Barnaby Rudge* is incorrect, but because it seems to apply an early twentieth-century frame of reference to the work of a writer who lived and died long before fascism rose to prominence. The result is that Glavin's essay must constantly fight against the inclination of a reader like myself to distrust his analogies because they seem improbable. Despite this, Glavin makes a valiant case for interpreting *Barnaby Rudge* in fascistic terms, noting that Dickens's contemporaries were more prone to admire Sparta than Athens, and suggesting that the novel may be read as a cautionary tale about the dangers of fascism.

Nevertheless, it does seem to me that Glavin occasionally overstates his case. For instance, he claims that "throughout [Dickens's] fiction, surrogation, constantly plotted, just as constantly fails" (109). What about Betsey Trotwood in *David Copperfield,* or Mr. Brownlow in *Oliver Twist,* both of whom function as successful surrogate parents? Glavin further suggests that "No one can take anyone's place in Dickens, and no place can replace the lost original. No one can change, and live" (109). This is a broad generalization and certainly open to refutation. Both *David Copperfield* and *Great Expectations* are about heroes who change during the course of their lifetimes. Neither David nor Pip is the same at the end of his respective novel as he was at the beginning. What about them? One could cite other objections to this overly broad claim.

However, when Glavin applies his contention about the lack of change in Dickens's fiction specifically to *Barnaby Rudge,* he is on far surer ground. "It is this protofascist resistance to surrogation that frustrates any attempt to read *Rudge*—or any other Dickens fiction—as political" (109), he writes, adding that "all the novel's sympathetic movements are retro. *Rudge* has only one goal for the future, to erase all difference and change" (110). Again, one can think of a counter-argument, but it seems to me that here Glavin is essentially right. Dickens does like to end his novels by hinting at repetitions of the past.

Glavin ends his essay by returning us to the present and suggesting that *Barnaby Rudge* should be read in terms of its implications for our own era. At the same time, he dismisses the notions of revival and restoration that he used at the beginning of his essay, suggesting that neither can account for *Barnaby Rudge.* In the end, writes Glavin, Dickens can neither restore nor revive, he can only retreat from the present into a past that never was.

Glavin's essay is followed by Michelle Mancini's informative but rambling "Demons on the Rooftops, Gypsies in the Street: The 'Secret Intelligence' of *Dombey and Son.*" Mancini argues that the plot of *Dombey and Son* is driven by what she calls "secret intelligence," that it is linked simultaneously to the new technology associated with the railway and to the older forms of knowing associated with gypsies and old witch-like women, the latter being exemplified in the person of Good Mrs. Brown. Beginning with an analysis of the famous passage from the novel that invokes "a good spirit who would take the housetops off," Mancini identifies the good spirit with Asmodeus, the title character of an eighteenth-century French novel by Alain René Le Sage, in which a Spanish aristocrat liberates the lame demon Asmodeus from a bottle. Asmodeus in return lifts the roofs off various Madrid houses to expose the human comedy being played out underneath. Asmodeus may thus be identified with the figure of an author peeping into the private lives of his characters, although Mancini more puzzlingly identifies him as well with the figure of the nineteenth-century flaneur. Because Asmodeus is both a demon and—in Dickens's version—a "good spirit," Mancini argues that he is an ambiguous role model for Dickens's own artistic practice (114).

However, although Mancini begins by suggesting that there is more to say about the good spirit passage than has hitherto been noticed by critics, the focus of her article is not on the limping demon but on Good Mrs. Brown. In fact, she seems to be arguing that the "good spirit" of the passage is subsumed into the figure of the haggish Mrs. Brown, who bears a certain physical resemblance to him with her yellow skin, shriveled arms, and limping gait. In the figure of Good Mrs. Brown, Mancini argues, Dickens ties together the novel's two thematic registers: the old world of fairy tale and romance, and the new world of trains, information, and capitalism. By associating the figure of Asmodeus with Good Mrs. Brown, Mancini intends to demonstrate the ways in which narrative knowledge is disfigured throughout *Dombey and Son.*

Towards this end, Mancini focuses attention on the gypsy quality of Dickens's depiction of Good Mrs. Brown, suggesting that she is a part of Dickens's "science of nomadology" (117), which strikes me as a rather dubious formulation. So do some of Mancini's other assertions, for instance, the statement that "like the blackmailing gypsy extortionist, the author too makes his living out of material that in other hands would have no value and endure only as trash" (118). Or the following: " . . . Why have authors and critics alike been so reluctant to acknowledge the elderly gypsy female as a prototype of the alienated and morally dubious (hard-boiled?) detective?" (125). These analogies suggest more discrepancies than concordances. Since Mancini does not really elaborate on these statements—I would love to know what Dickens's science of nomadology consists of—they never seem to be more than occasional authorial indulgences, which nonetheless are in danger of undermining at least some of the argument. And I am not sure what the assertion that "Good Mrs. Brown in fact knows more than the novel itself does or wants to" (132) is supposed to mean.

Despite such lapses, Mancini has some interesting things to say about Good Mrs. Brown as the purveyor of knowledge that has been somehow deformed and perverted. Mancini argues that this character has been badly served by critics. She has been routinely discussed as either Florence's abductor or Alice's mother, but Mrs. Brown, Mancini reminds us, has a story of her own—that of the seduced and abandoned country girl—and she knows how to manipulate the stories of others. Mancini thus discusses Good Mrs. Brown as a character who is privy to a certain kind of knowledge, a knowledge that appears limitless and that, to some extent, resembles that of the narrator. She is a trader in information, who sells what she knows—thus tying her themati-cally to the capitalistic element of the plot associated with Mr. Dombey. Mancini suggests that Dickens has it both ways with this character, depicting her as a gypsy because she wanders and as not a gypsy because she has a house. The ambiguity appropriately amplifies Mancini's analysis of this char-acter.

Regina Oost's essay on photography in *Bleak House,* entitled " 'More Like Than Life': Painting, Photography, and Dickens's *Bleak House,"* takes issue with Ronald R. Thomas's suggestion that photographic images in *Bleak House* are contrasted to the novel's many painted portraits, and that these portraits do not tell the truth. At first glance, any discussion of photography in *Bleak House* seems misplaced, since there are no photographs in the novel. But Oost is really out to disprove Thomas's contention that Bucket's ability to see things is akin to the workings of a camera, and that *Bleak House* is concerned with privileging this new technology. In order to anchor her argu-ment, Oost presents an informative overview of the way in which photogra-phy altered the cultural life of the mid-Victorian period by making the reproduction of family likenesses something even the middle class could aspire to. *Bleak House,* Oost notes, was written in the 1850s, a time when the photograph had largely replaced the painted portrait as a means of memo-rializing the middle class. However, while the novel was written in the 1850s, it is set in an earlier period, before the advent of photography. Oost argues that the novel shows considerable ambivalence about what any por-trait—painted or photographed—can convey.

One of Oost's most interesting observations is that readers of *Bleak House* in its serialized form, would have come across advertisements for Mayall's Daguerreotype Portrait Galleries, along with ads for other products aimed at enticing the middle class to raise its standard of living. Mayall was the man who in 1852 made the first known photographic images of Dickens. Oost also notes that two articles on the subject of photography appeared in *House-hold Words* in the early 1850s. Both of these articles articulated a position on the extent to which photography conveyed verisimilitude. Once it became possible in 1855 to retouch photographs, their documentary potential as re-corders of the truth was called into question. As with any new technology, photography evoked feelings of ambivalence, so that the writers in *Household*

Words were—in Oost's words—simultaneously excited by and wary of the new technology's potential (147).

This is a valuable essay that says much that is of interest about the history of photography, and about photography's ambiguous career as a recorder of reality. Oost relates this mid-century fascination with the photographed portrait to the multitude of painted portraits in *Bleak House* and to the various roles they play there—most especially as divulgers of secrets, as when Guppy guesses Esther's parentage from viewing the portrait of Lady Dedlock.

Regina Oost's essay is followed by two more on *Bleak House.* Robyn Schiffman's "Wax-Work, Clock-Work, and Puppet-Shews: *Bleak House* and the Uncanny" discusses Esther Summerson's relationship to her doll in light of Freud's 1919 essay on the uncanny. The young Freud had written to his fiancée Martha Bernays about *Bleak House* and about the character of Esther in particular, so that we know that he was familiar with Dickens's novel, although there is no overt connection between Freud's essay and *Bleak House.* And—as Schiffman informs us in an endnote—Freud did not like *Bleak House* and preferred *David Copperfield.*

Schiffman quotes an extract from Freud's essay which describes how, once, while sitting in a train compartment, Freud was startled by observing in the mirror the presence of a stranger in his compartment whom he only slowly recognized as being himself. Schiffman juxtaposes this passage with the oft-quoted scene from *Bleak House* of Esther's rediscovery of her own face in the mirror after her recovery from smallpox. In both cases, Schiffman argues, the uncanny is connected to a sense of estrangement from the self.

Schiffman's attention then shifts to a discussion of Esther's relationship to her doll. She notes that "Dolly lives and dies in the space of eight pages" (163), but that the doll remains important to the narrative as a figure of repetition, and as such demonstrates aspects of Freud's theory of the uncanny. Dolly, Schiffman suggests, is not only buried in the ground, she is buried as well in Esther's unconscious mind.

Schiffman has some excellent things to say about Esther's refusal of Guppy's marriage proposal, arguing that she is harsher with Guppy than is strictly necessary, and that her subsequent response of first laughing and then crying about the proposal can be explained by resorting to Freud's understanding of the uncanny as the revival of infantile complexes that have been repressed. Schiffman argues that Esther is afraid that she can only attract men like Guppy and like her father-figure John Jarndyce, because in her childhood the only figure who could give her love and acceptance had been a doll, a doll whom she had shamefully buried. Thus she views Guppy's proposal as a form of punishment, the inadequacy of Guppy as a suitor being related to Esther's assumption that her own hopes for fulfillment in love will never be satisfied by a lover worthy of her affections.

Dolly reappears again at a significant moment in Esther's life, when Esther first encounters Lady Dedlock and begins to inch towards the revelation that Lady Dedlock is her mother by remembering how, as a child, she used to first dress her doll before dressing herself, all the while gazing at her own reflection in the mirror. Here the doll mediates Esther's memory of herself as looking very much like Lady Dedlock, and in this way, "serves as the anchor during an emotional crisis" (167). Thus Schiffman's focus on the doll permits her to bring a new and illuminating perspective to some aspects of Esther's psychology. In the process, she also demonstrates just how multifarious a world Dickens created in his fiction, when even such an apparently marginal figure as a doll can be made to yield so many insights into the personality of a character whom one might have thought has already been analyzed to death.

In "Towards a Dickens Poetics: Indexical and Iconic Language in *Bleak House*," the third essay in the 2001 issue of *Dickens Studies Annual* to deal with *Bleak House*, James E. Marlow draws on the work of Charles Peirce, Ferdinand de Saussure, and Roman Jakobson to analyze some of Dickens's linguistic and rhetorical techniques in the novel. Marlow is especially fine on the inversion of tenses in *Bleak House*, noting that, contrary to what we might expect, the omniscient narrator uses the present tense, while Esther's narrative uses the past. Marlow also notes that the first three paragraphs of the novel indicate no tense at all, because the sentences there are missing their verbs.

While Marlow's discussion occasionally threatens to become too technical, he generally avoids this pitfall and is focused enough on the novel to make his remarks comprehensible. He has some particularly interesting things to say about Dickens's use of syntax, and I appreciated his method of taking passages from the text and then syntactically unpacking them in order to give a sense of Dickens's sophisticated use of the language.

Marlow's essay is followed by Barry Stiltner's "*Hard Times:* The Disciplinary City," which, not surprisingly given its title, draws on the work of D. A. Miller and the ever-present Foucault. Stiltner analyzes *Hard Times*, not as Dickens's industrial novel, but as "his most programmatic elaboration of mid-Victorian institutional circuits and disciplinary mechanisms" (193). Stiltner suggests that the usual criticism leveled against *Hard Times*—that it was inspired by Dickens's single weekend visit to Preston to see for himself the effects of the textile-workers strike, and that Dickens was writing about people and things outside the range of his own experience—misses the point of what Dickens was actually trying to do in this novel. Dickens's project, Stiltner argues, was "to construct a city based on disciplinary, Utilitarian ordering principles and follow the effects of those principles through both personal and institutional lenses" (196).

Stiltner's argument that *Hard Times* is about control rather than class, including the control of worker's bodies and schoolchildren's minds, certainly makes sense as a way of explicating the novel, but unfortunately his essay makes heavy-work of this thesis. It also seems to me, that despite the theoretical underpinning of Foucault and Miller, the essay says very little that is new about *Hard Times*. While the analytical focus here has shifted away from the novel's labor unrest, Stiltner's redirected emphasis on the regimentation and control that Dickens attributes to the school and the factory—as opposed to the "precapitalist" circus—have been noticed before.

Part of the problem may be that Stiltner relies too heavily on secondary sources. For instance, he quotes extensively from Foucault, but not always to convincing effect. And the extensive quotations tend to obscure whatever may be original in Stiltner's own interpretation. Furthermore, he suggests that Dickens's analysis of Utilitarian taxonomies is in accord with Foucault's elaboration of disciplinary taxonomies. Surely this is the wrong way round. It is Foucault who is in accord with Dickens. Dickens cannot be in accord with Foucault.

Mark M. Hennelly Jr.'s "'Like or No Like': Figuring the Scapegoat in *A Tale of Two Cities*" begins with an interesting premise, but then gets bogged down on its way to an argument. Hennelly's essay attempts to understand the *Tale* as a refiguring of the scapegoat motifs found in Leviticus. As a way of understanding the Victorian "culture value of self-sacrifice" (219), Hennelly begins with a discussion of Holman Hunt's 1854 painting *The Scapegoat*. Unfortunately, we are not shown a reproduction of this painting, so a reader who is unfamiliar with it is left floundering. Since a large part of Hennelly's argument rests on finding parallels between Dickens's novel and Hunt's painting, this makes for an analysis in the void.

Hennelly suggests that in Hunt's painting the scapegoat has become a double, representing both sin and salvation. He then goes on to apply these terms to the *Tale*. Too often, however, the analysis seems to be composed of a too-clever playing on words. For instance, Hennelly speaks of the "scapegoat's cross," and then suggests that other signs of the way in which Dickens's text "cross-examines" and "cross-questions" include the actual description of a cross, as well as the rape of Madame Defarge's sister, which Hennelly relates to Leviticus's injunction against cross-breeding. Furthermore, kissing, Hennelly writes, is also portrayed by an "X," "though the kiss may be la guillotine's Judas-kiss . . . of betrayal . . . " (224). All of this strikes me as too clever by half, and not particularly illuminating. The same is true for the rest of the essay, in which Hennelly's demonstration of erudition and his tendency towards over-interpretation get in the way of a coherent argument.

In "Monstrous Displacements: Anxieties of Exchange in *Great Expectations*," Clare Pettitt argues that *Great Expectations* is not a move away from the broad social criticism of the novels that immediately preceded it, but rather represents an investigation into "the mechanisms of market capitalism and the constituents of modernity" through the figure of the "restlessly aspiring" Pip. Pettitt suggests that *Great Expectations* may betray Dickens's feelings of unease about his own involvement in the capitalist marketplace. Noting that labor became more specialized in the nineteenth century, Pettitt focuses on Pip's dreams as manifestations of his anxiety about work and its meanings. She argues that Dickens's interest in dreams, states of conscious- ness, identity, and the freedom of will reflect contemporary scientific debate around these subjects. Her wide-ranging analysis draws, not surprisingly, on Marx, as well as on Mary Shelley's *Frankenstein* and Samuel Smiles's *Self-Help*.

Pettitt is very good on the scenes of literacy in the novel, suggesting, for instance, that Dickens is playing linguistic games by juxtaposing the forgeries of the convict Compeyson with the "honest forging" of Joe. However, I am not convinced by her argument that the several "sites of reading" in the novel really indicate that Dickens was nostalgic for a preliterate society. It seems to me that just the opposite is true.

Jonathan Taylor's " 'Servants' Logic' and Analytical Chemistry: George Eliot, Dickens, and Servants" suffers from the assumption that readers are familiar with the George Eliot essay called "Servants' Logic." I'm not sure that this is necessarily the case, and I for one would have welcomed an attempt on Taylor's part to put this essay into some kind of context. It would also be helpful to know why Eliot wrote her essay and for whom, as well as what is in it. Because Taylor's study assumes a familiarity with "Servants' Logic," it loses much of its interest right at the beginning. However, once the focus shifts to a discussion of the butler known as the Analytical Chemist in *Our Mutual Friend,* Taylor's essay begins to pick up steam.

In fact, he has some interesting things to say about the power dynamics between servants and masters in the later decades of the nineteenth century, and especially about the role of the butler. For instance, throughout the nine- teenth century the social distance between masters and servants tended gener- ally to increase. The sole exception to this distancing was the butler, who worked upstairs among his masters and was in the public eye. For this reason, according to Taylor, the public duties of the butler were relatively light, so as not to throw into relief the idleness of his masters.

Using the Analytical Chemist as his exemplar, Taylor analyzes the role of the butler within the Veneering household. Despite the fact that he is visibly present at the Veneering dinners, the purpose of the Analytical is to remain an absent presence. When he speaks it is to everyone, not to anyone. He is not permitted any interior feelings, yet he is the guardian of his masters against the insurgent proletariat, as represented in Dickens's novel by a coach- man who tries to deliver a message to one of the guests and is prevented from thus trespassing into the higher social realms by the Analytical.

Taylor ends his article by striving to unpack the term "analytical chemist." He suggests that Dickens confers this epithet on the Veneerings' butler, because he alone has a "subversive" knowledge of what the chablis is made of, since butlers were in charge of the wine cellars. Taylor then launches into a digression on the role of science in bourgeois psychology. The result is that his essay ends a little up in the air, without any clear-cut summation of where we have just been, suggesting that this is part of a larger work that has been unsuccessfully refashioned into an extract meant to stand on its own. However, despite the fact that " 'Servants' Logic' and Analytical Chemistry" could have used more shaping, much of the material here is informative and of more than passing interest.

Todd F. Davis and Kenneth Womack. *"Saints, Sinners and the Dickensian Novel: The Ethics of Storytelling in John Irving's* The Cider House Rules.*" John Irving.*

Finally, there is Todd F. Davis and Kenneth Womack's "Saints, Sinners and the Dickensian Novel: The Ethics of Storytelling in John Irving's *The Cider House Rules,*" which appears in a volume of The Modern Critical Views series devoted to John Irving. In his perfunctory editor's note to this volume, Harold Bloom suggests that Davis and Womack's essay discusses Irving's *The Cider House Rules* "as a successful instance of a modern Dickensian novel." Unfortunately, the essay is a disappointment, saying little of interest about Irving's novel and even less of value about "the Dickensian novel." The definition of the latter gets boiled down to some rather simplistic formulae, as for example, "the essential formulation of the Dickensian novel as a narrative form finds its origins in Dickens's dynamic approach to literary character" (122). Well, yes, but I'm not sure that's saying very much.

Noting that Irving himself has often acknowledged his debt to Dickens, and that nowhere is that debt more evident than in *The Cider House Rules,* the authors go on to suggest that, "In *The Cider House Rules* (1985), Irving avails himself of many of the Dickensian form's classic narratological elements, including its intentionally conflicted mélange of characters, its intricate layering of plots, its penchant for the detective story, and even its frequent depiction of orphans . . . ." Again, the outline itself is fine, but the level of discussion never does go beyond these superficial generalities. We are told, for instance, that the Dickensian novel is "ethical," but never get an explanation of the ways in which it is so. The result is an assertion like the following that never bothers to particularize its premise: "The Dickensian novel functions in *The Cider House Rules* as the ethical vehicle via which Irving challenges his readers to consider the abortion debate from a host of vantage points, rather than merely adopting a 'correct political vision' " (123–24). I would love to know how the Dickensian novel could function as an "ethical vehicle" for the abortion debate, but there is no clarification beyond the initial assertion.

The essay is full of such generalized and meaningless gestures in the direction of "the Dickensian novel" or "the Dickensian tradition." Nowhere is this tradition explained or spelled out. The authors' discussion of Dickens seems limited to superficialities, with the result that what might have been an illuminating juxtaposition of the Dickensian novel with Irving's twentieth-century attempt to refashion and adapt Dickens to his own purposes falls flat.

Essays and Articles in Periodicals

Dickens Quarterly

The year 2001 saw a number of fine essays appearing in *Dickens Quarterly*. While the topics of these essays touched on diverse aspects of Dickens's oeuvre, three of the best dealt with Dickens and America, a topic that seemed to be undergoing a renaissance in 2001, perhaps as a run-up to the Dickens and America conference that was held in Lowell, Massachusetts, in April 2002. All the essays published in the *Quarterly* on this subject were first-rate, beginning with Nancy Aycock Metz's " 'FEVERED with Anxiety for Home': Nostalgia and the 'New' Emigrant in *Martin Chuzzlewit*" in the June issue. This was followed in September by Jerome Meckier's essay on the parodies of *Great Expectations* that Mark Twain inserted into his *Life on the Mississippi* and by Iain Crawford's "Dickens in the Whaling City" in December 2001. The last of these is a fascinating account of Dickens's visit to New Bedford in March 1868, containing much information that was new to me—for instance, that in the mid-nineteenth century New Bedford boasted the highest per capita income in the world and was a vital, bustling place. Fleshing out his account with newspaper articles and private correspondence, Crawford gives a vivid snapshot of both New Bedford and the ailing Dickens at the time of his second American tour.

Jerome Meckier's essay was one of three in the 2001 issue of the *Quarterly* that dealt with intertextuality. The other essays connecting two authors were H. M. Daleski's "Dickens and Kipling: An Unexpected Intertextuality" in the September issue, and Anny Sadrin's " 'In the Name of the King': From Dickens's *Great Expectations* to Hugo's *L'Homme qui rit.*" It is curious that *Great Expectations* is the novel that all three of the writers on intertextuality cite as having influenced the work of other writers. Also noteworthy is the geographical range of influence, from the American Twain to the English

Kipling and the French Hugo. This far-flung impact suggests that *Great Expectations* presented a prototype of the bildungsroman plot that had a particular appeal to writers of the mid-to-late nineteenth century.

The September issue of the *Quarterly* also contained a superb essay by Natalie McKnight on "Dickens's Philosophy of Fathering," which treats of a topic that one might have thought had already been done to death. What McKnight's essay proves is that while fathering would appear to be a natural subject for Dickens criticism, in fact it has received relatively little analytical attention. Her essay provides an overdue corrective that is also most illuminating.

Other notable contributions to *Dickens Quarterly* in 2001 include George Goodin's "Competitive Conversation in the Dialogue of Dickens," Barbara Witucki's "*Hard Times:* Dickens's Ode to Saint Cecilia," Wendy Jacobson's "Freedom and Friendship: Women in *The Mystery of Edwin Drood,*" and a fascinating essay by Stanley Tick on "Autobiographical Impulses in *The Haunted Man* (1848)," which goes over some of the same ground covered by Rosemarie Bodenheimer in her essay on "Knowing and Telling in Dickens's Retrospects." Like Bodenheimer, Tick's focus is on Dickens's autobiographical writings of the years between 1846 and 1850. However, where Bodenheimer's emphasis was primarily on *David Copperfield,* Tick's is on the *The Haunted Man,* the last of Dickens's Christmas books. While conceding that the principle characters in this story are lifeless and that Dickens's prose is uninspiring, Tick concentrates his attention instead on the story's theme, suggesting that Dickens's fictional failures here are pregnant with biographical meaning. Tick then proceeds to provide a reading of *The Haunted Man* that is thoroughly suggestive, noticing, for instance, that in Part 1, Dickens composes thirty-two sentences in a row that begin with the word "when." Tick labels this "a kind of rhetorical eruption without cause or purpose . . . as though Dickens were concerned with a thought he could not bring himself to finish" (65). It is this kind of close attention to the details of language and nuance that makes this essay a pleasure to read.

Studies in English Literature

There were three essays on Dickens in the nineteenth-century issue of *SEL* in 2001. In "Bentham, Dickens and the Uses of the Workhouse," Peter Stokes argues that the Victorian workhouse has come to symbolize, on the one hand, systematic, institutional cruelty inspired by abstract economic principles, and, on the other, the moral heroism of social critics who saw through the inhumane dogma. Those who underline the cruelty of the workhouse associate it with Jeremy Bentham, who plays the role of the villainous theorist whose principles resulted in the Poor Law Amendment Act of 1834. The moral hero

who saw through the inhumane dogma of the workhouse is, of course, Charles
Dickens, the crusading novelist.

Stokes's article suggests that our polarized conception of the positions of
these two men requires rethinking and that each understood and portrayed
the workhouse in a more complicated fashion than at first appears. Bentham,
for instance, was not motivated by cruelty or even by utilitarianism so much
as by a wish to find a humane solution to the problem of poverty. Since he
rejected private charity as not only ineffectual, but also harmful, in that it
interfered with and nullified the will to work, he saw his own system as the
"true charity," because it created an environment that enabled the poor to
be deserving by compelling them to work. Bentham believed that charity
should be institutional. While Stokes acknowledges the validity of some of
the charges leveled against Bentham, he insists that to reject all of Bentham's
ideas is to overlook his rigorous critique of moral judgments of the poor.
Bentham's institution was meant to nurture as much as to control. For Bentham the humane was synonymous with the institutional.

Dickens is certainly the most famous critic of the Benthamite position,
especially in two of his novels, *Oliver Twist* and *Our Mutual Friend.* Stokes
argues that for Dickens "the social itself is fictional" (713)—a phrase I am
not sure I understand—and that while Dickens's novels are obviously critical
of the workhouse as an institution, they are not unreservedly so. It has not
generally been noticed, Stokes contends, that Dickens's portrayal of the workhouse is interwoven with plots of love as well as those of suffering.

According to Stokes, Dickens described Oliver's relationship with little
Dick as "a gently childish, public school kind of romance . . . not unlike that
of the lawyer roommates in *Our Mutual Friend,* Eugene and Mortimer"
(720). At the end of *Oliver Twist,* Oliver still remembers little Dick, which
indicates, "a nostalgia for the time when Oliver was in the workhouse" (720).
The workhouse may persecute children, but it also throws them together
(721). Thus Stokes argues that Dickens's workhouse can generate meaning
in contradictory ways, incorporating plots of violence and of love. This is an
interesting way of reading the workhouse in *Oliver Twist,* but it ignores a
more plausible understanding of the loving relationship between Oliver and
little Dick. Surely, we are meant to understand this relationship as existing
despite the workhouse, not because of it. It functions as an assertion of
the humanity possible in each individual, despite the deadening effects of
the institution.

Stokes also argues that Betty Higden in *Our Mutual Friend* is terrified of
ending up in the workhouse, not because of any direct experience of that
institution, but because of what she has read and heard about it from others.
Higden herself, Stokes argues, functions as a kind of substitute-workhouse
when she keeps Sloppy constantly turning the mangle. What Stokes is suggesting here is that Dickens was not as opposed to the ideology behind the

establishment of the workhouse as has generally been thought, that his novels construct the workhouse as both nurturing and restrictive. In this sense Dickens's position on the poor is not very far removed from Bentham's. While not all of Stokes's arguments convince me, his essay shines enough new light on Dickens's attitude towards the workhouse as to make it very much worth reading.

Susan Ferguson's excellent ''Dickens's Public Readings and the Victorian Author'' revisits the familiar terrain of Dickens's public readings in order to suggest new ways of understanding this aspect of Dickens's career. In lucid prose that is a pleasure to read, Ferguson suggests three ways of looking at Dickens's role in these readings—as actor, as reader, and as author. Ferguson analyzes all three of these roles in great detail, but the heart of her essay lies in the suggestion that the readings permitted Dickens the author to put himself in the position of his readers and thereby establish a bond with them, ''as one among a fellowship of readers with a mutual affection for the characters'' (730). By doing so, Ferguson suggests, Dickens transformed the role of the author from distant authority to the reader's intimate companion. It is this new sense of intimacy and shared endeavor that is the primary focus of Ferguson's essay.

Many of Ferguson's insights are quite striking. For instance, the fact that one of the props Dickens took on stage with him was a paper knife, and not, as one might expect, a pen, suggests his identification with the audience as a reader among readers, rather than as an author (or even an actor) delivering a text to his readership. Furthering her contention that Dickens's readings established a new intimacy between author and audience by downplaying the author's role, Ferguson turns to an examination of the prompt copies that Dickens used for his readings of *A Christmas Carol*. These show that the narrator's part has been consistently cut down from what it is in the printed text. This depersonalization of the narrator, Ferguson's suggests, again shows Dickens attempting to distance himself from the part one would most naturally attribute to him—that of the authorial narrator. The result of cutting down the role of narrator in the readings is to enable Dickens as actor to bring the characters themselves more strongly to life by giving them voice, intonation, and gesture. In this way, Dickens on the platform played the role of all his characters in much the same way as a reader reading his fiction reads from the heteroglossic point of view of all the characters. Yet Dickens's function during these readings is not analogous to that of a playwright. Playwrights, as Ferguson acutely observes, do not give readings. According to Ferguson, the purpose of Dickens's readings was not to lecture the audience, but to please them, to befriend and entertain them. The pleasing had, of course, a monetary component, since the more successful he was at pleasing, the more

money Dickens made. But the readings were also necessary to Dickens psychologically—pleasing an audience was as necessary to his emotional well-
being as pleasing a readership. In the process of feeding both his psychological
and his financial needs, Dickens changed the role of writer and reader, bringing both into a level of intimacy previously unknown.

The third article on Dickens in *SEL* is Anthea Trodd's "Messages in Bottles
and Collins's Seafaring Man," which, like Lillian Nayder's more extensive
study, is about the collaboration of Dickens and Wilkie Collins. While Trodd
makes some of the same points as Nayder about the tensions in the Dickens-
Collins relationship, Trodd's focus is necessarily narrower than Nayder's,
and she deals with only one of the collaborative stories, the nautical "A
Message from the Sea," the penultimate story on which Dickens and Collins
collaborated after a visit to Devon and Cornwall. Dickens wrote the third-
person frame of this story, while Collins wrote the first person account,
angering Dickens by seeming to repeat the same narrative techniques that he
had used in *The Woman in White,* which had appeared earlier that year.

Much of Trodd's focus is on Collins's contribution to the story, and she,
like Nayder, notices that Collins's path diverged markedly from that of his
senior partner. Collins, Trodd argues, dissociates his figure of the seafaring
man from the archetypal figure of the sailor and so disappoints expectations
of a seafaring yarn in the traditional manner. Instead, Trodd argues, Collins
incorporates into the figure of his sailor "the story of someone who does not
understand stories" (755).

Dickens's irritation with the original beginning of "The Seafaring Man,"
Trodd writes, was directed at Collins's shaping of the seaman's story as
written testimony rather than oral storytelling. "The frame narrative celebrated the values of oral storytelling, while Collins directed his section according to his very different interest in the awkward individuality of those
unfamiliar with reading or writing" (755).

Trodd contrasts Collins's rendering of the diffident seaman Hugh with
Dickens's rendering of a far more typical sailor in the frame story, the American Captain Jorgan, who has "a sagacious weather-beaten face," and slaps
his knees as a sign of openness of feeling. Trodd further suggests that, "The
different attitudes of the two seamen toward storytelling are further exemplified in the treatment of the message. Dickens's narrative concerns are for
delivery and decipherment, Collins's for the original circumstances of writing" (757). Trodd then goes on to give a fascinating history of the tradition
of leaving messages in bottles, returning to the Dickens-Collins relationship
to say that while Collins was writing within parameters set by Dickens,
plugging in the holes in Dickens's narratives—these holes usually being first-
person accounts—he was also establishing his own independent voice, a voice
that increasingly diverged from Dickens's expectations as Collins himself
became more established as a writer.

Nineteenth-Century Literature

Nineteenth-Century Literature published only one article on Dickens in 2001, but that article is a gem. In " 'Received, a Blank Child': John Brownlow, Charles Dickens, and the London Foundling Hospital—Archives and Fictions,'' Jenny Bourne Taylor gives an account of the London Foundling Hospital, chronicling its changes in policy and ideology from the days of its founding in the early eighteenth century by the retired sea captain Thomas Coram, to its heyday in the nineteenth century. These changes in policy echoed changing attitudes towards illegitimacy. In the early years, children were admitted anonymously to the Hospital with no questions asked. But during the nineteenth century, and especially after the passage of the Poor Law of 1834, the admissions policy became more restrictive, and the sexual history of the mother began to be taken into account as a criterion for admission. By the middle of the nineteenth century, admission was restricted to illegitimate children only, whose mothers were otherwise of good character, despite their one lapse.

This is a long and impressive essay, which will be indispensable to anyone working on issues of illegitimacy, child care, or the history of corporate and/ or charitable institutions in the nineteenth century. Bourne Taylor states that her intention is to "explore some of the myths, histories, and fictions that circulated around . . . the London Foundling Hospital'' (293). In order to do this, she takes a close look at the Hospital's archives and the history of the institution written by its Secretary, John Brownlow. But her inquiry is not limited to this. She also has interesting things to say about the paintings in the Foundling Museum's collection. Two paintings in particular—painted over a century apart by Hogarth and Emma Brownlow King—offer different perspectives on the role of the foundling. Hogarth himself had been one of the Hospital's original founders when it opened its doors in 1739 and was closely involved in its day-to-day operations.

Bourne Taylor's essay chronicles Dickens's involvement with the Hospital. In fact, her title, "Received, a Blank Child'' is a direct steal from the title of Dickens's own account of his visit to the Foundling Hospital, which he published in *Household Words* in 1853. The title is an allusion to the Hospital's official receipt, given to mothers when they deposited their children at its doors. (The blanks would have been filled in with the sex and date of admission of the child.)

Bourne Taylor's reading of Dickens is full of insight and is a potential gold mine for anyone working on related themes in Dickens's fiction. Not only does she describe Dickens's philanthropic involvement with the Hospital, but she also suggests the ways in which this involvement influenced his fiction. Her analysis of both the *Household Words* article and *Oliver Twist* is excellent. She is particularly good on the blankness associated with Oliver's "twisty" name, which alludes to the ambiguity inherent in all the names conferred on the foundlings by the Hospital. Just as illuminating is her discussion of Tattycoram from *Little Dorrit*. *Little Dorrit* is the first of two fictions by Dickens in which the Foundling Hospital makes an explicit appearance, the second being the 1867 Christmas story "No Thoroughfare." Bourne Taylor focuses on the obsessive pattern of self-assertion and destruction that Tattycoram manifests in her daily life, suggesting that," . . . she brings together and extends the novel's concerns with social and psychic confinement" (348). Bourne Taylor also maintains that Tattycoram's "overt sexuality is tacitly linked to her racial ambiguity" (349), that the girl is a double of "the other daughter of a total institution," Amy Dorrit. Both young women are introduced as servants, both are given childlike names, both excite Clennam's curiosity. But Amy manages to transcend the taint of prison in a way that Tattycoram cannot transcend the Foundling Hospital.

Bourne Taylor's essay also introduces John Brownlow, the secretary of the Foundling Hospital and a foundling himself, who may well have given his name to the benevolent Mr. Brownlow in *Oliver Twist*. Dickens knew John Brownlow and gave him a walk-on part in his essay on the hospital. It appears that Brownlow too wrote novels and Bourne Taylor discusses his *Hans Sloane, a Tale Illuminating the History of the Foundling Hospital in London* (1831) in relation to Dickens's *Oliver Twist*, suggesting where the two narratives agree and where they part company.

There is much more to Bourne Taylor's article than I have space to go into here, but in both its wide-ranging scope and its depth of analysis, this is an extraordinary essay, and I believe will prove a seminal one.

Articles in Miscellaneous Periodicals and Journals

The year 2001 saw the publication of two important articles on Dickens's short story "The Signalman." Although Norris Pope's "Dickens's 'The Signalman' and Information Problems in the Railway Age" and Jill Matus's "Trauma, Memory and Railway Disaster: The Dickensian Connection" go off in different directions, both use Dickens's short story as the springboard for informative essays on specific scientific and technological aspects of the Victorian era.

Norris Pope's essay is a fascinating discussion of the importance of signalling and signalmen to the safe functioning of the railway in nineteenth-century Britain. Focusing on two mid-century train disasters, the Clayton Tunnel wreck and the Staplehurst derailing, Pope's essay gives a comprehensive and very informative account of how these railway accidents highlighted issues of safety for the Victorian traveling public, and how Dickens's short story, "The Signalman," published a year after Dickens's own traumatic experience of surviving the Staplehurst crash, tapped into the problem of train safety, an issue that was already a matter of widespread public concern. More specifically, however, Pope is interested in "the information ambiguities and information failures within complex systems" (441) that caused the two wrecks as well as the fictional disaster in Dickens's story, and his essay gives a good idea of the potential for catastrophe that dogged the safety of all trains during the mid-nineteenth century.

But while Pope takes Dickens's short story as his starting point, and includes a brief synopsis of the plot, his focus in this article is not on literary analysis. Rather he is interested in examining how signaling technology provided advance information about traffic and line conditions on which the safe and smooth running of the trains depended. Signaling and information failure, he writes, were almost always the cause of collisions between trains at this time. While Pope's subject is the railway technology of the mid-Victorian era, it is impossible to read his essay and not make comparisons to the air traffic accidents of today and to the crucial role of air traffic controllers. Planes and trains are obviously not the same technologies, but the problems associated with directing air traffic today are not much different from what was involved in the smooth functioning of train traffic in Dickens's time, especially if one considers the heavy duties and responsibilities of railway signalmen and their complaints about the stress of their working conditions. While Pope himself does not make the analogy to the present day, the fact that he is writing about technological problems still relevant today gives his essay a contemporary edge.

Because Pope's essay is primarily factual rather than analytical, anyone looking for a literary analysis of Dickens's story will be disappointed. Not so readers with an interest in trains and railway technology of the nineteenth century. This is a thorough, readable, and fascinating account of trains and train safety during the middle decades of the nineteenth century, which uses the work of the century's most prominent novelist to illustrate and augment its contentions.

In "Trauma, Memory and Railway Disaster: The Dickensian Connection," Jill Matus too uses Dickens's "The Signalman" as a starting point for her discussion, but this time the focus is on the Victorian understanding of trauma and on the role that memory was understood to play in this psychological condition. Matus begins with an account of the Staplehurst crash, which left Dickens with all the symptoms of acute psychological distress; he lost his voice for two weeks, was subject to sudden rushes of terror, and was afraid to travel by train. By an odd coincidence, Dickens's death five years later occurred on the exact anniversary of the crash date.

Matus argues that ''The Signalman,'' published a year after the Staplehurst disaster, may be profitably read through the lens of current trauma theory, because in this story Dickens ''uncannily apprehends the heart of traumatic experience in its focus on the uncoupling of event and cognition, on belatedness, repetitive and intrusive return, and on a sense of powerlessness as impending disaster'' (414). Matus asserts that Dickens's sensitivity to altered states and to the literary possibilities of the ghost story ''helped him to articulate what the nascent study of trauma at this time was not quite yet posed to formulate'' (416). Such a reading in turn raises the question of how trauma was understood in the pre-Freudian 1860s, and what was the relationship between literature and the psychological and medical discourse of the day.

Like Pope, Matus points to the importance of the railway in the mid-nineteenth century, claiming that trains not only revolutionized travel, but they altered previously held conceptions of time and space. The new technology also carried with it the potential for accidents on a scale previously unknown to travelers, accidents which provoked claims against the railway companies, which in turn led to the need for insurance companies. Matus's essay provides an absorbing analysis of how psychological damage, specifically the damage caused by shock and trauma, gradually became accepted as causing as much harm as physical injury, although insurance companies remained reluctant to pay damages for emotional trauma. Beginning with a history of the mid-Victorian concepts of psychic shock, Matus then goes on to explore the debate around memory and its role in traumatic shock.

She suggests that Freud was the first to notice that the dreams of shell-shocked soldiers were different from the dreams of those who had not lived through traumatic experiences, and that this difference was attributable to memory. The knowledge of the traumatized is inaccessible to ordinary memory, but makes itself felt as an intrusive return into the life of the sufferer. Matus then gives an account of the various theories of memory held by Freud's Victorian predecessors. She suggests that the Victorian fascination with states of altered consciousness, as expressed in mesmerism, hypnotism, spiritualism, and somnambulism was another form of this debate on the nature of memory and its relationship to brain function and physiology.

Dickens, of course, was fascinated by mesmerism, and Matus devotes the last section of her discussion to Dickens's attraction to this phenomenon and to the ways in which ''The Signalman'' expresses some of Dickens's understanding of the unconscious capacities of the mind. She suggests that because Dickens was sympathetic to the possibility of unconscious knowledge and because he was adept at manipulating the conventions of the ghost story, he was able to articulate in this story the relationship between trauma and memory. Matus gives a suggestive reading of ''The Signalman'' filtered through the prism of the trauma theory set out in the earlier sections of her essay. One of her most intriguing suggestions is that the genre of the ghost story mimics the intrusiveness of traumatic memory because ghost stories are ipso facto about the imposition of the past on the present. Thus Matus suggests that "based structurally on the principle of repetition, 'The Signalman' reveals the hallmark of trauma as unbidden repetition and return" (429). And to the extent that trauma is a "disease of time," then traumatic memory is the return that does not recognize itself as a return (430).

One of the strengths of Matus's essay is its lucid organization, which makes it easy to follow each one of the separate strands of her argument. She is one of the few essay writers who lays out her plan of procedure in the introduction, with detailed comment on what she expects to demonstrate in each section. I particularly like the way that Matus's prose draws attention to the use of railway metaphors in everyday speech, without being overly aware of the fact. Matus writes of "laying tracks" for her argument, or of "switching tracks," and of "trains of thought." She writes that because the railway was "such a visible aspect of modernity in Victorian life, it is not surprising that railway tracks, networks, trains of thought . . . [should] influence the very way in which the mind's operations could be visualized" (422). This is a remarkable essay on several counts, and not least for the contribution it makes to our understanding of how the Victorians regarded trauma and memory.

Jerome Meckier's "*Great Expectations* and *Self-Help:* Dickens Frowns on Smiles" reads *Great Expectations* as Dickens's answer to the philosophy of Samuel Smiles, as enunciated in Smiles's mid-Victorian best-seller *Self-Help.* David Copperfield, Meckier argues, was the Smilesian hero par excellence, the young man, who, despite his erring, undisciplined heart, never lost sight of what he needed to lead a successful life—economic prosperity and literary fame. Ten years later, a more cynical and disillusioned Dickens "corrected"—the word is Meckier's—*David Copperfield* by writing *Great Expectations,* "the autobiography of a failure" (537).

Smiles's *Self-Help*—which created the genre of self-help books that is still with us today—argued that hard work and perseverance will inevitably lead to wealth and worldly success. He documented his philosophy of self-improvement with a series of biographies of those who began life with nothing and went on to build railroads, earn titles, and amass fortunes. Meckier accounts for the enormous success of *Self-Help*—which sold 20,000 copies in its first year of publication, and 160,000 in Smiles's lifetime—by suggesting that its doctrine mirrored the self-definition of England itself, a country that considered its rise in the world as on a par with Cinderella's (538). By chronicling the lives of the men responsible for England's industrial greatness, Smiles implied that such success was possible for all, that individuals make their own destinies.

Meckier argues that Dickens distrusted Smiles's doctrine because it permitted his followers to ignore the possibility of failure and tempted them to deny the existence of their own shortcomings. It also encouraged the calculation of self-worth chiefly in terms of material success (538). The result of Dickens's disapproval is that—as Meckier writes—where *Self-Help* disowned failure, *Great Expectations* is preoccupied with it (553). By Smiles's standards, Pip is a failure, who not only loses the advanced standing in life that Magwitch's money originally enabled him to enjoy, but also loses the two women in his life. Meckier thus reads *Great Expectations* as Dickens's answer to Smiles, and he sees Dickens's criticism as residing in three of the novel's plot strands: Pip's rise and fall, Joe's refusal to raise himself or be raised by Pip, and Magwitch's "unsettling transformation from powerless convict to vengeful Croesus" (543).

Meckier provides an instructive discussion of each of these plot strands, focusing in particular on how each refutes Smiles's doctrine of self-help, which Meckier also equates with the fairy tale plot of Cinderella. Specifically, Meckier claims, Dickens faulted Smiles's doctrine for raising unrealistic expectations and for suggesting that material success made people better human beings. *"Great Expectations,"* Meckier writes, "reveals that England is Pip writ large," reflecting "the communal myth of Victorian England as modern history's greatest success story, a rise of unprecedented importance that made self-satisfaction irresistible and self-scrutiny unpatriotic" (545).

Meckier suggests that there was also a more personal dimension to Dickens's disapproval of the self-help doctrine, namely, that Dickens regarded Smiles as a rival. More than such fellow novelists as Thackeray, Lever and Collins, Smiles posed a danger to Dickens's sense of himself as the era's premier social realist, critic, and setter of values (552). Interestingly, Meckier attributes this rivalry to the fact that Smiles uses the biographies of the successful to illustrate his philosophy, thus impinging on Dickens's novelistic territory.

Yet, Meckier points out, Dickens himself would never have given up all the advantages that his own rise in the world had bestowed on him, so that in a sense *Great Expectations* lets him have it both ways. Without forfeiting his own preeminence, Dickens in *Great Expectations* enjoys the luxury of overhauling the value system he promoted in *David Copperfield*. The later novel permits him to explore his misgivings about all risings, his own included, and to critique the philosophy attendant on defining success in entirely material terms. It does so, however, without obliging Dickens to question his own rise in any practical way.

Shorter essays on Dickens in 2001 include June Foley's argument in *Women's Studies* that the model for Fagin in *Oliver Twist* is not Bob Fagin, or any other character who has been previously proposed, but Dickens's mother. Noting that it is not uncommon for authors to reach across gender boundaries for their inspirational models, as Flaubert did in claiming that Mme. Bovary was himself, or as George Eliot did in claiming that she alone was the model for the male Casaubon in *Middlemarch,* Foley argues that Elizabeth Dickens has tended to be overlooked as a possible model for Fagin, because women have traditionally been effaced from the father/son plot. Pointing out that Fagin's feminine characteristics have been well documented by a variety of critics, Foley links these characteristics to contemporary descriptions of Mrs. Dickens as an extraordinary mimic with a strong sense of the ludicrous. This side of Dickens's mother is particularly described in a letter by Mrs. Daveys, with whom Elizabeth Dickens lived for a time. Foley believes that Elizabeth Dickens's role as the inspiration for Fagin has been obscured by Fagin's masculinity and by his Jewishness. In many other respects, she argues, Fagin and Elizabeth Dickens resemble each other. The fact that Dickens never overcame his animosity towards his mother for wanting to keep him working at Warren's Blacking Factory adds fuel to Foley's argument that Elizabeth Dickens inspired the characterization of Fagin. Foley's contention, while at first appearing improbable, is backed up by a secure knowledge of Dickens's biography and by an ability to argue persuasively.

Malcolm Pittock's "Peebles V. Plainstanes: Jarndyce V. Jarndyce: Scott V. Dickens" is yet another attempt to finger a source for Dickens's fiction. This time the originary text is argued to be Walter Scott's *Redgauntlet,* which Pittock claims gave Dickens the idea for the interminable case of Jarndyce versus Jarndyce in *Bleak House.* Certainly, it is not news that Dickens was a fan of Walter Scott's and was clearly influenced by him, an influence especially evident in *Barnaby Rudge.* So Pittock's claim is not farfetched, and he makes a good case. His essay also serves as a good introduction to a Scott novel that is no longer very widely read.

Dickens is only a secondary actor in Tim Marshall's "Not Forgotten: Eliza Fenning, *Frankenstein,* and Victorian Chivalry," a fascinating essay on the case of Eliza Fenning, a young servant girl who was hanged in London in 1815 on charges of having tried to poison her employer by putting arsenic into the dumplings that she served him. Fenning was convicted on very little evidence, and there was a strong perception, even at the time of her trial, that she was innocent of the charges. Adding to the poignancy of her story was the fact that she was hanged in her wedding gown on what was to have been her wedding day. *All the Year Round* revisited the Fenning case in its edition of July 18, 1867. But Marshall's focus is not primarily on Dickens, nor on the article that Dickens published about the case, but rather on the similarity between the Fenning case and that of the fictional Justine in Mary Shelley's *Frankenstein,* who is similarly innocent when she is hanged for murder in the novel. Marshall returns to Dickens only at the end of his essay, when he notes that Dickens approved of the Anatomy Act, which stipulated that the bodies of the poor and destitute be sent to the anatomy schools for dissection after death, rather than limiting this fate to the bodies of the executed. Eliza Fenning's body had not been dissected after her execution because her father had bought it back from the hangman. Marshall suggests that Fenning's staying power in Victorian memory was due to the fact that she was not dissected after death, and that this permitted Victorians like Dickens to feel righteous compassion on her behalf, while simultaneously ignoring the 57,000 poverty-stricken individuals whose bodies were delivered to the anatomy schools until the repeal of the Anatomy Act after the Second World War. As Marshall puts it, "The crime of poverty did not rouse Dickens to speak up on their behalf."

Finally, in "Defense of Flat Characters," George R. Clay suggests that—pace Forster—the flatness of flat characters often makes them the most interesting among an author's creations. His favorite author in this regard is, not surprisingly, Dickens. Clay suggests that a character's very flatness may also imply a complication: for instance, Mrs. Micawber's oft-repeated "I never will desert Mr. Micawber" suggests that at some point she may well have thought of deserting him, but had not gone through with it. Furthermore, Clay points out that the very obsession that makes Mrs. Micawber reiterate this tag-line also makes her memorable as a character. Clay then turns his attention to the flat characters in Jane Austen's novels and in Tolstoy's, but essentially his argument is the same, namely, that the opprobrium that has attached itself to flat characters is misplaced, and that in the hands of a writer like Dickens, flatness becomes a virtue.

If the flatness of Dickens's characters is a virtue, it is only one of the numerous virtues of this extraordinary writer, as displayed in his prodigious output of novels, stories, journalism, plays, and letters. However, it is not the quantity of Dickens's creation that is so remarkable, but rather the fact that so much of it is so good. Even his failures are interesting. Dickens's productivity and the quality of his writing has called forth a similar productivity from those who are inspired by his work and life, and seek to comment on it. I have tried in this essay to give a sampling of such commentary on the Inimitable from one particular year. I know that I have omitted mention of many other fine essays on Dickens, for which omission I hope their authors will forgive me. Writing about writing on Dickens is a little like trying to catch the sea in a sieve—much escapes, but there is plenty of nutrient in what remains behind.

WORKS CITED

Barber, Nicola. *Dickens* (Great Writers, 2). Tunbridge Wells, Kent: Ticktock Publishing, 2001.

Baumgarten, Murray. "Fictions of the City." *The Cambridge Companion to Charles Dickens.* Ed. John O. Jordan. Cambridge: Cambridge UP, 2001.

Bodenheimer, Rosemarie. "Knowing and Telling in Dickens's Retrospects." *Knowing the Past: Victorian Literature and Culture.* Ed. Suzy Anger. Ithaca: Cornell UP, 2001. 215–34.

Bourne Taylor, Jenny. " 'Received, a Blank Child': John Brownlow, Charles Dickens, and the London Foundling Hospital—Archives and Fictions." *Nineteenth-Century Literature* 56, 3 (Dec. 2001): 293–363.

Bradbury, Nicola. "Dickens and the Form of the Novel." *The Cambridge Companion to Charles Dickens.* Ed. John O. Jordan. Cambridge: Cambridge UP, 2001. 152–67.

Brantlinger, Patrick. "Did Dickens Have a Philosophy of History? The Case of *Barnaby Rudge.*" *Dickens Studies Annual* 30 (2001): 59–75.

Cheadle, Brian. "The Late Novels: *Great Expectations* and *Our Mutual Friend.*" *The Cambridge Companion to Charles Dickens.* Ed. John O. Jordan. Cambridge: Cambridge UP, 2001.

Clay, George R. "In Defense of Flat Characters." *The Midwest Quarterly* 42, 3 (Spring 2001): 271–80.

Crawford, Iain. "Dickens in the Whaling City." *Dickens Quarterly* 18, 4 (Dec. 2001): 173–86.

Daleski, H. M. "Dickens and Kipling: An Unexpected Intertextuality." *Dickens Quarterly* 18, 3 (Sept. 2001): 113–21.

Davis, Todd F. and Kenneth Womack. "Saints, Sinners and the Dickensian Novel: The Ethics of Storytelling in John Irving's *The Cider House Rules.*" *Modern Critical Views: John Irving.* Ed. Harold Bloom. Broomall, PA: Chelsea, 2001.

Ferguson, Susan L., "Dickens's Public Readings and the Victorian Author." *SEL* 41, 4 (Autumn 2001), 729–51.

Flint, Kate. "The Middle Novels: *Chuzzlewit, Dombey* and *Copperfield.*" *The Cambridge Companion to Charles Dickens.* Ed. John O. Jordan. Cambridge: Cambridge UP, 2001.

Foley, June. "Elizabeth Dickens: Model for Fagin." *Women's Studies* 30 (2001): 225–35.

Garcha, Amanpal. "Styles of Stillness and Motion: Market Culture and Narrative form in *Sketches by Boz*" *Dickens Studies Annual* 30 (2001): 1–23.

Glavin, John. "Politics and *Barnaby Rudge:* Surrogation, Restoration, and Revival." *Dickens Studies Annual* 30 (2001): 95–113.

———. "Dickens and Theatre." *The Cambridge Companion to Charles Dickens.* Ed. John O. Jordan. Cambridge: Cambridge UP, 2001. 204–24.

Goodin, George. "Competitive Conversation in the Dialogue of Dickens." *Dickens Quarterly* 18, 1 (March 2001): 21–37.

Hennelly Jr., Mark M., "Like or No Like": Figuring the Scapegoat in A Tale of Two Cities." *Dickens Studies Annual* 30 (2001): 217–43.

John, Juliet. *Dickens's Villains: Melodrama, Character, Popular Culture.* Oxford: Oxford UP, 2001.

Jordan, John O. Ed. *The Cambridge Companion to Charles Dickens.* Cambridge: Cambridge UP, 2001.

Mancini, Michelle. "Demons on the Rooftops, Gypsies in the Streets: The 'Secret Intelligence' of *Dombey and Son." Dickens Studies Annual* 30 (2001): 113–41.

Marlow, James E. "Towards a Dickens Poetics: Indexical and Iconic Language in *Bleak House." Dickens Studies Annual* 30 (2001): 173–93.

Marsh, Joss. "Dickens and Film." *The Cambridge Companion to Charles Dickens.* Ed. John O. Jordan. Cambridge: Cambridge UP, 2001. 224–30.

Marshall, Tim. "Not Forgotten: Eliza Fenning, Frankenstein, and Victorian Chivalry." *Critical Survey* 13, (2001): 98–114.

Matus, Jill. "Trauma, Memory and Railway Disaster: The Dickensian Connection." *Victorian Studies* 43, 3 (Spring 2001), 413–37.

McKnight, Natalie. "Dickens's Philosophy of Fathering." *Dickens Quarterly* 18, 3 (Sept. 2001): 129–39.

Meckier, Jerome. "*Great Expectations* and *Self-Help:* Dickens Frowns on Smiles." *Journal of English and Germanic Philology* (Oct. 2001): 537–55.

———. "What Noble Horseshoes This Man Might Have Made": Mark Twain Comments on *Great Expectations* in *Life on the Mississippi." Dickens Quarterly* 18, 3 (Sept. 2001): 121–29.

Mengham, Rod. *Charles Dickens.* Horndon, Tavistock: Northcote, 2001.

Metz, Nancy Aycock. *The Companion to Martin Chuzzlewit.* Mountfield, East Sussex: Helm Information Ltd., 2001.

———. " 'FEVERED with Anxiety for Home': Nostalgia and the 'New' Emigrant in *Martin Chuzzlewit." Dickens Quarterly* 18, 2 (June 2001): 49–62.

Miller, J. Hillis. "Moments of Decision in *Bleak House." The Cambridge Companion to Charles Dickens.* Ed. John O. Jordan. Cambridge: Cambridge UP, 2001.

Morgentaler, Goldie. "Dickens and the Aesthetics of Death." *Dickens Studies Annual* 30 (2001): 45–59.

Nayder, Lillian. *Unequal Partners: Charles Dickens, Wilkie Collins and Victorian Authorship.* Ithaca: Cornell UP, 2002.

Newsom, Robert. "Fictions of Childhood." *The Cambridge Companion to Charles Dickens.* Ed. John O. Jordan. Cambridge: Cambridge UP, 2001.

Oost. Regina B. " 'More Like Than Life': Painting, Photography, and Dickens's *Bleak House.*" *Dickens Studies Annual* 30 (2001):141–59.

Parker, David. *The Doughty Street Novels: Pickwick Papers, Oliver Twist, Nicholas Nickleby, Barnaby Rudge.* New York: AMS Press, 2002.

Patten, Robert. "From *Sketches* to *Nickleby.*" *The Cambridge Companion to Charles Dickens.* Ed. John O. Jordan. Cambridge: Cambridge UP, 2001. 16–34.

Peck, John. *Maritime Fiction: Sailors and the Sea in British and American Novels.* London: Palgrave, 2001.

Pettitt, Clare. "Monstrous Displacements: Anxieties of Exchange in *Great Expectations.*" *Dickens Studies Annual* 30 (2001), 141–59.

Pittock, Malcolm. "Peebles V. Plainstanes: Jarndyce V. Jarndyce: Scott V. Dickens." *Neophilologus* 85 (2001): 457–75.

Pope, Norris. "Dickens's 'The Signalman' and Information Problems in the Railway Age." *Technology and Culture* 42, 3 (2001): 436–61.

Robbins, Bruce. "How to Be a Benefactor without Any Money: The Chill of Welfare in *Great Expectations.*" *Knowing the Past: Victorian Literature and Culture.* Ed. Suzy Anger. Ithaca: Cornell UP, 2001. 171–92.

Sadrin, Anny. 'In the Name of the King': From Dickens's *Great Expectations* to Hugo's *L'Homme qui rit.*" *Dickens Quarterly* 18, 4 (Dec. 2001): 217–26.

Schiffman, Robyn L. "Wax-Work, Clock-Work, and Puppet-Shews: *Bleak House* and the Uncanny." *Dickens Studies Annual* 30 (2001): 159–73.

Schor, Hilary. "Novels of the 1850s: *Hard Times, Little Dorrit,* and *A Tale of Two Cities.*" *The Cambridge Companion to Charles Dickens.* Ed. John O. Jordan. Cambridge: Cambridge UP, 2001.

Shuman, Cathy. *Pedagogical Economies: The Examination and the Victorian Literary Man.* Stanford: Stanford UP, 2000.

Smith, Grahame. "The Life and Times of Charles Dickens." *The Cambridge Companion to Charles Dickens.* Ed. John O. Jordan. Cambridge: Cambridge UP, 2001. 1–16.

Stein, Richard L. "Dickens and Illustration." *The Cambridge Companion to Charles Dickens.* Ed. John O. Jordan. Cambridge: Cambridge UP, 2001. 167–89.

Stewart, Garret. "Dickens and Language." *The Cambridge Companion to Charles Dickens.* Ed. John O. Jordan. Cambridge: Cambridge UP, 2001. 136–52.

Stiltner, Barry. "*Hard Times:* The Disciplinary City." *Dickens Studies Annual* 30 (2001): 193–217.

Stokes, Peter. "Bentham, Dickens and the Uses of the Workhouse." *SEL* 41, 4 (Autumn 2001): 711–27.

Tambling, Jeremy. *Lost in the American City: Dickens, James, Kafka.* Houndmills: Palgrave, 2001.

Taylor, Jonathan. " 'Servants' Logic' and Analytical Chemistry: George Eliot, Dickens and Servants." *Dickens Studies Annual* 30 (2001): 263–85.

Tick, Stanley. "Autobiographical Impulses in *The Haunted Man.*" *Dickens Quarterly* 18, 2 (June 2001): 62–70.

Tracy, Robert. "Clock Work: *The Old Curiosity Shop* and *Barnaby Rudge.*" *Dickens Studies Annual* 30 (2001), 23–43.

Trodd, Anthea. "Messages in Bottles and Collins's Seafaring Man." *SEL* 41, 4 (Autumn 2001): 751–65.

Waters, Catherine. "Gender, Family and Domestic Ideology." *The Cambridge Companion to Charles Dickens.* Ed. John O. Jordan. Cambridge: Cambridge UP, 2001.

Wilt, Judith. "Masks of the English in *Barnaby Rudge.*" *Dickens Studies Annual* 30 (2001): 75–95.

Witucki, Barbara. "*Hard Times*: Dickens's Ode to Saint Cecilia." *Dickens Quarterly* 18, 4 (Dec. 2001): 203–17.

Wood, Jane. *Passion and Pathology in Victorian Fiction.* Oxford: Oxford UP, 2001.

Our Mutual Friend:
An Annotated Bibliography,
Supplement I—1984-2000

Robert J. Heaman

This annotated bibliography of Our Mutual Friend *supplements an earlier volume,* Our Mutual Friend: An Annotated Bibliography, *by Joel J. Brattin and Bert G. Hornback, and includes entries from 1984 through 2000. As in the earlier volume, the entries are numerically listed and indexed. So that annotations may be easily cross-referenced with the 1984 bibliography, the numbered entries are consecutive from that volume, and thus the present work begins with # 684. As in the 1984 volume, the bibliography is divided into three sections—Text, Studies, and Biography and Bibliography—and each of these sections is divided into subsections. As in the earlier bibliography, the following categories have been limited or omitted: condensations or editions of the novel that do not include a critical introduction, doctoral dissertations whose published abstracts do not call attention to the dissertation's treatment of* Our Mutual Friend, *translations of the novel, or criticisms written in foreign languages. Because single items are not generally listed in more than one section, users interested in subjects such as historical backgrounds or literary sources, parallels, and influence should consult the index for further references to those subjects in other subsections of the bibliography. With the exception of doctoral dissertations, for which the compiler has relied upon* Dissertation Abstracts International, *the editor has worked directly with the materials described.*

Our Mutual Friend

An Annotated Bibliography Supplement I—1984-2000

Robert J. Heaman

Contents

Part I. Text

Part II. Studies

Preface

How To Use This Bibliography

This bibliography supplements an earlier volume, *Our Mutual Friend: An Annotated Bibliography*, by Joel J. Brattin and Bert G. Hornback, and includes entries from 1984 through 2000. As in the earlier volume, the entries are numerically listed and indexed. So that annotations may be easily cross-referenced with the 1984 bibliography, the numbered entries are consecutive from that volume, and thus the present work begins with #684. Cross-references within the present volume are indicated by parentheses ( ). For ease of use, some materials (such as critical introductions to new editions) are multiply listed as well as cross-listed. As in the 1984 volume, the bibliography is divided into three sections—Text, Studies, and Biography and Bibliography—and each of these sections is divided into subsections. The entries in each subsection are arranged alphabetically, except for the subsections on Editions, Audio Adaptations, Film and Video Adaptations, and Stage Adaptations, all of which are arranged chronologically. Listings of commentary, arranged alphabetically, follow the items in the subsections on Audio Adaptations, Film and Video Adaptations, and Stage Adaptations. The entries are numbered consecutively throughout the bibliography, and the subject index refers to entries by item number, not by page number.

As in the earlier bibliography, the following categories have been limited or omitted: condensations or editions of the novel that do not include a critical introduction, doctoral dissertations whose published abstracts do not call attention to the dissertation's treatment of *Our Mutual Friend*, translations of the novel, or criticism written in foreign languages.

Because single items are not generally listed in more than one section, users interested in subjects such as historical backgrounds or literary sources, parallels, and influence should consult the index for further references to those subjects in other subsections of the bibliography.

With the exception of doctoral dissertations, for which the compiler has relied upon *Dissertation Abstracts International*, the editor has worked directly with the materials described.

Acknowledgements

I am deeply indebted to the staff of the Wilkes University Library, and in particular to Jon Lindgren and Brian Sacolic for their patience and guidance. I am grateful to Joel J. Brattin and Bert Hornback for their earlier volume, upon which this study is based; additionally to Joel for his generous support and suggestions on the introduction; and additionally to Bert for being a master teacher, scholar, and friend. I am also grateful to Richard Dunn and Ann M. Tandy for providing in *David Copperfield: An Annotated Bibliography, Supplement I* an excellent model for the update of a bibliography. To Duane DeVries, general editor of the Dickens Bibliographies series, I owe deep thanks not only for his generous encouragement and support, but also for his splendid editing and thoughtful suggestions. Finally, I want to suggest the debt of my gratitude and express my love for Patricia by dedicating this work to her.

Introduction

Out Mutual Friend, Dickens's last complete novel, explores the possibility of human redemption in a society bankrupt of value and meaning. Dickens had the title in mind as early as 1860 and had settled on it in the fall of 1862, two years before the first installment appeared in 1864. The novel itself had been percolating in his mind for some time; he wrote to Wilkie Collins on 9 August 1863 that he was "always thinking about writing a long book" but "never beginning to do it" **(684)**. He had difficulty composing the novel, complaining to Forster on 29 July 1864 that although he had "not been wanting in industry" he had been "wanting in invention and [had] fallen behind with the book" **(684)**. He was beset by personal, physical, and marital problems as well as artistic difficulties when he wrote to Forster at the end of May 1865 that work and "worry without exercise, would soon make an end" of him **(684)**. His marriage had broken up, his energy was failing, and his clandestine relationship with Ellen Ternan no doubt took its toll on his health. Many of his friends, including Frank Stone, Thackeray, and John Leech, had died recently, and Dickens himself may have been hearing Time's winged chariot hurrying near as he was writing *Our Mutual Friend.*

Despite these distractions, Dickens was thinking in large terms at the time of *Our Mutual Friend.* He told Collins that he "felt at first quite dazed in getting back to the large canvas and the big brushes" **(684)**. He is referring, of course, to writing a long book, and the scope of the world he is surveying is large indeed: society and money, poverty and exploitation, beauty and truth, love and death and resurrection. Joel J. Brattin and Bert G. Hornback's introduction to the 1984 annotated bibliography of *Our Mutual Friend* provides an admirable survey of the criticism of the novel from early contemporary reviews through the early 1980s. They note that recent criticism at the time of their survey had "demonstrated an increasing tendency to treat extraordinarily limited aspects of Dickens's artistic techniques, goals, and achievements," and they express hope that future studies will "come to grips with the large, complex, and often elusive social and human realities that so engrossed Dickens's attention.'' The best of the studies since Brattin and Hornback's bibliography have, I believe, done just that: they examine the large canvas of *Our Mutual Friend* to search for the sources of hope Dickens discovers in a morally bankrupt society.

The tension in recent criticism from 1984 to 2000, the years under consideration in this bibliography, is between those who are primarily concerned with Dickens's social analysis and those who are primarily concerned with his artistic technique in this novel. Steven Connor, Pam Morris, Juliet McMaster, and John P. Farrel best exemplify those who study Dickens as social critic; Angus Collins, Lawrence Frank, Gregg Hecimovich, J. Hillis Miller, and Peter Smith best exemplify those who deal with Dickens as artist.

Steven Connor **(745)** argues that *Our Mutual Friend* is Dickens's ''most radical and provoking examination of the determination of the individual by the system'' and concludes that ''this is a novel in which the only way for consciousness or identity to survive is to attempt a withdrawal from the encroaching life of systematic change.'' He sees the ''recurrent pattern'' of the novel as the ''shift from self to context, from being to being-in-relationship.''

In her thoughtful analysis of the effect of social forces of the 1860s on *Our Mutual Friend,* Pam Morris **(836)** argues that the ending of the novel, in which the marriage of Lizzie and Eugene brings together ''patrician disaffection'' with the ''dialect-working classes,'' offers the resolution to the problem of finding cultural self-renewal in a society that has ''devalued its own expressive currency'' through the degeneration of language resulting from Podsnappery. She sees the bringing together of the Boffins, the Harmons, the Wrayburns, Jenny Wren and Sloppy as representing a ''utopian community: lower-class trueness of heart, responsibly administered wealth, cultural refinement and working-class artistry and craftsmanship in the form of Jenny Wren's dolls and Sloppy's carpentry.'' However, she fears this community is removed from the ''common streets'' and points out that the product of the educated working class, Bradley Headstone, has been cast back to ''primal slime and mud,'' and excluded from the regenerated society.

Juliet McMaster **(823)** addresses the Victorian concern about the tendency of great civilizations to fragment, arguing that Dickens ''presents a vision of a world and a society that are disintegrating'' in *Our Mutual Friend.* She asserts that Dickens forces us to see the fragmentation and incoherence through his visual images but concludes that while he can make us see the incoherence, he does not ''convince us that the incoherent is coherent after all.'

John P. Farrell **(769)** argues that Dickens's social imagination is not as ideologically incoherent as many critics claim. Instead of simply identifying social problems and then taking his heroes and heroines off to safe enclaves where they are protected from these problems—as those who accuse Dickens of sentimental radicalism insist he is doing—Dickens is interested in the "expressive forms of human action and their interplay." He sees in Dickens's novels relationships among people that are more powerful than the negative effects of the war between "the system and the self," and demonstrates how the relationships among various sets of partners in *Our Mutual Friend* reveal that "the protest against the social system, emerging from the dialogic experience of social agents, is itself dialogic—an occasion, multiplied many times over, for the local practice of mutuality to redeem us from the monological discourse of the state."

Among those critics looking to Dickens's art as the source of his hope, Angus Collins **(744)** is concerned with the "possible exhaustion" of Dickens's creative energies as he was writing *Our Mutual Friend*. He argues that in the novel "Dickens's preoccupation with the terms of his art is rooted in his personal and creative situation and testifies in particular to his longing for some sort of human permanence." He concludes that through the very act of composing *Our Mutual Friend,* Dickens moves "into the life of the work as it will outlast and preserve the man."

Lawrence Frank **(774)** changes the focus from Dickens's personal concern about permanence to Dickens's desire to see his character achieve a sense of fulfillment. He argues that the self becomes a narrative construct and in the "urban labyrinth of *Our Mutual Friend,* man remains the novelist of himself."

Gregg Hecimovich **(794)**, in a splendid analysis, shifts from the focus on art and the imagination from the text to the reader. He argues convincingly that *Our Mutual Friend* is elaborately constructed as a riddle drawing the "reader into the narrative through revelations and deceptions in syntax, narrative perspective, and plot." What is often perceived as the disjunctive structure of the novel is, he believes, not a result of Dickens's weakness but of his society's sickness, which Dickens is reflecting in the novel. Hecimovich concludes that Dickens analyzes this disintegrating society and exposes it to the reader who "negotiates uncertainties of surface and substance" and, through the process of reading creatively, achieves the capacity to reorder the fallen world imaginatively.

J. Hillis Miller **(832)** comes to a similar conclusion, although he arrives at it from a very different place. Miller argues that the characters in the novel are "trapped within Victorian assumptions about class and gender." The only possibility for a "change in the bad condition of society is some extreme event that breaks up petrified class institutions and begins again after immersion" in an "impersonal energy" that lies beneath the "ideological matrices" of which characters cannot be aware. "This power underlies each person and, for Dickens, is present everywhere in nature, too," according to Miller.

He concludes that Dickens's capacity to force a happy ending in improbable circumstances comes from his own "histrionic invention in response to the demand made on him by the realm of otherness that, within the fiction, drives all his characters and, in the 'real world,' drives him to create them." Miller cautions us that in the end "Dickens's theatre will not, however, come alive without the reader's collaboration."

It is precisely this notion of the reader's collaboration that Peter Smith **(876)** insists is necessary for proper appreciation of *Our Mutual Friend,* a novel whose theme, in Smith's analysis, is beauty. Smith shows that Dickens is postulating an aesthetic that avoids the extremes of the bourgeois, on the one hand, and the avante-garde, on the other. He examines Jenny Wren to show how she creates beauty out of suffering and harsh experience—not by transforming the harshness but by carrying it along "into the realm of beauty, and there preserv[ing] it as a permanent source of beauty's vital strength."

When Joel J. Brattin **(732)** claims, in the introduction to his recent edition of *Our Mutual Friend,* that Dickens is "completely serious about the power of love to move the world—and to transform it utterly," we see that we have moved back to the larger canvas. The love that becomes identified with imagination, with the perception and creation of beauty, with self-denial, creativity, renewal, with the art that Blake insists is charity, is the self-annihilating power that allows the artist to enable those who are willing to see what needs to be done to bring about a new Earth and a new Heaven. The very capacity that allows us to see the coherent beauty of *Our Mutual Friend* is the same that can utterly transform the world it subjects to critical analysis. The best criticism on *Our Mutual Friend* over the past two decades has helped us to understand how Dickens is dealing with the large canvas and has given proper recognition to the importance of the interconnections among love, art, and the imaginations in Dickens's treatment of society.

Part I. Text

OUR MUTUAL FRIEND IN PROGRESS:
LETTERS, NUMBERS, PLANS

684. *The Letters of Charles Dickens.* Vols. 10 (1862–1864) and 11 (1865–1867). Ed. Graham Storey et al. Oxford: Clarendon Press, 1998–1999.

This meticulously edited, annotated, and indexed edition incorporates and supersedes all previous editions of Dickens's letters.

Vol. 10 (1862–1864). Ed. Graham Storey. Oxford: Clarendon Press, 1998.

This volume contains many letters relative to the genesis, composition, contractual arrangements, directions to Marcus Stone on illustrations, proof corrections, the dedication, and reception of *Our Mutual Friend* as well as Dickens's thoughts about *Our Mutual Friend* in its various stages of completion.

Dickens had chosen the title for the novel as early as 1861, according to Storey's preface. On 9 August 1863 Dickens wrote to Wilkie Collins that he was "always thinking of writing a long book" but "never beginning to do it." However, on 30 August 1863 he told Forster that he was "full of notions besides for the new twenty numbers," and indicated to Forster on 12 October 1863 that he was "exceedingly anxious to begin" his book. After completing the first two numbers, he wrote to Collins on 25 January 1864 that the book "is a combination of drollery with romance" and confessed that he believed it to be "very good," although he "felt at first quite dazed in getting back to the large canvas and the big brushes." He wrote to Marcus Stone on 23 February 1864 that he thought "the design for the cover, *excellent,*" and did "not doubt its coming out to perfection." The novel proceeded slowly: in a letter to Forster 29 March 1864, he wrote "I have grown hard to satisfy, and write very slowly. And I have so much-not fiction-that *will* be thought of, when I don't want to think of it, that I am forced to take more care than I once took." He reported to Forster on 3 May 1864, however, that "Nothing can be better than *Our Mutual*

Friend, now in its thirtieth thousand, and others flowing in fast.'' He continued to have problems with composing the novel, however, as he indicated to Forster on 29 July 1864: ''Although I have not been wanting in industry, I have been wanting in invention, and have fallen back with the book.'' In a letter to Mrs. Eliza Davis on 16 November 1864 he wrote that he hoped to ''be the best of friends with the Jewish people'' and assured her that an error he had made with regard to Riah would do ''no harm'' because Dickens was fusing together the ''peculiarities of dress and manner . . . for the sake of picturesqueness.''

Vol. 11 (1865–1867). Ed. Graham Storey. Oxford: Clarendon Press, 1999.

This volume contains many letters relative to *Our Mutual Friend*, including the composition, directions to Marcus Stone on illustrations, proof corrections, dedication, reception, adaptations, pirated editions, US publication, presentation copies, and Dickens's thoughts about *Our Mutual Friend* in its various stages of completion.

On 17 January 1865 Dickens expressed his amusement to Charles Kent for not seeing his ''way with a certain Mutual Friend of ours'' and suspects that he ''may begin to be fearfully knowing at somewhere about No. xii or xiii. But you shan't, if I can help it.'' In a letter to Lady Molesworth, 19 May 1865, he feared they ''shall not meet'' because between his writing and his social engagements he is ''gone a 'coon.' '' He told Peter Cunningham on 15 February 1865 that he hoped he ''will not like Our Mutual Friend worse, when you get to know him better.'' And on 23 May 1865 he assured Rev. William Harness that he had been ''hard at work at your conversion—to the opinion that the story of Our Mutual Friend is very interesting and was from the first tending to a purpose which you couldn't foresee until I chose to take you into my confidence. Modest this.—But true.'' However the work took its toll on him, and he told Forster at the end of May 1865 that work and ''worry, without exercise, would soon make an end'' of him and that ''no one knows as I know to-day how near to [a breakdown] I have been.'' In a letter to Thomas Mitton on 13 June 1865 he related the horrible experience of the Staplehurst railway accident and reported that he ''remembered that I had the MS. of a number with me, and clambered back into the carriage for it,'' anticipating his Postscript. He expressed his amazement to Forster in early July 1865 that he has ''under-written number sixteen by two and a half pages—a thing I have not done since *Pickwick*.'' He wrote to Bulwer Lytton on 20 July 1865 to decline an invitation on the grounds that he was ''tied by the leg'' to his book, and expressed his hope that

Lytton "will find the purpose and plot of my book very plain when you see it as a whole piece." He wrote to George Childs on 31 July 1865 that he was "but now finishing Our Mutual Friend," and indicated to W. H. Wills on 27 August 1865 that he was "working like a Dragon" on the novel and hoped "something near a week may bring me through it." He told Thomas Beard on 21 September 1865 that he had "been working my head off, but finished my book on the Second of this month," considerably before the final double Numbers appeared on 31 October 1865. A letter from Lytton "praising *Our Mutual Friend*, but registering some criticism, prompted one of Dickens's rare letters justifying his own writing," according to Storey's preface. Dickens wrote Lytton on 28 November 1865 that "I work slowly and with great care, and never give way to my invention recklessly, but constantly restrain it; and that I think it is my infirmity to fancy or perceive relation in things which are not apparent generally. Also I have such an inexpressible enjoyment of what I see in a droll light, that I dare say I pet it as if it were a spoilt child."

685. Stone, Harry, ed. *"Our Mutual Friend."* In his *Dickens' Working Notes for His Novels*. Chicago: Chicago University Press, 1987, pp. 329–73.

This handsome volume provides full-size facsimiles of the number plans to the novels with complementary typographic transcriptions, a general introduction, and an introduction and commentary on the number plans to *Our Mutual Friend*.

Stone demonstrates that the composition of *Our Mutual Friend* was "hard, slow, demanding, laborious work." He points out that Dickens was concerned "about how a motif should unfold as a novel progresses," indicating that Dickens needed to balance the bold effects that would be remembered from month to month in the serial publication with the "subtler meanings, easily forgotten or missed in the broken course of a long serial, but necessary for the rich rendering of a theme, and absolutely essential to the integrity of a novel in its completed, uninterrupted form." He asserts that the number plans "highlight how Dickens managed to keep a purpose 'unsuspected, yet always working itself out.' "

TEXTUAL COMMENTARY: SCHOLARSHIP CONCERNING PUBLICATION, TEXTUAL MATTERS, CHARACTER PROTOTYPES, ILLUSTRATIONS

686. Brattin, Joel. "Dickens's Creation of Bradley Headstone." *Dickens Studies Annual*, 14 (1985), 147–65.

Through a careful and intelligent examination of the holograph manuscript of *Our Mutual Friend* along with the number plans, Brattin
"reveal[s] Dickens's imagination in the process of creating a complex,
hauntingly memorable character," Bradley Headstone. Brattin shows
how interlinear additions in the manuscript demonstrate Dickens's
concern to capture Headstone's awkwardness, his superficial decency,
his repressed nature, and his uncontrollable depth of feeling. He concludes that the great care Dickens took in "reworking Headstone's
language, gestures, and 'state of mind' shapes both Bradley's villainy
and his humanity, and results in a convincing and frightening portrayal
of Bradley's inner life."

687. Brattin, Joel J. " 'I will not have my words misconstrued': The Text
of *Our Mutual Friend.*" *Dickens Quarterly*, 15 (1998), 167–76.
Brattin carefully analyzes the Charles Dickens edition (published in
1867–68) of *Our Mutual Friend*, which had long been assumed to be
the most carefully revised edition of Dickens's works but whose revisions have recently been challenged as minimal or "fitful." He discovers 2,203 variants in his collation of the 1868 Charles Dickens
edition with the first edition of 1864–65, and argues that "not a single
one of the over 2200 changes was necessarily by Dickens himself;
though Dickens may have revised other volumes in the edition which
bears his signature as imprimatur, *Our Mutual Friend* bears no trace of
authorial revision." Brattin indicates that the Charles Dickens edition
"offers many useful corrections of errors in the first edition" but
"fewer than 5% of the 2,203 new readings cry out for emendation."

688. Brattin, Joel J. "Reading Between the Lines: Interpreting Dickens's
Later Manuscripts." *Dissertation Abstacts International*, 47 (1986),
534A (Stanford University).
Brattin examines the "extraordinarily complex" holographs of several
of Dickens's late novels, including *Our Mutual Friend*, in order to
"illuminate different aspects of Dickens's work, and confirm in new
ways that explorations of character and theme are of central importance to Dickens."

689. Cayzer, Elizabeth. "Dickens and His Late Illustrators: A Change in
Style: *Two Unknown Artists.*" *Dickensian*, 87 (1991), 3–16.
Cayzer argues that although Marcus Stone seems "moderately capable" through his "matter-of-fact style" to illustrate Dickens's "more
restrained manner in writing" in *Our Mutual Friend*, he is not able to
capture the dramatic moment, and his pictures are full of inaccuracies.
Cayzer believes that Dickens was disappointed with the illustrator and
therefore employed Luke Fildes to illustrate *The Mystery of Edwin
Drood.*

690. Cotsell, Michael. "Mr. Venus Rises from the Counter: Dickens's Taxidermist and his Contribution to *Our Mutual Friend*." *Dickensian*, 80 (1984), 105–13.

Cotsell points out that Mr. Venus's shop in *Our Mutual Friend* is based on an actual business located at 42 St Andrew Street, off Holborn Circus. He indicates that the smells of the shop are the smells of the substances used by taxidermists according to Captain Thomas Brown's *The Taxidermist's Manual* (1836), and he analyzes the objects in the shop. Cotsell consults the South American explorer and popular author Charles Waterton's descriptions of proper articulation methods to evaluate Mr. Venus's work. He concludes that Mr. Venus is one of Dickens's "greatest comi-grotesque conceptions, humorously touching on a popular element of Victorian taste."

691. Dessner, Lawrence Jay. "A Possible Source for Dickens's Lammles." *Dickensian*, 85 (1989), 105–07.

Dessner offers Captain Frederick Marryat's *Japhet in Search of a Father* (1833–34) as the source for the Lammles in *Our Mutual Friend*. Japhet's parents had deceived one another, discovered their mutual deception, and agreed to separate, keeping the marriage a secret. Although Marryat's treatment of "deliberate sexual immorality" is amusing, the "moral astringency" of the coming Victorian culture can be seen in the fates of the couple, who are sufficiently punished, according to Dessner.

692. Knowles, Owen. "Veneering and the Age of Veneer: A Source and Background for *Our Mutual Friend*." *Dickensian*, 81 (1985), 88–96.

Knowles points to five articles by an anonymous author in *Fraser's Magazine* (1850–51) on the nineteenth century as "The Age of Veneer" as a probable source for the society scenes in *Our Mutual Friend*. These articles explain what the process of veneering is and apply the term metaphorically to "an age of meretricious sham which no longer knows itself for what it is." Knowles shows parallels among the five articles and Dickens's use of the metaphor throughout the novel, concluding that both the "novel and articles seem less concerned with political jobbery, acquisitiveness and inequalities of wealth as evils in themselves than with the systematic and interlocking pretexts which arise from all of these things and affect the rich and poor alike." *Our Mutual Friend*, he shows, "exploit[s] to richly poetic effect some of the structural properties" of the Victorian essay.

693. O'Hea, Michael. "Hidden Harmony: Marcus Stone's Wrapper Design for *Our Mutual Friend*." *Dickensian*, 91 (1995), 198–208.

O'Hea demonstrates that Stone cleverly provides clues that identify Harmon as Rokesmith and that in other details he followed Dickens's directions to ''give a 'vague idea' of the novel's plot'' in the cover design of *Our Mutual Friend*.

SUBSEQUENT EDITIONS CONTAINING NEW INTRODUCTIONS OR ILLUSTRATIONS

694. *Our Mutual Friend*. Champaign, Ill: Project Gutenberg, 1992. Electronic text.
http://www.netLibrary.com/urlapi.asp?action=summary&v=1&bookid=1032500.
This electronic version includes the text, but there are no notes, illustrations, indication of edition, or other apparatus.

695. *Our Mutual Friend*. Everyman Edition. Introduction by Andrew Sanders with illustrations by Marcus Stone. New York: A. A. Knopf, 1994. xliii + 832 pp.
This edition includes text, introduction (**864**), select bibliography, chronology, list of illustrations, list of characters, and the introduction to the original Everyman edition of *Our Mutual Friend* by G. K. Chesterton.

696. *Our Mutual Friend*. New Oxford Illustrated Edition. Introduction by Andrew Sanders (**864**). London: David Campbell, 1994. xliii + 832.
This edition is identical to the Everyman Edition (**695**).

697. *Our Mutual Friend*. Penguin Edition. Edited with an introduction and notes by Adrian Poole and illustrations by Marcus Stone. Harmondsworth: Penguin Books, 1997. xxxiii + 884 pp.
This paperback edition includes text, introduction (**856**), notes, chronology, a list of ''Further Reading,'' an appendix on Marcus Stone's illustrations (citing eight useful commentaries), and an appendix of Dickens's number plans.

698. *Our Mutual Friend*. New Oxford Illustrated Edition. Edited with an introduction by Michael Cotsell. New York: Oxford UP, 1998. xxvi + 852 pp.
This paperback edition includes text, chronology, introduction (**748**), list of characters, ''Explanatory Notes,'' and ''Further Reading.''

699. *Our Mutual Friend*. Everyman Edition. Edited with an introduction by Joel J. Brattin. With illustrations by Marcus Stone. London: J. M. Dent, 2000. xxxviii + 930 pp.
This paperback edition includes text, chronology, introduction (**732**), notes on the text and illustrations, notes, an appendix on ''*Our Mutual Friend* and Dickens's Book of Memoranda,'' an appendix on ''Running Titles in the Charles Dickens Edition,'' an appended commentary

on "Dickens and his Critics," "Suggestions for Further Reading," a selected bibliography, and a text summary.

AUDIO ADAPTATIONS

700. "A Lecture on Charles Dickens: *Little Dorrit* and *Our Mutual Friend.*" Delivered by John Holloway. Battle, Sussex: Norwich Tapes, 1984. 1 cassette, 90 minutes.
701. "The Bio-economics of *Our Mutual Friend.*" Lecture delivered by Catherine Gallagher, 29 July 1986, as part of the Lecture Series at the School of Criticism and Theory at Dartmouth. 1 cassette. See also **(777)**.
702. *Our Mutual Friend.* Read by Paul Scofield. Studio City, CA: Dove Books on Tape, 1987. 2 cassettes, 169 minutes.
703. *Our Mutual Friend.* Read by Jim Killavey. Portsmouth, RI: Jimcin Recordings, 1988. 27 cassettes, 40.5 hours.
704. *Our Mutual Friend.* Read by Jim Killavey. Newport Beach, CA: Books on Tape, 1989. 27 cassettes, 40.5 hours.
705. *Our Mutual Friend.* Read by Robert Hardy. New York: Penguin Audiobooks, 1997. 4 cassettes, 315 minutes.
706. *Our Mutual Friend.* Read by David Case. Newport Beach, CA: Books on Tape, 1998. Unabridged. 24 cassettes, 36 hours.
707. *Our Mutual Friend.* Read by Robert Whitfield. Ashfield, OR: Blackstone Audiobooks, 1999. 23 cassettes, 2007 minutes.
707a. "BBC Radio Presents *Our Mutual Friend.*" Narrated by Simon Cadell with a full cast of characters. Directed by Jane Morgan; dramatized by Betty Davies. New York: Bantam Doubleday Dell Audio, 1998. 6 cassettes, 530 minutes.
      Review: J. Wain, *Listener*, 111 (10 May 1984), 33.

COMMENTARY ON AUDIO ADAPTATIONS

708. See Bolton **(722)**. *Dickens Dramatized.*
     Bolton lists three radio dramas, including the BBC centennial celebration featuring Emlyn Williams. The bulk of Bolton's fifty-two entries on *Our Mutual Friend* refer to stage versions; see the entries under "Commentary on Film and Video Adaptations" **(712)** and "Commentary on Stage Adaptations" **(722)**.

FILM AND VIDEO ADAPTATIONS

709. *Our Mutual Friend.* Catherine Wearing, producer, and Julien Farino, director. Beverly Hills, CA: BBC Video, 1998. 3 videocassettes, 339 minutes.
   See reviews by Leonard (714), Reynolds (718), and Smith (719).
710. *A Charles Dickens Reading.* Read by Malcolm Andrews, 1986. 2 videocassettes, 102 minutes.
   Malcolm Andrews reads selections to a live audience from *Pickwick Papers, Oliver Twist, Little Dorrit,* and *Our Mutual Friend* (Mr. Podsnap).
711. *Phillip Collins: A Repertoire: Selected Readings from Charles Dickens.* Santa Cruz, CA; Presentation Unit of Media Services, the University Library, University of California, Santa Cruz, 1991. 1 videocassette, 1 hour 14 minutes.
   Phillip Collins presents excerpts from various works by Dickens, including Mr. Podsnap from *Our Mutual Friend.*

COMMENTARY ON FILM AND VIDEO ADAPTATIONS

712. See Bolton (722). *Dickens Dramatized.*
   Bolton lists two films and two teleplays. The bulk of Bolton's fifty-two entries on *Our Mutual Friend* refer to stage versions; see the entries under "Commentary on Audio Adaptations" (708) and "Commentary on Stage Adaptations" (722).
713. *Charles Dickens,* Our Mutual Friend: *A Viewer's Guide.* London: BBC Education, 1998. 46 pp.
   Published to accompany the BBC 2 Television adaptation of *Our Mutual Friend,* produced by Catherine Wearing (709), broadcast in Spring 1998.
714. Leonard, John. "*Our Mutual Friend.*" *New York,* 31 (4 January 1999), 75–76.
   Leonard praises Farino's 1998 BBC production (709) as "incredible television, worth every one of its six dark hours."
715. "*Our Mutual Friend*: The Scholarly Pages." Jon Michael Varese and David A. Perdue. Santa Cruz, Ca.: The Dickens Project, 1998. Posted December 1998. Accessed February 2002. *http://.ucsc.edu/dickens/ OMF/index.html.*
   The Scholarly Pages is an electronic archival resource dedicated to gathering and providing scholarly information on *Our Mutual Friend,*

designed to complement the BBC 1998 dramatization. The site includes links to e-text of the novel at Project Gutenberg; scans of the Marcus Stone illustrations; samplings of the original advertisements; a selected bibliography; a scholarly article archive; links to biographical accounts, sources on the history of composition, and contemporary reviews; links to the London Map from the BBC "Viewer's Guide"; "A Virtual Ramble of the London of *Our Mutual Friend*" led by David Parker; an excerpt of an essay on "Dust" from *Household Words* and on "Dustmen" by Henry Mayhew; essays on "Schools of Education" and "Life in the Victorian City"; and "A Photographic Archive" of thematically related nineteenth-century photographs.

716. Petrie, Graham. "Dickens in Denmark: Four Danish Versions of his Novels." *Journal of European Studies*, 26 (1996), 185–93.

Petrie points out that *Our Mutual Friend* was one of four films made by the Nordisk Company in Denmark between 1921 and 1924 based on Dickens novels, the others being *Great Expectations, David Copperfield*, and *Little Dorrit*. The films were favorably reviewed at the time: the British *Kinematograph Weekly* "claimed that 'Nordisk has proved its ability to translate the works of Charles Dickens to the language of the screen in fine productions of *Our Mutual Friend* and *Great Expectations . . . .*' " Although *Our Mutual Friend*, the longest of the films, exists only in an incomplete version today, it has several settings that capture very well the sense of "decay and rottenness that is central to the novel."

717. Pointer, Michael. *Charles Dickens on the Screen: The Film, Television, and Video Adaptations*. Lanham, MD; London: Scarecrow Press, 1996. vii + 207 pp.

Pointer provides introductory essays on dramatizing, condensing, and reconstructing Dickens, and offers commentary on several productions of his works. He then provides a catalogue of Dickens screen dramatizations that lists motion picture films, television productions, and videos, including "parodies, pastiches, and spoofs." He provides shortened cast lists of large productions. The 1976 BBC production of *Our Mutual Friend* "ranks as one of television's finest adaptations of Dickens and was an opportunity to see a dramatization of one of the less-popular of his novels. The whole production was so finely mounted that it raised the standard of quality in costume drama serials on TV," according to Pointer.

718. Reynolds, Matthew. "*Our Mutual Friend* BBC2." *Times Literary Supplement, 27* March 1998, p.20.

Reynolds finds the 1998 BBC adaptation **(709)** "full of things to praise, not least of which it makes real for us the teeming London of the novel.'' He regrets that Eugene and Bella "have been, not dumbed down but niced up," and finds that "the script is to a remarkable extent a work of inspired cutting and pasting, rather than of rewriting; the characters almost always speak the words which Dickens penned for them," for which he is grateful.

719. Smith, Grahame. "Television Review: *Our Mutual Friend.*" *Dickensian*, 94 (1998), 145–46.

Smith sees the 1998 BBC adaptation of *Our Mutual Friend* **(709)** as a "triumphant version"; he praises the "depth and range" of acting and the compensation of the loss of narrative prose "by a daring substitution of visual and aural alternatives."

STAGE ADAPTATIONS

720. *Our Mutual Friend.* Directed by Mike Patterson. Leeds University Theatre Production, 1986.

Review: G. Wild, *Dickensian*, 83 (1987), 61–62.

721. "Wooman, Lovely Wooman." Performed by Miriam Margoyles and David Timson. Directed by Sonia Fraser. Devised by Miriam Margoyles and Sonia Fraser. Performed at the Edinburgh International Festival, 22–27 August 1989.

Reviews: M. Slater, *Dickensian*, 85 (1989), 185–87; S. Raitt, "Dickens's Sick Fancies." *Times Literary Supplement*, 21 June 1991, p. 16.

COMMENTARY ON STAGE ADAPTATIONS

722. Bolton, H. Phillip. *Dickens Dramatized.* London: Mansell; Boston: G. K. Hall, 1987, pp. 430–36.

Bolton provides a chronological list of dramatic productions of Dickens's works, ranging from contemporary stage adaptations to more recent films, radio and television dramas and readings. He provides introductory essays on "Dickens's Dramatic Fame and Posterity," "Historical Background," "The Contemporary Context," "Playmakers: Playwrights," and "Playmakers: Actors and Actresses." He focuses on each novel chronologically, studying the dramatic history of each work.

Bolton points out that *Our Mutual Friend* "spawned no theatrical imitations during its initial serial issue," and only thirty staged versions after its completion, compared to 400 staged versions of *Oliver Twist* and 250 of *Nicholas Nickleby.* He lists fifty-two dramatizations of *Our Mutual Friend*, including two films, three radio dramas, and three teleplays.

Reviews: A. Sanders, *Times Literary Supplement*, 21 August 1987, p. 908; J. Parker, *Choice*, 25 (November 1987), 451–52; B. Bell, *Theatre Review*, 13 (Spring 1988), 60–61; J. Brattin, *Dickensian*, 84 (Spring 1988), 50–51; S. James, *Library Review*, 36 (Winter 1987), 295–96; G. deSousa, *American Reference Books Annual*, 19 (1988), 545; J. Ellis, *Nineteenth-Century Theatre Research*, 16 (Summer 1988), 68–72; P. Schlicke, *Theatre Notebook*, 43, i (1989), 44; G. Worth, *Victorian Studies*, 32 (Winter 1989), 255–57; A. Shelston, *New Theatre Quarterly,* 5 (1989), 306.

PART II. STUDIES

CRITICISM

723. Abrahams, Emily Linda. "Charles Dickens and the Projects of Narrative: *Oliver Twist* and *Our Mutual Friend*." *Dissertation Abstracts International*, 45 (1984), 3133A (Columbia University).

Abrahams considers the "multiple narrative projects" in *Oliver Twist* and *Our Mutual Friend*. She argues that Dickens's inconsistency in insisting on writing about things as they really are while at the same time attempting to portray absolute goodness in *Oliver Twist* is avoided in *Our Mutual Friend* "by recognizing that conflicting codes of representation are an inevitable part of novel-writing and by everywhere insisting on the fictiveness of all projects."

724. Ackroyd, Peter. *Dickens*. New York: Harper-Collins, 1990, passim.

A novelist himself, Ackroyd's extensively researched biography is animated by his own historical imagination. He argues, in his unique style, that Dickens "sensed in the change of London, a change in the nature of civilization itself. A civilization that he anatomized in *Our Mutual Friend* with the Veneerings and the Podsnaps. Speculation. Peculation. Overseas investment. Short-term money markets. Brokering. Joint stock banking. Discount companies. Limited liability. Credit. A world in which human identity was seen in terms of monetary value. A world of barter and exchange. And thus, in the houses of the middle-class and the upper middle-class, the fake 'marbling.' Veneer. Imitation wood. Chinoiserie. Exaggerated ornamentation. Blankets of fabric. Stifled silent rooms. Death. Gold. Filth. This is the world of his last complete novel." Ackroyd sees Dickens portraying his characters as actors in an "unreal game, its unreality confirming Dickens's sense of waking life as kind of a dream which must be 'dreamed out' before we dead awaken." In such a world, only those who "have gone through something like the loss of identity can be restored to anything like integrity."

Reviews: S. Gill, *Times Literary Supplement*, 31 August 1990, p. 911; S. Shatto, *Dickens Quarterly*, 7 (1990), 392–95; J. Kincaid, *New*

York Times Book Review, 13 January 1991, pp. 1, 24; G. Wills, *New York Review of Books*, 16 May 1991, pp. 8–12; W. Pritchard, *Hudson Review*, 44 (1991), 301–08.

725. Alter, Robert. "Reading Style in Dickens." *Philosophy and Literature*, 20 (1996), 130–37.

Alter demonstrates through wonderful close readings of a passage from *Dombey and Son* and two passages from *Our Mutual Friend* that Dickens, "above all the great master of figurative language in English after Shakespeare," deserves to be read slowly. Alter claims that Dickens's "particular stylistic feature" is metaphor and that he is "preeminently a performer."

726. Barloon, James Patrick. "Charting Boundaries: Secrets in the Novels of Charles Dickens." *Dissertation Abstracts International*, 56 (1995), 4404A (University of Kansas).

Barloon looks at the role secrets play in Dickens's novels, arguing that in *Our Mutual Friend* "secrets play an ineluctable role in Dickens's anatomization of society and approach toward characterization; what began primarily as a means to inject mystery and suspense into his stories, secrets came to constitute a defining element of Dickens's articulation of Victorian society and reality generally" in his last completed novel.

727. Baumgarten, Murray. "Seeing Double: Jews in the Fiction of F. Scott Fitzgerald, Charles Dickens, Anthony Trollope, and George Eliot." In *Between Race and Culture: Representations of "The Jew" in English and American Literature*. Ed. Bryan Cheyette. Stanford: Stanford University Press, 1996, pp. 44–61.

Baumgarten argues that in attempting to offer a positive portrayal of "the Jew" in response to Eliza Davis's urgings to "atone for the great wrong" of encouraging prejudice against "the despised Hebrew . . . Fagin," Dickens merely repeats in his creation of Riah the error he commits in *Oliver Twist*. To make Riah the only Jew in the novel, Baumgarten shows, is once again to scapegoat the Jew as a Jew. Because Riah is not seen in his "Jewish reference group" he is "non-narratable. Even in *Our Mutual Friend*, the Jew is outside discourse and thus in his or her isolation vulnerable to caricature."

728. Baumgarten, Murray. "The Imperial Child: Bella, *Our Mutual Friend*, and the Victorian Picturesque." In *Dickens and the Children of Empire*. Ed. Wendy S. Jacobson. New York: Palgrave, 2000, pp. 54–66.

Baumgarten analyzes two passages in *Our Mutual Friend* that associate Bella Wilfer with imperial imagery: "An Innocent Elopement" and "The Feast of the Three Hobgoblins." In the first, Bella takes her father away from Chicksey Veneering and Stobble's, buys him a complete outfit of clothes, takes him on a cruise to Greenwich, and provides him with an extravagant feast. In her fantasy Bella transforms the "elopement" into "an heroic, imperial adventure, yet one we recognize as part of the exploitative side of British nineteenth-century commerce." By the time of the second passage, in which John and Bella go to the Counting House to announce their love to Bella's father, Bella has renounced her mercenary ways and exchanged money and status for love and apparent poverty. Her father greets the declaration of love with joy, but, Baumgarten points out, the language he uses echoes Bella's imperial fantasies of the previous passage. Bella's stereotypical vision of the China house where John tells Bella he works after they are married reinforces for Baumgarten that "the Empire and her fantasies continue to be present" and that imperial images and concern for economic power remain as "traces" in Bella, " as picturesque details." The Boffin-miser plot turns out to be "picturesque" as well, the picturesque being an "artistic mode that emphasizes the transformative power of personal feeling," according to Baumgarten. The picturesque is set against the panoramic in *Our Mutual Friend* (Baumgarten points to the panoramic opening of the novel and follows the camera-eye of the narrator to close-up in that scene). Baumgarten wonders in this provocative essay if the horror Lizzie feels as she watches her father exploit the dead is not the same horror Dickens feels as he considers the impact of Empire on his characters.

729. Beiderwell, Bruce. "The Coherence of *Our Mutual Friend.*" *Journal of Narrative Technique,* 15 (1985), 234–43.
Beiderwell carefully analyzes the grammatical and lexical features of first two chapters of *Our Mutual Friend* to examine Dickens's "strategy of opposition and repetition" in those chapters, and goes on to argue convincingly that this pattern extends throughout the novel to provide coherence for the narrative threads.

730. Bird, Toby Anne. "Dickens and the Tradition of Comedy: A Study of *Pickwick Papers* and *Our Mutual Friend.*" *Dissertation Abstracts International,* 46 (1985), 3356A (City University of New York).
Bird examines Dickens's use of comic technique, particularly of farce derived from the stage, in *Pickwick Papers* and *Our Mutual Friend,* arguing that he draws on traditional elements of comedy in both works but that in *Our Mutual Friend* he "invests these comic techniques with symbolic resonance meant to suggest that deceit has corrupted all levels of society."

731. See Brattin **(686)**. "Dickens's Creation of Bradley Headstone."

732. Brattin, Joel J. "Introduction." In 2000 Dent Edition **(699)**, pp. xxiii-xxxi.

Brattin discusses the great care Dickens took in writing *Our Mutual Friend* and analyzes how comedy illuminates a reality of social life in the novel. He indicates that all the major themes of the mature Dickens appear here, particularly the important theme of transformation. He analyzes the various presentations of love in the novel—family, friendship, romantic—, discusses riches and the condition of the various economic classes in the novel, and concludes that the novel is largely about dissolution and fragmentation. *Our Mutual Friend* is "not, finally, about greed and selfishness as much as it is about love." Dickens, Brattin insists, "is completely serious about the power of love to move the world—and to transform it utterly."

733. See Brattin **(687)**. " 'I will not have my words misconstrued': The Text of *Our Mutual Friend*."

734. See Brattin **(688)**. "Reading Between the Lines: Interpreting Dickens's Later Manuscripts."

735. Brennan, Joseph Anthony. "Carlyle, Dickens, and the Gospel of Work." *Dissertation Abstracts International*, 57 (1995), 228A (State University of New York at Buffalo).

Brennan examines *Our Mutual Friend* in the context of Carlyle's "gospel of work," arguing that Dickens demonstrates the social and psychological damage resulting from obsessive work. Dickens presents the home in opposition to the economic world, "presenting it as a place where commodity consumption can reverse the alienation and reification of the subject which occurs in work." However, Dickens undercuts this opposition by showing that the consumption of commodities creates waste, which in turn becomes commodity.

736. Budd, Dona. "When So, Not So: Voice and Gender in Dickens's Fiction." *Dissertation Abstracts International*, 55 (1993), 1963A (Berkeley: U of California).

Budd argues that the patriarchal voice dominates Dickens's fiction but is not fully adequate to accommodate his sympathies with the poor and the oppressed. Dickens thus appropriates a feminine voice in *David Copperfield*, *Bleak House*, and *Our Mutual Friend* that compensates for the inadequacies of this patriarchal voice and destabilizes its narrative authority.

737. Burns, Deborah Hughes. "Marriage and Money in Charles Dickens's *Our Mutual Friend*." *Dissertation Abstracts International*, 54 (1993), 3445A (University of Rhode Island).

Burns considers *Our Mutual Friend* in the context of how economic conditions shaped love and marriage in Victorian times. She analyzes the marriage of John and Bella as a failed instance of an attempt to establish a new kind of marriage, one based on equality and freedom from financial considerations. Finally, in the marriage of Eugene and Lizzie, Dickens is able to create an ideal marriage based on love and respect rather than money. Burns concludes that at the end of his career Dickens comes to "reject the middle-class ideas about love and marriage he had always been so strongly associated with."

738. Busch, Frederick. "Suitors by Boz." *Gettysburg Review*, 6 (1993), 561–78.

Busch draws a comparison between Ellen Ternan and *Our Mutual Friend*'s Pleasant Riderhood. He is "tempted to think that when Mr. Venus, the artist-of-sorts, is rejected by his beloved, he is an emblem for Dickens." Pleasant's self-consciousness and desire for privacy are, he believes, projections of Dickens's clandestine relationship with Ellen Ternan. An interesting, if not altogether convincing, parallel.

739. Calvino, Italo. "Charles Dickens, *Our Mutual Friend*." In his *Why Read the Classics?* Trans. Martin McLaughlin. New York: Pantheon Books, 1999, pp. 145–50.

Calvino regards *Our Mutual Friend* as "an unqualified masterpiece, both in its plot and in the way it is written," giving examples of similes and descriptions from the novel to make his case. He also praises Dickens's portrayal of society and class conflict in the novel.

740. See Cayzer **(689)**. Dickens and His Late Illustrators: A Change in Style: *Two Unknown Artists*.

741. Černý, Lothar. Life in Death: Art in Dickens's *Our Mutual Friend*. *Dickens Quarterly*, 17 (2000), 22–36.

Černý points out that Dickens presents two worlds in *Our Mutual Friend*, the mechanical, lifeless world of the Veneerings and Podsnaps, and the world of art, created from apparently worthless and useless debris. He examines Jenny Wren, Mr. Venus, and Sloppy as artists and sees reading itself as an articulation through which lifeless letters are transformed into living material for Noddy Boffin. The art of Jenny Wren and Lizzie Hexam, Černý concludes, transforms the world by 'articulation' and 'reparation,' it imitates the world but delivers a more nearly perfect image at the same time."

742. Chlebek, Diana Arlene. "Money and Its Effects in the Novels of Balzac and Dickens." *Dissertation Abstracts International*, 45 (1984), 2865A (Cornell University).

Chlebek studies the influence of social and economic changes in the nineteenth-century on Balzac and Dickens. She "examines how *Our Mutual Friend* presents the quest for identity through both a testing of individual and social values and an unmasking of the money myth."

743. Cohen, Monica Feinberg. "Home Inc: Professional Domesticity at Work in the Victorian Novel." *Dissertation Abstracts International*, 55 (1994), 1567A (Columbia University).

Cohen examines home life as the basis for "aesthetic structure" in the Victorian novel and analyzes *Our Mutual Friend* to consider "the *professionalization* of domesticity whereby home life, depicted as 'amateur' professional work, meets the Protestant criteria Max Weber uses to characterize a vocational calling."

744. Collins, Angus. "Dickens and *Our Mutual Friend*: Fancy as Self-Preservation." *Etudes anglaises*, 38 (1985), 257–65.

Collins argues that Dickens was facing the "possible exhaustion" of his creative energies as he was writing *Our Mutual Friend* and shows how in the novel "Dickens's preoccupation with the terms of his art is rooted in his personal and creative situation, and testifies in particular to his longing for some sort of human permanence." Collins focuses on the rooftop scene where Jenny and Lizzie "go to book-learning" and where Jenny calls out to "Come up and be dead," a scene he reads as "a conscious moment apart that is also a preparation for return, a return that is clearly perceived and accepted in the knowledge that it can now be borne more easily." Collins reads this as a "form of therapy that [Dickens] found now increasingly unavailable, but which out of the pressures of his own situation he continued to wish to make available to others." Thus, according to Collins, through the very act of composing *Our Mutual Friend*, Dickens moves "into the life of the work as it will outlast and preserve the man."

745. Connor, Steven. "*Our Mutual Friend*." In his *Charles Dickens*. New York: Basil Blackwell, 1985, pp. 145–58.

Connor explores *Our Mutual Friend* from the point of view of Marxist and psychoanalytic theory. He finds *Our Mutual Friend* Dickens's "most radical and provoking examination of the determination of the individual by the system" and argues convincingly that "this is a novel in which the only way for consciousness or identity to survive is to attempt a withdrawal from the encroaching life of systematic exchange." He forcefully concludes that the "shift from self to context, from being to being-in-relationship . . . is the recurrent pattern of the novel."

Reviews: L. Mackinnon, *Times Literary Supplement*, 5 July 1985, p. 752; E. Sando, *Choice*, 22 (July-August 1985), 1631; P. Conrad, *Observer*, 31 March 1985, p. 27; P. Dean, *Use of English*, 37 (Spring 1986), 89–92; F. Rosslyn, *Cambridge Quarterly*, 15, ii (1986), 164–67; V. Rumbold, *Cambridge Review*, 107 (May 1986), 96; D. Shanker, *Literary Half-Yearly*, 28 (January 1987), 134–36; M. Gantz, *Dickens Quarterly*, 4 (September 1987), 172–74; L. Lane, *Indian and Foreign Review*, 14 (Summer 1987), 92–98; P. Preston, *Notes and Queries*, 43, i (1989), 545–48.

746. Cotsell, Michael. "The Book of Insolvent Fates: Financial Speculations in *Our Mutual Friend.*" *Dickens Studies Annual*, 13 (1984), 125–42.

Cotsell demonstrates that Dickens's treatment of financial speculation in *Our Mutual Friend* reflects the reports of contemporary newspapers and journals, and in particular a series of articles by M. R. Meason that appeared in *All the Year Round* in 1864 and 1865. Cotsell examines these articles and shows that the connection between Dickens's handling of financial speculation is "aided by the appearance within the articles of observations, imagery and character types similar to those in the novel." After demonstrating convincingly the parallels between the novel and Meason's series of articles, Cotsell points out that Veneering's "resounding smash," unlike Merdle's fall which is the central catastrophe *Little Dorrit*, is postponed until after the novel concludes. Cotsell speculates that Dickens may have doubted the soundness of the "apparent 'cornerstone' of the British financial system, the great discount house Overend, Gurney," whose collapse in May 1866 he may, indeed, have anticipated.

747. Cotsell, Michael. *The Companion to Our Mutual Friend.* Dickens Companions. London: Allen & Unwin, 1986. xii + 316 pp.

According to the General Preface, "The Dickens Companions series offers the most comprehensive annotations of the works of Dickens ever undertaken." Factual rather than critical, the "annotation identifies allusions to current events and intellectual and religious issues, and supplies information on topography, social customs, costume, furniture, transportation, the illustrations to the novel, and so on. Identifications are provided for allusions to plays, poems, songs, the Bible, the Book of common Prayer, and other literary allusions." The work plans are also included. This exhaustive study is a valuable background resource.

Review L. J. Clipper, *Choice*, 24 (December 1986), 622–23; M. Slater, *Times Higher Education Supplement*, 5 December 1986, p.18; P. Collins, *Times Literary Supplement*, 16 January 1987, p. 66; J. Brattin, *Dickens Quarterly*, 5 (March 1988), 31–33; A. Sadrin, *Etudes anglaises,* 40 (October-December 1987), 475–76; T. Cribb, *Review of English Studies,* NS 39 (February 1988), 136–38; S. Monod, *Modern Language Review*, 83 (October 1988), 979–80.

748. Cotsell, Michael. "Introduction." In 1998 New Oxford Illustrated Edition **(698)**.

Cotsell points out that *Our Mutual Friend* is the "last major Victorian novel to deal with the subject of London until George Gissing's working-class novels of the 1880's." The new generation of writers, Trollope, George Eliot, and Henry James had new standards and were more interested in "the new ethos of high Victorianism, that 'middle class affair,' as Bernard Shaw was to call it." Cotsell sees Dickens choosing "passion and freedom" over "respectable married domesticity" at a time when he was having a liaison with Ellen Ternan, and finds new "notes of the subterranean, the private, the elemental enter into the writing." He sees Dickens searching for "community from an intensified perception of both our psychological depths and our social dispersal." Since Dickens's "art is premissed on the possibility of social change," according to Cotsell, and since his society did not provide the happy endings, the fact that Dickens's "characters have the capacity for sunny goodness and for surprising change" makes them seen by his successors as "unrealistic, belonging to the world of fairy tale, not to that of the modern intellect." But, Cotsell argues compellingly, while Dickens's characters may not seem convincing to the modern world of the 1880's, the artist figures he created, Venus and Jenny Wren, and the "literariness of the basic organization" of the novel make *Our Mutual Friend* the novel in which Dickens "most successfully transcends the limitations of realism: it is closer to the creativity of Joyce's *Ulysses* than to the cold eye of Gissing's fiction."

749. See Cotsell (**690**). "Mr Venus Rises from the Counter: Dickens's Taxidermist and his Contribution to *Our Mutual Friend*."

750. Cotsell, Michael. "Secretary or Sad Clerk? The Trouble with John Harmon." *Dickens Quarterly*, 1 (1984), 130–36.

Cotsell argues that Dickens has "two contradictory intentions" with John Harmon: he presents him as strong, energetic, and in control of the events in the novel, on the one hand, and, on the other, as the fairy tale, Cinderella-type, complete with fairy godparents (the Boffins), who transform him and provide him with the princess, Bella. After Harmon is rejected by Bella in the proposal scene, we see him as resolute and accepting of his lot, Cotsell indicates. Not until the end of the novel do we learn that John had been discovered by Mrs. Boffin "and that she and Boffin had given him money and won Bella for him." The Boffin plot, according to Cotsell, although presented as motivated for Bella's sake, is actually for Harmon's, "the caressed child" of the novel.

751. Cotsell, Michael. " 'The Sensational Williams': A Mutual Friend in 1864." *Dickensian*, 81 (1985), 79–85.

Cotsell begins with an article in *All the Year Round*, "The Sensational Williams," (XI, 14–18) which "ridicules the notion of the anti-sensational school of criticism that literature must be only about the ordinary doings of ordinary people"; otherwise it is "Sensational." The article makes its point by reviewing Shakespeare in the style of the anti-sensational school, and dismissing him for his exaggeration, improbability, and violence. Cotsell notes that the article demonstrates that, among other things, Mr. Podsnap represents a satire on the anti-sensational school of criticism, and he speculates that Dickens had James Fitzjames Stephen in mind as a representative of the school. Stephen objected to Dickens's sentimental comedy and found Dickens decidedly "Not English" in his attack on British institutions in *Little Dorrit*. Cotsell concludes that Podsnappery was responsible for " impos[ing] its respectable and repressive routine on Bradley Headstone, with the consequent violent reaction. It causes Bradley's Shakespearean passions and then declares their representation illegitimate." In the tercentenary year of Shakespeare's birth, while the nation was celebrating Shakespeare, and itself "for speaking the language Shakespeare spoke," Dickens, Cotsell points out, "was contending for . . . the right to . . . an equivalent language for his own time."

752. Currie, Richard A. "Dickens and Internalized Aggression." *Dissertation Abstracts International*, 49 (1988), 1148A (New York University). Currie examines the repression of angry, aggressive feelings in several female protagonists in Dickens, including Lizzie Hexam in *Our Mutual Friend*. "By representing hidden anger" that Currie points to in these characters, "Dickens deepens his portrayal of the female protagonists into one of psychological complexity rather than sentimentality."

753. Curry, Mary Jane Chilton. "Anaphoric and Cataphoric Reference in Dickens's *Our Mutual Friend* and James's *The Golden Bowl*." In *The Text Beyond: Essays in Literary Linguistics*. Ed. Cynthia Goldin Bernstein. Tuscaloosa: U of Alabama P, 1994, pp. 30–55. Curry offers linguistic analysis to help define the boundaries that distinguish realist, modernist, and postmodernist novels, hoping to "construct another section of the bridge between literary theoretical and text linguistic approaches to the novel." While accepting with some qualifications the arguments of theoretical critics who categorize novels concerned primarily with questions of epistemology as realist or modernist, and those concerned primarily with ontology as postmodernist, Curry proposes that these theoretical constructs can be reinforced by linguistic analysis of the types and degree of referentiality embedded in the language of texts. By close analysis of the "bird of prey" metaphor in *Our Mutual Friend* and the "pagoda" metaphor in *The Golden Bowl*, Curry shows that Dickens achieves textual cohesion through the accumulation of meaning provided by "anaphoric" or backward-pointing referentiality that enables both characters and readers to solve mysteries to arrive at a largely stable understanding,

whereas James creates emotional and epistemological instability by using "cataphoric" or forward-pointing referentiality that is frequently ambiguous or elliptical. She suggests that such an analysis indicates that a continuum of referentiality—from explicit to ambiguous—reflects the development of the novel from realist to postmodernist and parallels the changing focus from epistemology to ontology posited by theoretical critics. Not surprisingly, her analysis reveals that *Our Mutual Friend* reflects Dickens's movement from realism toward modernism, and *The Golden Bowl* reflects James's movement from modernism toward postmodernism.

754. Daldry, Graham. *"Our Mutual Friend* and the Art of the Possible." In his *Charles Dickens and the Form of the Novel.* Totowa, NJ: Barnes and Noble, 1986, pp. 164–93.
  Daldry explores Dickens's voice in "both fictive and narrative novel" and discovers that in *Our Mutual Friend* "his voice is that detached one represented, not within the novel, but within the whole texture and composition, within what I have called the landscape of its substance. This landscape is a larger and more potent source of energy and authority than any single voice in the novel could be." Daldry argues that *Our Mutual Friend* "brings these opposing views" of fiction and narrative together "to achieve, not unity or the realization of a fairy tale, but the novel at its most extensive and comprehensive," and to provide us with a landscape that includes and extends those of the earlier novels. This novel demonstrates a mature vision of the world between fiction and narrative and "shows us the meaning of a world governed by accident." Daldry concludes that in *Our Mutual Friend* "Dickens withdraws from both narrative and fiction, and allows them to take their own place in the landscape of the novel, to do what they can to bring about coherence. The interaction they provide does produce . . . the unity of reality. It is accidental, precarious, but . . . it is possible."
  Reviews: L. Clipper, *Choice,* 24 (April 1987), 1217; N. Russel, *Dickensian,* 83 (Summer 1987), 115–16; S. Monod, *Modern Language Review,* 84 (January 1989), 137–39; T. Cribb, *Review of English Studies,* 40 (1989), 281–83.

755. Daleski, H. M. "Imagining Revolution: The Eye of History and Fiction." *Journal of Narrative Technique,* 18 (1988), 61–72.
  Daleski compares Carlyle's *The French Revolution* with *A Tale of Two Cities.* He refers briefly to *Our Mutual Friend* to indicate that Dickens tags his characters with an epithet used in an early description of the character, as with "The Analytical," Mr. Veneering's butler.

756. Darby, Margaret Flanders. "Fault Lines in Dickens." *Dissertation Abstracts International*, 49 (1988), 825A (State University of New York at Binghamton).

Darby challenges the notion that Dickens could not portray women, arguing, from a feminist perspective, that underneath Dickens's "use of popular codes of Victorian expectation for fictional women, a complex sense of sexual politics struggles for resolution and clarity." Dickens captures the seething violence in repressed women and "seized on their discomfort to reveal his sense of patriarchal injustice and of a dominant masculine consciousness in conflict with itself." Darby provides a close reading of five Dickens novels, including *Our Mutual Friend*, to make the argument.

757. Darby, Margaret Flanders. "Four Women in *Our Mutual Friend*." *Dickensian*, 83 (1987), 24–39.

In this thoughtful essay that explores Dickens's ambivalence toward women, Darby examines the treatment of Bella Wilfer, Lizzie Hexam, Sophronia Lammle, and Georgiana Podsnap in *Our Mutual Friend* to argue that "Dickens's explicit presentation of them does not match their implicit development." Bella becomes a heroine at the expense of her "liveliness." Lizzie's love is able to conquer Eugene's lust only through the "cataclysmic intervention" of her rescuing him and reducing him to "nearly total dependence on his wife." Sophronia is trapped in an unhappy marriage but changes her mind about ensnaring Georgiana, and demonstrates strength of character we had not suspected in her. And Georgiana herself "makes money shine as brightly as Bella does" in offering Sophronia money "yet the novel clearly does not give her the same credit." The novel's "indirections," Darby argues—more convincingly in the cases of Sophronia and Georgiana than in the cases of Bella and Lizzie—give these women "a subtle strength" and reveal the "richness" of Dickens's ambivalence.

758. See DeMarcus **(900)**. "Wolves Within and Without: Dickens's Transformation of 'Little Red Riding Hood' in *Our Mutual Friend*."

759. Denny, Apryl Lea. "Women's Discourse and Social Change: A Psychological Study of Charles Dickens's *Oliver Twist, Hard Times, Little Dorrit,* and *Our Mutual Friend*." *Dissertation Abstracts International*, 53 (1992), 1922A (University of Colorado, Boulder).

In examining orphaned heroines in four of Dickens's novels, Denny argues that Dickens presents a "causal connection between individual and social development." Thus through her visions in the fireplace Lizzie Hexam modifies her world to accommodate her public and private needs.

760. See Dessner **(691)**. "A Possible Source for Dickens's Lammles."

761. Dillon, Nancy Agnes. " 'Wondrous Secrets of Nature' and Uncanny
     Ones: *Macbeth* as a Context for Sexual Identity in the Novels of
     Charles Dickens." *Dissertation Abstracts International*, 57 (1996),
     1630A (Fordham University).
     Dillon examines *Our Mutual Friend* as an instance of Dickens's use
     of images of the "uncanny" and elements of carnival in ways that
     "subvert belief in the possibility of such a definable entity as the self."

762. Dvorak, Wilfred P. "Dickens and Popular Culture: Silas Wegg's Ballads
     in *Our Mutual Friend*." *Dickensian*, 86 (1990), 142–57.
     Dvorak demonstrates that Dickens uses ballads to expose Wegg's char-
     acter and to reinforce his major themes in *Our Mutual Friend*. Wegg
     sings his ballads in his initial greed to gain money from the Boffins;
     as his greed becomes compulsive, he sings ballads to enlist the support
     of Venus against Boffin after the discovery of the Harmon will; finally,
     when his greed has deranged him, Wegg sings ballads to celebrate his
     power over Boffin.

763. Dyer, James Harold, Jr. "Charles Dickens and Victorian England:
     His Benevolent Response in Fiction to the First Modern Society."
     Dissertation Abstracts International, 53 (1992), 2823A (South Caro-
     lina University).
     Dyer argues that Dickens's fame was due largely to his "sustained
     message of benevolence in response to the rapid transformation of his
     country from agrarianism to urbanism." He claims that Dickens's
     compassion came from two sources: the blacking warehouse experi-
     ence and the New Testament. Dyer sees "the Galilean" as the "perfect
     role model . . . an ethical guide for individuals in a changing, disorient-
     ing society," and traces the "benevolent mission" of "the Inimitable"
     throughout his career, examining several novels including *Our Mutual
     Friend*. "Benevolence," he concludes, "is the unifying theme of the
     oeuvre."

764. Edgecombe, Rodney S. "Middle-Class Erasures: The Decreations of
     Mrs. General and Mr. Podsnap." *Studies in the Novel*, 31 (1999),
     279–95.
     Edgecombe argues that Dickens "mocks the pillars of a repressive
     society" through the presentations of Mrs. General in *Little Dorrit*
     and Mr. Podsnap in *Our Mutual Friend*. He points out that Bradley
     Headstone's "decent" exterior demonstrates the extent to which Pods-
     nappery reaches as Bradley assumes the propriety of middle-class
     norms to mask his seething, frustrated emotions. Dickens represents
     middle-class "piety as try[ing] to mask its working-class needs with
     its own version of decency" and thus moving backward in time rather
     than progressing, according to Edgecombe.

765. Edgecombe, Rodney Stenning. "Personification in the Late Novels of Dickens." *Dickensian*, 95 (1999), 230–40.

Edgecombe examines Dickens's use of personification in the late novels, including *Our Mutual Friend*, arguing that his "unsympathetic characters are always staging themselves, stepping into allegorical functions, and appropriating personification as a means of self-advancement." He offers Wegg, Fledgeby, and Lady Tippins as examples.

766. Edgecombe, Rodney Stenning. " 'The Ring of Cant': Formulaic Elements in *Our Mutual Friend*." *Dickens Studies Annual*, 24 (1996), 167–84.

Edgecombe shows that the "moral debility" that results from an obsessive concern for money in Dickens's chracters is often attended by a "linguistic debility," a debility Dickens mimics throughout *Our Mutual Friend*. Edgecombe offers several instances of Dickens's use of clichéd and tired language to expose emotional and moral enfeeblement in the novel.

767. See Edgecombe (**902**). "Two Oblique Allusions in *Our Mutual Friend*."

768. See Edgecombe (**903**). "The 'Veiled Prophet' in *Our Mutual Friend*."

769. Farrell, John P. "The Partner's Tale: Dickens and *Our Mutual Friend*." *English Literary History*, 66 (1999), 759–99.

Using Mikhail Bakhtin's and Charles Taylor's models of "dialogism" and the "dialogical structure of identity," Farrell explores the relationship of "self, society and mutuality by tracing the intricate interplay [*Our Mutual Friend*] constructs between its reflections on performance and its diagnosis of social being." He argues that Dickens's social imagination is not as ideologically incoherent as many have claimed. Instead of simply identifying social problems and then taking his heroes and heroines off to safe enclaves where they are protected from these problems, as those who accuse Dickens of sentimental radicalism insist he is doing, Dickens is rather, according to Farrell, interested in "the expressive forms of human action and their interplay." He sees relationships in Dickens's novels among people that are more powerful than the negative effects of the war between "the system and the self," and goes on to demonstrate how in *Our Mutual Friend* the relationships among various partners reveal that "the protest against the social system, emerging from the dialogic experiences of social agents, is itself dialogic—an occasion, multiplied many times over, for the local practice of mutuality to redeem us from the monological discourses of the state." The essay provides particularly valuable insight into the partnering of John Harmon and George Radfoot (whom

Harmon throws off) as contrasted with Bradley Headstone and Rogue Riderhood (whom Headstone clings to) and Eugene Wrayburn and Mr. Dolls ("Mr. Doll's in debility forecasts Eugene in catastrophe. But, in the end, Eugene is able to defeat his demon"). In spite of the jargon that sometimes gets in the way, this is a valuable essay.

770. Ferguson, Kathleen. " 'A Very Pleasant, Profitable Little Affair of Private Theatricals?' A Study of the Changing Narrative Voice in the Novels of Charles Dickens." *Dissertation Abstracts International*, 49 (1985), 257A (University of Ulster, Northen Ireland).

Ferguson argues that Dickens adopted a series of "narrative personae" in his novels that reflect the dramatic aspects of the stories. In *Our Mutual Friend*, Ferguson claims, John Harmon, in establishing an identity "finds himself," just as Dickens himself "was probably trying to do" in his personal life at the time.

771. Fielding, K. J. "The Spirit of Fiction—The Poetry of Fact." *Dickens Studies Annual*, 14 (1984), 147–65.

Fielding examines the article on "The Spirit of Fiction" in *All the Year Round* (18 [28 July 1867], 118–20), an article that Richard Stang had attributed to Dickens in his *The Theory of the Novel in England 1850–1870* (1959) but that Fielding argues was probably written by Henry Morley. The article demonstrates "that members of Dickens's inner circle were ready to discuss the 'spirit of fiction' " and that they often associated it with a comparison between the world of fancy as shown at one extreme by the folk tale or fairy tale and at the other by what is termed "the poetry of fact." Fielding considers the failure of institutional education as it is represented in *Our Mutual Friend* to be opposed to the faith Dickens shows in the "positive qualities of the illiterate human imagination" as demonstrated in Lizzie, Jenny, and the Boffins. He concludes that the fairy tale union of Eugene and Lizzie may well point to a time when the sympathy between classes is achieved, but points out that "Dickens is essentially a novelist, whose allusions to and treatment of the conflict between the school-master and storyteller is largely a literary device." Morley's essay shows how conscious Dickens's circle was of fairy tale elements in contemporary fiction at a time when they were concerned about institu-tional education; Fielding insists that what is important is that we make the "connections between one work and another, between his [Dickens's] life and thought, and with the culture out of which he wrote."

772. Flood, Tracy Seeley. "Gnostic Romance: Dickens, Conrad, and the Advent of Modernism." *Dissertation Abstracts International*, 49 (1988), 3368A, (University of Texas).

Flood considers *Our Mutual Friend* as a romance, a form that "is a permanent imaginative response to social change and disorder." Dickens's central characteristics of romance are revealed in *Our Mutual Friend*: "the essentially narrative and dialectic structure of its role in human experience; its potential for subverting authority and creating change; its power to create a coherent community in opposition to the dominant culture."

773. Fox, Warren Frederick. "Better to be Abel than Cain? The Figure of the Murderer in Mid-Victorian Britain." *Dissertation Abstracts International*, 57 (1996), 2047A, (University of California, Irvine).

Fox examines the representation of an actual murder case, that of Franz Muller, in Victorian newspapers, along with *Daniel Deronda*, *The Ring and the Book*, and *Our Mutual Friend*, in order to demonstrate the difference between moral and aesthetic reactions to the murderer.

774. Frank, Lawrence. "Dickens's Urban Gothic: *Our Mutual Friend* and *The Mystery of Edwin Drood*." In his *Charles Dickens and the Romantic Self*. Lincoln: U of Nebraska P, 1984, pp.185–201.

Frank employs psychoanalytic and phenomenological critical methods to explore the role the self plays in *Our Mutual Friend*, in which "Dickens has returned to the pilgrimage of being, to the enduring paradox within the romantic conception of the self." The self becomes a narrative construct and in "the urban labyrinth of *Our Mutual Friend*, man remains the novelist of himself," according to Frank. He argues compellingly that "Wrayburn and Headstone seek to affirm their own existence in their pursuit of Lizzie: they wish her to acknowledge them, and reassure them of the presence of their inaccessible selves."

Reviews: M. Timko, *Choice*, 22 (June 1985), 1492; N. Auerbach, *New York Times Book Review*, 17 March 1985, p. 43; D. Walder, *Times Literary Supplement*, 31 January 1986, p. 125; R. Levine, *Studies in the Novel*, 17 (Winter 1995), 423–24; M. Steig, *Dickens Quarterly*, 3 (June 1986), 95–100; S. Tick, *Victorian Studies*, 29 (Spring 1986), 475–77; C. Dudt, *Culture and Literature*, 35 (Winter 1986), 41–42; C. Rzepka, *Studies in Romanticism*, 25 (Winter 1986), pp. 585–89; J. Carter, *Victorians Institute Journal*, 15 (1987), 158–62.

775. Freeland, Natalka. "Trash Fiction: The Victorian Novel and the Rise of Disposable Culture." *Dissertation Abstracts International*, 59 (1998), 1177A (Yale University).

Freeland analyzes *Our Mutual Friend* in the context of the problem of dealing with garbage in Victorian England, claiming that descriptions of refuse in Victorian fiction reflect a shift "from a culture

based on permanence to one valuing innovation.'' *Our Mutual Friend*
reflects the fragments of dust and garbage in the disconnectedness of
plots and voices in the story, and this fragmentation poses threats to
the characters in the novel and to the coherence of the novel itself,
threats that Dickens must deal with by looking for ''radically new
representational forms.''

776. Fulweiler, Howard W. '' 'A Dismal Swamp': Darwin, Design, and
Evolution in *Our Mutual Friend.*'' *Nineteenth-Century Literature*, 49
(1994), 51–74.

Fulweiler argues that as he was writing *Our Mutual Friend* Dickens
had in mind Darwin's *The Origin of Species*, a work that provides a
comprehensive presentation of the mutual relationship of living organ-
isms to one another and their environment as they struggle for dominance. Dickens presents a world that has many affinities with *Origin*
and shares much of the same ground but differs sharply in its basic
principles: ''design and teleology are at the core of its [*Our Mutual
Friend's*] fictional intent and thus diametrically opposed to the special
vision of Darwin.'' Dickens may accept Darwin's theory of evolution
as a theoretic idea and yet not accept its Malthusian premise. Fulweiler
concludes that ''the teleological tradition of natural theology . . . touched his imagination and led to a deeper reality behind the multitudinous array of phenomenon.''

777. Gallagher, Catherine. ''The Bioeconomics of *Our Mutual Friend.*'' In
Subject to History: Ideology, Class, Gender. Ed. David Simpson. Ithaca, NY: Cornell UP, 1991, pp. 47–64.

Gallagher points out similarities between *Our Mutual Friend* and Ruskin's *Unto This Last* to make the point that for mid-Victorians economic health was often thought of in terms of bodily health. However,
Gallagher argues, the attempt ''to rewrite economic discourse so that
it constantly referred back to the body's well-being paradoxically
tended to do what it accused unreconstructed political economists of
doing: separating value from flesh and blood, conditioning value on a
state of suspended animation or apparent death.'' She analyzes John
Harmon's decision to remain in a state of suspended animation in
order to do good with the Harmon estate, Mr. Venus's articulation,
Jenny Wren's dolls' dressmaking work, Gaffer Hexam's making a
living off the dead bodies in the river, and the dust mounds themselves
to argue that ''[a]pparent death becomes the only direct access to the
essence and value of life.'' Eugene Wrayburn's life assumes value
when he is in a state of suspended animation and, like John Harmon,
is then ''able to give and receive love.'' Gallagher concludes this
complex but provocative essay with the observation that the suspended

and discarded bodies in the novel are male because the plots "are driven by attempts to save women from becoming commodities . . . . The state of suspended animation is thus exclusively masculine in *Our Mutual Friend* because it is so naturally feminine." See also **(706)**.

778. Garnett, Robert R. "Dickens, the Virgin, and the Dredger's Daughter." *Dickens Studies Annual*, 28 (1999), 45–65.

Garnett argues convincingly that in *Our Mutual Friend* Dickens creates in Lizzie Hexam a fully realized, sexually vital woman whose dark sensuality informs her moral beauty. After Mary Hogarth's death Dickens developed a spiritualized personal religion that was embodied in the feminine purity and innocence of Rose Maylie and Agnes Wickfield. "By the time of *Our Mutual Friend*'s Lizzie Hexam," Garnett demonstrates in this thoughtful analysis, "Dickens's rarefied ideal had acquired a body, and become a woman with both a physical and moral nature." Lizzie's moral strength "emerges from [her experience of] river slime and corpse dredging."

779. Gaughan, Richard T. "Prospecting for Meaning in *Our Mutual Friend*." *Dickens Studies Annual*, 19 (1990), 231–46.

Because characters are trapped by society into playing roles, meaningful action is almost impossible in *Our Mutual Friend*, according to Gaughan. The human will to subdue reality to a coherent order is the source of this problem, and Dickens uses the passivity of John Harmon's character "to find in the negation of will the human qualities that have been lost in its exercise." Harmon suspends his own will and is thus freed from his socially defined identity to establish an identity based on his relationships with other characters, relationships created outside of socially prescribed rules. Harmon's use of symbolic disguise differs from Headstone's in that Harmon uses "symbolic form as a way of responding to and understanding a world that is not defined entirely by social will" whereas Headstone imposes "symbolic forms as realistic in and of themselves." Harmon creates a new identity outside the social system. Headstone, in accepting society's notion of respectability as an end in itself and attempting to impose that value on Lizzie, refuses to "establish a relationship between himself and his own inner reality and the reality of others." Gaughin concludes, convincingly, that for Dickens the search for meaning is itself the real value in *Our Mutual Friend*.

780. Gibbon, Frank. "Myths of Dismemberment in *Our Mutual Friend*." *Meridian*, 3 (1984), 13–22.

Gibbon analyzes the underlying mythic structure of *Our Mutual Friend* as "based on the notion of dismemberment and reassembly and reanimation of human corpses." He argues persuasively that Dickens's main source is the Egyptian myth of Osiris, and that the "ambivalent attitudes thus embodied in the Osiris story held a deep attraction for Dickens and encouraged many ironic uses of the myth in *Our Mutual Friend*." Gibbon goes on to indicate several parallels between the myth and the novel.

781. Gibbon, Frank. "R. H. Horne and *Our Mutual Friend*." *Dickensian*, 81 (1985), 140–44.

Gibbon points out that the essay that Humphry House refers to in *Household Words* as the probable source for the dust mounds in *Our Mutual Friend*, an essay we now know to have been written by R. H. Horne ("Dust; or Ugliness Redeemed," *Household Words*, 13 July 1850), contains "a great deal more of the symbolism of the novel than that of the mounds . . . ." Gibbon goes on to summarize this story recounted in *Household Words* of a man who attempts to drown himself but is rescued by three dust sifters and to show how the story suggests much of the symbolism of the novel, particularly that between "dead matter and regeneration."

782. Gikandi, Simon Eliud. "Charles Dickens and the Art of the Ironic." *Dissertation Abstracts International*, 47 (1986), 2594A (Northwestern University).

Gikandi examines Dickens's use of irony in several novels, arguing that irony is "ultimately geared toward defamiliarization." In *Our Mutual Friend* Dickens "confounds his readers with 'unstable' ironies and denies them a stable narrative center." However irony does not leave everything in a void at the end of the novel, Gikandi asserts: "it trains us to be critical readers who are cognizant of the dubious authority of language."

783. Gindele, Karen. "Desire and Deconstruction: Reclaiming Centers." *Dickens Studies Annual*, 29 (2000), 269–301.

Gindele argues against the ideas of "lack," the claims that we desire what we do not possess, that inform desire and meaning as theorized by Freud, Lacan, and Derrida. She claims that we can find positive models of desire in literary and cultural theory and in discourses of physics and biology. She examines *Our Mutual Friend* as a work that "marks the beginning . . . of the shift towards models of desire that qualify concepts of lack," analyzing Bradley Headstone, Lizzie Hexam, and Eugene Wrayburn as representing three models of desire: "Bradley represents the model of lack; Eugene's desire begins by the exercise of power; and Lizzie's desire is imaginative, connecting her not only to a lover but to the world." She concludes that "Lizzie would have chosen Eugene whether Bradley was there or not because she desired him and had to act. This is the human predicament: people imagine, and then must make choices because they must act. If we have any capacity to choose, even the illusion of choosing, we have the capacity to act.'' Thus, for Gindele, *Our Mutual Friend* demonstrates that desire originates from energy, and ''meaning is not founded on lack or absence.''

784. Ginsburg, Michel Peled. ''The Case Against Plot in *Bleak House* and *Our Mutual Friend*.'' In her *Economies of Change: Form and Transformation in the Nineteenth-Century Novel*. Stanford: Stanford UP, 1996, pp. 138–56.

Ginsburg contrasts the plots of *Our Mutual Friend* and *Bleak House*, seeing the latter as a novel whose organizing principle is one of ''restoration'' while the former is based on ''transformation.'' The key symbols capturing this distinction are Krook's Rag and Bottle Warehouse and the hoarding instinct that it represents in *Bleak House* on the one hand and the recycling of waste materials in the dust mounds and in Jenny Wren's dolls' dressmaking work in *Our Mutual Friend* on the other. The symbols also represent ''a different notion of transformation, of plot, of temporality, of what constitutes beginning, middle, and end, causality, motivation, and logic.'' Whereas *Our Mutual Friend* is in ''the constant process of recycling, without beginning or end . . . the plot of *Bleak House* has a marked, catastrophic end and a marked, simple beginning.'' Ginsburg demonstrates that although *Our Mutual Friend* is far more radical than the conservative *Bleak House*, within the plot models of *Our Mutual Friend* the stories of Eugene, Lizzie, Harmon, Bella, and Boffin show differing degrees of transformation, ''none of which fully conforms to'' the plot models of *Bleak House* or *Our Mutual Friend*. Ginsburg concludes that ''formalization is not simply an expression; form does not simply perform an ideological task. From the moment something like the ideology of justice gets formalized . . . a certain space is opened up in which these features and elements can combine in many different ways.'' She sees *Our Mutual Friend* as demonstrating ''precisely this freedom of combination'' in her thoughtful and insightful analysis.

Review: M. Hollington, *Dickens Quarterly*, 16 (1999), 55–58.

785. Grant, David Abram. ''Emotional Prisons: Dickens and the Fallacies of Family Behavior.'' *Dissertation Abstracts International*, 53 (1992), 3536A (Ohio State University).

Grant considers Dickens's treatment of family in three novels to argue that Dickens anticipates modern family behavioral theory, ''particularly the Bowen Family Systems Theory . . . [that] emphasizes the 'web of interconnection and influences that repeat themselves within a family cluster of individuals.' '' He argues that Dickens's treatment of corrupt institutions in *Our Mutual Friend* exposes like weaknesses "of the allegedly salubrious family institution."

786. See Green (**904**). "Two Venal Girls: A Study in Dickens and Zola."

787. Greenstein, Michael. "Mutuality in *Our Mutual Friend*." *Dickens Quarterly*, 8 (1991), 127–34.

Through a close reading of *Our Mutual Friend*, Greenstein demonstrates that the redundancy of the title of the novel itself highlights the "excessive mutuality that pervades the novel." Looking at structure, chapter titles, relationships, recurrent images, and the role of commerce and of education, Greenstein argues that the meaning of mutuality is itself ambiguous throughout the novel. He concludes, not surprisingly, that we cannot arrive at a conclusion with regard to a satisfactory resolution of the novel.

788. Grose, Janet Lynne. "The Sensation Novel and Social Reform: Revising Prescriptions of Gender, Marriage, and Domesticity." *Dissertation Abstracts International*, 56 (1995), 2248A (University of South Carolina).

Grose examines *Our Mutual Friend* in the context of the sensation novel of the 1860s and sees it as an instance of novels that attempt to "redefine accepted gender roles in less polarized terms and to see marriage as an egalitarian rather than hierarchical relationship" as well as to recognize women's "need for autonomy."

789. Grossman, Jonathan H. "The Absent Jew in Dickens: Narrators in *Oliver Twist, Our Mutual Friend*, and *A Christmas Carol*." *Dickens Studies Annual*, 24 (1996), pp. 37–57.

Grossman argues that Dickens does not create a convincing Jewish character in his novels and reads the representation of Riah in *Our Mutual Friend* not as a demonstration of Dickens's failure to present Riah convincingly but as a success in "terms of Dickens's attempt not to depict a Jew, but rather to represent the impossibility of doing so." Riah demonstrates that Jewish identity is formed as a response to Christian representation and, Grossman concludes, that Jews in Dickens's society "will always be both literally and metaphorically in public spaces; the home of the Jews remains off-stage, a vague place where Lizzie Hexam can find refuge, but the narrator cannot follow."

790. See Hackenberg (**905**). " 'Loitering Artfully': Reading Flânerie in *Our Mutual Friend*."

791. Hake, Stephen. "Becoming Poor to Make Many Rich: The Resolution of Class Conflict in Dickens." *Dickens Studies Annual*, 26 (1998), 107–20.

Hake takes issue with the assumption that the upper classes elevate the condition of the lower classes in Dickens, arguing that in fact the lower classes actually humanize those above them. He shows as an example that, in *Our Mutual Friend*, Eugene is redeemed by Lizzie.

792. Hale, Keith. "Doing the Police in Different Voices: The Search for Identity in Dust Heaps and Waste Lands." *Dickens Studies Annual*, 29 (2000), 303–21.

Hale argues that the concern with the question of identity makes *Our Mutual Friend* Dickens's most modern novel and *The Waste Land* Eliot's "quintessentially 'modern' poem." He points out identity confusion in both the novel and the poem, arguing that maintaining one's identity amidst the dissolution of contemporary society is a modern theme. Hale also points to the death-in-life and life-in-death motifs and the death and resurrection by water themes in both works. He concludes that Dickens establishes identity by having his characters tell their own story. "It is as if the breaking up of identities is a necessary first step in being reborn. It may be that the multiplicity of human life must face itself through the controlled social surface for characters to confront themselves in ways that allow them to tell their own stories."

793. Hayward, Jennifer. "Mutual Friends: The Development of the Mass Serial." In her *Consuming Pleasures: Active Audiences and Serial Fictions from Dickens to Soap Opera*. Lexington: UP of Kentucky, 1997, pp. 21–84.

Hayward studies *Our Mutual Friend* as "Dickens's working through of serial tropes and techniques still in use today." Hayward points out many parallels between the tropes and techniques that define the serial form today and those in the novel: return from the dead, character transformation, concealed secrets, along with many reverberations of the news of the day. In an exhaustive, perhaps exhausting, survey of the running reviews of *Our Mutual Friend* in four London newspapers as the novel was published in installments, she argues that the readers affected the development of the novel by letting their reactions, predictions, likes, and dislikes be known.

Reviews: R. Keefe, *Dickens Quarterly*, 16 (1999), 120–23; L. Hughes, *Nineteenth- Century Literature*, 53 (1999), 539–42; J. Glavin, *Victorian Studies*, 42 (2000), 702–04.

794. Hecimovich, Gregg A. "The Cup and the Lip and the Riddle of *Our Mutual Friend*." *English Literary History*, 62 (1995), 955–77.

Hecimovich argues trenchantly that *Our Mutual Friend* is elaborately constructed as a riddle drawing the "reader into the narrative through revelations and deceptions in syntax, narrative perspective, and plot." What is often seen as the disjunctive structure of the novel is, he believes, not due to Dickens's weakness but to his society's sickness, which Dickens is reflecting in the novel. In this insightful and penetrating essay, Hecimovich concludes that Dickens analyzes this fallen society and exposes it to the reader who "negotiates uncertainties of surface and substance" and achieves the capacity to reorder the fallen world imaginatively.

795. Hecimovich, Gregg A. "Waking the Reader: Riddles in Nineteenth-Century British Literature." *Dissertation Abstracts International*, 58 (1997), 4279A (Vanderbilt University).

Hecimovich examines *Our Mutual Friend* in the context of the place of the riddle in nineteenth-century British culture, arguing that riddles promote cohesion in a culture but also transgress barriers, and thus expose the boundaries that establish "imagined communities." He argues that *Our Mutual Friend* is elaborately constructed as a riddle.

796. Heller, Deborah. "The Outcast as Villain and Victim: Jews in Dickens's *Oliver Twist* and *Our Mutual Friend*." In *Jewish Presences in English Literature*. Ed. Derek Cohen and Deborah Heller. Montreal: McGill-Queen's UP, 1990, pp. 40–60.

Heller argues that in *Our Mutual Friend* Dickens attempts to balance Fagin (from *Oliver Twist*), "the bad Jew," with Riah, "the good Jew." Riah, the "epitome of integrity and benevolence," befriends the innocent victims in the novel and is thus identified with his own victimization by Fledgeby. He is, like Fagin, a social outcast, but he is not an outlaw. Society itself is morally flawed in *Our Mutual Friend*, Heller asserts, while the outcasts, Riah, Jennie, Lizzie, and Betty Higden, together represent the moral center of the novel. Heller associates Fledgeby, not Riah, with the devil, and Fledgeby is identified with the Society Dickens condemns. Eugene's anti-Semitism, Heller points out, is not addressed in his moral reform, and Riah is never seen with Lizzie, whom he has supported, after she leaves London. That Riah is not integrated into "the larger social fabric" serves for Heller "to intensify the darkness that hovers over the world of *Our Mutual Friend*."

797. Hennelly, Mark M., Jr. "Toy Wonders in *Our Mutual Friend*." *Dickens Quarterly*, 12 (1995), 60–72, 95–107.

Hennelly argues compellingly that play motifs in *Our Mutual Friend* offset the negative cultural values of pretence, class, and concern for money with the traditional values of self-sacrifice, love, and mutuality. He provides a thoughtful analysis of the elements of play in the novel in the context of Victorian education play theory compared to modern play theory. Hennelly concludes convincingly that Sloppy's courtship of Jenny Wren and Twemlow's "courtly courage" at the end of the novel demonstrate the importance of play in dealing with the pain of existence.

798. Heyns, Michiel. " 'Oh, 'tis love, 'tis love . . . ': Privileged Partnership in Dickens." In Heyns's *Expulsion and the Nineteenth-Century Novel: The Scapegoat in English Realist Fiction.* Oxford: Clarendon Press, 1994, pp. 90–135.

Heyns argues that Dickens "privileges . . . the archetypal partnership of marriage, reducing his vast social order to a vision of two people happily exempt from the exploitation and greed he sees everywhere." The "scapegoat" figure isolated from "the companionship of others, remains the unacknowledged mainspring propelling the narratives." Thus Heyns reads *Our Mutual Friend*, "in many ways Dickens's most powerful novel," as owing "much of its energy to the presence of Bradley Headstone, in whom Dickens at last fully dramatizes the darkest possibilities of his fiction, the most destructive potential of partnership and of love." Bradley, the scapegoat, who is driven as much by his hatred of Eugene as by his love of Lizzie, is the "bearer . . . of much of the novel's pain."

799. Holbrook, David. "Finding One Another's Reality: Lizzie Hexam and Her Love Story in *Our Mutual Friend.*" In his *Charles Dickens and the Image of Woman.* New York: New York UP, 1993, pp. 147–63.

Holbrook sees Lizzie and Eugene's relationship as being based on mutual respect and equality after Eugene has suffered and nearly drowned and thus "become fit to marry Lizzie." He reads the Thames as representing the "unconscious and primal passion. It is in this dark river of the unconscious that one encounters the ultimate existential challenge—and it is through immersion in this river that Lizzie fulfills her marvelous moral integrity and Eugene finds himself as a real man."

800. Hollington, Michael. "Opium and the Grotesque: *Our Mutual Friend* and *Edwin Drood.*" In his *Dickens and the Grotesque.* London: Croom Helm; Totowa, NJ: Barnes and Noble, 1984, pp. 231–46.

Hollington demonstrates that "in *Our Mutual Friend* continual reference is made to narcotics and opiates, and that these . . . form a persistent theme whose dimensions are primarily sociological rather than psychological." He explores the humorous side of the narcotics theme in the novel, focusing particularly on Mr. Venus. Observing that "the theme of narcotics, of opiates to deaden pain, relates of course to this torment from the past that seems to have already been in Dickens's mind," he concludes that by reading *Edwin Drood* in the light of *Our Mutual Friend* we reach a corrective to the many "thoroughly privatizing readings" of *Drood.*

Reviews: B. F. Fisher, *Choice,* 22 (1985), 1332; D. Parker, *Meridian,* 4 (1985), 62–64; W. Palmer, *Dickens Quarterly,* 4 (1987), 26–28.

801. Hotz, Mary E. "On the Bodies of the Poor: English Representations on Death Rituals, 1835–1865." *Dissertation Abstracts International*, 58 (1997), 173A (University of Chicago).

Hotz argues that burial ceremonies in the nineteenth-century reflect the nature of social relations and that in *Our Mutual Friend* Dickens, "understanding the power of the corpse to mediate social change, expropriates literal burial to argue for the resurrection of the gentlemanly ideal and the death and burial of the self-help philosophy."

802. Hustvedt, Siri Ellen. "Figures of Dust: A Reading of *Our Mutual Friend*." *Dissertation Abstracts International*, 47 (1986), 2595A (Columbia University).

Hustvedt examines the language of *Our Mutual Friend* closely to argue that the metaphorical structure reveals images of ambiguity that obscure all boundaries. Dust acts metaphorically not only to indicate physical fragmentation but also to signify erosion in the symbolic realm. "This loss of significance is directly associated with characters who are in positions of authority—with fathers and officials," Hudvesdt asserts. The novel is shaped by characters struggling against this "nonsensical patriarchy," which is "countered by an idyllic conception of community grounded in memory and fantasy."

803. Jaffe, Audrey. "Omniscience in *Our Mutual Friend*: On Taking the Reader by Surprise." *Journal of Narrative Technique*, 17 (1987), 91–101.

Jaffe analyzes point of view in *Our Mutual Friend* to argue that the reader who, because of the narrative structure of the novel, "has considered himself omniscient finds that he has been misled, exposed, and taken in." Jaffe states that the novel establishes a "pattern of one-upmanship" in which characters try to entrap other characters into their own plots to control their world. In allowing the reader to share Harmon's interior monologue, Jaffe argues, Dickens establishes an illusion of omniscience on the reader's part. Boffin thus misleads the reader as he misleads Bella in his pretence to be a miser. And it is precisely this kind of surprise, this reversal of the reader's role from omniscience to "character"—to one who, like the Bradley Headstone who believes he is in control in hunting Eugene through the streets of London only to have Eugene turn suddenly and pass him, demonstrating Eugene's control as hunter—that entraps the reader, according to Jaffe.

804. Jaffe, Audrey. "*Our Mutual Friend*: On Taking the Reader by Surprise." In her *Vanishing Points: Dickens Narrative, and the Subject of Omniscience*. Berkeley: U of California P, 1991, pp.150–67.

A reworked presentation of "Omniscience in *Our Mutual Friend*: On Taking the Reader by Surprise" (**803**).

805. Jaffe, Audrey Anne. " 'Vanishing Points': The Dickens Narrator and the Fantasy of Omniscience."*Dissertation Abstracts International*, 47 (1985), 912A (Berkeley: U of California).

Jaffe explores narrative omniscience in Dickens's work, including *Our Mutual Friend*, arguing that omniscience is a "fantasy about knowledge, which depends upon a narrator's demonstrating the limitations of characters' and sometimes readers' knowledge." She shows how the assumption of omniscience "affects Dickens's work both structurally and thematically."

806. Kaplan, Fred. "The Sons of Toil." In his *Dickens: A Biography*. New York: William Morrow, 1988, pp. 467–76.

In this indispensable biographical study of Dickens, Kaplan argues that in the world of *Our Mutual Friend* "society shapes the individual into unnatural contortions. This society that unnatural people create embodies their preoccupation with money, power, exclusion, exploitation, and cannibalism." However, "Dickens implies that there are special people whose innate moral sentiments are so strong that they are invulnerable to deformation." Kaplan traces patterns of redemption and rebirth in the novel and notes parallels between characters in the novel and figures in Dickens's personal life.

Reviews: J. Bayley, *New York Review of Books,* 19 January 1989, pp. 11–12; G. Beer, *New York Times Book Review,* 13 November 1988, pp. 3, 67; J. Carey, *Sunday Times Books,* 20 November 1988, pp.1–2; J. Gross, *New York Times,* 25 October 1988, p. C20; R. Heller, *Mail on Sunday,* 11 December 1988, p. 26; A. Hutter, *Los Angeles Times Book Review,* 23 October 1988, pp. 3, 8; P. Kemp, *Listener,* 22 December 1988, p. 64; R. Martin, *Washington Post Book World*, 23 October 1988, pp. 1, 18; J. Mortimer, *Spectator*, 261 (3 December 1988), 40–41; A. Quinn, *New Statesman & Society*, 1 (16 December 1988), 23; E. Turner, *Punch,* 295 (2 Dec. 1988), 49–50; W. West, *Washington Times,* 24 Oct 1988; R. Brown, *Library Journal*, 113 (1 September 1988), 169; L. Clipper, *Choice*, 26 (March 1989), 1158; P. Collins, *Times Higher Education Supplement*, 3 March 1989, p. 21; P. Rogers, *Times Literary Supplement*, 7 April 1989, pp. 360–61; J. Sutherland, *London Review of Books*, 2 February 1989, pp. 19–22; B. Allen, *Smithsonian,* 20 (1989), 243; R. Coles, *Virginia Quarterly Review,* 65 (1989), 569; M. Slater, *Dickensian,* 85 (1989), 181–83; J. Meckier, *Albion,* 21 (1989), 509–12; S. Monod, *Victorian Studies,* 33 (1990), 513.

807. Keh, Wonbong. "Father-Daughter Relationships in Selected Novels by Charles Dickens." *Dissertation Abstracts International*, 57 (1996), 2048A (Iowa University).

Keh examines *Our Mutual Friend* as an instance of Dickens's "tendency to waver between his sharp criticism of fathers and his sentimentalization of abusive father-daughter relationships [that] constitutes one of the major weaknesses of his social criticism."

808. Kelly, Mary Ann. "From Nightmare to Reverie: Continuity in *Our Mutual Friend*." *Durham University Journal*, 48 (1986), 45–50.

Kelly demonstrates that the imagination serves as a saving force in *Our Mutual Friend* for those who have suffered intense pain, loss, and deprivation. Lizzie and Jenny Wren are able to imagine a better life by creating vivid fantasies and to assume invented lives for periods of time in order to cope with their pain. Furthermore they are able to "prompt change in others by living according to one's imagined idea of a better existence." Lizzie is able to influence Bella, and Lizzie and Jenny are able to change Eugene. "In *Our Mutual Friend*," Kelly concludes, "fantasy whose necessity springs from pain and whose substance is woven from memory, helps change the world."

809. Kim Tag-Jung. "Ghosts of the Past in Dickens' Later Novels: Transformation of Memory in Author and Characters." *Dissertation Abstracts International*, 58 (1997), 884A (Texas Tech University).

Kim argues that Dickens's "present" unhappiness with his failed marriage is reflected in his later novels and considers *Our Mutual Friend* as representing a reconciled view with regard to the past.

810. King, James Roy. "Defense Mechanisms in *Our Mutual Friend*." *Dickens Quarterly*, 12 (1995), 45–49.

King examines defense mechanisms of characters who are beaten down in *Our Mutual Friend* in the context of Freudian psychology, particularly the numerous defense mechanisms Freud identified and described. King shows how these "buffeting mechanisms" fit together and strengthen the organic quality of the novel.

811. Klemp, Annette Doblix. "Dickens and Melodrama: Character Presentation and Plot Motifs in Six Novels." *Dissertation Abstracts International*, 45 (1984), 3646A (Penn State University).

Klemp examines Dickens's use of melodramatic motifs in three early novels and three later novels, arguing that he deliberately undercuts the melodramatic formulas in the later novels thus presenting a "pessimistic social vision and a complex treatment of character." *Our Mutual Friend*, she concludes, contrasts a melodramatic conflict in the Boffin-Harmon-Wilfer plot with one that undermines melodramatic expectation in the Wrayburn-Headstone-Hexam plot, the latter of which she sees as presenting more complex characters.

812. See *Knowles* (**692**). "Veneering and the Age of Veneer: A Source and Background for *Our Mutual Friend*."

813. Kubasak, Sharon. "Reflexive Delight." *Dickensian*, 90 (1994), 25–35. Kubasak argues that when "Dickens's details work with a self-incorporating action . . . the details work like reflexes *and* they work reflexively." She considers Mr. Wegg of *Our Mutual Friend* briefly as an example of her thesis.

814. Kucich, John. "Dickens's Fantastic Rhetoric: The Semantics of Reality and Unreality in *Our Mutual Friend.*" *Dickens Studies Annual*, 14 (1985), 167–89.

Kucich analyzes the realistic and anti-realistic—or fantastic—elements in Dickens in the context of the semantics of Dickens's rhetoric. Meaning and un-meaning are not merely mixed in Dickens, according to Kusick; they can be seen as "dynamically related." Kucich makes a distinction between the "economical" in Dickens, that language which is a "complete folding together of rhetoric and meaning," on the one hand, and the "non-economical," that language that "exuberantly wastes itself." These two kinds of rhetoric, real and unreal, economic and non-economic, "are ultimately enclosed by a second-order economy that puts them into an efficient and perfectly well defined relationship in terms of meaning." In the second-order economy, the significant and "extra-significant" come together in a new way, a way in which non-sense "produces its own particular kind of meaning." Kucich goes on to analyze how "mode," an efficient lexical system, and "style," an "inefficient" lexical system, interact in *Our Mutual Friend* in ways that produce not a mixture but a fragmentation of the modes and which reflect "constantly shifting and explicit authorial judgments about meaning." He concludes, after acknowledging that "the concept of second-order economy is very complex," that "this structural tension in Dickens can carry us beyond the reach of both psychology and linguistics, into a greater appreciation of Dickens's concern with the relationship of all human energy to limiting systems, and to ways in which dialectical relationships can be represented in art." This ambitious and complex essay deserves careful reading.

815. Kucich, John. "Repression and Representation: Dickens's General Economy." *Nineteenth-Century Fiction,* 38 (1984), 62–77. Reprinted in *Charles Dickens*. Ed. Steven Connor. London: Longman, 1996, pp. 197–210.

Kucich revisits the critical commonplace that Dickens's work is divided between the forces of violence and repression. He argues that the self must be seen as "figural" or linguistic in nature and this self is created out of a linguistic interchange, an "economy," of both repression and violence which together work "in a nonoppositional way" not to divide but rather to reinforce individual identity. Kucich analyzes *Our Mutual Friend* to show how Dickens "solves the problem of restrictively economic violence by incorporating violence metonymically" with themes that are associated with repression: self-sacrifice, self-control, disinterest. He contrasts Harmon and Wrayburn with Headstone to demonstrate "not that they are immune to self-conflict but that their doubleness represents a general psychic economy in which both the radical violence of desire and the self-denial of moral coherence are exercised at the same time rather than suffered as an opposition." Kucich concludes that for Dickens's heroes and heroines to be redeemed they must "be incorporated in a social—and a narrative—economy rather than a merely self-enclosed and subjective one"; to center the violence and repression in a linguistic relationship within the "emotional range of the self-and not to represent it as a singular image of public action—is to prevent any collective experience of psychological rupture."

816. Lamarque, Peter. "Learning from Literature." *Dalhousie Review*, 77 (1997), 7–21.

Lamarque investigates the extent to which it can be said that "learning, acquiring beliefs about the world at large, is an integral or even important feature of our response to literature." He goes to *Our Mutual Friend* to demonstrate that the value of the novel lies not in its central theme but in the way that the details of plot, setting, and characters "cohere around the theme and make it vivid." The "imaginative immersion" and "exploration of the vision of the work through its themes," not the truth of the proposition itself, is what allows us to appreciate a literary work as literature. He concludes, sensibly, that "we do not capture the essence of literature by appeal to terms like knowledge, truth, or understanding." Great literature is a product of the creative imagination that "treats of the deepest human concerns through verbal artifice which invites a distinctive mode of appreciation unlike that associated with philosophy or science."

817. Langland, Elizabeth. "*Our Mutual Friend*: Bella Wilfer's Reformation by Housekeeping." In her *Nobody's Angels: Middle-Class Women and Domestic Ideology in Victorian Culture*. Ithaca, NY: Cornell UP, 1995, pp. 104–12.

Langland takes a feminist/new historicist approach to investigate the changing conception of bourgeois woman, particularly the middle-class housewife and her development in the Victorian period. By examining domestic novels as well as "nonliterary representations of domesticity," she challenges the stereotype of the Victorian housewife as passive and dependent. Bella Wilfer demonstrates that she is a worthy wife by competently managing the modest resources she has as housekeeper. Langland convincingly analyzes the tension between the serious and the trivial in the representation of Bella's household management, concluding that *Our Mutual Friend* "represents but cannot finally assess the complex contribution of a man's wife to the middle-class venture." In the end, Dickens "required a helpmeet fit not only to love but to labor by his side." Dickens's novels, Langland asserts, "dramatize the clash between patriarchal ideology with its gender bifurcations and bourgeois ideology with its class bifurcations." The middle-class wife is the "figure whose mystifications protect patriarchal privilege with its rhetoric of dominance and subservience, while her disciplining presence at home and colonizing effect abroad secure England as a haven for the bourgeoisie."

818. Lesser, Wendy. "From Dickens to Conrad: A Sentimental Journey." *English Literary History*, 52 (1985), 185–208.

Lesser compares Conrad's *The Secret Agent* (1907) with Dickens's *Our Mutual Friend* to argue that Conrad's irony is an "outgrowth of Dickens's complex form of sentimentality." She analyzes reports of child abuse in *The Times* in October 1851 and in November 1901 and demonstrates that the earlier account is far more concerned with issues of character, moral sentiment, and personal elements than the later, more objective, account, and claims that the language of the earlier account establishes a "community of moral agreement" among the reporter, the readers, the magistrate, and even the "good" side of the abusive mother. Dickens, according to Lesser, both "exploits [sentimentality] and undercuts it, uses it to make people feel and then questions the value of that feeling." This "dual vision" develops "so completely as to become unadulterated irony" in Conrad's *The Secret Agent*. The two newspaper accounts represent the opposing poles of Dickens's and Conrad's sentimental rhetoric: "Dickens is likely to gush where Conrad mocks, and Dickens judges lavishly where Conrad refrains from judgment." Nonetheless, both Dickens and Conrad "offer a complex mix of sentimental immersion and ironic alienation." Lesser concludes that Conrad is "still writing for an audience schooled in the novelistic functions of sentimentality."

819. Lucas, John. "*Our Mutual Friend*: Instruments in their Places." In his *Charles Dickens: The Major Novels*. London and New York: Penguin Books, 1992, pp. 145–59.

Lucas reads *Our Mutual Friend* as presenting a society "dominated by the facts of class and capital, [in which] people must appear to each other as surfaces reflecting or instantiating the evidence of both these facts, for it is by that people wish to be known. To put it simply, they become their images." He goes on to examine how the self becomes an object in the novel and how people use one another as instruments. The presentation of "fixed" characters in the novel "represents [Dickens's] marvelous and imaginative way of exploring the cost of class consciousness in a society which can conceive of itself in no other way."

820. McCarthy, Patrick. "Designs in Disorder: The Language of Death in *Our Mutual Friend.*" *Dickens Studies Annual*, 17 (1998), 129–44.

McCarthy considers the importance of death in the context of reading Dickens's stories as "embodiments of his primordial myth of the nature of existence." Dickens's world is one in which each entity struggles to affirm itself in opposition to forces that threaten its existence. In *Our Mutual Friend* McCarthy points out four verbal patterns that capture this opposing turbulence: "animal imagery, animism, odd collocations, and superlative expressions." The novel faces down the dark side of the myth of destruction and affirms death as a release from the imprisoning forces of life. "Death, the end-point of the myth of life, the final dissolver of the individual life, opens or re-opens the myth to new constructions, to new life." Betty Higden sets a positive standard for dying, while Gaffer Hexam, Mr. Dolls, and Rogue Riderhood "point the moral by negative example." Harmon and Wrayburn are able to free themselves from the imprisoning will of their fathers by "consenting" to their deaths. In this novel, McCarthy argues convincingly, Dickens is focusing on death, but not negatively: "he looks at life through death and finds it sad but not an enemy of happiness."

821. McClure, Joyce Kloc. "Vulnerability and Obligation: The Ethical Relevance of Contingency and Finitude." *Dissertation Abstracts International*, 59 (1998), 1628A (Yale University).

McClure examines *Our Mutual Friend* in the context of considering "contingency and finitude as conditions of existence." For Dickens "acceptance, in particular self-acceptance," is the proper moral response to human vulnerability; by thus looking at the "moral task in response to vulnerability as self-acceptance" we gain new insights into the nature of obligation that raise questions about obligations to ourselves and others.

822. McMaster, Juliet. "Dickens and David Copperfield on the Act of Reading." *English Studies in Canada*, 15 (1989), 288–304.

McMaster argues that Dickens makes reading itself a subject in his novels and examines *David Copperfield* closely to support the claim. She considers briefly *Our Mutual Friend*, where, she points out, language "crumbles and disintegrates."

823. McMaster, Juliet. "*Our Mutual Friend*: 'A Heap of Broken Images.' "
In her *Dickens the Designer*. London: Macmillan; Totowa, N J: Barnes
and Noble, 1987, pp. 193–221.

McMaster demonstrates that the "great Victorian anxiety about the
tendency of a complex civilization to divide and subdivide, and in the
process to destroy and dehumanize, is made literal and visual" in *Our
Mutual Friend*, where Dickens "presents a vision of a world and a
society that are disintegrating." McMaster traces the motif of disintegration in Dickens's presentation of both people and landscape as
falling apart and shows how this is reinforced in the language itself.
She finds the novel "somber and almost tragic in its view of life" but
concludes that her concern is with Dickens's "power to make us
see . . . . Dickens as a painter with words instinctively speaks through
visual images, and communicates by dramatizing ways of seeing. The
world of *Our Mutual Friend* . . . is splintered and incoherent. The artist . . . can make a coherent picture of incoherence, but he cannot—at
least he does not—convince us that the incoherent is coherent after
all."

824. McMullen, Buck. "Allergies of Reading: Some Ambiguities of Literacy in Nineteenth-Century British Fiction." *Dissertation Abstracts International*, 53 (1992), 3538A (University of Colorado, Boulder).

McMullen examines the representations of literacy in several nineteenth-century British novels, including *Our Mutual Friend*, and discovers that reading and writing "have no one consistent meaning or
developmental pattern of representation." Literacy "is a deeply
clouded issue, of which little of historical, cultural, psychological or
literary importance can be reliably concluded."

825. MacKay, Carol Hanbery. "The Encapsulated Romantic: John Harmon
and the Boundaries of Victorian Soliloquy." *Dickens Studies Annual*,
18 (1989), 255–76.

MacKay analyzes John Harmon's long soliloquy in *Our Mutual Friend*
in which he debates about whether or not to resume his own identity
in the context of Romantic and Victorian elements. She argues that
"some of the aesthetic, formal and psychological elements of Romanticism" that are expressed in the soliloquy "can be contained or encapsulated by a Victorian emphasis on social concerns," also discovered
in a close reading of the soliloquy. She sees that the Romantic struggle
to go beyond formal boundaries is encapsulated by the Victorian concern for socializing vision in Harmon's decision to "stay dead."

826. Maglavera, Soultana. "*Our Mutual Friend*." In Maglavera's *Time Patterns in Later Dickens: A Study of the Thematic Implications of **Bleak***

House, Hard Times, Little Dorrit, A Tale of Two Cities, Great Expectations, and Our Mutual Friend. Amsterdam: Rodolpi, 1994, pp. 163–81.

This narratological analysis focuses on the temporal organization of the events in *Our Mutual Friend* in their chronological order and their arrangement in the narrative. Using the distinctions and categories put forward by Gerard Genette, Maglavera analyzes the relationship between appearance and reality, and the inability to reach truth solely through logical reasoning. This useful reading of *Our Mutual Friend* concludes that we cannot escape our past and reinforces the "good that permeates the novel." Maglavera discovers that destructive consequences of past events can be reformulated "through redeeming actions of love and goodness." Maglavera reads *Our Mutual Friend* as espousing a Christian view of time, one in which love and compassion give final meaning to all forms of time.

827. Marks, Patricia. "Storytelling as Mimesis in *Our Mutual Friend*." *Dickens Studies Newsletter*, 5 (1988), 23–30.

Marks sees *Our Mutual Friend* as exploring the relationship between aesthetics and life, arguing that the storytelling in the novel imposes a pattern on random events and suggests that life itself is grounded in pattern. The characters who engage in "monologic storytelling"—self-referential, close-ended, and selfish—fail, because they are too narrow, Marks asserts; those who tell "dialogic" stories—focused on the good of others, open-ended, and pluralistic—are successful. The latter, Marks shows, are concerned with integrating many selves in a confused world; the former with self-aggrandizement. She also believes that the male storytellers tend to be more dramatic while the female storytellers are more verbal. Marks demonstrates in this valuable essay that those who attempt to protect their identities through close-ended fictions are not as successful as those who engage human variety through open-ended fictions that redeem others from a lack of pattern in life.

828. Michie, Helena. " 'Who is this in Pain?': Scarring, Disfigurement, and Female Identity in *Bleak House* and *Our Mutual Friend*." *Novel*, 22 (1989), 199–212.

Michie argues that although women's bodies and desires seem to have no place in Dickens's novels generally, his "novels do provide one space for women, one means of textual entrance for their bodies; sickness, pain, and the rooms in which sickness and pain unfold, locate the heroine and her body in Dickens's verbal labyrinths." In this provocative article, Michie claims that Dickens's heroines come into their being through scarring, pain, and disfigurement and that "for Dickens, the process of making and unmaking is itself foregrounded in the illnesses of his heroines, and that pain necessarily both temporarily reproduces female physicality and makes any notion of the stable and fully representable female self impossible.'' Michie considers Jenny Wren as an instance of Dickens's attempt to ''transcend the passive one-dimensionality'' of his usual portrayals of young women, arguing that, like other Dickens heroines, she comes ''to textuality'' through scarring and pain, but that she turns her affliction to ''specifically narrative power.'' For Jenny, physical pain is not merely the ''condition through which she must pass, but the structuring idiom of her life, the force that produces her language and experiences.''

829. Milbank, Alison. ''Daughters of the House: Modes of the Gothic in the Fiction of Wilkie Collins, Charles Dickens, and Sheridan Le Fanu.'' *Dissertation Abstracts International*, 50 (1988), 3238A (University of Lancaster, UK).

Milbank considers the treatment of women in relation to the domestic house in the fiction of Dickens, Collins, and Le Fanu drawing on ''male'' and ''female'' gothic conventions, and argues that by the time of *Our Mutual Friend* Dickens has shifted from the male to the female gothic mode, and that his desire to free the imprisoned male from female ''domestic confinement results in a weakened concept of social regeneration.''

830. Miller, Andrew H. ''The Solicitudes of Material Culture: Victorian Novels and the Commodity Form.'' *Dissertation Abstracts International*, 52 (1991), 928A (Princeton University).

Miller considers the position of four Victorian novelists, including Dickens, in relation to the culture of goods manufactured in their society. He argues that Dickens sees ''the home as free from the desiccation of the public sphere, and in *Our Mutual Friend* its representation is implicated in the representation of writing.'' While domesticity and writing are seen as havens from material desiccation in the novel, only the home provides safe harbor in the end, according to Miller; ''writing is finally inadequate to this task.''

831. Miller, Andrew. ''Rearranging the Furniture in *Our Mutual Friend*.'' In his *Novels Behind Glass: Commodity Culture and Victorian Narrative*. Cambridge: Cambridge UP, 1995, pp. 119–59.

Miller attempts to demonstrate that in an effort to forestall the fragmentation, alienation, and commodification attendant upon urban capitalism, Dickens created a space for himself where he could have the imaginative freedom to work his will on his universe. Dickens is able to control his domestic situation as well as his novels in the domestic space in which they are written: ''The creation of the home, this imaginary space, must be rigorously defended, its order maintained so that the sovereign will residing within it can exercise its desires and picture things in their places.'' Miller argues, not convincingly, that the Dickens who controlled his wife and her domestic space likewise took pleasure in treating women as objects in his novels.

832. Miller, J. Hillis. ''The Topography of Jealousy in *Our Mutual Friend*.'' In *Dickens Refigured: Bodies, Desires, and Other Histories*. Ed. John Schad. Manchester: Manchester UP, 1996, pp. 218–35.

Miller points out that Dickens is intentionally vague in his mapping of *Our Mutual Friend* so that it is not always clear ''how to get from there to here'' in the novel, offering Harmon's confusion about where he was drugged and thrown into the river as the most obvious example of this ''failure in mapping.'' Unlike *Bleak House*, where ''everything and everybody is interconnected and interdependent,'' characters in *Our Mutual Friend* share stories in a mediated and indirect form, through mutual friends. The mutual friendships in the novel are often doubled, the most extreme form of this doubling being in Eugene Wrayburn and Bradley Headstone and their love of Lizzie Hexam. Miller analyzes Bradley's jealousy, arguing trenchantly that jealously is ''a way of being tormentedly related to the wholly other by way of curiosity about the other's other.'' Bradley's frustrated rage to know the other person wholly and also to know the ''other's relation to the other's others, the beloved's supposed secret lovers,'' stirs up otherness within himself and leads him to self-destruction.

The otherness in *Our Mutual Friend*, Miller points out, is expressed ''in the river's dark depths,'' depths which figuratively express the ''anonymous and unnameable energy within each person.'' Miller argues that the characters in the novel are ''trapped within Victorian assumptions about class and gender,'' thus Mrs. Wilfer's ''crazy imitation of genteel speech'' or Podsnap's ''inane nationalist stupidities.'' The only possibility for a ''change in the bad condition of society is some extreme event that breaks up petrified class institutions and begins again after immersion'' in an ''impersonal energy'' that lies beneath the ''ideological matrices'' of which characters cannot be aware. ''This power underlies each person and, for Dickens, is present everywhere in nature too,'' Miller asserts. This ubiquitous force resists rational mapping. It interferes with the reader's efforts always to locate every person and every milieu in *Our Mutual Friend* in some place that might be identified according to familiar spatial coordinates.''

Miller concludes that Dickens's capacity to force a happy ending in improbable circumstances comes from his ''own histrionic invention in response to the demand made on him by the realm of otherness that, within the fiction, drives all his characters and, in the 'real world,' drives him to create them.'' Miller sees Bella's ''transformation of her relation with her father'' and Jenny Wren's dolls as examples of Dickens's own ''benign, life-giving theatrical creativity in the novel''; but, Miller cautions us in this powerful and moving essay, ''Dickens's theatre will not, however, come alive without the reader's collaboration.''

833. Miller, Michael. '' 'The Fellowship-Porters and the Veneerings': Setting, Structure and Justice in *Our Mutual Friend.*'' *Dickensian,* 85 (1989), 30–38.

Miller contrasts the Six Jolly Fellowship-Porters in *Our Mutual Friend* with the Veneerings' home to argue that in ''almost certainly a sustained counterpoint'' between the coziness of the one and the coldness of the other, Dickens is helping to unify his work. By examining judgments made in both places we learn something about Dickens's notion of justice. Miller considers the misjudgments (Gaffer's guilt, Harmon's death) and drownings made at the Six Fellowship-Porters which help to unify the novel and contrasts them with the misjudgments at the Veneerings', particularly the judgment of Eugene's marrying Lizzie. The pronouncement that Harmon is alive made at The Fellowship-Porters signals that he deserves to be alive; the mocking of Eugene at the Veneerings' for marrying Lizzie indicates he has done the right thing.

834. Moon, Sangwha. ''Dickens in the Context of Victorian Culture: An Interpretation of Three of Dickens' Novels from the Viewpoint of Darwinian Nature.'' *Dissertation Abstracts International,* 57 (1996), 3039A, (North Texas University).

Moon examines *Our Mutual Friend* in the context of *The Origin of Species,* pointing out that money is ''the central metaphor of the novel, the characters kill and are killed like the nature of Darwin in which animals kill each other.''

835. Morgentaler, Goldie. *Dickens and Heredity: When Like Begets Like.* Basingstoke, Eng.: Macmillan; New York: St. Martin's Press, 2000, passim.

Morgentaler examines heredity in Dickens and concludes that by the time he is writing *Our Mutual Friend* Dickens ''jettisons heredity'' and replaces it with ''metaphors of disintegration and dispersal.'' Dickens does present Riah as inheriting the traits of ''the Jews [construed] as tribally and racially all of a piece,'' but does not ''conceive of Jews as individuals. They exist in his mind merely as particles of one collective stereotyped whole.'' Otherwise, for Dickens biological heredity has been replaced by wills: ''they represent an obstruction to the present imposed by the past, played out as an attempt to regulate biological destiny.'' To some degree, life is seen as coming from death, as in Harmon's and Wrayburn's resurrections, but even Jenny Wren's and Mr. Venus's creations never really come alive. Thus, Morgentaler concludes, the ''process of disintegration and regeneration which so fascinates Dickens in *Our Mutual Friend* may substitute for his earlier interest in heredity, but cannot replace it.''

836. Morris, Pam. ''A Taste for Change in *Our Mutual Friend*.'' In *Rethinking Victorian Culture*. Ed. Juliet John and Alice Jenkins. Houndmills, Eng.: Macmillan; New York: St. Martin's Press, 2000, pp. 179–95.

Morris examines the ''complex ways in which *Our Mutual Friend* expresses some of the main currents of feeling and social forces of the 1860s,'' in the context of what Raymond Williams described as a ''structure of feeling'' in *The Long Revolution*. She refers to Max Müller's lectures at the Royal Institute on the ''Bow-wow'' theory of language that dismisses the notion that language originates in attempts to imitate natural sounds, to discussions of evolutionary theory and cultural regeneration and degeneration, and particularly to Marx's *The Eighteenth Brumaire of Louis Bonaparte* (1852), which argues that the bourgeoisie must become an increasingly repressive and reactionary force culturally and politically in order to preserve its own freedoms to pursue its economic interests. Marx hopes that by educating the working classes to meet the needs of capitalist expansion, the proletariat will be provided with the wherewithal to overthrow the oppressive capitalist class. Müller hopes that language will be revitalized by the linguistic energy from the dialect-speaking classes. ''The disease of language,'' Morris argues, ''is shown as indissolubly linked to the financial venality of economic Darwinism.''

The ending of the novel implies, Morris indicates, that Müller's hope prevails: the marriage of Lizzie and Eugene brings together ''patrician disaffection'' with the ''dialect-speaking classes,'' and thus offers a resolution to the problem of finding cultural self-renewal in a society that has ''devalued its own expressive currency'' through the degeneration of language resulting from Podsnappery. But Morris points out that ''unlike Marx and Müller, *Our Mutual Friend* does not represent the poor as untouched by the culture of commodity capitalism.'' She shows how Mrs. Frank Milvey and Jenny Wren, for example, express interests that demonstrate ''taste,'' which is associated with an ''inherent desire for transcendence.'' Morris refers to Pierre Bourdieu's analysis of taste (in *Distinction: A Social Critique of the Judgement of Taste*) in a commodity culture where economic capital, represented by

Podsnap and the new rich, competes against cultural capital, represented by Eugene Wrayburn. Educational capital, represented by Bradley Headstone, offers no hopeful transcendence; Bradley receives certificates "but his body stays relentlessly lower class." The confrontation between Eugene and Bradley is, for Morris, "a confrontation between oppositional values: those based upon the common needs of bodily life and those that claim transcendence from those needs, in disembodied spiritual distinction."

The ending of the novel, for Morris, offers sexual dominance as the answer to the Darwinian struggle for survival and a union of cultural capital with the dialect-speaking classes as the answer to the problem of cultural self-renewal in a society suffering from a degeneration of language. She sees those characters who are brought together at the end of the novel, the Boffins, the Harmons, the Wrayburns, Jenny Wren and Sloppy, as representing a "utopian community: lower-class trueness of heart, responsibly administered wealth, cultural refinement and working-class artistry and craftsmanship in the form of Jenny Wren's dolls and Sloppy's carpentry." However she sees this community as removed from the "common streets" and points out that the product of the educated working class, in the person of Bradley Headstone who has been cast back to "primal slime and mud," is excluded from the regenerated society.

Morris concludes this thoughtful, complex, and provocative essay with the observation that Headstone insists to Lizzie that he is in earnest. She sees the earnest claims of the aspiring working class as having been denied as a result of the educational provisions of the late nineteenth century; looking toward the twentieth century, she wonders if Dickens wasn't being prescient "when he so grimly seals Headstone off from the possibility of a regenerative future." She finishes with the disturbing observation that the value system based on transcending the common necessities of life—not the value system based on the common necessities of life—"still organizes our educational hierarchies and, frequently, our aesthetic judgments."

837. Morris, Pam. "*Our Mutual Friend*: The Taught Self." In her *Dickens's Class Consciousness: A Marginal View*. London: Macmillan, 1991, pp. 120–40.

Morris argues that although the surface of political, social, and religious life in Victorian England appeared to be untroubled, there was corruption beneath that surface. She demonstrates that in *Our Mutual Friend* Dickens "constructs a parodic mockery of national progress in a search for origins in dust and mud, and the siting of patriotic pride in the desert of cultural and political life." She analyzes the "speech image constructed by Wrayburn's character discourse," along with Headstone's and Jenny Wren's, and discovers that in "its multiple resourcefulness, its hard-bitten cynicism as to intentions behind rhetoric, and its positive impulse of anger, . . . the speech image constructed by Jenny Wren's discourse achieves a more powerful and convincing counterforce than that of Wrayburn's to the social chorus of bombast and deceit." Morris concludes that "it is the 'vulgar' discourse of Jenny Wren's speech image which is the locus of a positive, non-hegemonic, perspective based upon material cultural practice and which engages in a sustained dialogic critique of the imaginary solutions offered by the plot structure." Despite the jargon, this is a useful study.

Reviews: R. Edmond, *Dickensian*, 87 (1991), 171–72; F. Schwartzbach, *Dickens Quarterly*, 9 (1992), 32–34.

838. Murray, Brian. "Money and Mystery: *Little Dorrit, Great Expectations, Our Mutual Friend, The Mystery of Edwin Drood.*" In his *Charles Dickens*. New York: Continuum Publishing Company, 1994, pp. 155–86.

Murray "aims to provide students and general readers with an introduction to Dickens's life and writings" in this study. He finds that *Our Mutual Friend*, "although brilliant in many ways, is often all but unreadable. Its related plots are particularly convoluted, and it is repeatedly slowed by wordiness and pretentious phrasing—by sentences that are often more flabby than firm."

839. See Myer (**908**). "Dickensian Echoes in Shaw: *Our Mutual Friend* and *Pygmalion.*"

840. Newey, Vincent. "Dickensian Decadents." In *Romancing Decay: Ideas of Decadence in European Culture.* Ed. Michael St. John. Aldershot, Eng.: Ashgate, 1999, pp. 64–82.

Newey analyzes Steerforth in *David Copperfield*, Harthouse in *Hard Times*, and Eugene Wrayburn in *Our Mutual Friend* as characters who anticipate the decadence at the end of the century. He sees Steerforth and Harthouse as unredeemed, but argues that Wrayburn, who has many of their qualities, also possesses a "capacity for self-scrutiny and for reflecting upon his own situation and behavior" that distinguishes him from his predecessors. The crisis Eugene finds himself in—"out of the question" to marry Lizzie or to leave her—"is so emphatic and summary as to suggest a deliberate contrivance by Dickens, a coil from which to launch a definitive movement in the text, which thereafter drives toward patent affirmation of 'domestic virtues,' or, that is, of 'domestic ideology.'" Newey concludes, not altogether convincingly, that this subordination of Lizzie and Eugene to the purposes of domestic ideology represents a sacrifice of Dickens's "imaginative art." He sees the ending of *Our Mutual Friend* as a repetition of Dickens's siding with the world of the Brownlows and Maylies at the expense of Fagin, Sikes, and the gang: the world "of order against energy, or of narrative—that is the teleology of middle-class values—against the life of fiction."

841. Newman, S. J. "Decline and Fall Off? Towards an Appreciation of *Our Mutual Friend.*" *Dickensian*, 85 (1989), 99–104.

Newman asserts that *Our Mutual Friend* is a "broken book" but one that poses the problem of how seriously to take the novel itself. Newman asks if we are to take the "Decline-and-Fall-Off-the Rooshan-Empire" as a symbol of the decline of Victorian England or as a symbolic joke, and examines the novel in the context of Gibbon's work. He concludes that as deep as the joke may be and as "deep as Dickens has sunk his Victorian theme, the novel still feels essentially Victorian, in the official sense of the word. Dickens has not broken the grip of his age even though he has deepened our understanding of it." Not an altogether convincing argument.

842. Nielsen, Margaret Worthen. "Dickens's Prevaricating Piece of Goods: Liars and Truthtellers in *Dombey and Son, Little Dorrit,* and *Our Mutual Friend.*" *Dissertation Abstracts International*, 53 (1991), 162A (Iowa University).

Nielsen examines liars and truth tellers in three of Dickens's novels, arguing that whether or not characters tell the truth is not as important as "their innate morality." She points to Mr. Boffin and the narrator in *Our Mutual Friend* to demonstrate that motivation is the "most important insight into Dickens's moral vision."

843. O'Donnell, Patrick. " 'A Speech of Chaff': Ventriloquy and Expression in *Our Mutual Friend.*" *Dickens Studies Annual*, 19 (1990), 247–79.

O'Donnell examines identity in *Our Mutual Friend* in the context of ventriloquy, comparing Dickens's use of voice to the performance of the popular ventriloquist, Mr. Love. The ventriloquist destroys his own identity to create his characters, and the success of the spectacle depends on the suppression of the self and the multiplication of the self into other characters. After an elaborate analysis of voice in the novel, O'Donnell concludes not very convincingly that as Dickens throws his voice in *Our Mutual Friend*, he "finds that to be an author—a father of identities—is to confront the facelessness of one's own identity . . . and to acknowledge identity's groundless origins even as writing it down marks its entrance into the world."

844. Oeler, Karla Beth. "Murder and Narrative in Balzac, Dostoevsky and Dickens." *Dissertation Abstracts International*, 61 (2000), 1831A (Yale University).

Oeler examines murder in Balzac, Dostoevsky, and Dickens to demonstrate how the "representation of murder gives rise to narrative ruptures and semantic instabilities that both reveal narrative limitations and profoundly reflect a larger historic world." She argues that in *Our Mutual Friend* "the almost modernist fragmentation of the text reflects a murderous economic violence and that the story of Bradley Headstone, in particular, disrupts the teleological functioning of the legitimization narrative and the marriage plot."

845. See O'Hea **(693)**. "Hidden Harmony: Marcus Stone's Wrapper Design for *Our Mutual Friend*."

846. O'Hea, Michael Patrick. "Inclusion and Exclusion in Dickens's Comedy." *Dissertation Abstracts International*, 57 (1996), 3040A (University of Alberta).

O'Hea examines "the importance of surprise and insight in the comic" in Dickens and considers the riddle-like nature of *Our Mutual Friend*; he concludes that Dickens is only moderately successful in achieving "comic elucidation" in that novel.

847. O'Sullivan, Sean Lawrence. "The Reader's Purchase: Anticipating Scott, Dickens, and Hardy." *Dissertation Abstracts International*, 61(2000), 4008A (Yale University).

O'Sullivan argues that after the failure of "reconsidering models of transactions with his public" in *Master Humphrey's Clock* in an attempt to provide a fresh narrative approach, Dickens returned to the "templates" that had made him famous, and in *Our Mutual Friend* "he inscribed this metanarrative as the very plot" of the novel. The "questions of freshness vs. familiarity, expectation vs. surprise, and identity vs. disguise that propel the stories of that novel also describe the burden of maintaining an instantly recognizable writing persona."

848. Oxenford, Rosemary Ann. "Narrative Structure and the Pursuit of Identity in *Nicholas Nickleby, David Copperfield,* and *Our Mutual Friend*." *Dissertation Abstracts International*, 52 (1991), 3942A (Harvard University).

Oxenford examines identity in four of Dickens's novels, seeing *Our Mutual Friend* as structured upon John Harmon's recovering his name by piecing together the story and establishing his self through clues. The attempt to create meaning for the hero of the novels under consideration mirrors the "narrative's attempt to establish itself as a closed system." While working to establish closure, "the novels reaffirm the perpetual dialect between order and disorder. Hence, the contrivances in bringing about the happy ending should be seen . . . as sophisticated calibrations of the problematics of individuation and closure.''

849. Page, Norman. *"Our Mutual Friend.''* In his *A Dickens Companion.* New York: Schocken Books, 1984, pp. 225–38.

Page provides valuable background on composition, serialization, and publication information, an overview of critical reception, and an annotated list of characters in Dickens's works, including *Our Mutual Friend.*

850. Palmer, William J. "Dickens and Shipwreck." *Dickens Studies Annual,* 18 (1989), 39–92.

Palmer examines Dickens's use of shipwreck scenes and metaphors of shipwreck to demonstrate that Dickens found a "metaphor for his age, that of a generation of shipwrecked mariners." In *Our Mutual Friend* Dickens presents society as an "apocalyptic shipwreck" that must be survived if there is to be a more enlightened society. The generally sound thesis is sometimes strained, as when Eugene is argued to be the lighthouse keeper who protects Lizzie from the "shoals of exploitation both by Headstone and by himself."

851. Park, Hyungji. "The Empire Within: Masculinity and Colonial Travel in the Victorian Novel." *Dissertation Abstracts International,* 57 (1996), 181A (Princeton University).

Park considers the influence of the British Empire on its colonizers, in particular on the young travelers who embark on colonial journeys, as reflected in the Victorian novel. He analyzes *Our Mutual Friend* as a novel that "negotiate[s] the tension between Orientalist fantasies of the East and realist views of colonial careers."

852. Paulson, Linda Louise. "A Capital Reaction: Changing Patterns in the City Novels of Dickens and Balzac." *Dissertation Abstracts International,* 45 (1984), 2867A (UCLA).

Paulson examines the family in the context of the sprawling incoherence of the metropolitan areas in the novels of Dickens and Balzac. She sees *Our Mutual Friend* as portraying the family as "less and less a satisfying or relevant resolution to the difficulties that the city poses."

853. Petch, Simon. "The Sovereign Self: Identity and Responsibility in Victorian England." In *Law and Literature.* Ed. Michael Freeman and Andrew D. E. Lewis. Oxford: Oxford UP, 1999, pp. 397–415.

Petch examines the concept of sovereignty in Victorian moral discourses and in areas in which the concept of self-sovereignty "can be focused and interrogated through the interaction of law and literature." He claims that the breaking of promises and bargains drives the action of *Our Mutual Friend.* "As people barter and exchange 'bits of selves,' their fragmented selves spin out of control and thrash around in the social economy of a post-contractual world—a world, that is, in which contract no longer functions as a principle of social discipline.'' He considers Venus's owning Wegg's leg, which was bought ''in open contract,'' as an instance of open contract functioning as the ''law of the market''; Riderhood's blackmailing Headstone as an inversion of contract; the Lammles's agreement to work together in any scheme that will bring them money as their true marriage contract, demonstrating that for them marriage was a business partnership all along. Furthermore, ''the implications of the Lammle marriage contract'' point beyond that marriage to the generally subservient status of a woman in ''the relation of sovereign and subject.''

854. See Petrie (716). ''Dickens in Denmark: Four Danish Versions of his Novels.''

855. Philpotts, Harvey Lewis, III. '' 'Active Resignation': A Study of the Late Work of Charles Dickens (1855–1865) in Biographical and Social Context.'' *Dissertation Abstracts International*, 52 (1990), 171A (Delaware University).

Philpotts sees the historical events between 1855–1865 as putting added pressure on Dickens's fiction, including *Our Mutual Friend*, in such a way that the normative values that should counter the pressures are suspect and appear ''as consoling illusions.'' Each ''solution'' becomes increasingly inadequate ''mandating additional fictional strategies. From behind these constant modifications, however, a dialect can be seen to emerge, a logical progression of thought reflecting Dickens's own changing attitude toward the reality of his world.''

856. Poole, Adrian. ''Introduction.'' In 1997 Penguin Edition (697), pp. ix-xxiv.

Poole regards life in *Our Mutual Friend* as tending to ''a state of suspended animation'' and Dickens's anatomy of this corrupt society as ''more somber, more muted, and more appalled than ever before.'' He discusses the circumstances of Dickens's personal life at the time of writing the novel, and emphasizes the importance of repetition, which he regards as the novel's ''keynote.'' He considers the rich variety of character and scenes in the novel, analyzes the influence of the popular dramatist John Sheridan Knowles on the novel, examines the role of fathers, of the river and dust-heaps, of partnerships, fairy tales, popular ballads, and religious allusions, of reading and writing, and concludes that *Our Mutual Friend* ''asks some large questions about the life and the soul of the society it represents'' but offers answers that ''do not always agree with each other.'' It ''boasts less confidence than earlier works in its last judgements.''

857. Poovey, Mary. ''Reading History in Literature: Speculation and Virtue in *Our Mutual Friend*.'' In *Historical Criticism and the Challenge*

of Theory. Ed. Janet Levarie Smarr. Urbana: U of Illinois P, 1993, pp. 42–80.

Poovey sees the return to literary history and the rise of New Historicism as a challenge to the neoformalism of deconstruction. She offers a model of historical criticism that deploys principles of and differs from both ''New'' and traditional historical approaches by relying on close textual analysis to uncover the ''network of connotations and associations'' to which the language of literary texts belongs and which point to the ideological projects in which texts participated at the times of their production. She also relies on a range and variety of historical materials that, although not originally textual, involve representational systems that can be ''read'' through contemporary critical lenses. She describes this ambitious and extensive undertaking as a collective, interdisciplinary project through which scholars and critics put readers and the past in a relationship of mutual construction in order to ''reconstruct the debates and practices in which texts originally participated as well as the contemporary interpretive practices that make these debates visible now.'' Her textual analysis of *Our Mutual Friend*, set against the reconstruction of historical narratives of the Victorian period, seeks to demonstrate how Dickens participates in Victorian debates involving race, gender, and virtue through his representation of financial, legal, and ethical questions posed by new forms of economic organization and investment in which Alfred Lammle, Fledgeby, Twemlow, Wrayburn, Riah and others are players or victims. Poovey further claims that Dickens reflects unresolved fears and anxieties of Victorian England regarding ''the other''—seen as the black man or the strong independent woman—that underlie an ideology of wishful thinking in which good women, like Lizzie, Mrs. Boffin, and the reformed Bella, and the domestic sphere represent virtue divorced from monetary interests and so act as antidotes to the harsh demands and deceits of the marketplace. Her careful textual analysis reveals how the complexity of Dickens's narrative, with its intricate plotting and range of characters, challenges the apparent stability of solutions he advances to complex ideological issues.

858. Puccio, Paul M. ''Brothers of the Heart: Friendship in the Victorian and Edwardian Narrative.'' *Dissertation Abstracts International*, 56 (1995), 4409A (University of Massachusetts).

Puccio examines the fictional representation of friendship in all-male public boarding schools in nineteenth- and early twentieth-century England. He indicates that Dickens alludes to Eugene and Mortimer's school days together in order to reinforce the depth of their adult friendship.

859. Rebeck, Theresa. "Your Cries are in Vain: A Theory of the Melodramatic Heroine." *Dissertation Abstracts International*, 50 (1989),1668A, (Brandeis University).

Rebeck examines nineteenth-century stage melodrama, considering the aesthetics of the melodrama and studying stage adaptations of several Victorian novels. She then reads *Our Mutual Friend* in the context of her discoveries about stage melodrama, finding it a "high melodramatic" novel of late nineteenth-century England.

860. Reed, John R. "*Our Mutual Friend*." In his *Dickens and Thackeray: Punishment and Forgiveness*. Athens: Ohio UP, 1995, pp. 289–303.

Reed argues that "the rights and wrongs are intentionally confounded in *Our Mutual Friend*," a novel in which Dickens partly attempts to "recuperate the original Christian scheme of punishment and forgiveness." The "good people . . . must not punish directly" but the "narrator can dispense justice and punishments prohibited to his good characters because, like God, he is the creator of their story and knows its real meaning in the end." Reed insists that "although any text can be deconstucted simply because language itself is so complex and so intricately involved with social structures and other signs, texts can nonetheless . . . sustain a larger coherence that can be dissolved only through willful or capricious misreading, or through innocent ignorance of the language's contextual meaning." He concludes, convincingly, "that searching for these larger patterns of coherence is a worthwhile critical endeavor."

861. Robson, John M. "Crime in *Our Mutual Friend*." In *Rough Justice: Essays on Crime in Literature*. Ed. M. L. Frieland. Toronto: U of Toronto P, 1991, pp. 114–40.

Robson analyzes the extent to which Dickens offers a Victorian view of crime and the law in *Our Mutual Friend*. By juxtaposing selections from the novel with contemporary accounts in the newspaper and Mayhew's *London Labor and the London Poor*, Robson demonstrates convincingly that Dickens accurately portrays the real world of crime in the London of his time. He argues that neither the police nor the legal system "offers a reliable version of 'To Serve and Protect' " in *Our Mutual Friend*. However, Dickens does mete out proper rewards and punishments in the novel, he concludes, and with the important exception of Society, all criminals are duly punished.

862. Royce, Nicholas. "*Our Mutual Friend*." In *Dickens Refigured: Bodies, Desires, and Other Histories*. Ed. John Schad. Manchester: Manchester UP, 1996, pp. 39–54.

Royce considers *Our Mutual Friend* as "radically different from other contemporaneous English novels . . . and much closer to being a vast phantasmagoric sort of verbal 'Glue Monge' to half-inch Young Blight's mispronunciation.'' He analyzes Joycean and Beckettian elements in the novel, and concludes by agreeing with Eve K. Sedgwick **(867)** that the text is "about anality" but suggests "more radically that it is *about* the relations between anality and language, anality and writing.''

863. Sadrin, Anny. "Inheritance or Death." In her *Parentage and Inheritance in the Novels of Charles Dickens*. Cambridge: Cambridge UP, 1994, pp. 121–47.

Sadrin argues compellingly that *Our Mutual Friend* has "only one objective—that of giving back to the hero both his patrynomic and his patrimony and of establishing a direct link between what he has, who he is, and where he comes from." John Harmon's return as the prodigal son demonstrates again the "omnipotence of the father-figure" in Dickens and "gives expression here to [Dickens's] own oedipal torments (which remain unresolved long after his father's death)." Harmon returns "because it is necessary that the ambiguous drama of the revolt against the father and filial submission should once again be acted out so that, in the long term, the father's will might be done." Boffin plays the role of the surrogate father to Harmon, who "gets nothing in direct succession from his old sire; everything comes to him from the hands of Boffin, Boffin the servant, the ungenteel, illiterate man who, by divesting himself of his inheritance, ensures the 'genuine' succession." Sadrin concludes insightfully that "Boffin's mediation is, after Magwitch's, the greatest ideological revolution in the Dickens plot."

Reviews: T. Loe, *Choice ,*32 (April 1995), 1304–05; L. Litvack, *Dickensian*, 92 (1996), 52–55.

864. Sanders, Andrew. "Introduction." In 1994 Knopf Edition **(695)** pp. xi-xxv.

Sanders discusses the difficulty of composing *Our Mutual Friend*, particularly the serious disruption caused by the Staplehurst railway accident. He indicates that the influence of Dickens's liaison with Ellen Ternan may be reflected in the disguises and assumed identities in the novel. He gives an historical account of "real" dust in nineteenth-century England, but argues that "Dickens's central metaphor for the confused and disjointed condition of England," and for the consequent alienation of its "scrunched citizens," is not the dust heaps but Mr. Venus's "little dark greasy shop" where Venus's "trade, like Dickens's own, is somehow associating the dissociated."

865. Schiefelbein, Michael E. "Dickens's Characters and the Revision of Spiritual Fictions." *Dissertation Abstracts International*, 52 (1990), 929A (University of Maryland).

Schiefelbein examines the development of Dickens's religious and moral values by studying the characters from six novels, including *Our Mutual Friend*. He argues that Dickens creates "a new materialist vision powerful enough" to replace religious and romantic fictions while at the same time retaining his belief in a human spirit represented in these "transcendent fictions." By the time of his later novels, according to Schiefelbein, Dickens considers " 'larger social forces that shape an individual's destiny."

866. Scoggin, Daniel Paul. "Gothic Capital: Speculation, Specters, and Atonement in the Victorian Novel." *Dissertation Abstracts International*, 59 (1998), 1181A (Claremont College).

Scoggin considers *Our Mutual Friend* in the tradition of the gothic novel, which, he argues, in part deals with returning inheritances to their rightful heirs. Dickens uses the metaphor of "living-deadness" to demonstrate the attempt of the avaricious to control the future, he points out. Only by playing dead rather than trading in death can characters claim their inheritance and "escape an economy that thrives by recycling selves and things."

867. Sedgwick, Eve Kosofsky. "Homophobia, Misogyny, and Capital: The Example of *Our Mutual Friend*." In *Modern Critical Views. Charles Dickens*. Ed. Harold Bloom. New York: Chelsea House, 1987, pp. 245–61.

Sedgwick claims that *Our Mutual Friend*, a novel "about anality," is "about the whole issue of anal eroticism, and not merely a sanitized invective against 'filthy lucre' or . . . the dust-money equation . . . [and] concerns itself with other elements in the chain Freud describes: love between man and man, for instance; the sphincter, its control, and the relation of these to sadism; the relations among bodily images, material accumulation, and economic status." She sees the "erotic fate of every female or male . . . [as] cast in the terms and propelled by the forces of class and economic accumulation" and concludes that "[s]entient middle-class women of this time perceive the triangular path of circulation that enforces patriarchal power as being routed through them . . . while capitalist man . . . is always deluded about what it is that he pursues . . . . His delusion is . . . blindest, and closest to real empowerment, in his triangular transactions through women with other men." A creative reading, filled with impressive insights, but tendentious and unconvincing.

868. Shuman, Cathy Elizabeth. "Different for Girls: Gender and Professional Authority in Mill, Ruskin, and Dickens." *Dissertation Abstracts International*, 55 (1994), 1971A (Yale University).

Shuman examines how *Our Mutual Friend* "demystifies" the opposition between public and private that Mill and Ruskin set up in their works. Dickens does this "using a series of jokes about intellectual labor to create contradictions in distinctions between labor and leisure, past and present, and public and private." He goes on to establish a "new binarism to replace those it debunks, one based on the gendering of different pedagogical techniques."

869. Shuman, Cathy. " 'In the Way of School': Dickens's *Our Mutual Friend.*" In her *Pedagogic Economies: The Examination and the Victorian Literary Man.* Stanford, CA: Stanford UP, 2000, pp. 123–69.

In this essay largely drawn from her "Invigilating *Our Mutual Friend*: Gender, and Legitimation of Professional Authority" **(870)**, Shuman adds an interesting analysis on the parallels between the roles played by the novel's scavengers, like Gaffer Hexam and Jenny Wren, and its intellectual workers, lawyers, secretaries, and schoolteachers. "Scavengers and intellectual laborers are similar, *Our Mutual Friend* seems to argue, because both obtain access to traditional capital by untraditional methods, methods that problematize the division between the economic and the extraeconomic."

870. Shuman, Cathy. "Invigilating *Our Mutual Friend*: Gender and the Legitimation of Professional Authority." *Novel*, 28 (1995), 154–72.

Shuman examines the relationship between professional and domestic authority and argues convincingly that "domesticity's doctrine of separate spheres" is replaced in *Our Mutual Friend* by "pedagogic authority." The division between professional and domestic life is replaced by the division between teacher and student. Shuman insightfully demonstrates that Bella succeeds not by becoming a "good bourgeois wife, but by *passing a test* as a good bourgeois wife." After looking at the male and female "test takers," Shuman shows that "the banking-teacher's promiscuous transmission of knowledge [is] countered by a midwife pedagogy, where no transmission of knowledge takes place." Bella's value in the end is not based on the "labor theory of value" but "is a treasure buried within the heart." A thoughtful and convincing analysis. See also Shuman **(869)**.

871. Sirabian, Robert H. "Playing Play and Games: Structure and Meaning in the Novels of Charles Dickens." *Dissertation Abstracts International*, 55 (1994), 3855A, (Purdue University).

Sirabian considers "play as a theory of cultural and literary interpretation" in examining Dickens's novels, arguing that questioning play involves questioning reality and culture. In *Our Mutual Friend* he sees Jenny Wren as mediating "her identity with the reality of an urban environment through play."

872. See Slater, **(909)**. "Letter to the Editor."

873. Smith, John Robert. "Prominent Backgrounds: Visions of Class and Desire in Dickens's Illustrated Novels." *Dissertation Abstracts International*, 59 (1999), 4155A, (Boston University).

Smith examines characters in Dickens who try to raise themselves into a higher class but are anxious about blemishes in their social backgrounds preventing them from doing so. He focuses on illustrations in the novels, and in *Our Mutual Friend* he examines "the criminality of Bradley Headstone in light of the illustrations . . . to explore Dickens's continued dissatisfaction with a class system that offered only the illusion of social advancement."

874. Smith, Jonathan. "Heat and Modern Thought: The Forces of Nature in *Our Mutual Friend*." *Victorian Literature and Culture*, 23 (1995), 37–69.

Smith demonstrates in this thoughtful essay that in *Our Mutual Friend* Dickens uses the language and theories of the first law of thermodynamics—the law that affirms that the total energy of the universe is constant—to create a fiction of order. By the time of the writing of *Our Mutual Friend*, the dissemination of the second law of thermodynamics—that the universe will eventually run out of usable energy—had made the "comfortable, optimistic, ordered first-law mode" difficult to support. Smith argues convincingly that Dickens uses the language of the first law to provide meaning for a society that seems moving toward decay and stasis. According to Smith, Dickens is saying we have to act as though we live in a first-law world even if we know we live in a world dominated by the second law.

875. Smith, Monika Rydygier. "The W/Hole Remains: Consumerist Politics in *Bleak House*, *Great Expectations*, and *Our Mutual Friend*." *Victorian Review*, 19 (1993), 1–21.

Smith argues that through the figurative language of eater and eaten Dickens is able to describe the reality of nineteenth-century social life that does not conform to the "world of 'appearances': the illusion that England was a nation of equally prosperous classes." Smith claims that the "code of silence" prevented novelists—male as well as female—from pointing out the "appalling" nature of Victorian England's social problems, and so many authors "couch their criticism in 'covert, symbolic form.' " She argues that Dickens employs metaphors of consumption to expose the evils of England's social problems. However, rather than "contradict[ing] the world of 'appearance' constructed through the management of silences," as Smith claims Dickens's figurative language does in *Our Mutual Friend*, it would seem that his figurative language in fact reinforces a very loud shriek of outrage against the hypocrisy and Podsnappery he is exposing in that work.

876. Smith, Peter. "The Aestheticist Argument of *Our Mutual Friend*."
   Cambridge Quarterly, 18 (1989), 362–82.
   Smith argues splendidly that the theme of *Our Mutual Friend* is beauty.
   In this thoughtful and convincing analysis, Smith shows that Dickens
   is postulating an aesthetic that avoids the extremes of the bourgeois
   and the avant-garde: "there must be enough of the avant-garde element
   to prevent utility from bearing the slightest resemblance to the dull
   and all too familiar mode of Ruskinian edification, yet at the same
   time enough of the bourgeois to inhibit any tendency towards solipsis-
   tic over-refinement." He examines Jenny Wren closely to show how
   she creates beauty out of suffering and harsh experience—not by transforming the harshness but by carrying "it along into the realm of
   beauty, and there preserv[ing] it as a permanent source of beauty's
   vital strength." Smith claims that Dickens is dealing with the same
   issues that Pater treats in the close of the Winckelmann chapter of *The
   Renaissance* and that Dickens finally recognized that he "was an artist
   and nothing else." A valuable reading.

877. Solomon, J. Fisher. "Realism, Rhetoric, and Reification: Or the Case
   of the Missing Detective in *Our Mutual Friend*." *Modern Philology*,
   86 (1988), 34–44.
   Solomon analyzes the Harmon mystery plot, and particularly Dickens's abandonment of "both his mystery and his detective at the risk
   of disappointing his readers" in *Our Mutual Friend*. The mystery
   element is not merely a "tactical error" or simply "clumsy," as has
   been claimed, Solomon argues; rather it is "a calculated aesthetic
   strategy in Dickens's social criticism."
       Solomon sees the Harmon plot as an attempt to undermine the very
   logic of the detective novel. As the nineteenth-century city "fills up
   with objects—that is, with reified subjects and depersonalized (as well
   as depersonalizing) things and institutions—it ceases to appear to us
   as a construct designed for human purposes by human wills and begins
   to appear more as a mysterious sequence of mere signs, of objective
   signifiers with no apparent signified meanings." The detective novel
   seeks to make meaning of this meaningless world and to discover
   telltale signs of human purpose in it, Solomon asserts. John Harmon's
   resistance to the Harmon Will "can be interpreted as a kind of 'realistic' allegory of subjective resistance to the naturalistic determination
   of signs," and those who refuse to accept the conditions of the Will
   dramatize "a deliberate rebellion by a group of people who refuse to
   be manipulated by their world." Harmon's inversion of the detective
   story, Solomon argues convincingly, can be read as an "attack on
   urban reification." Harmon does not accede to the signs of the past

as represented in the Will but escapes from "the circle of signs precisely *by* building a family." This family "includes the creatively imaginative members of London, the Lizzie Hexams and Jenny Wrens rather than the readers of dead signs." Solomon concludes persuasively that the hero of the novel "is not the reader of signs, not the Silas Weggs or the Night Inspectors or even the passive reader of its tale: it is the active reader who in reading the story resolves to create a better world."

878. Sroka, Kenneth. "Dickens's Metafiction: Readers and Writers in *Oliver Twist, David Copperfield*, and *Our Mutual Friend*." *Dickens Studies Annual*, 22 (1993), 35–65.

Sroka argues that the readers and writers in Dickens's novels can be regarded as examples of "Victorian metafiction, fiction whose matter is the nature of fiction, the phenomenon of reading and writing, and the interrelationship of writer, text, and reader." In *Our Mutual Friend* he divides the readers into three different categories: mercenary readers, escapists, and those whose reading affects them and causes them to bring about change in other characters. The argument becomes strained at times, such as when Jenny Wren is regarded as reader/ writer because she is doing work that resembles the work of the artist/ novelist, but is valuable and convincing overall. Sroka concludes that Dickens is reminding us, particularly in his "Postscript," of the important relationship between reading and living and the "need to keep Fancy alive."

879. Stewart, Garrett. "Signing Off: Dickens and Thackeray, Woolf and Beckett." In *Philosophical Approaches to Literature: New Essays on Nineteenth- and Twentieth-Century Texts*. Ed.William E. Cain. Lewisburg, PA: Bucknell UP, 1984, pp. 117–39.

Stewart investigates "the philosophy of literary discourse implicit in the way certain novels choose to desist from inscription." He argues that Dickens and Thackeray anticipate Derrida and Barthes in understanding that closure "opens us up to all questions of literary significance." Stewart claims that in the postscript to *Our Mutual Friend* Dickens establishes Mr. and Mrs. Boffin's reality as no more or less real than Dickens's own reality may be if he were "a divine artificer's own invention" and goes on to argue that Dickens "verges" here on "a model of selfhood that will become predominant in Virginia Woolf and Samuel Beckett, an understanding of identity psychologically as well as linguistically deconstructive."

880. Stone, Harry. *The Night Side of Dickens: Cannibalism, Passion, Necessity*. Columbus: Ohio State UP, 1994, passim.

Stone discusses the fascination of Dickens and his age with cannibalism, passion, and necessity, examining the "many contrapuntal variations" of the cannibalism motif in *Our Mutual Friend*, a novel in
which all "humankind is compromised by a social order that must
sustain itself by feeding each one on the other." In his analysis of
passion, Stone examines Bradley Headstone as an instance of "what
can happen when we (with the connivance and through the impositions
of society) deny our deepest emotions. Those neglected emotions, once
evoked, will not go away; when they do emerge, they emerge mon-
strously transformed."

881. Surridge, Lisa. " 'John Rokesmith's Secret': Sensation, Detection, and
the Policing of Women in *Our Mutual Friend.*" *Dickens Studies Annual*, 26 (1998), 265–84.
Surridge demonstrates that *Our Mutual Friend* reproduces many of
the ingredients of the sensation novel only to frustrate the expectations
raised by that genre by revealing its own plot secrets prematurely. The
real concern of *Our Mutual Friend*, Surridge argues, is to confront,
"through an inverted sensational plot, two of the anxieties of the
sensation novel: the instability of the middle-class home, and the unre-
liability of the women at its center." Surridge claims that the disciplining of Bella into "absolute compliance to a wifely role" brings about
not self-fulfillment but "a revelation of the self predicated on the
absolute moral authority of the male." See Ginsburg **(784)** for another
point of view on the testing of Bella.

882. Suter, Anthony. "*Our Mutual Friend*: Mistaken Identity and the Hollow Centre." *Words International*, April 1988, pp. 12–15.
Suter argues that because Dickens was himself "imprisoned in his
own image . . . and found himself implicated in a profound conflict
between what was expected of him and his real character" as a result
of his liaison with Ellen Ternan, the center of *Our Mutual Friend* "is
deliberately false." The novel "depicts a whole series of characters
who are not what they seem," and Dickens, in turning "Victorian
novel conventions against themselves, . . . was working out his problems as an artist and hoping his readers would one day guess what he
really was and would have liked to be." Suter does not indicate what
that is.

883. Thomas, Sydney Joseph. "Imperial Pretexts: Nineteenth-Century Narratives and the Shaping of Empire." *Dissertation Abstracts International*, 57 (1995), 1155A, (State University of New York,
Binghamton).
Thomas considers *Our Mutual Friend* from a "non-Western anti-peri-
alist" [sic] point of view and "explores the way domination of women

is presented and critiqued'' by Dickens; he discovers that although most critics think John Harmon is ''self-sacrificing and benevolent toward his future spouse,'' Dickens finds him to be a ''presumptuous even reprehensible'' manipulator. Evidence of this is found in the ''imperialistic gaze'' of certain minor characters, according to Thomas.

884. Thomas, Syd. '' 'Pretty Woman, Elegantly Framed': The Fate of Bella Wilfer in Dickens's *Our Mutual Friend*.'' *Dickens Quarterly*, 14 (1997), 3–23.

Thomas argues that Mr. Venus shares symbolic roles with the Thames and dust heaps in *Our Mutual Friend*, claiming that the ''story at its most significant level is a process of life-into-death.'' Venus is able to make ''the lifelike appear to be living,'' and his articulating of once live flesh and bone is paralleled by Harmon's articulating Bella from a live, vital person into a doll in a doll's house. In this strained, unconvincing argument, Harmon is seen as deceptive and rationalizing, one whose ''pretenses are in some ways the most vile of all'' as he reduces Bella to ''essentially a stuffed woman.''

885. Thomson, Graeme. ''A Waste of Time: Vitalism and Virtuality in *Our Mutual Friend*.'' In *Dickens: The Craft of Fiction and the Challenges of Reading*. Ed. Rossana Bonadei et al. Milan: Unicopli, 1998, pp. 93–101.

Thomson reads Bella Wilfer and John Harmon as characters who do not actualize their identities but rather engage in a process of ''virtualization, a change of identity, a displacement of the center of ontological gravity of the subject.'' Thus Bella develops a ''multiplicity of virtual selves . . . which she traverses in an indescribable movement of pure desire. In other words, a life.'' Thomson argues that Lizzie and Eugene, on the other hand, are trapped in the ''realm of the possible'' and so their relationship is ''altogether different'' from John and Bella's: they must discover their authenticity.

886. Tiffany, Grace. ''*Our Mutual Friend* in Eumaeus: Joyce Appropriates Dickens.'' *Journal of Modern Literature*, 16 (1990), 643–46.

Tiffany argues that the ''Eumaeus'' chapter of *Ulysses* can ''be read as Ironic Modernist commentary on Dickens's Victorian sentimentality'' in pointing out the parallels between *Ulysses* and *Our Mutual Friend*. Tiffany concludes that Joyce ''invokes Dickens only to depart from him, rejecting the specious harmony with which his predecessor resolved all forms of human conflict.''

887. Trotter, David. *Circulation: Defoe, Dickens, and the Economies of the Novel*. Basingstoke, Eng.: Macmillan; New York: St. Martin's Press, 1988, pp. 133–36.

Trotter concludes his book, in which he demonstrates how Defoe and Dickens, among others, use the metaphor of the circulation of blood through the body to describe economic and social processes such as wealth, trade, transportation, information, and urban development, with a subsection entitled *"Our Mutual Friend*: The Exhaustion of Medical Police.'' He argues that both literary and nonliterary texts adopted the discourse of a body nourished and cleansed by healthful circulation, unless impeded by blockage and contagion, to diagnose and propose cures for social organizations. The nineteenth-century discourse of Medical Police—a program of social action to improve public health by searching out sources of blockage, contagion, infection, and rupture—is represented in Dickens's novels of the 50s and 60s as he sought to diagnose the health of the nation, locating sources of physical and moral disease in the densely populated and ''blocked'' slums, courts, prisons, urban graveyards, and centers of crime in London. By the time he wrote *Our Mutual Friend*, Trotter claims, Dickens's belief in the efficacy and use of the vocabulary of Medical Police had become exhausted by a social organization in which the possibility of ''blockage'' or stagnation was denied (Podsnap's assumption that poverty has been taken care of) and meaningless or corrupt ''circulation'' (of ''shares,'' credit, debt, orphans): ''In a world where everyone and everything circulates, or ceases to exist, circulation will no longer serve to distinguish a state of health from a state of collapse.''

Reviews: J. Sutherland, *London Review of Books*, 10 November 1988, pp. 22–23; J. Mullan, *Times Literary Supplement,* 3 March 1989, p. 218.

888. Tuss, Alex Joseph. ''The Inward Revolution: Troubled Young Men in Victorian Fiction, 1850–1880.'' *Dissertation Abstracts International*, 52 (1991), 1345A (Fordham University).

Tuss considers the presentation of the young middle-class male in novels and periodicals in Victorian England, showing the diversity of presentations and arguing that the figure ''reflects the debate during the period'' until this figure ''eventually questions commonly held positions, openly opposes society's conventions, and finally chooses voluntary exile from England.'' He examines the presentation of the figure in *Our Mutual Friend*.

889. Vita, Paul Anthony. ''The Epitaph in Victorian England.'' *Dissertation Abstracts International*, 59 (1998), 1587A (Columbia University).

Vita examines *Our Mutual Friend* as an instance of Dickens's conflict with the ''language of commemoration'' in a study of how the ''Victorians transferred their anxieties about death onto the purpose, effect, and value of epitaphs.''

890. Waters, Catherine. *"Our Mutual Friend."* In her *Dickens and the Politics of the Family*. Cambridge: Cambridge UP, 1997, pp. 175–202.

Waters employs feminist and new historicist methodologies to argue, unpersuasively, that *Our Mutual Friend* "betrays a disjunction between form and ideology, ultimately suggesting Dickens's ambivalence about his own novelistic activity." She claims that the "reassuring triumph of the middle-class family is put into question by the very narrative methods used to secure it, for the novel relies upon the representation of gender difference to overcome the problems seen to be generated by economic and social inadequacies." She concludes that "the very split between productive and reproductive realms, supposedly determined by the value of capitalism, becomes visible as an ideological formation that is already shaped by gender and class difference. A more trenchant examination of the relationship between capitalism and the family in *Our Mutual Friend* demonstrates some of the ways in which Dickens's representation of the family enabled the construction of the very ideology that the form of the novel would seem to subvert." For other points of view on this, see Ginsburg **(784)** Morris **(836)**, and Shuman **(870)**.

Reviews: A. Sadrin, *Dickensian*, 94 (1998): 56–58; B. Rosenberg, *Dickens Quarterly*, 15 (1998), 226–28; P. Faulkner, *Review of English Studies*, 50 (Feb. 1999), 119–20.

891. Watts, Alan. "Dickens and Pauline Viardot." *Dickensian*, 91 (1995), 171–78.

In examining the relationship between Dickens and the French mezzo-soprano, Pauline Viardot-Garcia, Watts quotes a letter to Madame Viardot from Dickens in which he indicates that he is completing *Our Mutual Friend*.

892. See Westbrook **(912)**. "Dickens's Secret Sharer, Conrad's Mutual Friend."

893. Wheeler, Michael. "Dickens: *Our Mutual Friend*." In his *Death and Future Life in Victorian Literature and Theology*. Cambridge: Cambridge UP, 1990, pp. 265–304.

Wheeler argues that John's gospel in the New Testament and the orders of Baptism, Matrimony, and the Burial of the Dead in the prayer book provide the basis for the baptism and resurrection themes in *Our Mutual Friend*. He sees that "the novel's central conceit of rising and falling, worked out in social climbing and abrupt descents, the amassing and removal of dust, a cityscape of airy rooftops and dark labyrinthine streets, and a river of drownings and rescues, is underpinned with a theological understanding of the fall and of man's redemption through love, worked out in the here-and-now as an earnest of a future heavenly state." Wheeler sees Dickens as sympathetic to Anglican Broad Church opinion on most of the doctrinal issues at the time in this thoughtful analysis.

894. Wiesenthal, C. S. "Anti-Bodies of Disease and Dickens: Spirit-Body Relations in Nineteenth-Century Culture and Fiction." *Victorian Literature and Culture*, 22 (1994), 187–220.
    Wiesenthal explores the relationship between "the sphere of the body or soma and the affective realm of the psyche or spirit," mentioning *Our Mutual Friend* in passing as an example of the nineteenth-century's awareness of the "presence of death in its midst."

895. Wilkes, David Michael. "Dickens and the Pastoral Ethic." *Dissertation Abstracts International,* 51 (1990), 3759A (Rhode Island University).
    Wilkes asserts that "pastoral signification in Dickens is polyphonic." He traces the "discordant or confrontational range of pastoralism" throughout Dickens's career, claiming that by the time of *Our Mutual Friend* "moral conflict is both initiated and resolved in ideographic sites of struggle."

896. Worthington, Pepper. "The Religious Issues of Materialism, Love, and God in Dickens's Last Novel, *Our Mutual Friend* (1865)." *Mount Olive Review*, 5 (1991), 61–73.
    Worthington illustrates through exhaustive citing of the text that in *Our Mutual Friend* Dickens opposes materialism, supports the "fundamental ingredients of love," and sees God's providence as being worked out in what happens to the characters in the novel.

897. Yoon, Hyee-Joon. "Capital in Dickens: A Dialectical Study." *Dissertation Abstracts International*, 53 (1992), 3228A (State University of New York, Buffalo.)
    Yoon traces the "configuration of capital" in the writings of Dickens, and analyzes *Our Mutual Friend* as one instance of "idiosyncratically critical articulations of the problems of capital."

TOPOGRAPHY

898. See *Our Mutual Friend*: The Scholarly Pages **(715)**.

LITERARY INFLUENCES AND PARALLELS

899. See Cotsell **(747)**. *The Companion to Our Mutual Friend.*
900. DeMarcus, Cynthia. "Wolves Within and Without: Dickens's Transformation of 'Little Red Riding Hood' in *Our Mutual Friend.*" *Dickens Quarterly*, 12 (1995), 11–17.
    Demarcus examines *Our Mutual Friend* in the context of "Little Red Riding Hood," arguing that the fairy tale helps to unify the novel and

allows Dickens to capture the terrors of modern life as well as to force readers to explore the depths of their own dark unconsciousness. DeMarcus points out that several of the characters in the novel are portrayed as wolves but the ''Thames River—and consequently death—is the Arch Wolf of 'Little Red Riding Hood.' '' The solution Dickens offers in this brutal universe involves using fairy tales to interpret life, DeMarcus insists. She concludes that Dickens's use of fairy tales in *Our Mutual Friend* demonstrates that he is aware of their therapeutic value in dealing with life.

901. See Dvorak (762). ''Dickens and Popular Culture: Silas Wegg's Ballads in *Our Mutual Friend*.''

902. Edgecombe, Rodney Stenning. ''Two Oblique Allusions in *Our Mutual Friend*.'' *Notes and Queries*, 41 (1994), 352–53.

Edgecombe looks at a passage in *Our Mutual Friend* describing the Podsnaps' protectiveness of Georgiana and points to Thompson's *The Seasons* and Corinthians 13:12 as possible sources for ''buried'' allusions for Dickens.

903. Edgecombe, Rodney Stenning. ''The 'Veiled Prophet' in *Our Mutual Friend*.'' *Dickensian*, 92 (1996), 208–09.

Edgecombe claims that the reference to Veneering as a ''Veiled prophet, not prophesying'' derives from Ezekiel 13:17–18 and 21, a description of ''would-be sybils'' who conceal their fraudulence through the use of veils. This is an inversion of Exodus 34:33, where Moses's veil is a covering for radiance too powerful for the human eye. Edgecombe speculates that the reference may have come by way of an intermediate source, Archbishop Whately. See Slater (909).

904. Green, Paul. ''Two Venal Girls: A Study in Dickens and Zola.'' *Recovering Literature,* 19 (1993), 21–35.

Green compares Bella Wilfer with Berthe Josserand in Zola's *Pot-Bouille*. Bella remains likable even in her ''venal stage'' because she intuits her own limitations self-critically, Green points out. He then goes on to argue, not very convincingly, that Bella becomes an ''idealization'' after she has been tested by Harmon, not because she is cured of her venality but because Dickens takes the spirit out of her in so curing her.

905. Hackenberg, Sara. '' 'Loitering Artfully': Reading Flânerie in *Our Mutual Friend*.'' In *Dickens: The Craft of Fiction and the Challenges of Reading*. Ed. Rossana Bonadei et al. Milan: Unicopli, 1998, pp. 230–39.

Hackenberg argues that the scene in *Our Mutual Friend* where Eugene leads Bradley through the streets of London at night is based on Poe's ''The Man of the Crowd'' (1845), the story in which a convalescent man has the uncanny ability to "read" people who appear in the crowd but comes across someone he cannot read and pursues him, looks him squarely in the face, only to be ignored by him. She indicates that this "reader" is the *flâneur*, "the nineteenth-century spectator who begins to unravel the mysteries of urban space through active reading of its inhabitants." She goes on to consider several other characters in the novel as more or less successful "readers."

906. See Hecimovich **(794)**. "The Cup and the Lip and the Riddle of *Our Mutual Friend*."

907. See Lesser **(818)**. "From Dickens to Conrad: A Sentimental Journey."

908. Myer, Michael Grosvner. "Dickensian Echoes in Shaw: *Our Mutual Friend* and *Pygmalion*." *Notes and Queries*, 31 (1994), 508.
Myer points out convincing parallels between Doolittle's conversation in *Pygmalion* and Riderhood's in *Our Mutual Friend* and indicates other parallels in the works, including the fact that Doolittle is a dustman.

909. Slater, Michael. "Letter to the Editor." *Dickensian*, 93 (1997), 47.
Slater disagrees with Edgecombe **(903)** that the description of Veneering in the second chapter of *Our Mutual Friend* as "a veiled-prophet, not prophesying" is from *Ezekiel*; he calls attention to Cotsell's *Companion to Our Mutual Friend* **(747)**, where he points out that the image is derived from Moore's popular *Lalla Rookh* (1817).

910. See Stewart **(879)**. "Signing Off: Dickens and Thackeray, Woolf and Beckett."

911. See Tiffany **(886)**. "*Our Mutual Friend* in Eumaeus: Joyce Appropriates Dickens."

912. Westbrook, Wayne W. "Dickens's Secret Sharer, Conrad's Mutual Friend." *Studies in Short Fiction*, 5 (1992), 61–73.
Westbrook points out similarities between *Our Mutual Friend* and Conrad's "Secret Sharer," tentatively suggesting that Dickens's novel "is a possible source for many of the psychological aspects and details of plot" in Conrad's story.

TEACHING AND STUDY MATERIALS

913. Carter, Jane. *Charles Dickens, Our Mutual Friend: Notes.* Harlow: Longman, 1984. 72 pp.
This study was not available.

914. Charles Dickens, *Our Mutual Friend: A Viewer's Guide*. London: BBC Education, 1998. 46 pp.
Published to accompany the BBC 2 Television adaptation of *Our Mutual Friend*, produced by Catherine Wearing, broadcast in Spring 1998.

915. See Cotsell **(747)**. *The Companion to Our Mutual Friend.*
916. Davis, Paul. *Charles Dickens A to Z: The Essential Reference to His Life and Work.* New York: Checkmark Books, 1999. ix + 432 pp.
    This is a "guide to Dickens's life, works, characters, the Victorian context in which he wrote, and critics and scholars who have commented upon it." It includes over 2,500 cross-referenced entries, alphabetically arranged.
917. The Dickens Project. Santa Cruz: University of California. John O. Jordan, Director. http://humwww.ucsc.edu/dickens/index.html.
    As announced on its website, "The Dickens Project of the University of California is a scholarly consortium devoted to promoting the study and enjoyment of the life, times, and work of Charles Dickens. Internationally recognized as the premier center for Dickens studies in the world, the Project consists of faculty and graduate students from the eight general campuses of the University of California as well from other major American and international universities." In addition to sponsoring an annual week-long conference on a topic related to Dickens, the Project maintains a Dickens electronical archive, provides links to other on-line resources, makes available publications and teaching resources on Dickens, and maintains *"Our Mutual Friend:* The Scholarly Pages" **(715)** among other things.
918. Hawes, Donald. *Who's Who in Dickens.* London: Routledge, 1998. xxv + 278 pp.
    Hawes gives "fuller accounts of the major characters than are found in many reference books, noting some of Dickens's possible sources and referring, in limited ways, to critical opinion, especially when questions of influence and interpretation have arisen."
919. Matsuoka, Mitsuharu. "The Dickens Page." *http://lang.nagoya-u.ac.jp/~matsouka/Dickens.html#New.* Accessed Feb. 2002.
    Contains e-texts of Dickens's works, including *Our Mutual Friend,* links to the Dickens Fellowship, the Japan Branch of the Dickens Fellowship, the Dickens Society, the Dickens Project, bibliographies, biography, filmography, concordances, Dickens Home Pages, among several other things. The best website on Dickens.
920. *Our Mutual Friend.* Margaret Tanner. Oxford, Eng., and Portsmouth, NH: Heinemann, 1992, 127 pp.
    Heinemann guided reader; textbook for foreign speakers. This study was not available.
921. See *Our Mutual* Friend: The Scholarly Pages **(715).**
922. Newlin, George. *Every Thing in Dickens: Ideas and Subjects Discussed by Charles Dickens in His Complete Works, A Topicon.* Westport, CT: Greenwood Press, 1996. lviii + 1,102 pp.

From Newlin's *Window into Dickens* series. This "can be read for pleasure, for casual browsing in the distinctiveness of Victorian things and thoughts; but it can also be mined for selective gold by the social historian, the political historian, and by those who simply need or want to know something specific about Dickens himself or about Victorian manners, morals, thoughts and things,'' according to Fred Kaplan's Forward.

923. Page, Norman. *"Our Mutual Friend.''* In his *A Dickens Companion.* New York: Schoken Books, 1984, 225–38.

Page provides valuable background on composition, serialization, and publication information, an overview of critical reception, and an annotated list of characters in Dickens's works, including *Our Mutual Friend.*

Reviews: A. Sanders, *Times Literary Supplement,* 6 April 1984, p. 379; C. Bishop, *Library Journal,* 109 (1 May 1984), 901; K. Flint, *Times Higher Education Supplement,* 4 May 1984, p. 24; S. Gill, *British Book News,* June, 1984, pp. 372–73; B. Tadman, *Times Education Supplement,* 18 May 1984, p. 33; E. Wexler, *Booklist,* 80 (15 April 1984), 1145; *Choice,* 21 (June 1984), 1468; J. Rettig, *Wilson Library Bulletin,* 58 (June 1984), 753; S. Shatto, *Dickensian,* 80 (Summer 1984), 118–19; R. Dunn, *Studies in the Novel,* 16 (Winter 1984), 458–60.

924. Watts, Alan S. *"Our Mutual Friend.''* In his *The Life and Times of Charles Dickens.* New York: Crescent Books, 1991, pp.125–30.

Watts introduces Dickens to general readers, especially younger readers, in this elaborately illustrated book that includes photographs, stills from theater and film productions, paintings, prints, engravings, antique collectibles, and a variety of book illustrations.

BIOGRAPHICAL STUDIES

925. See Ackroyd **(724)**. *Dickens.*

926. See Kaplan **(806)**. "The Sons of Toil.''

927. Page, Norman. *"Our Mutual Friend.''* In his *"A Dickens Chronology.* London: Macmillan, 1988, pp. 114–18.

According to Page's General Editor's Preface, the Chronology Series "aims at providing a means whereby the chronological facts of an author's life and career . . . can be seen at a glance.'' We are thus able to know what Dickens "was doing in each month and week, and almost on each day, of his prodigiously active working life; and the student is . . . likely to find it fascinating as well as useful just when

Dickens was at work on each part of [a] novel, what other literary
enterprises he was engaged in at the same time, whom he was meeting,
what places he was visiting, and what were the relevant circumstances
of his personal and professional life." Of course, given the delicate
nature of Dickens's personal life at the time of writing *Our Mutual
Friend*, we have "sparse records of some of Dickens's later years
when his secret liaison with Ellen Ternan was presumably absorbing
much of his time, but from which no correspondence between the two
lovers has come to light."

Author and Subject Index

(Characters in *OMF* are indexed under their first names.)

VOLUME INDEX

515